PHILOSOPHY OF RELIGION
A Global Approach

Stephen H. Phillips
University of Texas at Austin

Under the general editorship of

Robert C. Solomon
University of Texas at Austin

Harcourt Brace College Publishers

Fort Worth   Philadelphia   San Diego   New York   Orlando   Austin   San Antonio
Toronto   Montreal   London   Sydney   Tokyo

Publisher	Ted Buchholz
Editor-in-Chief	Christopher P. Klein
Senior Acquisitions Editor	David Tatom
Developmental Editor	Laurie Runion
Senior Project Editor	Margaret Allyson
Project Editor	Juliet George
Production Manager	Diane Gray
Art Director	Garry Harman

ISBN 0-15-501753-5

Library of Congress Catalog Card Number 95-78855

Address for Editorial Correspondence: Harcourt Brace College Publishers, 301 Commerce Street, Suite 3700, Fort Worth, Texas 76102

Address for Orders: Harcourt Brace & Company, 6277 Sea Harbor Drive, Orlando, Florida 32887. 1-800-782-4479, or 1-800-433-0001 (in Florida)

To
Charles Hartshorne

PREFACE

"But what about Buddhism? Is Nirvana the meaning of life?"

"Why do you never talk about Islam?"

"It's because of karma from previous lifetimes why people suffer."

"I'm a Taoist."

"You spent too much time on God. What about Eastern religions?"

During the last fifteen years, students have expressed these and similar comments about a course I have taught in philosophy of religion. Gradually, I began to include Eastern materials, when I could find them in appropriate formats, and began regularly announcing my disappointment with the philosophy discipline that specialists in philosophy of religion were not doing their job with respect to religious concepts and claims other than those growing out of Christianity. But the counter-complaint sounded hollow, and I decided to make a globalist collection of readings, which now with introductions comprise this volume.

Philosophy of Religion was written for the introductory course in philosophy of religion; the readings have been selected for freshmen and sophomores who have not previously studied philosophy. There are, however, more difficult selections that could be used in a course for third- and fourth-year philosophy majors, or in an introductory course as a final reading on a given topic. The more advanced selections are marked with a » in the Table of Contents.

This book has pedagogical features that should prove particularly helpful given that students, and probably some instructors, are unfamiliar with non-Western traditions. First, there is an extensive glossary, where crucial foreign words (from Sanskrit, Chinese, etc.) are defined along with technical terms standardly used in philosophy of religion. Second, instructors who have taught philosophy of religion without making use of non-Western materials will find a familiar arrangement of topics. Non-Western selections have been placed in a manner that extends the usual treatment of a topic and require, normally, no special familiarity with non-Western traditions beyond the introductory remarks provided for each individual reading. In some cases, an earlier selection may be referred to in the introductory discussion as important background, and in these cases the earlier selection should be read first. The non-Western materials and introductions included in the subsections of the first section, Divine Reality, are especially important in that they provide overviews of the major religious philosophies worldwide. But, for example, the Confucius reading in the section Religion and Ethics depends on no previous selection, nor does the Hindu selection from M. Hiriyanna on rebirth in the section Personal Destiny. Brief material histories for each of the major religions are provided in the book's general introduction, and probably many students would profit by becoming apprised of that background if only better to appreciate the difference between the material and intellectual dimensions of religions.

Thus this book is organized to make possible a gradual expansion beyond customary Western discussions. In fact, the book is sufficiently long and comprehensive to be used as a textbook for a course in which no non-Western material was required. I would not want to encourage such use, but a virtue of having a wide range of selections—whichever particular readings are chosen for a particular course—is that students can easily see for themselves how a discussion might be extended.

A convention used for glossary items is that the first time a glossary term appears in an introductory discussion, it is highlighted.

Study questions follow each section and subsection, there being fifteen sets in all. The order of questions follows, generally, the order of selections in each section or subsection. But there is also a second ordering principle that in most cases dovetails with the first, a principle having to do with inviting different kinds of student response. Let me explain.

Some questions target specific views and arguments, suggesting rather specific answers. Other questions raise issues for reflection where there is no clearly right or wrong answer with respect to the readings. As far as possible, while honoring the order of the readings, I have tried to organize each set of study questions to range from those presented first, where a rather definite answer is expected, to those presented last, where it is more appropriate to respond creatively. Since in philosophy no issue is so elementary or decided that we should discourage original thought and since a "wrong" answer that is well-thought-out can often merit an "A," no hard and fast line can be drawn dividing questions into two neat groups. Nevertheless, questions appearing earlier tend to test students' comprehension of readings, whereas those appearing later tend to invite students to think on their own about issues and arguments.

In addition to a glossary, the book includes a Guide to Further Reading and a Pronunciation Guide written for native speakers of English in North America with respect to classical Arabic, Sanskrit, and Chinese. The Guide to Further Reading lists both classical and contemporary material, primarily the well-recognized pivotal and seminal works usually mentioned in philosophy of religion textbooks. Additionally, as is appropriate for this textbook, much scholarship concerning non-Western traditions is also listed.

ACKNOWLEDGMENTS

My wife Hope Schlorholtz heads a long list of persons to whom I am especially grateful. She has been my partner in this project, handling in particular the permissions requests, patiently logging publishers' and authors' responses. She also listened and provided appropriate advice about a wide range of editorial decisions. Philosophy colleagues at the University of Texas at Austin who suggested readings or helped me digest them include Bob Solomon, Al Martinich, Tom Seung, Dan Bonevac, Rob Koons, Bob Kane, Kelly Oliver, and Louis Mackey. I am also grateful to the Department for allowing me to teach a couple of upper-division courses where I experimented with some of the readings here. The reviews solicited by Harcourt Brace proved helpful, and I appreciate the sensitive responses we received from professionals not accustomed to a global approach to the field. Of this group Nancy Frankenberry of Dartmouth College must be singled out. She suggested several additional or alternative readings, many of which have been included and have made this a better book. Suggestions from other reviewers were followed as well, and I am grateful to Joram Graf Haber, Bergen Community College; David Hall, University of Texas at El Paso; Christine Holmgren, Santa Monica College; James Huchingson, Florida International University; Charles Kielkopf, Ohio State University; George Mavrodes, University of Michigan; and S. N. Tagore, University of Texas at San Antonio. At Harcourt Brace, David Tatom, Laurie Runion, and Juliet George were a pleasure to work with; the production process was made very easy. The expertise of Harcourt colleagues Diane Gray and Garry Harman is appreciated, as well as that of J. R. Peacock and Susan Swain. Finally, a heartfelt thanks goes to Linda Webster, who diligently compiled the index.

CONTENTS

→ know the fundamentals

» denotes more advanced reading selection

INTRODUCTION

Globalism in Philosophy of Religion

In Western civilization, religion and philosophy have had a complex relationship ranging from philosophy conceived as "the handmaiden of faith" to philosophers trying to debunk religious beliefs. In the twentieth century, philosophic questions growing out of or associated with Western religions—"Does God exist?" "What is God's nature?" "Is there a soul that survives death?"—have not been at the center of philosophy as a field or academic discipline. Nevertheless, professional, academic philosophers have continued to scrutinize religious beliefs, clarifying issues and older arguments and, occasionally, innovating a new line of reasoning. But it has been almost exclusively Western religious claims and concepts that have been examined, views associated with Judaism, Christianity, and (though the association has not been so well understood) Islam. Rarely within philosophy of religion have Hindu or Buddhist or Taoist conceptions been examined, especially at an introductory level.

This book is intended to broaden philosophy of religion at an introductory level, or, more precisely—since interest is widespread and much scholarship has already occurred—to reflect a broadening that is taking place as we humans begin to realize that we belong to a global civilization. The topics, issues, and arguments of traditional Western-oriented philosophy of religion are thoroughly represented here. But claims and concepts growing out of Eastern religions are considered also.

Philosophers writing in Western languages of research (English, French, etc.) have been among the better students and commentators on Eastern religious thought. Although usually their work has appeared under the banner of comparative philosophy or Chinese or Indian philosophy, it has helped widen philosophy of religion. Some of their work is presented here. Also presented is work by scholars in the field of religious studies, who, I daresay, as a group have been a little more inclined to look in an Eastern direction.

Most importantly, philosophy considered from a global perspective is not limited to the West. In particular, in classical India and in classical China traditions of abstract speculation on clearly philosophic topics as well as critical analysis of a range of views developed from an early date, uninfluenced by anything Greek or Western. Eastern philosophy includes much religious speculation but also ethical and political theorizing, logic, scrutiny of canons of debate, and theory of knowledge. Classics of Eastern thought, particularly that associated with the great Eastern religions, along with some Eastern critiques of religious perspectives, are excerpted and discussed in just about every section here.

In the final section, selections are drawn from thinkers—some committed to a particular religion, some not—who have attended to the fact of religious diversity. What does religious diversity import for the claims of individual religions? Is there common ground among the belief systems? If not, is the debunking perspective of the sociology of religion reinforced? This book reflects religious pluralism in each of its ten sections. In the tenth, questions targeting that pluralism itself are asked.

RELIGION, PHILOSOPHY, RELIGIOUS PHILOSOPHY, AND PHILOSOPHY OF RELIGION

Each religion has an intellectual dimension, but beliefs are hardly all there is to a religion. Rituals or ceremonies celebrating birth, marriage, death, and so forth, as well as practices of worship and meditation, larger patterns of social behavior, that is, religious mores and ethics, temples and an order of priests, as well as each religion's material history are important to what a religion is, not just its characteristic intellectual positions.

Even the intellectual dimension of religions includes more than the concepts and claims that typically serve as grist for the mills of philosophy. For example, Scripture, according to Southern Buddhism—called (in Pāli) the *Tipiṭaka,* "Three Baskets,"— comprises (1) sermons attributed to the Buddha, (2) regulations for monks, and (3) doctrinal discussions. Philosophers, whether in classical India or modern Germany or France or Japan, or wherever (and whether themselves Buddhist or non-Buddhist), have rarely if ever been concerned with the second "basket," the regulations for monks, since philosophers tend to be interested in questions which the regulations presuppose—such as, whether *nirvāṇa* or "enlightenment" as traditionally conceived is really possible, what is its relation to our ordinary experience of self and world, what is real and what not, and so forth. Philosophers are interested above all in theoretical questions and in arguments purported to justify one view over others. The intellectual dimension of religion includes some of this, but it also includes specifications of rituals, sometimes a recorded history of a lineage of priests or monks, and other written work further from the concerns of philosophers. There are also sometimes such materials as canons of interpretation of scripture that some philosophers see as rich veins to mine for certain purposes but that cannot be said to be near the heart of philosophic affection.

What, then, is philosophy? What are its interests and topics? What are its methods? What is its point? These are difficult questions and hotly debated. The word 'philosophy' derives from two Greek words, *philos* and *sophia,* which compounded mean "love of wisdom." With arguably the first philosopher within the Greek tradition, Socrates (469–

399 BCE), philosophy was something like love of knowledge, implying love of truth, especially truths about ourselves as knowers (what it is to know, what makes it possible), also truths about the world including human agency and society. Socrates taught that when we self-consciously apprehend such truths we become able to lead the best sorts of lives.

Socratic and later Greek philosophy have enormous importance for almost all subsequent Western philosophy, shaping its contours and providing resources for on-going reflection. But the Greeks did not establish once and for all the issues or the methods of Western philosophy, much less a set of standard views. Moreover, as suggested, anyone who has a sense of philosophy from its long history in the West and who also knows even a little about Eastern literature knows that philosophic reflection abounds in non-Western traditions. It is difficult to provide a nutshell definition of philosophy since so much of human wisdom—and possibly, foolishness (though foolishness backed up with argument)—falls under the title. But any argument or systematic speculation about truths or claims—especially the wide-ranging or general—that would impact importantly our lives counts as philosophy. It should be added that philosophy would make its impact through a direct appeal to our first-person perspectives, not as science through technology. (See also the glossary entry, *philosophy*.) Among the more central issues of philosophy are how we know, what are the canons of justification, what is real and why should we think so, what is the best that life has to offer, and should we trust the teachings of religion.

Although philosophers speculate and forge new theories (sometimes with mysterious motives), we may identify *argument,* to be construed broadly, as the method of philosophy, or the premier and least disputable method. Philosophic argument includes generalization from experientially based premises as well as teasing out ramifications from a given assumption along with analysis of meaning of terms and drawing out presuppositions. The marshalling of reasons for or against a position may be taken as a working definition of philosophic argument. The sections, Arguments for a Divine Reality and Faith Against Reason, include selections, and introductions to selections, where further general remarks about argument in philosophy are made. A range of arguments in favor of a Divine Reality are presented in the former of these two sections, along with several counterarguments. In the section, Religion Debunked, important broad arguments against religious perspectives are considered. (See also the glossary entries, *argument* and *cogency*.)

Religious philosophy is systematic theorizing associated with individual religions and committed defense (by argument) of religious beliefs. All theology is religious philosophy, but so too is Buddhist speculation about how the teaching of the Buddha connects with things we know in everyday life. *Theology* implies a commitment to theism; not all religious philosophy is theistic (for example, Buddhist philosophy is not). Religious philosophy is particularly important to the field of philosophy of religion because it is the systematic expressions of beliefs and philosophic defenses that philosophers, whatever their religious or areligious precommitments, find "user-friendly," to use a computer metaphor. Again, philosophers typically want to know what general-most beliefs are espoused, and on what grounds. (And they care little about ritual, etc.) Learning a religious philosophy, they are able to entertain evaluative questions.

It would be wrong to suppose that a theologian—or any religious philosopher precommitted to a particular religion as a Christian, Hindu, Muslim, and so on—does not himself or herself carry out evaluative tasks with respect to an intellectual heritage. Details change, and indeed large-scale theological innovations are sometimes achieved by committed religious philosophers. It would be difficult to identify a belief that a Christian theologian, for example, would have to accept in order to remain Christian. Religious philosophy and broader philosophy of religion interpenetrate, the latter in effect including the whole of the former. There is speculation in religious philosophy and of course argument.

Philosophy of religion is the subfield of philosophy that includes religious philosophy and all efforts of evaluation of religious beliefs, all the attacks and defenses from whatever party, as well as attempts to debunk religious practices (and not only beliefs) by psychologists (for example, Sigmund Freud) or sociological theorists (for example, Karl Marx), and so forth. This book is an introduction to the subject where as little as possible about philosophy or world religions has been presupposed.

World religions—according to academics within the field of religious studies for whom the expression has proved useful—are the religions that have both a universal message and established institutions that to an extent transcend national and non-religious cultural boundaries. Scholars identify other standard features: rituals, a priestly order, mosques, churches, temples, or the like, texts regarded as scripture, as well as beliefs centering on a transmundane reality. World religions are sometimes called the high religions or the major religions. Usually they are counted as five: Judaism, Christianity, Islam, Hinduism, and Buddhism. Taoism is sometimes added to the list, though as an institution Taoism is practically a phenomenon of the past. (And some find misleading the exclusion of African and Amerindian religions, which have numerous practitioners, if few by comparison with Christianity, Islam, and Hinduism, and which also have, in some cases, a universal message.) It is to be stressed that although scholars are able to identify several features that world religions have in common, not every aspect of Judaism, for example, has a parallel within, for example, Hinduism. Each religion is also unique.

This is not a textbook on world religions. Most of the history of world religions and most matters of daily religious practice are well beyond our purview. A textbook on world religions would be primarily descriptive, ranging over all dimensions, including rituals and architecture as well as characteristic beliefs. In contrast, we shall be concerned almost exclusively with religious beliefs and attempts to evaluate them.

Fortunately, it does not seem as though philosophers need to know much, if any, of the material history, rituals, and so forth, of a religion in order to carry out their examinations; they need to know only the most general beliefs. (A contrary view is presented in the section Faith Against Reason, specifically the selection from D. Z. Phillips entitled "Wittgensteinian Fideism.") Nevertheless, it may be helpful to look at each of the major religious traditions in broad outline before going on to the issues proper to philosophy of religion. For this reason I present the following sketches. See the Guide to Further Reading for references to several fuller, and much superior, treatments. The following provide overall context. Core beliefs, the centralmost planks of the religious philosophies that have developed in association with each tradition, will be elaborated in later sections, especially the first, Divine Reality. Directions to specific selections will be given at appropriate places.

Judaism

Judaic scripture, the *Torah,* largely overlaps with that part of Christian scripture called the Old Testament. The first five books, or Pentateuch, are particularly important for Judaic practices as well as Judaic theology. Scholars believe that they became set in their canonical form at the time of the prophet Ezra (ca. 428 BCE), well after the destruction of Solomon's temple by Babylonians in 586 BCE. At least a century earlier, a written narrative seems to have been composed concerning the dealings of YHWH (mistranslated "Jehovah," usually pronounced "Yahweh") with a Jewish patriarch Abraham and the tribes of Israel, including the revelation to Moses known as the Ten Commandments. And an oral tradition is very early, presumably from the second millennium BCE. But priestly editors in the fifth century BCE apparently put together the Pentateuch as we have it today. The great prophets Amos, Hosea, Micah, and (the most important theologically) Isaiah probably lived in the eighth century BCE. Additions to the Pentateuch called books of the prophets, along with a second, more disputed group of books called the writings (e.g., Psalms, Job, Ruth, Tobit, and I and II Maccabees) came to be officially regarded as scripture after the Roman destruction of Jerusalem in 70 CE.

In the second century CE, a great leader named Judah ha-Nasi (Judah the Prince) collected all the legal commentary written since Ezra. This massive text is the *Mishnah,* which together with subsequent subcommentary written in Palestine and in Babylon up to the fifth century, called *Gemara,* comprises the *Talmud.* The Talmud is central to the practices of Orthodox Judaism. Conformity to God's revealed law is of paramount importance.

In the nineteenth century, Reform Judaism emerged, at first in Germany, endorsing practices—such as diet and observance of the Sabbath—not as strict as in Orthodox Judaism. Reform Judaism accepts continuity with all earlier Judaism but rejects the authority of the Talmud. Also, while a promise of a Messiah, or Anointed Redeemer, is normally viewed as part of a covenant between God and Abraham—a covenant that has been reaffirmed through subsequent generations—in Reform Judaism the idea that the Messiah will secure a specific homeland is explicitly renounced.

Another departure from Orthodox Judaism, which is, like Reform Judaism, mainly a matter of practices but which also involves a somewhat different attitude towards God, is the Hasidic movement inaugurated by Israel ben Eliezer (1699–1760) who became known as Baal Shem Tov ("master of the good name"). His followers, the Hasidim, were urged not to toil in Talmudic scholarship but to try to approach God with a simple, heartfelt faith. This world is not significant in comparison with an afterlife paradise, and God according to His own counsel will someday send a Messiah. (See also the selection from Martin Buber under Mysticism.)

Diversity of Judaic practice, particularly in modern times, has become pronounced. But though subordinate doctrines do vary, departure from a fundamental religious philosophy is rare. Judaism is theistic at its core, as are its sister religions, Christianity and Islam. The selection from the theologian Philo in the section Divine Reality elaborates the classical and mainstream theism associated with Judaism for more than two thousand years.

In portions of the Pentateuch and other scriptural passages reflecting early Judaic belief, YHWH appears to be thought of as a local deity, a tribal or national deity, whose residence was the temple built by King Solomon (tenth century BCE?). After the temple was destroyed and many Jews made captives in Babylon, the conception of YHWH was apparently broadened; no longer was the deity thought to be confined to a particular locale. The prophet Isaiah made pellucidly clear that the God of the Israelites was the one true God of the entire world, God eternal and infinite, the Creator, transcendent and holy. (See the selection "Biblical Theology" in the section Divine Reality.)

Christianity

Jesus of Nazareth (4 BCE–29 CE), the founder of Christianity, lived in Palestine during the height of the Roman Empire. The Mediterranean world as well as much of Europe and Western Asia were unified politically under Roman rule. Previously, much of this territory had been conquered by the Greek emperor, Alexander (356–323 BCE), and a Hellenistic culture, including Greek philosophy, had spread, with Greek as the language of intellectual exchange as well as of commerce and legal administration. Judaic scripture, for example, was translated into Greek by 250 BCE. Under the Romans, Greek culture and ideas were gradually reclothed, with Latin emerging as the cosmopolitan language. But it was mainly through the medium of Greek that the religious teaching of Jesus was conveyed—by Paul and other disciples—throughout the Roman world.

Christianity began as a sect of Judaism. Jesus and all his immediate disciples followed Judaic practices, and Judaic scripture was accepted almost in its entirety as part of the Christian Bible. Jesus proclaimed himself the Messiah promised by God according to Isaiah and other prophets, although the Christian interpretation of the Messiah as God incarnate does appear radical by Judaic standards. And Christian theology, particularly early Christian theology (sometimes called the philosophy of the Church Fathers), owes much to the Judaic theologian Philo (see under Divine Reality).

Judaic opposition to Christianity has not been a result of the Christian claim that Jesus is the Messiah; several figures have been accepted as the Messiah within minority sects of Judaism throughout its long history without being repudiated by the mainstream. Judaic opposition to Christianity seems to have stemmed from the admission of Gentiles (non-Jews or non-practitioners) into the Christian fold without circumcision (for males) or adherence to other requirements of Judaic law.

On the Christian side, Jesus and his early disciples (especially Paul) saw their mission as so transcending traditional Judaism that following the old law seemed no longer to be of importance. According to the four Gospels which appeared within a century of Jesus' death, Jesus preached a new law of inner relation to God, through acceptance of himself as the Son of God, or God incarnate, and love of all humanity. The New Testament—composed of these Gospels and writings by Paul and other disciples—is accordingly supposed to supercede Judaic scripture, the Old Testament, with a new teaching of reliance on God through Jesus and an ethics of brotherly love. (From the Judaic perspective, however, Jesus' teaching does not seem to be so different from that of other priests, or rabbis, recorded in the Mishnah.) God's endorsement of Jesus' message is said to be secured by miracles performed by Jesus and his disciples, in particular, Jesus' rising from the dead and direct ascension to heaven, that is, God's company.

Paul and many of Jesus' immediate disciples made great effort to carry Jesus' teaching abroad, using the Jewish communities that had grown up in many cities as sanctuaries, and corresponding extensively, usually in Greek. On the whole, their success has to be judged outstanding. However, Christianity's spread through the Roman world was chequered in the early centuries by opposition by some of the Roman emperors. Persecution was severe at times—for example under Emperor Decius (249–251), who tried to reestablish pre-Christian worship of Roman gods, which by that time had been eclipsed by the new religion, and Diocletian (284–305), whose edicts targeted first Christian writings, then clergy, and finally laity as well, causing widespread suffering. In 313, Emperor Constantine in the West and Lucinius in the East issued a joint decree demanding tolerance of all religions. In 380, Christianity became the official religion of the Roman Empire by the Edict of Theodosius I, and other religions were suppressed with varying degrees of harshness.

The divisions between the Eastern Orthodox and the Roman Catholic, which occurred early in the history of Christianity, and between the Protestant Reformation and the Catholic Church, which occurred in the sixteenth century, grew more out of political factors than any dispute over doctrine, though there are some doctrinal differences that are noteworthy. Early Christian communities apparently exhibited several types of leadership: elders, deacons, and bishops or patriarchs were all prominent. The overall organization among communities was loose at best. But when Christianity became the official religion of the Roman Empire, institutional organization became tighter, mirroring that of the Empire itself, with a bishop, or patriarch, as the head official in each major city. When Constantine moved his capital to Constantinople (modern Istanbul), a power vacuum was left in the West, which the patriarch of Rome filled, gradually gaining ascendency over other bishops in the West. It was this the "pope" who negotiated with the conquerors of Rome as the Roman Empire declined in the West. A similar concentration of ecclesiastical power did not occur in the East. The Eastern Orthodox and Roman Catholic Churches divided principally over the issue of the papacy. Each side found scriptural texts apparently in support of its stance. Differences in modes of worship—particularly in the use of Latin or Greek—also emerged. Doctrinally, the most important disagreement occurred concerning the nature of Jesus Christ as both human and divine. The Eastern Church emphasized Jesus' divinity, while the Western, his humanity. We may note that the topic of the mystery of the Trinity (God, Son, and Holy Spirit) was in general hotly debated in theological circles. For a sampling of the controversy, see the selection from Augustine under Divine Reality.

In 1517, Martin Luther (1483–1546) tacked his famous *Ninety-five Theses* on the door of the castle church in the German town of Wittenburg. This act has come to symbolize the inception of the Protestant Reformation, though there were precursors. Among the political factors contributing to the extensive rallying around Luther's protests were the growth of nationalism and a corresponding anti-papalism in England, France, Germany, and Bohemia, the financial burdens imposed by Rome on outlying parishes, and widespread condemnation of clerical excesses, particularly the selling of so-called indulgences that supposedly atoned in advance for contemplated sins. The Protestant movement threw almost the whole of Europe into war throughout most of the sixteenth and much of the early seventeenth centuries. The final divisions of Protestant and Catholic were mainly determined by the religious affiliation of the individual princes and kings who emerged victorious. France, for example, remained Catholic, and the numerous city-states of Germany formed a patchwork of Protestant and Catholic enclaves.

Despite the politics of the conflict's resolution, greater freedom of individual conscience was probably the most important outgrowth of the Reformation movement, considering in particular subsequent intellectual history. Concerning Christian doctrines, continuity was more pronounced than change, although central to Protestantism is defense of the freedom of the individual to interpret Scripture for herself or himself, a freedom denied in Catholicism. The principal Protestant churches continued to maintain trinitarianism, the two natures of Christ, and other longstanding doctrines such as the infallibility of Scripture as the result of the inspiration of the Holy Spirit. But there was one point of true revolution, centering on a new understanding of faith. Luther saw faith as the key to salvation, a faith that he understood not so much as a matter of intellectual assent as of personal trust. Others amplified, sometimes redirecting, this valuation. In the section Faith Against Reason, several selections reflect the new Protestant emphasis and understanding of faith.

Other developments in the history of Christianity blend with the larger material and intellectual history of Europe and the Americas, also Asia and Africa, where beginning as early as the sixteenth century there were vigorous missionary movements. These diminished in the twentieth century as African and Asian nations asserted their national independence, often identifying missionary work as threatening their cultural identities. The Americas, of course, became predominantly Christian—Protestant or Catholic—primarily according to the religious affiliation of colonists. Recently, there has been an Ecumenical movement both among Catholics and Protestants to further unity among Christians worldwide, and the emergence of Liberation Theology—mainly among priests in Latin America, who read the New Testament with the eyes of the poor and dispossessed and who call for wholesale social change.

Islam

Like Christianity and Buddhism, Islam has a historical founder, Muhammad (570–632), an illiterate orphan of the Arab Quraish tribe, a remarkable leader, whose inspired recitations became the Koran (or Quran), Scripture (the word of God), and who galvanized his followers to unite the Arab world under an Islamic banner, and, in time, vast populations primarily in Asia and Africa. According to Islamic tradition, after a marriage to a wealthy widow named Khadija at the age of twenty-five, Muhammad started going into the hills around Mecca to pray and meditate. There a series of revelations from God began, first a message conveyed by the angel Gabriel, later inspirations that came to him in sleep or ecstatic trance. These were Divine statements for which Muhammad was only a passive receiver. The word "Koran" means literally "recitation," and after Muhammad's death, his inspired recitations were collected to comprise holy writ. For Muslims (adherents to Islam), a secondary authority is the *hadīth,* or "sayings," attributed to Muhammad but not deemed the word of God.

Muhammad was aware of the teachings and practices of both Judaism and Christianity, as well as of an Arab religion that probably was predominant among the peoples of the Arabian peninsula at his time. He felt in particular called to revolutionize the religion of

Mecca, an important center of trade—an intercontinental crossroads—and a pilgrimage site even in pre-Islamic days. We know practically nothing about this religion except through the Koran and Islamic folklore, but scholars have constructed a fairly detailed picture. It was polytheistic, but a highest god, called Allah, was recognized. Lesser spirits included angels and *jinn* (genies), the latter usually hostile to humans. Mecca's religious importance was at least in part due to a large meteoric stone that had fallen there centuries earlier and that was regarded as sacred and capable of spiritually enlivening the totems of various tribal gods. A building known as the Kaaba housed the stone, and was full of totem symbols and sundry relics and objects deemed sacred by pilgrims. Muhammad with a message of strict monotheism ("There is no god but God") cleared away all the idols and relics, though he left the stone. This act is taken to be symbolic of his being recognized as God's prophet by the population at large.

Muhammad came to view himself and Judaism and Christianity as forming a single sacred lineage, with himself as the last or the "seal" of the prophets as well as a descendent of Abraham through Ishmael. (According to Islamic legend, Ishmael and his father built the Kaaba.) Before Muhammad, Jesus was the last and greatest prophet, whose mistake was to encourage worship of himself as God. Christian worship remained idolatrous. The Judaic revelations were incomplete. But the Gospel of Jesus, the Psalms of David, the Torah (in the sense of the Pentateuch) of Moses, and so on, were accepted truly as revelations, each the word of God which God had given previous prophets for the guidance of humanity. According to later Islamic theologians, not even the Koran exhausts the Word of God, considered eternal and uncreated. (Compare Philo's view of the Divine Logos, under Divine Reality, and the inclusivist polemics of the modern Islamic philosopher, S. H. Nasr, under Religious Pluralism.) Jews and Christians are "people of the Book" (i.e. the uncreated Divine Word), whose religious practices are thus due a respect not to be afforded to atheists, polytheists, animists, and the like. Nevertheless, Judaism and Christianity are obsolete, and Jews and Christians to be urged to see the Koran as superceding the earlier teachings.

Theologically, however, there is little departure from the core theism forged by Philo and the Greek Church Fathers, though there is considerable polishing and of course rejection of Christian trinitarianism. During a five-hundred-year ascendency of an Abbasid dynasty (750–1258) whose capital was Baghdad, scholarship and cosmopolitanism flourished, with Judaic, Eastern Christian, and Islamic theologians together debating the nature of God. Greek science was studied and improved upon; Plato and Aristotle were translated into Arabic; and, according to some, Islamic civilization reached a peak. Islamic savants travelled widely, from Persia to Spain, advising lesser princes and rulers and educating the Western world. The great Judaic philosopher Maimonides (1135–1204), for example, lived in Spain and yet wrote in Arabic. Is is not an overstatement to say that Islamic theologians such as Avicenna (980–1087) are as responsible as any for the cast of classical Western theism, whether Judaic, Christian, or Islamic. His and other Arabic works were studied closely by Christian scholars in the emerging culture of Europe. (See the selection from Avicenna, under Divine Reality.)

It is likely that, broadly considered, the history of Islam particularly after the decline of the Abbasids has more to do with political factors (such as the Christian Crusades to conquer Jerusalem, the emergence of the Mamelukan and then Ottoman Turks, the conquest of Egypt by Napoleon, and so on) than with any intellectual development. However, a conflict between the rationalist philosophers, such as Avicenna, and traditionalists, such as al-Ghazali (see under Mystical Experience)—a conflict that, it seems, the philosophers lost—may have had some bearing on the fundamentalist direction of much of subsequent Islam. Avicenna and his colleagues felt that both God and the world could be known through rational interpretations of sensory experience which did not conflict with a right reading of Scripture. Al-Ghazali upheld both scripture and mystical experience against reason, arguing (in the style of the philosophers though against their conclusions) that faith should not be placed in the human mind but rather in God.

The simplicity of Islamic teaching is striking. One does not have to form an opinion on hairsplitting doctrinal issues or achieve a personal transformation by long hours of meditation and prayer to be a good Muslim. The Arabic word *islam* in fact means simply "submission." In the religious sense, it is a faithful submission to a simple creed—"There is no god but God; Muhammad is God's messenger"—and the faithful performance of common practices of morality along with ritual prayer, almsgiving, and a few other observances that make a good Muslim—who is guaranteed by God the Just and Compassionate of a place in an eternal paradise.

On the other hand, sectarianism and departures from the mainstream within Islam should not be underestimated. Even the principal divisions, such as the Shiah and Sunni, are beyond our purview. But we should be mindful of the enormity of the Islamic phenomenon, which exhibits considerable diversity along most of the important dimensions of religion. For example, within the minority world of the Shiah there are views close to that of Christian—and Hindu—incarnationism (with the successors of the Prophet, called imams, thought to be imbued with Divine light, and deemed worthy of an absolute trust and devotion). There also developed throughout the Islamic world profound mysticism, called Sufism, where the goal in some cases has been not only to emulate the Prophet in having direct ecstatic communion with God, but to achieve union with God (compare the discussion of monistic mystical experience under Mystical Experience).

Hinduism

Hinduism and Buddhism, along with several less well-known religions and religious philosophies (such as Jainism and Yoga), have common cultural origins in the ancient and classical civilization of the South Asian Subcontinent. The Subcontinent is a rather natural geographic unit, bordered to the west by the mountains of Afghanistan, the Great Indian Desert, and the Arabian Sea, to the north and east by the Himalayas and the Bay of Bengal, and to the south by a vast expanse of the Indian Ocean. The Subcontinent includes what are now Pakistan, India, Bangladesh, and Nepal. The ancient and classical civilization, whose texts are largely in the language Sanskrit, produced religious, philosophical, literary, judicial, musical, and other traditions of arts and science, stretching, in some cases, for more than three thousand years.

Some of the religious beliefs and practices that grew up in this civilization are now called Hinduism. But the term "Hinduism" presents a difficulty. The words "Hindu" and

"Hinduism" are not Sanskrit, and they were not used by anyone to refer to his/her own religious identity until rather recently. Their usage derives from a contrast with Islam and the coming of Muslims to India, who arrived late in classical times. The word "Hindu" seems to have been first used by Arab traders of the ninth and tenth centuries to designate any person who lived near the Indus River. Then "Hindustan" came to be the Arabic word for greater India, and from Arabic to pass into wider usage. Until recently, all that distinguished Hinduism was a certain difficult-to-specify unity of culture in the Subcontinent before the Muslim invasion (c. 1100, earlier in the Sind and Punjab). Now in our global age, millions do think of themselves as Hindu, but Hinduism is still at best only an umbrella religion, with little overall unity.

Many if not most Hindus adhere to at least some of the social codes known as caste. A person's caste is a matter of birth. Caste is not very important now, unlike centuries ago, in restricting choice of occupation. But caste is still widespread considering marriage—who weds whom. On the other hand, there are many now who see themselves as Hindu and who have renounced caste entirely.

The problem of defining Hinduism is even more problematic with regard to religious beliefs. The dominant religious philosophy of Hinduism is theistic. But not only is the theism much more diverse and complex than any tradition of Western theology, many Hindus are outright atheists while others are Absolutists espousing an illusionism where only the One (called Brahman) is real. Some Hindu belief should be called polytheistic, and henotheism is a label that scholars of Hinduism are prone to use. This complexity will be sorted out in two subsections of the section Divine Reality, the first entitled Absolute Brahman, the second, Polytheism and Henotheism.

At the risk of oversimplification, let me say now that the dominant view is that the Absolute (= God) is both the stuff of all things and a determining will, loosing forth progressively forms of itself as gods and goddesses, human souls, plants and animals, and matter. Hindu theists choose to worship a Divine form—that is, god or goddess—that they see as best matching their personal dispositions and needs. Each god and goddess is thought to represent the one Supreme—scholars call this *henotheism.*

However, for the present it is probably best to think of Hinduism not in terms of such a religious philosophy—there are so many others—that is, not as defined by beliefs so much as by broader cultural developments and, in particular, certain social practices including caste. So considered, Hinduism emerges at about the same time as Buddhism, or a little earlier, that is to say, in the sixth and fifth centuries BCE. There is a considerable religious literature in Sanskrit stretching for four or five hundred years before this date, the Vedas and Upanishads, whose themes are broadly Hindu (see the first two selections under Absolute Brahman). But it is at the time of the (earliest stratum of) the Great Indian Epic, or *Mahābhārata*—around the sixth century BCE—that characteristic Hindu patterns of society become established. Moreover, probably the most revered religious text among the many scriptures of the Subcontinent is the *Bhagavad Gītā* ("Song of God": see the selection under Absolute Brahman). The *Gītā* is a portion of the Great Indian Epic.

"Right living," *dharma,* is the key concept in *Brāhminism,* a conservative strand of Hinduism, the strand most closely tied to the social regulations that define duties according to a person's caste, sex, age, and stage of life in general. Every Hindu—according to this now far from universally adhered-to prescription—is born into a particular caste and sub-caste, and along with gender, this brings with it far-reaching expectations about proper behavior. The most stringent expectations, and privileges, accrue to those born Brāhmins, the "priests," the highest of a fourfold classical division that includes Kṣatriyas, "warriors," Vaiśyas, "merchants," and Śūdras, "peasants." Over time other categories were added, as well as a perplexing variety of subcastes.

To focus on the classical rules for a Brāhmin to get just a taste of what these social regulations are like: a youngster is introduced to a ritual regimentation from birth, when his or her naming is carried out according to certain precepts. A sense of what constitutes sanctified behavior is instilled all through a child-rearing process, including such visible signs as tonsure and the wearing of a sacred thread.

Boys and girls have distinct *dharma*s, here "duties." A girl will, or should, become a loving and obedient wife and a good mother, and she develops the skills to make her husband happy—with whom, we may note, if *dharma* is upheld, she will enjoy a place in a blissful afterlife in a non-material heaven, and felicitous earthly rebirths for him, herself, and, with qualifications, her children. A more complex plan of life is enjoined for a male Brāhmin, traditionally broken into four stages, each with specific and characteristic rules:

(1) study

(2) marriage and "householding"

(3) "forest-dwelling," a period of retirement when there is preparation for death, and

(4) "world-renunciation," when a Brāhmin strives for "liberation" and cessation of the round of rebirths.

Here in particular the Brāhminical strand begins to blend with another, namely mysticism, which we shall review in a later paragraph.

A theory of *karma* ("action" or "disposition to act"—in other usages, "sacrifice" or "ritual performance") underlies and supports a Brāhminic concept of *dharma*. The thesis is that any course of action creates a psychological tendency—a habit, conceived as a real though unconscious force—to repeat it. One's life, one's status as well, thus becomes largely determined by one's unconscious dispositions to act, dispositions that continue even into a new birth. By performing actions, *karma,* in accordance with "duty," *dharma,* "the right way to live," thus making them in the Brāhminic conception all *karma* in the sense of "ritual performances," one develops the best sort of karmic disposition. In fact, actions in the exemplary case would all be prescribed sacrifices and rituals, and thus would instantiate *dharma,* here conceived as a substantive "Law" or "Way" (somewhat similar to the Chinese *tao:* see p. 15 below). Thus the exemplary Brāhmin's course of birth, marriage and householding, asceticism, death, and then rebirth in a heaven or on earth, would be guaranteed to be the best and most privileged course available, as it would instantiate the magical universal structure that is *dharma* in its highest sense, the "Cosmic Law."

Another important strand of Hinduism is its mysticism. In the section Mystical Experience, there are three selections from Hindu (or non-Buddhist Indian) sources along with introductory discussion. Here I shall be brief. In the *Gītā* and other religious texts—some as early as 800 BCE, that is in *Upanishads* (see the glossary entry) that precurse the *Gītā*—

the teaching centers on a mystical experience called liberation and enlightenment and, in Sanskrit, *brahma-vidyā,* "mystical knowledge of the Absolute, Brahman." Through meditation and various practices of *yoga,* one comes to know directly the Divine Reality. Mysticism is prominent in almost every development of the almost three thousand years of Indian religion since being first stressed in early Upanishads.

One final strand of Hinduism that I shall mention is a widespread devotionalism called *bhakti* ("love of God"). Devotional practices tie up theologically with Hindu henotheism, the view that the one supreme God animates various Divine forms. This notion is extended in an *avatāra* theory found in the *Gītā:* God assumes earthly births, while maintaining a native awareness, power, and bliss, whenever circumstances demand special intervention. In popular Hinduism, Jesus, Muhammad, Mahatma Gandhi, and even John F. Kennedy are sometimes worshiped as Avataras. In the *Gītā,* the warrior and hero of the larger epic, Krishna, reveals himself as a such a Divine person. Religious devotion, *bhakti,* is often focused on an Avatara, not only on a god or goddess. One prominent sect holds the Avataras to number precisely ten, with the last not yet having appeared. But in the long and diverse history of Hinduism, hundreds of persons have been regarded as, if not Avataras by birth, at least Avataras by works and by an enlightenment experience that have made them living and conscious vessels of the Divine.

Buddhism

A teaching of a mystical supreme good that has had enormous importance not only for the history of Indian religion but also Sri Lankan, Chinese, Korean, Japanese, Southeast Asian, and now also Western developments, belongs to the Buddha. The Buddha taught the supreme goal of life to be *nirvāṇa,* an "extinction" or "blowing out" of suffering and desire, and an awakening to what is most real. In Sanskrit, the word *buddha* means literally "awakened."

The Buddha was a historical person. He lived in the sixth century BCE in the Gangetic valley in what is now Nepal. He was born Siddhārtha Gautama of the Śākya clan. According to the oldest versions of his life, he was a prince destined to inherit his father's ruling mantle, leading as a young man a life of pleasure and enjoyment. In this he was encouraged by his father who feared a prophesy that his son would become a religious mendicant. The father tried to protect him from the sight of anything unpleasant or evil. But one day the Buddha-to-be journeyed some distance from the royal gardens and pleasure-grounds, and encountered first a diseased person, then a wrinkled and decrepit old man, and finally a corpse. (Buddhists view these conditions as the "three evils.") Inquiring about each in turn and being told that all persons are subject to such infirmities, the prince renounced his enjoyments, vowing to search tirelessly for the origin and cause of these evils and the power to root them out. His experience of enlightenment, or awakening, did not occur right away, however; he tried out various paths of asceticism before arriving at the Middle Way, a way of life he later proclaimed to disciples. Finally, after a long ordeal in meditation under a Bodhi tree, he achieved the *summum bonum,* an extinction of evil at its roots. The remainder of his life he spent travelling and preaching, helping others to reach the supreme good, called *nirvāṇa.*

The Buddha himself did not write anything, and we are left to reconstruct his teachings from disciples' writings. According to the Southern tradition, records of his sermons were kept, and during the reign of the Buddhist emperor Aśoka in the third century BCE an enormous canon sacred to Southern Buddhists was compiled. In the contemporary world, Southern Buddhism is prevalent in Sri Lanka, Burma, Thailand, and other parts of Southeast Asia. Northern Buddhism, known as Mahāyāna (prevalent in Nepal, Tibet, China, Korea, and Japan), recognizes a distinct literature as sacred, though it does not entirely reject the teachings of the Southern Canon. The distinct Mahāyāna literature was composed centuries after the oldest sections of the Southern Canon.

Though the Northern and Southern traditions should not be thought of as a schism, there have been, over the centuries, disputes about the Buddha's views. That a mystical enlightenment or awakening is possible and is the one possibility in life that should be sought is a thesis on which all Buddhists agree. Moreover, most accept doctrines known as The Four Noble Truths (though variously interpreted) as integral to the Buddha's teaching. These are:

(1) All is suffering;

(2) The root of suffering is desire, attachment, or personal clinging;

(3) There is a way to eliminate desire, and thereby eliminate suffering, namely, *nirvāṇa* experience;

(4) The experience is achieved by following The Eightfold Noble Path—right thought, right resolve, right speech, right conduct, right livelihood, right effort, right mindfulness, and right concentration or meditation.

Other core doctrines include "no soul" (*anātman*)—false identification with the body and the mind being an impediment to enlightenment—and "interdependent origination" (*pratītya-samutpāda*), a causal doctrine, variously interpreted, that apparently would underpin teachings about the way to enlightenment. It is the way to enlightenment that is the greatest preoccupation of the literature that seems the most directly influenced by the Buddha, much of which is ethical in tone and concerned with requirements of a mystic path. In the subsection entitled The Vibrant Void, Emptiness, of the section, Divine Reality, we shall closely survey ideas about what the reality is like that is, according to Buddhists, revealed by the enlightenment experience at the core of all Buddhist teaching.

Anticipating that discussion, we may look now at a personalistic dimension of what is probably the principal intellectual or doctrinal division between Northern and Southern Buddhists. According to the schools of Southern Buddhism, the "saint," *arhat,* loses all individual personality in a universal, impersonal, unconceptualizable bliss and awareness that somehow underlies all appearance. According to Mahāyāna Buddhism in contrast, the truest aim is to become a *bodhisattva,* who, unlike the Arhat, turns back from the final Bliss and extinction of personality in *nirvāṇa* to help every conscious being attain it. From the perspective of a Mahāyānist, the Southern Canon presents, by and large, a course of spiritual discipline and a goal that are not the best and highest since they are personally oriented. If one strives for one's own personal salvation alone, intending to have no career (*yāna*) helping others to the supreme good, one would belong to the Hīnayāna, and would be "one with no career," a term used by Mahāyānists in deprecation of such a path. Mahāyānists, "those with wide and great careers," in contrast, seek not only their own personal salvation but "deliverance of every sentient being from suffering and ignorance." A follower of this, the wide path attempts to acquire six moral, intellectual, and spiritual perfections (*pāramitā;* see the selection from the *Surangama Sūtra* under Divine Reality) considered possessed by the Buddha. He or she endeavors to become a bodhisattva, a person who has one foot in the bliss of *nirvāṇa,* so to say, but who is naturally turned through compassion toward the welfare of all beings.

Buddhism matured in India for about a thousand years before being exported to China. There, and in other Eastern cultures, it took on some color and flavor according to local customs. However, Chinese pilgrims from about the sixth century CE often travelled to India to visit shrines and to study and translate Buddhist texts. And now of course Buddhism, though diminished in the East, has become a global phenomenon.

Chinese Religion

Religious practices were as prevalent in ancient Chinese civilization as in other early cultures. Evidence of early Chinese religious beliefs consists chiefly of inscriptions on oracle bones and bronze sacrificial vessels dating to a period (1500–1050 BCE) prior to the unification of China under the Chou dynasty (1050 BCE). Prominent is the notion of a Supreme Lord who presides over an afterlife kingdom including human souls as well as lesser deities that govern rain, wind, rivers, and other natural phenomena. Under Chou, the anthropomorphic notion of a Supreme Lord apparently gave way to that of an impersonal Heaven. Chou emperors claimed the right to rule as the "mandate of Heaven."

Confucius (551–479 BCE) may be taken to be the first great Chinese philosopher shaping not only much of the course of Chinese thought but also determining much in Chinese government and morals, a veritable father of Chinese culture. Confucius speaks often of Heaven but never mentions a Supreme Lord. His teaching stresses the importance of religious ritual for personal character development (see the selection from A. C. Graham under Religion and Ethics) and views Heaven as grounding the moral law. But Confucius's philosophy is decidedly humanist, oriented to questions about social and political relations and containing little that is expressly theological.

Taoism, which stretches back almost as far as Confucianism, is both a religion and a philosophy. As a philosophy it has to be understood within a broadly Confucian context. It is a reaction to the Confucian outlook, a championing of the individual and the reclusive against a Confucian insistence on right social practice. The individual has connections to the universe's spiritual ground, called *tao,* that society does not. The individual transcends society. A subsection of the section Divine Reality surveys Taoist philosophy with selections from the earliest Taoist texts.

Taoism developed alongside Confucianism as a philosophy, and, in later centuries, alongside and competing with Buddhism as an official religion of the Chinese state. Taoist rituals, a priestly order, temples, a pantheon of gods and goddesses, and a series of later scriptural revelations gave Taoism the multiple dimensions characteristic of what some call world religions or the high religions. Mysticism, centering on a vital force called *ch'i,* was also prominent during the later Chinese dynasties. And there was much mutual influence among Taoism and Buddhism. In particular Zen Buddhism, which originated in China and is now prominent in Japan, incorporates Taoist pastoral and anti-intellectual themes.

African and Amerindian Religion

With the exception of Mayan writing, which has been deciphered recently, there are no texts of either African or Amerindian religion that predate the excursions into the Americas of European conquistadors and colonizers and into sub-Saharan Africa of Muslim and Christian traders and missionaries and, later, colonizers. Many of the post-Columbian texts in the Americas and texts post-contact with Islam and Christianity in Africa are colored by missionary polemics—although we find in the case of Zera Yacob, an astute Ethiopian philosopher of the seventeenth century (whose writing is excerpted in the section Religion and Ethics), insistence on an ethical perspective from which the teachings of Christianity and Islam are rightly criticized. And of course there are many modern African philosophers whose views transcend the presuppositions of whatever religion. Nevertheless, with regard to the vast and diverse religious phenomena of the American and (sub-Saharan) African continents, archeology and anthropology assume premier importance, that is, respecting pre-modern times. Currently there are few in Africa practicing religions other than Christianity, Islam, Judaism (principally in Ethiopia), and Hinduism (in eastern and southern Africa). It is estimated that practitioners of other religions now number less than ten percent of the sub-Saharan population. Practice of native Amerindian religion is now similarly not widespread.

Thus because of various factors, concepts and claims of pre-modern African and Amerindian religions cannot have a prominent place in an introductory philosophy of religion textbook such as this. That may be unfortunate, because especially with respect to mysticism these religions may well have much to offer philosophic reflection (see in particular works by Mircea Eliade and Wade Davis, under "Mysticism" in the Guide to Further Reading). But our purview has to be largely determined by the major traditions and by philosophic *texts* (as opposed to oral folklore, etc.), texts focused on religious claims, although we shall not ignore African and Amerindian religion entirely. In the section Divine Reality, there is a selection from the Ghanian philosopher, Kwame Gyekye, who reconstructs from oral accounts and observations of religious ceremonies the religious belief system of the Akan, a prominent Ghanian tribe. And in the section Religion and Ethics, we shall look at the work of philosophers J. B. Callicott and Thomas Overholt who champion traditional Amerindian religious attitudes as possible resources for a new environmental ethic—as well as at the writings of the Ethiopian Zera Yacob as already mentioned. But compared with the amount of attention paid to Christian theology, Buddhist philosophy, and so forth, it may seem as though African and Amerindian religious claims and concepts are given here short shrift. Again, this is an introductory textbook in philosophy of religion, not in the study of religion, where African and Amerindian religions would naturally call for much more detailed treatment. See the Guide to Further Reading.

CHAPTER ONE

Divine Reality

GOD

The three great Western religions—Judaism, Christianity, and Islam—embrace *theism* as the core of a doctrinal system. Theism with respect to the great Western religions may be taken to be equivalent to *monotheism;* that is to say, the proposition that there is a single God is central to the theism of Judaism, Christianity, and Islam. Two further claims embraced by mainstream Western theists are: (a) God is the creator of the universe, and (b) God is the supremely excellent or perfect being and thus the sole being worthy of unqualified adoration or worship. Other doctrines fill out a picture of God by providing details of God's relation to the universe or details of God's intrinsic nature apart from the world.

Theism advanced alongside wider developments in the history of Judaism, Christianity, and Islam. Theistic theory was expressed by theologians drawing on scriptural revelation and on philosophic reflection, in particular that of the early Greek reasoners, Plato (427–347 BCE) and Aristotle (384–322 BCE). Jewish, Christian, and Muslim philosophers integrated a theological inheritance into a more tightly unified view or innovated or clarified a method of thinking about God.

In the modern period, there has been much concern with *conceptual atheism,* the position that God as traditionally conceived is impossible, like a "square circle." Conceptual atheism differs from *factual atheism* in the latter's conceding the possibility of God but denying that God exists in fact.

A related debate occurs between advocates of *classical theism* and *process theology.* Subscribers to the process view contend that the classical view of God is incoherent, that is, that there is no possibility of God as traditionally conceived, whereas the process view does not suffer such a devastating defect. Defenders of classical theism thus try to show the possibility of God as traditionally conceived. Three voices in this controversy that we shall listen to are those of Richard Gale, Charles Hartshorne, and William Alston.

Biblical Theology

From the Bible, Revised Standard Version, 1952

The first readings in this section are taken from the Bible, from both the Old and New Testaments as delineated in Christianity and thus including some of Judaic scripture. The Bible does not present a theoretically refined view of God. The attributes of God that come to be spelled out by philosophers and theologians—omnipotence, omniscience, and omnibenevolence (lovingness), and so forth—are not explicitly declared in the words of the Bible itself. Nevertheless, most of the attributes traditionally ascribed to God are grounded in various "proof-texts," some of which are presented here.

As noted, in modern philosophy—also in some pre-modern thinking—concern is expressed whether all that is traditionally said about God could possibly be true. That is to say, is every attribute traditionally ascribed consistent or compatible with every other? Is God's holiness compatible with omnipotence? Can God sin? And if God cannot, is God omnipotent? The Bible does not concern itself with such questions. In fact, there are passages—particularly in Job and Isaiah (see certain of the following selections)—where it is implied that such questioning would be impertinent and those asking them impudent at best.

GOD AS ALMIGHTY

When Abram was ninety-nine years old the Lord appeared to Abram, and said to him, "I
   am God Almighty; walk before me, and be blameless."
(Genesis 17.1)

The Lord makes poor and makes rich;
he brings low, he also exalts.
He raises up the poor from the dust;
he lifts the needy from the ash heap,
to make them sit with princes
and inherit a seat of honor.
For the pillars of the earth are the Lord's,
and on them he has set the world. (1 Samuel 2.7–8)

Jesus looked at them and said, "With men it is impossible, but not with God; for all things
   are possible with God." (Mark 10.27)

GOD AS ALL-KNOWING

. . . he looks to the ends of the earth,
and sees everything under the heavens. (Job 28.24)

Great is our Lord, and abundant in power;
his understanding is beyond measure. (Psalms 147.5)

GOD AS ETERNAL

> For thus says the high and lofty One
> who inhabits eternity, whose name is Holy; . . . (Isaiah 57.15)

GOD AS OMNIPRESENT

> Whither shall I go from thy Spirit?
> Or whither shall I flee from thy presence?
> If I ascend to heaven, thou art there!
> If I make my bed in Sheol,
> thou art there! (Psalms 139.7–8)

GOD AS ONE, SINGLE

> I am the Lord, and there is no other,
> besides me there is no God . . . (Isaiah 45.5)

> . . . there is no God but one. (1 Corinthians 8.4)

GOD AS TRANSCENDENT AND HOLY

> To whom then will you liken God,
> or what likeness compare with him? . . .
> Have you not known? Have you not heard?
> Has it not been told you from the beginning?
> Have you not understood from the foundations of the earth?
> It is he who sits above the circle of the earth,
> and its inhabitants are like grasshoppers; . . .
> To whom then will you compare me,
> that I should be like him?
> says the Holy One.
> Lift up your eyes on high and see:
> who created these? . . . (Isaiah 40.18, 21–22, 25–26)

GOD AS MERCIFUL, LOVING

> For the mountains may depart and the hills be removed,
> but my steadfast love shall not depart from you,
> and my covenant of peace shall not be removed,
> says the Lord, who has compassion on you. (Isaiah 54.10)

> . . . God is love. (1 John 4.16)

Platonic Theology: God as Immutably Good and as the Creator Insuring Harmony

From *The Republic, The Timaeus,* and *The Laws* by Plato in *The Dialogues of Plato,* B. Jowett, translator, 1892

Among classical Greek thinkers, Plato (427–347 BCE) may be credited with originating a moral theism roughly in the monotheistic sense appropriate to the great Western religions. Although Plato sometimes uses the plural 'Gods', he usually does not mean to refer to the popular gods of Olympus but to the Divine, single in nature as perfectly good. Plato's idea of God is that God is the supreme exemplar of righteousness and beauty, who through contemplation of absolute value is moved to create harmony among finite things. Probably Plato's greatest theological contribution is his rejection of the stories of immoral gods of Olympus—with their lusts, jealousies, quarrels, and so forth—in favor of a view of a thoroughly moral Divine.

Now although God transcends the universe, so too for Plato does the Ideal Good (said to be equivalent to Ideal Beauty). The Good as a Form or Ideal is independent of God (see also the selection from Plato under Mysticism). Thus in Plato's view, unlike the mainstream theology of later Western religions, God is responsible for certain actualities but not for possibilities. Ideals or Forms delineate possibilities separately from the creative activity of God. The possibility of a human being, for example, exists eternally as a Form, namely, as the Humanity Form, which is exemplified in individual human beings. The Form underpins our knowledge of particular individuals as all human, as all creatures of the same type. For Plato, God exemplifies the Good and is guided by it in arranging the harmonies of our world.

Concerning a question of the mutability of God, Plato appears to be of two minds. In his earlier writings, the emphasis is on immutability, the unchangeableness of God's nature as perfectly good. But in his later writings, the emphasis is on God's stewardship and care for all things great or small. Presumably, God's knowledge of the interactions of finite things compels a view of God (or at least of God's knowledge) as changing as things change, although God's concern and care for this world may be said to be constant. Classical Western theism, we may note, insists on an absolute immutability of God, whereas process theism (as in the view of Charles Hartshorne) insists on the changeableness of God corresponding to worldly changes.

Later Western orthodoxy has viewed God's creation as "out of nothing" (ex nihilo). Plato, in contrast, views matter as pre-existing, or eternal, like God. In creating, God shapes matter according to the Forms. Some followers of Plato (called Neoplatonists) embrace a third view, emanationism, a creationist doctrine that is endorsed by Avicenna (see p. 40) and other rationalists as opposed to creationists within Islamic theology, and that resonates with Indian theism (see Absolute Brahman). It is the Judaic theologian Philo who, though often following Plato, established as orthodox the "creation ex nihilo" view.

The first passage excerpted—from the Republic—*may be taken as an argument for the immutability of God, with the crucial, and most controversial, premise that any change in*

God be only for the worst. That supposition is backed up in turn by the view that any will to change would betray a deficiency (and God, of course, has no deficiency). In the next excerpt—from the Timaeus—*Plato puts forth his conception of God's creation as the "fairest and best." In the excerpt from the* Laws, *Plato, in the voice of an "Athenian," articulates a view of the ordering of parts with respect to the good of the whole, arguing that God though not negligent of anything great or small arranges things for the "excellence of the whole."*

FROM *THE REPUBLIC*

. . . Do you think that God is a magician, and of a nature to appear insidiously now in one shape, and now in another—sometimes really changing and passing into many forms, sometimes deceiving us with the semblance of such transformations; or is he one and the same immutably fixed in his own proper image?

I [Adeimantus] cannot answer you, he said, without more thought.

Well, I [Socrates] said; but if we suppose a change in anything, that change must be effected either by the thing itself, or by some other thing?

Most certainly.

And things which are at their best are also least liable to be altered or discomposed; for example, when healthiest and strongest, the human frame is least liable to be affected by meats and drinks and fatigue, and the plant which is in the fullest vigour also suffers least from winds or the heat of the sun or any similar causes.

Of course.

And will not the bravest and wisest soul be least confused or deranged by any external influence?

True.

And the same principle, as I should suppose, applies to all composite things—furniture, houses, garments: when good and well made, they are least altered by time and circumstances.

Very true.

Then everything which is good, whether made by art or nature, or both, is least liable to suffer change from without?

True.

But surely God and the things of God are in every way perfect?

Of course they are.

Then he can least of all be compelled by external influence to take many shapes?

Certainly.

But may he not change and transform himself?

Clearly, he said, that must be the case if he is changed at all.

And will he then change himself for the better and fairer, or for the worse and more unsightly?

If he change at all he can only change for the worse, for we cannot suppose him to be deficient either in virtue or beauty.

Very true, Adeimantus; but then, would anyone, whether God or man, in your opinion deliberately make himself worse in any respect?

Impossible.

Then it is impossible that God should ever be willing to change; being, as is supposed, the fairest and best that is conceivable, every one of the gods remains absolutely and for ever in his own form.

That necessarily follows, he said, in my judgement.

FROM *THE TIMAEUS*

TIMAEUS: Let me tell you then why the creator made this world of generation. He was good, and the good can never have any jealousy of anything. And being free from jealousy, he desired that all things should be as like himself as they could be. This is in the truest sense the origin of creation and of the world, as we shall do well in believing on the testimony of wise men: God desired that all things should be good and nothing bad, so far as this was attainable. Wherefore also finding the whole visible sphere not at rest, but moving in an irregular and disorderly fashion, out of disorder he brought order, considering that this was in every way better than the other. Now the deeds of the best could never be or have been other than the fairest; and the creator, reflecting on the things which are by nature visible, found that no unintelligent creature taken as a whole could ever be fairer than the intelligent taken as a whole; and again that intelligence could not be present in anything which was devoid of soul. For which reason, when he was framing the universe, he put intelligence in soul, and soul in body, that he might be the creator of a work which was by nature fairest and best. On this wise, using the language of probability, we may say that the world came into being—a living creature truly endowed with soul and intelligence by the providence of God.

FROM *THE LAWS*

ATHENIAN: Surely God must not be supposed to have a nature which He Himself hates?—he who dares to say this sort of thing must not be tolerated for a moment.

KLEINIAS: Of course not. How could He have?

ATHENIAN: Should we not on any principle be entirely mistaken in praising anyone who has some special business entrusted to him, if he have a mind which takes care of great matters and no care of small ones? Reflect; he who acts in this way, whether he be God or man, must act from one of two principles.

KLEINIAS: What are they?

ATHENIAN: Either he must think that the neglect of the small matters is of no consequence to the whole, or if he knows that they are of consequence, and he neglects them, his neglect must be attributed to carelessness and indolence. Is there any other way in which his neglect can be explained? For surely, when it is impossible for him to take care of all, he is not negligent if he fails to attend to those things great or small, which a God or some inferior being might be wanting in strength or capacity to manage? . . .

. . . Sensation and power are in an inverse ratio to each other in respect to their ease and difficulty.

KLEINIAS: What do you mean?

ATHENIAN: I mean that there is greater difficulty in seeing and hearing the small than the great, but more facility in moving and controlling and taking care of small and unimportant things than of their opposites.

KLEINIAS: Far more.

ATHENIAN: Suppose the case of a physician who is willing and able to cure some living thing as a whole—how will the whole fare at his hands if he takes care only of the greater and neglects the parts which are lesser?

KLEINIAS: Decidedly not well.

ATHENIAN: No better would be the result with pilots or generals, or householders or statesmen, or any other such class, if they neglected the small and regarded only the great;—as the builders say, the larger stones do not lie well without the lesser.

KLEINIAS: Of course not.

ATHENIAN: Let us not, then, deem God inferior to human workmen, who, in proportion to their skill, finish and perfect their works, small as well as great, by one and the same art; or that God, the wisest of beings, who is both willing and able to take care, is like a lazy good-for-nothing, or a coward, who turns his back upon labour and gives no thought to smaller and easier matters, but to the greater only.

KLEINIAS: Never, Stranger, let us admit a supposition about the Gods which is both impious and false.

ATHENIAN: I think that we have now argued enough with him who delights to accuse the Gods of neglect.

KLEINIAS: Yes.

ATHENIAN: He has been forced to acknowledge that he is in error, but he still seems to me to need some words of consolation.

KLEINIAS: What consolation will you offer him?

ATHENIAN: Let us say to the youth:—The ruler of the universe has ordered all things with a view to the excellence and preservation of the whole, and each part, as far as may be, has an action and passion appropriate to it. Over these, down to the least fraction of them, ministers have been appointed to preside, who have wrought out their perfection with infinitesimal exactness. And one of these portions of the universe is thine own, unhappy man, which, however little, contributes to the whole; and you do not seem to be aware that this and every other creation is for the sake of the whole, and in order that the life of the whole may be blessed; and that you are created for the sake of the whole, and not the whole for the sake of you. For every physician and every skilled artist does all things for the sake of the whole, directing his effort toward the common good, executing the part for the sake of the whole, and not the whole for the sake of the part. . . .

true is a
simple q-a

Classical Theism (Judaism)

From *On the Allegories of the Sacred Laws, On the Posterity of Cain, On the Account of the World's Creation Given by Moses* by Philo in *The Works of Philo Judaeus,* C. D. Yonge, translator, 1909

Philo Judaeus, also known as Philo of Alexandria (20 BCE–40 CE), was born into a wealthy and prominent family in Alexandria when that city was a center of Hellenistic culture. Philo became steeped in both Judaism and Greek philosophy. Though it appears he did not know Hebrew, Judaic scripture had been translated into Greek by his time. By drawing mainly on themes from Plato as well from the Torah, Philo forged a synthetic theism which he expressed in voluminous writings. These include an influential commentary on Scripture, now lost but studied by early theologians of the Christian Church. Philo may be counted as the first Western classical theist, a thinker of the first class responsible for the earliest articulation of much that became orthodox within Judaism, Christianity, and Islam.

For Philo, God is absolutely simple in the sense of non-composite. Thus God does not change because there is no variety in God's nature. Moreover, God transcends time. God also transcends the Forms that God uses as a pattern in creating the visible world. Here the theologian departs from Plato. According to Philo, creation occurred in two stages. First, God created the Forms as well as matter out of nothing; then God created the visible world according to the Forms. Before the second stage of creation, the Forms existed as ideas in the mind of God. Afterward, they were exemplified in objects. Philo calls the mind of God the Word (logos), and it appears to be his innovation to locate the Forms there. The Word is not only the pattern of creation but also the archetype of human reason. This view of Philo's became enormously influential in Christianity—witness the (Greek-composed) Gospel of John: "In the beginning was the Word (logos), and the Word was with God, and the Word was God."

The implicit tension between the view of God as absolutely simple or non-composite in nature on the one hand, and God's mind as filled with Forms, on the other, does not appear to be addressed by Philo. It is addressed, however, by later Christian theologians such as Augustine, who talks about it as part of the problem of understanding God as a Trinity (see the discussion of Augustine on p. 28).

There is a prominent strand of negative theology in Philo's thinking. While humans may know the Forms—that is, the Divine Mind—it is impossible to know what God is in Himself, God's essence. Moreover, we know God's existence, but this too, is distinct from his essence. In other words, we know that God is, but we know not what God is. Our ability to comprehend essences stops with the Forms, and God is transcendent to these and, indeed, to everything. "Nowhere is there His likeness." Philo seems to have originated—in Greek thought at least—the view that God, though knowable as existing, is ineffable and indescribable in Himself. Later, another Judaic philosopher, Maimonides (see Religious Language), develops a theory of predication in consonance with Philo's negative theological view.

*Philo talks about the Word (*logos*) in a second sense, namely as revealed Scripture. Philo believes that we can infer the existence of God from natural observations and thus attain an indirect knowledge. A more direct knowledge of God comes by divine inspiration apparently mediated by the Word in the sense of Scripture.*

FROM *ON THE ALLEGORIES OF THE SACRED LAWS*

"And the Lord God said, It is not good for man to be alone: let us make him a help meet for him." Why, O prophet, is it not good for man to be alone? Because, says he, it is good, that he who is alone should be alone. But God is alone, and by himself, being one; and there is nothing like unto God. So that, since it is good that he who only has a real existence should be alone (for that which is about itself alone is good), it cannot be good for man to be alone. But the fact of God being alone one may receive in this sense; that neither before the creation was there anything with God, nor, since the world has been created, is anything placed in the same rank with him; for he is in need of absolutely nothing whatever.

But the better way of understanding this passage is the following: God is alone: a single being: not a combination: a single nature: but each of us, and every other animal in the world, are compound beings: for instance, I myself am made up of many things, of soul and body. Again, the soul is made up of a rational part and an irrational part: also of the body, there is one part hot, another cold; one heavy, another light; one dry, another moist. But God is not a compound being, nor one which is made up of many parts, but one which has no mixture with anything else; for whatever could be combined with God must be either superior to him, or inferior to him, or equal to him. But there is nothing equal to God, and nothing superior to him, and nothing is combined with him which is worse than himself; for if it were, he himself would be deteriorated; and if he were to suffer deterioration, he would also become perishable, which it is impious even to imagine. Therefore God exists according to oneness and unity; or we should rather say, that oneness exists according to the one God, for all number is more recent than the world, as is also time. But God is older than the world, and is its Creator.

FROM *ON THE POSTERITY OF CAIN*

For the great Cause of all things does not exist in time, nor at all in place, but he is superior to both time and place; for, having made all created things in subjection to himself, he is surrounded by nothing, but he is superior to everything. And being superior to, and being also external to the world that he has made, he nevertheless fills the whole world with himself; for, having by his own power extended it to its utmost limits, he has connected every portion with another portion according to the principles of harmony.

When, therefore, the soul that loves God seeks to know what the one living God is according to his essence, it is entering upon an obscure and dark subject of investigation, from which the greatest benefit that arises to it is to comprehend that God, as to his essence, is utterly incomprehensible to any being, and also to be aware that he is invisible. . . .

. . . the whole heaven was made by God; and the maker always goes before that which is made. So that, of necessity, not only the other things which exist among us, but also that which has the most rapid motion of all, namely, the mind, may fall short of a proper comprehension of the great cause of all things by an undescribable distance.

But the stars, as they are themselves in motion, pass by all things that move; but, though it seems incredible, God, while standing still, outstrips everything. And it is said that he, at the same moment, is close to us and at a great distance, touching us with his creative or his punishing powers, which are close to each individual, and yet at the same time driving away the creature to an excessive distance from his nature as existing according to its essence, so that it cannot touch him without even the unalloyed and incorporeal efforts of the intellect. Therefore we sympathise in joy with those who love God and seek to understand the nature of the living God, even if they fail to discover it; for the vague investigation of what is good is sufficient by itself to cheer the heart, even if it fail to attain the end that it desires. . . .

FROM *ON THE ACCOUNT OF THE WORLD'S CREATION GIVEN BY MOSES*

We must mention as much as we can of the matters contained in his account, since to enumerate them all is impossible; for he embraces that beautiful world which is perceptible only by the intellect, as the account of the first day will show: for God, as apprehending beforehand, as a God must do, that there could not exist a good imitation without a good model, and that of the things perceptible to the external senses nothing could be faultless which was not fashioned with reference to some archetypal idea conceived by the intellect, when he had determined to create this visible world, previously formed that one which is perceptible only by the intellect, in order that so using an incorporeal model formed as far as possible on the image of God. He might then make this corporeal world, a younger likeness of the elder creation, which should embrace as many different genera perceptible to the external senses, as the other world contains of those which are visible only to the intellect.

But that world which consists of ideas, it were impious in any degree to attempt to describe or even to imagine: but how it was created, we shall know if we take for our guide a certain image of the things which exist among us.

When any city is founded through the exceeding ambition of some king or leader who lays claim to absolute authority, and is at the same time a man of brilliant imagination, eager to display his good fortune, then it happens at times that some man coming up who, from his education, is skilful in architecture, and he, seeing the advantageous character and beauty of the situation, first of all sketches out in his own mind nearly all the parts of the city which is about to be completed—the temples, the gymnasia, the prytanea, the markets, the harbour, the docks, the streets, the arrangement of the walls, the situations of the dwelling houses, and of the public and other buildings. Then, having received in his own mind, as on a waxen tablet, the form of each building, he carries in his heart the image of a city, perceptible as yet only by the intellect, the images of which he stirs up in memory which is innate in him, and, still further, engraving them in his mind like a good workman, keeping his eyes fixed on his model, he begins to raise the city of stones and wood, making the corporeal substances to resemble each of the incorporeal ideas. Now we must form a somewhat similar opinion of God, who, having determined to found a mighty state, first of all conceived its form in his mind, according to which form he made a world perceptible only by the intellect, and then completed one visible to the external senses, using the first one as a model.

As therefore, the city, when previously shadowed out in the mind of the man of architectural skill had no external place, but was stamped solely in the mind of the workman, so in the same manner neither can the world which existed in ideas have had any other local position except the divine reason which made them; for what other place could there be for his powers which should be able to receive and contain, I do not say all, but even any single one of them whatever, in its simple form? And the power and faculty which could be capable of creating the world, has for its origin that good which is founded on truth; for if any one were desirous to investigate the cause on account of which this universe was created, I think that he would come to no erroneous conclusion if he were to say as one of the ancients did say: "That the Father and Creator was good; on which account he did not grudge the substance a share of his own excellent nature, since it had nothing good of itself, but was able to become everything." For the substance was of itself destitute of arrangement, of quality, of animation, of distinctive character, and full of all disorder and confusion; and it received a change and transformation to what is opposite to this condition, and most excellent, being invested with order, quality, animation, resemblance, identity, arrangement, harmony, and everything which belongs to the more excellent idea.

And God, not being urged on by any prompter (for who else could there have been to prompt him?) but guided by his own sole will, decided that it was fitting to benefit with unlimited and abundant favours a nature which, without the divine gift, was unable of itself to partake of any good thing; but he benefits it, not according to the greatness of his own graces, for they are illimitable and eternal, but according to the power of that which is benefited to receive his graces. For the capacity of that which is created to receive benefits does not correspond to the natural power of God to confer them; since his powers are infinitely greater, and the thing created being not sufficiently powerful to receive all their greatness would have sunk under it, if he had not measured his bounty, allotting to each, in due proportion, that which was poured upon it. And if any one were to desire to use more undisguised terms, he would not call the world, which is perceptible only to the intellect, any thing else but the *reason* of God, already occupied in the creation of the world; for neither is a city, while only perceptible to the intellect, anything else but the *reason* of the architect, who is already designing to build one perceptible to the external senses, on the model of that which is so only to the intellect—this is the doctrine of Moses, not mine. Accordingly he, when recording the creation of man, in words which follow, asserts expressly, that he was made in the image of God—and if the image be a part of the image, then manifestly so is the entire form, namely, the whole of this world perceptible by the external senses, which is a greater imitation of the divine image than the human form is. It is manifest also, that the *archetypal seal,* which we call that world which is perceptible only to the intellect, must itself be the *archetypal model,* the idea of ideas, the Reason of God.

Classical Theism (Christianity)

From *The City of God* and *Confessions* by Augustine in *Saint Augustine*, Marcus Dods, translator, 1872

Saint Augustine (354–430), a late Church Father or founder of Christian doctrine, was, like Philo, learned both with respect to religious teachings and to Greek philosophy, which he, as an African-born Roman citizen, studied in Latin translation. Plato, among pre-Christian Greeks, had decidedly the most influence on Augustine, as he did too with other Fathers of the Church. Augustine made several outstanding contributions to Christian theism, but his fame is perhaps mostly due to his standing as the last great Christian theologian before Rome fell to the Vandals (455). Augustine was a prolific writer, renowned for masterful prose (especially in his Confessions *where he recounts a less than saintly early life) as well as for his breadth and depth as a theistic philosopher.*

The selections excerpted concern, first, God's unity and simplicity of nature in the context of the Christian teaching of the Trinity (God as Father, Son, and Holy Spirit), and, second, God's eternality and, in general, the nature of time. Augustine faces a challenging problem to defend God's simplicity in the face of the Christian commitment to a Trinity, but he manages, through insisting on God's incorruptibility or unchangeableness, to show a disanalogy that helps him make his case: God is what God is incorruptibly whereas a body can lose its color or a cup what it holds. With God's eternality, the problem concerns less the nature of God than the meaningfulness of viewing creation as occurring at a specific time. What could be before, in the sense of a temporal series, creation itself? Augustine sees God's being eternal and before creation as a matter of God's timelessness, not as God's standing at an earlier point in a series.

FROM *THE CITY OF GOD*

OF THE SIMPLE AND UNCHANGEABLE TRINITY, FATHER, SON, AND HOLY GHOST, ONE GOD, IN WHOM SUBSTANCE AND QUALITY ARE IDENTICAL

There is, accordingly, a good which is alone simple, and therefore alone unchangeable, and this is God. By this Good have all others been created, but not simple, and therefore not unchangeable. "Created," I say,—that is, made, not begotten. For that which is begotten of the simple Good is simple as itself, and the same as itself. These two we call the Father and the Son; and both together with the Holy Spirit are one God; and to this Spirit the epithet Holy is in Scripture, as it were, appropriated. And He is another than the Father and the Son, for He is neither the Father nor the Son. I say "another," not "another thing," because He is equally with them the simple Good, unchangeable and co-eternal. And this Trinity is one God; and none the less simple because a Trinity. For we do not say that the nature of the good is simple, because the Father alone possesses it, or the Son alone, or the Holy Ghost alone; nor do we say, with the Sabellian heretics, that it is only nominally a Trinity, and has no real distinction of persons; but we say it is simple, because it is what it has, with the exception of the relation of the persons to one another. For, in regard to this relation, it is true that the Father has a Son, and yet is not Himself the Son; and the Son has a Father, and is not Himself the Father. But, as regards Himself, irrespective of relation to the other, each is what He has; thus, He is in Himself living, for He has life, and is Himself the Life which He has.

It is for this reason, then, that the nature of the Trinity is called simple, because it has not anything which it can lose, and because it is not one thing and its contents another, as a cup and the liquor, or a body and its colour, or the air and the light or heat of it, or a mind and its wisdom. For none of these is what it has: the cup is not liquor, nor the body colour, nor the air light and heat, nor the mind wisdom. And hence they can be deprived of what they have, and can be turned or changed into other qualities and states, so that the cup may be emptied of the liquid of which it is full, the body be discoloured, the air darken, the mind grow silly. The incorruptible body which is promised to the saints in the resurrection cannot, indeed, lose its quality of incorruption, but the bodily substance and the quality of incorruption are not the same thing. For the quality of incorruption resides entire in each several part, not greater in one and less in another; for no part is more incorruptible than another. The body, indeed, is itself greater in whole than in part; and one part of it is larger, another smaller, yet is not the larger more incorruptible than the smaller. The body, then, which is not in each of its parts a whole body, is one thing; incorruptibility, which is throughout complete, is another thing;—for every part of the incorruptible body, however unequal to the rest otherwise, is equally incorrupt. For the hand, *e.g.,* is not more incorrupt than the finger because it is larger than the finger; so, though finger and hand are unequal, their incorruptibility is equal. Thus, although incorruptibility is inseparable from an incorruptible body, yet the substance of the body is one thing, the quality of incorruption another. And therefore the body is not what it has. The soul itself, too, though it be always wise (as it will be eternally when it is redeemed), will be so by participating in the unchangeable wisdom, which it is not; for though the air be never robbed of the light that is shed abroad in it, it is not on that account the same thing as the light. I do not mean that the soul is air, as had been supposed by some who could not conceive a spiritual nature; but, with much dissimilarity, the two things have a kind of likeness, which makes it suitable to say that the immaterial soul is illumined with the immaterial light of the simple wisdom of God, as the material air is irradiated with material light, and that, as the air, when deprived of this light, grows dark, (for material darkness is nothing else than air wanting light), so the soul, deprived of the light of wisdom, grows dark.

According to this, then, those things which are essentially and truly divine are called simple, because in them quality and substance are identical, and because they are divine, or wise, or blessed in themselves, and without extraneous supplement. In Holy Scripture, it is true, the Spirit of wisdom is called "manifold" because it contains many things in it; but what it contains it also is, and it being one is all these things. For neither are there many wisdoms, but one, in which are untold and infinite treasures of things intellectual, wherein are all invisible and unchangeable reasons of things visible and changeable which were created by it. For

God made nothing unwittingly; not even a human workman can be said to do so. But if He knew all that He made, He made only those things which He had known. Whence flows a very striking but true conclusion, that this world could not be known to us unless it existed, but could not have existed unless it had been known to God. . . .

FROM *CONFESSIONS*

Seeing then Thou are the Creator of all times, if any time was before Thou madest heaven and earth, why say they that Thou didst forego working? For that very time didst Thou make, nor could times pass by, before Thou madest those times. But if before heaven and earth there was no time, why is it demanded, what Thou then didst? For there was no "then," when there was no time.

Nor dost Thou by time, precede time: else shouldest Thou not precede all times. But Thou precedest all things past, by the sublimity of an everpresent eternity; and surpassest all future because they are future, and when they come, they shall be past; but Thou art the Same, and Thy years fail not. Thy years neither come nor go; whereas ours both come and go, that they all may come. Thy years stand together, because they do stand; nor are departing thrust out by coming years, for they pass not away; but ours shall all be, when they shall no more be. Thy years are one day; and Thy day is not daily, but To-day, seeing Thy To-day gives not place unto to-morrow, for neither doth it replace yesterday. Thy To-day, is Eternity; therefore didst Thou beget The Coeternal, to whom Thou saidst, This day have I begotten Thee. Thou hast made all things; and before all times Thou art: neither in any time was time not.

At no time then hadst Thou not made any thing, because time itself Thou madest. And no times are coeternal with Thee, because Thou abidest; but if they abode, they should not be times. For what is time? Who can readily and briefly explain this? Who can even in thought comprehend it, so as to utter a word about it? But what in discourse do we mention more familiarly and knowingly, than time? And, we understand, when we speak of it; we understand also, when we hear it spoken of by another. . . .

But whence had it this degree of being, but from Thee, from Whom are all things, so far forth as they are? But so much the further from Thee, as the unliker [more unlike] Thee; for it is not farness of place. Thou therefore, Lord, Who art not one in one place, and otherwise in another, but the Self-same and the Self-same, and the Self-same, Holy, Holy, Holy, Lord God Almighty, didst in the Beginning, which is of Thee, in Thy Wisdom, which was born of Thine own Substance, create something, and that out of nothing. For Thou createdst heaven and earth; not out of Thyself for so should they have been equal to Thine Only Begotten Son, and thereby to Thee also; whereas no way were it right that aught should be equal to Thee, which was not of Thee. And aught else besides Thee was there not, whereof Thou mightest create them, O God, One Trinity, and Trine Unity; and therefore out of nothing didst Thou create heaven and earth; a great thing, and a small thing; for Thou art Almighty and Good, to make all things good, even the great heaven, and the petty earth. Thou wert, and nothing was there besides, out of which Thou createst heaven and earth; things of two sorts; one near Thee, the other near to nothing, one, to which Thou alone shouldest be superior; the other, to which nothing should be inferior.

But that heaven of heavens was for Thyself, O Lord; but the earth which Thou gavest to the sons of men, to be seen and felt, was not such as we now see and feel. For it was invisible, without form, and there was a deep, upon which there was no light; or, darkness was above the deep, that is, more than in the deep. Because this deep of waters, visible now, hath even in his depths, a light proper for its nature; perceivable in whatever degree unto the fishes, and creeping things in the bottom of it. But that whole deep was almost nothing, because hitherto it was altogether without form; yet there was already that which could be formed. For Thou, Lord, madest the world of a matter without form, which out of nothing, Thou madest next to nothing, thereof to make those great things, which we sons of men wonder at. . . . But this same earth which Thou madest, was formless matter, because it was invisible and without form, and darkness was upon the deep, of which invisible earth and without form, of which formlessness, of which almost nothing, Thou mightest make all these things of which this changeable world consists, but subsists not,[1] whose very changeableness appears therein, that times can be observed and numbered in it. For times are made by the alterations of things, while the figures, the matter whereof is the invisible earth aforesaid, are varied and turned.

And therefore the Spirit, the Teacher of Thy servant,[2] when It recounts Thee to have In the Beginning created heaven and earth, speaks nothing of times, nothing of days. For verily that heaven of heavens which Thou createdst in the Beginning, is some intellectual creature, which, although no ways coeternal unto Thee, the Trinity, yet partaketh of Thy eternity, and doth through the sweetness of that most happy contemplation of Thyself, strongly restrain its own changeableness; and without any fall since its first creation, cleaving close unto Thee, is placed beyond all the rolling vicissitude of times. Yea, neither is this very formlessness of the earth invisible, and without form, numbered among the days. For where no figure nor order is, there does nothing come, or go; and where this is not, there plainly are no days, nor any vicissitude of spaces or times.

Koranic Theology

From the Koran, in *The Koran Interpreted*, A. J. Arberry, translator, 1955

Like the Bible, the Koran does not present a systematic exposition of theology but rather contains statements that ground theological constructions. Also, God is often referred to in the Koran by epithets capturing various attributes; theologians' identification of these is thus much facilitated. God is called the Omnipotent, the Everlasting, the All-glorious, the Compassionate and All-merciful, as well as the Creator and Lord of the heavens and earth upon whom all depend. From these epithets have been compiled a list of the "ninety-nine most beautiful names of God" familiar to devout Muslims. In addition to the epithets, a few

---

[1] Constat, et non constat. St. Aug. takes occasion of the word to say, that in its full sense it cannot belong to matter, which has no intrinsic consistency. Martin supposes the antithesis to be between its present and any future form which it may take, "consists and (as yet) consists not."

[2] Moses.

sūras, or chapters, are commonly identified as particularly significant from a doctrinal point of view. One of these is the "Throne Verse" excerpted here, along with other passages about the nature of God or God's relation to the universe.

Clearly, the doctrine that there is "No god but God" is theologically central; monotheism is repeatedly proclaimed. God generally seems to be conceived in consonance with biblical theology, though, of course, the Koran brooks no trinitarianism. The Koran explicitly endorses Judaic and Christian revelations, but only with qualifications (see the discussion of Islam in the general introduction).

THE THRONE-VERSE:
GOD AS SINGLE, THE ALL-RULER,
AND TRANSCENDENT

> God
> there is no god but He, the
> Living, the Everlasting.
> Slumber seizes Him not, neither sleep;
> to Him belongs
> all that is in the heavens and the earth.
> Who is there that shall intercede with Him
> save by His leave?
> He knows what lies before them
> and what is after them,
> and they comprehend not anything of His knowledge
> save such as He wills.
> His Throne comprises the heavens and earth;
> the preserving of them oppresses Him not;
> He is the All-high, the All-glorious. (Sūra 2)

OTHER THEOLOGICAL PASSAGES:
GOD AS THE OMNIPOTENT
CREATOR AND LORD

> God is He who raised up the heavens
> without pillars you can see. . . .
> It is He who stretched out the earth
> and set therein
> firm mountains and rivers, . . .
> Say: 'God is the Creator of everything, and He is the One, the Omnipotent.' (Sūra 13)

> Him who created the earth and the high heavens; the
> All-compassionate
> sat himself upon the Throne;
> to Him belongs
> all that is in the heavens and the earth
> and all that is between them, and
> all that is underneath the soil.

GOD AS THE ALL-KNOWING, ALL-WISE

So God makes clear to you His signs; and God is
All-knowing, All-wise. (Sūra 24)

He is the All-subtle, the All-aware. (Sūra 67)

GOD AS THE ALL-MERCIFUL

The All-merciful has taught the Koran.
He created man
and He has taught him the Explanation. . . .

And earth—He set it down for beings,
therein fruits, and palm-trees with sheaths,
and grain in the blade, and fragrant herbs. (Sūra 55)

GOD AS ABSOLUTE, PERFECT

He is God;
there is no god but He.
He is the knower of the Unseen and the Visible;
He is the All-merciful, the All-Compassionate.

He is God;
there is no god but He.
He is the King, the All-holy, the All-peaceable,
the All-faithful, the All-preserver,
the All-mighty, the All-compeller
the All-sublime. . . .

To Him belong the Names Most Beautiful.
All that is in the heavens and the earth magnifies Him;
He is the All-mighty, the All-wise. (Sūra 59)

Classical Theism (Islam)

From "On the Nature of God" by Avicenna in *Avicenna on Theology,* Arthur J. Arberry,
translator, 1951

*That Islamic doctrine derives from the Koran supplemented by traditional "sayings of
the prophet," or* hadīth, *cannot be denied. But, as in Judaism and Christianity, Islamic philosophers forged a systematic theism drawing on Greek thought as well as on
sacred texts.*

Avicenna, or Ibn Sīnā (980–1037), was a theologian and philosopher of the first rank as well as an accomplished physician and medical theorist. His books, revered throughout Islamic civilization, were also translated into Latin and studied closely for several centuries in Europe. The Qānūn, *Avicenna's comprehensive treatise on medicine, was not supplanted as the chief university textbook in European medicine for five hundred years. Much of Avicenna's theology was similarly influential, both within Islam and outside, particularly his thoughts on the nature of God. Thomas Aquinas (1225–74) repeated many of his ideas, and the view of Anselm (1033–1109) that God is the only necessary being is clearly precursed by the Muslim thinker.*

Avicenna knew the works of Plato, and, as mentioned above, he embraces the emanationist doctrine pioneered in Neoplatonism. In this he was opposed by Islamic creationists who, like Philo, viewed creation as ex nihilo.

Despite instances of dependence on Plato, it was Aristotle, Plato's more systematic pupil, that Avicenna adored. Aristotle's doctrine of four types of cause—active, material, formal, and final—finds clear expression in the passage excerpted here. Avicenna was in fact the leading commentator on Aristotle studied in medieval European universities.

Although the passage excerpted here concerns the nature of God, it opens with an argument for the existence of God known as the cosmological argument, *or the argument from contingency (see the discussion under Arguments for a Divine Reality, "Aristotelian Rational Theology"). However, concerned as we are now with views of God's nature, the point may be taken to be that God's mode of being is necessary as opposed to contingent. The way God exists is different from the way a chair, for example, exists, in that the chair, but not God, could possibly not be. Avicenna takes pains to show that God cannot be an effect in any way: not receptively (as the effect of an active or instrumental cause, as a pot of a potter), not materially (as a pot of clay), not formally (as clay coming to possess the form of a pot), and not finally or completively (as a pot exists for the sake of the uses to which it can be put). As with Aristotle, argument dominates Avicenna's writing; there is little exposition of views that is not presented in the form of tight deductive reasoning.*

THAT THERE IS A NECESSARY BEING

Whatever has being must either have a reason for its being, or have no reason for it. If it has a reason, then it is contingent, equally before it comes into being (if we make this mental hypothesis) and when it is in the state of being—for in the case of a thing whose being is contingent the mere fact of its entering upon being does not remove from it the contingent nature of its being. If on the other hand it has no reason for its being in any way whatsoever, then it is necessary in its being. This rule having been confirmed, I shall now proceed to prove that there is in being a being which has no reason for its being.

Such a being is either contingent or necessary. If it is necessary, then the point we sought to prove is established. If on the other hand it is contingent, that which is contingent cannot enter upon being except for some reason which sways the scales in favour of its being and against its not-being. If the reason is also contingent, there is then a chain of contingents linked one to the other, and there is no being at all; for this being which is the subject of our hypothesis cannot enter into being so long as it is not preceded by an infinite succession of beings, which is absurd. Therefore contingent beings end in a Necessary Being.

OF THE UNICITY OF GOD

It is not possible in any way that the Necessary Being should be two. Demonstration: Let us suppose that there is another necessary being: one must be distinguishable from the other, so that the terms "this" and "that" may be used with reference to them. This distinction must be either essential or accidental. If the distinction between them is accidental, this accidental element cannot but be present in each of them, or in one and not the other. If each of them has an accidental element by which it is distinguished from the other, both of them must be caused; for an accident is what is adjoined to a thing after its essence is realized. If the accidental element is regarded as adhering to its being, and is present in one of the two and not in the other, then the one which has no accidental element is a necessary being and the other is not a necessary being. If, however, the distinction is essential, the element of essentiality is that whereby the essence as such subsists; and if this element of essentiality is different in each and the two are distinguishable by virtue of it, then each of the two must be a compound; and compounds are caused; so that neither of them will be a necessary being. If the element of essentiality belongs to one only, and the other is one in every respect and there is no compounding of any kind in it, then the one which has no element of essentiality is a necessary being, and the other is not a necessary being. Since it is thus established that the Necessary Being cannot be two, but is All Truth, then by virtue of His Essential Reality, in respect of which He is a Truth, He is United and One, and no other shares with Him in the Unity: however the All-Truth attains existence, it is through Himself.

THAT GOD IS WITHOUT CAUSE

A necessary being has no cause whatsoever. Causes are of four kinds: that from which a thing has being, or the active cause; that on account of which a thing has being, or the final and completive cause; that in which a thing has being, or the material cause; and that through which a thing has being, or the formal cause.

The justification for limiting causes to these four varieties is that the reason for a thing is either internal in its subsistence, or a part of its being, or external to it. If it is internal, then it is either that part in which the thing is, potentially and not actually, that is to say its matter; or it is that part in which the thing becomes actually, that is to say its form. If it is external, then it can only be either that from which the thing has being, that is to say the agent, or that on account of which the thing has being, that is to say its purpose and end.

Since it is established that these are the roots and principles of this matter, let us rest on them and clarify the problems which are constructed upon them.

Demonstration that He has no active cause: This is self-evident: for if He had any reason for being, this would be adventitious and that would be a necessary being. Since it is established that He has no active cause, it follows on this line of reasoning that His Quiddity is not other than His Identity, that is to say, other than His Being; neither will He be a subsistence or an accident. There cannot be two, each of which derives its being from the other; nor can He be a necessary being in one respect, and a contingent being in another respect.

Proof that His Quiddity is not other than His Identity, but rather that His Being is unified in His Reality: If His Being were not the same as His Reality, then His Being would be other than His Reality. Every accident is caused, and every thing caused requires a reason. Now this reason is either external to His Quiddity, or is itself His Quiddity: if it is external, then He is not a necessary being, and is not exempt from an active cause; while if the reason is itself the Quiddity, then the reason must necessarily be itself a complete being in order that the being of another may result from it. Quiddity before being has no being; and if it had being before this, it would not require a second being. The question therefore returns to the problem of being. If the Being of the Quiddity is accidental, whence did this Being supervene and adhere? It is therefore established that the Identity of the Necessary Being is His Quiddity, and that He has no active cause; the necessary nature of His Being is like the quiddity of all other things. From this it is evident that the Necessary Being does not resemble any other thing in any respect whatsoever; for with all other things their being is other than their quiddity.

Proof that He is not an accident: An accident is a being in a locus. The locus is precedent to it, and its being is not possible without the locus. But we have stated that a being which is necessary has no reason for its being.

Proof that there cannot be two necessary beings, each deriving its being from the other: Each of them, in as much as it derives its being from the other, would be subsequent to the other, while at the same time by virtue of supplying being to the other, each would be precedent to the other: but one and the same thing cannot be both precedent and subsequent in relation to its being. Moreover, if we assume for the sake of argument that the other is nonexistent: would the first then be a necessary being, or not? If it were a necessary being, it would have no connexion with the other: if it were not a necessary being, it would be a contingent being and would require another necessary being. Since the Necessary Being is One, and does not derive Its being from any one, it follows that He is a Necessary Being in every respect; while anything else derives its being from another.

Proof that He cannot be a Necessary Being in one respect and a contingent being in another respect: Such a being, in as much as it is a contingent being, would be connected in being with something else, and so it has a reason; but in as much as it is a necessary being, it would have no connexions with anything else. In that case it would both have being and not have being; and that is absurd.

Demonstration that He has no material and receptive cause: The receptive cause is the cause for the provision of the place in which a thing is received; that is to say, the place prepared for the reception of being, or the perfection of being. Now the Necessary Being is a perfection in pure actuality, and is not impaired by any deficiency; every perfection belongs to Him, derives from Him, and is preceded by His Essence, while every deficiency, even if it be metaphorical, is negated to Him. All perfection and all beauty are of His Being; indeed, these are the vestiges of the perfection of His Being; how then should He derive perfection from any other? Since it is thus established that He has no receptive cause, it follows that He does not possess anything potentially, and that He has no attribute yet to be awaited; on the contrary, His Perfection has been realized in actuality; and He has no material cause. We say "realized in actuality," using this as a common term of expression, meaning that every perfection belonging to any other is non-existent and yet to be awaited, whereas all perfection belonging to Him has being and is present. His Perfect Essence, preceding all relations, is One. From this it is manifest that His Attributes are not an augmentation of His Essence; for if they were an augmentation of His Essence, the Attributes would be potential with reference to the Essence and the Essence would be the reason for the Attributes. In that case the Attributes would be subsequent to a precedent, so that they would be in one respect active and in another receptive; their being active would be other than the aspect of their being receptive; and in consequence they would possess two mutually exclusive aspects. Now this is impossible in the case of anything whatsoever; when a body is in motion, the motivation is from one quarter and the movement from another.

If it were to be stated that His Attributes are not an augmentation of His Essence, but that they entered into the constitution of the Essence, and that the Essence cannot be conceived of as existing without these Attributes, then the Essence would be compound, and the Oneness would be destroyed. It is also evident, as a result of denying the existence of a receptive cause, that it is impossible for Him to change; for the meaning of change is the passing away of one attribute and the establishment of another; and if He were susceptible to change, He would possess potentially an element of passing-away and an element of establishment; and that is absurd. It is clear from this that He has no opposite and no contrary; for opposites are essences which succeed each other in the occupation of a single locus, there being between them the extreme of contrariety. But He is not receptive to accidents, much less to opposites. And if the term "opposite" is used to denote one who disputes with Him in His Rulership, it is clear too on this count that He has no opposite. It is further clear that it is impossible for Him not to be; for since it is established that His Being is necessary, it follows that it is impossible for Him not to be; because everything which exists potentially cannot exist actually, otherwise it would have two aspects. Anything which is receptive to a thing does not cease to be receptive when reception has actually taken place; if this were not so, it would result in the removal of both being and not-being, and that is untenable. This rule applies to every essence and every unified reality, such as angels and human spirits; they are not susceptible to not-being at all, since they are free from corporeal adjunctions.

Demonstrations that He has no formal cause: A formal, corporeal cause only exists and is confirmed when a thing is possessed of matter: the matter has a share in the being of the form, in the same way that the form has a part in the disposition of the matter in being in actuality; such a thing is therefore caused. It is further evident as a result of denying this cause to Him, that He is also to be denied all corporeal attributes, such as time, space, direction, and being in one place to the exclusion of all other; in short, whatever is possible in relation to corporeal things is impossible in relation to Him.

Proof that He has no final cause: The final cause is that on account of which a thing has being; and the First Truth has not being for the sake of anything. Rather does everything exist on account of the perfection of His Essence, being consequent to His Being and derived from His Being. Moreover the final cause, even if it be posterior in respect of being to all other causes, yet it is mentally prior to them all. It is the final cause which makes the active cause become a cause in actuality, that is to say in respect of its being a final cause.

Since it is established that He is exalted above this last kind of cause too, it is clear that there is no cause to His Attributes. It is also evident that He is Pure Benevolence and True Perfection; the meaning of His Self-Sufficiency likewise becomes manifest, namely that he approves of nothing and disapproves of nothing. For if He approved of anything, that thing would come into being and would continue to be; while if He disapproved of anything, that thing would be converted into not-being and would be annulled. The very divergency of these beings proves the nullity of such a proposition; for a thing which is one in every respect cannot approve of a thing and of its opposite. It is also not necessary for Him to observe the rule of greater expediency or of expediency, as certain Qualitarians have idly pretended; for if His acts of expediency were obligatory to Him, He would not merit gratitude and praise for such acts, since He would merely be fulfilling that which it is His obligation to perform, and He would be to all intents and purposes as one paying a debt; He would therefore deserve nothing at all for such benevolence. In fact His acts proceed on the contrary from Him and for Him, as we shall demonstrate later.

HIS ATTRIBUTES AS INTERPRETED
ACCORDING TO THE FOREGOING PRINCIPLES

Since it is established that God is a Necessary Being, that He is One in every respect, that He is exalted above all causes, and that He has no reason of any kind of His Being; since it is further established that His Attributes do not augment His Essence, and that He is qualified by the Attributes of Praise and Perfection; it follows necessarily that we must state that He is Knowing, Living, Willing, Omnipotent, Speaking, Seeing, Hearing, and Possessed of all the other Loveliest Attributes. It is also necessary to recognize that His Attributes are to be classified as negative, positive, and a compound of the two: since His Attributes are of this order, it follows that their multiplicity does not destroy His Unity or contradict the necessary nature of His Being. Pre-eternity for instance is essentially the negation of not-being in the first place, and the denial of causality and of primality in the second place; similarly the term One means that He is indivisible in every respect, both verbally and actually. When it is stated that He is a Necessary Being, this means that He is a Being without a cause, and that He is the Cause of other than Himself: this is a combination of the negative and the positive. Examples of the positive Attributes are His being Creator, Originator, Shaper, and the entire Attributes of Action. As for the compound of both, this kind is illustrated by His being Willing and Omnipotent, for these Attributes are a compound of Knowledge and the addition of Creativeness.

GOD'S KNOWLEDGE

God has knowledge of His Essence: His Knowledge, His Being Known and His Knowing are one and the same thing. He knows other than Himself, and all objects of knowledge.

He knows all things by virtue of one knowledge, and in a single manner. His Knowledge does not change according to whether the thing known has being or not-being.

Proof that God has knowledge of His Essence: We have stated that God is One, and that He is exalted above all causes. The meaning of knowledge is the supervention of an idea divested of all corporeal coverings. Since it is established that He is One, and that He is divested of body, and His Attributes also; and as this idea as just described supervenes upon Him; and since whoever has an abstract idea supervening upon him is possessed of knowledge, and it is immaterial whether it is his essence or other than himself; and as further His Essence is not absent from Himself; it follows from all this that He knows Himself.

Proof that He is Knowledge, Knowing and Known: Knowledge is another term for an abstract idea. Since this idea is abstract, it follows that He is Knowledge; since this abstract idea belongs to Him, is present with Him, and is not veiled from Him, it follows that He is Knowing; and since this abstract idea does not supervene save through Him, it follows that He is Known. The terms employed in each case are different; otherwise it might be said that Knowledge, Knowing and Known are, in relation to His Essence, one. Take your own experience as a parallel. If you know yourself, the object of your knowledge is either yourself or something else; if the object of your knowledge is something other than yourself, then you do not know yourself. But if the object of your knowledge is yourself, then both the one knowing and the thing known are your self. If the image of your self is impressed upon your self, then it is your self which is the knowledge. Now if you look back upon yourself reflectively, you will not find any impression of the idea and quiddity of your self in yourself a second time, so as to give rise within you to a sense that your self is more than one. Therefore since it is established that He has intelligence of His Essence, and since His Intelligence is His Essence and does not augment His Essence, it follows that He is Knowing, Knowledge and Known without any multiplicity attaching to Him through these Attributes; and there is no difference between "one who has knowledge" and "one who has intelligence," since both are terms for describing the negation of matter absolutely.

Proof that He has knowledge of other than Himself: Whoever knows himself, if thereafter he does not know other than himself this is due to some impediment. If the impediment is essential, this implies necessarily that he does not know himself either; while if the impediment is of an external nature, that which is external can be removed. Therefore it is possible—nay, necessary—that He should have knowledge of other than Himself, as you shall learn from this chapter.

Proof that He has knowledge of all objects of knowledge: Since it is established that He is a Necessary Being, that He is One, and that the universe is brought into being from Him and has resulted out of His Being; since it is established further that He has knowledge of His Own Essence, His Knowledge of His Essence being what it is, namely that He is the Origin of all realities and of all things that have being; it follows that nothing in heaven or earth is remote from His Knowledge—on the contrary, all that comes into being does so by reason of Him: He is the causer of all reasons, and He knows that of which He is the Reason, the Giver of being and the Originator.

Proof that He knows all things by virtue of one knowledge, in a manner which changes not according to the change in the thing known: It has been established that

His Knowledge does not augment His Essence, and that He is the Origin of all things that have being, while being exalted above accident and changes; it therefore follows that He knows things in a manner unchanging. The objects of knowledge are a consequence of His Knowledge; His Knowledge is not a consequence of the things known, that it should change as they change; for His Knowledge of things is the reason for their having being. Hence it is manifest that Knowledge is itself Omnipotence. He knows all contingent things, even as He knows all things that have being, even though we know them not; for the contingent, in relation to us, is a thing whose being is possible and whose not-being is also possible; but in relation to Him one of the two alternatives is actually known. Therefore His Knowledge of genera, species, things with being, contingent things, manifest and secret things—this Knowledge is a single knowledge.

ACTS EMANATING FROM GOD

Since you now know that He is a Necessary Being, that He is One, and that He has no Attribute which augments His Essence (for that would imply a succession of various acts, whereas the Act of God is the vestiges of the Perfection of His Essence); this being so, it follows that His First Act is one. For if there had emanated from Him two acts, the emanation would have been in two different manners, for duality in the act implies duality in the agent. He who acts by virtue of his own essence, if his essence is one only one act emanates from it; whereas if he has a duality of essence, he must be a compound; and we have proved the impossibility of this as regards God. It follows necessarily that the first thing to emanate from God was not a body; for every body is compounded of matter and form, and these require either two causes, or a single cause with two aspects; this being so, it is impossible that these two should have emanated from God, it having been established that there is no compounding in God whatsoever. Since the first thing to emanate from God was not a body, it follows that it was an abstract substance, namely, the First Intelligence. This has been confirmed by the true religion, for the Prophet said, "The first thing God created was Intelligence," and again, "The first thing God created was the Pen." The phrase *Thou shalt not find any change in the Way of God* (Koran xxxiii. 62) refers to the perpetuity of the Creation: the phrase *Thou shalt not find any alteration in the Way of God* (Koran xxxv. 41) refers to the perpetuity of the Command. Certainly, the Universe emanated from Him in due succession of order and media. So when we say that this Act emanated from Him through a reason, and that that reason was of Him also, this implies no imperfection in His Activity; on the contrary, totality emanated from Him, through Him, and unto Him. Therefore all things having being emanated from Him according to a known order and known media: that which came later cannot be earlier, and that which came earlier cannot be later, for it is He Who causes things to be earlier and later. Indeed, the first thing having being that emanated from Him was the noblest; thereafter came a descent from the nobler to the lower, until the lowliest of all was reached. First was Intelligence; then Soul; then the Body of Heaven; then the materials of the four Elements with their forms (for their materials are common to all, only their forms differ). Then there is a mounting up from the lowliest to the noblest; the noblest of all ending at a degree parallel to the degree of the Intelligence. Through this process of origination and returning back, God is said to be the Originator and the Returner.

Perfect Being

From *Proslogion* by Anselm in *St. Anselm's Proslogion,* M. J. Charlesworth, translator, 1965

Anselm (1033–1109), Archbishop of Canterbury, is most famous for an argument he presents for the existence of God, the ontological argument *(see Arguments for a Divine Reality). A much less talked about feature of Anselm's thought is his method of thinking about God, which may be called* apriorist theology. *Anselm presents a definition of God as "that, nothing greater than which can be conceived," or, in a word, perfection. Thus from the idea of God,* a priori *or apart from experience, attributes or features of God can be known: God is whatever it is better to be than not to be, and that to the highest degree. The method is like deducing from the idea or definition of a triangle that a triangle has three sides. Of course, the procedure is present in Avicenna and other earlier theologians. But it was Anselm who standardized it within Christian thought.*

THAT GOD TRULY EXISTS

Well then, Lord, You who give understanding to faith, grant me that I may understand, as much as You see fit, that You exist as we believe You to exist, and that You are what we believe You to be. Now we believe that You are something than which nothing greater can be thought. . . .

THAT GOD IS WHATEVER IT IS BETTER TO BE THAN NOT TO BE
AND THAT, EXISTING THROUGH HIMSELF ALONE,
HE MAKES ALL OTHER BEINGS FROM NOTHING

What then are You, Lord God, You than whom nothing greater can be thought? But what are You save that supreme being, existing through Yourself alone, who made everything else from nothing? For whatever is not this is less than that which can be thought of; but this cannot be thought about You. What goodness, then, could be wanting to the supreme good, through which every good exists? Thus You are just, truthful, happy, and whatever it is better to be than not to be—for it is better to be just rather than unjust, and happy rather than unhappy.

Puzzles Concerning God's Attributes

From *On the Nature and Existence of God* by Richard Gale, 1991

Richard Gale, a professor of philosophy at the University of Pittsburgh, presents a new version of an old conundrum about God's attributes: Can God create a stone too heavy for God to lift? Whether God can or cannot, it would seem that God is not, strictly speaking, omnipotent.

After showing a theological way out of this difficulty, Gale examines further problems concerning God's omnipotence and the overall coherence of the traditional concept of God. For example, a "Pinrod," defined as a being with only one of God's perfections, for example, omnipotence—in contrast with God, who is omnibenevolent as well as omnipotent—would seem to have greater freedom or even power. A Pinrod, but not God, could possibly sin.

Gale examines some proposed solutions to such difficulties that arise in trying to defend the coherence of classical theism's concept of God, and in the excerpted selection he provides a good introduction, and much more than just a taste, a solid bite, into the controversy. But of course there are other problems, and other proposed solutions, depending on what attributes are taken up—simplicity and immutability, omniscience, aseity, and so on. Below, Gale focuses on omnipotence and simplicity, although other attributes figure in the discussion. Problems that flow from a conception of God as both omnipotent and omnibenevolent (all-loving), we may note, will be more closely examined below in the section entitled Evil.

The first divine attribute to be taken up is omnipotence. God is supposed to have this attribute, like all of his other attributes, essentially, meaning that it is logically or conceptually impossible that God exist without having this attribute. His possession of omnipotence is an example of a de re necessity, since it follows from his nature, not our way of referring to God, that he has it. This contrasts with de dicto necessity claims, the truth of which depend upon the mode of reference; for instance, it is true that it is necessary that God is omnipotent but not that Augustine's favorite individual is omnipotent, even though God is in fact Augustine's favorite individual.

Probably the most famous atheological argument is the one that deduces a contradiction from the initial set containing only the proposition that God is omnipotent. The trick in the argument is to require of an omnipotent being that he can do anything without restriction. The following is my version of the paradox of the stone, which differs from the standard version in that it is not mounted as a dilemma argument, thereby avoiding needless complications. It begins with an initial set containing only

    7. It is necessary that God is omnipotent;

and then proceeds as follows:

    8. It is necessary that an omnipotent being can do anything [by definition];

    9. It is necessary that God can do anything [from 7 and 8];

    10. It is necessary that God can create a stone so heavy that God cannot lift it [from 8 and 9];

    11. It is necessary that (if God can create a stone so heavy that God cannot lift it, then it is possible that there is something God cannot do) [conceptual truth];

    12. It is possible that there is something God cannot do [from 10 and 11];

    13. It is not necessary that God can do anything [from 12]; and

14. It is necessary that God can do anything and it is not necessary that God can do anything [from 9 and 13].

Since a contradiction has been deduced from 7, with appeal only to necessarily true additional premises, it follows that 7 is necessarily false.

There is a variant of the "stone" argument in which "commit suicide," rather than "create a stone so heavy that God cannot lift it," is substituted for "anything" in 9. If God can commit suicide, it is possible that an omnipotent being cease to exist. If you find nothing conceptually absurd about this, try an absolutely perfect being, which is what God essentially is, ceasing to exist. This, certainly, is not possible. This variant on the suicide argument is not directed exclusively at God's omnipotence but at his being essentially both omnipotent and absolutely perfect. Accordingly, we will call it the "omnipotence–perfection argument." Another mixed-bag atheological argument involving omnipotence is the "omnipotence–benevolence argument" in which "commit an immoral action" is substituted for "anything" in 9. Because God is omnipotent, he can commit an immoral action; but, since he is essentially benevolent, he cannot. Thus, one of the two properties must be jettisoned.

What is the theist to do in response to these atheological arguments? Plainly, unless we are Kierkegaards, some response is necessary, since we do not want to accept a logically inconsistent creed. There is considerable room for conceptual reform here, since the theologian's notion of God's omnipotence is a theoretical reconstruction of the biblical notion of God Almighty. From the idea of a God who is sovereign over all there is comes that of a God whose power knows no limitations, not even of a logical or conceptual sort.[1] To escape the stone and suicide arguments, a religiously acceptable restriction must be placed upon God's omnipotence. The mixed-bag arguments—the omnipotence–perfection and omnipotence–benevolence arguments—provide the theist more latitude, since either omnipotence or the other concerned attribute can be reconceived. It is interesting to note that usually it is omnipotence that is restricted by the theist rather than perfection or benevolence, since one of God's hard-core properties is being eminently worthy of worship and obedience, and it would seem that only a being that is essentially perfect and benevolent without restriction could qualify as such, at least according to the theist's own moral pecking order. This is quite consistent with the fact that there are nontheists who worship a being solely on the basis of his power. Since they give primary importance to power, it if turns out to be the case that the devil is the most powerful being, then he is on pragmatic grounds the most appropriate object of worship. But, for the theist, he still is not *eminently* worthy of worship because of his moral imperfection.

An obvious way to neutralize the stone argument is to restrict God's omnipotence as follows:

O_1. God can do or bring about anything that is logically possible.

While the O_1 account of God's omnipotence works for the stone argument, since "creating a stone so heavy that God [an omnipotent being] cannot lift it" is contradictory, it does not work for the suicide argument, "committing suicide" being a consistent-act description.

[1] Thomas Aquinas, *Summa Theologiae,* Iae, Q. 45, art. 1.

Nor does it work for the omnipotence–benevolence argument, since "committing an immoral action" describes a possible action. The problem with O₁ is that there are many things that are logically possible to do but which God cannot do since it is not logically possible that God performs these actions.

This suggests a way of further restricting O₁ so as to get around this difficulty, namely, as

O₂. God can do anything that it is logically consistent for God to do.

There are many possible actions that God, in virtue of being absolutely perfect, cannot perform, such as playing football. Only a being possessed of a body could do this, but God "ain't got nobody," since to have a body makes one subject to the possibilities of corruption and death, which certainly would disqualify one from being an absolutely perfect being. Notice that some properties are great making in a sortally relative, but not absolute fashion, such as being well coordinated, which is great making relative to an animal but not absolutely, since to have it one must be possessed of a body and thus not be absolutely perfect.

God's actions are confined to bringing things about in his own inimitable supernatural fashion by simply willing them. Thus, a more perspicuous way of rendering O₂ is as

O₃. For any proposition *p,* if it is logically possible that God bring it about that *p,* then God can bring it about that *p,*

in which "can bring it about" is to be understood in the full-blooded sense of having the power, ability, opportunity, and so on of bringing about the state of affairs in question. The "can" must not be understood in the weak, logical-possibility sense, for this would render O₃ vacuously tautological. Again, there are logically possible propositions, for instance, that there exists an uncreated stone (assuming that it is not necessary that God exists) that God cannot bring about, since it would be logically inconsistent for him to do so. Another example is the proposition that God exists, and this he cannot bring about even if his existence is necessary because entailed by his essence.

. . . there is a more serious difficulty with a sortally relativized account of God's omnipotence; it creates a paradox of perfection consisting in such a being having a lesser degree of power than that possessed by some possible nonperfect being. Let a Pinrod be a possible being who has only one of the divine perfections—omnipotence—and thereby does not qualify as an absolutely perfect being. Anything that God can do or bring about, our Pinrod can do or bring about, and then some. Not being burdened with being absolutely perfect, our Pinrod, in addition to having all of God's powers, for instance, being able to create a universe ex nihilo and perform other parlor tricks, can be possessed of a body and thereby be able to play football. Since he is not absolutely perfect, he is not barred from committing suicide. Furthermore, since he lacks benevolence, he is able to perform an immoral action. Thus, this lesser being has a greater degree of freedom than that possessed by God, an absolutely perfect being. It looks as if no one is perfect, not even an absolutely perfect being!

The great medieval theists would have had a ready response to the paradox of perfection based on the doctrine of the divine simplicity. It will be worthwhile to consider this doctrine, not only as offering a way out of this paradox, but for its own intrinsic interest. God's status as an absolutely perfect being precluded either there being any distinctions within his nature or his being dependent upon anything. The former entails that there is no distinction between God's properties: His omnipotence is identical with his omniscience, which is identical with his omnibenevolence, and so on. Were there to be any compositeness in his nature, he would face the possibility of destruction through decomposition. . . .

[An] instance identity version would seem plausible, since it is by now a familiar story that two referring expressions can be coreferential though differing in sense, for instance, "the morning star" and "the evening star." Thus, it might be possible that "an instancing of omnipotence" and "an instancing of omnibenevolence" are coreferential, although differing in sense, in that God's instancing of the one property is identical with his instancing of the other. Before we consider the possibility of this being so, it must be stressed that this instance identity version of the divine simplicity violates God's absolute aseity or independence, since it conceives of God as instantiating properties and thus as dependent upon them. Still, it is interesting to consider this version, since, if it proves viable, the theist might want to go with it and accept a restricted version of God's aseity. . . .

It would seem that we have the same intuitive grounds for denying the identity of an *instance* of perfect power with an instance of perfect knowledge as we previously had for denying the identity of the *property* of omnipotence with that of omnibenevolence. Because an instance of ordinary power is obviously not identical with an instance of ordinary benevolence, there is all the more reason to hold that instances of increasing degrees thereof are not identical, and thus to deny that an instance of an unlimited degree of the one is identical with an unlimited degree of the other.

In opposition to this line of reasoning, [Eleonore] Stump and [Norman] Kretzmann offer an analogy to show how (an instance of) perfect power can be identical with (an instance of) perfect knowledge although no instance of ordinary finite power is identical with an instance of ordinary finite knowledge. The former identity "does not entail that power is identical with knowledge any more than the fact that the summit of a mountain's east slope is identical with the summit of its west slope entails the identity of the slopes."[2] This spatial analogy is most unfortunate for their purpose, since, when it is pushed, it results in a view of God's omniproperties that is the opposite of what they intend. The common summit limits each of the slopes by serving as their common point of termination. Analogously, God's (instancing of) perfect power and perfect knowledge would also represent a limitation on ordinary power and knowledge. But this is the opposite of what they mean by these divine perfections, which are supposed to be ideal or unlimited instancings of power and knowledge. "The single summit is indeed the perfection of all the slopes"

---

[2] A crucial part of my support for this is contained in the next section, where I argue that temporarily is not required by relativity, potentiality, etc. For if God is temporal, creation ex nihilo is difficult to maintain.

and "suggests that the idea that perfect phi and perfect psi might be identical despite the plain difference between phi and psi." It might be objected that I have leaned too heavily on the spatial aspect of their analogy in drawing out the absurdity that God's omnipotence, and so on, represents a limitation rather than a perfection of ordinary power. But if we are not allowed to press their analogy in this way, it has no value.

Even if the instance identity version of the doctrine of the divine simplicity could somehow be made to work, it would still not succeed in neutralizing the paradox of perfection; for it would fail to show that one could not have one of God's perfections without having all of them, as was the case with our Pinrod. Let us assume for the sake of argument that God's instancing omnipotence is identical with his instancing benevolence. This does not entail that any instancing of omnipotence is identical with some instancing of benevolence. A token identity proposition does not entail a type identity proposition. That my instancing pain on some occasion is identical with a specific firing of my C-fibers does not entail that every instancing of pain is identical with some firing of C-fibers, no less a firing of my C-fibers. . . .

I have not tried to show that there could not be an acceptable version of the doctrine of the divine simplicity, only that none of the leading contemporary accounts are adequate. Thus, the paradox of perfection still awaits a resolution. Maybe the best strategy for the theist is to bite the bullet and take back the requirement that an absolutely perfect being have every perfection to an unlimited or unsurpassable degree. That such a being, unlike a Pinrod, cannot commit suicide or an immoral action does not dislodge it from its privileged place in the religious language game and form of life that is involved in it; for it still retains its status as the being most eminently worthy of worship and obedience and so on. Giving up the requirement that the Deity be absolutely simple in no way destroys the identity of the religious community over time and causes subsequent uses of "God" not to be coreferring with earlier uses. Not only is no real harm done, but it helps us to escape from a devastating atheological argument.

Failings of Classical Theism (and Corresponding Merits of Process Theism)

From *Omnipotence and Other Theological Mistakes* by Charles Hartshorne, 1984

Charles Hartshorne for more than fifty years has vigorously defended a philosophic theism that contrasts with classical theism. The latter's problems he often traces to what he sees as prejudices of early Greek reasoners. For example, Plato, as we saw, sometimes implied that if God were to change, God would be imperfect. But Charles Hartshorne finds serious difficulties with a view of God as immutable. In general, the problems of classical theism are problems of coherence, not only, according to Hartshorne, of internal coherence but also of compatibility with other things that we know or firmly believe. If God were omni-

scient, then God would know right now, for example, what color socks I will wear tomorrow. But if God knows that now, then the fact of the matter is already determined and I have no choice and in general no free will.

As a replacement conception, Hartshorne offers a process view of God (pioneered by Alfred North Whitehead: see the selection under Speculative Spiritual Metaphysics), emphasizing God's "dual transcendence." God transcends the world atemporally, but the world is also intimate to God, as intimate as we are to our bodies. As the world changes, so too does God, feeling or responding appropriately with every creaturely feeling. Thus God transcends each moment what God was before, thereby, according to the process metaphysics, continually becoming more valuable—or continuing the process of a dynamic perfection.

THE MISTAKES BRIEFLY PRESENTED

In this section I introduce, with a minimum of criticism or argument, . . . ideas about God which have been held by a great number of learned and brilliant philosophers and theologians through many centuries and in many religious traditions, but which I and many others, including some distinguished modern theologians and philosophers, have found quite unacceptable. In other words, what we attack is an old tradition, but we attack it standing within a somewhat newer tradition. In this newer tradition there is a partial appeal (with reservations) to still a third tradition which is old indeed, expressed in various sacred writings, including the Old and New Testaments of the Bible. For it is our contention that the "theological mistakes" in question give the word *God* a meaning which is not true to its import in sacred writings or in concrete religious piety. This result came about partly because theologians in medieval Europe and the Near East were somewhat learned in Greek philosophy and largely ignorant of any other philosophy. This happened in both Christianity and Islam, to a somewhat lesser extent in Judaism. In all three religions there was a development of mysticism, which was different still and in some ways partially corrective of the all-too-Greek form taken by the official theologies. . . .

First Mistake: God Is Absolutely Perfect and Therefore Unchangeable. In Plato's *Republic* one finds the proposition: God, being perfect, cannot change (not for the better, since "perfect" means that there can be no better; not for the worse, since ability to change for the worse, to decay, degenerate, or become corrupt, is a weakness, an imperfection). The argument may seem cogent, but it is so only if two assumptions are valid: that it is possible to conceive of a meaning for "perfect" that excludes change in any and every respect and that we must conceive God as perfect in just *this* sense. Obviously the ordinary meanings of perfect do not entirely exclude change. Thus Wordsworth wrote of his wife that she was a "perfect woman," but he certainly did not mean that she was totally unchangeable. In many places in the Bible human beings are spoken of as perfect; again the entire exclusion of change cannot have been intended. Where in the Bible God is spoken of as perfect, the indications are that even here the exclusion of change in any and every respect was not implied. And where God is directly spoken of as strictly unchanging ("without shadow of turning"), there is still a possibility of ambiguity. God might be absolutely unchangeable in righteousness (which is what the context indicates is the intended meaning), but changeable in ways compatible with, neutral to, *or even required by,* this unswerving constancy in righteousness. Thus, God would be in no degree, however slight, alterable in the respect in question (the divine steadfastness in good will) and yet alterable, not necessarily in spite of, but even because of, this steadfastness. If the creatures behave according to God's will, God will appreciate this behavior; if not, God will have a different response, equally appropriate and expressive of the divine goodness.

The Biblical writers were not discussing Greek philosophical issues, and it is at our own peril that we interpret them as if they were discussing these, just as it is at our peril if we take them to be discussing various modern issues that had not arisen in ancient Palestine. It may even turn out on inquiry that perfection, if taken to imply an absolute maximum of value *in every conceivable respect,* does not make sense or is contradictory. In that case the argument of the *Republic* is an argument from an absurdity and proves nothing. Logicians have found that abstract definitions may seem harmless and yet be contradictory when their meanings are spelled out. Example, "the class of all classes." Similarly, "actuality of all possible values," to which no addition is possible, may have contradictory implications. If perfection cannot consistently mean this value maximum, then the Platonic argument is unsound. Nor was it necessarily Plato's last word on the subject.

Second Mistake: Omnipotence. God, being defined as perfect in all respects must, it seems, be perfect in power; therefore, whatever happens is divinely made to happen. If I die of cancer this misfortune is God's doing. The question then becomes, "Why has God done this to me?" Here everything depends on "perfect in power" or "omnipotent." And here, too, there are possible ambiguities. . . .

Third Mistake: Omniscience. Since God is unchangeably perfect, whatever happens must be eternally known to God. Our tomorrow's deeds, not yet decided upon by us, are yet always or eternally present to God, for whom there is no open future. Otherwise (the argument goes), God would be "ignorant," imperfect in knowledge, waiting to observe what we may do. Hence, whatever freedom of decision we may have must be somehow reconciled with the alleged truth that our decisions bring about no additions to the divine life. Here perfect and unchanging knowledge, free from ignorance or increase, are the key terms. It can be shown that they are all seriously lacking in clarity, and that the theological tradition resolved the ambiguities in a question-begging way.

It is interesting that the idea of an unchangeable omniscience covering every detail of the world's history is not to be found definitely stated in ancient Greek philosophy (unless in Stoicism, which denied human freedom) and is rejected by Aristotle. It is not clearly affirmed in the Bible. It is inconspicuous in the philosophies of India, China, and Japan. Like the idea of omnipotence, it is largely an invention of Wesern thought of the Dark or Middle Ages. It still goes unchallenged in much current religious thought. But many courageous and competent thinkers have rejected it, including Schelling and Whitehead.

Fourth Mistake: God's Unsympathetic Goodness. God's "love" for us does not, for classical theists, mean that God sympathizes with us, is rejoiced or made happy by our joy or good fortune or grieved by our sorrow or misery. Rather God's love is like the sun's way of doing good, which benefits the myriad forms of life on earth but receives no benefits from the good it produces. Nor does the sun lose anything by its activity (we now know that this is bad astronomy). Or, God's beneficial activity is like that of an overflowing fountain that remains forever full no matter how much water comes from it, and without receiving any from outside. Thus it is not human love, even at its best, that was taken as the model for divine love but instead two inanimate phenomena of nature, fictitiously conceived at that. Bad physics and astronomy, rather than sound psychology, were the sources of the imagery.

In short, argument from an insufficiently analyzed notion of perfection and a preference for materialistic (and prescientific) rather than truly spiritual conceptions were for almost two thousand years dominant in Western theology. . . .

THE PRINCIPLE OF DUAL TRANSCENDENCE

The first four of the mistakes dealt with above are "one-sided" views in that they seek to distinguish God from all else by putting God on one side of a long list of contraries: finite-infinite, temporal-eternal, relative-absolute, contingent-necessary, physical-spiritual, and still others. But this is a species of idolatry, implying that what we worship is infinity, eternity, absoluteness, necessity, mere spirituality, or disembodied mind. But these are empty abstractions. So is love, if you only mean the mere quality of lovingness. What is really worshipful is the love which is inifinite in whatever sense that is an excellence and is finite in whatever sense that, too, is an excellence. God contrasts with creatures, not as infinite with finite, but as *infinite-and-finite* (*both in uniquely excellent ways,* beyond all possible rivalry or relevant criticism) contrasts with the merely fragmentary and only surpassably excellent creatures. God contrasts with creatures, not as the merely absolute contrasts with the relative, but as the absolute-and-relative in uniquely excellent ways contrasts with the creatures as neither relative nor absolute, except in senses in which they are surpassable by others. God is similarly both eternal and temporal in all-surpassing ways; God alone has an *eternal individuality,* meaning unborn and undying, and God alone has enjoyed the entire past and will enjoy all the future. He-She is both physical and spiritual, and the divine body is all-surpassing and all-inclusive of the creaturely bodies, which are to God as cells to a supercellular organism. His-Her spirit embraces all the psychical there is with all-surpassing, unstinted love.

The idea of omnipotence, as usually construed, contradicts dual transcendence; for it means that God is wholly active, independent, or absolute in relation to the creatures and that the creatures are wholly passive in relation to God. It means that God does either everything or nothing. If everything, then the creatures do nothing and are nothing. The divine excellence is a uniquely excellent way of interacting with others, of being active *and* passive in relation to them. We do things to God by deciding our own being, with necessary help from God, as setting limits to the disorder inherent in freedom, and as inspiring us to take our place in the cosmic order as best we can. God loves us as we partly make ourselves to be, not simply as we are divinely made to be. To say that a lover is uninfluenced by a partly self-made loved one is nonsense or contradiction. Omnipotence was often taken in a way that amounts to that contradiction.

The formula "dual transcendence" is mine. The basic idea is in Whitehead and still others, but in some respects less sharply formulated. The criticism, made for instance by a conservative English theologian, that it is contradictory to attribute both finitude and infinity, for example, to the same deity is nothing but the neglect of an elementary logical truth, which is that the description of something as both P and not-P (where P is some predicate or property) is contradictory *only* if the predicate and its negation are applied in "the same respect" to the something in question. And dual transcendence does not make or permit such an application. Moreover, it offers a definite explanation of how the difference in the two respects is possible. The absolute, infinite side is abstract and concerns the divine potentiality or capacity to have values, while the finitude or relativity concerns the divine actuality. If you or I had made different decisions, God would have enjoyed (or suffered) these other decisions. Anything that could be actual God could divinely have, but what God actually has depends partly on creaturely decisions. This is the social structure of existence. The primacy of love means that there is no possible value that any being could have simply in and by itself, or simply by its own decision.

Aristotle said that the abstract or universal is real only in the concrete and individual. But he failed to realize how abstract and merely universal was his idea of God, defined as unmoved mover changelessly thinking—thinking what? The divine thinking, Aristotle said, was simply thinking thinking itself. Particular things or individuals, such as you or me, are not worth knowing about. Only eternal essences, universals, are worth knowing. And so if we know both the universal essence human, and this or that particular human person, we know what God does and something more besides. The Greek fascination with abstractions and disparagement of the concrete could not have been better displayed than in this paradox. Of course few theologians, least of all Christian theologians, could so disparage the worth of individuals when even a sparrow is said in the Gospels to be of interest to the Heavenly Father. But the theologians failed, on their part, to realize what Aristotle had seen very clearly, that if, contrary to Aristotle's opinion, God is aware of particular individuals and their careers, then the entire fullness of reality must be embraced in divine knowledge. But this concrete fullness is not eternal, it receives new items moment by moment. Also some at least of the items are contingent, results of free decisions, divine or creaturely, or both. Hence it will no longer do to hold that God is exclusively eternal and necessary, rather than also temporal and contingent. Like it or not, the door to the doctrine of dual transcendence has been opened.

We do not contradict ourselves if we say that a certain person is unchanging in being always (reasonably) "kind," although of course in concrete particulars responding differently to take changing circumstances into account. The idealized form of this contrast can be applied to God, who alone can unfailingly conform to the ideal of kindness.

That there are really different aspects of the divine nature, as dual transcendence implies, will be rejected by some thinkers on the ground that God is "simple," a traditional doctrine. But as used against dual transcendence, this argument would be purely question-begging. God is both simple and complex, the one in abstract, the other in concrete aspects. For instance, the divine cognitive infallibility is not really different (illustrating simplicity) from the divine ethical infallibility. But the aesthetic value actualized in God is no mere infallibility of the divine aesthetic capacity to respond. Aesthetic value, unlike merely cognitive or ethical value, depends in part upon what is responded to. It is concrete. There is a real difference (illustrating complexity) between the absolutely unsurpassable cognitive perfection of God's knowing, or the absolute rightness of the divine decision-making about the creatures, and the beauty of the actual, cosmic poem (the "verses" of which are partly self-decided) as divinely enjoyed.

Paul Tillich's "God is being but not *a* being," that is, universal but not individual, violates dual transcendence and is open to the objections to be made against all such violations, that they either make God an empty abstraction, or else make Him-Her a fetish, a *merely* finite, relative, and changeable individual. A merely finite God of course will not do. The only infinity some of us can see as making sense we do attribute to God, but not the meaningless, contradictory, or empty *mere* infinity of the traditional view.

Classical Theism Defended (in Part)

From "Hartshorne and Aquinas: A Via Media" by William P. Alston in *Existence and Actuality,* John B. Cobb, Jr., and Franklin I. Gamwell, editors, 1984

William Alston, a professor of philosophy at Syracuse University and another leading professional, brings into sharper focus the contrast between Hartshorne's process view and classical theism. The former he calls neoclassical and the latter he talks about as Thomistic (referring to Thomas Aquinas, a late medieval Christian philosopher: see under Arguments for a Divine Reality and Religious Language).

Alston purports to find a middle ground concerning many of the attributes under dispute, and where there is direct opposition, and no possibility of mediation—for example, with immutability—he spells out the considerations that seem to underlie the alternatives. He also proposes a psychological model drawing on human perception where the classical conception of God as atemporal becomes, he says, intelligible.

Here [see p. 52] is a tabular presentation of the oppositions between what Hartshorne calls the "classical" position, paradigmatically represented by Aquinas, and his own, "neoclassical," position.

I shall go about my task as follows. I shall examine Hartshorne's arguments against the Thomistic attributes in the first group (absoluteness, simplicity, etc.), and show that they cut no ice against the Thomistic attributes in the second group. In order to carry this through, I will have to show that the classical attributes in the latter group are in fact consistent with the neoclassical features in the first group. In discussing the classical attributes in the second group, I shall cast a cursory glance at Hartshorne's other arguments against those attributes and suggest that they lack cogency. I would like to go on to argue for the religious adequacy of my "mixed" conception, but for that I will have to wait for another occasion.

CLASSICAL	NEOCLASSICAL
GROUP 1 ATTRIBUTES	
1. Absoluteness (absence of internal relatedness)	Relativity. God is internally related to creatures by way of His knowledge of them and His actions toward them.
2. Pure actuality. There is no potentiality in God for anything He is not.	Potentiality. God does not actualize everything that is possible for Him.
3. Total necessity. Every truth about God is necessarily true.	Necessity *and* contingency. God *exists* necessarily, but various things are true of God (e.g., His knowledge of what is contingent) that are contingently true of Him.
4. Absolute simplicity.	Complexity.
GROUP 2 ATTRIBUTES	
5. Creation ex nihilo by a free act of will. God could have refrained from creating anything. It is a contingent fact that anything exists other than God.	Both God and the world of creatures exist necessarily, though the details are contingent.
6. Omnipotence. God has the power to do anything (logically consistent) He wills to do.	God has all the power any one agent could have, but there are metaphysical limitations on this.
7. Incorporeality.	Corporeality. The world is the body of God.
8. Nontemporality. God does not live through a series of temporal moments.	Temporality. God lives through temporal succession, but everlastingly.
9. Immutability. This follows from 8. God cannot change since there is no temporal succession in His being.	Mutability. God is continually attaining richer syntheses of experience.
10. Absolute perfection. God is, eternally, that than which no more perfect can be conceived.	Relative perfection. At any moment God is more perfect than any other individual, but He is surpassable by Himself at a later stage of development.

Before starting on this task let me make explicit what I will not be challenging in the Hartshornean theology. First I readily and unreservedly grant that Hartshorne has made a powerful positive case for his conception of God as one that (a) is internally coherent, (b) has philosophical merit, (c) has important roots in the practice of theistic religion, and (d) nicely handles some nasty problems. Thus I allow that the full Hartshornean conception is an important alternative that must be seriously considered by contemporary theology, even though it is not my preferred alternative. Second, I acknowledge that theological thought during most of its history has been seriously hampered by the fact that the

Hartshornean alternative has been almost totally ignored. Hartshorne has repeatedly shown how this neglect of an important alternative has led to bad reasoning. Finally, I grant that Hartshorne has shown the classical conception not to be required by the practice of theistic religions. . . .

. . . Hartshorne argues effectively that, in any case of knowledge, the knowledge relation is internal to the subject, external to the object, and, indeed, that cognitive relations are *more* constitutive of the subject, the more certain, comprehensive, and adequate the knowledge. Whenever I know something, the fact that I know it goes toward making me the concrete being I am. If at this moment I see a tree across the street, I would not be just the *concrete* being I am at this moment (though I might be the same enduring individual or substance, according to standard criteria of identity for such beings) if I were not seeing that tree in just the way I am. I would be different from what I am in a significant respect. But the tree would still be just what it is if I did not see it.

This being the case, how can we both maintain that God has complete and perfect knowledge of everything knowable, including beings other than Himself, and still hold that God is not qualified to any degree by relations to other beings? I wholeheartedly agree with Hartshorne that we cannot. Classical theology has typically responded to this difficulty by alleging that, since all things other than God depend on God for their existence, their relations to the divine knower are constitutive of them rather than of God. The usual order of dependence is reversed. But Hartshorne effectively replies that, even if finite beings depend for their existence on the creative activity of God, it still remains true that if God had created a different world then He would have been somewhat different from the way He actually is by virtue of the fact that His perfect knowledge would have been of that world rather than of this world; and so the point still holds that divine cognitive relations to the creatures are partially constitutive of God.[1]

Now for the other traditional attributes in the first group. On reflection we can see that the above argument for the internal relatedness of God as cognitive subject *presupposes* that there are alternative possibilities for God, at least with respect to what creatures, or what states of creatures, He has as objects of knowledge. For if, as both Thomas and Hartshorne hold, it is necessary that God know perfectly whatever there is to know, and if there were no alternative possibilities as to what there is to know (whether by way of alternative possibilities for divine creativity or otherwise), then there would be no possible alternatives to the actual state of knowledge. And in that case the question as to whether God would be in any way different if He did not know what He does know would not arise. It would be like asking whether God would be different if *He* were not God, or like asking if the number 6 would be different if *it* were not 3 × 2. But if there are alternative possibilities for divine knowledge, then this implies both that there are unrealized potentialities for God, e.g., knowing some world (as actual) that He might have created but did not, and that

---

[1] The matter is further complicated by the Thomistic principle that there is no distinction between God's knowing and willing. However, even if that extraordinary claim were accepted, it is not clear that it would negate the point that God would be different from what He is, in his concrete reality, if He did not know what He knows.

some of the things true of God are true of Him contingently, e.g., that He knows what He knows about creatures. Hartshorne's denial of absoluteness really presupposes the denial of pure actuality and of total necessity.

Thus there is an intimate connection between these three oppositions to the classical scheme. But in showing this we have also been exhibiting a vulnerability in the argument for relativity. For unless we are justified in the attribution of potentiality and contingency to God, the argument for relativity is lacking in cogency. Fortunately Hartshorne can, and does, argue independently for divine potentiality and contingency. Again he proceeds from premises admitted by his opponents, namely, that the world is contingent and that God freely creates the world He creates (and, therefore, could have created some other world instead).[2] From the first premise we have the following argument.

1. (A) *God knows that W exists* entails (B) *W exists.*

2. If (A) were necessary, (B) would be necessary.

3. But (B) is contingent.

4. Hence (A) is contingent.

In other words, if what God, or any other subject, knows might not have existed, then God, or the subject in question, might not have had that knowledge. For if the object had not existed, it would not have been known. Hence God's knowledge of the contingent is itself contingent. Therefore we can totally exclude contingency from God only by denying of God any knowledge of anything contingent, a step none of the classical theologians were willing to take.

From the thesis that God could have created some other world it follows that there are unrealized potentialities for God, namely, His creating worlds that He does not create. Thomas' distinction between active and passive potentialities[3] does nothing to invalidate this point. Of course unrealized potentialities also follow from the first argument, and contingency from the second; for these notions are strictly correlative. If it is contingent that I am in state S, then I might have been in some other state or had some other property instead (at a minimum, state non-S); that is, there are potentialities for me that I did not realize. And if there are potentialities that I might have realized but did not, then my not realizing them, and my realizing some alternative, is a contingent fact about me; it is one that might not have obtained.

Thus, starting from points insisted on by classical theology, Hartshorne has effectively shown that these points require the theologian to give up the classical attributes of nonrelativity, pure actuality, and total necessity. The final member of this group, simplicity, falls as well, since its main support was the absence of any unrealized potentialities in God.

---

[2] And, as the classical theologian would add, could have refrained from creating any world at all. Hartshorne does not accept this addition; I will deal with that issue below. For now I am exploring implications of the common ground—that God could have created a world different from the one He did create.

[3] *Summa Theologiae,* Iae, Q. 45, art. 1.

Now let us turn to the classical attributes in Group 2, which I do not take Hartshorne to have succeeded in discrediting. I shall start with creation ex nihilo, since this is a fundamentally important element in classical theology, one I take to have deep roots in religious experience and practice. On this point there is a clear and sharp issue between Hartshorne and the classical tradition. For the latter not only is it the case, as Hartshorne would agree, that every finite individual owes its existence to the free creative activity of God, in the sense that apart from that creative activity *that* individual would not exist; in addition, it is wholly due to the free creative activity of God that anything other than Himself exists: it is contingent, and contingent on the will of God, that any created world at all exists. Whereas, for Hartshorne, it is a metaphysical necessity that there be a world of finite creatures, though not that there be just the one we have. This constitutes a significant difference in the area allotted to divine voluntary choice over against the area fenced round by impersonal metaphysical necessities.

Is the position of each party on this point in any way tied up with its position on the attributes of the first group? I cannot see that it is.[4] Why should we suppose that a deity with unrealized potentialities and contingent properties, and qualified by His cognitive relations with contingent objects, *must* be in relation with some world of entities other than Himself? Why should it not be one of His contingent properties that He has created beings other than Himself? Why should the fact that He *is* qualified by his relations to other beings imply the *impossibility* of there being no other beings to which He is related and thereby qualified? I cannot see that the neoclassical properties in our first group are incompatible with the correctness of the suggestions just broached. In fact, it seems that the traditional doctrine of creation is much more attractive, plausible, and coherent in Hartshornean than in Thomistic garb. When decked out in the medieval fashion, it is saddled with just those difficulties exposed so effectively by Hartshorne in the arguments canvassed [earlier]. It has to struggle to combine creation by a free act of will with the absence of alternative possibilities for God, and to combine the contingency of the world with the necessity of God's act of creation and with the necessity of God's knowledge of that world. Freed from those stultifying bonds it can display its charms to best advantage. It can mean what it says by "free act of will," by "contingency," by "knowledge," and so on. I would say that in exposing the internal contradictions of classical theology Hartshorne has done it a great service and rendered its doctrine of creation much more defensible. . . .

Now for temporality and mutability. I shall take it that these stand or fall together. God undergoes change *if* [if and only if] he is in time. The possibility of existing completely unchanged through a succession of temporal moments I shall dismiss as idle. Divergence in the other direction—change, in some sense, without temporal succession—deserves more of a hearing, and I shall accord it that shortly. However, since Hartshorne is clearly thinking of the sort of change that consists of first being in one state, and then at some temporally

---

[4] A crucial part of my support for this is contained in the next section, where I argue that temporality is not required by relativity, potentiality, etc. For if God is temporal, creation ex nihilo is difficult to maintain.

latter moment being in a different state, I shall use the term in that way. Hence I shall be taking temporality and mutability to be coextensive. . . .

I cannot see that contingency (in the sense of that which is not necessary, that the opposite of which is possible) is intelligible only for a temporal being that successively realizes various possibilities. It is true that a nontemporal being has no "open future" before it; once it exists then whatever is true of it is fixed, in a way in which that need not be the case for a temporal being. The latter can exist at a certain time, while it is yet undetermined which of various possibilities for its future will be realized. At least this is true if, as Hartshorne supposes, what is future is not yet determined. Nevertheless it can be true of a nontemporal being that although it is R it might not have been R; that, to put it in currently fashionable terms, there is a possible world in which it is not R. This is sufficient to make the fact that it is R a contingent fact. Moreover this sense or kind of contingency, there being some possible world in which it is not the case, is the basic one. Alternative possibilities for an as yet undetermined future constitute a particular subsense or subtype. Its being contingent at this moment whether I shall finish writing this essay this week, is just a special case of the phenomenon of alternative states of affairs holding in different possible worlds. The additional feature in this case is that at this moment it is not yet determined which of these possible worlds is the actual world.

One who is indisposed to accept contingency without an open future should consider whether one could say that the past of a temporal being could be contingent in any respect. Is it now a contingent or a necessary truth that I went to bed at 10:15 P.M. last evening? In whatever sense we can recognize that to be a contingent truth we can also recognize various truths concerning a nontemporal being to be contingent.

Finally, let me point out that this "not true in all possible worlds" sense of contingency is the only one in which Hartshorne has given reason for supposing God to exhibit contingency without presupposing that God is temporal. Without that presupposition his argument simply amounts to the following. "The existence of the created world (or, less question-beggingly, things other than God) and any part thereof is contingent. Therefore it (they) might have been otherwise. Therefore any relation in which God stands to the world, e.g., creating it or knowing it, might have been otherwise, and so is contingent." The conclusion of this argument is simply that any relation in which God stands to the world *might have been otherwise*. There is no license for drawing the further conclusion that God exists at a succession of temporal standpoints relative to each of which there is an open future.

But, it will be said, we are still faced with the apparent unintelligibility of a nontemporal being qualified by its relations to temporal beings. Is it possible to make sense of this? As far as knowledge is concerned, it seems to me that the psychological concept of the specious present provides an intelligible model for a nontemporal knowledge of a temporal world. In using the concept of the specious present to think about human perception, one thinks of a human being as perceiving some temporally extended stretch of a process in one temporally indivisible act. If my specious present lasts for, e.g., one-twentieth of a second, then I perceive a full one-twentieth of a second of, e.g., the flight of a bee "all at once." I don't *first* perceive the first half of that stretch of the flight, *and then* perceive the second. My perception, though not its object, is without temporal succession. It does not unfold successively. It is a single unified act. Now just expand the specious present to cover all of time, and you have a model for God's awareness of the world. . . .

DISCUSSION QUESTIONS

1. What do Plato's views about God have in common with biblical theology? What are the similarities between Koranic and biblical theology?

2. Reconstruct Plato's argument that God must be immutable.

3. (a) Reconstruct Avicenna's argument for what he calls God's unicity (and what others call God's simplicity). (b) Also, find foreshadowing of the argument with Philo. (c) To what extent does Augustine embrace, or reject, the doctrine of simplicity in upholding trinitarianism? Carefully retrace his reflection.

4. Using the definition of *negative theology* in the Glossary, find negative theological statements in the readings from the Bible and from Philo. How is Philo's negative theology softened or mollified?

5. Compare the views of creation of Plato, Philo, Augustine, and Avicenna.

6. Citing any of the premodern readings in this section (any selection up to that from Richard Gale), present a list of commonly identified attributes of God. Do Gale's arguments show that one or another of these attributes is *incompatible* with any other? Explain.

7. In the light of Richard Gale's reflections, alternatively of Charles Hartshorne's, how would you interpret (as sympathetically as possible, for the purpose of this exercise) the biblical statement that "all things are possible with God"?

8. What mistakes do classical theists make about God, according to Charles Hartshorne? What is Hartshorne's alternative conception of God? Do you find it indeed a superior theological view? Why or why not?

9. Both Augustine and William Alston (among others) hold that God is atemporal, that is to say, that God is not in time. Trace the reflection of each on this score. Does the atemporal position mitigate any of the difficulties in classical theism alleged by Charles Hartshorne? What does Alston have to say about this? What is your own view?

10. Draw together all the strands of reflection in this section on the issue of whether God (supposing God to exist) is immutable or mutable, paying special attention to Charles Hartshorne's arguments. What is the best position and why?

ABSOLUTE BRAHMAN

[handwritten margin note: ultimate reality — univ. soul through all the deities]

As noted in the general introduction, there is more diversity of fundamental philosophic opinion within Hinduism than within any Western religion or tradition of theology. Probably the dominant view is what has been called *henotheism,* which is in essence a type of monotheism but which also admits a plurality of gods and goddesses. Henotheism is the view that there is one God who takes many forms, one God enlivening and appearing as each god or goddess. But there is also the distinct albeit minority position that the different divinities are separate and not unified.

Another position, prevalent among high-brow Indian philosophers, emphasizes an absoluteness of God, or , more properly, of Brahman: Brahman, the single reality, is so utterly real and simple that all appearance of diversity must be unreal—including the gods and goddesses. Even God is unreal insofar as God is thought of as personal or in any way determinate. There is only the Absolute, the One, called Brahman. This position finds its clearest articulation in the Indian classical school known as *Advaita* (Non-Dualism).

Hindu or *Indian theism* has been influenced by the absolutist conception. However, it is crucial to all Indian *theo*logians (as opposed to Advaitins, or philosophers of Brahman understood as the One, the Absolute) to regard the forms taken by Brahman (=God) as real. Similarly, the world is real. The influence of the absolutist conception has meant that, first, emanationism is the preferred doctrine of creation (God creating, or manifesting, the world out of God's own self), and, second, levels of degrees of reality are proposed, from God, the Supreme, through the lesser gods and goddesses and human souls to material things. Thus Indian theism is similar to Neoplatonism in the West (compare what Avicenna says, for example, about the acts of God—although no Indian theist would be quite so insistent about what Avicenna calls God's unicity, i.e. simplicity).

Indian theists use the Sanskrit word for God (*īśvara*) and that for the Absolute (*brahman*) interchangeably. Classical philosophers of the Absolute (Advaitins) are at pains, then, to differentiate their notion of Brahman from the theists' notion of God. In the modern period, intellectuals trying to explain the outlook of Hinduism to the larger world have tended to minimize this dispute, and to find in the notion of Brahman, the Absolute, room for the more specific conceptions of other religions, including, it is important to note, the impersonalistic views of Buddhism (see the selection from Vivekananda under Religious Pluralism).

The complexity of Indian religious metaphysics—with its poles of strict Absolutism, on the one end, polytheism, on the other, and several henotheistic compromises in between—urges here a dual treatment. in this section, after observing the basic henotheistic idea in Hindu Scriptures, we shall tend to focus on the Absolutist pole and consider views about Brahman as understood in Advaita. In the section Polytheism and Henotheism, we shall return to Indian theism and look more closely at the idea of many gods and goddesses unified as a single Divine.

The Gods as Faces of God (Henotheism)

From the *Ṛg Veda,* Swami Prakash Sarasvati and Satyakam Vidyalanakr, translators, 1977–1980. • From *The Bhagavad Gītā*, Franklin Edgerton, translator, 1944

The Ṛg Veda is the oldest text in Sanskrit (the language of classical Indian philosophy and religion), and indeed the oldest in any language of the Indo-European family (which includes Greek, Latin, German, and English). Some Vedic hymns date back probably to 1200 BCE. Few Vedic gods continued to be worshipped in classical and modern India. But the Vedic theme of a pervasive divinity moving the gods and responsible for harmony in the universe shaped most later Indian religion. In the verses excerpted here we find that theme, sometimes called henotheism.

The most popular text of devotional Hinduism—or popular theism in India—is clearly the Bhagavad Gītā, "Song of God," a short poem in Sanskrit set in the middle of an epic about a war over a kingdom and rightful succession. Immediately prior to what proves to be the decisive battle, Krishna, prince of a neighboring land, reveals himself as God incarnate to Arjuna, an archer and brother to the throne's rightful heir. In the Gītā, Krishna teaches Arjuna about many theological as well as practical matters. In the verses excerpted, again we find henotheism expressed.

FROM THE *ṚG VEDA*[1]

They have styled Him Indra (the Chief of the gods), Mitra (the Friend), Varuṇa (the Venerable), Agni (Fire), also the celestial, great-winged Garutmā; for although one, poets speak of Him diversely; they say Agni, Yama (Death), and Mātarīśvan (Lord of breath). (*RV* 1.164.46)

The divine architect, the impeller of all, the multiform, has begotten and nourished a numerous projeny, since all these worlds belong to Him. . . . (*RV* 3.55.19)

The ten hundreds stand there as one; I have beheld the most excellent form of the gods. (*RV* 5.62.1)

His steady light, swifter than the mind, stationed throughout the moving world, indicates the way to happiness. All the gods are of one accord and one intention; they proceed unobstructed according to a single Will. (*RV* 6.9.5)

---

[1] Some alterations have been made—ed.

FROM *THE BHAGAVAD GĪTĀ*[2]

[Krishna said:]
In whatsoever way any come to Me,
In that same way I grant them favor.
People on all sides
Follow a path that is mine. (*Gītā*, 4.11)

Even those who are devotees of other gods,
And worship them permeated with faith,
It is only me, son of Kuntī (Arjuna), that even they
Worship, (tho) not in the enjoined fashion.
For I of all acts of worship
Am both the recipient and the lord; . . . (*Gītā* 9.23–24a)

[Arjuna said:]
I see the gods in Thy body, O God,
All of them, and the hosts of various kinds of beings too,
The Creator sitting on the lotus-seat,
And the seers all, and the divine serpents.
With many arms, bellies, mouths, and eyes,
I see Thee, infinite in form on all sides; . . . (*Gītā*, 11.15–16a)

[Arjuna said:]
O infinite Lord of Gods, in whom the world dwells,
Thou the imperishable, existent, non-existent, and beyond both!
Thou art the Primal God, the Ancient Spirit,
Thou art the supreme resting-place of this universe;
Thou art the knower, the object of knowledge, and the highest station,
By Thee the universe is pervaded, Thou of infinite form! (*Gītā* 11.37b–38)

The Absolute in the Upanishads

From *The Life Divine* by Sri Aurobindo, 1973

The Upanishads are predominantly mystic texts composed after the Veda. The earliest twelve or thirteen Upanishads range in date from 800 to 300 BCE. Upanishadic teachings center on Brahman, that is, the Absolute or God. They do not, however, speak with a single voice, at least not indisputably. Some Upanishads seem to favor the Advaita conception; others the theistic—although that Brahman is in some sense a Unity appears a common theme.

In the passage below, the twentieth-century philosopher Aurobindo (about whom, see Speculative Spiritual Metaphysics) echoes several Upanishadic passages in presenting the idea of Brahman as the Absolute and the One. But in line with his own theological inclu-

---

[2] Some alterations have been made—ed.

*sivism, he does not echo passages that suggest that the reality of Brahman means the illu-
sion of diversity in the world. With the following selection—from Śaṅkara—we encounter
the pure Advaita Absolutism. Here with Aurobindo we get a more moderate view.*

. . . The Upanishads affirm that all this is the Brahman; Mind is Brahman, Life is Brahman, Matter is Brahman; addressing Vayu, the Lord of Air, of Life, it is said "O Vayu, thou art manifest
Brahman"; and, pointing to man and beast and bird and insect, each separately is identified with
the One,—"O Brahman, thou art this old man and boy and girl, this bird, this insect." Brahman
is the Consciousness that knows itself in all that exists; Brahman is the Force that sustains the
power of God and Titan and Demon, the Force that acts in man and animal and the forms and energies of Nature; Brahman is the Ananda, the secret Bliss of existence which is the ether of our
being and without which none could breathe or live. Brahman is the inner Soul in all; it has taken
a form in correspondence with each created form which it inhabits. The Lord of Beings is that
which is conscious in the conscious being, but he is also the Conscious in inconscient things, the
One who is master and in control of the many that are passive in the hands of Force-Nature. He
is the Timeless and Time; he is Space and all that is in Space; he is Causality and the cause and
the effect: He is the thinker and his thought, the warrior and his courage, the gambler and his
dice-throw. All realities and all aspects and all semblances are the Brahman; Brahman is the Absolute, the transcendent and incommunicable, the Supracosmic Existence that sustains the cosmos, the Cosmic Self that upholds all beings, but It is too the self of each individual: the soul or
psychic entity is an eternal portion of the Ishwara [the Lord]; it is his supreme Nature or Consciousness-Force that has become the living being in a world of living beings. The Brahman
alone is, and because of It all are, for all are the Brahman; this Reality is the reality of everything
that we see in Self and Nature. Brahman, the Ishwara, is all this by his Yoga-Maya, by the power
of his Consciousness-Force put out in self-manifestation: he is the Conscious Being, Soul, Spirit,
Purusha, and it is by his Nature, the force of his conscious self-existence that he is all things; he
is the Ishwara, the omniscient and omnipotent All-ruler, and it is by his Shakti, his conscious
Power, that he manifests himself in Time and governs the universe. These and similar statements
taken together are all-comprehensive: it is possible for the mind to cut and select, to build a
closed system and explain away all that does not fit within it; but it is on the complete and many-
sided statement that we must take our stand if we have to acquire an integral knowledge.

Classical Non-Dualism (Advaita)

From *The Bṛhadāraṇyaka Upaniṣad: With the commentary of Śaṅkara,* Swami
Madhavananda, translator

*The most renowned proponent of the Absolutism known as Non-Dualism, or Advaita, is
Śaṅkara (c. 725 CE). Śaṅkara interprets the Upanishads as proclaiming the sole reality of
Brahman, who is identical with our self-awareness aware only of itself. The apparent theism and emanationism of some passages he explains as meditational aids. Thus there are
some Upanishadic passages closer to Śaṅkara's heart than others. Below is excerpted a
portion of his commentary on the* Bṛhadāraṇyaka Upaniṣad *where we find pretty clearly*

presented the Advaita—or Non-Dualist—understanding of Brahman as identical with self-awareness aware of nothing but itself.

Little is known with certitude about Śaṅkara's life, partly because in inaugurating an important monastic order and achieving great fame in Indian culture at large considerable legend grew up around him. It is difficult to separate the apocryphal from fact. Still, it seems sure that Śaṅkara was a great public speaker, vanquishing opponents in public debate. Śaṅkara is also famed—most deservedly—as a master of Sanskrit prose. Few if any classical Indian philosophers have been more widely read.

In the selection below from Śaṅkara's Upanishadic commentaries, the great Advaitin explains how all is illusory except the self, which is self-aware but aware of nothing other than itself. The self is the sole reality, Brahman. The individual, everyday self emerges like a bubble on the sea, but the bubble, in this conception, has no independent reality. Śaṅkara claims that in the mystical experience of Brahman all diversity disappears, and that there is, strictly speaking, nothing other than Brahman, the One and self-aware.

[*Bṛhadāraṇyaka Upaniṣad* 2.4.12:] . . . As a lump of salt dropped into water dissolves with (its component) water, and no one is able to pick it up, but from wheresoever one takes it, it tastes salt, even so, my dear, this great, endless, infinite Reality is but Pure Intelligence. (The self) comes out (as a separate entity) from these elements, and (this separateness) is destroyed with them. After attaining (this oneness) it has no more consciousness.[1] . . .

[Śaṅkara's commentary:] An illustration on the point is being given: '*As a lump of salt,*' . . . *From wheresoever,* from whichsoever part, *one takes* the water and tastes *it, it* is *salt.* But there is no longer any lump.

Like this illustration . . . is *this great Reality* called the Supreme Self, from which you have been cut off by ignorance as a separate entity, through your connection with the limiting adjuncts of the body and organs, and have become mortal, subject to birth and death, hunger and thirst, and other such relative attributes, and identified with name, form and action, and think you are born of such and such a family. That separate existence of yours, which has sprung from the delusion engendered by contact with the limiting adjuncts of the body and organs, enters its cause, the great Reality, the Supreme Self, which stands for the ocean, which is undecaying, immortal, beyond fear, pure and homogeneous like a lump of salt, and which Pure Intelligence, infinite, boundless, without a break and devoid of differences caused by the delusion brought on by ignorance. When that separate existence has entered and been merged in its cause, in other words, when the differences created by ignorance are gone, the universe becomes one without a second, 'the great Reality.' . . . There may be things in the relative world as big as the Himalayas, for instance, created by a dream or illusion, but they are not true; hence the text adds the qualifying word 'true.' . . .

Question: If It is one without a second, really pure and untouched by the miseries of the relative world, whence is this separate existence of the individual self, in which it is

---

[1] That is, particular consciousness.

born and dies, is happy or miserable, possessed of the ideas of 'I and mine,' and so on, and which is troubled by many a relative attribute?

Reply: I will explain it. There are the elements transformed into the body, organs and sense-objects, consisting of name and form. They are like the foam and bubbles on the limpid water of the Supreme Self. The mergence of these elements down to sense-objects in Brahman, which is Pure Intelligence, through a discriminating knowledge of the Truth has been spoken of—like the emptying of rivers into the ocean. *From these elements* called 'truth,' i.e., with their aid, the self *comes out* like a lump of salt. As from water reflections of the sun, moon, etc. arise, or from the proximity of such limiting adjuncts as a red cotton-pad a transparent crystal turns red and so forth, so from the limiting adjuncts of the elements, transformed into the body and organs, the self comes out clearly as an individualised entity. These elements, transformed into the body, organs and sense-objects, from which the self comes out as an individual, and which are the cause of its individualisation, are merged, like rivers in the ocean, by the realisation of Brahman through the instruction of the scriptures and the teacher, and are destroyed. And when they are destroyed like the foam and bubbles of water, this individualised existence too *is destroyed with them.* As the reflections of the sun, moon, etc. and the colour of the crystal vanish when their causes, the water, the red cotton-pad, and so on, are removed, and only the (sun), moon, etc., remain as they are, so the endless, infinite and limpid Pure Intelligence alone remains.

. . . No more is there such particular consciousness as, 'I so and so am the son of so and so; this is my land and wealth; I am happy or miserable.' For it is due to ignorance, and since ignorance is absolutely destroyed by the realisation of Brahman, how can the knower of Brahman, who is established in his nature as Pure Intelligence, possibly have any such particular consciousness? Even when a man is in the body,[2] particular consciousness is (sometimes) impossible; so how can it ever exist in a man who has been absolutely freed from the body and organs? . . .

[*Bṛhadāraṇyaka Upaniṣad* 2.4.14:] Because when there is duality, as it were, then one smells something, one sees something, one hears something, one speaks something, one thinks something, one knows something. (But) when to the knower of Brahman everything has become the Self, then what should one smell and through what, what should one see and through what, what should one hear and through what, what should one speak and through what, what should one think and through what, what should one know and through what? Through what should one know That owing to which all this is known—through what, should one know the Knower?

[Śaṅkara's commentary:] Why then is it said that after attaining oneness the self has no more consciousness? Listen. *Because when,* i.e. in the presence of the particular or individual aspect of the Self due to the limiting adjuncts, the body and organs conjured up by ignorance, *there is duality, as it were,* in Brahman, which really is one without a second, i.e. there appears to be something different from the Self. . . .

---

[2] For instance, in the state of deep sleep.

Then, just because there is duality as it were, therefore, *one,* he who smells, viz the un-real individual aspect of the Supreme Self, comparable to the reflection of the moon etc. in water, *smells something* that can be smelt, through something else, viz the nose. 'One' and 'something' refer to two typical factors of an action, the agent and object, and 'smells' sig-nifies the action and its result. As, for instance, in the word 'cuts.' This one word signifies the repeated strokes dealt and the separation of the object cut into two; for an action ends in a result, and the result cannot be perceived apart from the action. Similarly he who smells a thing that can be smelt does it through the nose. The rest is to be explained as above. *One knows something.* This is the state of ignorance. But when ignorance has been destroyed by the knowledge of Brahman, there is nothing but the Self. *When to the knower of Brahman everything,* such as name and form, has been merged in the Self and *has* thus *become the Self, then what* object to be smelt *should one smell,* who should smell, *and through what* instrument? Similarly *what should one see* and *hear?* Everywhere an action depends on certain factors; hence when these are absent, the action cannot take place; and in the absence of an action there can be no result. Therefore so long as there is ignorance, the operation of actions and their factors and results can take place, but not in the case of a knower of Brahman. For to him everything is the Self, and there are no factors or results of actions apart from That. Nor can the universe, being an unreality, be the Self of anybody. Therefore it is ignorance that conjures up the idea of the non-Self; strictly speaking, there is nothing but the Self. Therefore when one truly realises the unity of the Self, there cannot be any consciousness of actions and their factors and results. Hence, because of contradic-tion, there is an utter absence of actions and their means for the knower of Brahman. . . .

DISCUSSION QUESTIONS

1. According to the readings from the *Ṛg Veda* and the *Gītā,* there is a Divine Unity although there are also multiple gods and multiple forms of appropriate worship. How could this be?

2. According to Aurobindo's interpretation of the Upanishads, Brahman is the One, an Absolute Reality of all things. Is it also suggested that the appearance of diverse things is unreal? Explain.

3. How does Śaṅkara understand Brahman? Why, in his view, is individualized exis-tence unreal?

THE VIBRANT VOID, EMPTINESS (ŚŪNYATĀ)

It is problematic whether any notion in Buddhist philosophy stakes out remotely the same ground as concepts of God found in Western religions, or concepts of Brahman in Hinduism. Compared with Buddhist ideas, even the "matter" of materialism could be viewed as more directly competing with the notions of a Divine Reality that so far we have reviewed. A materialism, like any theology, endorses something as an "ultimate reality," namely matter. In Buddhism, we find, in contrast, outright denial that there is any God or anything like God (even matter) as an enduring objective reality.

The message of Buddhism is thoroughly mystical. Its doctrines are woven around a sense of the supreme importance of a special experience called *nirvāṇa*. Moreover, from the earliest Buddhist Scriptures to modern lamas and Zen masters, rational cogitation, as demanded in philosophy, is said to hinder progress toward that goal. There is a vigorous anti-intellectualism in Buddhist teachings, a tradition of opposition to speculative philosophy. Still, if we insist on viewing Nirvana as an experience that is *of* something, as sight is of things with shape and color, then think of that something as Nothingness, say Buddhist theorists. The Nothingness revealed by Nirvana is not the void of a nihilism; it is instead, paradoxically, a Vibrant Void, a Void brimming with compassion, so it is sometimes said. The term most commonly used, when one must be used, is the Sanskrit *śūnyatā*, literally, "Emptiness." In this way, the indications, if any, of Nirvana experience are not objectified, or only minimally objectified, and the salvific value of the experience is underscored, Buddhist philosophers have claimed. The term "Emptiness" also resonates with the central Buddhist teaching of "no-self" or "no-soul" (Sanskrit: *an-ātman*). Let me try to explain.

The "no-soul" doctrine is repeated throughout the Sermons of the Buddha as preserved in the Southern Canon (recall the discussion in the general introduction). As we shall see below with the selection from the Sri Lankan scholar, Walpola Rahula, the doctrine remains central in the Southern tradition, and is key, as Dr. Rahula explains, to the notion of an "Unconditioned Reality." The notion of an Unconditioned Reality comes close to a concept of a Divine Reality, at least as close as one can find in Southern Buddhism. Still, "no-soul" is to be understood in the context of a Buddhist path or discipline since it is to provide underpinnings for non-attachment or transcending desire, which, according to the Second Noble Truth, is key to attaining Nirvana (again, see the discussion in the general introduction).

In Mahāyāna or Northern Buddhism, the Nirvana experience seems cosmicized: the Awakened Mind—the Buddha Mind—fills all quarters of the universe. The selection below, from the *Suraṅgama Sūtra,* presents this conception. Here too, however, a transformational or soteriological teaching is paramount; led through a process of self-transcending by the Lord Buddha, Ānanda (traditionally the closest of the Buddha's disciples) gradually becomes prepared for the cosmic splendor related at the selection's end.

The modern Japanese philosopher, Keiji Nishitani, presents the Buddhist notion of a reality, or no-reality, "Emptiness," also within a soteriological context. To be empty of self-regard is to live on the "home ground" of oneself and of all things. This home ground is unlike anything we encounter in everyday life; it is "no-thing." But it is, in Nishitani's conception, as in the centuries-old Buddhist teachings he draws on, a supreme value, and indeed—or so it is intimated if not expressly declared—a supreme reality of everything.

"Unconditioned Reality" and "No-Soul"

From *What the Buddha Taught* by Walpola Rahula, 1974

Walpola Rahula is a Buddhist monk in the Southern tradition as well as a renowned scholar of early Buddhism, that is, of the doctrines and practices expressed in the Southern Canon. Trained first as a monk in the traditional manner in Sri Lanka and then as a scholar at the University of London and the University of Ceylon, he knows his tradition, we may say literally, both inside and out. He is currently Chancellor of the University of Kelaniya, Sri Lanka. In the selections excerpted below, Dr. Rahula translates several of the Buddha's Sermons (referred to as suttas) in explaining Nirvana (Pali: nibbāna) as Absolute Truth along with the doctrine of "No-Soul."

According to Rahula, Nirvana is positive. However, it has to be expressed negatively, apparently because of its transcendent character. This view echoes the negative theology of Philo and others, although it may well be that the transcendence of Nirvana and that of God are not conceived at all similarly.

What in general is suggested by Soul, Self, Ego, or to use the Sanskrit expression Ātman, is that in man there is a permanent, everlasting and absolute entity, which is the unchanging substance behind the changing phenomenal world. According to some religions, each individual has such a separate soul which is created by God, and which, finally after death, lives eternally either in hell or heaven, its destiny depending on the judgment of its creator. According to others, it goes through many lives till it is completely purified and becomes finally united with God or Brahman, Universal Soul or Ātman, from which it originally emanated. This soul or self in man is the thinker of thoughts, feeler of sensations, and receiver of rewards and punishments for all its actions good and bad. Such a conception is called the idea of self.

Buddhism stands unique in the history of human thought in denying the existence of such a Soul, Self, or Ātman. According to the teaching of the Buddha, the idea of self is an imaginary, false belief which has no corresponding reality, and it produces harmful thoughts of 'me' and 'mine', selfish desire, craving, attachment, hatred, ill-will, conceit, pride, egoism, and other defilements, impurities and problems. It is the source of all the troubles in the world from personal conflicts to wars between nations. In short, to this false view can be traced all the evil in the world.

Two ideas are psychologically deep-rooted in man: self-protection and self-preservation. For self-protection man has created God, on whom he depends for his own protection, safety and security, just as a child depends on its parent. For self-preservation man has conceived the idea of an immortal Soul or Ātman, which will live eternally. In his ignorance, weakness, fear, and desire, man needs these two things to console himself. Hence he clings to them deeply and fanatically.

The Buddha's teaching does not support his ignorance, weakness, fear, and desire, but aims at making man enlightened by removing and destroying them, striking at their very root. According to Buddhism, our ideas of God and Soul are false and empty. Though highly developed as theories, they are all the same extremely subtle mental projections, garbed in an intricate metaphysical and philosophical phraseology. These ideas are so deep-rooted in man, and so near and dear to him, that he does not wish to hear, nor does he want to understand, any teaching against them.

The Buddha knew this quite well. In fact, he said that his teaching was 'against the current' (*paṭisotagāmi*), against man's selfish desires. Just four weeks after his Enlightenment, seated under a banyan tree, he thought to himself: 'I have realized this Truth which is deep, difficult to see, difficult to understand . . . comprehensible only by the wise . . . Men who are overpowered by passions and surrounded by a mass of darkness cannot see this Truth, which is against the current, which is lofty, deep, subtle and hard to comprehend.' . . .

And further, referring to Nirvāṇa the Buddha says:

'O bhikkhus, there is the unborn, ungrown, and unconditioned. Were there not the unborn, ungrown, and unconditioned, there would be no escape for the born, grown, and conditioned. Since there is the unborn, ungrown, and unconditioned, so there is escape for the born, grown, and conditioned.'[1]

'Here the four elements of solidity, fluidity, heat and motion have no place; the notions of length and breadth, the subtle and the gross, good and evil, name and form are altogether destroyed; neither this world nor the other, nor coming, going or standing, neither death nor birth, nor sense-objects are to be found.'[2]

Because Nirvāṇa is thus expressed in negative terms, there are many who have got a wrong notion that it is negative, and expresses self-annihilation. Nirvāṇa is definitely no annihilation of self, because there is no self to annihilate. If at all, it is the annihilation of the illusion, of the false idea of self.

It is incorrect to say that Nirvāṇa is negative or positive. The ideas or 'negative' and 'positive' are relative, and are within the realm of duality. These terms cannot be applied to Nirvāṇa, Absolute Truth, which is beyond duality and relativity.

A negative word need not necessarily indicate a negative state. The Pali or Sanskrit word for health is *ārogya,* a negative term, which literally means 'absence or illness'. But *ārogya* (health) does not represent a negative state. The word 'Immortal' (or its Sanskrit equivalent *Amṛta* or Pali *Amata*), which also is a synonym for Nirvāṇa, is negative, but it does not denote a negative state. The negation of negative values is not negative. One of the well-known synonyms for Nirvāṇa is 'Freedom' (Pali *Mutti,* Skt. *Mukti*). Nobody would say that freedom is negative. But even freedom has a negative side: freedom is always a liberation from something which is obstructive, which is evil, which is negative. But freedom is not negative. So Nirvāṇa, *Mutti* or *Vimutti,* the Absolute Freedom, is freedom

---

[1] Ud. (Colombo, 1920), p. 129.
[2] Ibid. p. 128; D I (Colombo, 1929), p. 172.

from all evil, freedom from craving, hatred and ignorance, freedom from all terms of duality, relativity, time and space.

We may get some idea of Nirvāṇa as Absolute Truth from the *Dhātuvibhaṅga-sutta* (No. 140) of the *Majjhima-nikāya*. This extremely important discourse was delivered by the Buddha to Pukkusāti (already mentioned), whom the Master found to be intelligent and earnest, in the quiet of the night in a potter's shed. The essence of the relevant portions of the sutta is as follows:

A man is composed of six elements: solidity, fluidity, heat, motion, space and consciousness. He analyses them and finds that none of them is 'mine,' or 'me,' or 'my self'. He understands how consciousness appears and disappears, how pleasant, unpleasant and neutral sensations appear and disappear. Through this knowledge his mind becomes detached. Then he finds within him a pure equanimity (*upekhā*), which he can direct towards the attainment of any high spiritual state, and he knows that thus this pure equanimity will last for a long period. But then he thinks:

> 'If I focus this purified and cleansed equanimity on the Sphere of Infinite Space and develop a mind conforming thereto, that is a mental creation (*saṃkhatam*).[3] If I focus this purified and cleansed equanimity on the Sphere of Infinite Consciousness . . . on the Sphere of Nothingness . . . or on the Sphere of Neither-perception nor Non-perception and develop a mind conforming thereto, that is a mental creation.' Then he neither mentally creates nor wills continuity and becoming (*bhava*) or annihilation (*vibhava*). As he does not construct or does not will continuity and becoming or annihilation, he does not cling to anything in the world; as he does not cling, he is not anxious; as he is not anxious, he is completely calmed within (fully blown out within *paccattaṃ yeva parinibbāyati*). And he knows: 'Finished is birth, lived is pure life, what should be done is done, nothing more is left to be done.'

Now, when he experiences a pleasant, unpleasant or neutral sensation, he knows that it is impermanent, that it does not bind him, that it is not experienced with passion. Whatever may be the sensation, he experiences it without being bound to it (*visaṃyutto*). He knows that all those sensations will be pacified with the dissolution of the body, just as the flame of a lamp goes out when oil and wick give out.

'Therefore, O bhikkhu, a person so endowed is endowed with the absolute wisdom, for the knowledge of the extinction of all *dukkha* [suffering] is the absolute noble wisdom.

'This his deliverance, founded on Truth, is unshakable. O bhikkhu, that which is unreality (*mosadhamma*) is false; that which is reality (*amosadhamma*), Nibbāna, is Truth (*Sacca*). Therefore, O bhikkhu, a person so endowed is endowed with this Absolute Truth. For, the Absolute Noble Truth (*paramaṃ ariyasaccaṃ*) is Nibbāna, which is Reality.'

---

[3] Notice that all the spiritual and mystic states, however pure and high they may be, are mental creations, mind-made, conditioned and compound (*saṃkhata*). They are not Reality, not Truth (*sacca*).

Cosmic Enlightened Mind

From the *Surangama Sūtra,* in *A Buddhist Bible,* Dwight Goddard, editor, 1938

As explained, Northern or Mahāyāna Buddhism developed its own scriptural tradition. The Surangama Sūtra *is a part of it. Mahāyāna is distinguished from Southern Buddhism principally by the contrast between the Bodhisattva and Arhat (see the general introduction). But in Mahāyāna there is also a more substantive notion of what Nirvana experience reveals, a cosmicized Enlightenment, as we find expressed in the excerpted selection.*

THE MANY MANIFESTATIONS OF THE WONDERFUL ESSENCE-MIND, AND OF THE PERFECT PRINCIPLE OF THE THREE EXCELLENCIES WITHIN THE ALL-INCLUSIVE UNITY OF THE WOMB OF TATHĀGATA

Buddha trying to teach Ananda

(False Mind vs True Mind)

When Ānanda came into the presence of the Lord Buddha, he bowed down to the ground in great humility, blaming himself that he had not yet fully developed the potentialities of Enlightenment, because from the beginning of his previous lives, he had too much devoted himself to study and learning. He earnestly pleaded with the Lord Buddha and with all the other Tathāgatas from the ten quarters of the Universe, to support him in attaining perfect Enlightenment, that is, to support him in his practice of the Three Excellencies of Dhyāna, Samādhi and Samāpatti,* by some most fundamental and expedient means.

At the same time, all of the Bodhisattva-Mahāsattvas, as numerous as the sands of the river Ganges, together with all the Arhats, Pratyeka-Buddhas, from all the ten quarters, with one accord and with gladness of heart, prepared to listen to the instruction to be given to Ānanda by the Lord Buddha. With one accord they paid homage to the Lord and then resuming their seats, waited in perfect quietness and patience to receive the sacred teaching.

Then the Lord Buddha spoke to Ānanda, saying:— Ānanda, you and I are from the same ancestral blood and we have always cherished a fraternal affection for each other. Let me ask you a few questions and you answer me spontaneously and freely. When you first began to be interested in Buddhism what was it that impressed you in our Buddhist way of life and most influenced you to forsake all worldly pleasures and enabled you to cut asunder your youthful sexual cravings?

Ānanda replied:—Oh, my Lord! The first thing that impressed me were the thirty-two marks of excellency in my Lord's personality. They appeared to me so fine, as tender and brilliant, and transparent as a crystal.

---

* These are three types of mystic trance.—ed.

From that time I have constantly thought about them and have been more and more convinced that these marks of excellence would be impossible for anyone who was not free from all sexual passion and desire. And why? Because when anyone becomes inflamed by sexual passion, his mind becomes disturbed and confused, he loses self-control and becomes reckless and crude. Besides, in sexual intercourse, the blood becomes inflamed and impure and adulterated with impure secretions. Naturally from such a source, there can never originate an aureole of such transcendently pure and golden brightness as I have seen emanating fom the person of my Lord. It was because of this that I admired my Lord and it was this that influenced me to become one of thy true followers.

The Lord Buddha then said:—Very good, Ānanda! All of you in this Great Dharma Assembly ought to know and appreciate that the reason why sentient beings by their previous lives since beginningless time have formed a succession of deaths and rebirths, life after life, is because they have never realized the true Essence of Mind and its self-purifying brightness. On the contrary they have been absorbed all the time busying themselves with their deluding and transient thoughts which are nothing but falsity and vanity. Hence they have prepared for themselves the conditions for this ever returning cycle of deaths and rebirths. . . .

Ānanda then addressed the Lord Buddha, saying:—Noble Lord! Some time ago when my Lord was discussing the intrinsic Dharma with the four great Bodhisattva-Mahāsattvas, . . . I overheard my Lord to say, that the essence of the discerning, perceiving, conscious mind existed neither inside nor outside, nor between, in fact, that it had no location of existence. Since my Lord has interpreted this in his teachings just now, I have ceased to grasp any arbitrary conception as to the location of mind, but if this is true, and it is something intangible, in what sense can it be thought of as "my mind."

The Lord Buddha replied:—Ānanda, as to what you have just said that the essence of the discerning, perceptive, conscious mind has no definite location anywhere, the meaning is clear; it is neither in this world, in the vast open spaces, neither in water, nor on land, neither flying with wings, nor walking, nor is it anywhere. But when you say that your mind no longer grasps any arbitrary conception of the existence of the phenomena of mind, what do you mean by it? Do you mean that the phenomena have no true existence, or that they have no tangible existence? If you mean that they have no true existence, that would mean that they are like hair on a tortoise, or like horns on a rabbit. But so long as you retain this notion of not grasping, you cannot mean perfect non-existence. But what do you mean? Of course if your mind is perfectly blank, it must mean, as far as you are concerned, absolute non-existence, but if you are still cherishing some arbitrary conception of phenomena, you must mean some kind of existence. How is it then, that so long as the notion of not-grasping of anything, as for instance, the notion of "my mind," that you mean its non-existence? Therefore, Ānanda, you ought to see that what you have just said concerning the non-existence of anything just because you no longer cherish a conception of it within your mind, and that would mean the non-existence of a discerning, perceptive, conscious mind, would be quite absurd, would it not?

Thereupon, Ānanda rose from his place in the midst of the assembly, adjusted his ceremonial scarf, knelt upon his right knee, placed the palms of his hands together, and respectfully addressed the Lord Buddha, saying:—

My Noble Lord! I have the honor of being thy youngest relative and thou hast always treated me with affectionate kindness. Although I am now only one of your many converts, thou dost still continue to show thy affection for me. But in spite of all I have gained mentally, I have not become liberated from contaminations and attachments and consequently I could not overcome the magic spell at the home of a harlot. My mind became confused and I was at the point of drowning in its defilement. I can see now that it was wholly due to my ignorance as to the right realization of what is true and essential Mind. I pray thee, Oh my Lord, to have pity and mercy upon me and show me the right Path to the spiritual graces of the Samāpatti so that I may attain to self-mastery and become emancipated from the lure of evil myself, and be able to free all heretics from the bonds of their false ideas and craft.

When Ānanda had finished his plea, he bowed humbly before the Lord Buddha, with hands and forehead touching the ground, and the whole audience, awed into intense excitement, waited with earnest and reverential hearts for the response of the Blessed One.

Suddenly in the Meditation Hall, filled with its awed and expectant throng, there appeared a most marvelous sight that transcended everything that had ever been seen before. The Hall was filled with a radiant splendor that emanated from the moon-life face of the Blessed One, like hundreds of thousands of sunbeams scintillating everywhere, and wherever the rays reached immediately there were seen celestial Buddha-lands. Moreover, the person of the Lord Buddha was vibrant with the six transcendental motions simultaneously manifesting and embracing all the Buddha-lands of the ten quarters of all the universes, as numerous as the finest particles of dust in the sunlight. And this all-embracing, blessed and transcendent glory united all these unnumerable Buddha-lands into one single whole, and all the great Bodhisattvas of all these innumerable Buddha-lands were seen to be each in his own place with hands raised and pressed together expectantly waiting for the words of the Blessed One.

Then the Lord Buddha addressed the assembly, saying:—Ānanda, from beginningless time, from life to life, all sentient beings have had their disturbing illusions that have been manifested in their natural development each under the conditioning power of his own individual karma, such as the seed-pod of the okra which when opening always drops three seeds in each group. The reason why all devoted disciples do not at once attain to supreme enlightenment is because they do not realize two primary principles and because of it some attain only to Arhatship, or to Pratyekaship, and some to even lower attainments, to the state of devas and heretics, and some to Mārā kings and their dependents. The reason for these great differences is because, not knowing these two basic principles, they become confused in mind and fall into wrong practices. It is as if they were trying to cook fine delicacies by boiling stones or sand, which of course they could never do if they tried for countless kalpas.

What are these two fundamental principles, Ānanda? The First Fundamental Principle is the primary cause of the succession of deaths and rebirths from beginningless time. (It is the Principle of Ignorance, the outgoing principle of individuation, manifestation, transformation, succession and discrimination.) From the working out of this Principle there has resulted the various differentiation of minds of all sentient beings, and all the time they have been taking these limited and perturbed and contaminated minds to be their true and natural Essence of Mind.

The Second Fundamental Principle is the primary cause of the pure unity of Enlightenment and Nirvāṇa that has existed from beginningless time. (It is the Principle of integrating compassion, the in-drawing, unifying principle of purity, harmony, likeness, rhythm, permanency and peace.) By the in-drawing of this Principle within the brightness of your own nature, its unifying spirit can be discovered and developed and realized under all varieties of conditions. The reason why this unifying spirit is so quickly lost amongst the conditions is because you so quickly forget the brightness and purity of your own essential nature, and amid the activities of the day, you cease to realize its existence. That is why, Ānanda, you and all sentient beings have fallen through ignorance into misfortune and into different realms of existence. . . .

Thereupon the Blessed Lord laid his hand affectionately upon the head of Ānanda and proceeded to explain the true and Essence nature of Mind, desiring to awaken in them a consciousness of that which transcended phenomena. He explained to them how necessary it was to keep the mind free from all discriminating thoughts of self and not-self if they were to correctly understand it.

He continued:—Ānanda and all my Disciples! I have always taught you that all phenomena and their developments are simply manifestations of mind. All causes and effects, from great universes to the fine dust only seen in the sunlight come into apparent existence only by means of the discriminating mind. If we examine the origin of anything in all the universe, we find that it is but a manifestation of some primal essence. Even the tiny leaves of herbs, knots of thread, everything, if we examine them carefully we find that there is some essence in its originality. Even open space is not nothingness. How can it be then that the wonderful, pure, tranquil and enlightened Mind, which is the source of all conceptions of manifested phenomena, should have no essence of itself?. . . .

Emptiness

From *Religion and Nothingness* by Keiji Nishitani, Jan Van Bragt, translator, 1982

Keiji Nishitani, the elder statesman of the "Kyoto School" in Japan, has followed the lead of Kitarō Nishida (1870–1945) in using Western philosophical terms and insights to elucidate and defend a Buddhist outlook. Nishitani presents a Buddhist philosophy that at once speaks from Buddhist religious experience and expresses a modern sensibility. He is concerned above all with defending the value of the "Zen experience" and enlightenment, called in Japanese satori.

Born in 1900, Nishitani studied in the twenties with Nishida, and for a brief period just before World War II with Martin Heidegger in Germany. He had a distinguished career at the State University of Kyoto, as lecturer in ethics and German from 1928 to 1935, as professor of religion from 1935 to 1955, and as holder of the chair of modern philosophy from 1955 until his retirement in 1963.

Nishitani claims that the central failure of philosophy in our time is that it has not provided an adequate response to nihilism. With all life ending in death, with personal survival dubious, and with personalistic religions such as Christianity unable to explain, he claims, the cruel objectivity of scientific law, nihilism appears to be, Nishitani argues, an unavoidable conclusion for the serious thinker. This "nihilism" is the view that there is no ultimate meaning to our activities and lives; they go on in a meaningless content. Upon reflection, the meaninglessness of life encompassed by insentience and death infects all particular goals, snuffing out any apparent value, like a poisonous gas. But although the nihilist view appears warranted, it is not, he says, tenable "existentially." Instead, it pushes us toward the "standpoint" of śūnyatā, "emptiness," where one ecstatically and spontaneously acts for the welfare of all—in accordance with the classical Mahayana conception of a Bodhisattva.

In the passage excerpted here, Nishitani explores the relation between self-awareness and śūnyatā, which is said to be the self's "home ground" where everything surrounds and rests on everything else—called by Nishitani (and his translator) circuminsession (from the Latin sedere, *to rest or sit on). As revealed in the* satori *experience, "Emptiness" is thus the fundamental reality of ourselves and all things. It is, however—Nishitani stresses in line with earlier Buddhists—not to be regarded as itself a thing or as somehow substantial. Nishitani suggests that our own crises reflect Emptiness's transcendence (see also the selection from Stephen Phillips under Evil).*

That a thing actually *is* means that it is absolutely unique. No two things in the world can be completely the same. The absolute uniqueness of a thing means, in other words, that it is situated in the absolute center of all other things. It is situated, as it were, in the position of *master,* with all other things positioned relative to it as *servants.*

To our ordinary way of thinking, though, it is simply a contradiction to claim that this is how it is with everything that "is," and yet that the "world" is constituted through all such things being gathered into one. How is it possible that something in the position of master to other things can at the same time stand in the position of servant to all other things? If we grant that each and every thing, in its mode of being as what it is in itself, enjoys an absolute autonomy and occupies the rank of master seated at the center of everything, how are we to avoid thinking of such a situation as complete anarchy and utter chaos? Is this not diametrically opposed to conceiving of the world as an order of being?

This sort of objection arises because one is only thinking on the field of ordinary consciousness, which covers the expanse between sensation and reason and leaves the field of śūnyatā out of the picture. That beings one and all are gathered into one, while each one remains absolutely unique in its "being," points to a relationship in which, as we said above, all things are master and servant to one another. We may call this relationship, which is only possible on the field of śūnyatā, "circuminsessional." . . .

All things that are in the world are linked together, one way or the other. Not a single thing comes into being without some relationship to every other thing. Scientific intellect thinks here in terms of natural laws of necessary causality; mythico-poetic imagination perceives an organic, living connection; philosophic reason contemplates an absolute One. But on a more essential level, a system of circuminsession has to be seen here, according to which, on the field of śūnyatā, all things are in a process of becoming master and servant to one another. In this system, each thing is itself in not being itself, and is not itself in being itself. Its being is illusion in its truth and truth in its illusion. This may sound strange the first time one hears it, but in fact it enables us for the first time to conceive of a *force* by virtue of which all things are gathered together and brought into relationship with one another, a force which, since ancient times, has gone by the name of "nature" (*physis*).

To say *that a thing is not itself* means that, while continuing to be itself, it is in the home-ground of everything else. Figuratively speaking, its roots reach across into the ground of all other things and helps to hold them up and keep them standing. It serves as a constitutive element of their being so that they can be what they are, and thus provides an ingredient of their being. *That a thing is itself* means that all other things, while continuing to be themselves, are in the home-ground of that thing; that precisely when a thing is on its own home-ground, everything else is there too; that the roots of every other thing spread across into its home-ground. This way that everything has of being on the home-ground of everything else, without ceasing to be on its own home-ground, means that the being of each thing is held up, kept standing, and made to be what it is by means of the being of all other things; or, put the other way around, that each thing holds up the being of every other thing, keeps it standing, and makes it what it is. In a word, it means that all things "are" in the "world."

To imply that when a thing is on its own home-ground, it must at the same time be on the home-ground of all other things sounds absurd; but in fact it constitutes the "essence" of the existence of things. The being of things in themselves is essentially circuminsessional. This is what we mean by speaking of beings as "being that is in unison with emptiness," and "being on the field of emptiness." For this circuminsessional system is only possible on the field of emptiness or śūnyatā . . . .

For us, this field of emptiness is something we are aware of as an absolute near side. It opens up more to the near side than we, in our ordinary consciousness, take our own self to be. It opens up, so to speak, still closer to us than what we ordinarily think of as ourselves. In other words, by turning from what we ordinarily call "self" to the field of śūnyatā we become truly ourselves. The meaning of this turn to the field of śūnyatā has already been explained. Namely, when nihility opens up at the ground of the self itself, it is not only perceived simply as a nihility that seems to be outside of the self. It is drawn into the self itself by the subject that views the self as empty. It becomes the field of ecstatic transcendence of the subject, and from there turns once more to the standpoint of śūnyatā as the absolute near side where emptiness is self.

This means that the field of the so-called self, the field of self-consciousness and consciousness, is broken down. In a more elemental sense, it means that we take leave of the essential self-attachment that lurks in the essence of self-consciousness and by virtue of which we get caught in our own grasp in trying to grasp ourselves. It means also that we take leave of the essential attachment to things that lurks in the essence of consciousness and by virtue of which we get caught in the grasp of things in trying to grasp them in an objective, representational manner.

What does it mean, though, to say that "emptiness is self"? We said that emptiness is the field of the possibility of the world and also the field of the possibility of the existence of things. "Emptiness is self" means that, at bottom and in its own home-ground, the self has its being as such a field. The self is not merely what the self is conscious of as self. The field of śūnyatā within which the world and things become possible opens up at the home-ground of the self as a self that is truly on the home-ground of the self itself, that is, the *original self in itself.*

As a field of "possibility," the home-ground of the self in the self precedes the world and things. Of course, I speak here not of temporal precedence, since time, too, becomes possible on the field where the world becomes possible. For this reason, it is perfectly all right to claim that nothing can be conceived of as temporally prior to the world, and to regard the world as continuing infinitely in time. Still, the home-ground of the self and the self itself that is truly on its home-ground are still essentially *before* the world and things. The self has its home-ground at a point disengaged from the world and things and, at bottom, that is where it comes to rest. One might call this a "transcendence" in a sense similar to that found in contemporary existential philosophy (although there are differences as to how this is conceived).

In sum, when we are on our own home-ground and are truly ourselves, we are on a field—and have our being *as* that field—where the "world," in the sense of a circuminsessional system of being referred to in the preceding section, becomes possible and where "things" at the same time possess their possibility of existence. It may be said that all of us, as individual human beings, are also "things" in the world and that our existence is an illusory appearance precisely as the truly real beings that we are. And we may then go on to say that where this being of ours "is" at an elemental level at one with emptiness, the world and the totality of things become manifest from our own home-ground.

To be on such a home-ground of our own is, for us, true *self-awareness.* Of course, that self-awareness is not a self-consciousness or a self-knowledge, nor is it anything akin to intellectual intuition. We are used to seeing the self as something that knows itself, or intellectually intuiting itself. But what is called here "self-awareness" is in no sense the self's knowing of itself. Quite to the contrary, it is the point at which such a "self" and such "knowledge" are emptied. In what sense might this, then, be said to be our true self-awareness?

In speaking of things, it was observed that expressions such as "Fire does not burn fire" and "The eye does not see the eye itself" point to the non-objective mode of being of things as they are in themselves. An eye is an eye because it sees things, but when the eye is on the home-ground of the eye itself, there is an essential *not-seeing.* Could the eye see the eye itself, it would not be able to see anything else. The eye would cease to be an eye. The eye is an eye through that essential not-seeing; and because of that essential not-seeing, seeing is possible. Not being an eye (not-seeing) constitutes the possibility of being an eye (seeing). For that reason, the being of the eye, as mentioned earlier, can only be formulated in such terms as these: the eye is an eye because it is not an eye.

This means that the possibility of the existence of being rests in emptiness. Of course, what we here call "being" is the non-objective being of things as they are in themselves. In our example, the eye's not-seeing only comes to be a not-seeing in unison with the eye's activity of actually seeing something. Likewise, that activity of seeing only comes to be a seeing in unison with not-seeing. This contradictory state of affairs, in which seeing and not-seeing only come to be as a unity, constitutes the self-identity of the eye in its non-objective mode of being as what it is in itself.

Quite literally, then, we may speak of an essential "blindness" simultaneously present in seeing. The point of blindness comes at the very point that seeing is seeing as such: it is right at hand and manifest in the act of seeing. It is, of course, not a visual defect we speak of. It is not the objective phenomenon of sightlessness. What we have in mind is a not-seeing squarely positioned *within* the activity where seeing becomes manifest as seeing, a not-seeing that is there for the sake of the possibility of seeing to be seeing. It is not that sight in an objective, phenomenal sense is not present, but that in the non-objective way that it is what it is in itself, it is empty. Emptiness here means that the eye does not see the eye, that seeing is seeing because it is not-seeing. It means that the very sensation or perception called seeing (and consciousness as a whole) is, at bottom, empty. All consciousness as such is empty at its very roots: it can only become manifest on the field of emptiness. Consciousness is *originally* emptiness. Yet this original emptiness is not distinct from the fact, for instance, that seeing is seeing itself. That seeing is a groundless activity (empty already from its own-ground) means that seeing, strictly speaking, is seeing bottomlessly. Even the ordinary activity of sight is, as it were, an "action of non-action."

Put in more general terms, there is a *non-consciousness* at the base of all consciousness, though not in the sense of what is called the "unconscious." The realm of the unconscious, no matter how deeply it reaches into the strata underlying consciousness, remains after all continuous with the realm of consciousness and on a dimension where, together with consciousness, it can become the subject matter of psychology. We speak of non-consciousness here to indicate that the unconscious as such is also empty from its very roots up.

In that sense, as something that transcends the conscious and the unconscious, we might call the *non*-conscious a *trans*consciousness. But that would not mean, of course, that there is some "thing" that is a transconsciousness. We speak of emptiness but do not imply that there is some "thing" that is emptiness. Transconsciousness, as the original emptiness of consciousness, is one with consciousness itself. (Seeing is at one with seeing as the absolute negativity of seeing.) It is in that sense that we call it a *non*-consciousness. In the words of a haiku that comes to us from an unknown poet on his deathbed:

> Now that I am deaf
> it is clear for me to hear
> the sound of the dew

. . .

When Emperor Wu of the Liang Dynasty asked Bodhidharma, "What is the first principle of the holy teachings?" the Patriarch replied, "Emptiness, no holiness." The Emperor, confused by this answer, inquired further, "Who is this standing before me?" "No knowing," answered Bodhidharma. The story as such is well enough known, but what I should like to suggest here is that this "No knowing" that strikes out from beneath the very bottom of the universe like a bolt of lightning is quite the same thing we have been speaking of as the not-knowing in which the self is on its own home-ground as what it is in itself. . . .

I have called this nonobjective mode of being of things as they are in themselves—namely, the mode of being wherein things rest in the complete uniqueness of what they themselves are—a "middle"; I cited the saying, "If you try to explain something by comparing it with something else, you fail to hit the middle." If we grant that the field of śūnyatā, on which the possibility of the existence of the selfness of things takes hold of its ground, opens for us only when we return to our own home-ground, these words would apply in their most original sense to our own self in itself. Our self in itself is most elementally "middle." It resists all explanation because it is a being in unison with emptiness; because it is a being united with emptiness in a self-awareness according to which emptiness is self; and because, by virtue of that self-awareness, which is nearer to the elemental than anything else, it precedes the world and all things. Every human being in its selfness contains the field of that force by virtue of which the selfness of all things are gathered into one as a world. This field contains a roothold for the possibility of all things that become manifest in the world. And yet each human being, as such, is but one illusory thing in the world among others.

When we say that our self in itself is most elementally "middle," we are not thinking in terms of the "middle" that Aristotle, for instance, spoke of as the "mean" between two much and too little. Nor are we thinking of the role of go-between that Hegel attributed to reason as a "mediation" between contradictories. Whereas these are both "middles" projected on the field of reason, the "middle" seen as a mode of being on the field of emptiness cannot be projected on any other field whatsoever. It is immediately present—and immediately realized as such—at the point that we ourselves actually are. It is "at hand" for us and "underfoot." Just as no one else can see for us or hear for us, so too *none* of our actions can be performed by proxy. All actions imply, as it were, an absolute immediacy. And it is there that what we are calling the "middle" appears. . . .

> The ancients tell us that every man possesses a spiritual light. When the *Sutra of Perfect Enlightenment* speaks of the samādhi of the Storehouse of the Great Light, it means this spiritual light that belongs to the nature of all sentient beings. What is called the body-light, the wisdom-light, and the miracle-light of all the Buddhas, all are born out of this Storehouse of the Great Light. Down to the ordinary man's distinguishing of east from west and black from white, there is nothing that is not the marvellous work of that spiritual light. But fools forget this original light and turn to the outside in search of a worldly light.[1]

We noted earlier that the "natural light" is not the light of reason but the light of all things. What is here called "spiritual light" does not mean the light of the "soul" or the "spirit" in the ordinary sense of those words. It is rather a "samādhi of the Storehouse of the Great Light" out of which the light of all things (namely, the being itself of all things) is coming to birth; it belongs to the nature of every human being. When we say that our self in itself is the original and most elemental "middle," we are pointing to nothing other than just this.

---

[1] *The Muchū mondō* of Musō Kokushi.—ed.

DISCUSSION QUESTIONS

1. What is the Buddhist doctrine of "No-Soul"? How, according to Walpola Rahula, does the doctrine connect with that of Nirvana as "Absolute Truth"?

2. How is the Lord Buddha portrayed in the excerpt from the *Saraṅgama Sūtra?* What connection do you find between this portrayal and the Buddha's teaching of the "Second Fundamental Principle" of the "pure unity of Enlightenment of Nirvana"? Elaborate.

3. What is the relation, according to Keiji Nishitani, between, on the one hand, "emptiness of self" as the "homeground of the self," and, on the other, self-consciousness or self-knowledge?

THE TAO

As mentioned in the general introduction, Taoism contrasts with Confucianism in the classical Chinese context. As opposed to a Confucian emphasis on right social practice, Taoism exalts the individual. The Tao—the spiritual ground of all things—upholds each thing in its unique virtue and nature.

Tradition places Lao Tzu a generation before Confucius, but Lao Tzu's *Tao-te Ching,* the—or at least a—root text of Taoism, is clearly later than Confucius. The work mentions, and criticizes, several important Confucian doctrines. Scholars are unable to date the text with accuracy, but it is unlikely that the *Tao-te Ching* is later than the fourth century BCE or earlier than the fifth. A second root text for Taoism is the Chuang Tzu, attributed to Chuang Tzu, or Chuang Chou (fourth century BCE), and regarded by some scholars as the oldest Taoist text. With two foundational texts, there evolved a tradition of speaking of Lao Tzu and Chuang Tzu together as Lao-Chuang.

The concept of the Tao is central to the Taoist outlook. Usually rendered as Way, *tao* seems to have meant moral system or moral truth with Confucius and in other early Chinese thought. But with Lao Tzu and Chuang Tzu, the Tao is the One, a mystery ineffable and indescribable in itself but also the source and ground of diversity maintaining a complex harmony. The Tao is the fundamental reality that imparts to individuals their virtue or *te*, their deeply individual power, nature, and right way of being. In contrast with a Confucian emphasis on self-conscious, willful adherence to a set of moral rules and standards of social conduct, living in and by the Tao is said to be a matter of natural spontaneity and perfection—as is found in the crouch of the tiger, the flow of water, and so forth, that is, in nature uncorrupted by human (i.e. Confucian) moralizing.

Ineffable Unity

From *Tao-te Ching* by Lao Tzu, in *A Source Book in Chinese Philosophy*, Wing-Tsit Chan, translator and editor, 1963

Tradition has Confucius visiting an elderly Lao Tzu, but, as mentioned, scholars believe that this is improbable. We know little about Lao Tzu outside of legends, but the Tao-te Ching *as critical of Confucian doctrines and practices has to be later than Confucius.*

The Tao-te Ching opens with the paradox of declaring (telling) of the Tao that it cannot be told—the paradox of ineffability. Language makes distinctions, but the One transcends distinctions. It is difficult, however, to understand what "the One transcends distinctions" means. Lao Tzu suggests that this has to be known mystically, not through sentences.

The Tao is also the source of diversity providing harmony. Lao Tzu bases an ethics on this view. An individual embracing the One becomes a sage and the best sort of person, apparently by renouncing the ordinary ways of promoting his/her individuality and by being passively open to the Tao. Some have interpreted this as a teaching on non-action (wu-wei). But others have seen here a way to perfect action, as is found in phenomena of nature uncorrupted by human ambitions.

> The Tao (Way) that can be told of is not the eternal Tao;
> The name that can be named is not the eternal name.
> The Nameless is the origin of Heaven and Earth;
> The Named is the mother of all things.
> Therefore let there always be non-being so we may see their subtlety,
> And let there always be being so we may see their outcome.
> The two are the same,
> But after they are produced, they have different names
> They both may be called deep and profound
> Deeper and more profound,
> The door of all subtleties! . . .

> We look at it and do not see it;
>   Its name is The Invisible.
> We listen to it and do not hear it;
>   Its name is The Inaudible.
> We touch it and do not find it;
>   Its name is The Subtle (formless).
> These three cannot be further inquired into,
> And hence merge into one.
> Going up high, it is not bright, and coming down low, it is not dark.
> Infinite and boundless, it cannot be given any name;
> It reverts to nothingness.

This is called shape without shape,
Form without object.
It is The Vague and Elusive.
Meet it and you will not see its head.
Follow it and you will not see its back.
Hold on to the Tao of old in order to master the things of the present.
From this one may know the primeval beginning [of the universe].
This is called the bond of Tao. . . .

Act without action.
Do without ado.
Taste without tasting.
Whether it is big or small, many or few, repay hatred with virtue.
Prepare for the difficult while it is still easy.
Deal with the big while it is still small.
Difficult undertakings have always started with what is easy,
And great undertakings have always started with what is small.
Therefore the sage never strives for the great,
And thereby the great is achieved.
He who makes rash promises surely lacks faith.
He who takes things too easily will surely encounter much difficulty.
For this reason even the sage regards things as difficult,
And therefore he encounters no difficulty. . . .

Identity of Contraries

From the writings of Chuang Tzu, in *A Source Book in Chinese Philosophy*, Wing-Tsit Chan, translator and editor, 1963

Chuang Tzu and Lao Tzu have many themes in common. But Chuang Tzu insists more on the transcendence of the Tao and on mysticism than does Lao Tzu, who seems content with the expressions of the Tao in nature and in individuals' lives. It is the transcendence of the Tao that underpins its omnipresence, and seeing this omnipresence is crucial to a personal self-transformation, says Chuang Tzu. Natural oppositions are in balance. The Tao transcends oppositions and unifies them. Chuang Tzu tries to get us to appreciate this by attending to the nature of oppositions.

Chuang Tzu is at least as critical of Confucianists as is Lao Tzu. Another school of philosophy that had achieved prominence by Chuang Tzu's time is Mohism. Mohists stress the importance of pleasure and pain in determining value and right action. They are commonly called hedonists and utilitarians. They also develop a logic that emphasizes difference. 'A white horse is not a horse' (meaning, presumably, it's not just a horse) is one of their favorite

examples. Chuang Tzu attacks such a conception. The point for us is not to appreciate differ-
ence as such, he urges, but to appreciate the source of difference where differences disappear.

How can Tao be so obscured that there should be a distinction of true and false? How can
speech be so obscured that there should be a distinction of right and wrong? Where can
you go and find Tao not to exist? Where can you go and find speech impossible? Tao is obscured by petty biases and speech is obscured by flowery expressions. Therefore there
have arisen the controversies between the Confucianists and the Moists, each school regarding as right what the other considers as wrong, and regarding as wrong what the other
considers as right. But to show that what each regards as right is wrong or to show that
what each regards as wrong is right, there is no better way than to use the light (of Nature).

There is nothing that is not the "that" and there is nothing that is not the "this." Things
do not know that they are the "that" of other things; they only know what they themselves
know. Therefore I say that the "that" is produced by the "this" and the "this" is also caused
by the "that." This is the theory of mutual production. Nevertheless, when there is life
there is death, and when there is death there is life. When there is possibility, there is impossibility, and when there is impossibility, there is possibility. Because of the right, there
is the wrong, and because of the wrong, there is the right. Therefore the sage does not proceed along these lines (of right and wrong, and so forth) but illuminates the matter with
Nature. This is the reason.

The "this" is also the "that." The "that" is also the "this." The "this" has one standard
of right and wrong, and the "that" also has a standard of right and wrong. Is there really a
distinction between "that" and "this"? Or is there really no distinction between "that" and
"this"? When "this" and "that" have no opposites there is the very axis of Tao. Only when
the axis occupies the center of a circle can things in their infinite complexities be responded to. The right is an infinity. The wrong is also an infinity. Therefore I say that there
is nothing better than to use the light (of Nature). . . .

To take a mark (*chih*) to show that a mark is not a mark is not as good as to take a non-
mark to show that a mark is not a mark. To take a horse to show that a [white] horse is not
a horse (as such) is not as good as to take a non-horse to show that a horse is not a horse.
The universe is but one mark, and all things are but a horse. When [people say], "All
right," then [things are] all right. When people say, "Not all right," then [things are] not all
right. A road becomes so when people walk on it, and things become so-and-so [to people]
because people call them so-and-so. How have they become so? They have become so because [people say they are] so. How have they become not so? They have become not so
because [people say they are] not so. In their own way things are so-and-so. In their own
way things are all right. There is nothing that is not so-and-so. There is nothing that is not
all right. Let us take, for instance, a large beam and a small beam, or an ugly woman and
Hsi-shih (famous beauty of ancient China), or generosity, strangeness, deceit, and abnor-
mality. The Tao identifies them all as one. What is division [to some] is production [to oth-
ers], and what is production [to others] is destruction [to some]. Whether things are
produced or destroyed, [Tao] again identifies them all as one. . . .

1. Describe the best way of life according to, first, Lao Tzu, and, then, Chuang Tzu, that is, the way of life that would be most appropriate given the reality of the Tao. Do you find any important differences in this regard between the two Taoist teachers?

2. How do Lao Tzu and Chuang Tzu characterize the Tao? Is there anything in these characterizations that would motivate their apparent sense of the Tao's strict indescribability?

POLYTHEISM AND HENOTHEISM

In this section, we shall review contrasting opinions about *polytheism*—the worship of a plurality of gods and goddesses—one opinion debunking polytheism through finding connection with religions called pagan or primitive by anthropologists in the late nineteenth and early twentieth centuries, another opinion championing polytheism as enlightened religious belief. The "primitive" and "pagan" labelling has now been largely discredited (compare the selection from Callicott and Overholt under Religion and Ethics). But the anthropological perspective remains important in contemporary debate, no less than the sympathetic outlook.

First we take up an anthropological contribution, and, in particular, the hypothesis that polytheism has its origin in *animism.* Animism is the "primitive" outlook that finds plants and animals (and practically everything) as ensouled, as containing "spirit" and hidden sensitivities and psychical powers. This bit of anthropology is presented by Sir George Frazer (1854–1941), who, following E. B. Tylor and followed by many twentieth-century social scientists, charts a religious development that shows all religious ideas in an unfavorable light. (A selection from E. B. Tylor is included under Religion Debunked.) Western monotheism may be the highest stage of religion by these lights, but it, too, is immature in comparison with the worldview of science.

Next we turn to a presentation of an African religious belief system where there is not only polytheism but also *henotheism* (recall the discussion under Absolute Brahman). This presentation, by Professor Kwame Gyekye, who is from Ghana, is made sympathetically but without any apparent polemical end.

The following selection, by the French scholar, Alain Daniélou, is not only a presentation of Hindu polytheism and henotheism but an outright defense. Daniélou sees monotheism, not, as in the common anthropological view, as the highest refinement of religion, the final stage before replacement by science, but as a debasement, a glorification of a single divine form over others that are equally venerable. He sees the Hindu polytheistic attitude as the most commendable religious point of view.

Finally, William James presents a different kind of defense of polytheism, and indeed a rather different kind of polytheism. James sees the individual religious life, which is centered on religious emotion (and in some cases mysticism), as justifying religious beliefs.

But he also holds that such beliefs are justified only for an individual or a confined group, not universally. Thus a philosophic polytheism is the right overview.

Polytheism Viewed Anthropologically

From *The Golden Bough* by Sir James George Frazer, 1917

Early humans apparently thought of animals, plants, and even rivers and rocks as ani-mated, as enlivened, by some vague spirit or soul. According to Sir George Frazer—whose multi-volumed The Golden Bough *exerted enormous influence in this century not only in anthropology but in a broad intellectual swath—in the later stages of animism there is a disassociation of spirits from their physical abodes. Trees seemed to have held a special place for animists in Europe and South and Southeast Asia because of extensive forests there in early times. Frazer sees polytheism emerging when an ensouled tree becomes a tree spirit or tree divinity, with the god differentiated from his physical abode and con-ceived no longer in the form of a tree but anthropomorphically.*

BENEFICENT POWERS

When a tree comes to be viewed, no longer as the body of a tree-spirit, but simply as its abode which it can quit at leisure, an important advance has been made in religious thought. Animism is passing into polytheism. In other words, instead of regarding each tree as a living and conscious being, man now sees in it merely a lifeless, inert mass, ten-anted for a longer or shorter time by a supernatural being who, as he can pass freely from tree to tree, thereby enjoys a certain right of possession or lordship over the trees, and, ceasing to be a tree-soul, becomes a forest god. As soon as the tree-spirit is thus in a mea-sure disengaged from each particular tree, he begins to change his shape and assume the body of a man, in virtue of a general tendency of early thought to clothe all abstract spiri-tual beings in concrete human form. Hence in classical art the sylvan deities are depicted in human shape, their woodland character being denoted by a branch or some equally ob-vious symbol. But this change of shape does not affect the essential character of the tree-spirit. The powers which he exercised as a tree-soul incorporate in a tree, he still continues to wield as a god of trees. This I shall now attempt to prove in detail. I shall shew, first, that trees considered as animate beings are credited with the power of making the rain to fall, the sun to shine, flocks and herds to multiply, and women to bring forth easily; and, sec-ond, that the very same powers are attributed to tree-gods conceived as anthropomorphic beings or as actually incarnate in living men.

First, then, trees or tree-spirits are believed to give rain and sunshine. When the mis-sionary Jerome of Prague was persuading the heathen Lithuanians to fell their sacred groves, a multitude of women besought the Prince of Lithuania to stop him, saying that with the woods he was destroying the house of god from which they had been wont to get rain and sunshine. The Mundaris in Assam think that if a tree in the sacred grove is felled the sylvan gods evince their displeasure by withholding rain. In order to procure rain the inhabitants of Monyo, a village in the Sagaing district of Upper Burma, chose the largest tamarind-tree near the village and named it the haunt of the spirit (*nat*) who controls the rain. Then they offered bread, coconuts, plantains, and fowls to the guardian spirit of the village and to the spirit who gives rain, and they prayed, "O Lord *nat* have pity on us poor mortals, and stay not the rain. Inasmuch as our offering is given grudgingly, let the rain fall day and night." . . .

Again, tree-spirits make the crops to grow. Amongst the Mundaris every village has its sacred grove, and "the grove deities are held responsible for the crops, and are especially honoured at all the great agricultural festivals." . . . Swedish peasants stick a leafy branch in each furrow of their corn-fields, believing that this will ensure an abundant crop. The same idea comes out in the German and French custom of the Harvest-May. This is a large branch or a whole tree, which is decked with ears of corn, brought home on the last wag-gon from the harvest-field, and fastened on the roof of the farmhouse or of the barn, where it remains for a year. Mannhardt has proved that this branch or tree embodies the tree-spirit conceived as the spirit of vegetation in general, whose vivifying and fructifying influence is thus brought to bear upon the corn in particular. Hence in Swabia the Harvest-May is fastened amongst the last stalks of corn left standing on the field; in other places it is planted on the corn-field and the last sheaf cut is attached to its trunk. . . .

African (Akan) Polytheism and Onyame, the Absolute

From *An Essay on African Philosophical Thought* by Kwame Gyekye, 1987

Kwame Gyekye, a professor of philosophy at the University of Ghana and Howard University, presents the results of anthropological research and reconstruction in a markedly different fashion from Frazer and his school. There are no religious or philosophic texts expressing the Akan belief system that Gyekye reconstructs, but, he claims, "the religious language, attitude, and practices of the Akans provide a great deal of insight into their conceptions of reality."

The Akan conception turns out to have much in common with the henotheism most often associated with Hinduism: the Supreme God (Onyame) enlivens lesser deities and indeed all of nature with spirit. However, over the centuries the gods and goddesses of the Hindu pantheon come to be more clearly delineated, and there are tomes of religious and devotional literature in Hinduism and not just religious language and practices. Nevertheless, the notion of Onyame as portrayed by Gyekye seems quite similar to that of Brahman as understood by Indian theists. The school of Frazer and his followers would probably see this similarity as support for their debunking view. Whether it really is or not is a good question for reflection.

GOD AND THE OTHER CATEGORIES OF BEING

Quite often the impulse of philosophical reflection finds its first expression in religious life and thought. A philosophical idea may be found concealed in a religious perspective or expressed in religious language. This is the case with Akan ontology, that is, the doctrine of being. For the religious language, attitude, and practices of the Akans provide a great deal of insight into their conception of reality, that is, the sorts of entities considered to be real or to exist. It is the reality of an entity or object that in fact constitutes the ground of its being worshiped; the object of worship must be presumed to exist.

The language of the religious right of libation immediately reveals the entities that are considered real in Akan metaphysics. A typical prayer of libation runs as follows:

> Supreme God, who is alone great, upon whom men lean and do not fall, receive this wine and drink. Earth goddess, whose day of worship is Thursday, receive this wine and drink. Spirits of our ancestors, receive this wine and drink . . .

These words from the prelude of the libation prayer attest to the existence of a Supreme Being (Onyame, Onyankopōn), deities (*abosom:* lesser spirits), and ancestors (that is, ancestral spirits: *nsamanfo*), in descending order. Next after these entities are humans and the physical world of natural objects and phenomena. Thus the hierarchical character of Akan ontology is clear: the Supreme Being at the apex, and our phenomenal world at the bottom of this hierarchy. The Supreme Being, the deities, and the ancestors are spiritual entities. They are considered invisible and unperceivable to the naked eye: This is in fact the definition of the word "spiritual," for the Akans use the word *sunsum* ("spirit") generally to refer to the mystical, the unempirical, the nonphysical. Given the belief of most Akans that at least part of nature or the physical world is animated, and that man too is partly spiritual, we have to conclude that Akan ontology is essentially or primarily spiritual; the Akan universe is a spiritual universe, one in which supernatural beings play significant roles in the thought and action of the people. What is primarily real is spiritual. . . .

Onyame is the Absolute Reality, the origin of all things, the absolute ground, the sole and whole explanation of the universe, the source of all existence. Absolute Reality is beyond and independent of the categories of time, space, and cause. As *tetekwaframua* and *ōdomankoma,* Onyame transcends time and is thus free from the limitations of time, an eternity without beginning, without an end. The fact that Onyame dwells in an infinite time gives the lie to the supposition, made by Mbiti, that Africans do not have a concept of a long or infinite future, for surely a concept of an eternal infinite being implies a concept of an infinite time. If there were no concept of an infinite time the infinite being would be limited by time, and he would no longer be infinite. But *ex hypothesi* he is infinite; therefore, he must dwell in an infinite time. While containing space, Onyame is not held to be spatial. He is not bound or limited to any particular region of space. He is omnipresent (*enyiasombea*), all-pervading. The fact that Onyame is not confined to any particular locality is the basis of the proverb: "If you want to say something to Onyame, say it to the wind" (*wopē asēm aka akyerē Onyame a, ka kyerē mframa*). The Akans often draw an analogy between God, or for that matter any spiritual being, and the wind. Just as the wind is invisible and intangible—yet its effects are seen everywhere—so is Onyame invisible, intangible, and omnipresent. The analogy, however, is obviously incomplete, for the wind can be physically felt whereas Onyame cannot.

As the ultimate source of being, Onyame created the whole universe, including the deities or lesser spirits, out of nothing. He is the *ōbōadeē,* "the creator of the thing," the *bōrebōre,* originator. At some point in the distant past, Onyame created the world, and having brought the world into existence, he sustains it with his infinite power (*otumfo*). All things end up in him (*atoapem*), that is, into him all things are dissolved. Thus, a discussant stated: "Everything is from Onyame and ends up in Onyame." Onyame himself is uncaused (*ōdomankoma*). The Akan view here follows from the notion of infinity. Causality operates and is applicable in all matters of change in the world. But Onyame, being infinite and eternal, is not subject to change and *a fortiori* to causality. . . .

The Akan universe, essentially spiritual, is endowed or charged with varying degrees of force or power. This force or power is *sunsum,* usually translated as "spirit," which, as noted, is commonly used to refer to the mystical and nonempirical, as in *sunsum yare* (spiritual disease). In this metaphysic all created things, that is, natural objects, have or contain *sunsum;* every deity (*ōbosom*) is a *sunsum,* but not vice versa. This *sunsum* derives ultimately from Onyame who, as the Supreme Being, is the Highest Spirit or Highest Power. *Sunsum,* then, appears, on my interpretation, to be a generic concept; it appears to be a universal spirit, manifesting itself differently in the various beings and objects in the natural world. At the same time, the word *sunsum* is used in two different but related senses.

First, it is used to refer to any self-conscious subject whose activities are initiated self-consciously. In this sense, Onyame, the deities, and the ancestors are said to be spirits, that is, spiritual beings with intelligence and will. Second, it is used to refer to the mystical powers believed to exist in the world. These powers are held to constitute the inner essences or intrinsic properties of natural objects, and are believed to be contained in those objects. Thus, *sunsum* is used in both a specific sense, to refer to the essence of a particular deity or man, and a general sense, to refer to all beings and powers unperceived by man.

There are two ways in which the two senses of *sunsum* are related. The first is that the mystical powers in the world and in natural objects are categorically related to the deities, although they derive ultimately from Onyame. The second is that the deities are supposed to reside in natural objects such as trees, plants, rocks, mountains and hills, rivers and brooks.

Hindu Polytheism and Henotheism

From *Hindu Polytheism* by Alain Daniélou, 1964

Although Alain Daniélou does not use the term "henotheism", he brings the henotheistic idea into sharper focus. On the level of religious practices, "chosen deity" (Sanskrit: iṣṭa-devatā) is the operative notion. One chooses to worship one particular god while acknowl-

edging the others and the single God or Source enlivening them all. The "Immensity" of which Daniélou speaks as the source of equivalence among the Pervader (Vishnu), Destroyer (Shiva), etc., is called Brahman, as we have seen.

Apparently, the various gods and goddesses are thought to correspond to natural divisions of Divine manifestation. Throughout Hinduism, creation is viewed as emanation, which is practically the same idea as Divine manifestation. Thus each broad line of creative manifestation would be presided over, so to say, by a different divinity. Saraswatī, often represented as a beautiful four-armed woman playing a sitar, is considered to preside over learning and crafts, while Kālī, a frightful goddess usually represented as garlanded with severed human heads, is a war goddess. But it must be kept in mind that both Kālī and Saraswatī—the other gods and goddesses, too—are typically worshipped as the one Supreme, as the Absolute, Brahman.

Daniélou attacks monotheism (implicitly that of the great Western religions, Judaism, Christianity, and Islam), particularly the intolerance and proselytization that he sees fostered by an exclusivism in monotheistic worship. But Hindu henotheism is also a monotheism: Brahman is God, the One enlivening all, the Supreme. Exclusivism versus inclusivism seems to be what crucially differentiates the Hindu kind of monotheism from the Western. A presumption of superiority for inclusivism is, paradoxically (i.e., as excluding exclusivism), a rallying point for modern Hindu polemics (see the selection from Vivekananda under Religious Pluralism).

We can look at a sculpture from different angles. We grasp its whole form only when we have observed the front, the back, the profiles. Each of these views is different from the others; some of the elements of their description may seem incompatible. Yet from these contradictory reports of our eyes we can build up a general conception of the sculpture which we could hardly do if we had seen it from one angle only.

The apparent contradiction between the transcendent forms glimpsed through the diverse means of approach is really the key to the comprehension of the "Immense" reality, which can never be grasped as a whole. Thus divinity has been defined as "that in which opposites coexist." The more insights we can get, the more aspects of the Divine we can perceive, the more we see of divinities beyond the different aspects of the universe, the more elements we can assemble to build up some conception of the origin of things, of the destiny and purpose of life, the nearer we are to understanding something of what divinity is. . . .

In our time monotheism is often considered a higher form of religion than polytheism. People speak of God, pray to God, search for God rather than speak of gods, pray to a particular god, or acknowledge various divine incarnations. Individual monotheistic worshipers, however, usually worship a particularized form of their god and not his causal, unmanifest, formless aspect. There is a nearness, a response, in the formal aspect which is lacking in the abstract conception. But a causal, formless, all-pervading divinity, cause and origin of all forms, cannot be manifest in a particular form and would of necessity be equally at the root of all types of form. Divinity can only be reached through its manifestations, and there are as many gods as there are aspects of creation. The gods and the

universe are two aspects—the conscious powers and the unconscious forms—of an indefinite multiplicity.

In the polytheistic religion each individual worshiper has a chosen deity (*iṣṭa-devatā*)
and does not usually worship other gods in the same way as his own, as the one he feels
nearer to himself. Yet he acknowledges other gods. The Hindu, whether he be a worshiper
of the Pervader (Viṣṇu), the Destroyer (Śiva), Energy (Śakti), or the Sun (Sūrya), is
always ready to acknowledge the equivalence of these deities as the manifestations of distinct powers springing from an unknowable "Immensity." He knows that ultimate Being or
non-Being is ever beyond his grasp, beyond existence, and in no way can be worshiped or
prayed to. Since he realizes that other deities are but other aspects of the one he worships,
he is basically tolerant and must be ready to accept every form of knowledge or belief as
potentially valid. Persecution or proselytization of other religious groups, however strange
their beliefs may seem to him, can never be a defensible attitude from the point of view of
the Hindu. . . .

Monotheism is always linked with a culture, a civilization. It is not through its forms
but in spite of them that gifted individuals may reach spiritual attainment. We shall see that
monotheism is the projection of the human individuality into the cosmic sphere, the shaping of "god" to the image of man. Hence the monotheist commonly visualizes his "god" as
an anthropomorphic entity who shares his habits, patronizes his customs, and acts according to his ideals. Religion becomes a means of glorifying his culture or his race, or of
expanding his influence. He is one of the elect who follows the "Way of God" as if there
could be a Way that did not lead to "God." We can see all monotheistic religions fighting
to impose their god and destroy other gods as if God were not one as they claim. Monotheism is basically the absolute exaltation of the worshiper's own deity over all other aspects of the Divine, all other gods, who must be considered false and dangerous. The very
notion of a false god is, however, an obvious fallacy. If there is an all-powerful, all-
pervading divinity, how can there be a false god? How can we worship anything that is
not Him? Whatever form we try to worship, the worship ultimately goes to Him who is
everything.

"Those who piously worship other gods of whom they are the devotees, it is but myself they worship, [though] ignorant of the proper rites." (*Bhagavadgītā* 9.23.) . . .

The classification of the basic energies, of which the cosmological pantheon is an expression, is not an arbitrary creation of the mind but a rational effort to define the component elements of existence. As is the case for any form of knowledge, the classifications
first chosen in a particular country or time may have been inadequate, they may constitute
a first working hypothesis which can be perfected through deeper insight or later experience, or they may have defined all the essentials from the start. The only important thing,
however, is the nature of the permanent realities that these classifications try to represent.
This is the story of every science, of every philosophy, of all the ancient religions.

In the ancient world the Vedic Rudra could be equated with the Dravidian (?) Śiva, the
Greek Dionysos, or the Egyptian Osiris. Just as we can say, "The French call a spoon a

cuiller," the Hindu will say, "The Christians worship a form of Viṣṇu named Christ," because for him Viṣṇu is not an individual god pertaining to a particular religion but a general principle, as inevitably represented in any theology, in any code of symbols, as words representing objects (nouns), actions (verbs), and qualities (adjectives) are inevitably found in any language.

Hindu mythology acknowledges all gods. Since all the energies at the origin of all the forms of manifestation are but aspects of the divine power, there can exist no object, no form of existence, which is not divine in its nature. Any name, any shape, that appeals to the worshiper can be taken as a representation or manifestation of divinity.

The gods mentioned in the Vedas form only a small part of the Hindu pantheon, which gradually incorporated, and still is ready to incorporate, all the conceptions of divinity, all the gods, of all the religious groups, all new "incarnations" or representations of the supranatural powers which pervade the universe.

Many of the deities worshiped by the Hindus are not mentioned in the Vedas under their present names, and many Vedic gods are today known mostly to scholars. But it would be wrong to see a change in religion or a deviation from the Vedic idea of divinity in what is merely a matter of fashion, a way of representing the Divine that suited a particular time or country, a particular set of habits, or a different conception of the universe. The gods are universal principles; they are all-pervading realities. The words or forms we use to represent them are mere approximations, which can vary like the words of different languages used to represent the same object or like the different symbols used to represent the same mathematical facts.

All religions are based on the recognition of the existence of a suprasensorial reality. Very rarely can we find in any religion a positive assertion which is not to some extent justifiable. Error and conflict arise from exclusion, from negative elements. They appear whenever the door is closed to new discoveries, to the "revelation" of a new age. A religion reduced to a faith centered around fixed dogmas and refusing to equate its data with those of other creeds is to religion what the art of the primitive medicine man is to medical science, the mere practical utilization of some elements of knowledge accidentally assembled and used more for social supremacy than for real cure. This remains very short of the total search for the whole of truth. Thus, in many countries, the man of science, if he be true to himself, finds he has had to choose between reason and faith. This dilemma does not arise for the Hindu, for Hinduism does not claim any of its discoveries to be more than an approach. It rejects all dogma, all belief that reason and experience cannot justify; it remains ever ready to accept new and better expressions of the universal laws as they can be grasped through individual experience.

There is no doubt that superstition and ignorance have often superseded reason and enlightened thought in India just as elsewhere. Some of the modern Indian creeds have as little to be envied as foreign ones, so inadequate is their thinking. But the principle of a multiple approach, the recognition of the fundamental right of the individual to follow his own gods, his own code of behavior and ritual practice, has spared India so far the standardization of beliefs which is by its very nature the greatest obstacle on the path of Divine discovery.

Modern Philosophic Polytheism

From *The Varieties of Religious Experience* by William James, 1929

William James (1842–1910) figures prominently in this book, with selections from his works appearing in four different sections. For details about James' life, see the first selection from James under Faith Against Reason.

James is a philosopher of the very first rank, whose contributions to philosophy of religion are many. Probably the position of his that has attracted the most attention is his pragmatic, or modified, fideism, *which places faith beyond the canons of reason, common evidence, and philosophic scrutiny. We shall review that position later (under Faith Against Reason). First, we shall take up his defense of individualistic religious and mystical experience under the banner of a philosophic polytheism.*

In the selection here from James' classic Varieties, *his fideism is, nevertheless, relevant. For James, faith in personal possibilities of contact with a Divine—however more specifically conceptualized, as the God of Christians and others or as the Brahman of Hindus, or as the Emptiness of Buddhists, or even only vaguely as some More "continuous with one's higher self"—is justified by the occurrences of mystical and religious experiences as reported throughout the world and in all epochs. It does not matter, on this view, that we cannot arrive at common spiritual beliefs universally assertible. A "piecemeal supernaturalism" or polytheism is all we need espouse as a matter of broad philosophic position.*

Thus James would make a virtue out of vagueness in religious philosophy. His position is that through a specific faith a person opens himself or herself to the action of the supernatural. But, again, just how we should conceive of the Divine—beyond the vague designations "supernatural," the "More continuous with our higher self," a few others—it would be presumptuous and unphilosophic, he says, to try to specify. This type of limitation may be called philosophic polytheism—and polytheism of a radically pluralistic sort, not the inclusivism of Hinduism—since there is no justifiable overarching conception (except, perhaps, the negative conception that "there is no justifiable overarching conception").

We must next pass beyond the point of view of merely subjective utility, and make inquiry into the intellectual content itself.

First, is there, under all the discrepancies of the creeds, a common nucleus to which they bear their testimony unanimously?

And second, ought we to consider the testimony true?

I will take up the first question first, and answer it immediately in the affirmative. The warring gods and formulas of the various religions do indeed cancel each other, but there is a certain uniform deliverance in which religions all appear to meet. It consists of two parts:—

1. An uneasiness; and
2. Its solution.

1. The uneasiness, reduced to its simplest terms, is a sense that there is *something wrong about us* as we naturally stand.

2. The solution is a sense that *we are saved from the wrongness* by making proper connection with the higher powers.

In those more developed minds which alone we are studying, the wrongness takes a moral character, and the salvation takes a mystical tinge. I think we shall keep well within the limits of what is common to all such minds if we formulate the essence of their religious experience in terms like these:—

The individual, so far as he suffers from his wrongness and criticises it, is to that extent consciously beyond it, and in at least possible touch with something higher, if anything higher exist. Along with the wrong part there is thus a better part of him, even though it may be but a most helpless germ. With which part he should identify his real being is by no means obvious at this stage; but when stage 2 (the stage of solution or salvation) arrives,[1] the man identifies his real being with the germinal higher part of himself; and does so in the following way. *He becomes conscious that this higher part is conterminous and continuous with a* MORE *of the same quality, which is operative in the universe outside of him, and which he can keep in working touch with, and in a fashion get on board of and save himself when all his lower being has gone to pieces in the wreck. . . .*

I now turn to my second question: What is the objective 'truth' of their content?

The part of the content concerning which the question of truth most pertinently arises is that 'MORE of the same quality' with which our own higher self appears in the experience to come into harmonious working relation. Is such a 'more' merely our own notion, or does it really exist? If so, in what shape does it exist? Does it act, as well as exist? And in what form should we conceive of that 'union' with it of which religious geniuses are so convinced?

It is in answering these questions that the various theologies perform their theoretic work, and that their divergencies most come to light. They all agree that the 'more' really exists; though some of them hold it to exist in the shape of a personal god or gods, while others are satisfied to conceive it as a stream of ideal tendency embedded in the eternal structure of the world. They all agree, moreover, that it acts as well as exists, and that something really is effected for the better when you throw your life into its hands. It is when they treat of the experience of 'union' with it that their speculative differences appear most clearly. Over this point pantheism and theism, nature and second birth, works and grace and karma, immortality and reincarnation, rationalism and mysticism, carry on inveterate disputes. . . .

Originality cannot be expected in a field like this, where all the attitudes and tempers that are possible have been exhibited in literature long ago, and where any new writer can immediately be classed under a familiar head. If one should make a division of all thinkers into naturalists and supernaturalists, I should undoubtedly have to go, along with most

---

[1] Remember that for some men it arrives suddenly, for others gradually, whilst others again practically enjoy it all their life.

philosophers, into the supernaturalist branch. But there is a crasser and a more refined supernaturalism, and it is to the refined division that most philosophers at the present day belong. . . . Refined supernaturalism is universalistic supernaturalism; for the 'crasser' variety 'piecemeal' supernaturalism would perhaps be the better name. It went with that older theology which to-day is supposed to reign only among uneducated people. . . . It admits miracles and providential leadings, and finds no intellectual difficulty in mixing the ideal and the real worlds together by interpolating influences from the ideal region among the forces that causally determine the real world's details. In this the refined supernaturalists think that it muddles disparate dimensions of existence. For them the world of the ideal has no efficient causality, and never bursts into the world of phenomena at particular points. The ideal world, for them, is not a world of facts, but only of the meaning of facts; it is a point of view for judging facts. It appertains to a different '-ology,' and inhabits a different dimension of being altogether from that in which existential propositions obtain. It cannot get down upon the flat level of experience and interpolate itself piecemeal between distinct portions of nature, as those who believe, for example, in divine aid coming in response to prayer, are bound to think it must.

Notwithstanding my own inability to accept either popular Christianity or scholastic theism, I suppose that my belief that in communion with the Ideal new force comes into the world, and new departures are made here below, subjects me to being classed among the supernaturalists of the piecemeal or crasser type. Universalistic supernaturalism surrenders, it seems to me, too easily to naturalism. It takes the facts of physical science at their face-value, and leaves the laws of life just as naturalism finds them, with no hope of remedy, in case their fruits are bad. It confines itself to sentiments about life as a whole, sentiments which may be admiring and adoring, but which need not be so, as the existence of systematic pessimism proves. In this universalistic way of taking the ideal world, the essence of practical religion seems to me to evaporate. Both instinctively and for logical reasons, I find it hard to believe that principles can exist which make no difference in facts. But all facts are particular facts, and the whole interest of the question of God's existence seems to me to lie in the consequences for particulars which that existence may be expected to entail. That no concrete particular of experience should alter its complexion in consequence of a God being there seems to me in incredible proposition, and yet it is the thesis to which (implicitly at any rate) refined supernaturalism seems to cling. It is only with experience *en bloc,* it says, that the Absolute maintains relations. It condescends to no transactions of detail. . . .

I believe that a candid consideration of piecemeal supernaturalism and a complete discussion of all its metaphysical bearings will show it to be the hypothesis by which the largest number of legitimate requirements are met. That of course would be a program for other books than this; what I now say sufficiently indicates to the philosophic reader the place where I belong.

If asked just where the differences in fact which are due to God's existence come in, I should have to say that in general I have no hypothesis to offer beyond what the phenomenon of 'prayerful communion,' especially when certain kinds of incursion from the subconscious region take part in it, immediately suggests. The appearance is that in this phenomenon something ideal, which in one sense is part of ourselves and in another sense is not ourselves, actually exerts an influence, raises our centre of personal energy, and produces regenerative effects unattainable in other ways. If, then, there be a wider world of being than that of our every-day consciousness, if in it there be forces whose effects on us are intermittent, if one facilitating condition of the effects be the openness of the 'subliminal' door, we have the elements of a theory to which the phenomena of religious life lend plausibility. I am so impressed by the importance of these phenomena that I adopt the hypothesis which they so naturally suggest. . . .

The ideal power with which we feel ourselves in connection, the 'God' of ordinary men, is, both by ordinary men and by philosophers, endowed with certain of those metaphysical attributes which in the lecture on philosophy I treated with such disrespect. He is assumed as a matter of course to be 'one and only' and to be 'infinite'; and the notion of many finite gods is one which hardly any one thinks it worth while to consider, and still less to uphold. Nevertheless, in the interests of intellectual clearness, I feel bound to say that religious experience, as we have studied it, cannot be cited as unequivocally supporting the infinitist belief. The only thing that it unequivocally testifies to is that we can experience union with *something* larger than ourselves and in that union find our greatest peace. Philosophy, with its passion for unity, and mysticism with its monoideistic bent, both 'pass to the limit' and identify the something with a unique God who is the all-inclusive soul of the world. Popular opinion, respectful to their authority, follows the example which they set.

Meanwhile the practical needs and experiences of religion seem to me sufficiently met by the belief that beyond each man and in a fashion continuous with him there exists a larger power which is friendly to him and to his ideals. All that the facts require is that the power should be both other and larger than our conscious selves. Anything larger will do, if only it be large enough to trust for the next step. It need not be infinite, it need not be solitary. It might conceivably even be only a larger and more godlike self, of which the present self would then be but the mutilated expression, and the universe might conceivably be a collection of such selves, of different degrees of inclusiveness, with no absolute unity realized in it at all. Thus would a sort of polytheism return upon us—a polytheism which I do not on this occasion defend, for my only aim at present is to keep the testimony of religious experience clearly within its proper bounds.

Upholders of the monistic view will say to such a polytheism (which, by the way, has always been the real religion of common people, and is so still to-day) that unless there be one all-inclusive God, our guarantee of security is left imperfect. In the Absolute, and in the Absolute only, *all* is saved. If there be different gods, each caring for his part, some portion of some of us might not be covered with divine protection, and our religious consolation would thus fail to be complete. . . . [But] common sense is less sweeping in its demands than philosophy or mysticism have been wont to be, and can suffer the notion of this world being partly saved and partly lost. The ordinary moralistic state of mind makes the salvation of the world conditional upon the success with which each unit does its part. Partial and conditional salvation is in fact a most familiar notion when taken in the abstract, the only difficulty being to determine the details. Some men are even disinterested enough to be willing to be in the unsaved remnant as far as their persons go, if only they can be persuaded that their cause will prevail—all of us are willing, whenever our activity-excitement rises sufficiently high. I think, in fact, that a final philosophy of religion will have to consider the pluralistic hypothesis more seriously than it has hitherto been willing to consider it. For practical life at any rate, the *chance* of salvation is enough. No fact in human nature is more characteristic than its willingness to live on a chance. The existence of the chance makes the difference, as Edmund Gurney says, between a life of which the keynote is resignation and a life of which the keynote is hope. But all these statements are unsatisfactory from their brevity, and I can only say that I hope to return to the same questions in another book.

DISCUSSION QUESTIONS

1. Retrace the process whereby, according to George Frazer, the animism of tree spirits passes into a veritable polytheism of individualized deities.

2. Reconstruct (a) the theology of the Akan as presented by Kwame Gyekye, and (b) the polytheism, or henotheism, of Hinduism as presented by Alain Daniélou. What important similarities, and differences, do you find?

3. Does the similarity between the Akan conception of Onyame and the Hindu theistic, or henotheistic, conception of Brahman provide support for the anthropological view of Frazer and others, namely, that humans progress in religious views in definite stages until in the end they give up even monotheism, the penultimate stage, for the worldview of science?

4. What common intellectual content does William James find in mystical, or religious, experiences worldwide? What does he decide, and why, concerning the question of that content's truth? Based on this conclusion, a philosophic polytheism, called also a piecemeal supernaturalism, is defended by James. Just what is the virtue of this stance, (a) according to James, (b) as compared with the virtue Alain Daniélou finds in Hindu polytheism and a consonant rejection of the exclusivism of monotheism, and (c) in your own opinion?

SPECULATIVE SPIRITUAL METAPHYSICS

Not all theorizing about a Divine Reality has appeared under a religious banner. In the West, Baruch Spinoza (1632–1677), a Dutch philosopher, broke with orthodox Judaic theology in speculating about a divine One identical with nature. Several followed Spinoza in putting forth what we may call secular, though still spiritual, worldviews—most notably, in the nineteenth century, the German philosopher, G. W. F. Hegel (1770–1831).

The Hegelian philosophy centers on an Absolute known through a special method of reasoning designated dialectic. The philosophy was eclipsed—both in substance and method—in Anglo-American thought by the hard-headed pragmatism of William James, on the one hand, and the realism of G. E. Moore and Bertrand Russell, on the other, at the beginning of the twentieth century. On the Continent, Hegel's influence continued longer, finally displaced by the existentialist movement (see the selection from Albert Camus under Religion Debunked). James attacks Hegelian absolutism as incapable of handling the facts of everyday experience, not only the apparent plurality of things but, especially, all the evils alien to the Absolute so inspirationally conceived and divinely spoken of. (James' criticism is expanded—and answered, perhaps—below in selections under Evil.)

Aurobindo, an Indian mystic philosopher of the early twentieth century, and Alfred North Whitehead, a brilliant English metaphysician of approximately the same period, are both mindful of the challenge of evil, but speculate nevertheless in a spiritual vein. In contrast with Hegelians, however, these two recognize the reality of a pluralistic universe. Yet with Hegel and his followers, both find a Divine Reality insuring harmony and providing direction for emergent beings.

Both Whitehead and Aurobindo are theists. And they draw on traditional views of God. But neither feels called upon to defend a traditional theology. Each is philosophically creative, formulating a rather novel way of looking at things, transcending cultural precedent. The new worldview is, in each case, appreciated only with difficulty, with quite some effort of intelligence. We shall try to get only the broad lines of each philosopher's sense of a Divine Reality, leaving the entire theories for other occasions. (Selections from Aurobindo are included under Evil and Religion and Ethics.) We shall also look at Marjorie Suchocki's use of Whitehead's views to illumine Christian teachings.

Romantic Idealism

From *The Phenomenology of Spirit* by G. W. F. Hegel, A. V. Miller, translator, 1977

Georg Wilhelm Friedrich Hegel was the greatest philosopher of the Romantic Age, a period following the French Revolution that seemed a new dawn for humanity. It was a time when feudal institutions and sterile rational formula were disappearing or were being reformed in a more hopeful and joyous spirit of imagination and life. Although Hegel's philosophy is centered on an Absolute, it emphasizes change, orderly change through a dialectical process of opposition and re-integration.

There has been much controversy about Hegel's method of dialectic. According to the German metaphysician, inspection of just about any concept reveals an inadequacy, limitation, or negation. But the negation of the concept taken alone also proves inadequate, and a re-integration or synthesis becomes urged. This process of dialectic is not only of ideas (i.e., a method of philosophy) but also of social forms (i.e., historical progress). We, and indeed the Absolute itself (which is somehow everything), come to fuller and fuller awareness as we are carried ineluctably through a dialectic of social forms where inadequate social organizations give way to their negations and re-emerge in a new synthesis.

William James, we shall see, focuses on the intellectual process, as opposed to the social, finding the Hegelian method only a trick and no true way to proceed in metaphysics.

The need to represent the Absolute as *Subject* has found expression in the propositions: *God* is the eternal, the moral world-order, love, and so on. In such propositions the True is only posited *immediately* as Subject, but is not presented as the movement of reflecting itself into itself. In a proposition of this kind one begins with the word 'God'. This by itself is a meaningless sound, a mere name; it is only the predicate that says *what God is,* gives Him content and meaning. Only in the end of the proposition does the empty beginning become actual knowledge. This being so, it is not clear why one does not speak merely of the eternal, of the moral world-order, and so on, or, as the ancients did, of pure notions like 'being', 'the One', and so on, in short, of that which gives the meaning without adding the *meaningless* sound as well. But it is just this word that indicates that what is posited is not a being [i.e. something that merely *is*], or essence, or a universal in general, but rather something that is reflected into itself, a Subject. But at the same time this is only anticipated. The Subject is assumed as a fixed point to which, as their support, the predicates are affixed by a movement belonging to the knower of this Subject, and which is not regarded as belonging to the fixed point itself; yet it is only through this movement that the content could be represented as Subject. The way in which this movement has been brought about is such that it cannot belong to the fixed point; yet, after this point has been presupposed, the nature of the movement cannot really be other than what it is, it can only be external. Hence, the mere anticipation that the Absolute is Subject is not only *not* the actuality of this Notion, but it even makes the actuality impossible; for the anticipation posits the subject as an inert point, whereas the actuality is self-movement.

Among the various consequences that follow from what has just been said, this one in particular can be stressed, that knowledge is only actual, and can only be expounded, as Science or as *system;* and furthermore, that a so-called basic proposition or principle of philosophy, if true, is also false, just because it is *only* a principle. It is, therefore, easy to refute it. The refutation consists in pointing out its defect; and it is defective because it is only the universal or principle, is only the beginning. If the refutation is thorough, it is derived and developed from the principle itself, not accomplished by counterassertions and random thoughts from outside. The refutation would, therefore, properly consist in the further development of the principle, and in thus remedying the defectiveness, if it did not mistakenly pay attention solely to its *negative* action, without awareness of its progress and result on their *positive* side too—. The genuinely *positive* exposition of the beginning is thus also, conversely, just as much a negative attitude towards it, viz. towards its initially one-sided form of being *immediate* or *purpose.* It can therefore be taken equally well as a refutation of the principle that constitutes the *basis* of the system, but it is more correct to regard it as a demonstration that the *basis* or principle of the system is, in fact, only its *beginning.*

That the True is actual only as system, or that Substance is essentially Subject, is expressed in the representation of the Absolute as *Spirit*—the most sublime Notion and the one which belongs to the modern age and its religion. The spiritual alone is the *actual;* it is essence, or that which has *being in itself;* it is that which *relates itself to itself* and is *deter-*

minate, it is *other-being* and *being-for-self,* and in this determinateness, or in its self-externality, abides within itself; in other words, it is *in and for itself.* But this being-in-and-for-itself is at first only for us, or *in itself,* it is spiritual *Substance.* It must also be this *for itself,* it must be the knowledge of the spiritual, and the knowledge of itself as Spirit, i.e. it must be an *object* to itself, but just as immediately a sublated object, reflected into itself. It is *for itself* only for *us,* in so far as its spiritual content is generated by itself. But in so far as it is also for itself for its own self, this self-generation, the pure Notion, is for it the objective element in which it has its existence, and it is in this way, in its existence for itself, an object reflected into itself. The Spirit that, so developed, knows itself as Spirit, is *Science;* Science is its actuality and the realm which it builds for itself in its own element.

Against the Metaphysics of an Absolute

From *A Pluralistic Universe* by William James, 1909

In this excerpt, William James shows himself a great student of philosophy and an intellectual historian with wit and verve. The selection is best in its subtly sardonic presentation of Hegel's philosophy and the dialectical method. James's presentation is, if it can be presumed correct, much clearer than any exposition by Hegel himself. James, of course, endorses a view opposed to Hegel's, and he puts forth positive considerations in its favor, though not here. James's point below is to survey the absolutist metaphysics and to show where it goes wrong.

One of Hegel's arguments in support of his concept of an Absolute is that it makes no sense to imagine that the Absolute does not exist. That would be like claiming that 2 + 2 = 5. James is highly critical of such a line of thought, called ontological argument, *but the selection presented here omits most of that criticism (see the ontological argument selections under Arguments for a Divine Reality). The main problem, in any case, is, according to James, that, contrary to what Hegel claims, the philosophy of the Absolute is not the most rational. At least, it is not along some of the dimensions of rationality.*

. . . Hegel saw this undeniable characteristic of the world we live in [namely, its ever-changingness] in a non-empirical light. Let the *mental idea* of the thing work in your thought all alone, he fancied, and just the same consequences will follow. It will be negated by the opposite ideas that dog it, and can survive only by entering, along with them, into some kind of treaty. This treaty will be an instance of the so-called 'higher synthesis' of everything with its negative; and Hegel's originality lay in transporting the process from the sphere of percepts to that of concepts and treating it as the universal method by which every kind of life, logical, physical, or psychological, is mediated. Not to the sensible facts as such, then, did Hegel point for the secret of what keeps existence going, but rather to the conceptual way of treating them. Concepts were not in his eyes the static self-contained things that previous logicians had supposed, but were germinative, and passed beyond themselves into each other by what he called their immanent dialectic.

In ignoring each other as they do, they virtually exclude and deny each other, he thought, and thus in a manner introduce each other. So the dialectic logic, according to him, had to supersede the 'logic of identity' in which, since Aristotle, all Europe had been brought up.

This view of concepts is Hegel's revolutionary performance; but so studiously vague and ambiguous are all his expressions of it that one can hardly tell whether it is the concepts as such, or the sensible experiences and elements conceived, that Hegel really means to work with. The only thing that is certain is that whatever you may say of his procedure, someone will accuse you of misunderstanding it. I make no claim to understanding it, I treat it merely impressionistically.

So treating it, I regret that he should have called it by the name of logic. Clinging as he did to the vision of a really living world, and refusing to be content with a chopped-up intellectualist picture of it, it is a pity that he should have adopted the very word that intellectualism had already pre-empted. But he clung fast to the old rationalist contempt for the immediately given world of sense and all its squalid particulars, and never tolerated the notion that the form of philosophy might be empirical only. His own system had to be a product of eternal reason, so the word 'logic,' with its suggestions of coercive necessity, was the only word he could find natural. He pretended therefore to be using the *a priori* method, and to be working by a scanty equipment of ancient logical terms—position, negation, reflection, universal, particular, individual, and the like. But what he really worked by was his own empirical perceptions, which exceeded and overflowed his miserably insufficient logical categories in every instance of their use.

What he did with the category of negation was his most original stroke. The orthodox opinion is that you can advance logically through the field of concepts only by going from the same to the same. Hegel felt deeply the sterility of this law of conceptual thought; he saw that in a fashion negation also relates things; and he had the brilliant idea of transcending the ordinary logic by treating advance from the different to the different as if it were also a necessity of thought. The so-called maxim of identity, he wrote, is supposed to be accepted by the consciousness of everyone. But the language which such a law demands, "a planet is a planet; Magnetism is magnetism; Mind is mind," deserves to be called silliness. No mind either speaks or thinks or forms conceptions in accordance with this law, and no existence of any kind whatever conforms to it. We must never view identity as abstract identity, to the exclusion of all difference. That is the touchstone for distinguishing all bad philosophy from what alone deserves the name of philosophy. If thinking were no more than registering abstract identities, it would be a most superfluous performance. Things and concepts are identical with themselves only in so far as at the same time they involve distinction.[1]

The distinction that Hegel has in mind here is naturally in the first instance distinction from all other things or concepts. But in his hands this quickly develops into contradiction of them, and finally, reflected back upon itself, into self-contradiction; and the immanent self-contradictoriness of all finite concepts thenceforth becomes the propulsive logical force that moves the world.[2] "Isolate a thing from all its relations," says

[1] Hegel, *Smaller Logic.*
[2] Cf. Hegel's fine vindication of this function of contradiction in his *Wissenschaft der Logik,* Bk. ii, sec. 1, chap. ii, C., Anmerkung 3.

Dr. Edward Caird,[3] expounding Hegel, "and try to assert it by itself; you find that is has negated itself as well as its relations. The thing in itself is nothing." Or, to quote Hegel's own words: "When we suppose an existent A, and another B, B is at first defined as the other. But A is just as much the other of B. Both are others in the same fashion. . . . 'Other' is the other by itself, therefore the other of every other, consequently the other of itself, the simply unlike itself, the self-negator, the self-alterer," etc.[4] Hegel writes elsewhere: "The finite, as implicitly other than what it is, is forced to surrender its own immediate or natural being, and to turn suddenly into its opposite. . . . Dialectic is the universal and irresistible power, before which nothing can stay. . . . *Summum jus, summa injuria*—to drive an abstract right to excess is to commit injustice. . . . Extreme anarchy and extreme depotism lead to one another. Pride comes before a fall: Too much wit outwits itself. Joy brings tears, melancholy a sardonic smile."[5] To which one well might add that most human institutions, by the purely technical and professional manner in which they come to be administered, end by becoming obstacles to the very purposes which their founders had in view.

Once catch well the knack of this scheme of thought and you are lucky if you ever get away from it. It is all you can see. Let anyone pronounce anything, and your feeling of a contradiction being implied becomes a habit, almost a motor habit in some persons who symbolize a stereotyped gesture the position, sublation, and final reinstatement involved. If you say 'two' or 'many,' your speech bewrayeth you, for the very name collects them into one. If you express doubt, your expression contradicts its content, for the doubt itself is not doubted but affirmed. If you say 'disorder,' what is that but a certain bad kind of order? if you say 'indetermination,' you are determining just *that*. If you say 'nothing but the unexpected happens,' the unexpected becomes what you expect. If you say 'all things are relative,' to what is the all of them itself relative? If you say 'no more,' you have said more already, by implying a region in which no more is found; to know a limit as such is consequently already to have got beyond it; and so forth, throughout as many examples as one cares to cite.

Whatever you posit appears thus as one-sided, and negates its other, which, being equally one-sided, negates *it;* and, since this situation remains unstable, the two contradictory terms have together, according to Hegel, to engender a higher truth of which they both appear as indispensable members, mutually mediating aspects of that higher concept or situation in thought.

Every higher total, however provisional and relative, thus reconciles the contradictions which its parts, abstracted from it, prove implicitly to contain. Rationalism, you remember, is what I called the way of thinking that methodically subordinates parts to wholes, so Hegel here is rationalistic through-and-through. The only whole by which *all* contradictions are reconciled is for him the absolute whole of wholes, the all-inclusive reason to which Hegel himself gave the name of the absolute Idea, but which I shall continue to call 'the absolute' purely and simply, . . .

---

[3] *Hegel,* in *Blackwood's Philosophical Classics.*

[4] *Wissenschaft der Logik,* Bk. i, sec. 1, chap. ii, B, a.

[5] Wallace's translation of the *Smaller Logic,* p. 128.

Let us turn now at last to the great question of fact, *Does the absolute exist or not?* to which all our previous discussion has been preliminary. I may sum up that discussion by saying that whether there really be an absolute or not, no one makes himself absurd or self-contradictory by doubting or denying it. The charges of self-contradiction, where they do not rest on purely verbal reasoning, rest on a vicious intellectualism. I will not recapitulate my criticisms. I will simply ask you to change the *venue,* and to discuss the absolute now as if it were only an open hypothesis. As such, is it more probable or more improbable?

But first of all I must parenthetically ask you to distinguish the notion of the absolute carefully from that of another object with which it is liable to become heedlessly entangled. That other object is the 'God' of common people in their religion, and the creator-God of orthodox Christian theology. Only thoroughgoing monists or pantheists believe in the absolute. The God of our popular Christianity is but one member of a pluralistic system. He and we stand outside of each other, just as the devil, the saints and the angels stand outside of both of us. I can hardly conceive of anything more different from the absolute than the God, say, of David or of Isaiah. *That* God is an essentially finite being *in* the cosmos, not with the cosmos in him, and indeed he has a very local habitation there, and very one-sided local and personal attachments. If it should prove probable that the absolute does not exist, it will not follow in the slightest degree that a God like that of David, Isaiah, or Jesus may not exist, or may not be the most important existence in the universe for us to acknowledge. I pray you, then, not to confound the two ideas as you listen to the criticisms I shall have to proffer. . . .

The great claim made for the absolute is that by supposing it we make the world appear more rational. Any hypothesis that does that will always be accepted as more probably true than an hypothesis that makes the world appear irrational. Men are once for all so made that they prefer a rational world to believe in and to live in. But rationality has at least four dimensions, intellectual, aesthetical, moral, and practical; and to find a world rational to the maximal degree *in all these respects simultaneously* is no easy matter. Intellectually, the world of mechanical materialism is the most rational, for we subject its events to mathematical calculation. But the mechanical world is ugly, as arithmetic is ugly, and it is non-moral. Morally, the theistic world is rational enough, but full of intellectual frustrations. The practical world of affairs, in its turn, so supremely rational to the politician, the military man or the man of conquering business-faculty that he never would vote to change the type of it, is irrational to moral and artistic temperaments; so that whatever demand for rationality we find satisfied by a philosophic hypothesis, we are liable to find some other demand for rationality unsatisfied by the same hypothesis. The rationality we gain in one coin we thus pay for in another; and the problem accordingly seems at first to resolve itself into that of getting a conception which will yield the largest *balance* of rationality rather than one which will yield perfect rationality of every description. In general, it may be said that if a man's conception of the world lets loose any action in him that is easy, or any faculty which he is fond of exercising, he will deem it rational in so far forth, be the faculty that of computing, fighting, lecturing, classifying, framing schematic tabulations, getting the better end of a bargain, patiently waiting and enduring, preaching, joke-making, or what you like. Albeit the absolute is defined as being necessarily an embodiment of objectively perfect rationality, it is fair to its English advocates to say that those who have espoused the hypothesis most concretely and seriously have usually avowed the irrationality to their own minds of certain elements in it.

Probably the weightiest contribution to our feeling of the rationality of the universe which the notion of the absolute brings is the assurance that however disturbed the surface may be, at bottom all is well with the cosmos—central peace abiding at the heart of endless agitation. This conception is rational in many ways, beautiful aesthetically, beautiful intellectually (could we only follow it into detail), and beautiful morally, if the enjoyment of security can be accounted moral. Practically it is less beautiful; for . . . in representing the deepest reality of the world as static and without a history, it loosens the world's hold upon our sympathies and leaves the soul of it foreign. Nevertheless it does give *peace,* and that kind of rationality is so paramountly demanded by men that to the end of time there will be absolutists, men who choose belief in a static eternal, rather than admit that the finite world of change and striving, even with a God as one of the strivers, is itself eternal. For such minds Professor Royce's words will always be the truest: "The very presence of ill in the temporal order is the condition of the perfection of the eternal order. . . . We long for the Absolute only in so far as in us the Absolute also longs, and seeks, through our very temporal striving, the peace that is nowhere in Time, but only, and yet absolutely, in Eternity. Were there then no longing in Time, there would be no peace in Eternity. . . . God [*i.e.* the absolute] who here, in me, aims at what I now temporally miss, not only possesses, in the eternal world, the goal after which I strive, but comes to possess it even through and because of my sorrow. Through this my tribulation the Absolute triumph, then, is won. . . . In the Absolute I am fulfilled. Yet my very fulfilment demands, and therefore can transcend, this very sorrow."[6] Royce is particularly felicitous in his ability to cite parts of finite experience to which he finds his picture of this absolute experience analogous. But it is hard to portray the absolute at all without rising into what might be called the "inspired" style of language—I use the word not ironically, but prosaically and descriptively, to designate the only literary form that goes with the kind of emotion that the absolute arouses. One can follow the pathway of reasoning soberly enough,[7] but the picture itself has to be effulgent. This admirable faculty of transcending, whilst inwardly preserving, every contrariety, is the absolute's characteristic form of rationality. We are but syllables in the mouth of the Lord; if the whole sentence is divine, each syllable is absolutely what it should be, in spite of all appearances. In making up the balance for or against absolutism, this emotional value weights heavily the credit side of the account.

The trouble is that we are able to see so little into the positive detail of it, and that if once admitted not to be coercively proven by the intellectualist arguments, it remains only a hypothetic possibility.

On the debit side of the account the absolute, taken seriously, and not as a mere name for our right occasionally to drop the strenuous mood and take a moral holiday, introduces all those tremendous irrationalities into the universe which a frankly pluralistic theism escapes, but which have been flung as a reproach at every form of monistic theism or

---

[6] *The World and the Individual,* vol. ii.

[7] The best uninspired argument (again not ironical!) which I know is that in Miss M. W. Calkin's excellent book, *The Persistent Problems of Philosophy,* Macmillan, 1907.

pantheism. It introduces a speculative 'problem of evil' namely, and leaves us wondering why the perfection of the absolute should require just such particular hideous forms of life as darken the day for our human imaginations. If they were forced on it by something alien, and to 'overcome' them the absolute had still to keep hold of them, we could understand its feeling of triumph, tho we, so far as we were ourselves among the elements overcome, could acquiesce but sullenly in the resultant situation, and would never just have chosen it as the most rational one conceivable. But the absolute is represented as a being without environment, upon which nothing alien can be forced, and which has spontaneously chosen from within to give itself the spectacle of all that evil rather than a spectacle with less evil in it. Its perfection is represented as the source of things, and yet the first effect of that perfection is the tremendous imperfection of all finite experience. In whatever sense the word 'rationality' may be taken, it is vain to contend that the impression made on our finite minds by such a way of representing things is altogether rational. Theologians have felt its irrationality acutely, and the 'fall,' the predestination and the election which the situation involves have given them more trouble than anything else in their attempt to pantheize Christianity. The whole business remains a puzzle, both intellectually and morally.

A Modern Indian Mystic Metaphysics

From *The Life Divine* by Sri Aurobindo, 1973

Aurobindo (1872–1950) was a leading Indian nationalist at the beginning of the twentieth century who became a yogin *and spiritual leader as well as a philosopher crafting a modern worldview that draws on science as well as positions of classical Indian theism. Born in Calcutta, Aurobindo spent fourteen years in England from age seven until graduating from King's College, Cambridge University. Returning to India, he immersed himself in Indian culture, learning Sanskrit and several modern Indian languages. Aurobindo became a nationalist politician opposed to continued British colonialism and rule, and used the editorial columns of the newspaper,* Bande Mataram *("Hail to Mother India"), to call rather unreservedly for open rebellion. Arrested on charges of sedition and then "waging war," he spent a year in prison before being acquitted in a spectacular trial in 1909. Still harassed by British authorities, he retreated to the French colony of Pondicherry, in South India, retired from politics, and wrote voluminously while practicing meditation and yoga.*

Aurobindo intends his metaphysics to reflect both science and religion and to integrate several concerns of philosophy into a single vision. He understands the fundamental nature of matter to include an "evolutionary nisus" or urge that insures the emergence of individuals capable of mystical experience through which the supreme reality, Brahman (= God), is revealed.

Brahman—in essence perfect Being, Consciousness-Will, and Bliss or Value—involutes, or contracts, aspects of itself so that certain finite possibilities can emerge, a process that has an outer limit in the "inconscient" energies of matter. But Brahman (i.e., God) cannot create an entirely insentient world since God is constrained by the metaphysical law ex nihilo nihil fit ("nothing from nothing") to create out of God's own nature of Consciousness and Bliss. (Such emanationism, we noted above, is crucial to most Indian theism—as well as to Neoplatonism in the West.) Thus this world is destined to evolve sentient material beings and eventually a divine life conceived as a society where many have a rather direct experience of Brahman.

The selection excerpted is from Aurobindo's principal work of philosophy, The Life Divine *(a text running more than a thousand pages). Several broad theories are presented as candidate explanations of the cosmos: Chance, Necessity, a theism with an extracosmic Creator, and, finally, Aurobindo's own view of a theism where God is immanent in creation. The Indian metaphysician finds faults with each of the views except the last, thus paving the way for its acceptance. (His reasoning anticipates our discussion of the argument from design, with selections from David Hume and M. A. Corey, under Arguments for a Divine Reality.) In this excerpt, Aurobindo does not discuss what he sees as the most critical considerations supporting his view of the preeminent reality of Brahman. These are mystical occurrences. His task here is rather to survey potential broad explanations of the cosmos as revealed through common sense experience and as interpreted by science. (Several selections under Mysticism address the thesis that mystical experiences provide evidence for God or a spiritual reality like Aurobindo's Brahman.)*

We know also that certain combinations of certain invisible atomic infinitesimals produce or occasion new and visible determinations quite different in nature, quality and power from the constituent infinitesimals; but we fail to discover, for instance, how a fixed formula for the combination of oxygen and hydrogen comes to determine the appearance of water which is evidently something more than a combination of gases, a new creation, a new form of substance, a material manifestation of a quite new character. We see that a seed develops into a tree, we follow the line of the process of production and we utilise it; but we do not discover how a tree can grow out of a seed, how the life and form of the tree come to be implied in the substance or energy of the seed or, if that be rather the fact, how the seed can develop into a tree. We know that genes and chromosomes are the cause of hereditary transmissions, not only of physical but of psychological variations; but we do not discover how psychological characteristics can be contained and transmitted in this inconscient material vehicle. We do not see or know, but it is expounded to us as a cogent account of Nature-process, that a play of electrons, of atoms and their resultant molecules, of cells, glands, chemical secretions and physiological processes manages by their activity on the nerves and brain of a Shakespeare or a Plato to produce or could be perhaps the dynamic occasion for the production of a *Hamlet* or a *Symposium* or a *Republic;* but we fail to discover or appreciate how such material movements could have composed or necessitated the composition of these highest points of thought and literature: the divergence here of the determinants and the determination becomes so wide that we are no longer able to follow the process, much less understand or utilise. These formulae of Science may be pragmatically correct and infallible, they may govern the practical how of Nature's processes, but they do not disclose the intrinsic how or why; rather they have the air of the formulae of a cosmic Magician, precise, irresistible, automatically successful each in its field, but their rationale is fundamentally unintelligible.

There is more to perplex us. . . . What is the rationale of the determination, what is its original truth or its significance? What compels or impels this exuberant play of varying possibilities which seem to have no aim or meaning unless it be the beauty or delight of creation? A Mind, a seeking and curious inventive Thought, a hidden determining Will might be there, but there is no trace of it in the first and fundamental appearance of material Nature.

A first possible explanation points to a self-organising dynamic Chance that is at work,—a paradox necessitated by the appearance of inevitable order on one side, of unaccountable freak and fantasy on the other side of the cosmic phenomenon we call Nature. An inconscient and inconsequent Force, we may say, that acts at random and creates this or that by a general chance without any determining principle,—determinations coming in only as the result of a persistent repetition of the same rhythm of action and succeeding because only this repetitive rhythm could succeed in keeping things in being,—this is the energy of Nature. But this implies that somewhere in the origin of things there is a boundless Possibility or a womb of innumerable possibilities that are manifested out of it by the original Energy,—an incalculable Inconscient which we find some embarrassment in calling either an Existence or a Non-Existence; for without some such origin and basis the appearance and the action of the Energy is unintelligible. Yet an opposite aspect of the nature of the cosmic phenomenon as we see it appears to forbid the theory of a random action generating a persistent order. There is too much of an iron insistence on order, on a law basing the possibilities. One would be justified rather in supposing that there is an inherent imperative Truth of things unseen by us, but a Truth capable of manifold manifestation, throwing out a multitude of possibilities and variants of itself which the creative Energy by its action turns into so many realised actualities. This brings us to a second explanation,— a mechanical necessity in things, its workings recognisable by us as so many mechanical laws of Nature;—the necessity, we might say, of some such secret inherent Truth of things . . . governing automatically the processes we observe in action in the universe. But a theory of mechanical Necessity by itself does not elucidate the free play of the endless unaccountable variations which are visible in the evolution: there must be behind the Necessity or in it a law of unity associated with a coexistent but dependent law of multiplicity, both insisting on manifestation; but the unity of what, the multiplicity of what? Mechanical Necessity can give no answer. Again the emergence of consciousness out of the Inconscient is a stumbling-block in the way of this theory; for it is a phenomenon which can have no place in all-pervading truth of inconscient mechanical Necessity. If there is a necessity which compels the emergence, it can be only this, that there is already a consciousness concealed in the Inconscient, waiting for evolution and when all is ready breaking out from its prison of apparent Nescience. . . .

This opens the way for other explanations which make Consciousness the creator of this world out of an apparent original Inconscience. A Mind, a Will seems to have imagined and organised the universe, but it has veiled itself behind its creation; its first erection has been this screen of an inconscient Energy and a material form of substance, at once a disguise of its presence and a plastic creative basis on which it could work as an artisan uses for his production of forms and patterns a dumb and obedient material. All these things we see around us are then the thoughts of an extracosmic Divinity, a Being with an omnipotent and omniscient Mind and Will, who is responsible for the mathematical law of the physical universe, for its artistry of beauty, for its strange play of samenesses and variations, of concordances and discords, of combining and intermingling opposites, for the drama of consciousness struggling to exist and seeking to affirm itself in an inconscient universal order. The fact that this Divinity is invisible to us, undiscoverable by our mind and senses, offers no difficulty, since self-evidence or direct sign of an extracosmic Creator could not be expected in a cosmos which is void of his presence: the patent signals everywhere of the works of an Intelligence, of law, design, formula, adaptation of means to end, constant and inexhaustible invention, fantasy even but restrained by an ordering Reason might be considered sufficient proof of this origin of things. Or if this Creator is not entirely supracosmic, but is also immanent in his works, even then there need be no other sign of him,—except indeed to some consciousness evolving in this inconscient world, but only when its evolution reached a point at which it could become aware of the indwelling Presence. The intervention of this evolving consciousness would not be a difficulty, since there would be no contradiction of the basic nature of things in its appearance; an omnipotent Mind could easily infuse something of itself into its creatures. One difficulty remains; it is the arbitrary nature of the creation, the incomprehensibility of its purpose, the crude meaninglessness of its law of unnecessary ignorance, strife and suffering, its ending without denouement or issue. A play? But why this stamp of so many undivine elements and characters in the play of One whose nature must be supposed to be divine? To the suggestion that what we see worked out in the world is the thoughts of God, the retort can be made that God could well have had better thoughts and the best thought of all would have been to refrain from the creation of an unhappy and unintelligible universe. All theistic explanations of existence starting from an extracosmic Deity stumble over this difficulty and can only evade it; it would disappear only if the Creator were, even though exceeding the creation, yet immanent in it, himself in some sort both the player and the play, an Infinite casting infinite possibilities into the set form of an evolutionary cosmic order.

On that hypothesis, there must be behind the action of the material Energy a secret involved Consciousness, cosmic, infinite, building up through the action of that frontal Energy its means of an evolutionary manifestation, a creation out of itself in the boundless finite of the material universe. The apparent inconscience of the material Energy would be an indispensable condition for the structure of the material world-substance in which this Consciousness intends to involve itself so that it may grow by evolution out of its apparent opposite; for without some such device a complete involution would be impossible. If there is such a creation by the Infinite out of itself, it must be the manifestation, in a material disguise, of truths or powers of its own being: the forms or vehicles of these truths or powers would be the basic general or fundamental determinates we see in Nature; the particular determinates, which otherwise are unaccountable variations that have emerged from the vague general stuff in which they originate, would be the appropriate forms or vehicles of the possibilities that the truths or powers residing in these fundamentals bore within them. The principle of free variation of possibilities natural to an infinite

Consciousness would be the explanation of the aspect of inconscient Chance of which we are aware in the workings of Nature,—inconscient only in appearance and so appearing because of the complete involution in Matter, because of the veil with which the secret Consciousness has disguised its presence. The principle of truths, real powers of the Infinite imperatively fulfilling themselves would be the explanation of the opposite aspects of a mechanical Necessity which we see in Nature,—mechanical in appearance only and so appearing because of the same veil of Inconscience. It would then be perfectly intelligible why the Inconscient does its works with a constant principle of mathematical architecture, of design, of effective arrangement of numbers, of adaptation of means to ends, of inexhaustible device and invention, one might almost say, a constant experimental skill and an automatism of purpose. The appearance of consciousness out of an apparent Inconscience would also be no longer inexplicable.

All the unexplained processes of Nature would find their meaning and their place if this hypothesis proved to be tenable. . . . There would be no difficulty either in understanding on this principle how infinitesimals of a material character like the gene and the chromosome can carry in them psychological elements to be transmitted to the physical form that has to emerge from the human seed; it would be at bottom on the same principle in the objectivity of Matter as that which we find our subjective experience,—for we see that the subconscient physical carries in it a mental psychological content, impressions of past events, habits, fixed mental and vital formations, fixed forms of character, and sends them up by an occult process to the waking consciousness, thus originating or influencing many activities of our nature.

On the same basis there would be no difficulty in understanding why the physiological functionings of the body help to determine the mind's psychological actions: for the body is not mere unconscious Matter: it is a structure of a secretly conscious Energy that has taken form in it. Itself occultly conscious, it is, at the same time, the vehicle of expression of an overt Consciousness that has emerged and is self-aware in our physical energy-substance. The body's functionings are a necessary machinery or instrumentation for the movements of this mental Inhabitant; it is only by setting the corporeal instrument in motion that the Conscious Being emerging, evolving in it can transmit its mind formations, will formations and turn them into a physical manifestation of itself in Matter. The capacity, the processes of the instrument must to a certain extent reshape the mind formations in their transition from mental shape into physical expression; its workings are necessary and must exercise their influence before that expression can become actual. The bodily instrument may even in some directions dominate its user; it may too by a force of habit suggest or create involuntary reactions of the consciousness inhabiting it before the working Mind and Will can control or interfere. All this is possible because the body has a "subconscient" consciousness of its own which counts in our total self-expression; even, if we look at this outer instrumentation only, we can conclude that body determines mind, but this is only a minor truth and the major Truth is that mind determines body. In this view a still deeper Truth becomes conceivable; a spiritual entity ensouling the substance that veils it is the original determinant of both mind and body. On the other side, in the opposite order of process,—that by which the mind can transmit its ideas and commands to the body, can train it to be an instrument for new action, can even so impress it with its habitual demands or orders that the physical instinct carries them out automatically even when the mind is no longer consciously willing them, those also more unusual but well attested by which to an extraordinary and hardly limitable extent the mind can learn to determine the reactions of the body even to the overriding of its normal law or conditions of action,—these and other otherwise unaccountable aspects of the relation between these two elements of our being become easily understandable: for it is the secret consciousness in the living matter that receives from its greater companion; it is this in the body that in its own involved and occult fashion perceives or feels the demand on it and obeys the emerged or evolved consciousness which presides over the body. Finally, the conception of a divine Mind and Will creating the cosmos becomes justifiable, while at the same time the perplexing elements in it which our reasoning mentality refuses to ascribe to an arbitrary fiat of the Creator, find their explanation as inevitable phenomena of a Consciousness emerging with difficulty out of its opposite—but with the mission to override these contrary phenomena and manifest by a slow and difficult evolution its greater reality and true nature.

Process Metaphysics and Christian Theology

From *Process and Reality* by Alfred North Whitehead, corrected edition, David Ray Griffin and Donald W. Sherburne, editors, 1978 • From *God-Christ-Church* by Marjorie Hewitt Suchocki, 1982

We have already reviewed ideas pioneered in part by Lord Whitehead when we discussed the process concept of God (see the selections from Charles Hartshorne and William Alston). Here we shall survey Whitehead's thoughts about what is wrong with some concepts of God, and also how, very broadly, Whitehead understands God in the context of his overall theory. Although Whitehead holds that God is a concrete being, his presentation is exceedingly abstract. To help us understand just what his new concept is as well as to see how process theologians are able to use it to elucidate central positions of historical religions, in particular of Christianity, we turn next to a selection from Marjorie Suchocki, who is a professor of theology at Pittsburgh Theological Seminary.

First, a few words about the career of Whitehead (1861–1947) are appropriate. With a junior colleague named Bertrand Russell, he published early in the twentieth century Principia Mathematica, *a revolutionary masterpiece of mathematics and logic. Whitehead was also an accomplished physicist, and his early works in philosophy concerned interpretation of Einstein's discoveries and philosophy of science in general. It was later in his career that he turned to forging a new metaphysics.*

Proclaiming in the Introduction to Process and Reality *(first published 1929) that "Speculative Philosophy is the endeavor to frame a . . . system of general ideas in terms of which every element of our experience can be interpreted," Whitehead proceeds to lay out just such a system of interlocking categories and propositions. These are extremely abstract, as would be expected given the nature of the metaphysical project as Whitehead understands it. But as mentioned, God is not, for Whitehead, an abstract object, but is concrete—at least this is true for what Whitehead calls God's* consequent *nature. God's consequent nature is God understood as the omnipercipient being, feeling every creature's feeling as it happens: God, for Whitehead, as with Aurobindo, indwells the world, feeling with every being's feeling and experience. Marjorie Suchocki makes the idea come alive in elucidating the Christian doctrine of ressurrection.*

God's consequent nature contrasts with what Whitehead calls God's primordial *nature. This is a conception much like Philo's* logos, *or mind of God, filled with the Forms that provide the patterns for the visible world (see the earlier discussion of Philo). Whitehead does not understand there to be Forms in precisely the Platonic or Neoplatonic sense. But he does hold that God's primordial nature governs by necessity all possibilities of things coming to be.*

Yet despite such an element of necessitation, the central fact about things is their creativity. In Whitehead's view, we and God are in a continual process of creating ourselves, through original responses to what has occurred.

Marjorie Suchocki explains God's omnipercipience—*God's feeling every creature's feeling, or God's* consequent *nature—as God's feeling "the world precisely as it occurs, with the result that God's feeling can be described as crucifixion: our pain is ultimately God's pain as well." She goes on to explain, in Whiteheadian terms, the integration of pain in the redemptive power of God and the joy of ressurrection. God's primordial nature guarantees, according to Suchocki, that there is always present the possibility of integrating pain and suffering into a greater harmony and good, as we and God together move forward in creative interchange.*

FROM *PROCESS AND REALITY*

GOD AND THE WORLD

So long as the temporal world is conceived as a self-sufficient completion of the creative act, explicable by its derivation from an ultimate principle which is at once eminently real and the unmoved mover, from this conclusion there is no escape : the best that we can say of the turmoil is, 'For so he giveth his beloved—sleep.' This is the message of religions of the Buddhistic type, and some sense it is true. In this final discussion we have to ask, whether metaphysical principles impose the belief that it is the whole truth. The complexity of the world must be reflected in the answer. It is childish to enter upon thought with the simple-minded question, What is the world made of. The task of reason is to fathom the deeper depths of the many-sidedness of things. We must not expect simple answers to far-reaching questions. However far our gaze penetrates, there are always heights beyond, which block our vision [Islam].

The notion of God as the 'unmoved mover' is derived from Aristotle, at least so far as Western thought is concerned. The notion of God as 'eminently real' is a favourite doctrine of Christian theology. The combination of the two into the doctrine of an aboriginal, eminently real, transcendent creator, at whose fiat the world came into being, and whose imposed will it obeys, is the fallacy which has infused tragedy into the histories of Christianity and of Mahometanism [Islam].

When the Western world accepted Christianity, Caesar conquered, and the received text of Western theology was edited by his lawyers. The code of Justinian and the theology of Justinian are two volumes expressing one movement of the human spirit. The brief Galilean vision of humility flickered throughout the ages, uncertainly. In the official formulation of the religion it has assumed the trivial form of the mere attribution to the Jews that they cherished a misconception about their Messiah. But the deeper idolatry, of the fashioning of God in the image of the Egyptian, Persian, and Roman imperial rulers, was retained. The Church gave unto God the attributes which belonged exclusively to Caesar.

In the great formative period of theistic philosophy which ended with the rise of Mahometanism, after a continuance coeval with civilization, three strains of thought emerge which, amid many variations in detail, respectively fashion God in the image of an imperial ruler, God in the image of a personification of moral energy, God in the image of an ultimate philosophical principle. Hume's *Dialogues* criticize unanswerably these modes of explaining the system of the world.

The three schools of thought can be associated respectively with the divine Caesars, the Hebrew prophets, and Aristotle. But Aristotle was antedated by Indian, and Buddhistic, thought; the Hebrew prophets can be paralleled in traces of earlier thought; Mahometanism and the divine Caesars merely represent the most natural, obvious, theistic idolatrous symbolism, at all epochs and places.

The history of theistic philosophy exhibits various stages of combination of these three diverse ways of entertaining the problem. There is, however, in the Galilean origin of Christianity yet another suggestion which does not fit very well with any of the three main strands of thought. It does not emphasize the ruling Caesar, or the ruthless moralist, or the unmoved mover. It dwells upon the tender elements in the world, which slowly and in quietness operate by love; and it finds purpose in the present immediacy of a kingdom not of this world. Love neither rules, nor is it unmoved; also it is a little oblivious as to morals. It does not look to the future; for it finds its own reward in the immediate present.

Apart from any reference to existing religions as they are, or as they ought to be, we must investigate dispassionately what the metaphysical principles, here developed, require on these points, as to the nature of God. There is nothing here in the nature of proof. There is merely the confrontation of the theoretic system with a certain rendering of the facts. But the unsystematized report upon the facts is itself highly controversial, and the system is confessedly inadequate. The deductions from it in this particular sphere of thought cannot be looked upon as more than suggestions as to how the problem is transformed in the light of that system. What follows is merely an attempt to add another speaker to that masterpiece, Hume's *Dialogues Concerning Natural Religion*. Any cogency of argument entirely depends upon elucidation of somewhat exceptional elements in our conscious experience—those elements which may roughly be classed together as religious and moral intuitions.

In the first place, God is not to be treated as an exception to all metaphysical principles, invoked to save their collapse. He is their chief exemplification.

Viewed as primordial, he is the unlimited conceptual realization of the absolute wealth of potentiality. In this aspect, he is not *before* all creation, but *with* all creation. But, as primordial, so far is he from 'eminent reality,' that in this abstraction he is 'deficiently actual'—and this in two ways. His feelings are only conceptual and so lack the fulness of actuality. Secondly, conceptual feelings, apart from complex integration with physical feelings, are devoid of consciousness in their subjective forms.

Thus, when we make a distinction of reason, and consider God in the abstraction of a primordial actuality, we must ascribe to him neither fulness of feeling, nor consciousness. He is the unconditioned actuality of conceptual feeling at the base of things; so that, by reason of this primordial actuality, there is an order in the relevance of eternal objects to the process of creation. His unity of conceptual operations is a free creative act, untrammelled by reference to any particular course of things. It is deflected neither by love, nor by hatred, for what in fact comes to pass. The *particularities* of the actual world presuppose *it;* while *it* merely presupposes the *general* metaphysical character of creative advance, of which it is the primordial exemplification. The primordial nature of God is the acquirement by creativity of a primordial character.

His conceptual actuality at once exemplifies and establishes the categoreal conditions. The conceptual feelings, which compose his primordial nature, exemplify in their subjective forms their mutual sensitivity and their subjective unity of subjective aim. These subjective forms are valuations determining the relative relevance of eternal objects for each occasion of actuality.

He is the lure for feeling, the eternal urge of desire. His particular relevance to each creative act as it arises from its own conditioned standpoint in the world, constitutes him the initial 'object of desire' establishing the initial phase of each subjective aim. A quotation from Aristotle's *Metaphysics*[1] expresses some analogies to, and some differences from, this line of thought: "And since that which is moved and mover is intermediate, there is a mover which moves without being moved, being eternal, substance, and actuality. And the object of desire and the object of thought are the same. For the apparent good is the object of appetite, and the real good is the primary object of rational desire. But desire is consequent on opinion rather than opinion on desire; for the thinking is the starting point. And thought is moved by the object of thought, and one side of the list of opposites is in itself the object of thought; . . ." Aristotle had not made the distinction between conceptual feelings and the intellectual feelings which alone involve consciousness. But if 'conceptual feeling,' with its subjective form of valuation, be substituted for 'thought,' 'thinking,' and 'opinion,' in the above quotation, the agreement is exact.

There is another side to the nature of God which cannot be omitted. Throughout this exposition of the philosophy of organism we have been considering the primary action of God on the world. From this point of view, he is the principle of concretion—the principle whereby there is initiated a definite outcome from a situation otherwise riddled with ambiguity. Thus, so far, the primordial side of the nature of God has alone been relevant.

---

[1] Cf. *Metaphysics* 1072, trans. by Professor W. D. Ross. My attention was called to the appositeness of this particular quotations by Mr. F. J. Carson.

But God, as well as being primordial, is also consequent. He is the beginning and the end. He is not the beginning in the sense of being in the past of all members. He is the presupposed actuality of conceptual operation, in unison of becoming with every other creative act. Thus by reason of the relativity of all things, there is a reaction of the world on God. The completion of God's nature into a fulness of physical feeling is derived from the objectification of the world in God. He shares with every new creation its actual world; and the concrescent creature is objectified in God as a novel element in God's objectification of that actual world. This prehension into God of each creature is directed with the subjective aim, and clothed with the subjective form, wholly derivative from his all-inclusive primordial valuation. God's conceptual nature is unchanged, by reason of its final completeness. But his derivative nature is consequent upon the creative advance of the world.

Thus, analogously to all actual entities, the nature of God is dipolar. He has a primordial nature and a consequent nature. The consequent nature of God is conscious; and it is the realization of the actual world in the unity of his nature, and through the transformation of his wisdom. The primordial nature is conceptual, the consequent nature is the weaving of God's physical feelings upon his primordial concepts.

One side of God's nature is constituted by his conceptual experience. This experience is the primordial fact in the world, limited by no actuality which it presupposes. It is therefore infinite, devoid of all negative prehensions. This side of his nature is free, complete, primordial, eternal, actually deficient, and unconscious. The other side originates with physical experience derived from the temporal world, and then acquires integration with the primordial side. It is determined, incomplete, consequent, 'everlasting,' fully actual, and conscious. His necessary goodness expresses the determination of his consequent nature.

Conceptual experience can be infinite, but it belongs to the nature of physical experience that it is finite. An actual entity in the temporal world is to be conceived as originated by physical experience with its process of completion motivated by consequent, conceptual experience initially derived from God. God is to be conceived as originated by conceptual experience with his process of completion motivated by consequent, physical experience, initially derived from the temporal world.

FROM *GOD-CHRIST-CHURCH*

The edges of God are tragedy; the depths of God are joy, beauty, resurrection, life. Resurrection answers crucifixion; life answers death. If Jesus reveals the nature of God in his life and crucifixion, he most surely also reveals God through resurrection.

A curious aspect in speaking of resurrection is that the New Testament speaks about the results of resurrection, but not about resurrection itself. If we wish to talk of the way Jesus reveals God in his life, we can point to nearly any text in the gospels to see the content of that revelation. Likewise, to speak of God revealed in the crucifixion draws us to the long passion narratives that form the crux of each gospel. But when we wish to understand the glory of the resurrection, we are turned back. Not a single gospel account describes the details of the resurrection. There is no privileged discussion about the exact event. We must look instead to the results of resurrection, whether in the resurrection appearances or in the faith and zeal of the apostles as they proclaim the dawn of the new age heralded by the resurrection of Jesus. The resurrection itself is hidden from our view.

If the immediacy of the resurrection is hidden, the results are not. In fact, the resurrection might be considered through the metaphor of the sun. We cannot look directly at the sun, for the brightness would blind us—our eyes are not suited to that strength of light. Yet the sun, which we cannot see directly, illumines all else, and in its light we make our way in the world. We cannot look directly at the resurrection because it is not given for us to see. Nevertheless, it illumines the entire landscape of the New Testament: the resurrection is the confirmation of that which Jesus revealed in his life and death, and it is the catalyst that transforms the disciples, releasing the power that led to the foundation of the church.

Confirmation and transformation are thus both involved as results of the resurrection. There is an apparent tension between the two words, for confirmation appears to be an affirmation of that which has come to be, while transformation is a movement beyond. Both elements are clearly in the resurrection, and the resurrection, like the life and crucifixion of Jesus, must be taken as revelatory of the divine nature.

By focusing upon the story of the resurrection appearance to Thomas, we might understand these two facets as they apply to an understanding of God for us. In the gospel of John, Thomas plays the role of the misunderstanding disciple, first with regard to the raising of Lazarus, and second with regard to the resurrected Jesus. In both cases, Jesus' answer to Thomas underscores the purposes of God. In the Second account, Jesus has appeared to ten of the disciples, Thomas being absent. Upon being told of the appearance, Thomas scoffs, claiming that he will not believe until he sees the marks of the crucifixion on the one the others claim is Jesus. Accordingly, Jesus appears again and invites Thomas to touch the scars; Thomas' response is to exclaim "My Lord and my God," recognizing at last the presence of God in Jesus.

In the account, the scars of the crucifixion mediate the truth of the resurrection. But the scars belong to the preresurrection existence; the scars are the result of pain and death, yet they are present as well in the resurrection. The transformation of Jesus that occurred in resurrection is no *creatio ex nihilo,* no absolute new beginning. Rather, the transformation is fashioned through the experience of the crucifixion. Transformation bears the marks of the process leading to the very need for transformation; there is a continuity with the pain of the past in the resurrection life, for the pain of the past adds its shape to the transformation.

If the resurrection is both a confirmation and a transformation, the crucifixion appears to be a central link holding the two elements together. The resurrection power of God does not annihilate the past, it transforms the past. That which was, is affirmed, but given a new dimension, a new context, a new direction.

The dynamics of process thought can help us to express this. Remember the way in which the model describes God's feeling of any occasion in the world, and the unification of that feeling with the primordial vision:

God's feeling of the world ("A") is through the consequent nature. . . . God feels the world precisely as it occurs, with the result that God's feeling can aptly be described as a crucifixion: our pain is ultimately God's pain as well; the edges of God are tragedy. To continue with our illustration of an injured woman [injured in an assault and robbery], God feels her in that moment of pain as she feels herself; her suffering is God's suffering as well. But this moment at the edge of God is but the beginning of God's feeling of the world. In the process dynamic, every feeling must be integrated with all other feelings in terms of what

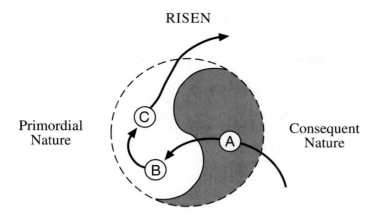

RISEN

Primordial
Nature

Consequent
Nature

the experiencer, the subject, chooses to be. With God, that choice of being is primordial, occurring eternally through the valuation of all possibilities in harmony. God does not decide the divine character on the basis of the consequent nature, but God *is* what God is through the primordial nature. The feelings of the world must be integrated into God's character. This means that "A"—the woman in pain—must be integrated into God's character. This means that "A"—the woman in pain—must be integrated with God's vision of harmony. In the process, resurrection *must* occur, for God *is* resurrection through the power of the primordial nature.

The woman is felt in relation to all other feelings in God—feelings of the young man [the robber, her assailant], feelings of the woman's past, feelings of all the world—and primarily, the woman is felt in relation to the eternal harmony of God. This integration moves God's feeling of the woman through the everlasting concrescence of God into the primordial harmony, the infinite resources of God ordered in goodness. This movement is represented by "B" on the diagram, and represents God's own inner redemption of that woman's pain. This redemptive process is resurrection in the sense that there has been a transformation of the woman from her finite context to her infinite context in God—the divine resources are brought to bear, integrating the feelings of that woman into divine harmony.

This integration is hidden in God, but the results of it are given to the world through what is marked on the diagram as "C." God feels a transformation for this woman in two respects: first with regard to her presence in God, but also with regard to the possibilities for her finite existence as her life continues in the world. "C" will be marked *both* by the reality of the woman's context—her age, her place in society, her past creation of herself in her personality and character—*and* by possibilities for her transformation; that is to say, those elements deeply within the resources of God which can apply to a finite form of transformation, mirroring in a finite way the divine transformation. God feels the resurrection of the woman both as actual within the divine nature and as possible for the world. The one will be perfect, the other will be an adaptation of that perfection to particularities of finite existence. There is a "best" for the woman, even in her harsh circumstances, and this "best" will bear the marks of both the world and God, leading her toward transformation.

The marks of pain cannot be abstracted in resurrection. Imagine the possible modes of resurrection which might be given to the woman: perhaps the most immediate would be the simple expedient of unconsciousness, blocking out the immediacy of pain. As we try to imagine further transformations open to the woman, we must be guided by the resurrection nature of God, which according to the revelation of Jesus is a depth and strength of love. It is possible that the woman might be taken to a hospital to receive care, and in that context encounter others who also need care. It is possible that because of her own pain, she might empathize with another in his or her pain; receiving care, she might give care. We might further speculate along the path of the reality of love to consider the possibility that upon release from the hospital, her attitude and actions with her family might be different.

The possibility of such paths would be finite reflections of the redemptive power of God, leading the woman toward a finite mode of resurrection living and loving. If the woman actualizes such possibilities, she will experience a transformation of her pain that is nevertheless purchased through pain. The shape of her sensitivities will be direct inheritors of the scars she has received, and will bear the imprint of pain transcended. Whether or not this happens would depend upon a complexity of circumstances, primarily the response of the woman to the opportunity. Her habituated responses might hinder her movement into transformation, or keep transformation to a low level—but insofar as it occurs, she will be living in the power of the resurrection, made available to her through the character of God. That God *is* this power is revealed by Jesus in the reality of his resurrection.

DISCUSSION QUESTIONS

1. Hegel says, "a so-called basic proposition of philosophy or principle of philosophy, if true, is also false, just because it is *only* a principle." Explain how this view connects with his sense that the Absolute as Spirit comes to be more than a spiritual Substance, namely, through a (dialectical) process, to move from the *in itself* to the *for itself.* (It may be helpful to consult the first couple of pages of the selection from James.)

2. Present the main lines of William James's criticism of Hegel's philosophy, both his attack on Hegel's dialectical method and his impugning the rationality of Hegel's philosophy of an Absolute.

3. Reconstruct Aurobindo's eliminative argument in favor of his view of matter as "structure of secretly conscious Energy" and as "the vehicle of expression of an overt Consciousness that has emerged and is self-aware in our physical energy-substance." That is to say, present Aurobindo's reasons that he takes to eliminate, first, a materialist explanation of consciousness (including an understanding of the universe as the work of a "self-organizing dynamic Chance") and, second, a theological explanation

centering on a notion of an "extracosmic Creator"—thus leaving his own view as the unobjectionable candidate.

4. Elucidate Whitehead's notions of God's primordial and consequent natures, making reference to Marjorie Suchocki's discussion of crucifixion and resurrection. What is your opinion about Suchocki's use of Whitehead's thought? In particular, given that Whitehead does not himself explicitly endorse Christian views, is Suchocki's borrowing legitimate?

CHAPTER TWO

Arguments for a Divine Reality

Philosophy professionals have classified reasons for accepting the existence of God as either (a) arguments of *rational theology* or (b) *revelation* or scripture. Rational theology has been divided, in turn, into two parts: (1) reasons known *a posteriori* or from experience (e.g., the argument to God as first cause, from a designed universe to God as designer, and so on) and (2) reasons known *a priori* or apart from experience (viz., various ontological arguments, as they are called).

One problem with this schema is that it leaves out mystical experience. Particularly with Buddhism and some Hindu schools but also in the West, mystical experience is often taken to be important evidence showing that there is a Divine Reality, though not necessarily God. Another problem with the schema is that revelation and scripture are excluded from rational theology. The exclusion implies that acceptance of religious doctrines on the basis of scripture is strictly *ir*rational. But interpreting scripture as testimony, or even as a miraculous revelation from God, could be a first step to an entirely rational acceptance of religious beliefs—at least it would seem, that the question, in advance of inquiry, should be treated as open.

Here simply for purposes of convenience we shall separate mystical experience off from other considerations offered in support of God or another Divine Reality, looking at mystic testimony in a global context in the next section. Now some would interpret scripture as authoritative because it is a record of mystical experience (this is a common view in Buddhist philosophy). Thus on such an interpretation, our survey of scripture as potential grounds for accepting God (etc.) will be postponed until the next section. But a question that is germane to disputes over scripture, namely, whether religious testimony can be relied on, launches this section. We shall also look at the justificational value of miracles. Then we shall proceed to arguments of traditional "rational theology," first the *a posteriori* arguments and finally the *a priori*.

Testimony and the Principle of Credulity

From *Belief* by H. H. Price, 1969

Epistemology *is that area of philosophy concerned with the sources and nature of our knowledge and warranted (or justified) belief. In this section, we shall chiefly be occupied with whether we can learn of the existence of a Divine Reality from argument, from considerations put before us formulable as* premises *in support of the* conclusion *that God (or the like) exists. Other ways in general that we come to know things are from our own experience and from peoples'* testimony *based on their experiences. The first selection, from a leading British epistemologist of the middle of the twentieth century, H. H. Price, concerns the epistemic value of testimony, a topic with obvious ramifications for philosophy of religion.*

    Price examines, and champions, what we may call a principle of credulity. *This is that one should believe what one is told unless there are grounds for doubt. Thus the default position concerning testimony would be innocence, or a presumption of truth.*

    Price does not dwell on the positive grounds there might be for doubting some particular bit of testimony. In the religious arena, where there is much conflicting testimony concerning what a Divine Reality is like, the very conflicts themselves seem grounds for doubt. We shall consider the issue of conflicts in testimony under Mysticism and Religious Pluralism. David Hume presents what he sees as grounds for doubting all testimony of miracles, as we shall see in an excerpt later in this section.

    Price's principle of credulity has had quite some influence in recent philosophy of religion. Richard Swinburne, the next author on our list, has promoted its importance, as have other professionals in the field.

THE EVIDENCE OF TESTIMONY

Epistemologists do not seem to have paid much attention to the evidence of testimony. But according to our ordinary way of thinking, testimony is one of our most important sources of knowledge. Everyone claims to know a very large number of geographical and historical truths, for which he has only the evidence of testimony. All of us here would claim to know that China is a very large and populous country, though none of us, perhaps, has been within three thousand miles of it. Every English schoolboy knows that Charles II was restored to the throne in 1660, and that Britain was once part of the Roman Empire, though these 'known facts' are facts about the remote past. The same applies to facts about the very recent past as well. If an important debate takes place in Parliament, millions of people claim to know about it next day, just by reading newspapers or listening to the wireless.

    To take an even more striking example, each of us would claim to know how old he is, that is, how many years have elapsed since he was born. But he has only the evidence of testimony to assure him that he was born in such and such a year; and equally he has only the evidence of testimony to assure him that this present year is 1967. How do I know, or what grounds have I for believing, that to-day is January 23, 1967? If it is a case of 'being sure and having the right to be sure', I have acquired this right by reading what is written on a calendar, or at the top of the front page of the newspaper which was delivered at my home this morning. I am often uncertain what day of the week it is. Is it Wednesday or Thursday? But in my ordinary unphilosophical moments, I assume that this question can be conclusively settled by consulting the appropriate written sources, such as to-day's newspaper.

Indeed, each of us depends on testimony for almost all that he claims to know about anything which is beyond the range of his own first-hand observation and memory; and one of the most important functions of memory itself is the remembering of what we have learned from other people by means of speech and writing. . . .

. . . our ordinary practice is to accept what we are told unless or until we see reason to doubt it. We do seem to follow the principle 'What there is said to be (or have been) there is (or was) more often than not'. There are of course certain special occasions when the principle is temporarily switched off as it were, or put into cold storage for a while. When someone says 'I am now going to tell you a story' he is warning us that what he is about to say is not to be taken as testimony. The principle 'What there is said to have been there was, more often than not' is to be ignored for the time being. A similar switching-off occurs when we begin to read a book which we have borrowed from the section marked 'Novels' in the library. The sentences uttered by characters in a play are not to be taken as testimony either, though may of them have the form of statements about empirical matters of fact, for instance, 'The wind bites shrewdly, it is very cold'. We are not to take this as a weather-report. But the important point to notice about these occasions is that they are special and exceptional ones. Special conventions and devices have to be used to convey to us that for the time being the principle we ordinarily follow is not to be applied. And that principle *is* something like 'What there is said to be, or to have have been, there is, or was, more often than not'.

. . . when we consider the enormous number and variety of the beliefs which each of us holds on the evidence of testimony alone, it is obvious that the amount of first-hand confirmation he has is tiny indeed in comparison. It is nothing like large enough to justify the generalisation 'what there is said to be, or have been, there is, or was, more often than not'. In a very simple and primitive society, where no one can read or write or listen to the radio, the situation would be easier. Then, if someone tells me that there was a wolf sitting beside the village well at midnight, I can go to the well myself this morning and see what look like the footmarks of a wolf in the mud beside it. But in a civilized and highly-educated community it is another matter. We have only to consider the vast mass of historical propositions which every educated person believes. I can personally remember a few of the events that happened in the reign of King Edward VII. But I certainly cannot remember anything that happened in the reign of King Edward the Confessor, to say nothing of the reign of Hadrian or Septimius Severus. Yet I do very firmly believe that both these Emperors visited Britain, and that Septimius Severus died at York. I hold this belief on nothing but the evidence of testimony. The best I have managed to do by way of 'checking' the testimony for myself is to read the Latin text of what I am told is a copy of *Historia Augusta*; and this hardly amounts to first-hand verification.

Suppose however that we re-stated our principle in a much weaker form: 'What there is said to be (or to have been) there is (or was) in at least one case out of every five.' This seems a very modest principle, even a rather sceptical one. But if it is supposed to be an inductive generalisation, the evidence which any one person has for believing it would still be quite insufficient. In a civilized and literate society, the amount of testimony which each of us has been able to test and verify for himself is far too small to justify any inductive estimate of the 'overall' reliability of testimony in general: too small, that is, in relation to the enormous number and variety of all the beliefs he has, which are supported partly or wholly by testimony spoken or written, or conveyed in other ways (for example, by means of maps). Whatever estimate any one person tried to make of its reliability, whether favourable or unfavourable, he would not have nearly enough first-hand evidence to justify it. Indeed, the habit of accepting testimony is so deep-rooted in all of us that we fail to realize how very limited the range of each person's first-hand observation and memory is. . . .

There is however another way of interpreting the principle we are discussing. Perhaps it is not itself a proposition which we believe, still less a proposition believed with complete conviction. Instead, it may be more like a maxim or a methodological rule. In that case, it is better formulated in the imperative than the indicative mood. We might put it this way: 'Believe what you are told by others unless or until you have reasons for doubting it.' Or we might say 'Conduct your thoughts and your actions as if what there is said to be (or to have been) there is (or was) more often than not'. If this is what our principle is, we no longer have to ask what evidence there is for believing it, because it is not itself something believed. It does of course concern believing, and could be described as a policy for forming beliefs. But a policy is not itself believable, since it is not itself either true or false. We could perhaps say that we believe 'in' it, in the sense in which some people believe in Classical Education and others believe in taking a cold bath every morning before breakfast. But believing in a policy or procedure is very different from believing that something is the case. . . .

. . . The moral aspect of it is only relevant in so far as the policy we are considering will not in fact succeed, unless there is at least a modicum of honesty and mutual trust among those who practise it. In a community of incorrigible liars or incurable romancers, the exchange of testimony would not help very much to solve the problem which arises from the scarcity of each person's first-hand experiences. And the testimony of incurable theorizers, who cannot report an observed fact without putting their own interpretation on it, would not be much better. Our policy will work best in a community of honest and hard-headed empiricists who have a respect for facts and for one another. It must also be assumed, I think, that the majority of the persons from whom one receives testimony are sane or in their right minds, and are usually capable of distinguishing between hallucinations and normal perceptions. . . .

Miracles and Revelation

From *Faith and Reason* by Richard Swinburne, 1981

Richard Swinburne, another British philosopher, has been a leading voice of late among professional philosophers defending the rationality of Christian belief. He holds that the occurrence of miracles is important for vindicating a prophet's message about divine matters (such as an afterlife) that are in principle unverifiable (by the living at least).

Carefully spelling out what a miracle is, namely, a non-repeatable exception to the operation of natural laws, Swinburne argues that without prejudging the case beforehand we might well find evidence showing the occurrence of miracles. (Apparently, he sees David Hume, the famous critic of miracles, making the mistake of discounting all possibility of such evidence: compare the selection from Hume.) Prima facie *examples of miracles that Swinburne cites are levitation, resurrection, and the turning of water into wine. Our learning of these would occur by the usual means: sense experience, others' testimony, and various traces (footprints, the smoking gun, etc.).*

For Swinburne, that God exists—God, the transcendent Creator of the universe—is established by some of the arguments of rational theology. Given the rationality of belief that there is such a Divine Reality, the best interpretation of miracles, Swinburne holds, is that they are acts of God. Presumably, Swinburne would also argue that such a view of miracles is the best explanation of their occurrence and that this is in itself a consideration in support of the rationality of theistic belief. Nevertheless, it is, on his view, arguments of rational theology, and not miracles vindicating a prophet's teaching, that carry the weight, in the first place, for showing that God exists. Miracles are important for giving us confidence about details of divine matters as provided by a prophet, such as, and especially, Jesus.

Here, in sum, we find interesting suggestions about the authority of scripture. But also, according to Swinburne, the importance of extra-scriptural arguments looms large.

. . . Revelations include, and can *a priori* be expected to include, things beyond human capacity independently to check. For example they typically assert the existence of a life after death; and they provide us with information about the sort of God who is to be worshipped in far more detail than a man could derive from examination of the created world, and they give us details of the way to worship him. Hence we need some evidence that what the prophet says is true when we cannot check independently whether it is or not. Analogy suggests the sort of evidence for which we ought to be looking. Suppose that in the days before wireless, telephones, and fast travel, a man claims to have visited a king of a distant country and to have brought back a message from him. What would show that the message comes from the king? First, the message may contain some prediction of an event of the future occurrence of which the messenger could have learnt only from the king; e.g. that the messenger's arrival would be followed by the arrival of some of the king's ships (the messenger having to all appearances travelled by land and so not having been able to meet such ships en route). Secondly, the messenger may bring some token which a man could only have obtained from the king, e.g. a precious stone of a kind only to be found in the king's country, and which is mined by the king alone and kept by him. The token might be the sort of token which people of the culture of those days traditionally gave to authenticate messages. By analogy, evidence that the prophet has his revelation from God and so is to be believed on deep matters where we have no independent means of checking, would be given, first, by his ability to predict some future event which he would have no means of predicting otherwise, i.e. by mere human powers. But any event in accordance with natural laws could be predicted by mere human powers. So this evidence needs to be evidence of an ability to predict events not in accordance with natural laws; and that, in a basically deterministic world, means violations of natural laws. The evidence would need also to suggest that the violations were brought about by God, and so were miracles. Secondly, evidence that the prophet had his revelation from God would be provided if the prophet's life was accompanied by events which, evidence suggested, were violations of natural laws produced by God in circumstances where such violations would naturally and by local convention be interpreted as vindicating the prophet's teaching. Both these further sources of evidence thus involve the occurrence of miracles.

Before taking the argument further, I need to spell out what I understand by a miracle and what would be evidence that an event was a miracle in my sense.[1] I understand by a miracle a violation of the laws of nature, that is, a non-repeatable exception to the operation of these laws, brought about by God. Laws of nature have the form of universal statements 'all *A*s are *B*', and state how bodies behave of physical necessity. Thus Kepler's three laws of planetary motion state how the planets move. The first law states that all planets move in ellipses with the sun at one focus. If this purported law is to be a law of nature, planets must in general move as it states.

What however is to be said about an isolated exception to a purported law of nature? Suppose that one day Mars moves out of its elliptical path for a brief period and then returns to the path. There are two possibilities. This wandering of Mars may occur because of some current condition of the Universe (e.g. the proximity of Jupiter drawing Mars out of its elliptical path), such that if that condition were to be repeated the event would happen again. In this case the phenomenon is an entirely regular phenomenon. The trouble is that what might have appeared originally to be a basic law of nature proves now not to be one. It proves to be a consequence of a more fundamental law that the original purported law normally holds, but that under circumstances describable in general terms (e.g. 'when planets are close to each other') there are exceptions to it. Such repeatable exceptions to purported laws merely show that the purported laws are not basic laws of nature. The other possibility is that the exception to the law was not caused by some current condition, in such a way that if the condition were to recur the event would happen again. In this case we have a non-repeatable exception to a law of nature. But how are we to describe this

---

[1] The following discussion of the nature and justification of claims that there has occurred a violation of a law of nature is an extremely brief extract from the short argument of Ch. 12 of *The Existence of God*. For fuller and more adequate discussion see my book, *The Concept of Miracle* (London, 1971).

event further? There are two possible moves. We may say that if there occurs an exception to a purported law of nature, the purported law can be no law. If the purported law says 'all As are B' and there is an A which is not B, then 'all As are B' is no law. The trouble with saying that is that the purported law may be a very good device for giving accurate predictions in our field of study; it may be by far the best general formula for describing what happens in the field which there is. (I understand by a general formula a formula which describes what happens in all circumstances of a certain kind, but does not mention by name particular individuals, times, or places.) To deny that the purported law is a law, when there is no more accurate general formula, just because there is an isolated exception to its operation, is to ignore its enormous ability to predict what happens in the field.

For this reason it seems not unnatural to say that the purported law is no less a law for there being a non-repeatable exception to it; and then to describe the exception as a 'violation' of the law. At any rate this is a coherent way of talking, and I think that it is what those who use such expressions as 'violation' of a law of nature are getting at. In this case we must amend our understanding of what is a law of nature. To say that a generalization 'all As are B' is a universal law of nature is to say that being A physically necessitates being B, and so that any A will be B—apart from violations.

But how do we know that some event such as the wandering of Mars from its elliptical path is a non-repeatable rather than a repeatable exception to a purported law of nature? We have grounds for believing that the exception is non-repeatable in so far as any attempt to amend the purported law of nature so that it predicted the wandering of Mars as well as all the other observed positions of Mars, would make it so complicated and *ad hoc* that we would have no grounds for trusting its future predictions. It is no good for example amending the law so that it reads: 'all planets move in ellipses with the Sun at one focus, except in years when there is a competition for the World Chess Championship between two players both of whose surnames begin with K.' Why not? Because this proposed law mentions properties which have no other place in physics (no other physical law invokes this sort of property) and it mentions them in an *ad hoc* way (that is, the proposed new law has the form 'so-and-so holds except under such-and-such circumstances', when the only reason for adding the exception clause is that otherwise the law would be incompatible with observations; the clause does not follow naturally from the theory.) What we need if we are to have a more adequate law is a general formula, of which it is an entirely natural consequence that the exception to the original law occurs when it does.

In these ways we could have grounds for believing that an exception to a purported law was non-repeatable and so a violation of a natural law. Claims of this sort are of course corrigible—we could be wrong; what seemed inexplicable by natural causes might be explicable after all. But then we could be wrong about most things, including claims of the opposite kind. When I drop a piece of chalk and it falls to the ground, every one supposes that here is an event perfectly explicable by natural laws. But we could be wrong. Maybe the laws of nature are much more complicated than we suppose, and Newton's and Einstein's laws are mere approximations to the true laws of mechanics. Maybe the true laws of mechanics predict that almost always when released from the hand, chalk will fall to the ground, but not today because of a slightly abnormal distribution of distant galaxies.

However although the true laws of nature predict that the chalk will rise, in fact it falls. Here is a stark violation of natural laws, but one which no one detects because of their ignorance of natural laws. 'You could be wrong' is a knife which cuts both ways. What seem to be perfectly explicable events might prove, when we come to know the laws of nature much better, to be violations. But of course this is not very likely. The reasonable man goes by the available evidence here, and also in the converse case. He supposes that what is, on all the evidence, a violation of natural laws really is one. There is good reason to suppose that events such as the following if they occurred would be violations of laws of nature: levitation, that is, a man rising in the air against gravity without the operation of magnetism or any other known physical force; resurrection from the dead of a man whose heart has not been beating for twenty-four hours and who counts as dead by other currently used criteria; water turning into wine without the assistance of chemical apparatus or catalysts; a man growing a new arm from the stump of an old one.

Since the occurrence of a violation of natural laws cannot be explained in the normal way, either it has no explanation or it is to be explained in a different way. The obvious explanation exists if there is a God who is responsible for the whole order of nature, including its conformity to natural laws, and who therefore can on occasion suspend the normal operation of natural laws and bring about or allow some one else to bring about events, not via this normal route. We should suppose that events have explanations if suggested explanations are at all plausible. If there is quite a bit of evidence that there is a God responsible for the natural order,[2] then any violations are plausibly attributed to his agency and so plausibly recognized as miracles—at least so long as those violations are not ruled out by such evidence as we may have from other sources about God's character.[3] God's permitting a law of nature to be violated is clearly necessary for this to occur if he is the author of Nature; and in the absence of evidence that any other agent had a hand in the miracle, it ought to be attributed to God's sole agency. But if there is evidence, say, that it happens after a command (as opposed to a request to God) for it to happen issued by another agent, then the miracle is to be attributed to a joint agency.

I have not considered here the kind of historical evidence needed to prove the occurrence of an event which if it occurred would be a violation, but clearly it will be of the same kind as the evidence for any other historical event. There is the evidence of one's own senses, the testimony of others (oral and written) and the evidence of traces (effects left by events, such as footprints, fingerprints, cigarette ash, etc.). I see no reason in principle why there should not be evidence of this kind to show the occurrence of a levitation or a resurrection from the dead.[4]

Now I claimed earlier that two further kinds of evidence for the genuineness of a prophet's revelation would be provided if there was evidence of the prophet's ability to

---

[2] As I claimed in *The Existence of God.*

[3] I argue in *The Coherence of Theism* that necessarily an omnipotent, omniscient, and perfectly free God must be perfectly good.

[4] Hume however thought otherwise. For discussion of his argument and for analysis of these kinds of evidence which we have for the occurrence of historical events and of their force, see my *The Concept of Miracle,* Ch. 4.

predict miracles, and if there was evidence that his teaching was vindicated by miracles. Christian theology has traditionally claimed both these further sources of evidence for the truth of what Christ said.

Against Miracles

From "Of Miracles" in *Enquiries Concerning Human Understanding and Concerning the Principles of Morals* by David Hume, 1777

David Hume (1711–1776), a Scottish philosopher, has a prominent place in the history of Western thought. It was his skepticism about necessity and causality the sparked Immanuel Kant (1724–1804), the pivotal thinker for Hegel and all nineteenth-century Western philosophy, to, by Kant's own account, "awaken from a dogmatic slumber," and to try to show causality's true ground. The selection below on miracles is taken from An Enquiry concerning Human Understanding, *written by Hume from age twenty-one to twenty-five. A much later book,* Dialogues Concerning Natural Religion, *published only after Hume's death, may be the most influential work ever written in the philosophy of religion; we shall review a couple of passages from it later, one in this section. (Also, recall Whitehead's reference to the work.) In any case, David Hume is an enormously important philosopher. And he is an adamant opponent of religion—or at least of all in it that he finds unfounded, superstitious, and atavistic, which is much.*

Hume's argument in "Of Miracles" is straightforward. He assumes that we are in the position of wondering whether to believe testimony concerning a miraculous occurrence. His conclusion is that we should not, for, given that a miracle is defined as a violation of a genuine natural law, it will be more probable that the testimony is false than that a miracle occurred. Hume does not say that it is improbable that what we presume to be a law of nature might prove not to be one. Rather, in effect he assumes, agreeing with Swinburne, that a miracle would be a non-repeatable violation of natural law.

There are also general reasons why a testifier to the miraculous might deceive or be deceived. Hume lists what he sees as a few of these, most notably, "surprise and wonder," which he says, people enjoy. He also alleges that reports of miracles occur chiefly among "ignorant and barbarous nations." Thus in this or another way, we might find an explanation why a miracle has been reported without admitting that one has actually occurred.

A miracle is a violation of the laws of nature; and as a firm and unalterable experience has established these laws, the proof against a miracle, from the very nature of the fact, is as entire as any argument from experience can possibly be imagined. Why is it more than probable, that all men must die; that lead cannot, of itself, remain suspended in the air; that fire consumes wood, and is extinguished by water; unless it be, that these events are found agreeable to the laws of nature, and there is required a violation of these laws, or in other words, a miracle to prevent them? Nothing is esteemed a miracle, if it ever happen in the common course of nature. It is no miracle that a man, seemingly in good health, should die on a sudden: because such a kind of death, though more unusual than any other, has yet been frequently observed to happen. But it is a miracle, that a dead man should come to life; because that has never been observed in any age or country. There must, therefore, be a uniform experience against every miraculous event, otherwise the event would not merit that appellation. And as a uniform experience amounts to a proof, there is here a direct and full *proof,* from the nature of the fact, against the existence of any miracle; nor can such a proof be destroyed, or the miracle rendered credible, but by an opposite proof, which is superior.

The plain consequence is (and it is a general maxim worthy of our attention), 'That no testimony is sufficient to establish a miracle, unless the testimony be of such a kind, that its falsehood would be more miraculous, than the fact, which it endeavors to establish; and even in that case there is a mutual destruction of arguments, and the superior only gives us an assurance suitable to that degree of force, which remains, after deducting the inferior.' When anyone tells me, that he saw a dead man restored to life, I immediately consider with myself, whether it be more probable, that this person should either deceive or be deceived, or that the fact, which he relates, should really have happened. I weigh the one miracle against the other; and according to the superiority, which I discover, I pronounce my decision, and always reject the greater miracle. If the falsehood of his testimony would be more miraculous, than the event which he relates; then, and not till then, can he pretend to command my belief or opinion.

In the foregoing reasoning we have supposed, that the testimony, upon which a miracle is founded, may possibly amount to an entire proof, and that the falsehood of that testimony would be a real prodigy: But it is easy to shew, that we have been a great deal too liberal in our concession, and that there never was a miraculous event established on so full an evidence.

For *first,* there is not to be found, in all history, any miracle attested by a sufficient number of men, or such unquestioned good-sense, education, and learning, as to secure us against all delusion in themselves; of such undoubted integrity, as to place them beyond all suspicion of any design to deceive others; of such credit and reputation in the eyes of mankind, as to have a great deal to lose in case of their being detected in any falsehood; and at the same time, attesting facts performed in such a public manner and in so celebrated a part of the world, as to render the detection unavoidable: All which circumstances are requisite to give us a full assurance in the testimony of men.

Secondly. We may observe in human nature a principle which, if strictly examined, will be found to diminish extremely the assurance, which we might, from human testimony, have, in any kind of prodigy. . . . The passion of *surprise* and *wonder,* arising from miracles, being an agreeable emotion, gives a sensible tendency towards the belief of those events, from which it is derived. And this goes so far, that even those who cannot enjoy this pleasure immediately, nor can believe those miraculous events, of which they are informed, yet love to partake of the satisfaction at second-hand or by rebound, and place a pride and delight in exciting the admiration of others.

With what greediness are the miraculous accounts of travellers received, their descriptions of sea and land monsters, their relations of wonderful adventures, strange men, and uncouth manners? But if the spirit of religion join itself to the love of wonder, there is an end of common sense; and human testimony, in these circumstances, loses all pretensions to authority. . . .

Thirdly. It forms a strong presumption against all supernatural and miraculous relations, that they are observed chiefly to abound among ignorant and barbarous nations; or if a civilized people has ever given admission to any of them, that people will be found to have received them from ignorant and barbarous ancestors, who transmitted them with that inviolable sanction and authority, which always attend received opinions. When we peruse the first histories of all nations, we are apt to imagine ourselves transported into some new world; where the whole frame of nature is disjointed, and every element performs its operations in a different manner, from what it does at present. Battles, revolutions, pestilence, famine and death, are never the effect of those natural causes, which we experience. Prodigies, omens, oracles, judgements, quite obscure the few natural events, that are intermingled with them. But as the former grow thinner every page, in proportion as we advance nearer the enlightened ages, we soon learn, that there is nothing mysterious or supernatural in the case, but that all proceeds from the usual propensity of mankind towards the marvelous, and that, though this inclination may at intervals receive a check from sense and learning, it can never be thoroughly extirpated from human nature.

It is strange, a judicious reader is apt to say, upon the perusal of these wonderful historians, *that such prodigious events never happen in our days. . . .*

I may add as a *fourth* reason, which diminishes the authority of prodigies, that there is no testimony for any, even those which have not been expressly detected, that is not opposed by an infinite number of witnesses; so that not only the miracle destroys the credit of testimony, but the testimony destroys itself. To make this the better understood, let us consider, that, in matters of religion, whatever is different is contrary; and that it is impossible the religions of ancient Rome, of Turkey, of Siam, and of China should, all of them, be established on any solid foundation. Every miracle, therefore, pretended to have been wrought in any of these religions (and all of them abound in miracles), as its direct scope is to establish the particular system to which it is attributed; so has it the same force, though more indirectly, to overthrow every other system. In destroying a rival system, it likewise destroys the credit of those miracles, on which that system was established; so that all the prodigies of different religions are to be regarded as contrary facts, and the evidences of these prodigies, whether weak or strong, as opposite to each other. . . .

One of the best attested miracles in all profane history, is that which Tacitus reports of Vespasian, who cured a blind man in Alexandria, by means of his spittle, and a lame man by the mere touch of his foot; in obedience to a vision of the god Serapis, who had enjoined them to have recourse to the Emperor, for these miraculous cures. The story may be seen in that fine historian;[1] where every circumstance seems to add weight to the testimony, and might be displayed at large with all the force of argument and eloquence, if anyone were now concerned to enforce the evidence of that exploded and idolatrous superstition.

---

[1] Hist. lib. iv. cap. 81. Suetonius gives nearly the same account *in vita* Vesp.

Aristotelian Rational Theology

From *The Works of Aristotle,* J. A. Smith and W. D. Ross, editors, 1908 • From *Proclus: The Elements of Theology,* E. R. Dodds, translator, 1933 • From *The Metaphysics of Avicenna* (ibn Sīnā), Parviz Morewedge, translator, 1973

>   *What seems to be the oldest argument within Western rational theology is based on causality, the first-cause argument. We see that an effect e_1 arises from a cause c_1, but c_1 is also an effect e_2 arising from another cause c_2, which is, in turn, an effect e_3, and so on. There cannot be an infinite backward series because there would be nothing to get the series started. Thus it would appear that there has to be a first cause for there to be any effect at all. This first cause, it is concluded, is God (presumably the best candidate), who is uncaused, having aseity, or is self-caused, as we find in some Indian theology.*
>   *The argument is adumbrated in Plato (Laws 10.884–889d). Aristotle gives it clearer expression, expanding it—in the first part of our selection—to include God as the ultimate final (or motivating) cause (the unmoved Mover) as well as the first in a series of active or efficient causes (recall the doctrine of four types of cause in the Avicenna selection in the previous section). One line of Aristotle's argument is reformulated by a Neoplatonist, Proclus (410?–485 CE)—see the second part of the excerpt—and then given classical formulation by several Islamic philosophers, al-Kindī (801–873?), al-Fārābī (c. 950), and the great Avicenna, from whose Metaphysica a final paragraph is also excerpted.*
>   *Critics have usually responded (a) by alleging there is no difficulty in admitting an infinite series of causes and effects, and/or (b) by claiming that without another source of information about the first cause such positing is worthless.*
>   *Avicenna's version of the first-cause argument uses the notions of necessity and contingency (again, see also the selection from Avicenna under Divine Reality). Anything that does not exist necessarily (i.e., that can be imagined not to exist) has to have a reason for existing (this axiom comes to be called the Principle of Sufficient Reason). An infinite backward series would mean that there would be no reason (or cause) to originate the series of contingencies, and so there would be nothing at all. Or, if there is supposed to be an infinite causal loop or circle, that would mean that two elements would have to be both cause and effect with respect to each other—an impossibility, Avicenna says. Thus without a necessary being, there would be no reason for the first contingency to come into being; similarly, there would be no reason for an entire causal chain (itself a contingency). Thus the chain of reasons (or causes) must terminate in a necessarily existing being, God. There cannot be an infinite series of contingencies, Avicenna implies in the earlier selection (under Divine Reality), since something exists.*
>   *A variation of this last argument has come to be known as the cosmological argument. (In a different usage, all of the arguments a posteriori are cosmological: see the Glossary.) Nothing that is brought about exists necessarily but, rather, contingently. The universe as a whole is an effect, and thus exists contingently. Such a contingency could*

come about only by being caused, or created, by God, who exists necessarily. Why is there something rather than nothing? (Since the world exists contingently, there could have been nothing, it seems.) Answer: God, who exists necessarily, creates a universe that did not have to be.

Further variations appear in the history of religious philosophy, as does further reflection on whether everything has to be intelligible, what is required for intelligibility, and the relevance of science. Thomas Aquinas, probably the most important rational theologian within Christianity, reworks Aristotle's argument into the first two of his "Five Ways" and Avicenna's into his third way; see the selection immediately following. William Lane Craig reworks a first-cause argument in the light of Big Bang cosmology: see the selection from Craig later in this section.

Critics have responded to the arguments about contingency as they have to the first-cause argument: (a) an infinite series of contingencies presents no difficulty, and/or (b) without information from another source about the supposedly necessary being, such a supposition is worthless.

FROM *THE WORKS OF ARISTOTLE*

Evidently there is a first principle, and the cause of things are neither an infinite series nor infinitely various in kind. For, on the one hand, one thing cannot proceed from another, as from matter, *ad infinitum,* e.g. flesh from earth, earth from air, air from fire, and so on without stopping; nor on the other hand can the efficient causes form an endless series, man for instance being acted on by air, air by the sun, the sun by Strife, and so on without limit. Similarly the final causes cannot go on *ad infinitum*—walking for the sake of health, this for the sake of happiness, happiness for the sake of something else, and so one thing always for the sake of another. And the case of the formal cause is similar. For in the case of an intermediate, which has a last term and a prior term outside it, the prior must be the cause of the later terms. For if we had to say which of the three is the cause, we should say the first; surely not the last, for the final term is the cause of none; nor even the intermediate, for it is the cause only of one. It makes no difference whether there is one intermediate or more, nor whether they are infinite or finite in number. But of series which are infinite in this way, and of the infinite in general, all the parts down to that now present are alike intermediates; so that if there is no first there is no cause at all.

FROM *PROCLUS: THE ELEMENTS OF THEOLOGY*

ALL THAT EXISTS PROCEEDS FROM A SINGLE FIRST CAUSE.

For otherwise all things are uncaused; or else the sum of existence is limited, and there is a circuit of causation within the sum; or else there will be regress to infinity, cause lying behind cause, so that the positing of prior causes will never cease.

But if all things were uncaused, there would be no sequence of primary and secondary, perfecting and perfected, regulative and regulated, generative and generated, active and passive; and all things would be unknowable. For the task of science is the recognition of causes, and only when we recognize the causes of things do we say that we know them.

And if causes transmit themselves in a circuit, the same things will be at once prior and consequent; that is, since every productive cause is superior to its product, each will be at once more efficient than the rest and less efficient. (It is indifferent whether we make the connexion of cause and effect and derive the one from the other through a greater or a less number of intermediate causes; for the cause of all these intermediaries will be superior to all of them and the greater their number, the greater the efficiency of that cause.)

And if the accumulation of causes may be continued to infinity, cause behind cause for ever, thus again all things will be unknowable. For nothing infinite can be apprehended; and the causes being unknown, there can be no knowledge of their consequents.

Since, then, things cannot be uncaused, and cause is not convertible with effect, and infinite regress is excluded, it remains that there is a first cause of all existing things, whence they severally proceed as branches from a root, some near to it and others more remote. For that there is not more than one such first principle has already been established, inasmuch as the subsistence of any manifold is posterior to the One.

FROM *THE METAPHYSICS OF AVICENNA* (IBN SĪNĀ)

FINDING THAT THE NECESSARY EXISTENT IS A UNITY IN REALITY AND THAT THE EXISTENCE OF ALL THINGS IS DUE TO IT

As we have stated, the Necessary Existent is in fact a unity, and all other things are non-necessary beings. Thus, they are contingent beings. All have a cause, and causes are infinite series. Accordingly, they either attempt to return to a primary cause, the Necessary Existent, or they return to themselves (i.e. the chain of causation is circular). For example, if A is the cause of B, B the cause of J, and J the cause of D, then D will be the cause of A. Taken together, therefore, this group will be a group of effects. Hence, it has become evident that there must be an external cause for them. The absurdity of the argument for the circularity of causes is also apparent in another proof. If D were the cause of A, then the effect of the effect of A, and the effect of the effect of the effect of A would be the effect of A. For the one thing, another thing would have to act both as cause and effect, which is impossible. Therefore, each effect must return to the Necessary Existent which is unique. Consequently, all effects and contingencies return to the one Necessary Existent.

Aquinas's "Five Ways"

From "Five Ways" in *Basic Writings of Saint Thomas Aquinas,* Anton C. Pegis, editor and translator, 1945

The most influential formulation of arguments a posteriori *in support of the existence of God is by Thomas Aquinas. Thomas (1225–1274) is an enormously important philosopher, a veritable consummator, we may say, of Christian theology after the reestablishment among Western Christians of familiarity with classical Greek thought. Thomas was a great student of Aristotle in particular, following that philosopher's metaphysics in working out Christian doctrines—in contrast with the Church Fathers who tended to follow Plato.*

All of Thomas's arguments proceed from a feature or features of the universe—very general features such as change and causal relations—to God as the ultimate ground or cause without whom change, etc., would not be. As mentioned, the first two arguments, which are very similar (focusing in the first instance on change and in the second on active or instrumental causality), are reworkings of Aristotle's first-cause argument for an unmoved Mover. The third "way" is Avicenna's argument for a necessary being given contingencies. The fourth is an argument from the fact of gradations of various values to perfection along each line, the maximum and ground of that value, namely God. The fifth argument is from purposefulness or design in nature to a designer or God, an argument that is usually called teleological.

We shall examine the teleological argument in later sections; we have already scrutinized, in effect, Thomas's first three ways. That leaves the fourth argument, from "degrees of perfection." Here the crucial premises are, first, that comparative terms describe varying degrees of approximation to a superlative, and, second, that the superlative has to be supposed a reality grounding the reality of all qualities exhibited to an imperfect degree. Thus qualities such as good are grounded in the goodness of God, who then must be assumed to be real.

However, it is far from clear that comparative qualities do have to be grounded in an actually existent superlative. There are a host of counterexamples to the contrary, for example, "being larger than" and even (were magnitude to be eliminated from the class of relevant analogues since magnitude is not considered by Thomas to be an attribute or quality of God in that it belongs only to corruptible things, then) "moral goodness." It seems to make perfectly good sense to hold that treating people with respect is morally better than murder without also subscribing to the existence of an absolute exemplar of moral virtue. This fourth argument, we may note, historically has not received as much attention as the other four "ways."

Finally, it is interesting that in the context of Thomas's magnum opus, *the* Summa Theologica, *the presentation of these five arguments is exceedingly brief, particularly given that the* Summa Theologica *is quite long. (Thomas does provide elaboration of the first argument in another work.) Here the important context appears to be a* fideist *challenge, that is, not the question whether God is known to be real, but the question whether God can be proven to be real. The fideist holds that God is known not by argument or proof but by faith alone. Thomas answers that the reality of God can be rationally shown, for example, in the following five ways.*

. . . The existence of God can be proved in five ways.

The first and more manifest way is the argument from motion. It is certain, and evident to our senses, that in the world some things are in motion. Now whatever is moved is moved by another, for nothing can be moved except it is in potentiality to that towards which it is moved; whereas a thing moves inasmuch as it is in act. For motion is nothing else than the reduction of something from potentiality to actuality. But nothing can be reduced from potentiality to actuality, except by something in a state of actuality. Thus that which is actually hot, as fire, makes wood, which is potentially hot, to be actually hot, and thereby moves and changes it. Now it is not possible that the same thing should be at once in actuality and potentiality in the same respect, but only in different respects. For what is actually hot cannot simultaneously be potentially hot; but it is simultaneously potentially cold. It is therefore impossible that in the same respect and in the same way a thing should be both mover and moved, *i.e.,* that it should move itself. Therefore, whatever is moved must be moved by another. If that by which it is moved be itself moved, then this also must needs be moved by another, and that by another again. But this cannot go on to infinity, because then there would be no first mover, and, consequently, no other mover, seeing that subsequent movers move only inasmuch as they are moved by the first mover; as the staff moves only because it is moved by the hand. Therefore it is necessary to arrive at a first mover, moved by no other; and this everyone understands to be God.

The second way is from the nature of efficient cause. In the world of sensible things we find there is an order of efficient causes. There is no case known (neither is it, indeed, possible) in which a thing is found to be the efficient cause of itself; for so it would be prior to itself, which is impossible. Now in efficient causes it is not possible to go on to infinity, because in all efficient causes following in order, the first is the cause of the intermediate cause, and the intermediate is the cause of the ultimate cause, whether the intermediate cause be several, or one only. Now to take away the cause is to take away the effect. Therefore, if there be no first cause among efficient causes, there will be no ultimate, nor any intermediate, cause. But if in efficient causes it is possible to go on to infinity, there will be no first efficient cause, neither will there be an ultimate effect, no any intermediate efficient causes; all of which is plainly false. Therefore it is necessary to admit a first efficient cause, to which everyone gives the name of God.

The third way is taken from possibility and necessity, and runs thus. We find in nature things that are possible to be and not to be, since they are found to be generated, and to be corrupted, and consequently, it is possible for them to be and not to be. But it is impossible for these always to exist, for that which can not-be at some time is not. Therefore, if everything can not-be, then at one time there was nothing in existence. Now if this were true, even now there would be nothing in existence, because that which does not exist begins to exist only through something already existing. Therefore, if at one time nothing was in existence, it would have been impossible for any to have begun to exist; and thus even now nothing would be in existence—which is absurd. Therefore, not all beings are merely possible, but there must exist something the existence of which is necessary. But every necessary thing either has its necessity caused by another, or not. Now it is impossible to go on to infinity in necessary things which have their necessity caused by another, as has been already proved in regard to efficient causes. Therefore we cannot but admit the existence of some being having of itself its own necessity, and not receiving it from another, but rather causing in others their necessity. This all men speak of as God.

The fourth way is taken from the gradation to be found in things. Among beings there are some more and some less good, true, noble, and the like. But *more* and *less* are predicated of different things according as they resemble in their different ways something which is the maximum, as a thing is said to be hotter according as it more nearly resembles that which is hottest; so that there is something which is truest, something best, something noblest, and consequently, something which is most being, for those things that are greatest in truth are greatest in being. Now the maximum in any genus is the cause of all in that genus, as fire, which is the maximum of heat, is the cause of all hot things, as is said in the same book. Therefore there must also be something which is to all beings the cause of their being, goodness, and every other perfection; and this we call God.

The fifth way is taken from the governance of the world. We see that things which lack knowledge, such as natural bodies, act for an end, and this is evident from their acting always, or nearly always, in the same way, so as to obtain the best result. Hence it is plain that they achieve their end not fortuitously, but designedly. Now whatever lacks knowledge cannot move towards an end, unless it be directed by some being endowed with knowledge and intelligence; as the arrow is directed by the archer. Therefore some intelligent being exists by whom all natural things are directed to their end; and this being we call God.

Classical Indian Rational Theology

From *An Offering of Flowers of Logic* by Udayana in *Hindu Theology: A Reader,* José Pereira, editor, 1976

For both the Buddhist "Emptiness" conception and "Brahman, the Absolute" within Hindu thought, mystical experience is the most commonly cited evidence. But other considerations are brought forward, particularly within the tradition of Indian theism where Brahman (or God) is thought of as a Creator and Sustainer of the universe. And among the classical Indian theists who try to prove the existence of God—beyond citing mystic evidence—Udayana (c. 1000 CE), a logician and realist about the objects of everyday life, is the outstanding figure.

Little is known about Udayana's life, but we have several texts, one of which, An Offering of Flowers of Logic, *is devoted exclusively to arguments for the existence of God.*

Udayana formulates his arguments pretty much according to a standardized logical pattern, although sometimes in elaborating he builds in wrinkles or sometimes skips steps, assuming that his audience will fill out what he has indicated but left unsaid. Also, the pattern he uses in the selection here is an abbreviated three-line form, with the general rule, which is stated in the longer form, left implicit. This abbreviated standardized pattern consists of: (a) a thesis to be proved comprised of two terms, a subject (which is to be understood as a thing, not a word) and a predicate, or attribute, to be established; (b) a supporting reason stating that the subject of the thesis exhibits an inferential mark or prover; and (c) an example showing a connection between the inferential mark and the attribute to be established. What is understood in the abbreviated or short form is the universal rule, namely that all things that exhibit the inferential mark also exhibit the attribute to be proved.

An example of the long form:

1. *There is fire on yonder hill.*
   (The conclusion to be proved. How? Because:)

2. *There is smoke rising from it.*

3. *Wherever there's smoke, there's fire, as in a kitchen hearth, and unlike on a lake.*

4. *This smoke-possessing hill is an example of the "wherever" of the universal proposition (3).*

   (Therefore:)

5. *There is fire on yonder hill.*

The short form makes implicit the universal proposition (3), as well as the application (4):

There is fire on yonder hill, because of smoke, as in a kitchen.

Most of Udayana's arguments are straightforward and can be understood without knowing context within Indian thought. Let me provide just a few words, however, about the second and seventh arguments, "from atomic combinations" and "from numerical augmentation." Buddhists had argued against the realism of Udayana's school, which proposes that material things with magnitude are made up of indivisible atoms, that if an atom has sides, then there is no reason why it should be indivisible. On the other hand, if it does not have sides, there is no way that it could be conjoined with another atom, forming a dyad and ultimately the things of magnitude that we touch and see. Udayana's school conveniently relies on God's miraculous power to avoid the difficulty; God brings about the combination of partless atoms resulting in a dyad with parts. Here Udayana goes further and tries to turn the difficulty to his advantage.

The first of Udayana's arguments is a teleological *argument. Though Udayana says "from effects," he elaborates that what he means is: effects produced "by someone possessed of the intent to produce," like a pot, which is produced by a potter. Such teleological argument has garnered extensive consideration in Western thought: see, for example, the selection from David Hume following that from Udayana.*

THE SEVEN WAYS

From (1) effects, (2) atomic combinations, (3) the suspension and other states of the world, (4) the existence of human skills, (5) the existence of authoritative knowledge, (6) the existence of Revelation and (7) the numerical combination of atoms—from all these we can prove the existence of the all-knowing, imperishable God.

1. *Argument from effects*

Things like the earth must have a cause.
Because they are effects.
Like a pot.

By having a cause I mean active production by someone possessed of the intent to produce, and a direct knowledge concerning the matter from which the production is to be.

2. *Argument from atomic combinations*

[The world, it must be remembered, is a combination of atoms, in different degrees of complexity.] Combination is an action, and hence an action occurring at the beginning of creation that brings about the bonding of two atoms, thus originating a dyad. Such a combination is always consequent on the activity of a conscious agent.

Because it is action.

As, for instance, the action of our bodies.

3. *Argument from the suspension of the world*

The world is supported by an active being which impedes it from falling.

Because it has the character of something suspended.

Like a twig held in the air by a bird.

By *"suspension"* I mean the absence of falling in things that possess weight. When I say "the suspension and *other states* of the world," I mean destruction. For the world is destructible by an active being; because its nature is destructible; like that of a torn cloth.

4. *Argument from the existence of human skills* . . . or the arts of life.

Traditional arts, like weaving, need to be launched by an independent person.

Because of their character as human usages.

Like modern writing and such other usages.

5. *Argument from the existence of authoritative knowledge.* Authoritative knowledge, that is, knowledge through authoritative norms.

The knowledge produced by the Veda is due to positive qualities in the cause of that knowledge.

Because of its character as normative knowledge.

As in a norm such as experience.

6. *Arguments from the existence of Revelation.* Revelation, that is to say, the Veda.

a. The Veda is personally originant.

Because of its capacity to instruct [instruction being conveyed through one person dialoguing with another].

Like the Veda of medicine [which all accept to have been humanly, or personally, produced].

b. Again, the Veda is personally originant.

Because it is composed of sentences.

Like the *Mahābhārata* [epic of the Great Indian War].

c. And the Veda's sentences are personally originant.

Because they are sentences.

Like our own sentences.

7. *Argument from numerical augmentation*

[Physical objects, which have measure, are produced from combinations of atoms, beginning with the dyads. But atoms themselves have no measure. How then do dyads? For the following reasons:]

a. A dyad's measure is produced by *number.*

Because, though not produced through the aggregation of measures, it still remains a *produced* measure.

As, for instance [of pot sections of equal size], the measure of a pot composed of three sections is greater than that of a pot composed of two such sections [the former's greater size thus being due to number alone].

b. An atomic measure does not produce measure.

Because its measure is eternal [and hence incapable of the temporal change that all production entails]; or because its measure is infinitesimal.

In this way, at the beginning of creation, the dual number—the reason for the dyad's measure—needs to be implanted in atoms. [According to the tenets of our combined Logicist-Atomist system, things exist singly, or monadically, and can be combined only by a faculty that reduces these monads to unity and order—the Methodizing Mind]. The combination cannot have been produced at that [primordial] time by the Methodizing Mind of beings like ourselves [then nonexistent]. Hence there exists such a Mind coeval with that time, that is to say, God's.

Finally, by the words "the all-knowing, imperishable God," I mean that the quality of imperishableness belongs to Him essentially [and is inconceivable apart]. It is certain then that an everlasting knowledge embracing all things exists.

FIVE OBJECTIONS TO THE ARGUMENT FROM EFFECTS

"There are five fallacies in your inferent sign, 'effectness.'

a. Causality is qualified by corporeity. [A cause always has a body; the body is thus the qualifier and the cause the qualified.] To negate the qualifier is to negate the qualified. [You deny that God is corporeal: so you must deny that He is a cause.]

b. And there is the counter-syllogism [that serves to neutralize your argument]:

There is no production by a cause [in the case of things like the earth].

Because the invariable concomitance between 'production by a cause' and 'production by a body' is there lacking.

c. 'The cause is always corporeal'—here is a concomitance that counters yours [that 'effects always have causes'].

d. From a concomitance unfolded by the perception of things as they are, we infer that a cause is corporeal [for experience shows us that causes always have bodies]. In your argument, however, the inherence of the inferent sign 'effectness' in the subject 'the earth,' does not serve to prove the inferendum ["God"] as qualified by incorporeity. There is, besides, a contradiction between qualifier [incorporeity] and qualified [the cause, always perceived as corporeal].

e. We can also introduce into your argument a vitiating contingency [a contingency which invalidates the concomitance, basic to your whole argument, between your inferent sign 'effectness' and your inferendum 'cause.' It is as if you were to assume the concomitance between fire and smoke, and argue that 'The mountain is smoky, because it has fire.' But the concomitance is vitiated by the contingency of wet fuel, and I could contend that 'The mountain is smoky, because it has wet fuel']. Here this vitiating contingency is 'being produced by a body' [and the argument could be presented thus: 'Things like the earth must have a cause, because they are produced by a body']. But then your concomitance between effect and causality [the causality of an incorporeal being] would be inconclusive."

REPLY TO OBJECTIONS

Our argument is not invalidated, because of the efficacity of its inferent sign; and it is not contraposed, because of the feebleness of the disproofs. But whether demonstrative or not, our reasoning is free of contradiction, and its inconclusiveness is baselessly alleged.

a. The negation of corporeity, the qualifier, in God, the subject qualified, does not imply negation of causality. Without knowledge about the subject, there cannot be knowledge about what the subject lacks. [God, the subject, is as you say not known: so it cannot be known whether He has a body.] Greater cogency has the effectness which both demonstrates the existence of the qualified subject and generates a knowledge of it, since it is a reason we are all constrained to recognize. Our argument is also not overridden by your syllogism "God is not a cause, because He has no body."

b. "Things like the earth have no cause, because they are not produced by a body." This is not a valid contraposition to our argument because, for the purposes of a countersyllogism, the qualification "body" has no probative relevance. [It is as if you argued: "The mountain is fiery, because it has golden-colored smoke." Smoke and fire are concomitant; the color qualifying the smoke is immaterial.] So qualified, your concomitant [between no production by cause and no production by body] is inconclusive; so your disproof is feeble.

c. As for your third objection, the effect-cause concomitance has the greater cogency, because of the inherence of the inferent sign "effectness" in the subject "earth," and because of the presence of reasons precluding all instances to the contrary [as there are no effects ever devoid of causes]. To this your own postulated concomitance "the cause is always corporeal" is too feeble to be a contrapositive.

d. As for your fourth objection [contradiction], the inherence of the inferent sign "effectness" in the subject "earth" either entails the incorporeity of the cause, in which case there cannot be contradiction, as the correlation between causality and incorporeity has been recognized; or it does not, in which case there can be no contradiction either, as there is no subject to which the contradiction can be predicated.

e. As for your fifth objection, since our argument has reasons preclusive of contrary instances, there cannot be any inconclusiveness in the shape of ignorance occasioned by their absence. Neither is there the inconclusiveness of concomitance [between cause and effect]. The vitiating contingency "being produced by a body," unable as it is to preclude contrary instances [such as God] can be disregarded.

HARMONY BETWEEN FAITH AND REASON

"If God is a cause, He must be corporeal. Thus we are confronted with adversative reasoning and the absence of supportive proof."

To this I say: the flawed reasoning of some thinkers has only the semblance of logic, and so is no refutation at all. But the supportive reasoning from the absence of effects [resulting from absence of causes] is our own position's enhancement.

The adversative arguments, supposing God as unproved, are devoid of a subject [to which they can predicate corporeity, in which the main force of their reasoning lies]. Hence they have only the semblance of logic. On the other hand "There is no effect without a cause—such a reasoning is an enhancement: in other words, efficacious.

Our view is supported by Sacred Tradition too:

I am the source of all: all things evolve from Me.
The wise know this, and filled with emotion worship Me.*

[And as the sage Manu says:]

A man who determines the sages' teachings on the Law through a logic not discordant with Revelation and the sacred sciences, only he, no other, knows that Law.†

These words evince the greater cogency of Sacred Tradition when reinforced by logic.

The Teleological Argument

From *Dialogues Concerning Natural Religion* by David Hume, 1778

The whole of classical and modern Western rational theology through the eighteenth century is surveyed in David Hume's masterpiece, Dialogues Concerning Natural Religion. *("Natural religion" means rational theology in Hume's usage.) We shall review here only the* teleological argument, *or argument from design.*

Three principal characters in the work are: Cleanthes, an advocate of the design argument and of an overall empiricist approach to religion; Demea, a traditional Christian of piety who voices a negative theology and distrust of Cleanthes' arguments; and Philo, usually taken to speak for Hume himself, who is skeptical, like Demea, about Cleanthes' arguments, but who also, unlike Demea, has little patience with traditional religious beliefs.

Cleanthes argues that so many features of the world—the human eye, the correspondences of the sexes, and so forth—appear designed that we are forced to accept a Designer, namely, God. In other words, the world seems to be an artifact. All artifacts have artificers. Thus the world has an artificer, namely, God. (Compare the first of Udayana's arguments excerpted earlier.)

Philo objects that the cause of the appearance of design in the universe need not be supposed to be similar in nature to a human artisan. There are many disanalogies between

---

* *Gītā* 8.10.
† *Mānava Dharma Śāstra* 12.106.

natural effects and human artifacts. Moreover, such a line of reasoning as Cleanthes' could not establish God as traditionally conceived, as infinite, single, simple, and so on.

At the time Hume was writing, Charles Darwin (1809–1882) had not revolutionized biology with his evolutionary theory. Many philosophers take evolutionary biology to put the final nails into the coffin of the teleological argument, since the origination of such marvelous instruments as the human eye can now be explained through natural selection, that is, without reference to any conscious intention. Some moderns, however, disagree. We shall review a post-Darwinian teleological argument later with a selection from M. A. Corey.

[CLEANTHES continued:] The declared profession of every reasonable skeptic is only to reject abstruse, remote, and refined arguments, to adhere to common sense and the plain instincts of nature, and to assent wherever any reasons strike him with so full a force that he cannot, without the greatest violence, prevent it. Now the arguments for natural religion are plainly of this kind, and nothing but the most perverse, obstinate metaphysics can reject them. Consider, anatomize the eye, survey its structure and contrivance, and tell me, from your own feeling, if the idea of a contriver does not immediately flow in upon you with a force like that of sensation. The most obvious conclusion, surely, is in favor [of] design, and it requires time, reflection, and study to summon up those frivolous though abstruse objections which can support infidelity. Who can behold the male and female of each species, the correspondence of their parts and instincts, their passions and whole course of life before and after generation, but must be sensible that the propagation of the species is intended by nature? Millions and millions of such instances present themselves through every part of the universe, and no language can convey a more intelligible, irresistible meaning than the curious adjustment of final causes. To what degree, therefore, of blind dogmatism must one have attained to reject such natural and such convincing arguments?

Some beauties in writing we may meet with which seem contrary to rules, and which gain the affections and animate the imagination in opposition to all the precepts of criticism and to the authority of the established masters of art. And if the argument for theism be, as you pretend, contradictory to the principles of logic, its universal, its irresistible influence proves clearly that there may be arguments of a like irregular nature. Whatever cavils may be urged, an orderly world, as well as a coherent, articulate speech, will still be received as an incontestable proof of design and intention.

It sometimes happens, I own, that the religious arguments have not their due influence on an ignorant savage and barbarian, not because they are obscure and difficult, but because he never asks himself any question with regard to them. Whence arises the curious structure of an animal? From the copulation of its parents. And these whence? From *their* parents? A few removes set the objects at such a distance that to him they are lost in darkness and confusion; nor is he actuated by any curiosity to trace them further. But this is neither dogmatism nor skepticism, but stupidity, a state of mind very different from your sifting, inquisitive disposition, my ingenious friend. You can trace causes from effects; you can compare the most distant and remote objects; and your greatest errors proceed not from barrenness of thought and invention but from too luxuriant a fertility, which suppresses your natural good sense by a profusion of unnecessary scruples and objections. . . .

Your instance, Cleanthes, said [DEMEA] drawn from books and language, being familiar, has, I confess, so much more force on that account; but is there not some danger too in this very circumstance, and may it not render us presumptuous by making us imagine we comprehend the Deity and have some adequate idea of his nature and attributes? When I read a volume, I enter into the mind and intention of the author; I become him, in a manner, for the instant, and have in immediate feeling and conception of those ideas which revolved in his imagination while employed in that composition. But so near an approach we never surely can make to the Deity. His ways are not our ways. His attributes are perfect but incomprehensible. And this volume of nature contains a great and inexplicable riddle, more than any intelligible discourse or reasoning. . . .

[PHILO continued:] The discoveries by microscopes, as they open a new universe in miniature, are still objections according to you, arguments according to me. The further we push our researches of this kind, we are still led to infer the universal cause of all to be vastly different from mankind, or from any object of human experience and observation.

And what say you to the discoveries in anatomy, chemistry, botany? . . . These surely are no objections, replied CLEANTHES; they only discover new instances of art and contrivance. It is still the image of mind reflected on us from innumerable objects. Add a mind *like the human,* said PHILO. I know of no other, replied CLEANTHES. And the liker the better, insisted PHILO. To be sure, said CLEANTHES.

Now, Cleanthes, said PHILO, with an air of alacrity and triumph, mark the consequences. *First,* by this method of reasoning you renounce all claim to infinity in any of the attributes of the Deity. For as the cause ought only to be proportioned to the effect, and the effect, so far as it falls under our cognizance, is not infinite, what pretensions have we, upon your suppositions, to ascribe that attribute to the divine Being? You will still insist that, by removing him so much from all similarity to human creatures, we give in to the most arbitrary hypothesis, and at the same time weaken all proofs of his existence.

Secondly, you have no reason, on your theory, for ascribing perfection to the Deity, even in his finite capacity, or for supposing him free from every error, mistake, or incoherence in his undertakings. There are many inexplicable difficulties in the works of nature which, if we allow a perfect author to be proved *a priori,* are easily solved, and become only seeming difficulties from the narrow capacity of man, who cannot trace infinite relations. But according to your method of reasoning, these difficulties become all real, and perhaps will be insisted on as new instances of likeness to human art and contrivance. At least you might acknowledge that it is impossible for us to tell, from our limited views, whether this system contains any great faults or deserves any considerable praise if compared to other possible and even real systems. Could a peasant, if the *Aeneid* were read to him, pronounce that poem to be absolutely faultless, or even assign to it its proper rank among the productions of human wit, he who had never seen any other production?

But were this world ever so perfect a production, it must still remain uncertain whether all the excellences of the work can justly be ascribed to the workman. If we survey a ship, what an exalted idea must we form of the ingenuity of the carpenter who framed so complicated, useful, and beautiful a machine? And what surprise must we feel when we find him a stupid mechanic who imitated others, and copied an art which, through a long succession of ages, after multiplied trials, mistakes, corrections, deliberations, and controversies, had been gradually improving? Many worlds might have been botched and bungled, throughout an eternity, ere this system was struck out; much labor lost, many fruitless trials made, and a slow but continued improvement carried on during infinite ages in the art of world-making. In such subjects, who can determine where the truth, nay, who can conjecture where the probability lies, amidst a great number of hypotheses which may be proposed, and a still greater which may be imagined?

And what shadow of an argument, continued PHILO, can you produce from your hypothesis to prove the unity of the Deity? A great number of men join in building a house or ship, in rearing a city, in framing a commonwealth; why may not several deities combine in contriving and framing a world? This is only so much greater similarity to human affairs. By sharing the work among several, we may so much further limit the attributes of each, and get rid of that extensive power and knowledge which must be supposed in one deity and which, according to you, can only serve to weaken the proof of his existence. And if such foolish, such vicious creatures as man can yet often unite in framing and executing one plan, how much more those deities or demons, whom we may suppose several degrees more perfect?

To multiply causes without necessity is indeed contrary to true philosophy, but this principle applies not to the present case. Were one deity antecedently proved by your theory, who were possessed of every attribute requisite to the production of the universe, it would be needless, I own (though not absurd), to suppose any other deity existent. But while it is still a question whether all these attributes are united in one subject or dispersed among several independent beings, by what phenomena in nature can we pretend to decide the controversy? Where we see a body raised in a scale, we are sure that there is in the opposite scale, however concealed from sight, some counterpoising weight equal to it; but it is still allowed to doubt whether that weight be an aggregate of several distinct bodies or one uniform united mass. And if the weight requisite very much exceeds anything which we have ever seen conjoined in any single body, the former supposition becomes still more probable and natural. An intelligent being of such vast power and capacity as is necessary to produce the universe, or, to speak in the language of ancient philosophy, so prodigious an animal, exceeds all analogy and even comprehension.

But further, Cleanthes, men are mortal, and renew their species by generation, and this is common to all living creatures. The two great sexes of male and female, says Milton, animate the world. Why must this circumstance, so universal, so essential, be excluded from those numerous and limited deities? Behold, then, the theogeny of ancient times brought back upon us.

And why not become a perfect anthropomorphite? Why not assert the deity or deities to be corporeal, and to have eyes, a nose, mouth, ears, etc.? Epicurus maintained that no man had ever seen reason but in a human figure, therefore the gods must have a human figure. And this argument, which is deservedly so much ridiculed by Cicero, becomes, according to you, solid and philosophical.

In a word, Cleanthes, a man who follows your hypothesis is able, perhaps, to assert or conjecture that the universe sometime arose from something like design, but beyond that position he cannot ascertain one single circumstance, and is left afterwards to fix every point of his theology by the utmost license of fancy and hypothesis. This world, for aught he knows, is very faulty and imperfect, compared to a superior standard, and was only the first rude essay of some infant deity who afterwards abandoned it, ashamed of his lame performance. It is the work only of some dependent, inferior deity, and is the object of derision to his superiors. It is the production of old age and dotage in some superannuated deity, and ever since his death has run on at adventures, from the first impulse and active force which it received from him. You justly give signs of horror, Demea, at these strange suppositions, but these, and a thousand more of the same kind, are Cleanthes' suppositions, not mine. From the moment the attributes of the Deity are supposed finite, all these have place. And I cannot, for my part, think that so wild and unsettled a system of theology is, in any respect, preferable to none at all.

These suppositions I absolutely disown, cried CLEANTHES; they strike me, however, with no horror, especially when proposed in that rambling way in which they drop from you. On the contrary, they give me pleasure when I see that, by the utmost indulgence of your imagination, you never get rid of the hypothesis of design in the universe, but are obliged at every turn to have recourse to it. To this concession I adhere steadily, and this I regard as a sufficient foundation for religion.

Rational Theology and the Big Bang

From "The Caused Beginning of the Universe" in *Theism, Atheism, and Big Bang Cosmology* by William Lane Craig and Quentin Smith, 1993

William Lane Craig during the last twenty years has been the leading professional student and champion of the first-cause argument and related cosmological reasoning. Craig has been especially devoted in this regard to bringing out the importance of the Arabic thought of Avicenna and others who had become neglected (see the Guide to Further Reading). But with the selection below, Craig focuses on recent findings of science, in particular the Big Bang cosmology that gradually has become widely accepted.

Craig's argument seems complicated since he defends its premises in the context of current physics. But in fact the argument is simple. Craig even declares, near the end of the piece, that the crucial premise, "Whatever begins to exist has a cause" is not a matter of probabilistic reasoning after all—that is, not an inductive generalization—but a "metaphysical intuition that something cannot come out of nothing." The Big Bang, by the way, is referred to as a singularity since it is a unique event. The remainder of the excerpt is straightforward.

One question about Craig's argument concerns "metaphysical intuitions." Do we share these, and should we feel very confident in speculating about what, if anything, caused the Big Bang? It would seem that we would require some other route to the divine cause, some other source of information about God or a Divine Reality. However, Craig, and others, would respond that this argument is part of a cumulative case *in favor of theism. We shall encounter this notion again with William Wainwright (under Religious Pluralism) and in the context of our examination of mysticism.*

. . . the following argument (which [Quentin Smith] incorrectly attributes to me) as a basis for inferring a supernatural cause of the universe's origin:

1. We have reason to believe that all events have a cause.

2. The Big Bang is an event.

3. Therefore, we have reason to believe that the Big Bang has a cause.

While admitting that this argument does not violate singularity theorems, since the cause is not conceived to be a spatiotemporal object, Smith maintains that the argument fails because (1) is false. Quoting me to the effect that 'the causal proposition may be taken as an empirical generalization enjoying the strongest support experience affords', Smith rejoins that quantum-mechanical considerations show that the causal principle is limited in its application, so that a probabilistic argument for a cause of the Big Bang cannot succeed. For according to Heisenberg's uncertainty principle, it is impossible to predict precisely the conditions of the values of momentum or position of some particle x at some time t_2 on the basis of our knowledge of the conditions of x at t_1. Since it is sufficient to understand causality in terms of a law enabling precise predictions of individual events to be deduced, it follows from Heisenberg's principle that there are uncaused events in this sense. Therefore, the causal proposition is not universally applicable and may not apply to the Big Bang.

But what exactly is the causal proposition which is at issue here? The proposition which I enunciated was not (1), as Smith alleges, but rather

(1') Whatever begins to exist has a cause.

The motions of elementary particles described by statistical quantum-mechanical laws, even if uncaused, do not constitute an exception to this principle. As Smith himself admits, these considerations 'at most tend to show that acausal laws govern the *change of condition* of particles, such as the change of particle x's position from q_1 to q_2. They state nothing about the causality or acausality of absolute beginnings, of beginnings of the existence of particles.

Smith seeks to rectify this defect in his argument, however, by pointing out that the uncertainty relation also permits energy or particles (notably virtual particles) to 'spontaneously come into existence' for a very brief time before vanishing again. It is therefore false that 'all beginnings of existence are caused' and, hence, 'the crucial step in the argument to a supernatural cause of the Big Bang . . . is faulty'.

But as a counter-example to (1'), Smith's use of such vacuum fluctuations is highly misleading. For virtual particles do not literally come into existence spontaneously out of nothing. Rather the energy locked up in a vacuum fluctuates spontaneously in such a way as to convert into evanescent particles that return almost immediately to the vacuum. As John Barrow and Frank Tipler comment, 'the modern picture of the quantum vacuum differs radically from the classical and everyday meaning of a vacuum—nothing. . . . The quantum vacuum (or vacua, as there can exist many) states . . . are defined simply as local, or global, energy minima ($V'(0) = 0$, $V''(0) > 0$).'[1] The microstructure of the quantum vacuum is a sea of continually forming and dissolving particles which borrow energy from the vacuum for their brief existence. A quantum vacuum is thus far from nothing, and vacuum fluctuations do not constitute an exception to the principle that whatever begins to exist has a cause. It seems to me, therefore, that Smith has failed to refute premise (1').

Let us pursue Smith's argument further, however. He proceeds to argue that there is no reason to think that the causal principle applies to the Big Bang, whether one adopts a model based exclusively on the General Theory of Relativity or whether one uses a model adjusted for quantum effects during the Planck era. Consider on the one hand a model in which quantum physics plays no role prior to 10^{-43} second after this singularity. Since the classical notions of space and time and all known laws of physics break down at the singularity, it is in principle impossible to predict what will emerge from a singularity. If we regard the Big Bang as the first physical state, then the particles that constitute that state must be regarded as being randomly and spontaneously emitted from nothing at all. Smith states,

> This means, precisely put, that if the Big Bang is the first physical state, then every configuration of particles that does constitute or might have constituted this first state is as likely on a priori grounds to constitute it as every other configuration of particles. In [this] case, the constitution of the Big Bang is impossible in principle to predict and thus is uncaused (for 'uncaused' minimally means 'in principle unpredictable').

Moreover, since the singularity is a point beyond which spacetime curves cannot be extended, it cannot have causal antecedents.

On the other hand, consider a model in which quantum processes do predominate near to the Big Bang. If the defender of the causal principle maintains that the proposition

4. There are some uncaused beginnings of existence *within* spacetime

is irrelevant to and thus cannot increase the probability of

5. The beginning of the existence of spacetime itself is uncaused,

then Smith will respond that the same holds for the parallel argument for a supernatural cause of four-dimensional spacetime. For the proposition

6. All beginnings of existence *within* spacetime are caused

would by the same token be irrelevant to and thus not increase the probability of

7. The beginning of the existence of four-dimensional spacetime is caused.

[1] J. Barrow and F. J. Tipler, *The Anthropic Cosmological Principle* (Oxford: Clarendon Press, 1986), 440.

So whether one adopts an unmodified relativistic model or a quantum model, there is no reason to postulate a cause, natural or supernatural, of the Big Bang.

Is this a sound argument? It seems to me not. To pick up on a point noted earlier, Smith's argument throughout his paper appears to be infected with positivism, so that it is predicated upon a notion of causality that is drastically inadequate. Smith assumes uncritically the positivistic equation between predictability in principle and causation.[2] But this verificationist analysis is clearly untenable, as should be obvious from the coherence of the position that quantum indeterminacy is purely epistemic, there existing hidden variables which are in principle unobservable, or even the more radical position of die-hard realists who are prepared to abandon locality (and perhaps even Special Relativity) in order to preserve the hidden variables. Clearly, then, to be 'uncaused' does not mean, even minimally, to be 'in principle unpredictable'.

This single point alone seems to me to vitiate Smith's entire argument for his conclusion and against the theistic hypothesis in particular. For now we see that Smith's argument, even if successful, in no way proves that the universe began to exist without a cause, but only that its beginning to exist was unpredictable. What is ironic about this conclusion is that it is one with which the theist is in whole-hearted agreement. For since according to classical theism creation is a freely willed act of God, it follows necessarily that the beginning and structure of the universe were in principal unpredictable even though they were caused by God. The theist will therefore not only agree with Smith 'That there are uncaused events *in this sense* follows from Heisenberg's uncertainty principle', but even more will insist that such uncaused events are entailed by classical theism's doctrine of creation. He will simply deny that this is the relevant sense when we are enquiring whether the universe could have come into being uncaused out of nothing.

When we ask that question, we are asking whether the whole of being could come out of non-being; and here a negative answer seems obvious. Concerning this question, even genuine quantum indeterminacy affords no evidence for an affirmative response. For if an event requires certain physically necessary conditions in order to occur, but these conditions are not jointly sufficient for its occurrence, and the event occurs, then the event is in principle unpredictable, but it could hardly be called uncaused in the relevant sense. In the case of quantum events, there are any number of physically necessary conditions that must obtain for such an event to occur, and yet these conditions are not jointly sufficient for the occurrence of the event. (They are jointly sufficient in the sense that they are all the conditions one needs for the event's occurrence, but they are not sufficient in the sense that they guarantee the occurrence of the event.) The appearance of a particle in a quantum vacuum may thus be said to be spontaneous, but cannot properly be said to be absolutely uncaused, since it has many physically necessary conditions. To be uncaused in the relevant sense of an absolute beginning, an existent must lack any non-logical necessary or sufficient condi-

---

[2] For a good example of this equation, see H. Bondi, 'Why Mourn the Passing of Determinism?' in Alwyn van der Merwe (ed.), *Old and New Questions in Physics, Cosmology, Philosophy, and Theoretical Biology* (New York: Plenum Press, 1983), 77–82.

tions whatsoever. Now at this juncture, someone might protest that such a requirement is too stringent; 'For how could *anything* come into existence without *any* non-logical necessary or sufficient conditions?' But this is my point exactly; if nothing existed—no matter, no energy, no space, no time, no deity—if there were absolutely nothing, then it seems unintelligible to say that something should spring into existence.

As for Smith's two cases, then, in the case of the classical relativistic theory, the fact that the universe originates in a naked singularity only proves that we cannot *predict* what sort of universe will emerge therefrom (and Smith does not claim otherwise), but it in no way implies that anything and everything can actually come into existence uncaused. Indeed, when we reflect on the fact that a physical state in which all spatial and temporal dimensions are zero is a mathematical idealization whose ontological counterpart is nothing, then it becomes clear why the universe is unpredictable and why its unpredictability in no way implies the possibility of its coming into being without a cause.[3] As for Smith's consideration that a singularity is a point beyond which spacetime curves cannot be extended, this only proves that the creation event cannot have been brought about by any natural cause; but it does not prove that a being which transcended space and time could not have caused it.

As for the quantum case, the problem with the inference from (4) to (5) is not that it moves from existents within the universe to the universe as a whole, but rather that Smith's faulty concept of causation makes the notion of 'uncaused' equivocal. For some beginnings of existence within spacetime are uncaused in the sense of being spontaneous or unpredictable, but one cannot conclude that therefore spacetime itself could come into being uncaused in the stronger sense of arising from nothing in the utter absence of physically necessary and sufficient conditions. But the inference from the necessity of causal conditions for the origin of existents in spacetime to the necessity of causal conditions for the origin of spacetime itself is not similarly equivocal. Indeed, our conviction of the truth of the causal principle is not based upon an inductive survey of existents in spacetime, but rather upon the metaphysical intuition that something cannot come out of nothing.[4] The proper inference, therefore, is actually from 'Whatever begins to exist has a cause' and 'The universe began to exist' to 'The universe has a cause', which is a logically impeccable inference based on universal instantiation. It seems to me, therefore, not only that Smith has failed to show that the Big Bang does not require a supernatural cause, but that,

---

[3] At the risk of seeming repetitious, I cannot refrain from referring again to G. E. M. Anscombe, '"Whatever Has a Beginning of Existence Must Have a Cause": Hume's Argument Exposed', *Analysis,* 34 (1973–4), 150. As she points out, we can form various pictures in our minds and give them appropriate titles, e.g., 'Superforce Emerging from the Singularity', 'Gravitons Emerging from the Singularity', or 'Rabbits Emerging from the Singularity', but our ability to do that says absolutely nothing about whether it is ontologically possible for something to come into being uncaused out of nothing.

[4] My defence of the causal proposition as an 'empirical generalization enjoying the strongest support experience affords' cited by Smith was in its original context a last-ditch defence of the principle designed to appeal to the hard-headed empiricist who resists the metaphysical intuition that properly grounds our conviction of the principle. (Craig, *The* Kalām *Cosmological Argument,* 141–8). It does seem to me that only an aversion to the theism implied by the principle in the present context would lead the empiricist to think that the denial of the principle is more plausible than the principle itself.

on the contrary, we see from these considerations that if the universe did originate from nothing, then that fact does point to a supernatural cause of its origin.[5]

Hence, I conclude that Smith has failed to show that there is no reason to regard the theistic hypothesis as true.

The Anthropic Design Argument

From *God and the New Cosmology* by M. A. Corey, 1993

In David Hume's Dialogues Concerning Natural Religion, *the character Philo argues that if a randomly changing universe is temporally infinite, then all possible material combinations should get realized. It is a commonplace that the winner of a lottery jackpot tends to believe that he or she has been personally favored by God; however, someone had to win. In our extensive universe, the planet earth may be the "lucky number," the fortuitous combination of physical circumstances that permitted evolution to get started and be sustained. The universe is enormously large relative to the mass of our planet and even the sun. Should not life have evolved somewhere, and wherever it evolved, would not the evolving beings tend to think that they have been chosen, intended, by something like themselves but controlling the entire universe?*

In recent physics, an anthropic principle *is appealed to to explain why the universe in our region of space-time looks as it does; if it did not, we could not have evolved. Other regions of space-time might obey different laws. But conditions essential to our evolution must be found here where we are, since we are here.*

M. A. Corey tries to turn the anthropic principle back into a theistic argument, the argument from design (or teleological argument). So many things could have gone wrong— and should have gone wrong given no other principle but chance (Corey calls this Murphy's Law)—that our universe seems entirely unlikely except on the theistic assumption.

Hardly all would be settled even given that this argument is successful. Aurobindo, as we saw (under Speculative Spiritual Metaphysics), advances Corey's argument in an overall defense not of God, but Brahman. And the anthropic principle is used just to the opposite effect in science, that is, to explain particular local features without relying on a cosmic intention.

. . . This Murphy's Law-breaking principle had to have been a power that was entirely sufficient for the infinitely complex anthropic takes being proposed, otherwise no such universe could have formed and we would not exist. The stature of this universal ordering principle can be inferred from the realization that in its absence, the precursors of life

---

[5] Such a cause would have to be uncaused, eternal, changeless, timeless, immaterial, and spaceless; it would, as I have argued elsewhere, also have to be personal and therefore merits the appellation 'God'. (Essay I, Sect. 4; William Lane Craig, 'The *Kalām* Cosmological Argument and the Hypothesis of a Quiescent Universe', *Faith and Philosophy,* 8 (1991), 492–503).

should have gone wrong trillions of times before life ever formed. After all, we're talking about the most complex thing known (a life-supporting universe), and billions of years in which these potential errors could have occurred. Yet no such errors can be identified, despite the universe's profound complexity and enormous age. Therefore, we can infer that an exceedingly competent organizing principle must have acted to keep life's precursors from malfunctioning during all the stages that initially led to our own evolution. While some have conceived of chance acting in this capacity, it is very difficult to see how chance processes could have repeatedly compensated for the universe's great tendency to go wrong over the thousands of millions of years of its formative evolution. The odds against the accidental formation of our present universe support us in this conclusion, as they have been calculated to be approximately 1 in $10^{10^{30}}$! This being the case, we are compelled to conclude that some sort of larger organizing power probably acted throughout cosmic history to keep the universe "on track" in its extremely straight and narrow anthropic trajectory.

This Argument from Murphy's Law reduces to the following:

1. Murphy's Law is applicable to all physical systems and to all stages of cosmic history.

2. Any system of infinite complexity requires an infinite amount of ingenuity in order to function properly.

3. Our present universe is infinitely complex in terms of its underlying structure and design.

4. Therefore, an infinite number of things had to have gone right for thousands of millions of years before intelligent life could have ever evolved on this planet.

5. Barring the activity of some sort of larger ordering influence, things *should* have gone wrong many times on the way to life, given the infinite complexity of our biocentric universe and the enormous amount of time in which it took to form.

6. Had things been capable of going significantly wrong in the distant past with respect to biogenesis and the evolution of intelligent life, they *would* have gone wrong at one time or another (especially given the tremendous age of the universe), and we would probably not be here.

7. But we *are* here.

8. Therefore, things must *not* have been capable of going significantly wrong in the early universe as far as the evolution of intelligent life is concerned.

9. Chance processes in the early universe were probably incapable of maintaining such a high degree of order in the universe over so many thousands of millions of years.

10. Therefore, some sort of larger organizing principle, entirely sufficient to the task, must have been at work throughout cosmic history to ensure that the universe did not descend into life-negating chaos at all stages of its evolution.

11. This universal organizing principle for all practical intents and purposes can be called God. . . .

The Overall Case for Intelligent Design

As we have seen, a grand conspiracy between a large number of seemingly unrelated events has been at work in the universe since its very inception. The purpose of this conspiracy has been, among other things, to make it possible for life to evolve on this planet.

While it is possible to "explain" the co-operation of these distinct elements in terms of chance alone, the more intuitive and probable explanation is to use the immense complexity and difficulty of life's evolution, along with the utterly remarkable nature of life itself, to conclude that these "coincidences" were deliberately planned and implemented by a Higher Power so as to enable life to come into being.

Most scientists, even the most hardened atheistic ones, will readily admit that this is the most natural and intuitive explanation for these remarkable "cosmic events." However, the notion of probability also greatly favors this intuitive explanation, since it is far more probable that these "coincidences" were the result of Intelligent Design than that they were the product of blind chance. But science operates primarily on the basis of recognized probabilities, since virtually nothing in science can be proved absolutely. Therefore, the most "scientific" conclusion with regard to these "coincidences" is undoubtedly the theistic one, since it is clearly the most probable explanation overall. The radically more improbable alternative—that life is merely the result of a stupendous cosmic accident—must therefore be dismissed as being a relatively unscientific form of self-deception, since it is sufficiently unlikely as to be virtually impossible.

Indeed, according to University of Montreal psychiatrist Karl Stern, the belief that our wondrous universe could have evolved by blind chance is ". . . crazy. And I do not at all mean crazy in the sense of a slangy invective but rather in the technical meaning of psychotic. Indeed such a view has much in common with certain aspects of schizophrenic thinking."

It takes a lot of faith to believe that our enormously complex universe could have arisen by chance alone—certainly a lot more faith than it takes to believe that it is the product of Intelligent Design. Since science, as we have seen, allies itself with probabilities and recognized analogies, and not heroic unsubstantiated faith, it follows that the notion of Intelligent Design is by far the most "scientific" explanation for the origin of our biocentric universe. The founding fathers of the modern scientific movement—Newton, Boyle, and a whole host of other brilliant thinkers—would have wholeheartedly agreed with this conclusion, as they were convinced beyond doubt that our universe was in fact Intelligently Designed. Given the strength of the Anthropic Design argument, perhaps we should return to their timeless fount of insight and wisdom.

An Axiological Argument

From *Philosophical Explanations* by Robert Nozick, 1981

Robert Nozick, a professor of philosophy at Harvard University, first became famous for an innovative political theory. He has done ground-breaking work as well in decision the-

ory and epistemology, also in ethics. The excerpt here is from a work in metaphysics. In the process of speculating about the meaning of life and the grounds of worth and value, Nozick formulates what we may call an axiological argument for God, or, as he says (using a Judaic term), the Ein Sof, the Absolute, which is, in his conception, very similar to the Indian theist's view of Brahman.

A starting point in Nozick's argument is the premise that the kind of meaning that implies value (as in "the meaning of life")—what we shall call axiological meaning—involves hooking up in an appropriate way with something larger than oneself, something that has value. Meaning is conferred by something valuable and larger than oneself. But then we can question what gives the meaning or value to that which confers it, as, for example, a family providing meaning and value to the life of a family member. It seems, then, that the question, "What provides meaning to a meaning-conferrer?" can be blocked (or answered) at a highest level only with reference to something that has meaning in and through itself. Only God (or the Ein Sof or Brahman) can have meaning in and through itself. This premise is a matter of definition, of the right understanding of God. A final premise is that meaning is indeed grounded, that is, there is no infinite regress. Thus the groundedness of meaning entails that there is God.

Nozick's tour de force *comes in a response to an objection; the objection, namely, that this is all wishful thinking. There is no reason to assume that meaning is grounded. Nozick replies that holding to austere epistemic standards in rejecting the argument would have to be, then, a meaningless act (in the axiological sense of "meaning"). This seems a forceful rebuttal in that it draws out a consequence of rejecting the view that meaning is grounded. On the other hand, we may ask: Is it right to pull in this way axiological meaning out of a hat?*

. . . we have glimpsed one way questions of meaning can be brought to a halt, with a self-sufficient unlimited being which is its own meaning and which we somehow connect with (as in the case of God) or are (as in the case of Brahman of Vedanta). There seems to be at least this one answer to the question of how meaning is possible. Thus, we can see how religion was thought to specify an answer to the question of the meaning of our life, and also why among the increasing numbers of those detached from religion in the past century, the question of meaning, suddenly unanswered, assumed great importance.

We have seen one way meaning is possible—if there were an unlimited and all-inclusive something which grounds meaning—but we have not yet discussed the question of whether it is actual. In specifying an alternative apparently so unviable in the minds of many at present, we appear to have made little progress. (Must the owl of Minerva insist on trying to fly from night back into the previous day?) This, despite the fact that the unlimited ground of meaning need not be some traditional religious alternative, western or eastern. Yet is the common belief that there is nothing anywhere that is infinite and unlimited an inductive inference from our limited experiences? Have we put this belief to its severest test by seeking out other experiences?

The task of evaluating what such experiences show, including those reported by mystics, is an intricate one. It is my judgment that these experiences do not demonstrate the existence of an unlimited entity; the experiences conflict, many of them can be explained away, the reports may be theory-laden, and so forth. Still, although the experiences by themselves may be insufficient, they do carry some weight. In contrast, the deductive arguments considered by philosophers of religion, the ontological, cosmological, teleological, and so on, seem to me, as to many others, fruitless.

Suppose there is no other route we can find to meaning, other than via something unlimited, no other way we can imagine that meaning is even possible. Is the fact that there apparently can be meaning to life only if there is such an unlimited being itself a reason to believe there is one? (If so, when this is combined with the weight of the experiences, do we then have a sufficient reason?) Or shall we dismiss this as wishful thinking, merely?

To this (wistful?) line of thought, we each know how to construct the reply. "Even if life can only have meaning when there is an unlimited being, nevertheless, perhaps there is no such entity and so life cannot have meaning. We must not confuse what we desire with what is the case; we must continue to base our beliefs on the evidence and reasons, to calibrate our degree of belief according to the evidence. That only thereby can life have meaning is no reason to think it is true that there is an unlimited being, unless there is independent reason to think it is true that life does or can have meaning."

This act of maintaining the most rigorous intellectual standards, uninfluenced by our hopes and aspirations, exhibits stern integrity in the face of temptation. The question is: does this scrupulous act have any *meaning?*

We were driven to speak of the unlimited by the nature of meaning as a transcending of limits, a connecting with something external. For how could a mere connection with something, no matter how trivial, establish the requisite meaning? That other thing, surely must itself have meaning, if meaning is to accrue to anything in virtue of being connected with it. Inexorably, we are led to iterate the question "and what is the meaning of that?", asking it of each wider context. Barring an infinite chain, we are led either to something itself without meaning, which seems to undercut the meaning of all the rest based upon it, or to something that somehow can constitute its own meaning. These structural possibilities are similar to the ones with explanatory chains we see elsewhere; the unlimited which is its own meaning, thereby anchoring the chain, corresponds to a fundamental self-subsuming principle which is its own explanation.

Refutation of the Ontological Argument

From *The Critique of Pure Reason* by Immanuel Kant, Norman Kemp Smith, translator, 1929

Earlier, in the subsection entitled God, the selection from Anselm expressed what has come to be known as an ontological argument, a conceptual or a priori *argument for the existence of God.*

(premise 1)   God is that, nothing greater (or better) than which can be conceived.
(premise 2)   God is (or can be) conceived. (Or, God exists in the mind.)
(premise 3)   To exist is greater (or better) than not to exist. (Or, to exist in reality is better than to exist only in the mind.)

(conclusion) God exists.
(logic)   *Imagine a God$_0$ that had every attribute that a God$_1$ has (omnipotence, omniscience, omnibenevolence, etc.) except existence. But by premise 3 having existence is better than not having it. So only God$_1$, not God$_0$, could be God according to Anselm's definition (premise 1).*

Several philosophers, including the so-called "father of modern philosophy," René Descartes (1596–1650), followed Anselm in putting forth a variation of the argument. A contemporary of Anselm's named Gaunilo was an early opponent; David Hume should be credited for the decisive empiricist critique. This is that only experience counts as ultimate evidence concerning any question of fact. Concepts in themselves articulate possibilities only. Experience tells us whether a concept is exampled in the world; in other words, experience tells us what exists.

Immanuel Kant (1724–1804) crystalized what Hume saw was wrong, and is commonly credited with a definitive refutation centering on the phrase "existence is not a predicate." A more accurate expression, however, would be that existence is not an attribute, at least not an attribute like any other.

The proposition, "All triangles have three sides," can be true even if there are no triangles, and we can know it is true. But only experience can tell us that there are indeed triangles in the universe. Similarly, we know that a unicorn would have a single horn whether or not there are in fact any unicorns. Kant uses the terms analytic *and* synthetic *to make this point. The concept of the subject of an analytic proposition includes that of its predicate. Thus to deny the predicate of an analytic proposition would be a patent falsehood, what Kant calls a contradiction: for example, "A puppy is not a young dog." A synthetic proposition adds something in the predicate that is not contained in the concept of the subject, and thus a denial of it would not be a contradiction: for example "Tame tigers growl" (tame tigers might not growl). According to Kant (and Hume and empiricism generally), only experience can tell us whether a synthetic proposition is true. Kant argues further that existence is not even a candidate for an attribute that could be indicated in the concept of a proposition's subject.*

Not all philosophers, however, find this line of thought conclusive against all ontological arguments. For example, Robert Kane—see the following selection—presents a sympathetic treatment of Anselm's reasoning, despite Kant's famous criticism.

My answer is as follows. There is already a contradiction in introducing the concept of existence—no matter under what title it may be disguised—into the concept of a thing which we profess to be thinking solely in reference to its possibility. If that be allowed as legitimate, a seeming victory has been won; but in actual fact nothing at all is said: the assertion is a mere tautology. We must ask: Is the proposition that *this or that thing* (which, whatever it may be, is allowed as possible) *exists*, an analytic or a synthetic proposition? If it is analytic, the assertion of the existence of the thing adds nothing to the thought of the thing; but in that case either the thought, which is in us, is the thing itself, or we have presupposed an existence as belonging to the realm of the possible, and have then, on the pretext, inferred its existence from its internal possibility—which is nothing but a miserable tautology. The word 'reality', which in the concept of the thing sounds other than the word 'existence' in the concept of the predicate, is of no avail in meeting this objection. For if all positing (no matter what it may be that is posited) is entitled reality, the thing with all its predicates is already posited in the concept of the subject, and is assumed as actual; and in the predicate this is merely repeated. But if, on the other hand, we admit, as every reasonable person must, that all existential propositions are synthetic, how can we profess to maintain that the predicate of existence cannot be rejected without contradiction? This is a feature which is found only in analytic propositions, and is indeed precisely what constitutes their analytic character.

. . . the illusion which is caused by the confusion of a logical with a real predicate (that is, with a predicate which determines a thing) is almost beyond correction. Anything we please can be made to serve as a logical predicate; the subject can even be predicated of itself; for logic abstracts from all content. But a *determining* predicate is a predicate which is added to the concept of the subject and enlarges it.

'*Being*' is obviously not a real predicate; that is, it is not a concept of something which could be added to the concept of a thing. \ . . .

Anselm's Modal Argument

From *Proslogion* by Anselm • From "Anselm's Second, or Modal, Ontological Argument" by Robert H. Kane, 1995

Robert Kane, a professor of philosophy at the University of Texas, Austin, who wrote the following piece expressly for this textbook, argues that crucial to the success of the ontological argument is the premise that God is coherently conceivable.

Kane draws on an important paper on the modal argument he published in the journal Mind *in 1984. There and here too he makes clear that a substitution marking the transition from the first, or non-modal, argument, criticized by Kant, to the second, or modal, argument does not appear vulnerable to Kant's criticism. For this substitution is that of necessary existence for plain existence as the attribute of God that the argument hinges upon. Necessary existence make God special, going hand-in-hand with God's eternity and non-dependence, which are, Kane argues (echoing Anselm and other scholastics), great-making characteristics that it would seem a perfect being would have. Kant makes it seem that existence is not an attribute. But what about eternity and non-dependence? Why should these have a different logical status than, say, omniscience?*

The second argument suggests that the conceivability of a perfect being is the crux of the issue; again, this is one of Kane's main points. Thus relevant to an examination would be the kind of discussion we surveyed in the first section with Richard Gale, Charles Hartshorne, and William Alston. Kane sees the question of whether God can be coherently conceived (i.e., the question of the possibility of a perfect being) as even embracing the problem of evil, where, as we shall see, the traditional approach has been, in the West, to try to find an explanation of evil given theistic premises. On Kane's reading, in contrast, evil is relevant to the ontological argument in that it can be viewed as eliminating the possibility of attributes such as omnibenevolence crucial to the idea of a perfect being. On such a construct, the ontological argument, far from being a way to begin rational theology, would be its copestone, the brick in the arch that holds everything in place.

FROM *PROSLOGION*

THAT GOD CANNOT BE THOUGHT NOT TO EXIST

And certainly this being so truly exists that it cannot be even thought not to exist. For something can be thought to exist that cannot be thought not to exist, and this is greater than that which can be thought not to exist. Hence, if that-than-which-a-greater-cannot-be-thought can be thought not to exist, then that-than-which-a-greater-cannot-be-thought is not the same as that-than-which-a-greater-cannot-be-thought, which is absurd. Something-than-which-a-greater-cannot-be-thought exists so truly then, that it cannot be even thought not to exist.

And You, Lord our God, are this thing. You exist so truly, Lord my God, that You cannot even be thought not to exist. And this is as it should be, for if some intelligence could think of something better than You, the creature would be above its creator and would judge its creator—and that is completely absurd. In fact, everything else there is, except You alone, can be thought of as not existing. You alone, then, of all things most truly exist and therefore of all things possess existence to the highest degree; for anything else does not exist as truly, and so possesses existence to a lesser degree. Why then did 'the Fool say in his heart, there is no God' [Ps. xiii. 1, lii. 1] when it is so evident to any rational mind that You of all things exist to the highest degree? Why indeed, unless because he was stupid and a fool?

FROM "ANSELM'S SECOND, OR MODAL, ONTOLOGICAL ARGUMENT"

When St. Anselm formulated his now famous "Ontological Argument" for the existence of God just after the year 1000 CE, it was like a bright flash of light at the end of what used to be called the "Dark Ages" in Western history. In the twentieth century, there has been a revival of interest in Anselm's argument and a discovery that he actually formulated a second ontological argument—often nowadays called the "Modal Ontological Argument"—even more powerful than the first. The discovery of this second argument was first made in the 1940s by Charles Hartshorne, one of the major philosophers of religion of the twentieth century, and then later, in the 1950s, independently by another philosopher, Norman Malcolm. Both Hartshorne and Malcolm were inspired by twentieth century developments in mathematical logic, particularly by what has come to be called "modal logic" (the logic of possibility and necessity). To Hartshorne and Malcolm, as to a number of other philosophers who came after them, modern developments in logic made Anselm's venerable argument even more interesting, and perhaps more plausible, than it had been before.

To understand Anselm's second or modal argument, it will help to consider a simple version of the original Ontological Argument which appears in chapter 2 of Anselm's *Proslogion.*

(1) God is a being than whom none greater can be thought.

This is Anselm's well-known definition of God as the most perfect conceivable, or maximally great, being.

(2) God "exists in the understanding" (we have an idea of God in our minds) even if it remains an open question whether God exists in reality.

This second premise adds to premise 1 that a being than whom none greater can be thought, *can be thought.* It is important to add this. For the definition in premise 1 might turn out to be a meaningless string of words for all we know, like "a round square" or "the non-existent elf who actually lives in your pants pocket." It is one thing to string words together like "a being than whom none greater can be thought" and another to be saying something meaningful.

The argument has one other premise, believed by many to be the most problematic. (We'll be discussing it shortly.)

(3) To exist in reality is greater than merely to exist in the understanding.

And from these three claims, the conclusion follows by relatively straightforward logical steps.

(4) If God existed only in the understanding and not in reality, God would not be a being than whom none greater can be thought,

which contradicts premise 1. So "God exists only in the understanding and not in reality" leads to a contradiction (of "reduces to absurdity") and must be false. Therefore,

(5) God exists also in reality.

Since steps 4 and 5 are logically valid, debate has focused on the three premises 1, 2 and 3. Premise 3 was especially troubling for many subsequent thinkers. Immanuel Kant held that "existence" (in reality) could not be considered a perfection, or great-making property, at all, like other perfections (all-knowing, almighty, all-loving, etc.) "Existence," Kant held, was not even a "predicate" that could characterize something as good or bad. Rather you first characterized something as good or bad (say, as all-knowing and all-loving) and then asked whether such a thing existed or not. The existence question was quite independent of whether the thing was good or bad, perfect or imperfect. It might be as perfect as it could be and still not exist.

Kant's criticism is itself problematic for many thinkers. But let's not worry about that because Anselm's second or Modal Ontological Argument replaces premise 3 altogether with another premise that many feel is stronger and more plausible.

(3') To be such that it is *not possible not to exist* is greater than to be such that it is *possible not to exist.* (*Necessary* existence is greater than merely contingent existence.)

When Anselm restated his original argument this way in chapter 3 of the *Proslogiun,* he changed premise (3) to (3') without apparently realizing what he was doing. But, in fact, he strengthened the argument by introducing "necessary existence" as a perfection rather than mere "existence." (This change also accounts for the designation "modal" of this second argument.) For, while one might debate the status of actual existence as a perfection or property, there is considerable plausibility in the claim that a being that cannot possibly not exist is greater than one that *could* possibly not exist. As Malcolm pointed out, a being whose existence is necessary is not dependent for its existence on anything else, since it cannot not exist. Moreover, such a being must always exist; it cannot exist at some times but not at others, or go out of existence or come into existence, like merely contingent things. But these properties of *non-dependent* and *eternal* existence are recognizable "perfections" that were traditionally ascribed to God in the scriptures.

Now if we add this modal premise 3' to the original premises 1 and 2 of Anselm's first argument, the rest of the second, or modal, argument follows by similarly non-controversial steps;

> (4') It is possible that God does not exist, then God is not a being than whom none greater can be thought.

which contradicts premise 1. So "it is possible that God does not exist" leads to a contradiction (reduces to absurdity), and must be false. Thus, it is *not* possible that God does not exist, and so

> (5') God exists.

Again, the logical steps to 4' and 5' look valid, so the argument depends on the premises. But premise 3' now looks unassailable because it ascribes great-making properties to God such as necessary, non-dependent and eternal existence. It seems that a perfect being would have such properties rather than their negations.

If something is wrong with this second argument then, it must be with the original premises 1 and 2 of both arguments. We did not question these first two premises earlier, but it looks like the case for the modal argument rests on them. Now, premise 1 is Anselm's well-known definition of God as "a being than whom none greater can be thought." How can we question a mere definition? Well, maybe Anselm got the idea of God wrong. Maybe God is not the most perfect conceivable being, or the sum of all perfections, or whatever else is meant by Anselm's formula. If you suspect that, here is a challenge you might want to accept. If you don't like, or don't agree with, Anselm's definition of God, suggest an alternative. Human history offers many alternatives, from ancient or pagan spirits, fertility deities and transcendent states to various gods or goddesses of ancient myths and cultures—great and powerful beings but not perfect in every way, not the greatest things that can be thought. Or perhaps you have some idea of your own of God or the ultimate reality that does not fit Anselm's formula. Well, then take your definition of God, whatever it is, and plug it into premise 1 in place of Anselm's.

Suppose the argument now no longer works when your definition is plugged in. Does that show Anselm's argument is unsound? Not at all. Anselm would say to you, "All you have shown is that you cannot prove the existence of *your* God. That does not mean one cannot prove the existence of my God. The point is that you have to get the *idea* of God *right* before you can prove the existence of God. If you get it wrong, if you believe in idols or false gods, something less than the most perfect being, you'll never be able to prove the existence of God." That is why Anselm put his proof in the context of a prayer or meditation. In effect, he said, "Oh (unknown) God whom I seek, help me to get the idea of You right, so I will understand that You exist. If I get it wrong, I will end up like the Fool who says in his heart 'There is no God.'"

This brings us to Premise 2. Can we really *have* an idea of the sum of all perfections, a being than whom none greater can be thought? This, I believe, is the most difficult question of the whole proof. It is no easy task to determine what perfections might be that a perfect being would possess (almighty, all-knowing, all-loving, eternal, infinite, transcendent, etc.). Can we really understand these traits, so far beyond our finite experience; and how do we know they all fit together rather than contradicting one another? In short, can we really understand what God is? And if not, can we ever be certain premise 2 is true?

Well, I think the answer must be that we cannot ever be *certain* that premise 2 is true. But neither can we be certain it is false. The Ontological Argument, by way of premise 2, places upon the person who takes it seriously the task which Anselm himself undertook in the rest of his writings—to search for a better understanding of God. It is the task of trying as best one can to determine whether there is coherent conception of God and what idea of perfection, or supreme reality, in the religions of mankind is the most coherent, if any are.[1] This is a large part of what the study of philosophy of religion is all about. (For example, the so-called "problem of evil" concerns whether we can coherently say that God is both almighty and all-loving, given the evil we see in the world. Does the existence of evil make the idea of an almighty *and* all-loving deity into something like a round square?) For such reasons, premise 2 of the Ontological Argument must remain an open question, one that depends on properly answering many other questions about religion, including the question of evil. But that does not necessarily undermine the Ontological Argument. The argument may then be understood as an invitation to address those other questions about the nature of God, realizing that, if they could be answered (so that a coherent idea of the most perfect being could be found), then the Ontological Argument would take one the rest of the way to the existence of such a being.

But what about the familiar objection that you can't get the existence of something out of a mere idea of it? It is obvious, isn't it, that from the idea of a rose you cannot get the existence of a rose, and from the idea of $100 in your pocket you can't get the actual existence of $100 in your pocket? And so it is for everything *else* in our experience *except* a perfect being. A perfect being is different because such a being possesses all perfections, and that is what allows one to get its existence from the mere idea of it. If you think God is

---

[1] You might end up disagreeing with Anselm on this score, arguing for example that some Eastern idea of Brahman, Nirvana or Tao (or some conception of the Western God different from Anselm's) was more perfect than Anselm's conception of God. But as long as you stayed with Anselm's general definition of the "most perfect being," or the "being than which none greater can be thought," the ontological argument would still work for the correct idea of the most perfect reality, whatever it is.

like everything else, roses and hundred dollar bills, so that you can't get existence from a mere idea of it—then *you don't get it.* God is different. Meditate on that fact, Anselm tells us. To think God is like a rose or a thunderbolt or a golden calf or any other finite thing is idolatry. You have to get over that to understand what God is *really* like, and if you understand what God is really like, a being than whom none greater can be thought, you'll get it: God exists.

But surely you can't become a believer on the basis of an abstract argument alone? No, of course not. But meditating on the right idea of God is a salutary religious undertaking. And making sure you have the right idea of the supreme reality rather than the wrong one is important. The Hindus say that one of the ways to approach the supreme reality is through what they call *Jnana Yoga*—the way of thought or philosophical meditation. This is what Anselm undertook when he made his "proof" part of a meditation on the nature of perfection. For the Hindus, such philosophical meditation is not the only way to the divine. There are other ways involving, for example, religious devotion, love and good works. (Anselm would have agreed with that also.) Different people may be better suited to different ways. This makes good sense. But the path of philosophical meditation would remain *a* path to the divine, perhaps along with other paths—and it is an important path, given that we are rational beings, who must make our beliefs cohere with everything else we believe. This is especially true in the present age, when belief faces continuous challenges from science and secular learning.

Such then is the goal of Anselm's argument. Maybe it doesn't work the way he thought it did. But in its own way, it has some of the qualities of the God it seeks to understand—awesome and fascinating.

EPILOGUE

Those who stop reading at this point will understand the gist of Anselm's second or Modal Ontological Argument. For those brave souls who want to learn more about it and are willing to wade into deeper waters, there is one other objection to be considered. Another well-known objection to Anselm's argument was made both by Saint Thomas Aquinas (regarded by many as the greatest of medieval philosophers who came after Anselm) and by Immanuel Kant (regarded by many as the greatest philosopher of the modern era). Both Aquinas and Kant argued that Anselm's original argument did not prove that God exists, but rather the far weaker claim that (X) *if God exists,* then God necessarily exists. Aquinas and Kant conceded that this claim X was no doubt true, indeed trivially true, by Anselm's definition of God. But, unfortunately, X is merely a hypothetical statement that falls far short of giving us God's *actual* existence.

Anselm's second, or modal, argument provides an answer to this objection also. To get an alternative version of the Modal Ontological Argument, take claim X (which Aquinas and Kant concede is trivially true and the real, but weak, *conclusion* of Anselm's original proof) and make claim X part of one of the *premises* of a second, or modal, version of the argument. That is to say, start with the claim that

(1') By definition (or necessarily), if God exists, then God necessarily exists.

Then add an alternative way of stating the original premise 2,

>   (2') God's existence is possible (i.e. thinkable, conceivable).

Each of these premises taken by itself is weak. The first says only that *if* God exists, God necessarily exists; and the second says that God's existence is merely possible. But what is surprising is that together these apparently weak premises have great power. For when put together, they yield an alternative version of the second or Modal Ontological Argument. (To compare this alternative version of the modal argument to the one given in the essay, note that the new premise 1' is an implication of the original premise 1—God is the most perfect being—together with 3'—necessary existence is a perfection. And the new premise 2' is another way of stating the original premise 2.)

From these two premises, 1' and 2', the argument proceeds as follows. From 1', we get

>   (3") If God's existence is possible, then it is possible that God necessarily exists.

For if God's existing entails by definition God's necessarily existing (which is what 1' says), then if the former is possible (God's existing), the latter will also be possible (God's necessarily existing). This result is both intuitive in itself and follows from a basic principle of modal logic which is in all the standard systems.[2] But, now, from 2' (God's existence is possible) and 3", we get

>   (4") It is possible that God necessarily exists.

Now we add a further principle of modal logic that is also part of some standard systems. (We'll discuss it further in a moment.)

>   (5") If something does not in fact exist, then it is not possible that it necessarily exists,

which gives us, for the special case of God's existence,

>   (6') If God does not in fact exist, it is not possible that God necessarily exists,

whose consequent clause contradicts 4" (it *is* possible that God necessarily exists). So the assumption that "God does not exist" of step 6" leads to a contradiction and is false. Therefore,

>   (7) God does in fact exist.

This is the more refined version of the Modal Ontological Argument that modern modal logics recognize. And the only additional problematic premise in it not previously discussed is 5"—"If something does not in fact exist, then it is not possible that it necessarily exists." This is an important and deep principle of modal logic sometimes called the B-principle (named after a German logician and mathematician named Brouwer). What can be said in its favor? First, the principle has some intuitive plausibility in the present context. If something does not in fact exist, how *could* it have necessary existence, since for something to have necessary existence, it must be such that it *could not* not exist.

---

[2] The principle is this: if P necessarily entails Q, then if P is possible, Q is possible also.

Second, the B-principle (5"), though it is not in all systems of modal logic, is in the most general system, called S5, which by common consensus expresses the standard idea of necessity in what Alvin Plantinga has called the "broadly logical sense." In this sense of necessity, what is necessarily true is true in all logically possible worlds whatever, without any further special conditions or qualifications attached. It is just such an "unconditional" sense of logical necessity that Anselm and other traditional thinkers most likely had in mind when they talked about God's necessary existence—that is, an unconditioned existence in all possible worlds whatever. Anything less than this unconditional necessity would not be worthy of a being than whom none greater can be thought. But, in this unconditional (S5) sense of logical necessity, the B-principle (or 5") is true; and so the Modal Argument as just stated is valid.

Now the Modal Ontological Argument as just stated has only two other premises besides the B-principle—(1') "By definition, if God exists, God necessarily exists" and (2') "God's existence is possible." Since 1' is the simple definitional truth acknowledged even by critics of the argument like Aquinas and Kant, we are brought back to premise 2' (or 2) as the only problematic premise.[3] Is God's existence possible or thinkable? Can we have a coherent idea of God? If so, says Anselm's argument, God exists.[4]

DISCUSSION QUESTIONS

1. What is the principle of credulity as explained by H. H. Price? How does Price defend it?

2. Belief in miracles is often taken to be *prima facie* irrational. Richard Swinburne takes a contrary stance. Explain his position, including his definition of a miracle and the types of evidence he sees as appropriate to warranted belief that a miracle has occurred.

3. Why does David Hume believe that, just by the definition of what a miracle is, we can be sure that no belief that a miracle has occurred could be rational or warranted? What is the key issue in an imagined dispute between Swinburne and Hume? And finally, list the reasons that Hume finds that people are prone to believe testimony of

---

[3] While 2' (or 2) may be the only problematic *premise* remaining, there is another possible difficulty for the Modal Ontological Argument that is similar to Gaunilo's well-known objection to Anselm's original argument. Suppose there could be "less-than-perfect" necessary beings—that is, beings that could not not exist, but lacked some of the other perfections assigned to God. Maybe these less-than-perfect beings were not all-knowing or all-powerful, or perhaps they sometimes did evil deeds. Since they nonetheless possessed necessary existence, their existence could be proved as well. Note that this objection is like Gaunilo's, except that while Gaunilo postulated *perfect* beings of different kinds (for example, a perfect island), whose existence could be proved if Anselm's argument worked, this objection postulates *less-than-perfect,* yet necessary, beings whose existence could be proved. What this objection shows is that, for Anselm's second, or modal, argument to work, it must not only be true that "a perfect being would be necessary" (premise 1'), but also that "a necessary being would be perfect." Anselm probably held this latter claim, but a case has to be made for it.

[4] For further discussion of the arguments of this article, see the author's essay: R. Kane, "The Modal Ontological Argument" *Mind* 93 (1984): 336–50, as well as other bibliographic references to the Ontological Argument in this volume.

miracles despite the fact that, in Hume's view, such belief is irrational. Is Hume convincing in this regard?

4. Reconstruct the following *a posteriori* arguments: (a) two first-cause arguments formulated by Aristotle, differentiating at least two different types of cause; (b) the first-cause argument of Proclus, and (c) the first-cause argument of Avicenna. Avicenna's argument could also be labeled an argument from contingencies; compare the argument in this section with Avicenna's reasoning in favor of a necessary being in the selection excerpted under Divine Reality. Optionally, say how (c) is distinct, if it is, from the *cosmological argument* (see the introductory discussion of Aristotelian Rational Theology).

5. Reconstruct Thomas's "Five Ways" that he takes to show God's existence. What is the most serious difficulty with each argument? Does the difficulty defeat the argument? Or is the argument successful anyway; that is to say, can the difficulty be answered?

6. Reformulate Udayana's first argument, the "Argument from Effects," using not the abbreviated, three-line form he uses but the longer form explained in the introductory discussion. Then focus on one or two of the objections to this argument that Udayana lists and on his replies. Is he successful in answering the complaint?

7. In the passages excerpted from David Hume's *Dialogues Concerning Natural Religion*, what are the considerations, if any, Cleanthes puts forward in support of the theses that the universe is designed, and that God is its designer, and what counter-considerations, if any, does Philo put forward to show that the universe need not be supposed designed, and that God need not be supposed to be its designer?

8. Reconstruct the first-cause argument advanced by William Lane Craig, who takes as a premise Big Bang cosmology. What do you see as the weakest point in the argument? If a challenger were to focus on that weakest point, what considerations would be relevant to decide the dispute? Or, could there be no resolution? Explain.

9. What is the *anthropic principle* used both by M. A. Corey in his "anthropic design argument" and by physicists to explain local features of the universe? What is the crucial consideration that Corey believes shows that God is the universe's designer? Is his argument cogent?

10. Reconstruct Robert Nozick's axiological argument. What is the theory of meaning that informs this argument, and is it plausible? Does Nozick successfully answer the objection that the supposition that meaning is grounded is wishful thinking?

11. Discuss Immanuel Kant's purported refutation of Anselm's (first, or non-modal) ontological argument, the refutation that centers on the claim that "existence is not a predicate." Just what does Kant mean? Why, if he is right, would this refute the ontological argument?

12. Why would the coherent conceivability of God or of a perfect being be the crucial issue in deciding the cogency of Anselm's second, or modal, ontological argument? What further issues are involved in the question of that conceivability? Could there be constructed such an ontological argument for the Tao, Buddhist "Emptiness," or Brahman? Explain.

CHAPTER THREE

Mystical Experience

In the philosophies associated with Hinduism, Buddhism, and Taoism, mystical experience is commonly cited as the—or at least a—foundation or source of claims about reality, and much more commonly than in Western religious philosophies. However, as early as Plato, Western spiritual speculation has exalted mystical ways of knowing, and mysticism is prominently expressed within Judaism, Christianity, and Islam. Furthermore, perceived response to prayer—and perceived lack of response—is often cited as the grounds for a personal faith, and for rejecting religion. Prayer is a form of mysticism, or of a mystic path, although some mystics would claim that it is not the most appropriate way to come into contact with Divine Reality.

Our study of mysticism can be divided roughly into two broad parts with a bridge in between. First, we shall become acquainted with important types of mystical experience, and distinct traditions, often by surveying first-hand mystic testimony, as with the writings of the theistic mystic Teresa and contemporary reportage of the Zen *satori* ("enlightenment") experience. Then beginning with a selection from C. B. Martin, we shall look at considerations philosophers have put forward to evaluate mystic claims. The selections from Martin Buber, a mystic philosopher out of the Judaic tradition, and from Kitaro Nishida, out of Zen Buddhism, are bridge selections in that they are self-consciously abstract and interpretive, not focused so much on experiences and their description but on the relation of mysticism to religion and daily life (Buber) or on cross-cultural harmony (Nishida). With the first group of selections—from Teresa and company—questions of interpretation and indeed of "theory-ladenness" inevitably arise, but the selections have been made for the experiences and individual perspectives expressed. Evaluative questions are engaged forthright with the second group—C. B. Martin, William Wainwright, Steven Katz, and Sallie B. King.

Crucial to the philosophic controversy is the question whether mystical experience provides evidence for God (or Brahman, or Emptiness, or the Tao) in any way similar to the evidence provided by sensory experience for physical objects and happenings. This question is discussed under the shorthand, "Is mystical experience cognitive?"

Opponents of mysticism as a reliable source of information about God or the like point to what they see as contradictory mystic testimony and indisputable broad divergences in mystic traditions. The great Catholic mystic Teresa says her special experience reveals God, the supreme reality, but Buddhists and others have experiences that they take to reveal something incompatible with Teresa's God—or at least of questionable compatibility. If the one is right, the other would seem to be wrong. Even in our initial survey of types of experience and distinct traditions worldwide, we should be mindful of the issue of the extent to which Buddhist mystic claims, for example, are compatible with the theistic. In two instances, similar mystic reportage has been grouped together across tradition. But in other cases, it seems the experiences, as expressed even in our rather narrow survey are quite different. Does such difference undermine the cognitive thesis?

The question of the cognitive value of mystical experience is not the only dimension of mysticism with possible ramifications for philosophy. With the selection from Martin Buber, and with some of the other selections as well, it is useful to think about questions of meaning and value. Defenders of mysticism typically find a deep connection between a mystical pursuit and life values. In Indian traditions (Hindu, Buddhist, also the minor traditions), a mystical experience is said to be a "person's supreme good" (Sanskrit: *parama-puruṣa-artha*), and, we shall see, this reverberates with some Western valuations of mysticism.

Perfect Beauty

From *Symposium* by Plato, Alexander Nehamas and Paul Woodruff, translators, 1989

Plato, we learned above, distinguishes God and the Ideal, or Form, of the Good, which is identical with Ideal Beauty. Crucial to his teaching about the possibilities for an individual is what has come to be called the Ladder of Love, climbing which a soul reaches a mystical contemplation and life's supreme good.

The individual soul learns to love the Good and Beautiful by first loving finite objects that are good and beautiful. Thus for Plato the Good and perfect Beauty explain the orientation of souls in work and all forms of self-initiated activity. (This idea informs one line of Aristotle's first-cause argument, where God would be the Unmoved Mover: see above.) Even when an individual attains to direct knowledge of the Ideal—as depicted in the passage excerpted here—activity does not cease. Rather, just as God creates in perfect love and harmony the great rhythms of the natural world, so does the mystic philosopher within the social universe.

[DIOTIMA continued:] "After this he must think that the beauty of people's souls is more valuable than the beauty of their bodies, so that if someone is decent in his soul, even though he is scarcely blooming in his body, our lover must be content to love and care for him and to seek to give birth to such ideas as will make young men better. The result is that our lover will be forced to gaze at the beauty of activities and laws and to see that all this is akin to itself, with the result that he will think that the beauty of bodies is a thing of no importance. After customs he must move on to various kinds of knowledge. The result is that he will see the beauty of knowledge and be looking mainly not at beauty in a single example—as a servant would who favored the beauty of a little boy or a man or a single custom (being a slave, of course, he's low and small-minded)—but the lover is turned to the great sea of beauty, and gazing upon this, he gives birth to many gloriously beautiful ideas and theories, in unstinting love of wisdom,[1] until, having grown and been strengthened there, he catches sight of such knowledge, and it is the knowledge of such beauty . . .

"Try to pay attention to me," [Diotima] said, "as best you can. You see, the man who has been thus far guided in matters of Love, who has beheld beautiful things in the right order and correctly, is coming now to the goal of Loving: all of a sudden he will catch sight of something wonderfully beautiful in its nature; that, Socrates, is the reason for all his earlier labors:

"First, it always *is* and neither comes to be nor passes away, neither waxes nor wanes. Second, it is not beautiful this way and ugly that way, nor beautiful at one time and ugly at another, nor beautiful in relation to one thing and ugly in relation to another; nor is it beautiful here but ugly there, as it would be if it were beautiful for some people and ugly for others. Nor will the beautiful appear to him in the guise of a face or hands or anything else that belongs to the body. It will not appear to him as one idea or one kind of knowledge. It is not anywhere in another thing, as in an animal, or in earth, or in heaven, or in anything else, but itself by itself with itself, it is always one in form; and all the other beautiful things share in that, in such a way that when those others come to be or pass away, this does not become the least bit smaller or greater nor suffer any change. So when someone rises by these stages, through loving boys correctly, and begins to see this beauty, he has almost grasped his goal. This is what it is to go aright, or be lead by another, into the mystery of Love: one goes always upwards for the sake of this Beauty, starting out from beautiful things and using them like rising stairs: from one body to two and from two to all beautiful bodies, then from beautiful bodies to beautiful customs, and from customs to learning beautiful things, and from these lessons he arrives in the end at this lesson, which is learning of this very Beauty, so that in the end he comes to know just what it is to be beautiful.

---

[1] "Love of wisdom": *philosophia.*

Mystical Experience Transcendent of Reason and Philosophy

From the autobiography of Al-Ghazzali in *The Varieties of Religious Experience* by William James (James' English translation from A. Schmölders' French translation), 1929

One might get the idea from Plato that mysticism amounts to a kind of intellectual contemplation. Platonic mysticism may indeed be of this type, and mystics of other traditions—for example, Teresa (see the next selection)—do sometimes assert the importance of an intellectual element. However, the predominant element is experiential, so much so that any adequate definition or account of mysticism would have to rule out any mere intellectualism. This is not to say that the question of how much the intellect (prior beliefs, expectations, etc.) inform or shape the experience is not important philosophically. But it is right to stress the experiential with all mysticism.

In this excerpt from the great Persian and Islamic mystic, al-Ghazālī (1058–1111), the predominance of the experiential over the intellectual is highlighted through an analogy of the difference between a medical understanding of intoxication and a first-person perspective of actually being intoxicated.

Al-Ghazālī belonged to the Islamic mystic order known as Sufism. In Sufism as in many mystic traditions, asceticism is encouraged as preparing one for, or making possible, a spiritual ecstasy. Al-Ghazālī renounced family and wealth, wore the simple wool robe of a Sufi, and wandered the Islamic world absorbed in prayer and meditation for a period of ten years.

In his writing, al-Ghazālī is critical of philosophy, of Avicenna and his followers in particular, who try through reason and argument to establish the existence of God, the eternity of the world, the "unicity" of God, and so on. Al-Ghazālī's intent seems to be that we should have less faith in reason and our own mental efforts and more faith in God.

This selection is taken from the classic, The Varieties of Religious Experience, *by William James, who made an English abridgment of a French translation to accentuate al-Ghazālī's anti-intellectual themes (which, by the way, accord well with James's own brand of mystic fideism: see the discussion under Faith and Reason).*

M[onsieur]. Schmölders has translated a part of Al-Ghazzali's autobiography into French:

"The Science of the Sufis," says the Moslem author, "aims at detaching the heart from all that is not God, and at giving to it for sole occupation the meditation of the divine being. Theory being more easy for me than practice, I read [certain books] until I understood all that can be learned by study and hearsay. Then I recognized that what pertains most exclusively to their method is just what no study can grasp, but only transport, ecstasy, and the transformation of the soul. How great, for example, is the difference between knowing the definitions of health, of satiety, with their causes and conditions, and being really healthy or filled. How different to know in what drunkenness consists—as being a state occasioned by a vapor that rises from the stomach—and *being* drunk effectively. Without doubt, the drunken man knows neither the definition of drunkenness nor what makes it interesting for science. Being drunk, he knows nothing; whilst the physician, although not drunk, knows well in what drunkenness consists, and what are its pre-disposing conditions. Similarly there is a difference between knowing the nature of abstinence, and *being* abstinent or having one's soul detached from the world.—Thus I had learned what words could teach of Sufism, but what was left could be learned neither by study nor through the ears, but solely by giving one's self up to ecstasy and leading a pious life.

"Reflecting on my situation, I found myself tied down by a multitude of bonds—temptations on every side. Considering my teaching, I found it was impure before God. I saw myself struggling with all my might to achieve glory and to spread my name. [Here follows an account of his six months' hesitation to break away from the conditions of his life at Bagdad [Baghdad], at the end of which he fell ill with a paralysis of the tongue.] Then, feeling my own weakness, and having entirely given up my own will, I repaired to God like a man in distress who has no more resources. He answered, as he answers the wretch who invokes him. My heart no longer felt any difficulty in renouncing glory, wealth, and my children. So I quitted Bagdad, and reserving from my fortune only what was indispensable for my subsistence, I distributed the rest. I went to Syria, where I remained about two years, with no other occupation than living in retreat and solitude, conquering my desires, combating my passions, training myself to purify my soul, to make my character perfect, to prepare my heart for meditating on God—all according to the methods of the Sufis, as I had read of them.

"This retreat only increased my desire to live in solitude, and to complete the purification of my heart and fit it for meditation. But the vicissitudes of the times, the affairs of the family, the need of subsistence, changed in some respects my primitive resolve, and interfered with my plans for a purely solitary life. I had never yet found myself completely in ecstasy, save in a few single hours; nevertheless, I kept the hope of attaining this state. Every time that the accidents led me astray, I sought to return; and in this situation I spent ten years. During this solitary state things were revealed to me which it is impossible either to describe or to point out. I recognized for certain that the Sufis are assuredly walking in the path of God. Both in their acts and in their inaction, whether internal or external, they are illumined by the light which proceeds from the prophetic source. The first condition for a Sufi is to purge his heart entirely of all that is not God. The next key of the contemplative life consists in the humble prayers which escape from the fervent soul, and in the meditations on God in which the heart is swallowed up entirely. But in reality this is only the beginning of the Sufi life, the end of Sufism being total absorption in God. The intuitions and all that precede are, so to speak, only the threshold for those who enter. From the beginning, revelations take place in so flagrant a shape that the Sufis see before them, whilst wide awake, the angels and the souls of the prophets. They hear their voices and obtain their favors. Then the transport rises from the perception of forms and figures to a degree which escapes all expression, and which no man may seek to give an account of without his words involving sin.

"Whosoever has had no experience of the transport knows of the true nature of prophetism nothing but the name. He may meanwhile be sure of its existence, both by experience and by what he hears the Sufis say. As there are men endowed only with the sensitive faculty who reject what is offered them in the way of objects of the pure under-standing, so there are intellectual men who reject and avoid the things perceived by the prophetic faculty. A blind man can understand nothing of colors save what he has learned by narration and hearsay. Yet God has brought prophetism near to men in giving them all a state analogous to it in its principal characters. This state is sleep. If you were to tell a man who was himself without experience of such a phenomenon that there are people who, at times swoon away so as to resemble dead men, and who [in dreams] yet perceive things that are hidden, he would deny it [and give his reasons]. Nevertheless, his arguments would be refuted by actual experience. Wherefore, just as the understanding is a stage of human life in which an eye opens to discern various intellectual objects uncompre-hended by sensation; just so in the prophetic the sight is illumined by a light which uncov-ers hidden things and objects which the intellect fails to reach. The chief properties of prophetism are perceptible only during the transport, by those who embrace the Sufi life. The prophet is endowed with qualities to which you possess nothing analogous, and which consequently you cannot possibly understand. How should you know their true nature, since one knows only what one can comprehend? But the transport which one attains by the method of the Sufis is like an immediate perception, as if one touched the objects with one's hand."

Theistic Mystical Experience

From *The Interior Castle* by Saint Teresa of Avila, John Venard, translator, 1988 • From *The Synthesis of Yoga* by Sri Aurobindo, 1973

Reports of theistic mystical experience come from both East and West, namely, from In-dian theistic mystic traditions as well as from the Christian, etc. Here are bits of mystic testimony from the great Spanish and Catholic mystic, Teresa of Avila (1515–1582), and the modern Indian mystic and philosopher, Aurobindo, whose life and metaphysics were sketched earlier (under Speculative Spiritual Metaphysics).

Teresa became Saint Teresa in 1622, canonized by Church procedure, and pro-claimed by Pope Paul VI in 1970 a "Doctor of the Church." William James refers to her often in his Varieties, *and several philosophers have followed James in scrutinizing her claims (see the Guide to Further Reading).*

The selection from Aurobindo comes from a book devoted to the teaching of yoga, not from Aurobindo's explicitly philosophic writings. Yoga (in Sanskrit: discipline) is a mystic path. Aurobindo calls the discipline he followed and recommends integral yoga, aiming at personal transformation in accordance with the spiritual metaphysics he advances (see above). Note that his interpretation of yogic experience, while perhaps not differing so entirely from Teresa's understanding of her special experiences, contrasts sharply with the mystic metaphysics found in the Yoga-sūtra: *see the selection from the* Yoga-sūtra *later in this section.*

FROM *THE INTERIOR CASTLE*

OCCASIONS WHEN GOD SUSPENDS THE SOUL IN RAPTURE, ECSTASY OR TRANCE

Because our nature is timid and lowly,
great courage is necessary
to achieve union with so great a Lord;
and the Lord, to encourage us,
and knowing our weakness,
continues to grant favors.
Unless God granted us the strength
it would be impossible to go on;
so God bestows raptures,
and it is of these that we shall now speak.

One kind of rapture is this:
though not actually engaged in prayer,
the soul is struck by some word,
which it either remembers
or hears spoken by God.
It seems to catch fire and spring to new life;
its sins are cleansed,
and God unites it with himself
in a way none can understand,
save the soul and God.
The soul is incapable
of speaking of it afterwards,
but at the time
is not deprived of the interior senses.
The soul has never before been so awake
to the things of God,
or had such light and knowledge of God;
even though both senses and faculties
were completely absorbed.

Also, if the soul has intellectual visions,
they cannot be described,
except perhaps after the soul
has regained its senses;
the profit to the soul is so great
that it cannot be exaggerated.
The favors are imprinted in the soul,
in its very depths,

and they are never forgotten.
Just as marvelous things
were revealed to Moses
when he saw the burning bush,
and these things gave him courage
to do what he did for the people of Israel,
and Jacob learned great secrets
in the vision of the ladder
ascending to the heavens,
so the soul is able to apprehend
supernatural truths
according to the pleasure of God revealing them,
without remembering in detail
all the things it has seen.

Remember, we are speaking of intellectual,
not imaginary visions,
and it is my belief
that if the soul does not understand
the secrets God is revealing,
they are not raptures at all,
but rather some form of absorption
proceeding from weakness.
If the soul is enraptured,
you can be sure
that God is taking the soul entirely to himself.
When He means to enrapture a soul,
it loses its power of breathing,
and cannot speak,
although the other senses
may remain active a little longer.
At other times,
it loses all the powers at once,
and the soul seems
to have departed from the body
and it seems not to breathe.
All this lasts only a short time,
but may be repeated again and again.
Complete ecstasy lasts only a short time.
This ecstasy, however,
has the effect of leaving the will
so completely absorbed,
and the understanding
so completely transported,
that the soul
seems incapable of grasping anything
that does not awaken the will to love.

When it comes to itself,
the soul is filled with ardent desires
to be used for God
in any way He pleases;
gladly it would give God a thousand lives,
and would wish every tongue on earth
to praise Him;
it has tremendous desires to do penances
and complains to God that it does not suffer.
With the aid of God, suffering becomes easy.

The soul suffers embarrassment from others
who notice this enraptured state;
this could be lack of humility,
but the Lord can bring comfort and reassurance;
it is certain that from now on
He intends to have the soul for himself,
whatever attacks may be made against her.
Henceforth the Lord will protect her
from the whole world
and indeed from hell itself.

SEVENTH MANSION

THE GREAT FAVORS IN THIS MANSION; THE DIFFERENCE BETWEEN SOUL AND SPIRIT

Before consummating the spiritual marriage,
our Lord brings the soul,
which He has now taken spiritually as His bride,
into this Mansion of His, the seventh.
He needs an abiding-place in the soul
as He has in heaven.
It becomes a second heaven.
In this Mansion,
everything is different from previous Mansions.
In those the soul was affected
only in its highest part;
the Lord united it with himself,
but He made it blind and dumb
to what was happening,
except for its vivid realization
of the nearness of God.

The faculties are all lost.
Now the scales are removed from its eyes;
it sees and understands something
of the favor given to it.
It is brought into this Mansion
by an intellectual vision,
in which the Most Holy Trinity reveals itself,
in all three Persons.
The spirit is enkindled and illumined
by a cloud of great brightness.
It sees these three Persons, individually,
yet, by a wonderful kind of knowledge,
it realizes that most certainly
all these three Persons
are one substance and one power
and one knowledge
and one God alone.
What we hold by faith,
the soul grasps by sight.
Nothing is seen by the eyes
either of the body or the soul;
it is not an imaginary vision,
but an intellectual vision.

All three Persons communicate themselves
to the soul, and speak to it,
explaining the words of the Gospel,
that "He and the Father and the Holy Spirit
will come to dwell
with the soul which loves Him
and keeps His commandments" (John 14:23).
What a difference between hearing these words,
and believing them,
and realizing how true they are!
The soul sees that these three Persons (of the trinity)
are in the interior of her soul,
in the most interior place.
She feels this divine companionship
within herself.

Not that she is unable to fix her mind on nothing else.
On the contrary,
she is in complete possession of her senses
and is more alert than before
in all that pertains to the service of God.
When not otherwise occupied,
she remains in this happy companionship.
She works more carefully than ever,

so as not to displease God,
but remains confident
that He will continue to give her
the most certain assurance of His presence.

This presence is not realized always
so fully or clearly
as when it first comes,
or as happens on certain occasions;
otherwise the soul could not go on living,
or think of anything else.
But it always has the awareness
of this companionship.

She is greatly assisted
to go onward to perfection
and to lose the fear
she had in the previous states;
she finds herself better in every way,
and the essential part of the soul
never moves from that dwelling place,
however numerous her trials and worries.
She seems to feel divided within herself,
but this is only apparent,
and is explained
by the division of soul and spirit,
which are different, though one.
Sometimes their operations seem to differ
just as the respective joys
which the Lord gives to the one and the other.
The soul is different from the faculties, too;
they are not one and the same.
All will be revealed about these things
in the life to come.

FROM *THE SYNTHESIS OF YOGA*

We may seek after him passionately and pursue the unseen beloved; but also the lover
whom we think not of, may pursue us, may come upon us in the midst of the world and
seize on us for his own whether at first we will or no. Even, he may come to us at first as
an enemy, with the wrath of love, and our earliest relations with him may be those of
battle and struggle. Where first there is love and attraction, the relations between the
Divine and the soul may still for long be chequered with misunderstanding and offense,
jealousy and wrath, strife and the quarrels of love, hope and despair and the pain of absence and separation. We throw up all the passions of the heart against him, till they are purified into a sole ecstasy of bliss and oneness. But that too is monotony; it is not possible
for the tongue of human speech to tell all the utter unity and all the eternal variety of the

Ananda [Bliss] of divine love. Our higher and our lower members are both flooded with it, the mind and life no less than the soul: even the physical body takes its share of the joy, feels the touch, is filled in all its limbs, veins, nerves with the flowing of the wine of the ecstasy, *amṛta.* Love and Ananda are the last word of being, the secret of secrets, the mystery of mysteries.

Monistic Mystical Experience

From *De Ornatu Spiritalium Nuptiarum* by Ruysbroeck in *Mysticism,* Evelyn Underhill, translator, 1930 • From *The Gospel of Sri Ramakrishna,* Swami Nikhilananda, translator, 1942

Earlier, under Absolute Brahman, we reviewed a selection from the Upanishads, along with the commentary of Śaṅkara, that seemed to be about a mystical experience revealing an identity between the individual consciousness and the supreme spiritual reality, Brahman or God. The passage reverberates in later Indian thought, both in mystical writing and in treatises that are more explicitly philosophical. But a unitive, or monistic, mystical experience is also reported, and glorified, in the West. Johannes Eckhart, or Meister Eckhart (1260–1327?), often said to be the founder of German mysticism, and Jan van Ruysbroeck (1293–1381), a Flemish mystic, are two of the more famous Western representatives of mysticism of the monistic variety. The first excerpt is a brief selection from Ruysbroeck (who, we may note, figures prominently in philosophic defenses of this type of mysticism: see the Guide to Further Reading, in particular books by W. T. Stace and Nelson Pike).

Ruysbroeck, like Eckhart before him, encountered Church pressure against his monistic themes. Although in his earlier writings it seems clear that he believes in the identity of God and soul and in the possibility of experience of the identity, in his later writings he travelled more the route of the Indian theist, finding analogies to illustrate simultaneous difference and identity. The selection here is from Ruysbroeck's earlier writing, and boldly suggests identity.

Ramakrishna (1834–1886) is India's most famous nineteenth-century mystic and religious figure, rivalled only by his eloquent and well-travelled disciple, Swami Vivekananda (about whom, see under Religious Pluralism). The second excerpt recounts a monistic experience of Ramakrishna's, and echoes Śaṅkara. But Ramakrishna, unlike Śaṅkara, believes in the reality of the world, seeing all religions as valid, as paths to a single Supreme, a Divine Mother in his preferred conception. Thus for Ramakrishna monistic experience shows only an aspect of the Divine. His overall view is that of henotheism, and he and the movement he launched through the missionary work of Vivekananda and other disciples are commonly acclaimed as spearheading a resurgence of Hindu philosophy in the late nineteenth century.

FROM *DE ORNATU SPIRITALIUM NUPTIARUM*

. . . Now this active meeting, and this loving embrace, are in their essence fruitive and un-conditioned; for the infinite Undifferentiation of the Godhead is so dark and so naked of all image, that it conceals within itself all the divine qualities and works, all the attributes of the Persons, in the all-enfolding richness of the Essential Unity, and brings about a divine fruition in the Abyss of the Ineffable. And here there is a death in fruition, and a melting and dying into the nudity of Pure Being; where all the Names of God, and all conditions, and all the living images which are reflected in the mirror of divine truth, are absorbed into the Ineffable Simplicity, the Absence of image and of knowledge. For in this limitless Abyss of Simplicity, all things are embraced in the bliss of fruition; but the Abyss itself re-mains uncomprehended, except by the Essential Unity. The Persons and all that which lives in God, must give place to this. For there is nought else here but an eternal rest in the fruitive embrace of an outpouring love: and this is the wayless Being that all interior souls have chosen above all other things. This is the dim silence where all lovers lose themselves."

FROM *THE GOSPEL OF SRI RAMAKRISHNA*   19th century Hindu scholar

Monday, March 15, 1886

About seven o'clock in the morning Sri Ramakrishna felt a little better. He talked to the devotees, sometimes in a whisper, sometimes by signs. Narendra, Rakhal, Latu, M., Gopal of Sinthi, and others were in the room. They sat speechless and looked grave, think-ing of the Master's suffering of the previous night.

MASTER (*to the devotees*): "Do you know what I see right now? I see that it is God Himself who has become all this. It seems to me that men and other living beings are made of leather, and that it is God Himself who, dwelling inside these leather cases, moves the hands, the feet, the heads. I had a similar vision once before, when I saw houses, gardens, roads, men, cattle—all made of One Substance; it was as if they were all made of wax.

"I see that it is God Himself who has become the block, the executioner, and the vic-tim for the sacrifice."

As he describes this staggering experience, in which he realizes in full the identity of all within the One Being, he is overwhelmed with emotion and exclaims, "Ah! What a vision!"

Immediately Sri Ramakrishna goes into samādhi. He completely forgets his body and the outer world. The devotees are bewildered. Not knowing what to do, they sit still.

Presently the Master regains partial consciousness of the world and says: "Now I have no pain at all. I am my old self again."

The devotees are amazed to watch this state of the Master, beyond pleasure and pain, weal and woe.

He casts his glance on Latu and says: "There is Loto. He bends his head, resting it on the palm of his hand. I see that it is God Himself who rests His head on His hand."

Yogic Mystical Experience

From *Yoga-sūtra*, Stephen H. Phillips, translator • From *Yoga: Immortality and Freedom* by Mircea Eliade, Willard R. Trask, translator, 1958

The word yoga *means "ascetic discipline" in Sanskrit, a discipline aimed at liberation (from rebirth and suffering), enlightenment, or an ecstatic transcendence of the world—according to several distinct religious and metaphysical systems advocating yogic practices. The selection from the* Yoga-sūtra, *the preeminent classical textbook of yoga practice (edited into its current shape, c. 400* CE*), provides one account, among many (Vedāntic, Buddhist, etc.), of the goal of yoga practice.*

The Yoga-sūtra *is both a "how-to" book on yoga practice, and a treatise of metaphysics interpreting yoga practice and experience in the terms of a simple dualism of consciousness and nature. There are many conscious beings, and a single nature. Normally, a conscious being is involved in nature, misidentifying himself (or herself: the conscious being in reality has no sex) with natural processes—bodily, emotional, and mental. The goal of yoga, according to the* Yoga-sūtra, *is disidentification, at least according to the* Yoga-sūtra's *metaphysical point of view.*

Some argue that the transcendence involved in yoga accomplishment—the experience itself—occurs independently of the dualist metaphysics, and may be understood in other terms. Among these scholars and philosophers is Mircea Eliade.

Eliade (1907–1991), a Romanian scholar and longtime professor at the University of Chicago who has had enormous influence within religious studies during the past several decades, characterizes such transcendence sympathetically, trying to stay close to his reading of what actually occurs to those accomplished in methods of yoga (principally, breath-control and meditation to the point of "mental silence").

According to Eliade's account, yogic mysticism seems to accord with unitive or monistic mysticism. However, as mentioned, the official metaphysics of the Yoga-sūtra *is a dualism of consciousness and nature. This teaching is not considered by Eliade in the excerpted passage. The* Yoga-sūtra *claims that the true person or self, discovered in yogic meditation and knowledge, is entirely aloof from the world, a purely witness self. In reality, consciousness and nature are disjoined. The summum bonum is* kaivalya, *"(self-rapt) aloneness."*

Nor is there a creator God. The Yoga-sūtra *uses the Sanskrit word for God,* īśvara, *but it is supposed to refer to the only conscious being that does not need to practice yoga in order to realize the truth of separateness from nature (*kaivalya*). God is thus an archetypally liberated yogin. The origin of the world and of awareness of the world is left unexplained. Eliade apparently wishes to ignore this metaphysical picture better to bring out what he sees as yoga experience.*

FROM *YOGA-SŪTRA*

1.1. Now instruction in yoga.

1.2. Yoga is cessation of the fluctuations of mind and awareness.

1.3. Then the seer (the conscious being) rests in the true self.

1.4. At other times, he identifies with the fluctuations.

1.5. The fluctuations are of five types, and are either detrimental or nondetrimental.

1.6. [The five are] (a) veridical awareness, (b) its opposite (illusion), (c) thought and imagination, (d) sleep, and (e) memory. . . .

1.12. The cessation of the fluctuations is accomplished through practice and disinterestedness.

1.13. Practice is effort to hold fast the cessation.

1.14. Practice is firmly grounded only through proper effort uninterrupted and stretching over a long time.

1.15. Disinterestedness is the intention to control on the part of someone who has no desire either for worldly or revealed objects. . . .

1.33. Calming illumination of the mind is furthered through friendship, compassion, happiness, and indifference to objects whether pleasant or painful, virtuous or full of vice.

1.34. Or, this can be brought about by controlled exhalation and retention of the breath.

1.35. Or, this (calming illumination) is brought about by particular activity centered on an object and arresting mentality.

1.36. Or, it is brought about by activity that is free from sorrow and luminous.

1.37. Or, it is achieved when the mind contemplates an object devoid of allure.

1.38. Another means involves the mind brought to a knowledge of sleep and dreams.

1.39. Or, from meditation as is appropriate. . . .

2.2. Yoga is practiced to achieve mystic trance as well as to attentuate the detrimental fluctuations or afflictions (*kleśa*).

2.3. The afflictions are spiritual ignorance, egoism, passion, hatred, and attachment to life. . . .

2.11. These (detrimental) fluctuations are banished through meditation.

2.12. (Action-inducing) karmic latencies, to be experienced in the current or in future births, are rooted in the afflictions.*

*The Yogic theory of karma supposes that every action creates a subliminal impression (or karmic latency) that impels future action, whether in this or a future lifetime.

2.13. So long as this root endures its fruit will endure, the (triple) fruit, namely, of birth, life, and apparent enjoyment.

2.14. These three bring joy or suffering according to the merit or lack thereof (in accumulated karmic latencies).

2.15. A person of discriminating judgment sees all as suffering because of the pain in continual change, in tortured states of mind, and in subliminal latencies. Suffering is caused by conflicting fluctuations.

2.16. Future suffering is to be banished.

2.17. That which is to be banished stands caused by a conjunction of the seer (the conscious being) and that to be seen (nature).

2.18. What is to be seen (i.e., nature) is characterized by the (three qualities or strands) of intelligence, activity, and inertia; it includes the gross elements and the sense organs, and has as its *raison d'être* enjoyments for or liberation of the conscious being. . . .   raison for being

2.22. Although destroyed (for the liberated) yogin whose purpose is accomplished, nature is not destroyed for others (who are not liberated), because she is common among them.

2.23. The conjunction between the power of phenomena and the power of their lord (the conscious being) is caused by a perception of the two's identity.

2.24. Spiritual ignorance is its reason (i.e., the reason the conjunction endures).

2.25. When spiritual ignorance is no longer, the conjunction is no longer. This is the relinquishment, the "aloneness" (*kaivalya*, i.e., salvation) of the seer (the conscious being).

2.26. Unbroken practice of discriminative discernment is the way to that relinquishment.

2.27. For such a yogin, sevenfold wisdom and insight (*prajñā*) arise as the highest foundation.

2.28. By practice of the "limbs of yoga," impurity is attentuated. Awareness is illuminated up to discriminative discernment.

2.29. (Ethical) restraints, constraints, *āsanas* [yogic postures, stretching exercises] breath control, withdrawal of the senses (and three stages of meditation, viz.,), concentration, "meditation," and mystic trance are the eight "limbs of yoga."

2.30. Of these, the restraints are noninjury (*ahiṃsā*), truthfulness, refraining from stealing, celibacy, and lack of avarice. (greed)

2.31. These practiced universally, irrespective of station and circumstance of time and place, constitute the "great vow."

2.32. The constraints are purity, contentment, asceticism, self-study, and focusing on God (as the archetypal liberated yogin). . . .

3.1. Concentration is binding the mind down to a single spot.

3.2. Of the three (stages of meditation), meditation proper (*dhyāna*) is a single ideational focus.

3.3. Mystic trance is this carried to the point where there is illumination only of the object as object, empty, as it were, of what it essentially is.

3.4. The three together are called "conscious power" (*saṃyama*).

3.5. Through its mastery comes the light of wisdom and insight (*prajñā*).

3.49. The yogin whose awareness is restricted to the perception of the difference between (the strand of nature called) intelligence (*sattva*) and the conscious being achieves lordship over all states of being and omniscience as well.

3.50. Through disinterest in that achievement arises aloneness (*kaivalya*) in the attenuation of the seeds of defects. . . .

3.55. When the intelligence (strand, i.e., *sattva*) and the conscious being are equal in purity, "aloneness" ensues. . . .

4.15. Since, with regard to one and the same object, mind (*citta*) differs (on different occasions of perception), the two (*citta* and objects) have a distinct mode of being.

4.16. And to exist a thing does not depend on a single mind or awareness (*citta*). When it is not cognized by that mind, what then would it be?

4.17. Something is known or unknown to a particular mind, depending on the coloring conferred.

4.18. The fluctuations of mind are always known to their lord (the conscious being), since the conscious being (*puruṣa*) is unchanging.

4.19. That (the *citta*) is not self-luminous, because it is something to be perceived.

4.20. And there is no possibility of cognizing both (objects and subject) at the same time.

4.21. It would be to assume too much to require one intelligence after another in order that a single mind or awareness be perceived. This would also mean memory's (impossibility because of) confusion.*

4.22. Self-awareness occurs when the mind assumes the form of consciousness that (as the nature of the conscious being) is transcendently unchanging.

*The argument seems to be that the unity of the conscious being accounts for our sense of mental unity, including memory.

4.23. A mind (*citta*) that is colored by both the seer and that to be seen is capable of cognizing anything.

4.24. Although the mind is moved by countless subliminal valences, it works by unifying (diversities) for the sake of the other (the conscious being).

4.25. For one who sees the distinction (between nature and the conscious being), the projection of sense of self in nature ceases.

4.26. Then the mind settling into deep discrimination is carried on toward (reflecting) the aloneness (of the conscious being).

4.27. In the gaps (or weaknesses) of discrimination, other ideational presentations (i.e., distractions) may arise by force of (unexhausted) subliminal valences.

4.28. These are banished like the afflictions, in the ways explained. . . .

4.34. Aloneness (*kaivalya,* the *summum bonum*) entails the reversal of the course of the strands or qualities of nature, now empty of meaning and value for the conscious being. Or, it may be understood as the power of consciousness returned and established in its own true self.

FROM *YOGA: IMMORTALITY AND FREEDOM*

Samādhi [mystic ecstasy] with all its tantric equivalents, is by its very nature a paradoxical state, for it is empty and at the same time fills being and thought to repletion.

Let us note that the most important yogic and tantric experiences realize a similar paradox. In *prāṇāyāma* [breath control], life coexists with holding the breath (a holding that is in fact in flagrant contradiction to life); in the fundamental tantric experience (the "return of semen"), "life" coincides with "death," the "act" becomes "virtuality." It goes without saying that the paradox is implied in the very function of Indian ritual (as, of course, in every other ritual); for, by the power of ritual, some ordinary object incorporates the divinity, a "fragment" (in the case of the Vedic sacrifice, the brick of the altar) coincides with the "Whole" (the god Prajāpati), nonbeing with Being. Regarded from this point of view (that of the phenomenology of paradox), *samādhi* is seen to be situated on a line well known in the history of religions and mysticisms—that of the coincidence of opposites. It is true that, in this case, the coincidence is not merely symbolic, but concrete, experiential. Through *samādhi,* the yogin transcends opposites and, in a unique experience, unites emptiness and superabundance, life and death, Being and nonbeing. Nor is this all. Like all paradoxical states, *samādhi* is equivalent to a reintegration of the different modalities of the real in a single modality—the undifferentiated completeness of precreation, the primordial Unity. The yogin who attains to *asamprajñāta samādhi* [the highest *samādhi*] also realizes a dream that has obsessed the human spirit from the beginnings of its history—to coincide with the All, to recover Unity, to re-establish the initial nonduality, to abolish time and creation (i.e., the multiplicity and heterogeneity of the cosmos); in particular, to abolish the twofold division of the real into object-subject.

It would be a gross error to regard this supreme reintegration as a mere regression to primordial nondistinction. It can never be repeated too often that Yoga, like many other mysticisms, issues on the plane of paradox and not on a commonplace and easy extinction of consciousness. . . . from time immemorial India has known the many and various trances and ecstasies obtained from intoxicants, narcotics, and all the other elementary means of emptying consciousness; but any degree of methodological conscience will show us that we have no right to put *samādhi* among these countless varieties of spiritual escape. Liberation is not assimilable with the "deep sleep" of prenatal existence, even if the recovery of totality through undifferentiated enstasis [*samādhi*] seems to resemble the bliss of the human being's fetal preconsciousness. One essential fact must always be borne in mind: the yogin works on all levels of consciousness and of the subconscious, for the purpose of opening the way to transconsciousness (knowledge-possession of the Self, the *puruṣa*). He enters into "deep sleep" and into the "fourth state" (*turīya*, the cataleptic state) with the utmost lucidity; he does not sink into self-hypnosis. The importance that all authors ascribe to the yogic states of *super*consciousness shows us that the final reintegration takes place in *this* direction, and not in a trance, however profound. In other words: the recovery, through *samādhi*, of the initial nonduality introduces a new element in comparison with the primordial situation (that which existed before the twofold division of the real into object-subject). That element is *knowledge* of unity and bliss. There is a "return to the beginning," but with the difference that the man "liberated in this life" recovers the original situation enriched by the dimensions of *freedom* and *transconsciousness*. To express it differently, he does not return automatically to a "given" situation; he reintegrates the original completeness after having established a new and paradoxical mode of being—*consciousness of freedom,* which exists nowhere in the cosmos, neither on the levels of life nor on the levels of "mythological divinity" (the gods, *devas*)—which exists only in the Supreme Being, Īśvara. It is here that we become better aware of the initiatory character of Yoga. For in initiation, too, one "dies" to be "reborn"; but this new birth is not a repetition of natural birth; the candidate does not return to the profane world to which he has just died during his initiation; he finds a sacred world corresponding to a new mode of being that is *inaccessible to the "natural" (profane) level of existence.*

One would be tempted to see in this ideal—the conscious conquest of freedom—the justification offered by Indian thought for the fact, the apparently cruel and useless fact, that the world exists, that man exists, and that his existence in the world is an uninterrupted succession of suffering and despair. For, by liberating himself, man creates the spiritual dimension of freedom, and "introduces" it into the cosmos and life—that is, into blind and tragically conditioned modes of existence.

Buddhist *satori* Experience

From *The Three Pillars of Zen* by Phillip Kapleau, 1965

The practice of meditation, or zazen, *according to precepts of Zen Buddhism is arduous, requiring heroic efforts of concentration. The difficulty of the path is portrayed in these excerpts from diaries and other personal writings from modern Zen novitiates from all over the world.*

*The editor of the book from which these reports are taken, Philip Kapleau, was for many years the resident monk and director of the Zen Meditation Center, Rochester, New York. Kapleau tells us that he has selected these accounts to show that enlightenment (*satori*) experience is a real possibility for people living now in our hectic age, not only for "monks isolated from the hurly-burly." Though two reports are from Americans, most were originally published in Japanese.*

MR. K. Y., A JAPANESE EXECUTIVE, AGE 47 / NOVEMBER 27, 1953 /

Dear Nakagawa-roshi:

Thank you for the happy day I spent at your monastery.

You remember the discussion which arose about Self-realization centering around that American. At that time I hardly imagined that in a few days I would be reporting to you my own experience. . . .

It so happened that that day my younger brother and his wife were staying at my home, and I told them about my visit to your monastery and about that American who had come to Japan again only to attain enlightenment. In short, I told them all the stories you had told me, and it was after eleven thirty before I went to bed.

At midnight I abruptly awakened. At first my mind was foggy, then suddenly that quotation flashed into my consciousness: "I came to realize clearly that Mind is no other than mountains, rivers, and the great wide earth, the sun and the moon and the stars." And I repeated it. Then all at once I was struck as though by lightning, and the next instant heaven and earth crumbled and disappeared. Instantaneously, like surging waves, a tremendous delight welled up in me, a veritable hurricane of delight, as I laughed loudly and wildly: "Ha, ha, ha, ha, ha, ha! There's no reasoning here, no reasoning at all! Ha, ha, ha!" The empty sky split in two, then opened its enormous mouth and began to laugh uproariously: "Ha, ha, ha!" Later one of the members of my family told me that my laughter had sounded inhuman.

I was now lying on my back. Suddenly I sat up and struck the bed[1] with all my might and beat the floor with my feet, as if trying to smash it, all the while laughing riotously. My wife and youngest, sleeping near me, were now awake and frightened. Covering my mouth with her hand, my wife exclaimed: "What's the matter with you? What's the matter with you?" But I wasn't aware of this until told about it afterwards. My son told me later he thought I had gone mad.

---

[1] This is not a Western but a traditional Japanese "bed," which consists of a quilted mattress two or three inches thick over the regular tatami mats.

"I've come to enlightenment! Shakyamuni and the Patriarchs haven't deceived me! They haven't deceived me!" I remember crying out. When I calmed down I apologized to the rest of the family, who had come downstairs frightened by the commotion.

Although twenty-four hours have elapsed, I still feel the aftermath of that earthquake. My entire body is still shaking. I spent all of today laughing and weeping by myself.

I am writing to report my experience in the hope that it will be of value to your monks, and because Yasutani-roshi urged me to.

Please remember me to that American. Tell him that even I, who am unworthy and lacking in spirit, can grasp such a wonderful experience when time matures. I would like to talk with you at length about many things, but will have to wait for another time.

P.S. That American was asking us whether it is possible for him to attain enlightenment in one week of sesshin. Tell him this for me: don't say days, weeks, years, or even lifetimes. Don't say millions or billions of *kalpa*. Tell him to vow to attain enlightenment though it take the infinite, the boundless, the incalculable future.

MIDNIGHT OF THE 28TH / [THESE DIARY ENTRIES WERE MADE DURING THE NEXT TWO DAYS]

Awoke thinking it 3 or 4 a.m., but clock said it was only 12:30.

Am totally at peace at peace at peace.

Feel numb throughout body, yet hands and feet jumped for joy for almost half an hour.

Am supremely free free free free free. . . .

The big clock chimes—not the clock but Mind chimes. The universe itself chimes. There is neither Mind nor universe. Dong, dong, dong!

I've totally disappeared. Buddha is! . . .

4 A.M. OF THE 29TH

Ding, dong! The clock chimed. This alone *is*! This alone *is*! There's no reasoning here.

Surely the world has changed [with enlightenment]. But in what way?

The ancients said the enlightened mind is comparable to a fish swimming. That's exactly how it is—there's no stagnation. I feel no hindrance. Everything flows smoothly, freely. Everything goes naturally. This limitless freedom is beyond all expression. What a wonderful world!

Dogen, the great teacher of Buddhism, said: "Zen is the wide, all-encompassing gate of compassion."

I am grateful, so grateful.

MR. P. K., AN AMERICAN EX-BUSINESSMAN, AGE 46 / DIARY EXTRACTS / NEW YORK, APRIL 1, 1953 /

. . . Belly aching all week, Doc says ulcers are getting worse. . . . Allergies kicking up too. . . . Can't sleep without drugs. . . . So miserable wish I had the guts to end it all.

APRIL 20, 1953

Attended S—'s Zen lecture today. As usual, could make little sense out of it. . . . Why do I go on with these lectures? Can I ever get satori listening to philosophic explanations of *prajñā* and *karuṇā** and why A isn't A and all the rest of that? What the hell is satori anyway? Even after four of S—'s books and dozens of his lectures, still don't know. I must be awfully stupid. . . . But I know this, Zen philosophy isn't ridding me of my pain or restlessness or that damn "nothing" feeling. . . .

Only last week a close friend complained: "You're forever spouting Zen philosophy, but you've hardly become more serene or considerate since you've begun studying it. If anything, it's made you supercilious and condescending. . . ."

SEPTEMBER 3, 1953

Quit business, sold apartment furniture and car. . . . Friends' unanimous judgment: "You're mad throwing up ten thousand a year for pie in the sky!" . . . Maybe. Or maybe they're the mad ones, piling up possessions and ulcers and heart disease. . . . I suspect some of them may even envy me. . . . If I didn't need to, I wouldn't be doing it, of this I'm positive, but I *am* frightened a little. Hope it's true about life at forty. . . . Bought ticket for Japan.

TOKYO, OCTOBER 6, 1953

How the features and mood of Japan have changed in seven years! The ghastly rubble and despairing faces have virtually disappeared. . . . Good to be back this time as a seeker instead of a carpetbagger with the Occupation. . . . Wonder what really brought me back? Was it the dignity of the Japanese, their patient endurance in the face of their untold sufferings that I marveled at? Was it the unearthly silence of Engaku Monastery and the deep peace it engendered within me whenever I strolled through its gardens or beneath its giant cryptomerias? . . .

DECEMBER 3, 1953

Pain in legs unbearable. . . . Why don't I quit? It's imbecilic trying to sit with this gruesome pain and taking these senseless wallops of the kyosaku plus Godo's insane shouting, it's masochism pure and simple. . . . Why did I leave Ryutaku-ji, why did I ever leave the United States? . . . But I can't quit now, what will I do? I must get satori, I must. . . .

What the devil is Mu, what can it be? . . . Of course! It's absolute prayer, the Self praying to itself. . . . How often as a student had I wanted to pray, but somehow it'd always seemed pointless and even silly to petition God for strength to cope with predicaments which He in his omniscience and omnipotence had allowed to arise in the first place. . . .

Tears welling up, how blissful is prayer for its own sake! . . . What do these tears mean? They're a sign of my helplessness, a tacit admission that my intellect, my ego, has reached the limit of its power. . . . Yes, tears are nature's benediction, her attempt to wash

---

*Sanscrit words meaning satori-wisdom and compassion, respectively.

away the grime of ego and soften the harsh outlines of our personalities become arid and tense through an egotistic reliance on the invincibility of reason. . . .

. . . What marvelous insights, I feel so good about them! I know I've progressed. I won't be surprised if satori hits me this very night!

Crack! Crack! "Stop dreaming! Only Mu!" roared the godo, walloping me. . . .

Dokusan! . . . "No, no, no! Didn't I tell you to concentrate simply on Mu? . . . Banish these thoughts! . . . Satori's not a matter of progress or regress, haven't I told you it's a leap? . . . You are to do this and only this: put your mind in the bottom of your belly and in-hale and exhale Mu. Is that clear?" . . . Why's he so harsh all of a sudden? . . . Even the hawks in the screen behind him have begun to glower at me. . . .

DECEMBER 5, 1953

. . . Am still aglow. . . . Satori will hit me any moment now, I know it, I feel it in my mar-row. . . . Won't my Zen friends in the United States be envious when I write I have satori! . . . Don't think of satori, you fool, think only of Mu! . . . Yes, Mu, Mu, Mu! . . . Damn it! I've lost it! . . . My excitement about satori has triggered off hundreds of thoughts—which leave me dispirited. . . . It's no use, satori's beyond me. . . .

OCTOBER 1, 1956

. . . In just two months three years will have elapsed since I first came to Hosshin-ji. . . . So much water has flowed under the stone bridge, or should I say so many stone bridges have flowed over the motionless water? . . . Have toiled with the monks in the heat of summer and shivered with them on snowy *takuhatsu,* felled trees, planted rice, cultivated the gar-dens, cleaned the outhouses, and worked in the kitchen with them. I've shared their heroic, dedicated moments, joined in their petty intrigues. . . .

Sitting sitting sitting one painful sesshin after another, then more zazen morning after morning, night after night and night into morning. . . . Dazzling insights and alluring visions have filed through my mind, but true illumination, satori, still eludes me. . . . Tangen-san, my wise monk-guide-interpreter-friend, solemnly assures me that just doing zazen wholeheart-edly each day brings greater rewards in serenity, clarity and purity than does a quickly at-tained satori which is unnurtured by further zazen. . . . Is this a consolation prize or another of Zen's paradoxes which needs the personal experience of enlightenment to be understood? . . . He insists I've gained in fortitude and purity, though I see little evidence of it. . . .

Every one of my allergies has disappeared, my stomach pains me only occasionally, I sleep well. . . . The dark fears which formerly haunted me, my cherished dreams and hopes, all these have withered away, leaving me lighter and with a clearer sense of the real. . . . But I'm still the hungry dog next to the tank of boiling fat that is satori: I can't taste it and I can't leave it. . . .

JULY 27, 1958

August 1 is my D-Day, the start of a one-week summer sesshin, my twentieth with Yasu-tani-roshi. . . . Sat two sesshin this month, one at Yasutani-roshi's temple and one at

Ryutaku-ji, besides day and night zazen in my own room, all in preparation for this Big Push. . . . My mind has a rare clarity and incisiveness. I must, I will break through. . . . For the first time I'm truly convinced I can.

AUGUST 1, 1958

. . . Sesshin's under way! . . . Quickly my concentration became strongly pitched. . . . Boring into Mu, thinking only Mu, breathing Mu. . . .

AUGUST 3, 1958

First two days passed quickly, uneventfully. . . .

AUGUST 4, 1958

Reached a white heat today. . . . Monitors whacked me time and again . . . their energetic stick wielding is no longer an annoyance but a spur. . . . Raced to the line-up with each clang of the dokusan bell to be first to see the roshi. . . . Hardly aware of pain in legs. . . . Was so eager to confront him that once or twice charged into his dokusan room without waiting for his signal. . . . When he asked me to show him Mu, I spontaneously seized his fan, fanned myself, picked up his handbell, rang it, and then left. . . .

At next dokusan he again asked for Mu. Quickly raised my hand as though to smack him. Didn't intend to really hit him, but the roshi, taking no chances, ducked. . . . How exhilarating these unpremeditated movements—clean and free. . . .

Animatedly the roshi warned: "You are now facing the last and toughest barrier between you and Self-realization. This is the time one feels, in the words of an ancient master, as though he were a mosquito attacking an iron bowl. But you must bore, bore, bore, tirelessly. . . . Come what may, don't let go of Mu. . . . Do zazen all night if you feel you may lose Mu in your sleep." . . .

"Mu'd" silently in temple garden till clock struck one. . . . Rose to exercise stiff, aching legs, staggered into nearby fence. Suddenly I realized: the fence and I are one formless wood-and-flesh. Mu. Of course! . . . Vastly energized by this . . . pushed on till the 4 a.m. gong.

AUGUST 5, 1958

Didn't intend to tell Roshi of my insight, but as soon as I came before him he demanded: "What happened last night?" . . . While I talked, his keen darting eyes X-rayed every inch of me, then slowly he began quizzing me: "Where do you see Mu? . . . How do you see Mu? . . . When do you see Mu? . . . How old is Mu? . . . What is the color of Mu? . . . What is the sound of Mu? . . . How much does Mu weigh?" . . .

Some of my answers came quickly, some haltingly. . . . Once or twice Roshi smiled, but mostly he listened in serene silence. . . . Then he spoke: "There are some roshi who might sanction such a tip-of-the-tongue taste as kensho, but—"

"I wouldn't accept sanction of such a picayune experience even if you wanted to grant it. Have I labored like a mountain these five years only to bring forth this mouse? I'll go on!" . . .

"Good! I respect your spirit."

Threw myself into Mu for another nine hours with such utter absorption that *I* completely vanished. . . . *I* didn't eat breakfast, *Mu* did. *I* didn't sweep and wash the floors after breakfast, *Mu* did. . . .

MRS. D. K., A CANADIAN HOUSEWIFE, AGE 35 / CANADA AND THE UNITED STATES

The early years of my life were quiet and uneventful. No tragedy touched me, and my parents were devoted to the bringing up of myself and my two sisters. It could almost be called an ideal childhood by most Western standards. Even from the first, though, there were recurrent periods of despair and loneliness which used to seep up from no apparent source, overflowing into streams of tears and engulfing me to the exclusion of everything else. At these times the painful feeling of being entrapped was overpowering, and simply to be a human being a wretched and ignominious lot. . . .

The following day, the seventh, I went before the roshi at dokusan once more. From the six or seven hours of continuous zazen I was so physically exhausted I could scarcely speak. Imperceptibly my mind had slipped into a state of unearthly clarity and awareness. I *knew,* and I knew I knew. Gently he began to question me: "What is the age of God? Give me Mu! Show me Mu at the railway station!" Now my inner vision was completely in focus and I responded without hesitation to all his tests, after which the roshi, my husband, who interpreted, and I all laughed joyfully together, and I exclaimed: "It's all so simple!" Whereupon the roshi told me that henceforth my practice in connection with succeeding koans was to be different. Rather than try to become one with a koan as heretofore with Mu, I was to ask myself profoundly: "What is the spirit of this koan?" When an answer came to me, I was to hang it on a peg, as it were, and do shikan-taza until my next dokusan provided me the opportunity to demonstrate my understanding of it.

Too stiff and tired to continue sitting, I slipped quietly from the main hall and returned to the bathhouse for a second bath. Never before had the road been so roadlike, the shops such perfect shops, nor the winter sky so unutterably a starry sky. Joy bubbled up like a fresh spring.

The days and weeks that followed were the most deeply happy and serene of my life. There was no such thing as a "problem." Things were either done or not done, but in any case there was neither worry nor consternation. Past relationships to people which had once caused me deep disturbance I now saw with perfect understanding. For the first time in my life I was able to move like the air, in any direction, free at last from the self which had always been such a tormenting bond to me.

SIX YEARS LATER

One spring day as I was working in the garden the air seemed to shiver in a strange way, as though the usual sequence of time had opened into a new dimension, and I became aware that something untoward was about to happen, if not that day, then soon. Hoping to prepare in some way for it, I doubled my regular sittings of zazen and studied Buddhist books late into each night.

A few evenings later, after carefully sifting through the *Tibetan Book of the Dead* and then taking my bath, I sat in front of a painting of the Buddha and listened quietly by candlelight to the slow movement of Beethoven's *A Minor Quartet,* a deep expression of man's self-renunciation, and then went to bed. The next morning, just after breakfast, I suddenly felt as though I were being struck by a bolt of lightning, and I began to tremble. All at once the whole trauma of my difficult birth flashed into my mind. Like a key, this opened dark rooms of secret resentments and hidden fears, which flowed out of me like poisons. Tears gushed out and so weakened me I had to lie down. Yet a deep happiness was there. . . . Slowly my focus changed: "*I*'m dead! There's nothing to call *me*! There never was a *me*! It's an allegory, a mental image, a pattern upon which nothing was ever modeled." I grew dizzy with delight. Solid objects appeared as shadows, and everything my eyes fell upon was radiantly beautiful.

These words can only hint at what was vividly revealed to me in the days that followed:

1. The world as apprehended by the senses is the least true (in the sense of complete), the least dynamic (in the sense of the eternal movement), and the least important in a vast "geometry of existence" of unspeakable profundity, whose rate of vibration, whose intensity and subtlety are beyond verbal description.

2. Words are cumbersome and primitive—almost useless in trying to suggest the true multi-dimensional workings of an indescribably vast complex of dynamic force, to contact which one must abandon one's normal level of consciousness.

3. The least act, such as eating or scratching an arm, is not at all simple. It is merely a visible moment in a network of causes and effects reaching forward into Unknowingness and back into an infinity of Silence, where individual consciousness cannot even enter. There is truly nothing to know, nothing that can be known.

4. The physical world is an infinity of movement, of Time-Existence. But simultaneously it is an infinity of Silence and Voidness. Each object is thus transparent. Everything has its own special inner character, its own karma or "life in time," but at the same time there is no place where there is emptiness, where one object does not flow into another.

5. The least expression of weather variation, a soft rain or a gentle breeze, touches me as a—what can I say?—miracle of unmatched wonder, beauty, and goodness. There is nothing to do: just to be is a supremely total act.

6. Looking into faces, I see something of the long chain of their past existence, and sometimes something of the future. The past ones recede behind the outer face like ever-finer tissues, yet are at the same time impregnated in it.

7. When I am in solitude I can hear a "song" coming forth from everything. Each and every thing has its own song; even moods, thoughts, and feelings have their finer songs. Yet beneath this variety they intermingle in one inexpressibly vast unity.

8. I feel a love which, without object, is best called lovingness. But my old emotional reactions still coarsely interfere with the expressions of this supremely gentle and effortless lovingness.

9. I feel a consciousness which is neither myself nor not myself, which is protecting or leading me into directions helpful to my proper growth and maturity, and propelling me away from that which is against that growth. It is like a stream into which I have flowed and, joyously, is carrying me beyond myself.

Theistic Mystic Philosophy

From *I And Thou* by Martin Buber, Walter Kaufmann, translator, 1970

All the selections we have so far reviewed in this section involve interpretation, at least in the sense that no experience itself is directly conveyed by words. Interpretation is involved even with just trying to say what an experience is like; all the more is it involved with trying to say what an experience indicates, is about, or reveals. All mystic reportage tries either to describe an experience from a first-person perspective—that is, phenomenologically—or to indicate what is taken to be revealed—for example, God, Brahman, "Emptiness." Some intellectual effort based on mystical experience is interpretive to a high degree in that it is concerned less with particular experiences than with a wide range of events, with deep context, perhaps with meaning for an entire society or multiple societies or whole epochs of human history. The selections from Martin Buber and Kitaro Nishida count as mystical writing in that they purport to be responsive to mystical experiences, but they are also interpretive efforts of the broader type.

Martin Buber (1878–1965) was professor of the philosophy of Jewish religion and ethics at Frankfurt-am-Main University from 1924 to 1933, holding during the period the only chair in Jewish religion at any German university. Buber was a principal spokesperson for and leader of German Jews during the rise of Hitler. Later, as professor of sociology of religion at Hebrew University in Israel he led the Yihud movement devoted to reconciliation between Arabs and Jews and to the formation of a binational state.

Buber is opposed to monistic mysticism, arguing that God is preeminently personal, a personal "other" that engages the "I" in a living and unpredictable relationship that demands complete authenticity, an entire presence to the other of one's self. Buber's classic, Ich und Du, *is usually translated "I and Thou," but it is really "I and You," since contemporary English, unlike German, does not differentiate between familiar and formal uses of a second-person pronoun. Buber takes the familiar "you" as symbolic of authentic personal engagement where our entire selves are involved in response. This "I-You" relationship contrasts with the "I-It," the impersonal, objectivist standpoint where we study others, theorize, and predict. It is comparatively easy, says Buber, to turn others—and God—into "it" or "it-s," to think and react to them impersonally, in that we do not then put ourselves, put the full "I," on the line. True mysticism involves personal encounter, according to this theistic philosopher and mystic, not immersion in some impersonal absolute. Buber takes monistic experience to be "physical delusion," spiritual error.*

All doctrines of immersion are based on the gigantic delusion of a human spirit bent back into itself—the delusion that spirit occurs in man. In truth it occurs from man—between man and what he is not. As the spirit bent back into itself renounces this sense, this sense of relation, he must draw into man that which is not man, he must psychologize world and God. This is the psychical delusion of the *spirit*. . . .

By its very nature the eternal You cannot become an It; because by its very nature it cannot be placed within measure and limit, not even within the measure of the immeasurable and the limit of the unlimited; because by its very nature it cannot be grasped as a sum of qualities, not even as an infinite sum of qualities that have been raised to transcendence; because it is not to be found either in or outside the world; because it cannot be experienced; because it cannot be thought; because we transgress against it, against that which has being, if we say: "I believe that he is"—even "he" is still a metaphor, while "you" is not.

And yet we reduce the eternal You ever again to an It, to something, turning God into a thing, in accordance with our nature. Not capriciously. The history of God as a thing, the way of the God-thing through religion and its marginal forms, through its illuminations and eclipses, the times when it heightened and when it destroyed life, the way from the living God and back to him again, the metamorphoses of the present; of embedment in forms of objectification, of conceptualization, dissolution, and renewal are one way, are *the* way.

The asserted knowledge and the posited action of the religions—whence do they come? The presence and strength of revelation (for all of them necessarily invoke some sort of revelation, whether verbal, natural, or psychic—there are, strictly speaking, only revealed religions), the presence and strength that man received through revelation—how do they become a "content"?

The explanation has two levels. The exoteric, psychic level is known when man is considered by himself, apart from history. The esoteric, factual one, the primal phenomenon of religion, when we afterward place him in history again. Both belong together.

Man desires to have God; he desires to have God continually in space and time. He is loath to be satisfied with the inexpressible confirmation of the meaning; he wants to see it spread out as something that one can take out and handle again and again—a continuum unbroken in space and time that insures life for him at every point and moment.

Life's rhythm of pure relation, the alternation of actuality and a latency in which only our strength to relate and hence also the presence, but not the primal presence, wanes, does not suffice man's thirst for continuity. He thirsts for something spread out in time, for duration. Thus God becomes an object of faith. Originally, faith fills the temporal gaps between the acts of relation; gradually, it becomes a substitute for these acts. The ever new movement of being through concentration and going forth is supplanted by coming to rest in an It in which one has faith. The trust-in-spite-of-all of the fighter who knows the remoteness and nearness of God is transformed ever more completely into the profiteer's assurance that nothing can happen to him because he has the faith that there is One who would not permit anything to happen to him.

The life-structure of the pure relation, the "lonesomeness" of the I before the You, the law that man, however he may include the world in his encounter, can still go forth only as a person to encounter God—all this also does not satisfy man's thirst for continuity. He thirsts for something spread out in space, for the representation in which the community of the faithful is united with its God. Thus God becomes a cult object. The cult, too, originally supplements the acts of relation, by fitting the living prayer, the immediate You-saying into a spatial context of great plastic power and connecting it with the life of the senses. And the cult, too, gradually becomes a substitute, as the personal prayer is no longer supported but rather pushed aside by communal prayer; and as the essential deed simply does not permit any rules, it is supplanted by devotions that follow rules.

In truth, however, the pure relation can be built up into spatio-temporal continuity only by becoming embodied in the whole stuff of life. It cannot be preserved but only put to the proof in action; it can only be done, poured into life. Man can do justice to the relation to God that has been given to him only by actualizing God in the world in accordance with his ability and the measure of each day, daily. This is the only genuine guarantee of continuity. The genuine guarantee of duration is that the pure relation can be fulfilled as the beings become You, as they are elevated to the You, so that the holy basic word sounds through all of them. Thus the time of human life is formed into an abundance of actuality; and although human life cannot and ought not to overcome the It-relation, it then becomes so permeated by relation that this gains a radiant and penetrating constancy in it. The moments of supreme encounter are no mere flashes of lightning in the dark but like a rising moon in a clear starry night. And thus the genuine guarantee of spatial constancy consists in this that men's relations to their true You, being radii that lead from all I-points to the center, create a circle. Not the periphery, not the community comes first, but the radii, the common relation to the center. That alone assures the genuine existence of a community.

The anchoring of time in a relation-oriented life of salvation and the anchoring of space in a community unified by a common center: only when both of these come to be and only as long as both continue to be, a human cosmos comes to be and continues to be around the invisible altar, grasped in the spirit out of the world stuff of the eon.

The encounter with God does not come to man in order that he may henceforth attend to God but in order that he may prove its meaning in action in the world. All revelation is a calling and a mission. But again and again man shuns actualization and bends back toward the revealer: he would rather attend to God than to the world. Now that he has bent back, however, he is no longer confronted by a You; he can do nothing but place a divine It in the realm of things, believe that he knows about God as an It, and talk about him. Even as the egomaniac does not live anything directly, whether it be a perception or an affection, but reflects on his perceiving or affectionate I and thus misses the truth of the process, thus the theomaniac (who, incidentally, can get along very well with the egomaniac in the very same soul) will not let the gift take full effect but reflects instead on that which gives, and misses both.

When you are sent forth, God remains presence for you; whoever walks in his mission always has God before him: the more faithful the fulfillment, the stronger and more constant the nearness. Of course, he cannot attend to God but he can converse with him. Bending back, on the other hand, turns God into an object. It appears to be a turning toward the primal ground, but belongs in truth to the world movement of turning away, even as the apparent turning away of those who fulfill their mission belongs in truth to the world movement of turning toward.

For the two basic metacosmic movements of the world—its expansion into its own being and returning to association [with God]—attain their supreme human form, the true spirit form of their struggle and conciliation, their mixture and separation, in the history of man's relation to God. It is in the return that the word is born on earth; in spreading out it enters the chrysalis of religion; in a new return it is reborn—with new wings.

Not caprice is at work here, although the movement toward the It may at times go so far that it holds down the movement of going forth again to the You and threatens to suffocate it.

Buddhist Mystic Philosophy

From *An Inquiry into the Good* by Kitarō Nishida, Masao Abe and Christopher Ives, translators, 1990

Like Martin Buber, the Japanese philosopher and mystic, Kitarō Nishida (1870–1945), finds a personal relationship at the heart of a religious life. Nishida achieves an intellectual accommodation among the major traditions by interpreting impersonalistic themes as an insistence on mystical knowledge, and by viewing mystical knowledge in turn as impossible without love and devotion.

Nishida has an important place in the history of modern Japanese thought as the founder of the "Kyoto School," the movement of professors of philosophy and religion who use Western philosophic terms and concepts to elucidate and defend a broadly Buddhist outlook (see the discussion of Keiji Nishitani under The Vibrant Void). Nishida's An Inquiry into the Good, *from which this selection is taken, is not Zen philosophy* per se, *but it is informed by Zen: Nishida was actively engaged in Zen practice while he was writing the book, and he says this helped him arrive at the views and insights he expresses.*

Nishida tries to take an entirely modern perspective, mindful of science and the difficulty of integrating philosophy and religion but insistent all the same that the two should not be split apart. He sees it as the chief error of the twentieth-century Western outlook to divide faith and intellect, religion and science, the mystical and the everyday. Nishida is a great synthesizer in the fullest sense of the word. And compared with his follower Nishitani (again, see above), Nishida emphasizes less the mystic object's transcendence and more the appropriateness of love.

I have discussed the relation between knowledge and love, and I will now consider this in connection with the facts of religion. Subjectivity is self-power and objectivity is other-power.[1] To

---

[1] By these terns Nishida is referring to faith in one's own ability (self-power) to achieve awakening as opposed to faith in Amida's power (other-power) as the only way to achieve rebirth in the Pure Land and eventual awakening.

know and love a thing is to discard self-power and embody the faithful heart that believes in other-power. If we assume that the work of one's life is not separate from knowledge and love, then day in and day out we are functioning upon faith in other-power. Both learning and morality are the glory of Buddha, and religion is the culmination of knowledge and love. In distinct individual phenomena, learning and morality are bathed in the glorious light of other-power, and religion touches the absolute, infinite Buddha extending throughout the universe. The ultimate meaning of religion is conveyed in such expressions as, "My Father, if it be possible, let this cup pass from me; nevertheless, not as I will, but as thou wilt,"[2] and, "Is the reciting of the name of Amida Buddha really the cause of rebirth in the Pure Land, or is it a karmic cause of falling into the lowest hell? Of such matters I know nothing."[3] We can moreover know this absolute, infinite God or Buddha only by loving God or Buddha; in other words, to love God is to know God, to love Buddha is to know Buddha. Vedantic teachings in India, Neo-Platonism, and Gateway of the Holy Path-type of Buddhism[4] refer to knowing God, whereas Christianity and Pure Land Buddhism refer to loving and relying on God. Both views have their own distinctive features, but they are identical in essence. We cannot know God through analysis and inference. If we assume that the essence of reality is personal, then God is that which is most personal. We can know God only through love, through the intuition of faith. So it is that those who love and believe in God without knowing God are the ones who best know God.

Against the Cognitive Thesis

From *Religious Belief* by C. B. Martin, 1959

With the selection from C. B. Martin, we turn to the question of whether mystic testimony makes rational a belief that God exists, or that Brahman is real, etc. Is mystical experience cognitive, that is, does it provide information about God or the like that a mystic through testimony can pass on to us, to non-mystics?

*Martin, a philosopher and prominent critic of religious belief and of the attempt to justify religious beliefs with reference to mysticism, argues that what makes mystical experience special also vitiates its justificational value for statements about anything other than the experiences themselves. Martin points out that if claims supposedly based on the special experiences are about nothing other than the experiences themselves, then no atheist need be troubled to deny them. Martin thus echoes a famous statement of Thomas Hobbes (1599–1679) that when a man says that God spoke to him in a dream, this "is no more than to say that he dreamed God spake to him" (*Leviathan*). The atheist can admit the dream occurred without admitting that God is real.*

---

[2] Matthew 26.39.

[3] *Tannishō*, section 2.

[4] Gateway of the Holy Path Buddhism refers to the Zen, Tendai, Shingon, and Kegon sects, which emphasize one's own power. This expression contrasts with "Gateway to the Pure Land," which refers to Pure Land Buddhism with its emphasis on other-power.

More is required, argues Martin, to have a right to claim that an experience reveals something objective—and for a mystic to say what that is—than just that others, following the same procedures (the same mystic path), have similar experiences. We could have similar delusions, as when any person with a finger on an eyeball tends to see double. "What would a photograph reveal?" Thus Martin implies that there is sufficient disanalogy between sense experience and its indications, on the one hand, and mystical experience and its indications, on the other, to deny that the latter is cognitive.

What makes a form of experience a way of knowing? It is often suggested that the mystic who "sees" God is like a man (in a society of blind men) who sees colors. It is claimed that each has a form of experience and a way of knowing that others lack. Let us now work out this analogy. A society of blind men is told by one of its members that he has come to have a form of experience and a way of knowing by means of which he has been able to discover the existence of things not discoverable by ordinary experience. He says that these things have a *kind* of size (not just like size as it is felt by the blind) and a *kind* of shape (not just like shape as it is felt by the blind); he further says that these things are somehow "everywhere" and that they cannot expect to understand what these things are like and what he means by experiencing them unless they themselves have these experiences. He then tells them of a procedure by which they will be able to discover for themselves the existence of these things. He warns them that these things do not always reveal themselves when the procedure is carried out, but, if a person is sufficiently diligent and believes strongly enough in their existence, he will probably come to know by means of unique and incomparable experiences of the existence of these things.

Some people, with faith and diligence, submit themselves to the required procedure, and some of these are rewarded by a kind of experience they have not known before. Color shapes float before them—things that they cannot touch or feel and that are beyond the reach of their senses, and things that may be present to one of their group and not experienced by the others, things that may as well be everywhere as anywhere, since they are locatable only in the sense of being "before" each observer to whom they appear. These people cannot correlate this new form of experience with the rest of experience, they cannot touch or smell these "things." Indeed, they "see" visions, not things. Or rather these people have no way of *knowing* the existence of the things that may or may not exist over and above the momentary experiences. May these experiences all the same be "cognitive"? Yes and no. Yes, there may be something, they know not what, responsible for their having these experiences. No, their experiences are not a way of *knowing* about this something. For the experience of a colored shape that needs no corroboration by the experience of others similarly placed, and that is not related to one's other senses, is not in itself a way of knowing what in the world is responsible for this experience even if there is something beyond the condition of the "observer" that is so responsible. So far, even the people concerned have no *way of knowing* what more is involved than the fact of their experiencing momentary "visions."

I have not denied that the religious mystic may have experiences that others do not. Neither have I denied that there might be some external agency responsible for these experiences. What I have denied is that the mystic's possession of these experiences is in itself a way of knowing the existence or nature of such an agency.

The argument . . . lies in an area in which confusion is common. I shall consider two cases of such confusion especially relevant to what I have been saying.

> You are acquainted with the distinction between feeling and emotion. Feeling, such as pleasure or pain, is in itself a purely subjective experience; emotion implies an objective situation within which there is something which arouses the emotion, and towards which the emotion is directed. The Divine is, it would seem, first experienced in such a situation; and is initially apprehended solely and exclusively as that which arouses certain types of emotion. If the emotion be awe, then the Divine is so far apprehended as the awesome, what Otto has so helpfully entitled the numinous.[1]

There are two questionable assumptions here: first, that whether or not an experience refers to an objective state of affairs can be read off from the experience itself; second, that emotions *must* do so.

The second claim that an emotion as such implies an objective situation can be refuted very simply. My feeling of pleasure while watching a game of football is related to something in my environment, but my feeling of pleasure at a tune running through my head is not. My emotion of awe in the presence of a particularly magnificent race horse is related to something in my environment, but my emotion of awe during a dream of a coronation service is not. Some people have aesthetic emotions aroused by the contemplation of mathematical proofs and theorems, and others have the emotion of fear toward ghosts and goblins.

In a criticism of the argument of the first part of this chapter (as originally published in "A Religious Way of Knowing," in *Mind,* October, 1952) Professor H. D. Lewis seems to be making the first claim, that a reference to an objective state of affairs can be read off from the experience itself.

> He [Martin] seems to think that the only claim to objectivity which an experience may have is that which is established by tests and checking procedures. A man's statement that he "seems to see a blue piece of paper" is thus said to be unassailable only because it is a "claim about his own state of mind." This I would doubt, for the colour expanse which we only seem to see is neither a mere appearance nor a state of mind. It is "out there before me" and real enough while I seem to see it, however many problems may be involved in distinguishing between it and physical entities. . . . "Having been stirred" by a religious ritual or act of worship, or having "certain sorts of emotions and feelings," is not the essential thing in religious experience; it is what we apprehend that comes first.[2]

However, "what we apprehend," if anything, is the whole problem and cannot "come first." Certainly, people have had special sorts of experience which incline them to claim with the greatest confidence that their expectations are of God. But whether the experiences are or are not of God is not to be decided by describing or having those experiences. For whether anything or nothing is apprehended by experiences is not to be read off from

[1] N. Kemp Smith, *Is Divine Existence Credible?,* British Academy Lecture (London: British Academy, 1931), p. 23.
[2] H. D. Lewis, "Philosophical Surveys X, The Philosophy of Religion, 1945–1952," *Philosophical Quarterly,* IV (July 1954), p. 263.

the experiences themselves. The presence of a piece of blue paper is not to be read off from my experience as of a piece of blue paper. Other things are relevant: What would a photograph reveal? Can I touch it? What do others see? It is only when I admit the relevance of such checking procedures that I can lay claim to apprehending the paper, and, indeed, the admission of the relevance of such procedures is what gives meaning to the assertion that I am apprehending the paper. *What I apprehend is the sort of thing that can be photographed, touched, and seen by others.*

It does not help when Lewis says:

> The colour expanse which we only seem to see is neither a mere appearance nor a state of mind. It is "out there before me" and real enough while I seem to see it, however many problems may be involved in distinguishing between it and physical entities.

Think now of a man who claims to see a blue piece of paper, and when we complain that we cannot, he replies, "Oh, it isn't the sort of thing that can be photographed, touched, or seen by others, but all the same, it is out there before me." Are we to think that he has come upon a special sort of object that is nevertheless "out there" as are desks and tables and the rest of the furniture of the world? No, ontological reference is something to be earned. We earn the designation "out there" of a thing by allowing its presence to be determined by the procedures we all know. We cannot just *say* "out there" of it, and we cannot just *say* "apprehended" of God.

It can be objected, "But God is different, and we never meant that our experiences of God should be checked by procedures relevant to physical objects." Of course not, but what *sort* of checks are there then, so that we are left with more than the mere experiences whose existence even the atheist need not deny?

The Cognitive Thesis Defended

From *Mysticism* by William J. Wainwright, 1981

William Wainwright, who is a leading professional voice in philosophy of religion, defends the possibility that a mystical experience is cognitive. Thus there would be a possibility of the truth of a claim stemming from a mystical experience, and the right, at least in principle, to believe mystic claims. Wainwright argues, contra Martin, that there is significant similarity between sense and mystical experience, and similarity in the ways that are crucial for an experience to be informative.

Clearly, mystics take their experiences to be informative (Wainwright, like William James in making a similar point, uses the term "noetic": both sense and mystical experiences are noetic in that they are taken to be informative about objects or objective states of affairs). This in itself does not entail that mystical experiences are veridical, that is, that their object (God, say) is in fact real and in fact exists in the ways indicated by the experience. Wainwright stresses that claims based on mystical experiences are corrigible, just as claims based on sense experiences. Because the experience seems to indicate something or

other about something beyond the experience itself, the experience does not count as infalli-
ble evidence. Other considerations could be overriding, as with the perception of a bent
pencil in a glass of water. Finally, Wainwright lists procedures whereby the indications of a
mystical experience might be checked, focusing in particular on Christian mysticism.

THE COGNITIVE STATUS OF MYSTICAL EXPERIENCE

. . . I shall argue that mystical experience is sufficiently similar to sense experience to create a presumption in favour of its cognitive validity. . . . The conclusion is that there are
good reasons for believing that mystical consciousness is a mode of cognitive experience.

Mystical experience is often said to involve a kind of 'seeing' or 'tasting' or 'touching'. We are told that mystical experience is an 'experimental knowledge' of the divine.
Mystical experiences are believed to involve a direct or immediate awareness of reality
or some aspect of reality which is normally hidden from us. It is clear that an analogy
with sense experience is intended and that part of what is implied in ascribing cognitive value to mystical experience is that these experiences are, in some important respects, like ordinary perceptual experience. In the opposite camp we find critics like C. B.
Martin who assume that ordinary perceptual experiences provide us with the paradigm of
a cognitive or perceptual experience and go on to argue that religious experiences cannot be cognitive or perceptual because they deviate in certain important ways from that
paradigm.

The analogy (or lack of it) between mystical experience and sense experience appears,
then, to be critically important both to those who ascribe cognitive value to mystical experiences and to those who refuse to do so.

Mystical experiences and sense experiences are alike in two important respects.
(1) Both types of experience are noetic. (2) On the basis of both types of experience claims
are made about something other than the experience itself. These claims are corrigible and
independently checkable. In each case there are tests for determining whether or not the
object of the experience is real and tests for determining whether or not an apparent perception of that object is a genuine one.

1. Sense experiences (whether veridical or not) have a noetic quality. This involves
two things. (a) The experiences have an object, i.e. they are experiences of something (real
or imagined). In this respect sense experiences are unlike pains, feelings of depression and
so on. The latter may have causes. They may be aroused or occasioned by certain kinds of
events or objects but . . . they are not experiences *of* those events or objects. . . . (b) Sense
experience typically involves the conviction that the object on which the experience is focused is 'really there', that it exists and that one 'experimentally' apprehends it. To use
Berkeley's language, the experience has 'outness'. This conviction is not an interpretation
which is placed upon the experience, but part of the experience itself.

In spite of the fact that some mystics speak as if their experiences transcended the
subject-object structure of ordinary perceptual experience, many mystical experiences
(and perhaps all of them) are noetic in this sense. (For example, monistic mystics by

and large agree that they experience something which transcends space and time, is devoid of distinctions and is supremely valuable. Theistic mystics believe that they experimentally perceive God.)

2. No type of experience can be called cognitive if it induces those who have it to make false claims. Thus, the experience of a mirage or the experiences one obtains by pressing one's eyeball and seeing double are called delusive because they are inherently misleading—the very nature of these experiences is such that (until one learns better) one is likely to base false claims upon them, (that water is really present or that there are two candles rather than one). There is no conclusive reason to suppose that mystical experiences are delusive in this sense. The mystic does not make false empirical statements on the basis of his experiences because he does not make empirical statements. Rather he claims to know, on the basis of his experience, that God is real and present to him or that there is an 'uncreated, imperishable Beyond', or something of the sort. It would therefore seem that we are entitled to assert that these experiences are delusive only if we have good independent reasons for believing that claims of this kind are false. It is by no means clear that we do.

But the fact that experiences are not delusive does not imply that they are cognitive. Pains are not delusive, but they are not cognitive either. One of the reasons for calling sense experiences cognitive is that not only do they not induce *false* claims, they also provide a basis for making *true* claims about something other than the experience itself. This involves two things. First, sense experiences are means of apprehending (some aspect of) reality. Those who have them are more likely to discern certain truths than those who do not, or can at least discern them more easily. Second, sense experiences can be appealed to, to justify the truths which have been made out by their means. For example, people with normal vision are more likely to discern truths about colours and shapes, and can do so more easily, than those who are blind, and they are entitled to appeal to their visual experiences to justify their claims.

Are mystical experiences like sense experiences in this respect? We can at least say this: on the basis of their experiences, mystics make claims about something other than their own experiences. They believe that they have directly apprehended a reality which others accept on faith, or on the basis of certain arguments, and they appeal to their experiences to justify their claims. Furthermore (assuming that there is no disproof of God's existence, or of the reality of the One, etc.) these claims are not known to be false. We seem therefore to have found a respect in which sense experiences and mystical experiences are like each other and unlike pains.

The analogy extends further. When a person claims to see, hear or touch something, his claim is not self-certifying. Things other than his own experience are relevant to a determination of the truth or falsity of his claim. C. B. Martin and others have asserted that sense experiences are radically unlike mystical experiences in this respect, for (they say) when the mystic claims to experience God or the Brahman, his claims are not corrigible—there are (to use Martin's phrase) no independent tests and check-up procedures which he and others would regard as relevant to a determination of the truth or falsity of the claims he makes. His claims are therefore private (like first-person psychological reports), not public (like ordinary perceptual claims).

This is simply false. Misled by the fact that certain familiar tests (for example, the appeal to the agreement of others) play at most a minor role in the evaluation of mystical experiences, critics like Martin have illicitly concluded that mystics, therefore, dismiss all tests and check-up procedures as irrelevant and regard their claims as incorrigible.

Suppose someone claims to have seen an elephant in his backyard. There are at least two ways in which his claim might be attacked. One might try to show that no elephant was there at all, or one might try to show that he could not have seen it because, for example, he was not in a position to observe it, or his sensory equipment was defective. When we turn to mystical experience we find both sorts of test and check-up procedure (at least in a rough and ready way), that is, we find independent procedures for determining whether its object is real and we find independent procedures for determining whether the experience is a genuine perception of its object.

Even when claims about such things as God or Nibbāna are grounded in mystical consciousness, they are not self-certifying. Things other than the experience itself are relevant to an evaluation of their truth. *Pace* [W. T.] Stace, these claims cannot be true if the concepts of God or Nibbāna are self-contradictory. Again, considerations adduced in arguments for and against the existence of God have some bearing on the truth of the claims made by theistic mystics. Even the statement that there is a One beyond distinctions does not appear to be self-certifying though, since what is claimed is relatively minimal, it would be harder to disprove. (Considerations of logic, and considerations adduced by positivists and naturalists, might count against it.) When the mystic asserts that he has experienced God (or Nibbāna, or Brahman) he implies that what he has experienced is real. He should therefore recognise that things besides his own experience are relevant to an evaluation of his claim. It is true that mystics are usually certain of the truth of the claims that they make, but this is no more incompatible with their corrigibility than the fact that I am certain that there is a red pen in front of me is incompatible with the fact that that claim is corrigible. In short, claims about God, or Nibbāna and other things of that kind are not self-certifying, and we have some idea of the sorts of things which count for and against them.

There are, then, independent tests for determining whether the object of mystical experience is real. There are also independent tests for determining whether an experience of this object is a genuine perception of it. Consider theistic mystical experiences, for example. Even if God exists and a direct experience of Him is possible, it does not follow that every claim to be immediately aware of God is justified. How, though, do we distinguish experiences of God which are veridical from those which are not? If we turn our attention to the communities in which theistic mysticism has flourished, we find that various tests have been used to distinguish the experiences which genuinely involve a perception of God from those which do not. Each of the following six criteria is employed in the Christian (particularly the Catholic) community. Similar criteria are used in other communities.

1. The consequences of the experience must be good for the mystic. The experience must lead to, produce, or reinforce, a new life marked by such virtues as wisdom, humility and charity. (Sanity should be subsumed under this criterion. A genuine experience of God

is believed to have a tendency to produce a life of rather extraordinary goodness. It seems reasonable to suppose that sanity is a necessary condition of such a life.) This criterion helps to explain why people are bothered by the presence of certain kinds of causes. Many people find it impossible to believe that the use of drugs, nervous and physical disorders and so on, can play a part in the best sort of life. Consequently, if they find that these things play a major role in the life of a mystic, they will tend to discount his experience.

2. One must consider the effect which the experience has on others. For instance, one should ask whether the mystic's words, actions and example tend to build up the community or weaken it.

3. The depth, the profundity and the 'sweetness' (Jonathan Edwards) of what the mystic says on the basis of his experience counts in favour of the genuineness of that experience. On the other hand, the insignificance, or the silliness, of what he says counts against it. (On the basis of this criterion many would reject the claims of Margery Kempe.)

4. We must examine what the mystic says on the basis of his experience and see whether it agrees or disagrees with orthodox talk. (It should be noted that this test is not circular. The statement being tested is a statement like 'Teresa saw God,' or 'John received heavenly consolations'. Statements of this kind are not Christian dogmas).

5. It will be helpful to determine whether the experience in question resembles other mystical experiences regarded as paradigmatic by the religious community. (In the Roman Catholic church, experiences are often compared with the experiences of Teresa of Avila or of John of the Cross.)

6. We must also consider the pronouncements of authority. In some communities (for example, Zen) the word of the spiritual director, guru or master is final. In other religious communities, the voice of the spiritual director is important though not conclusive. In some cases the relevant authority may be the community as a whole, or some special organ of it. (For example, the standing enjoyed by the experiences of John of the Cross and Teresa in the Roman Catholic community is largely a consequence of their acceptance by that community and its official representatives.) In some cases all of these authorities may be relevant.

If I am correct, these criteria are similar to the tests which we employ in ordinary perceptual cases to determine whether an apparent perception of an object is a genuine perception of it, that is, they are similar to the tests which take things into account like the position of the observer and the condition of his sensory equipment. Of course, the *nature* of the tests is not much alike. Nevertheless, the point of them is, viz., to show not that the object of the experience is real or unreal but that there is or is not a genuine perception of it. (One would not expect the nature of the tests to be much alike. For example, in the case of introvertive mystical experience there is no sensory equipment which can go awry because sense organs are not involved. Nor does there appear to be anything which clearly corresponds to the position of the observer in sense experience.)

Mystical Experience as Sociologically Determined

From "Language, Epistemology, and Mysticism" by Steven T. Katz in *Mysticism and Philosophical Analysis,* Steven T. Katz, editor, 1978

Gestalt psychologists have shown that beliefs, expectations, and various mental factors extraneous to the nature of an object perceived shape or determine sense perception. For example, doctors looking at x-rays are prone to see hairline fractures if they expect them. Told that the appearance of an old Western town is only a Hollywood facade, a person looking down at it will suddenly see it as a facade, and no longer, as before, as abandoned buildings, and so forth. Experience is not a private, isolated matter of what is occurring with a subject. Socially transmitted and reinforced beliefs alter the very nature or content of experience.

Steven Katz, a scholar in religious studies with a specialty in Jewish mysticism, applies this discovery to mystical experience and finds wide-ranging consequences. According to him, tradition shapes mystical experience to such an extent that its apparent indications are all dubious. Sufis are predisposed by belonging to a Sufi tradition to have a Sufi sort of mystical experience. And thus their testimony, and all mystic testimony, is unreliable.

The question remains whether the fact that experiences are in part determined by prior beliefs, expectations, etc., means that they lose all justificational value. Because sense experience is shapeable, is it then not cognitive? Mystical experience may well be determined to a greater extent than sense experience by mental factors. But if the analogy to sense experience is strong enough, then it might be cognitive all the same.

However, strengthening Katz's contention is the diversity of mystical experience and diversity of mystic claims, a diversity in some instances that borders on outright contradiction. Does this mean that mystical experiences are not informative? We shall consider the question further, in looking at a response to Katz, by Sallie B. King, a defender of the possible cognitive value of a mystical experience, and again in the section Religious Pluralism.

To get a clearer conception of what this paper is after when it speaks of the issue of 'Why mystical experiences are the experiences they are', let me state the single epistemological assumption that has exercised my thinking and which has forced me to undertake the present investigation: *There are* NO *pure (i.e. unmediated) experiences.* Neither mystical experience nor more ordinary forms of experience give any indication, or any grounds for believing, that they are unmediated. That is to say, *all* experience is processed through, organized by, and makes itself available to us in extremely complex epistemological ways. The notion of unmediated experience seems, if not self-contradictory, at best empty. This epistemological fact seems to me to be true, because of the sorts of beings we are, even with regard to the experiences of those ultimate objects of concern with which mystics have intercourse, e.g. God, Being, nirvāṇa, etc. This 'mediated' aspect of all our experience seems an inescapable feature of any epistemological inquiry, including the inquiry into mysticism, which has to be properly acknowledged if our investigation of experience, including mystical experience, is to get very far. . . . A proper evaluation of this fact leads to the recognition that in order to understand mysticism it is *not* just a question of studying the reports of the mystic after the experiential event but of acknowledging that the experience itself as well as the form in which it is reported is shaped by concepts which the mystic brings to, and which shape, his experience. To flesh this out, straightforwardly, what is being argued is that, for example, the Hindu mystic does not have an experience of *x* which he then describes in the, to him, familiar language and symbols of Hinduism, but rather he has a Hindu experience, i.e. his experience is not an unmediated experience of *x* but is itself the, at least partially, pre-formed anticipated Hindu experience of Brahman. Again, the Christian mystic does not experience some unidentified reality, which he then conveniently labels God, but rather has the at least partially prefigured Christian experiences of God, or Jesus, or the like. Moreover, as one might have anticipated, it is my view based on what evidence there is, that the Hindu experience of Brahman and the Christian experience of God are not the same. . . . The significance of these considerations is that the forms of consciousness which the mystic brings to experience set structured and limiting parameters on what the experience will be, i.e. on what will be experienced, and rule out in advance what is 'inexperienceable' in the particular given, concrete, context. Thus, for example, the nature of the Christian mystic's pre-mystical consciousness informs the mystical consciousness such that he experiences the mystic reality in terms of Jesus, the Trinity, or a personal God, etc., rather than in terms of the non-personal, non-everything, to be precise, Buddhist doctrine of nirvāṇa. . . .

. . . There is a clear causal connection between the religious and social structure one brings to experience and the nature of one's actual religious experience. . . . [some might argue however that] all mystics are wary about using language to describe their experience, and many are absolutely opposed to its employment, arguing a form of 'I don't mean what I say and I don't say what I mean'. Also, we are sure to be reminded of the well-known mystical penchant for paradox and ineffability as relevant at this point. However, this 'escape' is no escape at all. It fails to provide the desired way out because it fails to realize that, if the mystic does not mean what he says and his words have *no* literal meaning whatsoever, then not only is it impossible to establish my pluralistic view, but it is also logically impossible to establish any view whatsoever. If none of the mystics' utterances carry any literal meaning then they cannot serve as the *data* for any position, not mine, and certainly not the view that all mystical experiences are the same, or reducible to a small class of phenomenological categories. . . .

What is the 'given' or the 'suchness' or even the 'real'? Analysis of these terms indicates their relativity; they are applied to a variety of alternative and even mutually exclusive 'states of affairs' and 'states of no-affairs'. This variety itself should alert us to the real danger and arbitrariness involved in this gambit. Phenomenologists seem especially prone to this fruitless naivety—all intuit the 'given' but their intuitions differ significantly. It can fairly be said that no attempt to state clearly or individuate the 'given' has succeeded. Indeed, talk of the 'given' seems to be a move made to short-circuit the very sort of epistemological inquiry here being engaged in, but such a move fails because there is no evidence that there is any 'given' which can be disclosed without the imposition of the mediating conditions of the knower. All 'givens' are also the product of the processes of 'choosing', 'shaping', and 'receiving'. That is, the 'given' is appropriated through acts which shape it into forms which we can make intelligible to ourselves given our conceptual constitution, and which structure it in order to respond to the specific contextual needs and mechanisms of consciousness of the receiver. . . .

Mysticism as Irreducibly Experiential

From "Two Epistemological Models for the Interpretation of Mysticism" by Sallie B. King in *Journal of the American Academy of Religion,* Volume 56, Number 2, 1988

Sallie B. King, Chair of the Department of Philosophy and Religion at James Madison University, challenges an assumption of Katz's that appears to be crucial to his argument: experience is a social construct, not a private, subjective event. She counters with examples drawn from everyday life that suggest that there is an irreducibly experiential element in some experiences. The taste of coffee is what it is, and no tradition of talking about it could eliminate the peculiarly experiential quality of breathing in its aroma and sipping. Presumably, a mystical experience has such an experiential quality, securing its independence and irreducibility to doctrine.

    King goes on to speculate about what common ground, or object, could lie at the bottom of, or give rise to, the broad range of mystical experiences reported in mystic literature worldwide. She does not claim to produce a spiritual philosophy capable of integrating all the diverse mystical and religious philosophies. That is not her concern in the excerpted paper. But she says she sees enough that is in common in the reports of the experiences themselves to begin to delineate a possible common ground, which she explains mainly in terms of an axiological (value-grounding) dimension mystically encountered.

    What, finally, are the implications of the plurality of traditions for the cognitive question concerning mysticism? King leaves the question open. But she urges philosophers to take seriously the possibility that a theory about what she sees as the common (Divine) ground of mystical experiences might dull the edge of doctrinal differences. King provides such a theory's outlines, but only within the context of her epistemological enquiry, that is to say, of her defense of the possible cognitive status of a mystical experience. Large questions of theory, she would readily admit, remain. We shall review further efforts to overcome doctrinal divergencies in our last section, Religious Pluralism.

This essay is composed of two parts. The first offers a criticism of the pluralist conception of mysticism and the epistemological model on which it is based. I argue that this model is inadequate and improperly reduces mystical experiences to doctrine. The second part of the article proposes an alternative epistemological model and examines its implications for the study of mysticism.

To determine which phenomena to include in, and which to exclude from our analysis requires a definition of mysticism. But there is no generally accepted definition for this term. Recent studies which display the variety of phenomena normally included in the category of the mystical make it doubtful that any single essence pervades the various phenomena and furnishes the necessary unifying element for the construction of a definition. In practice scholars have employed Wittgenstein's notion of "family resemblances" and applied it to a definition of "mysticism." The basic idea of this approach is that some words, such as "religion," are instanced by members that share a whole set of characteristics, no one of which must be possessed by all or by any individual in order to justify its inclusion in the class. The set of characteristics is shared by the group of members in such a way that a whole list of characteristics might overlap among the group in endlessly varying ways. . . .

Steven Katz's work offers the clearest statement of the epistemological model that forms the foundation of the pluralist understanding of mysticism. Katz makes the "single epistemological assumption that . . . there are NO pure (i.e., unmediated) experiences." On this basis, he argues that mystical experience is conditioned by tradition and that therefore mysticism is irreducibly pluralistic.

Katz's straightforward statement of this presupposition is a key to the evaluation of the pluralist position it represents. This assumption ultimately derives from a post-Wittgensteinian epistemological model that holds that there are no "private languages," no purely private experiences, and no purely "private" realm at all because all of our experience derives its meaningfulness from the public realm of culture and language. A moment of sadness, for example, though apparently a private experience, is for Wittgenstein only meaningfully a moment of sadness because of the larger context within which that moment occurs. The larger context is the public world of language. In other words, the meaning of the "private" moment is not in fact private at all. Wittgenstein himself, in *Philosophical Investigations,* is ambiguous, but the book as a whole has been received as an attack on the concept of private experience.

In the philosophy of language, and in Katz's interpretation in particular, this thesis means that no experiences are free of the conditioning power of the public world of language and culture. This is what it means to say that there are no unmediated experiences.

An example or two may suffice to establish Katz's position. Having summarized the Jewish doctrine of *devekuth* and the Buddhist doctrine of *nirvāṇa,* Katz goes on to say, "Just setting this Buddhist understanding of the nature of things [i.e., doctrine] over against the Jewish should, in itself, already be strong evidence for the thesis that what the Buddhist experiences as *nirvāṇa* is different from what the Jew experiences as *devekuth.*" Here Katz claims that the doctrinal difference between Buddhism and Judaism is "strong evidence" that the experiences of the Jew and the Buddhist are also, and in a parallel fashion, different.

Note that there is no discussion of experience as such. Rather, Katz uses doctrinal evidence to draw conclusions about experience. Consequently, he reduces experience to doctrine. For Katz, the experience is so utterly conditioned by the training that precedes it that it becomes a mere reproduction of that training. Katz continues his argument as follows:

> Let us draw this out more clearly. To begin, when the Jewish mystic performs his special mystical devotions and meditations . . . he does so in order to *purify his soul* . . . in order to liberate it for its upward spiritual ascent culminating in *devekuth,* adhesion to God's emanations, the *Sefiroth.* The Buddhist mystic, on the other hand, performs his meditative practices . . . not in order to free the soul from the body and purify it, but rather in order to annihilate suffering by overcoming any notion of 'self'. . . .

But this is a comparison of doctrine and does not clarify for us anything about the experiences themselves. Surely this is a case of reducing mystical experience to doctrine. Katz explains that "*nirvāṇa* is also not a relational state, i.e., it is *not* the meeting of two distinct selves or realities who come together in loving embrace. *Nirvāṇa* is the absence of all relation, all personality, all love, all feeling, all individuality, all identity." This is a statement of early Buddhist doctrine; Katz misleads us to the extent that he conflates the doctrinal usage of the term *nirvāṇa* with the problematic usage of the term in connection with Buddhist mystical experience. *Nirvāṇa,* doctrinally, may be the "absence of all relation," etc., but what is it experientially? This is another matter indeed, though of course there is an important relation between the two. . . . Katz continues, "The losing of self is not equivalent to the finding of another. . . ." Elsewhere he writes, ". . . the Hindu experience of Brahman and the Christian experience of God are not the same." Here we are required to agree not only that we do not have evidence to establish that the experiences in question are the same, but also that we *do* have evidence to establish that they are different. This is a much broader thesis, which cannot be supported.

More is at issue here than the status of mysticism as a category with cross-cultural validity. The assumption that there are no unmediated experiences also negates the very foundation of yoga, most of Buddhism, large segments of Hinduism, and philosophical Taoism. The issue is not just one of cross-cultural analysis and understanding, but of the status of most of the great Asian religious traditions in and of themselves. At stake is not only what scholars . . . say about mystical experience, but what many great traditions say about themselves.

The pluralist account states variously that tradition conditions, shapes, and/or determines the form and content of mystical experience. So, for example, Katz asserts, "the forms of consciousness which the mystic brings to experience set structured and limiting parameters on what the experience will be." And again: "This much is certain: the mystical experience must be mediated by the kind of beings we are. . . . Thus experience of *x*—be *x* God or *nirvāṇa*—is conditioned both linguistically and cognitively by a variety of factors *including the expectation of what will be experienced.*" Though there are occasional exceptions (such as when Katz states "beliefs shape experience, just as experience shapes belief" the overall impression Katz leaves is that mysticism is a matter of a one-way street; a given religious tradition produces the experience of the mystic, and the mystical experience contains no elements that are unconditioned but is entirely the product of the teaching and training that the mystic has received prior to the mystical experience. The strongest language speaks of causality and indicates a cause and effect relationship between religious tradition and mystical experience. Thus Katz asserts, "What I wish to show is only that there is a clear causal connection between the religious and social structure one brings to experience and the nature of one's actual religious experience."

But consider some other forms of experience that are in some sense said to be ineffable. In particular, let us analyze the relationship between these experiences and the contexts in which they occur. Take, for example, the experience of drinking and tasting coffee. One who drinks coffee knows exactly what coffee tastes like but will be incapable of describing that taste. (This knowledge is, moreover, verifiable insofar as we can give the subject coffee, tea, and other drinks to taste and test the subject's ability to identify the correct drink as coffee.) What is the relationship between the first taste of coffee one acquires and the context of that experience—the "tradition" of coffee drinkers whom one has heard exclaiming that coffee is delicious, invigorating, relaxing, bitter, etc.; the advertisements for coffee with their visual images, jingles, slogans; the countless childhood experiences of watching one's parents drink their morning coffee and perhaps undergoing noticeable personality changes in the process—what is the relationship between all this and one's own first direct taste? Is it possible to say—as the pluralists do with respect to mystical experience—that this experience is produced, brought into being, caused by that pre-existing context of tradition?

Think about one's own experience of tasting coffee, or anything else for that matter. Certainly one may be predisposed to like or dislike coffee depending upon what one has heard and witnessed with respect to coffee. One may eagerly seek out an opportunity to acquire such experience or try to avoid it. Being told that coffee is bitter would certainly predispose one to find bitterness in the taste. But there, I claim, is where the conditioning power of the "coffee tradition" ends. It cannot cause the subject to have the total experience s/he has upon drinking coffee. Why? The main reason is that the taste of coffee is ineffable: in all the words, lifestyles, and art forms associated with the cult of coffee, there is nowhere even an approximation of an adequate description of the taste of coffee. The power of the coffee tradition to convey information about the taste of coffee is limited to the point of insignificance compared to the power of the sensation of tasting coffee in experience.

The same point is made, of course, with respect to the content of mystical experience: it cannot be adequately described. This is not to say that nothing is said about it or that the things that are said about it do not convey certain amounts of information. It is simply to emphasize that what is said is radically inadequate. For this reason, it is impossible for the tradition (religious or coffee) to produce or cause the experience in its fullness—its resources are radically inadequate. I emphasize this point: the coffee tradition in this country overwhelmingly invades our minds. The act of drinking coffee in its totality can by no means be said to be an unmediated experience. Nonetheless, before one drinks coffee one really has no idea what it tastes like; after one cup, one knows exactly. How far does the conditioning power of the coffee tradition extend? In the end, though drinking coffee is a mediated experience, that mediation is a relatively insignificant element of the experience itself. . . .

Let us take another example: the experience of listening to music. I would argue that, like the experience of drinking and tasting coffee, the experience of listening to and hearing music is an experience that occurs within a context, a musical tradition in this case, but that this context by no means can be said to determine, cause, or exhaust the experience of hearing music itself. To be sure, listening to music is an experience which is shaped by one's musical training. Clearly, a trained and experienced Japanese hears things in classical koto music that an untrained American does not. The experience is different for the two persons, moreover, in the very sense that the meaning and value of the experience is different for them. Does this mean that the training of the Japanese caused that experience with its accompanying sense of meaning and value, or that the experience of listening to that music can be *reduced* to that training? Certainly not. Despite the fact that a complex and extensive technical vocabulary has been developed within a given musical tradition, there is always more to the experience of hearing music than can be conveyed in words— sounds, rhythms and tones are not concepts. . . .

. . . A mystical experience is an encounter with that which grounds one's existence, one's phenomenal selfhood, one's values; it is an encounter, in other words, with that which, while it may or may not be an entity of any kind, constitutes the ground for the possibility and meaning of my finite experience. I purposely speak of a "ground" here in order to leave as open as possible the question of the extent to which this ground is self or other. One can insert into this formula language of creation by the Wholly Other or manifestation of finite form out of Absolute Being. Even radically apophatic (*via negativa*) language can be appropriate here, though this is more difficult. Tao as Nonbeing could be such a ground. The most difficult cases are the Buddhist. But since in Mahāyāna Buddhism *saṃsāra* is *nirvāṇa,* or in other words, supreme value is present in the particulars of mundane experience, seeing the "Thusness" of "what is" fits this description, as does Zen's pure awareness of this moment. The more negative language of Nāgārjuna or of Theravāda accounts of *nirvāṇa* reveal an absolute commitment to the apophatic path. But even these fit the present analysis, for all that my characterization of mystical experience requires is an existential grounding—a vivid experiential realization of that into which one fits as a cognizing, valuing, existing individual. Does not realization of the *Heart Sūtra*'s "form is emptiness and emptiness is form" entail grounding in such an existential sense? And when the Buddha, in speaking of *nirvāṇa,* says:

> O bhikkhus, there is the unborn, ungrown, and unconditioned. Were there not the unborn, ungrown, and unconditioned, there would be no escape for the born, grown, and conditioned. Since there is the unborn, ungrown, and unconditioned, so there is escape for the born, grown, and conditioned. (*Udāna,* cited in Rahula: 37)

are we not talking about existential grounding? Thus, even though a given tradition may deny, as Indian Buddhism does, that there is anything in any sense whatsoever that is either the basis or the source of the individual's being, that tradition in its mystical dimension still points towards an existential grounding of the individual. This, then, can serve as a cross-culturally valid component of mystical experience: an experience that leaves one existentially grounded.

There is also an element of axiological grounding: an encounter with absolute value. This is partly related to the factor of existential grounding and partly separable from it. As related to the above, it is clear that what grounds one existentially will possess superlative value for one. One may also, separately, speak of the non-existential qualities that emerge in mystical experience. Mystics frequently report feelings of bliss, ecstasy, or of serene joy, deep peace; Otto speaks of the fascination of the numinous. Such reports are evidence of a grounding in values produced by mystical experience, an experiential encounter with a source of superlative, intrinsic value. Again, such language fits the Tao even inasmuch as it is Non-being. It even fits emptiness—not in the sense that emptiness as such possesses value, which is impossible since it is only a tool, but in the sense that the transformation engendered by the discipline of emptiness possesses value.

This leaves us with a provisional definition of mystical experience: mystical experience is a form of primitive experience (a form of experience prior to the division of experience into subject and object components) in which there is radical transformation of the experiential self sense, and radical axiological and existential grounding. This definition, though, is inadequate insofar as it fails to include stages on the path (in some cases and traditions) towards such experience: the dropping of body and mind, the Great Death, the desert, etc.

What does our proposed epistemological model indicate about the possibility of unmediated experience? We first need to examine the concept "unmediated" as it is used in this context. I have argued that "primitive" and mystical experience is constituted by experiential unity prior to a subject-object split. The structure of such experience is "consciousness-of." In the language of phenomenology, this means we bring a "noetic correlate" with us to each moment of experience; we bring ourselves to experience *in some fashion*. But all of our sensory, perceptual, cognitive, emotive, and other faculties are not engaged in every momentary experience. If the primitive experience is a *concentrated* looking at a flower, then we bring ourselves as visual beings to the experience. If the primitive experience is a *concentrated* smelling of a flower, we bring ourselves as olfactory beings to the experience. By "concentrated" I mean the one-pointed mind spoken of in Buddhism; as mentioned above, concentration such as that cultivated in meditation entails the focusing of awareness on a single point. There is no need to posit the presence of ourselves as tactile, auditory, tasting, emotive, linguistic beings in these moments of concentrated use of other senses. These other functions are not engaged at this moment.

So the question becomes: What is engaged, what is "turned on" in a *given* mystical experience? Buddhists, who believe in psychophysical unity, sometimes make much of the fact that meditation is an embodied experience-process. In mysticism generally, there are auditions, visions, automatic speech, stigmata, etc.—obviously the mystic brings the corresponding noetic correlative along in these cases. (And, as mentioned above, we should recall that many mystics are negatively impressed with such sense-based experiences.) Moreover, our discussion above of the experiences of drinking coffee and listening to music established, I believe, that there can be non-verbal knowledge gained from non-verbal experience.

Do we then want to call this kind of thing "mediation"? Let us examine the term. The concept of mediation indicates the presence of something coming in between the subject experiencer and the object experienced, as in: the concepts of the tradition come between the mystical and the contents of the mystical experience. (Note that this model could correlate with either Stace's or Katz's view.) But on our epistemological model there is no division between subject and object; hence, it is misleading to think in terms of mediation. *However,* there is a noetic correlate in experience, whether sensorial, non-verbal cognitive, or whatever. Perhaps a better term than mediation is embodiment: all experience is embodied, in the sense that a noetic correlate is present.

In sum, this means that if we ask "can there be unmediated experience?" we must reply that there cannot be unembodied experience. But why should we suppose that there cannot be moments of experience free of the influence of ideas, concepts, words, philosophies, and religious traditions? We do not constantly have our linguistic functions turned on in every moment. Not only is the turning off of this function the very purpose of many forms of meditation, but we can think of many examples of secular experience in which the individual experiences in the "primitive" mode without the presence of verbal functions in the noetic correlate. When one gives oneself up completely to the present moment of physical exertion in sports, or the present moment of sound in listening to music, or the present moment of singing, there is no experiential sense of a separate self. There is just the event, in which one is "lost." We can all think of moments in which the sense of a separate self was absent and the events of the moment—musical, physical, or whatever—simply played themselves. If the event itself is not linguistic in nature, there is no need to assume a linguistic element in the noetic correlate. But one can look back on these experiences and say something about them, however inadequately in some cases; there was "consciousness-of" in these experiences. Here again, then, is evidence for non-verbal cognition. One learns from these experiences; the body and non-verbal components of awareness have knowledge that reflective consciousness can later examine and process in its own way.

In conclusion, from the vantage point of this proposed epistemological model, the very question of unmediated experience is misconceived. We need to examine more carefully what, in each *particular* case, the mystic brings to the experience as the noetic correlate of that experience. We do not need to assume in every case that the mystic brings along the baggage of her or his religious tradition and culture to each experience, though in some cases it is no doubt true. We do need to further examine the manner in which reflective consciousness inspects non-verbal knowledge and issues its report: this, it seems to me, is one of the key nuts to crack in understanding the phenomena of mystical experience. If I am right in suggesting that phenomenological data for such an inquiry can be found in both mystical experiences and the kinds of secular experiences discussed above, a resolution to this puzzle may not elude us indefinitely.

DISCUSSION QUESTIONS

1. Retrace the steps on Plato's "Ladder of Love." Try to fill out the conception with examples drawn from contemporary life.

2. Elaborate Al-Ghazālī's distinction between theory and practice with regard to his theistic mysticism and at least one example drawn from everyday life.

3. Portray as best you can the theistic experience of Teresa and of Aurobindo as well. What are important similarities and/or differences in their reports?

4. Portray as best you can the monistic experience of Ruysbroeck and of Rama-krishna as well. What are important similarities and/or differences in their reports?

5. Present yogic mystical experience in the light of the metaphysics of the *Yoga-sūtra*. Mircea Eliade tries to convey a more phenomenological, and less interpreted, account of yogic experience. Is what he says latent in some of the words of the *Yoga-sūtra*, extractable despite the metaphysics? Try to find particular verses (sūtras) that support Eliade's statements.

6. Portray as best you can the Zen experiences recounted from the book by Philip Kapleau. Do you find important similarities and/or differences between these reports, on the one hand, and any of the other types of mysticism we have surveyed, on the other?

7. Martin Buber argues that authentic mysticism involves a relationship to God that is thoroughly personal, engaging one's entire self. He sees monistic mysticism as a psychical delusion. Present his position and arguments. Do you agree?

8. Nishida takes himself to find grounds for accommodation of personal and impersonal mysticism. Just what is he recommending? Could this be compatible with the central teachings of all the traditions we have surveyed?

9. Reconstruct C. B. Martin's case against the cognitive value of a mystical experience.

10. Does William Wainwright successfully answer the arguments of C. B. Martin? What are the best, and weakest, points in his defense of the cognitive value of a mystical experience?

11. Experiences have been shown to be shaped to a significant extent by subjective factors such as expectation and prior belief. Mystical experiences usually occur within the context of a religious and ascetic tradition where there are inherited doctrines and mystic practices. Steven Katz argues that the diversity among mystical traditions has as a bottom-line philosophical ramification that mystical experiences are not cognitive. Present his argument. Do you agree?

12. Is Sallie B. King successful in answering Steven Katz on the question of the cognitive value of a mystical experience? What are the most important issues in this dispute?

CHAPTER FOUR

Religion Debunked

From the European Renaissance through the nineteenth century and, some would argue, now as much as ever, religion has opposed and been opposed by science. To take a scientific perspective was, or is, to renounce religion, and a goal of the special human sciences—anthropology, sociology, psychology—was, or is, to debunk religion, to show, assuming the falsity of religious beliefs, why it has arisen and thus to explain it away. Although many would contend that the best in religion should be preserved, that not all religious beliefs are incompatible with science, that only the superstitious and atavistic should be discarded, others hold than an atheism, an areligious *materialism,* or a *naturalism* and *agnosticism,* is the only reasonable view.

The principal focus of this section is the debunking effort of sociologists and psychologists of religion. But more broadly the concern is the status of religious beliefs in the context of science. This section may be seen as devoted to arguments against a Divine Reality. But there are also selections in other sections with that aim, so let me define debunking: a debunking effort vis-à-vis a belief P involves not only argument against the truth of P but also explanation why someone would hold P in spite of its falsity and a lack of good grounds. It is in the sciences of sociology and psychology in particular that such efforts directed against religious beliefs have flourished during the last hundred or so years. In the section Faith Against Reason, we shall look at attempts to dissociate the spheres of science and religion. Here we look at the two together—as we did with some of the theistic arguments. But this time we listen in particular to those who say that, first, science excludes religion, and, second, that science explains the tendency for persons to be religious despite the fact that religious beliefs lack solid supports.

The first selection, from the contemporary philosopher Michael Scriven, is aimed at showing atheism the appropriate attitude, given that arguments for the existence of God fail. Scriven's position is that when the existence of something is such that it should be discerned (that is, should leave discernible traces), then its not being discerned is decisive evidence that it does not exist. Next, we turn to a general piece by J. C. C. Smart on science and religion, a brief history of their conflict, and the main points of tension between science and Christianity in particular. The selections from Karl Marx, E. B. Tylor, and Sigmund Freud are debunking efforts, or outlines of theories that would explain the origins of religion as other than in a Divine ground. Materialist opposition to religion is not only a modern phenomenon, and not only a Western one, as the selection on classical Indian materialism shows. The atheistic existentialism expressed by Albert Camus may be read as a response and a counter both to the axiological reasoning of Robert Nozick (see above) and to the fideism of Soren Kierkegaard (see the selection under Faith Against Reason). Finally, Ernest Nagel shows that philosophical atheism need not be defined merely in opposition to religious perspectives but is a positive philosophy in its own right—if not a worldview, still a common outlook, with a moral dimension.

Lack of Evidence

From *Primary Philosophy* by Michael Scriven, 1966

A position popular among Protestant theologians in particular has been that while no argument shows conclusively that God exists, none shows that God does not exist. There is thus "room for faith"—and a call for faith as the appropriate attitude toward the propositions of religion. No less a philosopher than Immanuel Kant (see above) endorsed such a separation of (a) evidentially supported belief and (b) religious beliefs held not in opposition to evidence but without it. William James, too, promoted our right to believe what we will when evidence is indeterminate (e.g., ruling neither for nor against God) such that the hypothesis is "live" (see the second selection from James under Faith Against Reason).

Michael Scriven argues, in contrast, that religious hypotheses such as the theistic have no claim to such middle ground. Given the failure of theistic arguments, not even agnosticism is a live option, much less is there room for faith. Scriven asks us what evidence we should expect to find if something X exists. Answer: That depends on X's nature. Then God being omnibenevolent, etc., there would seem to be no reason why God should hide. It doesn't even seem possible. If we are reasonable, Scriven concludes, following evidence where it leads, as in science, atheism appears the only appropriate attitude.

The arguments are the only way to establish theism, and they must be judged by the usual standards of evidence—this we have argued. It will now be shown that if they fail, there is no alternative to atheism.

Against this it has commonly been held that the absence of arguments *for* the existence of something is not the same as the presence of arguments *against* its existence; so agnosticism or an option remains when the arguments fail. But insofar as this is true, it is irrelevant. It is true only if we restrict "arguments for the existence of something" to highly specific demonstrations which attempt to establish their conclusion as beyond all reasonable doubt. The absence of these is indeed compatible with the conclusion's being quite likely, which would make denial of its existence unjustified. But if we take arguments for the existence of something to include all the evidence which supports the existence claim to any significant degree, i.e., makes it at all probable, then the absence of such evidence means there is *no* likelihood of the existence of the entity. And this, of course, is a complete justification for the claim that the entity does not exist, provided that the entity is not one which might leave no traces (a God who is impotent or who does not care for us), and provided that we have comprehensively examined the area where such evidence would appear if there were any. Now justifying the claim that something does not exist is not quite the same as proving or having arguments that it doesn't, but it is what we are talking about. That is, we need not have a proof that God does not exist in order to justify atheism. Atheism is obligatory in the absence of any evidence for God's existence.

Why do adults not believe in Santa Claus? Simply because they can now explain the phenomena for which Santa Claus's existence is invoked without any need for introducing a novel entity. When we were very young and naively believed our parents' stories, it was hard to see how the presents could get there on Christmas morning since the doors were locked and our parents were asleep in bed. Someone *must* have brought them down the chimney. And how could that person get to the roof without a ladder and with all those presents? Surely only by flying. And then there is that great traditional literature of stories and songs which immortalize the entity and his (horned) attendants; surely these cannot all be just products of imagination? Where there is smoke, there must be fire.

Santa Claus is not a bad hypothesis at all for six-year-olds. As we grow up, no one comes forward to *prove* that such an entity does not exist. We just come to see that there is not the least reason to think he *does* exist. And so it would be entirely foolish to assert that he does, or believe that he does, or even think it likely that he does. Santa Claus is in just the same position as fairy godmothers, wicked witches, the devil, and the ether. Each of these entities has some supernatural powers, i.e., powers which contravene or go far beyond the powers that we know exist, whether it be the power to levitate a sled and reindeer or the power to cast a spell. Now even belief in something for which there is *no* evidence, i.e., a belief which goes *beyond* the evidence, although a lesser sin than belief in something which is *contrary* to well-established laws, is plainly irrational in that it simply amounts to attaching belief where it is not justified. So the proper alternative, when there is no evidence, is not mere suspension of belief, e.g., about Santa Claus; it is *disbelief*. It most certainly is not faith.

The situation is slightly different with the Abominable Snowman, sea serpents, or even the Loch Ness monster. No "supernatural" (by which, in this context, we only mean wholly unprecedented) kinds of powers are involved. Previous discoveries have been made of creatures which had long seemed extinct, and from these we can immediately derive some likelihood of further discoveries. Footprints or disturbances for which no fully satisfactory alternative explanation has yet been discovered (although such an explanation is by no means impossible) have been seen in the Himalayan snow and the Scottish lochs. It would be credulous for the layman to believe firmly in the existence of these entities. Yet it would be equally inappropriate to say it is certain they do not exist. Here is a domain for agnosticism (though perhaps an agnosticism inclined toward skepticism). For the agnostic does not believe that a commitment either way is justified, and he is surely right about strange creatures which, while of a new *appearance*, have powers that are mere extensions, proportional to size, of those with which we are already familiar on this Earth. There is some suggestive, if by no means conclusive, evidence for such entities; and the balance of general considerations is not heavily against them.

But when the assertion is made that something exists with powers that strikingly transcend the well-established generalizations we have formulated about animal capacities or reasonable extrapolations from them, then we naturally expect correspondingly better evidence before we concede that there is a serious likelihood of having to abandon those generalizations. It is entirely appropriate to demand much stronger support for claims of telepathy or levitation or miraculous cures than for new sports records or feats of memory in which previous levels of performance are merely bettered to some degree, in a way that is almost predictable. On the other hand, it is entirely prejudiced to reject all such evidence on the ground that it *must* be deceptive because it contravenes previously established generalizations. This is simply to deify the present state of science; it is the precise opposite of the experimental attitude. It is right to demand a stronger case to overthrow a strong case and to demand very strong evidence to demonstrate unprecedented powers. It is irrational to require that the evidence of these powers be just as commonplace and compelling as for the previously known powers of man or beast: one cannot legislate the exceptional into the commonplace.

Religion and Science

From "Religion and Science" by J. C. C. Smart in *Encyclopedia of Philosophy,* Paul Edwards, editor, 1967

Prominent philosopher of science J. C. C. Smart addresses not the question of the evidence of religious hypotheses, nor the question of the ramifications of lack of evidence, but whether religious beliefs are compatible with scientific findings. If they are not, then so much the worse for religious beliefs—unless one is prepared to take a radically fideist and anti-intellectual position (again, see Faith Against Reason). Incompatibility is a logical term: if two beliefs are incompatible, one must be false. By extension, whole outlooks are said to be incompatible if given that one—call it A—is largely correct, then another— call it B—must be largely in error. The presumption is that A and B are in competition, that they claim common territory. Those who argue that religion and science are compatible usually propose that their spheres are radically different. Smart, writing in the mid-sixties, disputes this proposal with regard to much contemporary Christianity and some other religious outlooks, too.

In an earlier day, science was seen as incompatible with religion, not, as in our times, principally from the side of science, but from the side of religion, or religious authorities. Professor Smart briefly traces the history of religious opposition to scientific advance. He then turns to his central concern, an anthropocentrism he sees at the core of Christianity, and wonders whether—as elaborated in beliefs about creation, incarnation, and souls and their immortality—it is compatible with what science teaches. A commit-

ment to the efficacy of prayer, or to the veridicality of mystical experience, stirs up more trouble with science, according to Smart, since each would demand supernatural agency.

Smart mentions the religious views of R. B. Braithwaite as a way to avoid conflict with science. Braithwaite proposes that religion—or Christianity at least—requires no assertion of fact but only ethical intention. We shall review his position under Religion and Ethics.

At the end of the selection, Smart considers briefly religions other than Christianity, and suggests that, whatever the problems, for example, of Hinduism and Buddhism, they do not suffer from the severely unscientific anthropocentrism of Christianity and, Smart adds casually, of Islam. But Smart's treatment here seems too unlabored and unscholarly to deserve much pause. Doubtless there is superstition and backwardness cloaked by religions of all flavors. The deep question is whether with each religion—anthropocentric Christianity no less than with any other—there is a core perspective that can live with science in (conjectural) peace and harmony.

The purpose of this article is to discuss the present relations between religion and science and to examine respects in which they may be held either to conflict with or to support one another. It is well known that in the nineteenth century scientists and theologians came into open conflict, the sharpness of which is apparent in, for example, T. H. Huxley's lively volumes of essays. It is often said nowadays that the conflict between religion and science is a thing of the past. Science is said to have become less materialistic and hence more favorable to theology, whereas theology has allegedly become more sophisticated and thus less vulnerable to attack by science. Scientists like Arthur Eddington and J. H. Jeans have tried to use the theories of modern physics to support a spiritual interpretation of the universe, whereas among theologians there has been a withdrawal, in that most of them would no longer wish to defend the literal truth of Biblical stories such as that of Adam and Eve or of Noah's ark. Those who still hold that there is a conflict between religion and science are quite commonly considered naive and old-fashioned. Nevertheless, it will be argued in the present article that although some of the conflicts between religion and science have disappeared, others are still present, and moreover that there are new areas of controversy which were not envisaged by previous generations or at least did not take a prominent place in their thought. It should be understood that in the following discussion "religion" will generally refer to the Christian religion, since Christianity has held a dominant place in the Western religious and intellectual tradition. In most cases it should be possible for the reader who is more interested in some other religion to see for himself whether similar considerations apply. At the end of this article, however, other religions will be briefly discussed, together with the question of whether or to what extent *any* religious outlook might be held to be incompatible with the scientific attitude.

Historical preliminaries. In the history of the conflict between religion and science we find a twofold theme. First, there is the spectacle of religion defending itself against the encroachments of science, and second, there is the spectacle of science hampered and even persecuted by religious organizations. The most celebrated example of religious interference with science is perhaps the humiliation of Galileo. Modern views about the position of the earth in the solar system, about sunspots, about comets, and about meteorology were all arrived at only in the face of theological opposition. In the nineteenth century the propagation of enlightened theories about the geological history of the earth and about the evolution of biological species was greatly hampered because Charles Lyell, Darwin, and others were apprehensive about exciting the animosity of the churches. The progress of medical science was considerably delayed on account of theological opinions about the causes of disease, which was regarded either as a rightful punishment for sins or as the malicious work of Satan. (Against this, of course, must be balanced the good practical effects of the impulse to carry on the healing work of Christ, for instance the founding of hospitals and of orders of nursing sisters.) Not only was the religious theory of the causes of disease inimical to those concerned with the development of theoretical medicine, but the study of anatomy itself was gravely handicapped by religious prohibition of the dissection of the human body. The belief in witches and the cruel use of the text "Thou shalt not permit a witch to live" held up the development of psychiatry, as did the religious opinion that insanity was due to an individual's being possessed by devils.

Happily, all these phenomena are now mainly of historical interest. The scientific spirit is presently so powerful, and scientists are so influential in modern society, that the persecution and intimidation of scientists by religious authorities are things of the past. Moreover, few religious apologists would wish to defend their churches' past hostility toward scientific ideas. They would argue that the persecution of science was a perversion of religion . . .

Finally, it should be noted that in the twentieth century it has frequently been claimed that while there may be a conflict between science and theology, science and religion are nevertheless compatible. This was also the position taken at the end of the nineteenth century by A. D. White in *A History of the Warfare of Science with Theology in Christendom,* in which he argued that a religion that is purified of antiscientific theological ideas will be all the stronger for it. As we shall note later on in this article, some modern philosophers carry this line of thought much further. They try to separate entirely religion and theology in the hope of making religion immune from any scientific criticism and indeed from any intellectual criticism whatever. We shall see that this attempt to remove religion from the intellectual arena is open to grave objections, and for the moment we shall adopt the more usual opinion that religion essentially involves theological ideas and that religion and theology must stand or fall together.

Theology and man's place in the universe. Any religion which, like Christianity, Judaism, and Islam, derives at least part of its authority from a body of scriptural writings that is thought to be divinely inspired, is likely to run into trouble when scriptural pronouncements contradict the findings of science. Thus, in the nineteenth century much ink was shed over the question of the literal truth of the story of the creation in Genesis and of the story of the deluge and Noah's ark, and so on. Some of T. H. Huxley's wittiest polemical essays turn on such issues. Today, however, theologians have generally given up the view of the Scriptures as being literally the word of God and have become content to think of them as inspired by God in some weaker sense, whereby the Scriptures can quite well be supposed to contain the outmoded cosmological, geological, biological, and historical speculations of prescientific man. It is this retreat on the part of the theologians that has made them safe from many of the attacks which T. H. Huxley and his contemporaries used to delight in making against them. This may in part explain the view that science and religion need no longer be in conflict.

Nevertheless, it is far from clear that the theologian has entrenched himself in a position that is safe from all attacks by science. The Christian religion contains at least two fundamental tenets—namely, those of immortality and of the efficacy of prayer—which seem to be particularly hard to reconcile with modern scientific ideas. It also contains tenets which would probably have to be considerably modified in order to be fitted into the modern scientific picture of the world, but which are so constituted that it is possible to suppose that the theologian might eventually be induced so to modify them. It will be convenient to review this latter sort of consideration first.

In its traditional form, Christianity is very much an anthropocentric doctrine. Man plays a central role in the Christian doctrine in a way that he does not, for example, in Hindu or Buddhist theology. The Christian system of ideas must have been more plausible when the earth was thought to be the center of the universe: above us was heaven, and below us was hell. It is true that various sorts of angels were supposed to exist and to be in some ways superior to human beings, but man was considered the lord of the material world. He was made in the image of God, and God became incarnate in the flesh of man. These considerations may pose two problems for theologians.

In the first place, modern astronomy has shown that our planet has no specially distinguished place in the universe. The earth rotates round the sun, which is a medium-sized star situated well away from the center of a vast galaxy of stars. Moreover, this galaxy is only one among countless similar systems of stars. There are probably hundreds of millions of such galaxies, and if certain cosmological speculations were to be accepted, we would have to say that there is an infinite number of them. It is quite probable that in our own galaxy alone there are perhaps hundreds of thousands of stars with planetary systems like that of our sun. Unless we think that the solar system is quite untypical, we must suppose that a fair proportion of these other systems contain planets on which life could develop; and modern speculations on the origin of life strongly suggest that where life can develop it will develop. The inhabitants of a small village may feel insignificant when they are made aware that the population of the earth is approximately three billion persons. Nevertheless, our own numerical insignificance relative to the population of the earth is negligible in comparison with the probable total population of inhabited planets in the universe.

In the second place, evolutionary considerations suggest other ways in which we may not be as important as we are apt to think we are. On our own planet (if we can avoid blowing ourselves up) evolution has perhaps hundreds of millions of years still to run. One who objects to the theological point of view may therefore urge that there may be distant planets on which there are living beings as far superior to *Homo sapiens* as *Homo sapiens* is superior to an insect or a worm. Therefore, is it not presumptuous of the theologian to claim that man is made in the image of God and that God became incarnate in man? . . .

Religious people often draw attention to their humility. However, as Bertrand Russell has often stressed, there is often an extraordinary vanity mixed with this humility: man was made in the likeness of God, God became man, and God concerns himself with our sins. A criminal feels flattered by the majesty and pomp of the law; although he may be executed, he has his name in the headlines. Similarly, there is something congenial to human vanity even in the thought that God considers us important enough to send us to hell, to say nothing of the belief that those of us who go to heaven find themselves in the very presence of God. . . .

 . . . It is quite likely that we may learn to direct the course of evolution by controlling the mechanisms of heredity. We may perhaps be able to induce favorable mutations in the hereditary material in human egg cells, thus transforming the human species. Some writers on evolution have hailed such a prospect with delight and optimism, but theologians on the whole have reacted with alarm and condemnation. Such experiments with the evolutionary process would indeed constitute a very great moral challenge, but apart from questionable theological premises, it is hard to see how such experiments would be morally wrong. Of course, we can easily feel outraged by the prospect of such evolutionary advances. The idea that we are not at the summit of the evolutionary process is a blow to our vanity. In this instance theological beliefs reinforce our natural human vanity, just as vanity may in part have determined the content of theological beliefs. As T. H. Huxley remarked in a slightly different context, in "The Evolution of Theology," "Men forgive all injuries but those which touch their self-esteem, and they make gods after their own likeness, in their own image make they them."

Therefore, even if theology has come to terms with modern ideas about the past evolution of the human species, as is commonly thought, it may have to face serious unresolved problems in connection with future evolution. It could also be argued that theologians have often been much too sanguine about the question of past evolution. Are modern evolutionary ideas quite so concordant with even a sophisticated theology as is usually supposed? The answer to this question, of course, depends on the particular theology in question. Roman Catholics are certainly allowed to believe in evolution, but there are some reservations. Pius XII, in his encyclical *Humani Generis* (1950), said that it is not permissible to believe that the human race does not descend from a single man. Conjectures about polygenism are incompatible with the doctrine of original sin. "Original sin," he wrote, "is the result of a sin committed, in actual historical fact, by an individual man named Adam, and it is a quality native to all of us, only because it has been handed down by descent from him." It would appear, then, that not only are Catholics committed to a monogenist theory of human evolution, but that they are involved in a serious biological unorthodoxy, for this doctrine of the inheritance of Adam's sinfulness seems to entail the acceptance of at least one instance of the inheritance of acquired characteristics.

When it is claimed that theology and evolutionary theory are compatible, it is always pertinent to inquire just what sort of evolutionary theory is meant. Many attempts to reconcile evolution with theology are in fact successful only in reconciling theology with a pseudoscientific evolutionary doctrine. The same can be said of evolutionary metaphysics of the type expounded by Bergson or, in a more popular form, by George Bernard Shaw, which provides a sort of substitute for religion. These romantic conceptions of evolution must be sharply distinguished from the properly scientific Neo-Darwinian theory, which is based on a mechanistic theory of natural selection that is in accordance with the theories of modern genetics. In modern biology, living creatures tend to be thought of as complicated self-maintaining and self-regulation systems, many of whose characteristics can be stimulated by means of physical artifacts. Modern theoretical biology has become more and more a matter of biochemistry. Through the work of A. I. Oparin, Harold Urey, and others, we are also beginning to be able to guess how life could have arisen naturally from inorganic matter. Few modern biologists, therefore, would wish to support the view of the Anglican theologian E. W. Barnes, bishop of Birmingham, England, who as recently as 1933 wrote that "the emergence of life must be regarded as a sign of creative activity" and that "the mystery of life is unsolved, probably unsolvable." It is extremely significant that Barnes, who in addition to being a noted mathematician was well known for his scientific and extremely modernist outlook in theology, should have said this. Even he, it seems, was impelled to believe in "the mystery of life." We must also remember that Roman Catholics hold that evolutionary theory is at the very least incomplete in that it cannot account of the emergence of the souls of men, which are believed to be created through the special agency of God.

Immortality. An important part of Christian belief is the doctrine of personal immortality. Most Christians, however, are committed to belief in the resurrection of the body. However, many Protestants do not take the doctrine of the resurrection of the body very seriously; they either deny it outright or interpret it in some figurative sense. They hold a doctrine of immortality according to which it is a purely immaterial self that survives death.

The doctrine of survival as purely immaterial spirit conflicts with many influential philosophical doctrines. Some philosophers elucidate mind in terms of bodily behavior, and others defend the doctrine that conscious experiences are brain processes. If such views are true, then there is clearly no such thing as an immaterial mind that could survive death. But even if some form of philosophical dualism is accepted and the mind is thought of as something over and above the body, the empirical evidence in favor of an invariable correlation between mental states and brain states is extremely strong: that is, the mind may be thought of as in some sense distinct from the body but also as fundamentally dependent upon physical states. Without oxygen or under the influence of anesthetics or soporific drugs, we rapidly lose consciousness. Moreover, the quality of our consciousness can be influenced in spectacular ways by appropriate drugs or by mechanical stimulation of different areas of the brain. In the face of all the evidence that is being accumulated by modern research in neurology, it is hard to believe that after the dissolution of the brain there could be any thought or conscious experience whatever.

The orthodox doctrine of the resurrection of the body clearly escapes the difficulties associated with the notion of the independent existence of the mind. However, it is beset with equally grave difficulties of another sort. In the early days of the Christian religion, the concept of the resurrection of the body was conceived crudely; the dead were thought to rise from the grave and live again in a heaven somewhere above the clouds. But where, in accordance with modern cosmological views, can the resurrected bodies exist? Any attempt to specify a location (or perhaps some "fifth dimension") seems subject to the sort of embarrassment that typically arises when we try to put the old wine of Christian theology into the new bottles of modern cosmology. There are also philosophical puzzles as to the sense in which the resurrected person would be the same as the earthly person. . . .

Prayer. A rather different issue, which may lead to conflict between science and religion, is the nature of prayer. At one time the efficacy of prayer was an issue decidable by experiment, as is shown by the Old Testament story of the contest between Elijah and the priests of Baal. Now, however, a more sophisticated attitude is likely to be adopted. The efficacy of prayer is not usually put forward as an empirical issue, for whatever happens is taken to be the will of God, and if a prayer is not answered it is presumably because God, in his own inscrutable way, knows better than we do what is best. Furthermore, the greater people's knowledge of how things actually happen, the less they tend to regard these things as capable of being affected by prayer. Even with all our knowledge of meteorology we cannot be sure what the weather is going to be; nevertheless, changes in the weather no longer strike us as being mysterious. Even many professed Christians have therefore come to feel that there is something about praying for rain that is akin to a belief in magic and superstition. Again, many religious people are not strongly inclined to pray for someone's recovery from disease when they have modern medical knowledge of its diagnosis and prognosis. Some will still continue to pray for a miracle, but many will not do so with any confidence. As weather and disease increasingly come within the scope of scientific law, so a prayer for rain or for the disappearance of a lesion comes more and more to seem like a prayer that the sun should stand still in the sky. Similarly, as our knowledge of human psychology increases, the mental states of human beings also lose their appearance of capriciousness, and the tendency to pray for someone's change of heart may go the way of the tendency to pray for good weather or for good health.

This is not to say, of course, that even the agnostic will regard all prayers as inefficacious. This is because prayer itself is a psychological process which has perfectly natural effects. Thus, one can deny the supernatural efficacy of prayer and still believe that a prayer for recovery can relieve a disease, if, for example, the disease is psychosomatic and the patient both believes in prayer and knows that he is being prayed for. This would be quite unlike the case of a prayer for the recovery of someone who was unaware of the prayer and who was entirely in the company of people who were likewise unaware of the prayer.

However, if prayer is to have supernatural efficacy (which it must have if the usual religious claims about prayer are correct), then its working must be at variance with our scientific beliefs about how things happen. For presumably, all the natural causes and effects of the behavior of the weather or of the human body or brain will be the same after a prayer has been offered as before. How, then, could the weather or the body or brain become different from what it would have been without the prayer? The entire matter is quite inexplicable and by suggesting that a sufficiently careful meteorological, physiological, or psychological investigation would reveal causal anomalies—that is, actual breaches of scientific law. This, however, would be a retreat to the old conception of the efficacy of prayer as a scientifically testable issue, and the theologian might be reluctant to re-enter the lists in this way.

Mysticism. In regard to the subject of the possibility of interaction between natural and supernatural agents, there is the question of whether religion can be based on mystical experience. It would seem that if mystical experiences are not mere aberrations of feeling, that are explicable in naturalistic terms, then they must be in some way miraculous. If mystical experiences exist and if they are the sort of thing that they are claimed to be, then how can they be explained in terms of modern psychology? In what way is the brain of the mystic affected by the supernatural with which he is in contact? Are the synapses in his brain changed by a purely supernatural agency, or must we believe that his mystical experiences are not correlatable with neuronal changes? Physics and physiology enable us to explain, in outline at least, how we can get in touch with rabbits or even with electrons. "Getting in touch" involves responses to physical stimuli, and it is clear that no naturalistic account could be given of mystical cognition of the supernatural. It would appear that either mystical experiences are not what they are claimed to be or else that there is a clash between the scientific and the theological ways of thinking about the mind.

Separation of religion and science. If the foregoing arguments are correct, it would appear that there are important areas in which science and religion impinge on each other. Some of the battlefields are indeed now deserted, and many of the polemics of nineteenth-century writers are no longer of interest. Nevertheless, it has been suggested in this article that in fundamental ways science does impinge on theology and that some of the conflicts between them are even sharper than they were a hundred years ago. It would be wrong to suppose that the peculiar characteristics of twentieth-century science make it necessarily less inimical to religion than was the science of the nineteenth century. It is true that Eddington and Jeans used to argue, on the basis of modern physics, for an idealist metaphysics, but their arguments would not be accepted by many contemporary philosophers. It is easy (although wrong) for a physicist to come to think of an electron as a mental construction out of sense experiences, but a biologist is not likely to be tempted in this way. For him, the animal is the concrete reality, and any experience which the animal has is something that happens to the animal: the animal can hardly be a construction out of things which happen to the animal.

Eddington, however, compared the scientist to an ichthyologist. Using a net of two-inch mesh, the ichthyologist catches fish that are never less than two inches long. Does this prove that there are no fish in the sea less than two inches long? Clearly not; but his net will never catch them. In the same way it is suggested that there are facts which the scientific method will never "catch."

This is an ingenious suggestion, but it will not help to resolve the sorts of controversy with which we have been concerned. These are not simply cases for scientific agnosticism, but cases in which the scientist would expect things to work out in one sort of way and the religious person would expect it to work out in another sort of way, or in which the religious person is at least likely to be disturbed by positive scientific facts, or the possibility of them. For example, it is hard to see how the idea that there are more things in the universe than science can know of could possibly affect theological worries about life on other planets.

Sometimes the theologian will point to art or morality as being outside the scope of science. However, since art and morality are concerned with evoking feelings and recommending actions, not with the cognition of facts, they would not appear to provide a counterinstance to the omnicompetence of science as a cognitive activity. The theologian, however, may be prepared to maintain that religion is not, in fact, a cognitive activity. An explicitly noncognitivist theory of religion has been put forward by R. B. Braithwaite and, in a slightly different form, by T. R. Miles. Clearly, if religion is essentially noncognitive, then, like morality and art, it cannot possibly conflict with science. These writers eliminate all factual content from religion: they interpret Christian doctrine purely as a collection of stories, myths, or parables that are used to inculcate a certain way of life—"agapeistic behaviour," as Braithwaite calls it. Certainly, if religious belief can be construed correctly in this way, then there can be no logical incompatibility between religion and science. (There may, of course, still be a psychological incompatibility, if the religious myths are uncongenial to the thought-forms of a scientific age.) However, it is unlikely that a religion thus construed is a religion that many religious people would recognize as such. Commonly, a religious creed is construed as making factual assertions. Most Christians would wish to say that in fact Christ rose from the dead, that in fact there is life after death, and so on. Moreover, if religion is not a matter of fact, there is the problem of how to decide rationally between Christianity, say, and Islam. Most religious people would probably not care to assert that the choice must be made on purely ethical or aesthetic grounds.

Other religions. It could plausibly be argued that Christianity is more vulnerable to objections drawn from cosmology, evolutionary theory, and other branches of science than is any other of the great religions. This is because Christianity is the most anthropocentric of the great religions. We have discussed possible ways in which the Christian theologian might react to this sort of challenge. However, in their conception of paradise popular forms of Islam would also appear to suffer from a crudely anthropocentric cosmology. The difficulties with respect to immortality apply to Judaism and Islam as well as to Christianity. Hinduism and Buddhism are easier to reconcile with science inasmuch as they do not give man a special place in the world and still less a place outside the purely natural order. In the case of Buddhism and some popular forms of Hinduism problems arise over the notion of reincarnation, which is contrary to the spirit of modern biology and psychology. Esoteric (Advaita) Hinduism is probably immune from scientific criticism, since its doctrine is on such a transcendental metaphysical level that it has no contact at all with the empirical level. However, such a form of Hinduism is perhaps more a form of metaphysics than of religion. In taking part in religious observances the devotee must abandon his austere metaphysics of nonduality in favor of a pluralism of god or gods and worshipers. In other words, he must return to the phenomenal level of māyā (illusion).

Finally, a critic of religious belief and practice might argue that any religion must inevitably conflict with science. This is because any religion, correctly so-called, relies heavily on the authority of tradition and ancient writings and perhaps of a priesthood. There will therefore be a tension in the mind of one who has leanings toward both science and religion. As a scientist he has scant respect for tradition or for the authority of old writings, and he is used to seeing the scientific theories of one generation rejected by the next. This is not to say that such tension is necessarily unsupportable, since there have always been devout men who have also been eminent scientists. Nevertheless, the tension is likely always to exist in the background, and in view of the great successes of science it may tend to bring about a progressive weakening of religious attitudes.

False Consciousness

From "Contribution to the Critique of Hegel's *Philosophy of Right:* Introduction" by Karl Marx in *The Marx-Engels Reader,* second edition, Robert C. Tucker, editor, 1978

The selection from Karl Marx (1818–1883) includes his famous statement, "religion is the opium of the masses." This is said as part of a debunking view that would explain the origin of religion and thus explain it away. Marx's theory of religion is historicist.

Philosophically, Marx took much from Hegel (see above), in particular Hegel's theory of history as dialectical progression. For Marx, however, in contrast to Hegel, the progression is not of an Absolute who is antecedent to human beings, but rather just of human consciousness and society. Historical progression will lead, Marx thinks, to true self-awareness, which is, according to him, a species awareness. A human being truly understands herself or himself when she sees herself not as an individual human being but as a human species being.

Religion is a symptom, and a cause, of self-deception, of an alienation from true self-understanding. Religion is escapism. It drains off the best of human energies in fantasy, energies that could be directed to the realization of what we are in ourselves and a construction of a common human home, a potential paradise where we would work together, seeing everyone as family, each having desires we would take as seriously as our own. This is Marx's utopian vision.

Thus religion is to be explained with reference to historical circumstances, economic circumstances, according to Marx, in particular. Human beings (subconsciously) invent religion; they people the heavens with supernatural beings to escape harsh economic realities. Such a view of historical determination of ideas and consciousness has had much influence among scholars and intellectuals all over the world since Marx, though few any longer accept (in good faith) the details of Marx's theory.

The basis of irreligious criticism is this: *man makes religion;* religion does not make man. Religion is indeed man's self-consciousness and self-awareness so long as he has not found himself or has lost himself again. But *man* is not an abstract being, squatting outside the world. Man is *the human world,* the state, society. This state, this society, produce religion which is an *inverted world consciousness,* because they are an *inverted world.* Religion is the general theory of this world, its encyclopedic compendium, its logic in popular form, its spiritual *point d'honneur,* its enthusiasm, its moral sanction, its solemn complement, its general basis of consolation and justification. It is *the fantastic realization* of the human being inasmuch as the human being possesses no true reality. The struggle against religion is, therefore, indirectly a struggle against *that world* whose spiritual aroma is religion.

Religious suffering is at the same time an *expression* of real suffering and a *protest* against real suffering. Religion is the sigh of the oppressed creature, the sentiment of a heartless world, and the soul of soulless conditions. It is the *opium* of the people.

The abolition of religion as the *illusory* happiness of men, is a demand for the *real* happiness. The call to abandon their illusions about their condition is a *call to abandon a condition* which *requires illusions*. The criticism of religion is, therefore, *the embryonic criticism of this vale of tears* of which religion is the *halo.*

The Anthropology and Sociology of Religion

From *Religion in Primitive Culture* by E. B. Tylor, 1958 • From *The Elementary Forms of Religious Life* by Émile Durkheim, 1915

Such "primitive" religious practices as propitiation of nature gods lies at the bottom of much contemporary worship, according to the anthropological perspective pioneered by E. B. Tylor (1832–1917). Tylor was an Oxford don at a time of great expansion of the social sciences. Continuity between early human societies and our own was the byword in anthropology, and Tylor at the end of his magnum opus, *excerpted here, speculates about the meaning of this for theology. Subsequent anthropologists understood Tylor's approach as debunking, as showing religion as a holdover from more primitive societies, though Tylor himself does not say as much in so many words. In a different direction, some theologians took Tylor's discoveries to show not only that religiosity is native to all society, but that the idea of God is innate to all human mentality. This* common consent argument *has been refuted decisively by evidence cited by later anthropologists, who have, I repeat, by and large seen Tylor as pioneering theories that would explain religion (away!) in the ritual practices of early societies.*

After Tylor, the science of sociology broke away from anthropology, and in some quarters a different understanding of religion emerged. Pioneered by the French scholar Émile Durkheim (1858–1917), the sociology of religion *finds the essential religious characteristic to be ritual binding together of social elements. Society thus requires religious practices just to be what it is. Now religious practices go hand-in-hand with religious beliefs. The meaning of the beliefs, however, usually unknown to the society or clan itself, are just the ideals that organize the society or clan. Religious symbols convey religious beliefs; all religious representation occurs through these. Religious symbols are essentially totems, and the gods of totems and the ideals of society and society itself are essentially one. Thus religion holds a society together, as the integrity of the totem, for example, is identified with the integrity of the clan. According to Durkheim, even the fundamental categories of mind, the fundamental forms of human understanding, are derived from ritual performances.*

We may wonder whether such explanation of religious practices and beliefs is, one, successful, and, two, if successful whether it means that the beliefs are false. Durkheim insists that to ask about truth or falsity is to miss the point about religion. But philosophers ask the question anyway—as shall I later, in introducing Freud, our final debunker, another who purports to unmask religion as an illusion or product of false consciousness.

FROM *RELIGION IN PRIMITIVE CULTURE*

It now remains, in bringing to a close these investigations on the relation of primitive to modern civilization, to urge the practical import of the considerations raised in their course. Granted that archaeology, leading the student's mind back to remotest known conditions of human life, shows such life to have been of unequivocally savage type; granted that the rough-hewn flint hatchet, dug out from amidst the bones of mammoths in a drift gravel-bed to lie on an ethnologist's writing-table, is to him a very type of primitive culture, simple yet crafty, clumsy yet purposeful, low in artistic level yet fairly started on the ascent toward highest development—what then? Of course the history and præ-history of man take their proper places in the general scheme of knowledge. Of course the doctrine of the world-long evolution of civilization is one which philosophic minds will take up with eager interest, as a theme of abstract science. But beyond this, such research has its practical side, as a source of power destined to influence the course of modern ideas and actions. To establish a connexion between what uncultured ancient men thought and did, and what cultured modern men think and do, is not a matter of inapplicable theoretic knowledge, for it raises the issue, how far are modern opinion and conduct based on the strong ground of soundest modern knowledge or how far only on such knowledge as was available in the earlier and ruder stages of culture where their types were shaped. . . .

The general study of the ethnography of religion, through all its immensity of range, seems to countenance the theory of evolution in its highest and widest sense. In the treatment of some of its topics here, I have propounded special hypotheses as to the order in which various stages of doctrine and rite have succeeded one another in the history of religion. Yet how far these particular theories may hold good, seems even to myself a minor matter. The essential part of the ethnographic method in theology lies in admitting as relevant the compared evidence of religion in all stages of culture. The action of such evidence on theology proper is in this wise, that a vast proportion of doctrines and rites known among mankind are not to be judged as direct products of the particular religious systems which give them sanction, for they are in fact more or less modified results adopted from previous systems. The theologian, as he comes to deal with each element of belief and worship, ought to ascertain its place in the general scheme of religion. Should the doctrine or rite in question appear to have been transmitted from an earlier to a later stage of religious thought, then it should be tested, like any other point of culture, as to its place in development. The question has to be raised, to which of these three categories it belongs—is it a product of the earlier theology, yet sound enough to maintain a rightful place in the later?—is it derived from a cruder original, yet so modified as to become a proper representative of more advanced views?—is it a survival from a lower stage of thought, imposing on the credit of the higher by virtue not of inherent truth but of ancestral belief? These are queries the very asking of which starts trains of thought which candid minds should be encouraged to pursue, leading as they do toward the attainment of such measure of truth as the intellectual condition of our age fits us to assimilate. In the scientific study of religion, which now shows signs of becoming for many a year an engrossing subject of the world's thought, the decision must not rest with a council in which the theologian, the metaphysician, the biologist, the physicist, exclusively take part. The historian and the ethnographer must be called upon to show the hereditary standing of each opinion and practice, and their enquiry must go back as far as antiquity or savagery can show a vestige, for there seems no human thought so primitive as to have lost its bearing on our own thought, nor so ancient as to have broken its connection with our own life.

FROM *THE ELEMENTARY FORMS OF RELIGIOUS LIFE*

In this book we propose to study the most primitive and simple religion which is actually known, to make an analysis of it, and to attempt an explanation of it. A religious system may be said to be the most primitive which we can observe when it fulfils the two following conditions: in the first place, when it is found in a society whose organization is surpassed by no others in simplicity;[1] and secondly, when it is possible to explain it without making use of any element borrowed from a previous religion.

We shall set ourselves to describe the organization of this system with all the exactness and fidelity that an ethnographer or an historian could give it. But our task will not be limited to that: sociology raises other problems than history or ethnography. It does not seek to know the passed forms of civilization with the sole end of knowing them and reconstructing them. But rather, like every positive science, it has as its object the explanation of some actual reality which is near to us, and which consequently is capable of affecting our ideas and our acts: this reality is man, and more precisely, the man of to-day, for there is nothing which we are more interested in knowing. Then we are not going to study a very archaic religion simply for the pleasure of telling its peculiarities and its singularities. If we have taken it as the subject of our research, it is because it has seemed to us better adapted than any other to lead to an understanding of the religious nature of man, that is to say, to show us an essential and permanent aspect of humanity.

But this proposition is not accepted before the raising of strong objections. It seems very strange that one must turn back, and be transported to the very beginnings of history, in order to arrive at an understanding of humanity as it is at present. This manner of procedure seems particularly paradoxical in the question which concerns us. In fact, the various religions generally pass as being quite unequal in value and dignity; it is said that they do not all contain the same quota of truth. Then it seems as though one could not compare the highest forms of religious thought with the lowest, without reducing the first to the level of the second. If we admit that the crude cults of the Australian tribes can help us to understand Christianity, for example, is that not supposing that this latter religion proceeds from the same mentality as the former, that it is made up of the same superstitions and rests upon the same errors? This is how the theoretical importance which has sometimes been attributed to primitive religions has come to pass as a sign of a systematic hostility to all religion, which, by prejudging the results of the study, vitiates them in advance.

There is no occasion for asking here whether or not there are scholars who have merited this reproach, and who have made religious history and ethnology a weapon against

---

[1] In the same way, we shall say of these societies that they are primitive, and we shall call the men of these societies primitives. Undoubtedly the expression lacks precision, but that is hardly evitable, and besides, when we have taken pains to fix the meaning, it is not inconvenient.

religion. In any case, a sociologist cannot hold such a point of view. In fact, it is an essential postulate of sociology that a human institution cannot rest upon an error and a lie, without which it could not exist. If it were not founded in the nature of things, it would have encountered in the facts a resistance over which it could never have triumphed. So when we commence the study of primitive religions, it is with the assurance that they hold to reality and express it; this principle will be seen to re-enter again and again in the course of the analyses and discussions which follow, and the reproach which we make against the schools from which we have separated ourselves is that they have ignored it. When only the letter of the formulae is considered, these religious beliefs and practices undoubtedly seem disconcerting at times, and one is tempted to attribute them to some sort of a deep-rooted error. But one must know how to go underneath the symbol to the reality which it represents and which gives it its meaning. The most barbarous and the most fantastic rites and the strangest myths translate some human need, some aspect of life, either individual or social. The reasons with which the faithful justify them may be, and generally are, erroneous; but the true reasons do not cease to exist, and it is the duty of science to discover them.

In reality, then, there are no religions which are false. All are true in their own fashion; all answer, though in different ways, to the given conditions of human existence. It is undeniably possible to arrange them in a hierarchy. Some can be called superior to others, in the sense that they call into play higher mental functions, that they are richer in ideas and sentiments, that they contain more concepts with fewer sensations and images, and that their arrangement is wiser. But howsoever real this greater complexity and this higher ideality may be, they are not sufficient to place the corresponding religions in different classes. All are religions equally, just as all living beings are equally alive, from the most humble plastids up to man. So when we turn to primitive religions it is not with the idea of depreciating religion in general, for these religions are no less respectable than the others. They respond to the same needs, they play the same rôle, they depend upon the same causes; they can also well serve to show the nature of the religious life, and consequently to resolve the problem which we wish to study. . . .

For a society to become conscious of itself and maintain at the necessary degree of intensity the sentiments which it thus attains, it must assemble and concentrate itself. Now this concentration brings about an exaltation of the mental life which takes form in a group of ideal conceptions where is portrayed the new life thus awakened; they correspond to this new set of psychical forces which is added to those which we have at our disposition for the daily tasks of existence. A society can neither create itself nor recreate itself without at the same time creating an ideal. This creation is not a sort of work of supererogation for it, by which it would complete itself, being already formed; it is the act by which it is periodically made and remade. Therefore when some oppose the ideal society to the real society, like two antagonists which would lead us in opposite directions, they materialize and oppose abstractions. The ideal society is not outside of the real society; it is a part of it. Far from being divided between them as between two poles which mutually repel each other, we cannot hold to one without holding to the other. For a society is not made up merely of the mass of individuals who compose it, the ground which they occupy, the things which they use and the movements which they perform, but above all is the idea which it forms of itself. It is undoubtedly true that it hesitates over the manner in which it ought to conceive itself; it feels itself drawn in divergent directions. But these conflicts which break forth are not between the ideal and reality, but between two different ideals, that of yesterday and that of to-day, that which has the authority of tradition and that which has the hope of the future. There is surely a place for investigating whence these ideals evolve; but whatever solution may be given to this problem, it still remains that all passes in the world of the ideal.

Thus the collective ideal which religion expresses is far from being due to a vague innate power of the individual, but it is rather at the school of collective life that the individual has learned to idealize. It is in assimilating the ideals elaborated by society that he has become capable of conceiving the ideal. It is society which, by leading him within its sphere of action, has made him acquire the need of raising himself above the world of experience and has at the same time furnished him with the means of conceiving another. For society has constructed this new world in constructing itself, since it is society which this expresses. Thus both with the individual and in the group, the faculty of idealizing has nothing mysterious about it. It is not a sort of luxury which a man could get along without, but a condition of his very existence. He could not be a social being, that is to say, he could not be a man, if he had not acquired it. It is true that in incarnating themselves in individuals, collective ideals tend to individualize themselves. Each understands them after his own fashion and marks them with his own stamp; he suppresses certain elements and adds others. Thus the personal ideal disengages itself from the social ideal in proportion as the individual personality develops itself and becomes an autonomous source of action. But if we wish to understand this aptitude, so singular in appearance, of living outside of reality, it is enough to connect it with the social conditions upon which it depends.

Fantasy and Wish Fulfilment

From *The Future of an Illusion* by Sigmund Freud, James Strachey, translator, 1961

Sigmund Freud (1856–1939), the founder of psychoanalysis, forged an explanation of religion (in its most general features) that draws on anthropological and sociological findings, supplemented by Freud's own psychological theories. For Freud, religion serves to maintain psychological health by providing the kind of fantastical wish-fulfilment accomplished by dreams. Religion also performs a socializing function.

Religion helps us cope with the difficulties of life and especially each of our impending deaths. This role dovetails with a socializing function. Individuals renounce individual satisfactions (subconsciously, in privation*) in subordinating their individual desires to social cohesion. Society repays in health and quality of life in ways continuous with religion, particularly in earlier stages of civilization. Thus society and its gods have, in Freud's words, a "threefold task: they must exorcise the terrors of nature, they must reconcile men to the cruelty of Fate, particularly as it is shown to them in death, and they must compensate them for the sufferings and privations which a civilized life in common has imposed on them."*

Propitiation of nature gods and like practices in early religion—along with a host of modern social phenomena (such as wartime public prayers)—make Freud's and similar outlooks on the origins of religion ring true. There is also the consolation that religions the world over, and in every age, bring to death, to the death of loved ones and to the imminence of one's own demise. Is it true that whether or not God exists, or whether anything like God is real, that people would invent religion?

The success of a Freudian or another debunking explanation of religion would suggest that religious beliefs are false. Debunking explanations make the beliefs debunked seem improbable. Different areas or fields of science support one another, interlocking to varying degrees. Thus the debunking explanations of the sociology and psychology of religion, though as theories not themselves as well established as theories in some areas, challenge world religions and entire sets or systems of beliefs that have grown up as their intellectual supports.

On the other hand, Freud, it should be pointed out, proceeds on the assumption that religious beliefs are false and unwarranted; he says expressly that the judgment that religious beliefs are not well-founded forms part of the block from which his explanation is carved. That is to say, he assumes that none of the arguments or mystic testimony successfully ground religious beliefs. We may ask, is this judgment correct?

Moreover, whereas Freud's theory helps us to understand how religions arise, or probably arise, namely, in individual and social needs, there is at least the possibility that a religious practice or belief be overdetermined. *That is, it could arise by a complex of causes C_1, with another complex C_2 such that if C_1 hadn't been operative C_2 would have done the trick. Eight clothespins could be holding up a shirt when one or two are all that are needed. There is also the possibility that Freud's views, or another debunker's, do not apply to a specific range of religious phenomena or specific set of religious beliefs. Moreover, sociological and psychological explanations of religious phenomena are much more speculative—much less well established—than theories in the physical and biological sciences, classifications in botany, for example. Finally, Durkheim's and Freud's views, in particular, face difficulties themselves, difficulties peculiar to the causal agencies they propose.*

Opponents and defenders of religion battle on anthropological, sociological, and psychological grounds and assumptions. There is surely in the science of religion (as opposed to a theology's theoretical bridges to science) much grist for philosophers' mills.

For the individual, too, life is hard to bear, just as it is for mankind in general. The civilization in which he participates imposes some amount of privation on him, and other men bring him a measure of suffering, either in spite of the precepts of his civilization or because of its imperfections. To this are added the injuries which untamed nature—he calls it Fate—inflicts on him. One might suppose that this condition of things would result in a permanent state of anxious expectation in him and a severe injury to his natural narcissism. We know already how the individual reacts to the injuries which civilization and other men inflict on him: he develops a corresponding degree of resistance to the regulations of civilization and of hostility to it. But how does he defend himself against the superior powers of nature, of Fate, which threaten him as they threaten all the rest?

Civilization relieves him of this task; it performs it in the same way for all alike; and it is noteworthy that in this almost all civilizations act alike. Civilization does not call a halt in the task of defending man against nature, it merely pursues it by other means. The task is a manifold one. Man's self-regard, seriously menaced, calls for consolation; life and the universe must be robbed of their terrors; moreover his curiosity, moved, it is true, by the strongest practical interest, demands an answer.

A great deal is already gained with the first step: the humanization of nature. Impersonal forces and destinies cannot be approached; they remain eternally remote. But if the elements have passions that rage as they do in our own souls, if death itself is not something spontaneous but the violent act of an evil Will, if everywhere in nature there are Beings around us of a kind that we know in our own society, then we can breathe freely, can feel at home in the uncanny and can deal by psychical means with our senseless anxiety. We are still defenceless, perhaps, but we are no longer helplessly paralysed; we can at least react. Perhaps, indeed, we are not even defenceless. We can apply the same methods against these violent supermen outside which we employ in our own society; we can try to adjure them, to appease them, to bribe them, and, by so influencing them, we may rob them of a part of their power. A replacement like this of natural science by psychology not only provides immediate relief, but also points the way to a further mastering of the situation.

For this situation is nothing new. It has an infantile prototype, of which it is in fact only the continuation. For once before one has found oneself in a similar state of helplessness: as a small child, in relation to one's parents. One had reason to fear them, and especially one's father; and yet one was sure of his protection against the dangers one knew. Thus it was natural to assimilate the two situations. Here, too, wishing played its part, as it does in dream-life. The sleeper may be seized with a presentiment of death, which threatens to place him in the grave. But the dream-work knows how to select a condition that will turn even that dreaded event into a wish-fulfilment: the dreamer sees himself in an ancient Etruscan grave which he has climbed down into, happy to find his archaeological interests satisfied.[1] In the same way, a man makes the forces of nature not simply into persons with whom he can associate as he would with his equals—that would not do justice to the overpowering impression which those forces make on him— but he gives them the character of a father. He turns them into gods, following in this, as I have tried to show,[2] not only an infantile prototype but a phylogenetic one.

In the course of time the first observations were made of regularity and conformity to law in natural phenomena, and with this the forces of nature lost their human traits. But man's helplessness remains and along with it his longing for his father, and the gods. The gods retain their threefold task: they must exorcize the terrors of nature, they must reconcile men to the cruelty of Fate, particularly as it is shown in death, and they must compensate them for the sufferings and privations which a civilized life in common has imposed on them.

---

[1] This was an actual dream of Freud's, reported in Chapter VI (G) of *The Interpretation of Dreams* (1900), *Standard Ed.*, 5, 454–5.

[2] See Section 6 of the fourth essay in *Totem and Taboo* (1912–13), *Standard Ed.*, 13, 146 ff.

Classical Indian Materialism

From *The Sarva-Darśana-Saṃgraha,* E. B. Cowell and A. E. Gough, translators, 1914

In classical India, opposition to religious views was prominent. A materialist school called Cārvāka—also called Lokāyata, a term meaning "those attached to the ways of the world"—became famous for debunking religious positions. Cārvāka philosophers held that physical matter is the only reality. To this metaphysical position, they attached an ethics of hedonism and "live for the day."

Seeing matter as the only reality, materialists brook no spiritual entities such as God or souls. Nor is there rebirth or any kind of an afterlife. Consciousness arises out of material elements somewhat like the "intoxicating power of grain (etc., processed into beer)." The Indian materialists were also sensationists, maintaining that we can know only what we perceive through our senses, namely, material elements and their combinations.

The selection here is taken from a late Sanskrit textbook (c. 1500) that presents a wide range of contending views, views of more than fifteen distinct philosophic schools (and in some cases several subschools, as with Buddhist philosophy). As we can see, the materialists were apparently known for wit in attacking religious beliefs.

The efforts of Cārvāka are indeed hard to be eradicated, for the majority of living beings hold by the current refrain—

> While life is yours, live joyously;
> None can escape Death's searching eye;
> When once this frame of ours they burn,
> How shall it e'er again return?

The mass of men, in accordance with the Śāstras of policy and enjoyment, considering wealth and desire the only ends of man and denying the existence of any object belonging to a future world, are found to follow only the doctrine of Cārvāka. Hence another name for that school is Lokāyata—a name well accordant with the thing signified.

In this school the four elements, earth, etc. are the original principles; from these alone, when transformed into the body, intelligence is produced, just as the inebriating power is developed from the mixing of certain ingredients; and when these are destroyed, intelligence at once perishes also. They quote the *śruti* [Vedic text] for this [*Bṛhadáraṇyaka Upanishad* ii.iv.12]: "Springing forth from these elements, itself solid knowledge, it is destroyed when they are destroyed—after death no intelligence remains." Therefore the soul is only the body distinguished by the attribute of intelligence, since there is no evidence for any self distinct from the body, as such cannot be proved, since this school holds that perception is the only source of knowledge and does not allow inference, etc.

The only end of man is enjoyment produced by sensual pleasures. Nor may you say that such cannot be called the end of man as they are always mixed with some kind of pain, because it is our wisdom to enjoy the pure pleasure as far as we can, and to avoid the pain which inevitably accompanies it; just as the man who desires fish takes the fish with their scales and bones, and having taken as many as he wants, desists; or just as the man who desires rice, takes the rice, straw and all, and having taken as much as he wants, desists. It is not therefore for us, through a fear of pain, to reject the pleasure which our nature instinctively recognises as congenial. Men do not refrain from sowing rice, because forsooth there are wild animals to devour it; nor do they refuse to set the cooking-pots on the fire, because forsooth there are beggars to pester us for a share of the contents. If any one were so timid as to forsake a visible pleasure, he would indeed be foolish like a beast, as has been said by the poet—

> The pleasure which arises to men from contact with sensible objects,
> Is to be relinquished as accompanied by pain—such is the reasoning of fools;
> The berries of paddy, rich with the finest white grains,
> What man, seeking his true interest, would fling away because covered with husk
> and dust?

If you object that, if there be no such thing as happiness in a future world, then how should men of experienced wisdom engage in the *Agnihotra*[1] and other sacrifices, which can only be performed with great expenditure of money and bodily fatigue, your objection cannot be accepted as any proof to the contrary, since the *Agnihotra,* etc., are only useful as means of livelihood, for the Veda is tainted by the three faults of untruth, self-contradiction, and tautology; then again the imposters who call themselves Vaidic [or Vedic] pandits are mutually destructive, as the authority of the *jñāna-khaṇḍa* (section on knowledge) is overthrown by those who maintain that of the *karma-khaṇḍa* (section on action), while those who maintain the authority of the *jñāna-khaṇḍa* reject that of the *karma-khaṇḍa;* and lastly, the three Vedas themselves are only the incoherent rhapsodies of knaves, and to this effect runs the popular saying—

> The Agnihotra, the three Vedas, the ascetic's three staves, and smearing oneself with
> ashes,—
> Bṛhaspati says these are but means of livelihood for those who have no manliness nor
> sense.

Hence it follows that there is no other hell than mundane pain produced by purely mundane causes, as thorns, etc.; the only Supreme is the earthly monarch whose existence is proved by all the world's eyesight; and the only liberation is the dissolution of the body. By holding the doctrine that the soul is identical with the body, such phrases as "I am thin," "I am black," etc., are at once intelligible, as the attributes of thinness, etc., and self-

---

[1] Sacrificial offering to fire.

consciousness will reside in the same subject (the body); and the use of the phrase "my body" is metaphorical like "the head of Rahu" [Rahu being really *all head*].

All this has been thus summed up—
In this school there are four elements, earth, water, fire, and air;
And from these four elements alone is intelligence produced,—
Just like the intoxicating power from *kinva*, etc., mixed together;
Since in "I am fat," "I am lean," these attributes abide in the same subject,
And since fatness, etc., reside only in the body, it alone is the soul and no other,
And such phrases as "my body" are only significant metaphorically. . . .

. . . phenomena can all be produced spontaneously from the inherent nature of things. Thus it has been said—

The fire is hot, the water cold, refreshing cool the breeze of morn;
By whom came this variety? from their own nature was it born. . . .
There is no heaven, no final liberation, nor any soul in another world,
Nor do the actions of the four castes, orders, etc., produce any real effect.
The *Agnihotra,* the three Vedas, the ascetic's three staves, and smearing oneself with ashes,
Were made by Nature as the livelihood of those destitute of knowledge and manliness.
If a beast slain in the *Jyotiṣṭoma* rite[2] will itself go to heaven,
Why then does not the sacrificer forthwith offer his own father?
If the *Śrāddha*[3] produces gratification to beings who are dead,
Then here, too, in the case of travellers when they start, it is needless to give provisions for the journey.
If beings in heaven are gratified by our offering the *Śrāddha* here,
Then why not give the food down below to those who are standing on the housetop?
While life remains let a man live happily, let him feed on gee even though he runs in debt;
When once the body becomes ashes, how can it ever return again?
If he who departs from the body goes to another world,
How is it that he comes not back again, restless for love of his kindred?
Hence it is only as a means of livelihood that *brāhmins* have established here
All these ceremonies for the dead—there is no other fruit anywhere.
The three authors of the Vedas were buffoons, knaves, and demons.
All the well-known formulas of the pandits . . .
And all the obscene rites for the queen . . . ,
These were invented by buffoons, and so all the various kinds of presents to the priests,
While the eating of flesh was similarly commanded by night-prowling demons.

---

[2] A Vedic sacrifice.
[3] Oblations to the dead.

Hence in kindness to the mass of living beings must we fly for refuge to the doctrine of Cārvāka. Such is the pleasant consummation.

Areligious Existentialism

From *The Myth of Sisyphus and Other Essays* by Albert Camus, Justin O'Brien, translator, 1955

The French existentialist, Albert Camus (1913–1960), a novelist as well as an essayist, won the Noble Prize for Literature. Along with Jean-Paul Sartre, Camus led the existentialist movement in the forties and fifties until his death in a car accident.

Camus's existentialist themes are revolt and freedom within an absurd universe, the social universe as well as the natural. He stresses the radical contingencies of life and a presumed inability of science and philosophy to explain human awareness. He is skeptical of any externally imposed system of values, and attacks science, as well as religion, when either would tell us who or what we are or what should be our values. Sartre insists that each of us makes our own meaning, and Camus views this as part and parcel of freedom. Choice is central in the existentialist view; it is our existence. Thus the existentialist slogan, "Existence before essence," means choice over idea—personal, arbitrary, individual choice before any explanation or imposed set of ideas or values.

Camus sees atheism as a matter of deep honesty and good faith. Near the end of his first novel, The Stranger, *the central character, Meursault, who is about to be executed, dramatically banishes a priest from his cell, refusing an offer of spiritual expiation. Camus sees the religious existentialist, who like himself views the world as absurd, but who unlike himself makes a leap of faith (see the selection from Kierkegaard under Faith Against Reason), as selling out, as abandoning the existentialist attitude because absurdity is too hard to live with. Camus's counsel is instead: "Everything considered, a determined soul will always manage."*

The selection here is excerpted from Camus's essay, The Myth of Sisyphus, *and is mainly occupied with what is wrong with the so-called religious existentialist, who arbitrarily leaps to God. For Camus, the titan Sisyphus of Greek mythology, condemned to push a rock up a hill only to have it roll back and to have to do it all over again, for an unforeseeable eternity, is the model of the true existentialist who triumphs in an inner attitude against the absurdity of his/her situation.*

If I accuse an innocent man of a monstrous crime, if I tell a virtuous man that he has coveted his own sister, he will reply that this is absurd. His indignation has its comical aspect. But it also has its fundamental reason. The virtuous man illustrates by that reply the definitive antinomy existing between the deed I am attributing to him and his lifelong principles. "It's absurd" means "It's impossible" but also "It's contradictory." If I see a man armed only with a sword attack a group of machine guns, I shall consider his act to be absurd. But it is so solely by virtue of the disproportion between his intention and the reality he will encounter, of the contradiction I notice between his true strength and the aim he has in view. Likewise we shall deem a verdict absurd when we contrast it with the verdict the facts apparently dictated. And, similarly, a demonstration by the absurd is achieved by comparing the consequences of such a reasoning with the logical reality one wants to set up. In all these cases, from the simplest to the most complex, the magnitude of the absurdity will be in direct ratio to the distance between the two terms of my comparison. There are absurd marriages, challenges, rancors, silences, wars, and even peace treaties. For each of them the absurdity springs from a comparison. I am thus justified in saying that the feeling of absurdity does not spring from the mere scrutiny of a fact or an impression, but that it bursts from the comparison between a bare fact and a certain reality, between an action and the world that transcends it. The absurd is essentially a divorce. It lies in neither of the elements compared; it is born of their confrontation.

In this particular case and on the plane of intelligence, I can therefore say that the Absurd is not in man (if such a metaphor could have a meaning) nor in the world, but in their presence together. For the moment it is the only bond uniting them. If I wish to limit myself to facts, I know what man wants, I know what the world offers him, and now I can say that I also know what links them. I have no need to dig deeper. A single certainty is enough for the seeker. He simply has to derive all the consequences from it.

The immediate consequence is also a rule of method. The odd trinity brought to light in this way is certainly not a startling discovery. But it resembles the data of experience in that it is both infinitely simple and infinitely complicated. Its first distinguishing feature in this regard is that it cannot be divided. To destroy one of its terms is to destroy the whole. There can be no absurd outside the human mind. Thus, like everything else, the absurd ends with death. But there can be no absurd outside this world either. And it is by this elementary criterion that I judge the notion of the absurd to be essential and consider that it can stand as the first of my truths. The rule of method alluded to above appears here. If I judge that a thing is true, I must preserve it. If I attempt to solve a problem, at least I must not by that very solution conjure away one of the terms of the problem. For me the sole datum is the absurd. The first and, after all, the only condition of my inquiry is to preserve the very thing that crushes me, consequently to respect what I consider essential in it. I have just defined it as a confrontation and an unceasing struggle.

And carrying this absurd logic to its conclusion, I must admit that struggle implies a total absence of hope (which has nothing to do with despair), a continual rejection (which must not be confused with renunciation), and a conscious dissatisfaction (which must not be compared to immature unrest). Everything that destroys, conjures away, or exorcises these requirements (and, to begin with, consent which overthrows divorce) ruins the absurd and devaluates the attitude that may then be proposed. The absurd has meaning only in so far as it is not agreed to.

There exists an obvious fact that seems utterly moral: namely, that a man is always a prey to his truths. Once he has admitted them, he cannot free himself from them. One has to pay something. A man who has become conscious of the absurd is forever bound to it. A man devoid of hope and conscious of being so has ceased to belong to the future. That is natural. But it is just as natural that he should strive to escape the universe of which he is the creator. All the foregoing has significance only on account of this paradox. Certain men, starting from a critique of rationalism, have admitted the absurd climate. Nothing is more instructive in this regard than to scrutinize the way in which they have elaborated their consequences.

Now, to limit myself to existential philosophies, I see that all of them without exception suggest escape. Through an odd reasoning, starting out from the absurd over the ruins of reason, in a closed universe limited to the human, they deify what crushes them and find reason to hope in what impoverishes them. That forced hope is religious in all of them. It deserves attention.

I shall merely analyze here as examples a few themes dear to Chestov and Kierkegaard. . . .

. . . To be sure, it is hard to outline clear propositions in so elusive a writer [as Kierkegaard]. But, despite apparently opposed writings, beyond the pseudonyms, the tricks, and the smiles, can be felt throughout that work, as it were, the presentiment (at the same time as the apprehension) of a truth which eventually bursts forth in the last works: Kierkegaard likewise takes the leap. His childhood having been so frightened by Christianity, he ultimately returns to its harshest aspect. For him, too, antinomy and paradox become criteria of the religious. Thus, the very thing that led to despair of the meaning and depth of this life now gives it its truth and its clarity. Christianity is the scandal, and what Kierkegaard calls for quite plainly is the third sacrifice required by Ignatius Loyola, the one in which God most rejoices: "The sacrifice of the intellect."[1] This effect of the "leap" is odd, but must not surprise us any longer. He makes of the absurd the criterion of the other world, whereas it is simply a residue of the experience of this world. "In his future," says Kierkegaard, "the believer finds his triumph."

It is not for me to wonder to what stirring preaching this attitude is linked. I merely have to wonder if the spectacle of the absurd and its own character justifies it. On this point, I know that it is not so. Upon considering again the content of the absurd, one understands better the method that inspired Kierkegaard. Between the irrational of the world and the insurgent nostalgia of the absurd, he does not maintain the equilibrium. He does not respect the relationship that constitutes, properly speaking, the feeling of absurdity. Sure of being able to escape the irrational, he wants at least to save himself from that desperate nostalgia that seems to him sterile and devoid of implication. But if he may be right on this point in his judgment, he could not be in his negation. If he substitutes for his cry of revolt a frantic adherence, at once he is led to blind himself to the absurd which hitherto enlightened him and to deify the only certainty he henceforth possesses, the irrational. The important thing, as Abbé Galiani said to Mme d'Epinay, is not to be cured, but to live with one's ailments. Kierkegaard wants to be cured. To be cured is his frenzied wish, and it runs throughout his whole journal. The entire effort of his intelligence is to escape the antinomy of the human condition. An all the more desperate effort since he intermittently perceives its vanity when he speaks of himself, as if neither fear of God

---

[1] It may be thought that I am neglecting here the essential problem, that of faith. But I am not examining the philosophy of Kierkegaard or of Chestov or, later on, of Husserl (this would call for a different place and a different attitude of mind); I am simply borrowing a theme from them and examining whether its consequences can fit the already established rules. It is merely a matter of persistence.

nor piety were capable of bringing him to peace. Thus it is that, through a strained subterfuge, he gives the irrational the appearance and God the attributes of the absurd: unjust, incoherent, and incomprehensible. Intelligence alone in him strives to stifle the underlying demands of the human heart. Since nothing is proved, everything can be proved.

Indeed, Kierkegaard himself shows us the path taken. I do not want to suggest anything here, but how can one fail to read in his works the signs of an almost intentional mutilation of the soul to balance the mutilation accepted in regard to the absurd? It is the leitmotiv of the *Journal.* "What I lacked was the animal which *also* belongs to human destiny. . . . But give me a body then." And further on: "Oh! especially in my early youth what should I not have given to be a man, even for six months . . . what I lack, basically, is a body and the physical conditions of existence." Elsewhere, the same man nevertheless adopts the great cry of hope that has come down through so many centuries and quickened so many hearts, except that of the absurd man. "But for the Christian death is certainly not the end of everything and it implies infinitely more hope than life implies for us, even when that life is overflowing with health and vigor." Reconciliation through scandal is still reconciliation. It allows one perhaps, as can be seen, to derive hope of its contrary, which is death. But even if fellow-feeling inclines one toward that attitude, still it must be said that excess justifies nothing. That transcends, as the saying goes, the human scale; therefore it must be superhuman. But his "therefore" is superfluous. There is no logical certainty here. There is no experimental probability either. All I can say is that, in fact, that transcends my scale. If I do not draw a negation from it, at least I do not want to found anything on the incomprehensible. I want to know whether I can live with what I know and with that alone. I am told again that here the intelligence must sacrifice its pride and the reason bow down. But if I recognize the limits of the reason, I do not therefore negate it, recognizing its relative powers. I merely want to remain in this middle path where the intelligence can remain clear. If that is its pride, I see no sufficient reason for giving it up. Nothing more profound, for example, than Kierkegaard's view according to which despair is not a fact but a state: the very state of sin. For sin is what alienates from God. The absurd, which is the metaphysical state of the conscious man, does not lead to God.[2] Perhaps this notion will become clearer if I risk this shocking statement: the absurd is sin without God.

It is a matter of living in that state of the absurd. I know on what it is founded, this mind and this world straining against each other without being able to embrace each other. I ask for the rule of life of that state, and what I am offered neglects its basis, negates one of the terms of the painful opposition, demands of me a resignation. I ask what is involved in the condition I recognize as mine; I know it implies obscurity and ignorance; and I am assured that this ignorance explains everything and that this darkness is my light. But there is no reply here to my intent, and this stirring lyricism cannot hide the paradox from me. One must therefore turn away. Kierkegaard may shout in warning: "If man had no eternal consciousness, if, at the bottom of everything, there were merely a wild, seething force producing everything, both large and trifling, in the storm of dark passions, if the bottomless void that nothing can fill underlay all things, what would life be but despair?" This cry is not likely to stop the absurd man. Seeking what is true is not seeking what is desirable.

---

[2] I did not say "excludes God," which would still amount to asserting.

If in order to elude the anxious question: "What would life be?" one must, like the donkey, feed on the roses of illusion, then the absurd mind, rather than resigning itself to falsehood, prefers to adopt fearlessly Kierkegaard's reply: "despair." Everything considered, a determined soul will always manage. . . .

All Sisyphus' silent joy is contained therein. His fate belongs to him. His rock is his thing. Likewise, the absurd man, when he contemplates his torment, silences all the idols. In the universe suddenly restored to its silence, the myriad wondering little voices of the earth rise up. Unconscious, secret calls, invitations from all the faces, they are the necessary reverse and price of victory. There is no sun without shadow, and it is essential to know the night. The absurd man says yes and his effort will henceforth be unceasing. If there is a personal fate, there is no higher destiny, or at least there is but one which he concludes is inevitable and despicable. For the rest, he knows himself to be the master of his days. At that subtle moment when man glances backward over his life, Sisyphus returning toward his rock, in that slight pivoting he contemplates that series of unrelated actions which becomes his fate, created by him, combined under his memory's eye and soon sealed by his death. Thus, convinced of the wholly human origin of all that is human, a blind man eager to see who knows that the night has no end, he is still on the go. The rock is still rolling.

I leave Sisyphus at the foot of the mountain! One always finds one's burden again. But Sisyphus teaches the higher fidelity that negates the gods and raises rocks. He too concludes that all is well. This universe henceforth without a master seems to him neither sterile nor futile. Each atom of that stone, each mineral flake of that night-filled mountain, in itself forms a world. The struggle itself toward the heights is enough to fill a man's heart. One must imagine Sisyphus happy.

Philosophical Atheism

From "Philosophical Concepts of Atheism" by Ernest Nagel in *Basic Beliefs,* Johnson E. Fairchild, editor, 1959

Ernest Nagel (born 1901), editor of the prestigious Journal of Philosophy *for almost twenty years, presents positive philosophic commitments or at least tendencies and themes that unite philosophical atheists beyond their opposition to theism and other religious points of view. These are three: first, a materialist tendency, materialist in the sense of a denial of incorporeal agencies and disembodied spirits or minds; second, empiricism, with controlled sensory evidence (i.e., the scientific experiment) viewed as the final court of appeal for any factual question; and third, a moral dimension of utilitarianism and libertarianism.*

The moral dimension of philosophical atheism is not usually brought out. Here Nagel shows moral parameters provided by atheism, and, perhaps more profoundly, the temperament of the philosophical atheist's approach to moral issues and human values. Nagel elo-

*quently expresses his sense of the philosophical atheist's typical courage and serene resig-
nation in the face of a nature hostile to many a "legitimate desire." It is interesting to compare such sentiment with that of probably the most famous philosophical atheist of the
twentieth century, Bertrand Russell (see the selection under Personal Destiny).*

. . . [I] will show how atheism belongs to the great tradition of religious thought. Needless
to say, this expectation is difficult to satisfy, and did anyone succeed in doing so he would
indeed be performing the neatest conjuring trick of the week. But the expectation nevertheless does cause me some embarrassment, which is only slightly relieved by an anecdote
Bertrand Russell reports in his recent book, *Portraits from Memory.* Russell was impris-
oned during the First World War for pacifistic activities. On entering the prison he was
asked a number of customary questions about himself for the prison records. One question
was about his religion. Russell explained that he was an agnostic. "Never heard of it," the
warden declared. "How do you spell it?" When Russell told him, the warden observed
"Well, there are many religions, but I suppose they all worship the same God." Russell
adds that this remark kept him cheerful for about a week. Perhaps philosophical atheism
also is a religion. . . .

. . . the question [arises] whether, apart from their polemics against theism, philosophical atheists have not shared a common set of positive views, a common set of philosophical convictions which set them off from other groups of thinkers. In one very clear sense of
this query the answer is indubitably negative. For there never has been what one might call
a "school of atheism," in the way in which there has been a Platonic school or even a Kantian school. In point of fact, atheistic critics of theism can be found among many of the con-
ventional groupings of philosophical thinkers—even, I venture to add, among professional
theologians in recent years who in effect preach atheism in the guise of language taken
bodily from the Christian tradition.

Nevertheless, despite the variety of philosophic positions to which at one time or another in the history of thought atheists have subscribed, it seems to me that atheism is not
simply a negative standpoint. At any rate, there is a certain quality of intellectual temper
that has characterized, and continues to characterize, many philosophical atheists. (I am
excluding from consideration the so-called "village atheist," whose primary concern is to
twit and ridicule those who accept some form of theism, or for that matter those who have
any religious convictions.) Moreover, their rejection of theism is based not only on the in-
adequacies they have found in the arguments for theism, but often also on the positive
ground that atheism is a corollary to a better supported general outlook upon the nature of
things. I want therefore to conclude this discussion with a brief enumeration of some
points of positive doctrine to which by and large philosophical atheists seem to me to subscribe. These points fall into three major groups.

In the first place, philosophical atheists reject the assumption that there are disembodied spirits, or that incorporeal entities of any sort can exercise a causal agency. On the contrary, atheists are generally agreed that if we wish to achieve any understanding of what
takes place in the universe, we must look to the operations of organized bodies. Accordingly, the various processes taking place in nature, whether animate or inanimate, are to be

explained in terms of the properties and structures of identifiable and spatio-temporally lo-cated objects. Moreover, the present variety of systems and activities found in the universe is to be accounted for on the basis of the transformation things undergo when they enter into different relations with one another—transformations which often result in the emer-gence of novel kinds of objects. On the other hand, though things are in flux and undergo alteration, there is no all-encompassing unitary pattern of change. Nature is ineradicably plural, both in respect to the individuals occurring in it as well as in respect to the processes in which things become involved. Accordingly, the human scene and the human perspective are not illusory; and man and his works are no less and no more "real" than are other parts of phases of the cosmos. At the risk of using a possibly misleading characteri-zation, all of this can be summarized by saying that an atheistic view of things is a form of materialism.

In the second place, atheists generally manifest a marked empirical temper, and often take as their ideal the intellectual methods employed in the contemporaneous empirical sciences. Philosophical atheists differ considerably on important points of detail in their account of how responsible claims to knowledge are to be established. But there is sub-stantial agreement among them that controlled sensory observation is the court of final ap-peal in issues concerning matters of fact. It is indeed this commitment to the use of an empirical method which is the final basis of the atheistic critique of theism. For at bottom this critique seeks to show that we can understand whatever a theistic assumption is al-leged to explain, through the use of the proved methods of the positive sciences and with-out the introduction of empirically unsupported *ad hoc* hypotheses about a Deity. It is pertinent in this connection to recall a familiar legend about the French mathematical physicist Laplace. According to the story, Laplace made a personal presentation of a copy of his now famous book on celestial mechanics to Napoleon. Napoleon glanced through the volume, and finding no reference to the Deity asked Laplace whether God's existence played any role in the analysis. "Sir, I have no need for that hypothesis," Laplace is re-ported to have replied. The dismissal of sterile hypotheses characterizes not only the work of Laplace; it is the uniform rule in scientific inquiry. The sterility of the theistic assump-tion is one of the main burdens of the literature of atheism both ancient and modern.

And finally, atheistic thinkers have generally accepted a utilitarian basis for judging moral issues, and they have exhibited a libertarian attitude toward human needs and im-pulses. The conceptions of the human good they have advocated are conceptions which are commensurate with the actual capacities of mortal men, so that it is the satisfaction of the complex needs of the human creature which is the final standard for evaluating the valid-ity of a moral ideal or moral prescription.

In consequence, the emphasis of atheistic moral reflection has been this-worldly rather than other-worldly, individualistic rather than authoritarian. The stress upon a good life that must be consummated in this world, has made atheists vigorous opponents of moral codes which seek to repress human impulses in the name of some unrealizable other-worldly ideal. The individualism that is so pronounced a strain in many philosophi-cal atheists has made them tolerant of human limitations and sensitive to the plurality of le-gitimate moral goals. On the other hand, this individualism has certainly not prevented many of them from recognizing the crucial role which institutional arrangements can play in achieving desirable patterns of human living. In consequence, atheists have made important contributions to the development of a climate of opinion favorable to pursuing the values of a liberal civilization and they have played effective roles in attempts to rectify social injustices.

Atheists cannot build their moral outlook on foundations upon which so many men conduct their lives. In particular, atheism cannot offer the incentives to conduct and the consolations for misfortune which theistic religions supply to their adherents. It can offer no hope of personal immortality, no threats of Divine chastisement, no promise of eventual recompense for injustices suffered, no blueprints to sure salvation. For on its view of the place of man in nature, human excellence and human dignity must be achieved within a finite life-span, or not at all, so that the rewards of moral endeavor must come from the quality of civilized living, and not from some source of disbursement that dwells outside of time. Accordingly, atheistic moral reflection at its best does not culminate in a quiescent ideal of human perfection, but is a vigorous call to intelligent activity—activity for the sake of realizing human potentialities and for eliminating whatever stands in the way of such realization. Nevertheless, though slavish resignation to remediable ills is not characteristic of atheistic thought, responsible atheists have never pretended that human effort can invariably achieve the heart's every legitimate desire. A tragic view of life is thus an uneliminable ingredient in atheistic thought. This ingredient does not invite or generally produce lugubrious lamentation. But it does touch the atheist's view of man and his place in nature with an emotion that makes the philosophical atheist a kindred spirit to those who, within the frameworks of various religious traditions, have developed a serenely resigned attitude toward the inevitable tragedies of the human estate.

DISCUSSION QUESTIONS

1. Reconstruct Michael Scriven's argument in favor of the exclusive rationality of atheism.

2. List and discuss at least three instances of doctrinal conflict, or of the semblance of doctrinal conflict, between science and religion, taking cues from J. C. C. Smart.

3. What does Marx mean when he says that religion is the opiate of the masses? And how does this tie in with his *historicist* debunking of religion?

4. Outline the anthropological understanding of religion suggested by E. B. Tylor, and the sociological understanding of religion pioneered by Émile Durkheim. Are these debunking theories?

5. Sketch the psychological theory of religion advanced by Sigmund Freud. What anthropolical or sociological proposals does Freud endorse and incorporate into his view? Does Freud's theory successfully debunk religious beliefs and practices? What, at least, are the important issues here?

6. Present Cārvāka's views of religion. What do you see as the most worrisome consideration raised in the reading, worrisome, that is, from the perspective of a religious advocate? How might it best be answered, or do you think that any attempted response is likely to fail?

7. What is the existentialist attitude championed by Albert Camus? Camus attacks religious existentialists for "leaping," for abandoning authenticity in choosing to have religious faith. What do you think of his complaints? (Optionally: after reading the selection from Søren Kierkegaard—under Faith Against Reason—construct a debate between Camus and Kierkegaard.)

8. Elaborate the positions, or themes, that, according to Ernest Nagel, unite philosophical atheists beyond their opposition to theism. Does the unity that Nagel finds make philosophical atheism a stronger or more attractive position? Explain.

CHAPTER FIVE

Evil

One challenge to religious beliefs questions their foundations. Are the beliefs warranted? On what grounds? On what grounds surviving scrutiny? Another challenge concerns compatibility with other things we know. Here the biggest problem seems to be science, which rules out superstition and some religious beliefs inherited from the past, though how much at the core of religious outlooks is opposed by science is a good question and a live one. In this section, we take up another source of worry about compatibility, namely, the compatibility of the evil in the world with beliefs about God and the like. Does the world with its evil rule out the possibility of the existence of, for example, a loving God?

Evil, in fact, has been identified from the earliest stirrings of philosophy, both in the East and in the West, as a problem for theism. The Greek philosopher Epicurus (342–270 BCE), a younger contemporary of Aristotle's, formulated an argument, based on evil, against a theology of an omnipotent and omnibenevolent deity, as David Hume notes in the first selection here. In the East, the Buddha is among several citing evil as evidence against the view that there is a personal Creator or God.

Gottfried Wilhelm von Leibniz (1646–1716) appears to deserve the credit for coining the term "theodicy" for that area of philosophical theology intent on explaining evil on theistic assumptions, that is to say, theology that would justify God's lovingness in the face of evil (see *theodicy* in the Glossary). The word "theodicy" is also used for any particular theory that would explain evil while maintaining the reality of God (or the like), and Leibniz himself formulated a theodicy.

Another contribution of Leibniz's was a threefold classification of evil that has stuck through later philosophic discussions: (a) *metaphysical evil,* the evil of anything in comparison with God, who is the most valuable entity (even morally perfect angels are evil in this sense); (b) *moral evil,* evil done intentionally by human beings or other moral agents, for example, Hitler's crimes; and (c) *natural evil,* evil in the universe for which no moral agent (other than perhaps God, the Creator) is responsible, for example, disease, old age, and death. (These, by the way, are evils cited by the Buddha according to Buddhist tradition, and for our purposes they will serve as good examples of natural evil.)

Leibniz reasoned that since (1) God is the omnipotent Creator of everything, and (2) God is omnibenevolent, or all-loving, then (3) this, the universe that God has created, is the best of all possible worlds. In other words, the conclusion (3) that this is the best of all possible worlds is entailed by the truth of premises (1) and (2), propositions that themselves follow from a definition of God as the perfect being along with the supposition that God in fact exists. Now if it follows from (4) there is evil that (5) this is not the best of all possible worlds, then there would be blatant incompatibility between (a) the existence of God as perfect (as both the omnipotent Creator of everything and omnibenevolent) and (b) the reality of evil. So either there is no evil or no God, that is, given that God has to be omnipotent and omnibenevolent.

But surely there is evil of some type or other, Leibniz reflected. There is metaphysical evil just in there being a universe at all. Thus God as omnipotent and omnibenevolent is compatible, he reasoned, with one type of evil, metaphysical evil; it would seem as though God out of God's omnibenevolence would create a universe just to let creatures have, so to say, their day in the sun. So metaphysical evil should be expected given an all-loving God. Thus metaphysical evil is not just compatible with an all-loving God, it is explained by God's all-lovingness as what we would expect from God.

Now moral evil brought about by agents other than God also presents no problem insofar as the precondition of moral action, namely, free will, is itself something good. It is, advocates of a free-will theodicy claim, indeed a most valuable attribute of a creature. God would do something good to create free beings, and thus, again, not only does God get off the hook—we may reconstruct Leibniz's (and many others') reasoning—for moral evil, but given a God who is omnibenevolent, and the assumption that some with free will are likely to sin, then moral evil is something that we should expect, too. Most critics of theism have accepted this line of reasoning, although there are some that question the assumption whether freedom need mean that some are likely to sin (e.g. J. L. Mackie and Ninian Smart in papers included in Nelson Pike's *God and Evil*: see the Guide to Further Reading). The main problem, then, is natural evil.

We shall look at several attempts to resolve the difficulty of natural evil to theism's advantage, both classical and modern efforts. We shall also look at some Eastern theories that are responses to similar problems. Indian theists face an obviously comparable difficulty, but there are parallel problems facing Hindu Absolutists (Advaitins) and Buddhists. With Buddhism, for example, there is the problem why I am not enlightened (and perhaps you, too, though I speak for myself alone). It would seem that I should have been born enlightened, since enlightenment is said to be the natural or native state, and the self-aware Void the supreme, or only, reality. As it is difficult to understand how there can be natural evil given the existence of a loving God, it is difficult to understand how any can fail to be enlightened (a specific evil) on Buddhist suppositions.

An Amoral Creator

From *Dialogues Concerning Natural Religion* by David Hume, 1778

We begin this section with a statement of the problem on the part of David Hume, or, rather, of Philo, Hume's mouthpiece in his classic dialogue. Recall from the "Teleological Argument" selection from Hume under Arguments for a Divine Reality that the three principal characters are Cleanthes, an advocate of rational theology (though not of the ontological argument), Demea, a theist and man of piety, and Philo, a skeptic and critic of religion who is usually taken to speak for Hume himself.

Hume's treatment of the problem of evil has to be seen in the context of his inquiry into rational theology as a whole, where the empiricist method is agreed to by both Philo and Cleanthes. Our selection occurs late in the work, and Philo has come around and granted a modified version of Cleanthes's contention that the source of the universe is something like a human mind. The question, Philo says, is of degree—an enormous, indeed unfathomably large, degree, according to Philo, whereas the source (namely, God) is rather personal, according to Cleanthes. Philo is now questioning whether this source (call it God) has any moral attribute. Because of evil, he reasons, clearly God is not omnibenevolent. The source of the universe seems amoral, to judge by the nature of the effect.

Ask yourself, ask any of your acquaintance, whether they would live over again the last ten or twenty years of their life. No! but the next twenty, they say, will be better:

> And from the dregs of life, hope to receive
> What the first sprightly running could not give.[1]

Thus at last they find (such is the greatness of human misery, it reconciles even contradictions) that they complain at once of the shortness of life and of its vanity and sorrow.

And is it possible, Cleanthes, said PHILO, that after all these reflections, and infinitely more which might be suggested, you can still persevere in your anthropomorphism, and assert the moral attributes of the Deity, his justice, benevolence, mercy, and rectitude, to be of the same nature with these virtues in human creatures? His power, we allow, is infinite; whatever he wills is executed; but neither man nor any other animal is happy; therefore he does not will their happiness. His wisdom is infinite; he is never mistaken in choosing the means to any end; but the course of nature tends not to human or animal felicity; therefore it is not established for that purpose. Through the whole compass of human knowledge

---

[1] Dryden, *Aureng-Zebe, Act* iv.

there are no inferences more certain and infallible than these. In what respect, then, do his benevolence and mercy resemble the benevolence and mercy of men?

Epicurus' old questions are yet unanswered.

Is he willing to prevent evil, but not able? Then is he impotent. Is he able, but not willing? Then is he malevolent. Is he both able and willing? Whence then is evil?

You ascribe, Cleanthes (and I believe justly), a purpose and intention to nature. But what, I beseech you, is the object of that curious artifice and machinery which she has displayed in all animals? The preservation alone of individuals, and propagation of the species. It seems enough for her purpose if such a rank be barely upheld in the universe, without any care or concern for the happiness of the members that compose it. No resource for this purpose; no machinery in order merely to give pleasure or ease; no fund of pure joy and contentment; no indulgence without some want or necessity accompanying it. At least, the few phenomena of this nature are overbalanced by opposite phenomena of still greater importance.

Our sense of music, harmony, and indeed beauty of all kinds gives satisfaction, without being absolutely necessary to the preservation and propagation of the species. But what racking pains, on the other hand, arise from gouts, gravels, megrims, toothaches, rheumatisms, where the injury to the animal machinery is either small or incurable? Mirth, laughter, play, frolic seem gratuitous satisfactions which have no further tendency; spleen, melancholy, discontent, superstition are pains of the same nature. How then does the divine benevolence display itself, in the sense of you anthropomorphites?

Classical Aesthetic Theodicy

From "The Nature of the Good: Against the Manichees" by Augustine in *Augustine: Earlier Writings,* John H. S. Burleigh, editor, 1953

See the discussion of Augustine earlier, under the title God, for a few details about the life of the Church Father.

Augustine accomplished an explanation of apparent evil that has had enormous influence over the centuries, and is still drawn upon by theologians of our day. All true evil is moral evil. Much that we see as natural evil is God's righting the natural balance in justly punishing moral evil (i.e., sin). Other natural evil is the work of Satan, a non-human moral agent, and thus really moral evil. Thus the appearance of natural evil is a mistake of regard that would disappear were one able to appreciate the universe as it really is.

Everything has its rightful place in the universe, and everything insofar as it exists is good. Sin is intentional corruption, a falling away from a proper role or place. It is justly punished; God is all-loving but also perfectly just. God secures the beauty of the whole, and punishment is required to maintain the cosmic harmony. Humans too often see only the part, only the punishment, for example, and think it is evil. There is in fact no other evil than sin and its deserts.

Augustine's theodicy is called aesthetic *because the beauty and harmony of the universe as a whole are key to the explanation of what we perceive as natural evil, for example, disease, old age, and death. Were we able to appreciate the whole—by ascending the Christian equivalent of Plato's "Ladder of Love" (see under Mysticism)—we would know that punishment of sin contributes to overall beauty and harmony, as does everything else we thought erroneously to be evil without being sin.*

Augustine makes some mistaken factual assumptions, such as that the universe is a plenum; that the universe be chock-full of every possible existent is required, too, for this to be the most perfect world by Augustine's aesthetic criterion. Critics have faulted his theodicy on these grounds. A more penetrating criticism, however, is that it seems dubious whether, as he sees it, the punishment fits the crime. Is God really perfectly just if God uses such horrors as disease, old age, and death—invested on innocent babies as well as on the Hitlers of the world—in punishment of sin? The payback for an "original sin" of Adam and Eve, our primordial forebears, seems a bit extreme. Finally, why should God allow Satan any power over human affairs? Could not God constrain the renegade angel? And would not God do so if God were really all-loving? Because of these last questions, many modern theologians who subscribe to Augustine's overall theodicy have dropped the bits about Satan.

If we ask whence comes evil, we should first ask what evil is. It is nothing but the corruption of natural measure, form or order. What is called an evil nature is a corrupt nature. If it were not corrupt it would be good. But even when it is corrupted, so far as it remains a natural thing, it is good. It is bad only so far as it is corrupted.

Of course it is possible that one nature even when corrupted may still be better than another nature which has remained uncorrupted, because the one has a superior, the other an inferior measure, form and order. According to the estimation of men, judging by what they see before them as they look, corrupted gold is better than uncorrupted silver, and corrupted silver is better than uncorrupted lead. Among spiritual natures of greater potency a rational spirit, even when corrupted by an evil will, is better than an irrational spirit that is uncorrupted; and any spirit, even when corrupted, is better than any body even when uncorrupted. For the thing which when present gives life to a body is better than the body to which it gives life. However corrupt the created spirit of life may become, it can still give life to its body. Hence even when corrupted it is better than its body though the latter be uncorrupted.

If corruption take away from corruptible things all measure, form and order, nothing at all will remain in existence. Similarly any nature which cannot be corrupted will be the supreme good, as God is. Any nature which can be corrupted has some good in it, for corruption could not harm it except by taking away or diminishing what is good in it.

To his most excellent creatures, that is to rational spirits, God has given the power not to be corrupted if they do not will to be; but remain obedient under the Lord their God and cleave to his incorruptible beauty. But if they will not remain obedient and are willingly corrupted by sin, they are unwillingly corrupted by penalties. God is the good, so that it can be well with no one who deserts him; and among his creatures the rational nature is so great a good that no other good save God can make it happy. Sinners are ordained to punishment. This order is contrary to their nature, and is therefore penalty. But it suits their fault and is therefore just.

Other things created out of nothing which are inferior to rational spirit can be neither happy nor miserable. Since they are themselves good, because of the degree of measure and form they possess, and since, though the good in them be small or even minimal, they could not have existed save by the act of the good God most high; they are so ordered that the weaker yield to the stronger, and the feebler to those that have greater might, and the less powerful to the more powerful. So terrestrial things have peace with celestial things, being as it were submissive to things which are more excellent than they are. When things pass away and others succeed them there is a specific beauty in the temporal order, so that those things which die or cease to be what they were, do not defile or disturb the measure, form or order of the created universe. A well-prepared speech is beautiful even though all its syllables and sounds pass in succession as if they are born and die.

The nature and quantity of the penalty due to each fault is determined by the judgment of God, not by that of man. When it is remitted to the converted, that is proof of the great goodness of God. When it is paid as due there is no inequity with God. It is a better order that a thing [*natura*] should suffer punishment justly than that it should rejoice in sin with impunity. So long as it retains some measure, form and order there is still some good in it no matter into what extremity it may come. If these were all together taken away and destroyed completely there would be no good because there would be nothing left.

Corruptible natures would not be natures at all unless they derived being from God. Nor would they be corruptible if they were part of him. They would then be as he is. The fact that they have some measure, form and order is due to their having been created by God. And they are not immutable because they were made out of nothing. It is sacrilegious audacity to equate nothing and God as we do if we want to make that which he created out of nothing equal to that which is born of God.

No hurt whatever can be done to the divine nature, nor can any other nature which is less than divine be hurt unjustly. No doubt some people by sinning do harm unjustly. Their will to harm unjustly is counted against them, but the power by which they are permitted to do the harm comes only from God, who knows, though they do not, what those ought to suffer whom he permits them to harm.

If those who want to introduce a nature other than that which God has made would only pay attention to these clear and certain facts, they would not be filled with such blasphemies as to impute so much good to the supreme evil, and to impute to God so many evils. As I said above, it is sufficient for their correction if they would only pay attention to what truth compels them to confess even against their will, that all good things come from God alone. Good things whether they are great or small all come from one source, that is from the supreme good, which is God.

Let us, therefore, recall all the good things we can which are worthy to be attributed to God as their author, and let us see whether when they are removed anything will remain in existence. All life, potency, health, memory, virtue, intelligence, tranquility, plenty, sense, light, sweetness, measure, beauty, peace—all these things whether great or small, and other similar things which may occur to one, and especially those things which are found universally in spiritual or corporeal existence, measure, form, and order, come from the Lord God. Whoever willingly makes a bad use of these good things will, by the divine judgment, pay the penalty. But wherever none of them is present at all, absolutely nothing will remain in existence.

Process Theodicy

From "Creation Out of Chaos and the Problem of Evil" by David R. Griffin in
Encountering Evil: Live Options in Theodicy, Stephen T. Davis, editor, 1981

*We encountered process theology first with Charles Hartshorne (under the title God) and
then with Alfred North Whitehead and Marjorie Suchocki (under Speculative Spiritual
Metaphysics). David Griffin presents a process theodicy, that is to say, a theodicy consonant with process philosophy's understanding of God.*

*As we saw with Hartshorne, God's power, which is maximal, is nevertheless con-
strained by general requirements for creation—for example, necessary connectedness between creatures and God, requirements of cosmic harmony (i.e. universal law), and
creaturely freedom and creativity, freedom that extends down to the lowliest entity or particle of matter. Moreover, the doctrine of* creation ex nihilo *is rejected by process philosophers. There is never a time when God is bereft of a body, so to say, when there is nothing
contingent and temporal. And God's love and goodness lures creatures. God does not
control them by overriding their choices.*

*Griffin has refined and amplified his process theodicy in several publications subsequent
to the paper excerpted here (see the Guide to Further Reading). It becomes clear in the sup-
plementary works that process theodicy is a modern aesthetic theodicy that, although not
embracing the classical concept of God, is like Augustine's theodicy; both find an aesthetic
criterion of harmony, beauty, and unity within complex diversity at the bottom of the explanation of apparent evil. According to the process view, creaturely freedom enriches God cosmologically, insuring a complex diversity. God and universal law insure unity and harmony.*

*Critics have complained that evil shows the process God to be rather pathetically
weak. Do you mean to say that God could not have saved a single person from Hitler's
chambers? And could not God help us speedily find a cure for AIDS, if it is true, as Griffin alleges, that God could not directly eliminate the virus? Other criticisms are focused
less on evil but on the overall process metaphysics. For example, is the process view consistent with Big Bang cosmology, which seems to indicate, contrary to the process view,
that the universe has a beginning?*

CREATION AND DIVINE POWER

I now turn to the solution I favor, to which the rejection of *creatio ex nihilo* is fundamental.
In fact, the problem of evil is uniquely a problem for those theistic positions that hold the
doctrine of omnipotence implied by the doctrine of creation out of nothing. For, the problem of evil can be stated as a syllogism validly entailing the non-existence of deity only if
deity is defined as omnipotent in the sense of having no essential limitations upon the exercise of its will. And it is precisely omnipotence in this sense that the speculative hypothesis of *creatio ex nihilo* is designed to support.

Two issues are involved. First, if God in creating our world necessarily worked with
some pre-existent actualities, these actualities might well have some power of their own

with which they could partially thwart the divine will. Second, there might be some eternal, uncreated, necessary principles (beyond purely logical truths) about the way these actualities can be ordered which limit the sorts of situations that are really possible. But if God created this world out of absolutely nothing, then the beings of this world are *absolutely* dependent upon God. Any power they have is not at all inherent, but is totally a gift of God, and as such can be overridden (or, which amounts to the same thing, withdrawn) at any time. And if there has not always been a multiplicity of finite actualities, it does not make sense to think of any uncreated and hence necessary principles as to how the actualities of the world can be ordered. Any such principles would be purely contingent ones, created along with the actualities whose behavior they describe, and hence alterable at (divine) will.

My solution dissolves the problem of evil by denying the doctrine of omnipotence fundamental to it. Of the various ways of denying deity's essentially unlimited power to effect its will, mine is to hypothesize that there has always been a plurality of actualities having some power of their own. This power is two-fold: the power to determine themselves (partially), and the power to influence others.

Traditional theism has always held that energy or power is eternal. But it hypothesized that this power all essentially belonged to God alone, and was at some point all embodied in God. I share the view of those who hold instead that power has always existed in non-divine actualities as well as in the divine actuality. No special philosophical problems are raised by this view: if it is intelligible to hold that the existence of God requires no explanation, since *something* must exist necessarily and "of itself," then it is not unintelligible to hold that that which exists necessarily is God *and* a realm of non-divine actualities. Nor is this a denial that our world is contingent and created by God. My view is that the beings making up our world, including the most primitive ones (such as quarks and electrons) are contingent, having been brought about and sustained through the creative providential activity of God. All that is necessary to the hypothesis is that power has always been and necessarily is *shared* power, that God has never had and could never have a monopoly on power, and that the power possessed by the non-divine actualities is inherent to them and hence cannot be cancelled out or overridden by God.

This last point is the most essential one. Some theologians might agree that we have power, even power in relation to God, and yet say that God could overpower us and hence totally determine our activities, including our willing and desiring. But that is excluded by what I mean by saying that we have inherent power in relation to God. The claim is precisely that our self-determining activity, and the consequent influence we have on others, *cannot* be totally controlled by God. Hence God cannot control but can only persuade what we become and how we affect others. . . .

THE GOODNESS OF GOD

What then is the upshot of my theodicy, my attempt to "justify the ways of God"? It is not to maintain that God is not responsible for any of the evil in the world. For, in a very real sense, God *is* ultimately responsible for all of those things that we normally think of when we refer to the problem of evil. For, if God had not persuaded the world to bring forth living cells and then animal life, there would be no significant suffering in the world. If God had not continued to draw the creation upward until creatures with the capacity for rational thought were evoked, there would be no moral evil, or sin, i.e., deliberate disobedience of the divine will; nor would the most awful forms of suffering exist—there would be no Holocausts.

The question then is, "Can God be thus responsible without being indictable, i.e., blameworthy?" I would say "Yes." In the first place, although God is ultimately responsible for the world's having reached a state in which significant evils can occur, God is never totally responsible for the evils that do occur. Each situation contains seeds for good and evil. God (by hypothesis) seeks to lure the creatures to realize the greatest good that is possible in that particular situation. When the creatures actualize a lesser possibility, this failure is due to their exercise of power, not God's.

In the second place the aim of a "morally good being" is more accurately stated positively than negatively. That is, the aim is first of all to produce good, not to avoid suffering. If the moral aim could be adequately expressed as the intention to avoid suffering, then moral adults would never have children—that would be the way to guarantee that they would never have children who would suffer or cause suffering. Analogously, a perfectly moral God would simply avoid bringing forth a world with any creatures capable of any significant degree of suffering. But—by hypothesis—this would mean that there would be *no world with any significant value in it.* Surely that cannot be our idea of what a perfectly moral being would do! The aim must be to create the conditions that allow for the greatest good while minimizing the evils.

In other words, suffering and sinful intentions resulting in suffering are not the only forms of evil. Any absence of good that could have been realized is evil even if no suffering is involved. Recall that the definition of genuine evil offered earlier was "anything which makes the world worse than it could have otherwise been." Any absence of good that makes the world worse than it could have been, all things considered, is an evil. Hence, for God to have failed to bring forth beings capable of experiencing significant value when this was possible would have made God indictable.

Unless, of course, the evils that were thereby made possible are so great that the goods that could be achieved are not worth the risk. That is a question that each of us can only answer for ourselves. Those of us who are among the most fortunate people who have ever lived on the face of the earth must of course be aware of our biased perspectives, and must be sensitive to the response that may come from the less fortunate. But, even when trying to take into account my biased perspective, I cannot imagine that I would ever conclude that the evils of life have been so great that it would have been better had life never emerged, or that the evils of human life, as horrendous as they have been (and quite possibly the worst is still to come!), are such that it would have been better had human life never been created.

There is one other theological conviction that reinforces my judgment on this matter. This is the conviction that God shares all our sufferings (analogously to the way that I share the pains of my bodily members). Accordingly, while every advance in the creative process has been a risk, since greater sufferings were thereby made possible as well as greater goods, this has never been a risk which God has urged us creatures to run alone. It has always been a risk for God too. In fact God is the *only* being who has experienced every single evil that has occurred in the creation. This means that God is the one being in position to judge whether the goods achievable have been worth the price.

Natural Evil

Thus far, insofar as I have discussed the *cause* of evil, I have focused attention primarily on *moral* evil, as I have sought to explain why human beings can cause so much evil. But the theological position being outlined here is equally capable of explaining so-called "natural evil," that which is caused by non-moral agents. And it is this form of evil that most theodicies find most problematical. For, they employ what I call a "hybrid free-will defense" to account for the evil caused by human beings. I call it a *hybrid* free-will defense because it does not say that freedom is inherent in the world as such, but instead says that God voluntarily bestows freedom upon the creation—and usually only to a select portion of creation, i.e., to human beings alone, or to them and other rational creatures (angels).

Accordingly, this hybrid free-will defense has a difficult time with evils apparently caused by sub-human nature, since the beings constituting this realm by hypothesis have no power with which to deviate from God's will. One way out is to say with Augustine that no genuine evil ever results from sub-human causes. But in the face of the enormous and non-rationalizable distribution of sufferings caused by tornadoes, earthquakes, droughts, germs, and cancer cells, this is a difficult assertion to make. Another way out is to affirm that all such evils are caused by a fallen angel (Satan). This is, of course, not readily falsifiable, but it does strain credulity (for me, at least, much more than the hypothesis that all creatures have some power of their own). Also it raises the question as to why God allows Satan to do things that make the universe worse than it could have been; hence it calls God's goodness or wisdom into question.

According to my theodicy, all creatures great and small have some power with which to deviate from the divine will for them. This means that there never has been a time at which we could say that the creation was necessarily "perfect" in the sense of having actualized the best possibilities that were open to it. Granted, very low-grade actualities cannot be thought to deviate *very much* from the divine aims for them. But over a period of billions of years very slight deviations occurring in each moment can add up to a state of the world that is very far removed from the state that would have resulted had the divine aims been actualized all the way along. Accordingly, if God has always worked with materials that were not necessarily in a perfect state, and which have some inherent power to deviate from God's aims and to influence their successors forevermore, there is no reason to infer that cancer, polio, tornadoes, and earthquakes exist because God wanted our world to have them.

Why God Does Not "Prevent" Some Evils

I will conclude with a discussion intended to drive home more clearly why God (according to my hypothesis) simply cannot prevent the major types of evils that usually lead people to question God's goodness or even reality. These questions can be phrased in the form: "Why didn't God prevent such and such?" For example, why didn't God prevent that bullet from striking my son? Why didn't God prevent that mine shaft from caving in? Why did God allow all the pain that occurred in the evolutionary process? Why didn't God prevent Hitler from murdering six million Jews?

The answer to questions of this type will be more evident to us if we think in terms of the way God can affect the following three types of entities: (1) low-grade enduring individuals; (2) high-grade enduring individuals; (3) aggregates of individuals. (For the sake of simplicity I have left out the whole spectrum of medium-grade individuals, from the lowest animals through the non-human primates.) These three types of entities differ from each other in having (1) very little power of self-determination, (2) very great power of self-determination, and (3) no power of self-determination, respectively.

(1) God acts in the world, by hypothesis, by seeking to persuade individuals to actualize the best possibilities that are *real* possibilities for them. (E.g., it is not a real possibility for a chipmunk to write a symphony.) Low-grade enduring individuals, such as electrons, atoms, molecules, having very little power of self-determination, and not having many real possibilities open to them, cannot change their behavior very quickly. Individuals at this level are largely the products of their inheritance and their environment. They essentially repeat the same patterns of behavior, century after century. Even as we move into the medium-grade level, with living cells, the capacity for novel self-determining behavior is very limited, compared with that of human beings.

The theological significance of this discussion is this: on the one hand, these low-grade individuals cannot deviate very much from the divine aims for them. On the other hand, the divine aims for them, since they can only be for possibilities that are *real* possibilities for these low-grade creatures, cannot be aims for very radical changes in behavior. Insofar as God can move these individuals to change their ways, it must be over a very long period of time. (This is why evolutionary change occurred so gradually until relatively recently on our earth.)

Accordingly, if the behavior of one or more of these individuals is causing destruction in its environment, God cannot do much quickly to change things. For example, if you have been exposed to radio-active materials, God cannot divert the alpha, beta, and gamma particles out of your body before they have done irreversible damage. If cancerous cells have developed in your body, God cannot lure them to leave voluntarily.

(2) By "high-grade enduring individuals" I am referring here exclusively to human beings. These individuals have much power of self-determination, and have many more real possibilities open to them than do the lower creatures. Hence, very rapid changes of behavior can occur with them. What is God's power to affect them? On the one hand, God can present quite novel aims to them, one after another. And God can seek to persuade them to change their behavior quite rapidly—for example to stop one's journey to help the victim of a crime. But on the other hand, these creatures have tremendous power with which to deviate from the divine aims for them, and they can deviate much more widely than can lower individuals. In a relatively short time after they learned to write, these individuals could discover that $E = mc^2$; and they can use this knowledge to destroy the world even more quickly.

Thus far I have been speaking of individuals. Most of these are *compound* individuals in which a number of individuals are ordered hierarchically, with one dominant member giving a unity of experience and activity to the whole society. The atom, the molecule, and the cell all have a unity of activity due to this hierarchical organization. Likewise the animal, by virtue of the dominating influence of its soul, has a unity of response to its environment.

(3) But some of the entities of this world seem to have no such unity. They are mere *aggregates*. Non-living things such as rocks, bodies of water, planets, automobiles, and timbers are obvious examples. Plants also probably have no dominant member, no soul. In any case, those things which are aggregates cannot, *as* aggregates, be directly affected by God. Since God acts by seeking to persuade individuals, and there is by definition no

individual dominating the other members of an aggregate, God cannot directly get an aggregate to do anything. God can move a living human body by persuading the soul to move; if the soul decides to cross the street, the rest of the body has little choice but to go along (assuming a healthy body). But there is no corresponding means by which God can directly move a rock—or get it to stop moving down the bank towards the highway. There is no way for God to stop that bullet speeding toward the heart of a man "too young to die." There is no way for God to stop the overburdened timbers in a mine shaft from caving in. There is no way God can stop the automobile with a sleeping driver from crashing into the oncoming cars. There is no way God can prevent that aggregate of molecules called a hurricane from devastating the towns in its paths.

In the earlier part of the paper I stressed what God has been doing in the world, by way of creating the conditions for good. With more space, I would describe some of the ways in which God seeks to overcome evil in the world. But I thought it best in these last few pages to stress the limitations on God's prevention of evil, since God's "failure" to prevent evil is usually the chief source of complaint, by theists and non-theists alike. This brief analysis of these limitations leads to the following three-fold conclusion:

1. Those things which cannot deviate much from the divine will also cannot be influenced by God very quickly.

2. Those things which can be influenced by God quickly can deviate drastically from the divine will.

3. Those things which can do nothing on their own cannot be directly influenced by God at all.

I could not, of course, in the brief space of this essay hope to justify the wide-ranging hypothesis outlined here. But I do hope that readers find the hypothesis potentially helpful enough to consider it worthy of further exploration. It (including variations on it) is the only hypothesis I have found that makes faith possible in the face of the horrendous evils that occur in our world.

Soul-Making Theodicy

From *Evil and the God of Love* by John Hick, revised edition, 1978

The Romantic poet John Keats (1795–1821) wrote in a letter to his brother and sister that this world is not "a vale of tears" but rather "the vale of Soul-making," with pain and suffering necessary to form a soul and a personality. Cognate notions were prevalent throughout the Romantic movement; Hegel's view of an Absolute evolving through a dialectic of history is probably the quintessential Romantic philosophy.

John Hick, a philosopher and theologian for many years at the University of Birmingham in England, has taken the Romantic idea and wedded it to views he has found in Irenaeus (130–202), a Greek Father of the Church, and has developed a soul-making Christian theodicy that is responsive to science and modern sensibilities. Hick's view has been prominent, if not dominant, in philosophic discussions of evil and God since the mid-sixties when his Evil and the God of Love *appeared.*

According to this view, evil is instrumental to soul-making. We make ourselves through our choices, through overcoming temptations and by responding to suffering with compassion. A person who has made herself into the person she is is much more valuable, says Hick, than would be someone without a personal history, who was created by God all-at-once, a person who had not undergone growth and personal development. And without evil, we would have no hurdles to jump over to make us strong, and to provoke moral responses. Hick is particularly concerned with our forging of our own moral character.

Now much evil is in fact instrumental to survival. Pain, for example, has demonstrable biological value. Pain teaches us the limits of our environment and not to damage tissue, for example, by carelessly putting our hands into fire. Suffering also seems sometimes to make stronger personalities, though often we do not see the gain while we are suffering. Hick's contention is that all this is integral to the creative process, a process in which we are in part self-creators, eventually deserving the right to enjoy God's company as having become Christ-like, in the "finite likeness of God."

Two questions are: first, dysteleological suffering, such as that of babies that die, or Hitler's victims, that do not plausibly lead to any benefit of soul or personality development; second, the implausibly complete development of almost anyone, except saints, at death. To the first problem Hick says that he has no solution except to recommend faith. Seeing that evil leads to good in many instances, those having faith that God redeems all evil would not be making a leap that is blind. To the second problem Hick, a Protestant, proposes something like the Catholic notion of Purgatory. Since except for a very few the soul-making process seems incomplete at death, there must be "other worlds" into which we are born at death and where we continue making ourselves.

Critics have alleged that this move is ad hoc *and unsupported by other evidence. And dysteleological suffering, say several critics, is not merely an occasional anomaly but rather such an extensive counterexample to Hick's theory as to refute it.*

Instead of regarding man as having been created by God in a finished state, as a finitely perfect being fulfilling the divine intention for our human level of existence, and then falling disastrously away from this, the minority report sees man as still in process of creation. Irenaeus himself expressed the point in terms of the (exegetically dubious) distinction between the 'image' and the 'likeness' of God referred to in Genesis i. 26: 'Then God said, Let us make man in our image, after our likeness.' His view was that man as a personal and moral being already exists in the image, but has not yet been formed into the finite likeness of God. By this 'likeness' Irenaeus means something more than personal existence as such; he means a certain valuable quality of personal life which reflects finitely the divine life. This represents the perfecting of man, the fulfilment of God's purpose for humanity, the 'bringing of many sons to glory',[1] the creating of 'children of God' who are 'fellow heirs with Christ' of his glory.[2]

[1] Hebrews ii. 10.

[2] Romans viii. 17.

And so man, created as a personal being in the image of God, is only the raw material for a further and more difficult stage of God's creative work. This is the leading of men as relatively free and autonomous persons, through their own dealings with life in the world in which He has placed them, towards that quality of personal existence that is the finite likeness of God. The features of this likeness are revealed in the person of Christ, and the process of man's creation into it is the work of the Holy Spirit. In St. Paul's words, 'And we all, with unveiled faces, beholding the glory of the Lord, are being changed into his likeness (εἰκών) from one degree of glory to another; for this comes from the Lord who is the Spirit',[3] or again, 'For God knew his own before ever they were, and also ordained that they should be shaped to the likeness (εἰκών) of his Son.'[4] In Johannine terms, the movement from the image to the likeness is a transition from one level of existence, that of animal life (*Bios*), to another and higher level, that of eternal life (*Zoe*), which includes but transcends the first. And the fall of man was seen by Irenaeus as a failure within the second phase of this creative process, a failure that has multiplied the perils and complicated the route of the journey in which God is seeking to lead mankind.

In the light of modern anthropological knowledge some form of two-stage conception of the creation of man has become an almost unavoidable Christian tenet. At the very least we must acknowledge as two distinguishable stages the fashioning of *homo sapiens* as a product of the long evolutionary process, and his sudden or gradual spiritualization as a child of God. But we may well extend the first stage to include the development of man as a rational and responsible person capable of personal relationship with the personal Infinite who has created him. This first stage of the creative process was, to our anthropomorphic imaginations, easy for divine omnipotence. By an exercise of creative power God caused the physical universe to exist, and in the course of countless ages to bring forth within it organic life, and finally to produce out of organic life personal life; and when man had thus emerged out of the evolution of the forms of organic life, a creature had been made who has the possibility of existing in conscious fellowship with God. But the second stage of the creative process is of a different kind altogether. It cannot be performed by omnipotent power as such. For personal life is essentially free and self-directing. It cannot be perfected by divine fiat, but only through the uncompelled responses and willing co-operation of human individuals in their actions and reactions in the world in which God has placed them. Men may eventually become the perfected persons whom the New Testament calls 'children of God', but they cannot be created ready-made as this.

The value-judgment that is implicitly being invoked here is that one who has attained to goodness by meeting and eventually mastering temptations, and thus by rightly making responsible choices in concrete situations, is good in a richer and more valuable sense than would be one created *ab initio* in a state either of innocence or of virtue. In the former case, which is that of the actual moral achievements of mankind, the individual's goodness has within it the strength of temptations overcome, a stability based upon an accumulation of

---

[3] II Corinthians iii. 18.

[4] Romans viii. 29. Other New Testament passages expressing a view of man as undergoing a process of spiritual growth within God's purpose, are: Ephesians ii. 21; iii. 16; Colossians ii. 19; I John iii. 2; II Corinthians iv. 16.

right choices, and a positive and responsible character that comes from commitment of costly personal effort. I suggest, then, that it is an ethically reasonable judgement, even though in the nature of the case not one that is capable of demonstrative proof, that human goodness slowly built up through personal histories of moral effort has a value in the eyes of the Creator which justifies even the long travail of the soul-making process.

The picture with which we are working is thus developmental and teleological. Man is in process of becoming the perfected being whom God is seeking to create. However, this is not taking place—it is important to add—by a natural and inevitable evolution, but through a hazardous adventure in individual freedom. Because this is a pilgrimage within the life of each individual, rather than a racial evolution, the progressive fulfilment of God's purpose does not entail any corresponding progressive improvement in the moral state of the world. There is no doubt a development in man's ethical situation from generation to generation through the building of individual choices into public institutions, but this involves an accumulation of evil as well as of good.[5] It is thus probable that human life was lived on much the same moral plane two thousand years ago or four thousand years ago as it is today. But nevertheless during this period uncounted millions of souls have been through the experience of earthly life, and God's purpose has gradually moved towards its fulfilment within each one of them, rather than within a human aggregate composed of different units in different generations.

If, then, God's aim in making the world is 'the bringing of many sons to glory',[6] that aim will naturally determine the kind of world that He has created. Antitheistic writers almost invariably assume a conception of the divine purpose which is contrary to the Christian conception. They assume that the purpose of a loving God must be to create a hedonistic paradise; and therefore to the extent that the world is other than this, it proves to them that God is either not loving enough or not powerful enough to create such a world. They think of God's relation to the earth on the model of a human being building a cage for a pet animal to dwell in. If he is humane he will naturally make his pet's quarters as pleasant and healthful as he can. Any respect in which the cage falls short of the veterinarian's ideal, and contains possibilities of accident or disease, is evidence of either limited benevolence or limited means, or both. Those who use the problem of evil as an argument against belief in God almost invariably think of the world in this kind of way. David Hume, for example, speaks of an architect who is trying to plan a house that is to be as comfortable and convenient as possible. If we find that 'the windows, doors, fires, passages, stairs, and the whole economy of the building were the source of noise, confusion, fatigue, darkness, and the extremes of heat and cold' we should have no hesitation in blaming the architect. It would be in vain for him to prove that if this or that defect were corrected greater ills would result: 'still you would assert in general, that, if the architect had had skill and good intentions, he might have formed such a plan of the

---

[5] This fact is symbolized in early Christian literature both by the figure of the Antichrist, who continually opposes God's purposes in history, and by the expectation of cataclysmic calamity and strife in the last days before the end of the present world order.

[6] Hebrews ii. 10.

whole, and might have adjusted the parts in such a manner, as would have remedied all or most of these inconveniences'.[7]

But if we are right in supposing that God's purpose for man is to lead him from human *Bios,* or the biological life of man, to that quality of *Zoe,* or the personal life of eternal worth, which we see in Christ, then the question that we have to ask is not, Is this the kind of world that an all-powerful and infinitely loving being would create as an environment for his human pets? or, Is the architecture of the world the most pleasant and convenient possible? The question that we have to ask is rather, Is this the kind of world that God might make as an environment in which moral beings may be fashioned, through their own free insights and responses, into 'children of God'?

Such critics as Hume are confusing what heaven ought to be, as an environment for perfected finite beings, with what this world ought to be, as an environment for beings who are in process of becoming perfected. For if our general conception of God's purpose is correct the world is not intended to be a paradise, but rather the scene of a history in which human personality may be formed towards the pattern of Christ. Men are not to be thought of on the analogy of animal pets, whose life is to be made as agreeable as possible, but rather on the analogy of human children, who are to grow to adulthood in an environment whose primary and overriding purpose is not immediate pleasure but the realizing of the most valuable potentialities of human personality.

The Free Will *Defense* (as opposed to *Explanation* of Evil)

From *God, Freedom, and Evil* by Alvin Plantinga, 1974

Alvin Plantinga has refined professional consideration of several issues in philosophy of religion by clarifying concepts using tools of logic. With regard to evil, Plantinga cleverly points out that defending the compatibility of God and evil is not so hard. What is hard is to explain why there is evil on theistic suppositions, the task of theodicy as traditionally conceived.

An explanation of X *says why* X *occurs. Or it allows us to predict* X. *A good explanation should be well-founded. There should be evidence for regarding the explanation as true. A good explanation should hook up with other things we know, especially laws and other general truths since a good explanation is by nature itself general, purporting to apply to a range of events or facts. A defense of* X, *on the other hand, need show only possibility, that, given what we definitely know,* X *is not ruled out. Thus, unlike a traditional theodicy purporting to explain evil, a defense of God in the face of evil purports to show only that it is possible that God be real and there be the evil there is. If it can be shown that the supposition that God is real is not strictly ruled out by the evil we perceive, then the reality of God is shown compatible with the evil we perceive. God has*

---

[7] *Dialogues Concerning Natural Religion,* pt. xi.

been defended. A defense need not be likely, need not be supported by evidence so that we ought to believe it. A defense can be imaginative, indeed wildly imaginative, so long as it is conceivable given what we know.

Plantinga's Free Will Defense, then, is not a theodicy, not a proposal why there really is evil, but an effort to show what evil might conceivably be due to, given a perfectly moral God. Plantinga's defense proposes that natural evil is due to Satan and his co-horts; in other words, he would make it a species of moral evil, moral evil brought about not by God but by non-human moral agents. Then the usual logic whereby God gets off the hook for moral evil would apply.

Critics say that this is facile, that natural evil cannot so easily be dismissed. Natural evil makes God's reality so unlikely that, failing a workable theodicy, belief in God could not be rational. Plantinga's retort is that there are arguments that establish the reality of God; the case for God rests on these. And since one of these is, according to Plantinga, the (modal) ontological argument, which concerns conceptual necessities, not empirical probabilities, a defense of God in the face of evil, and not a theodicy, is all that is called for. Of course, many would dispute that the ontological or any other argument makes a case for God. In the context of such controversy, Plantinga seems to be at least polemi-cally wrong to discount the importance of true theodicy.

But Plantinga seems right that it is not hard to show the compatibility of God and evil. One need not buy his speculations about the possibility of a Satan to see this. Here is what I call the Parallel Worlds Defense (which I thought of while contemplating Auro-bindo's attempt to explain evil: see below). Leibniz reasons that God should create the best of all possible worlds. The problem is that this world does not seem to be that world, because of evil. But suppose that God does create the best of all possible worlds. What about the second-best world, the runner-up in world competition? Should not God, out of lovingness, give the creatures in the second-best world their day in the sun? Why should some marginal flaw, in comparison with the champion world, prevent God from letting the runner-up world be. God, it seems, would create the second-best universe as a paral-lel universe, with its own space and time, and so forth, alongside the world with the blue ribbon. Similarly, with the third-place universe, the fourth, the fifth, and so on down to a universe where the balance of good and evil is so tenuous that God says, "Okay, this one and no more." That last universe is ours. Thus so long as we judge that there is not ab-solutely so much evil in this world that God would refuse to give us our day in the sun, then the evil here is compatible with God. (This defense has the further virtue that it matches our gratitude for being at all. That is, so long as we are, all told, glad that we exist, we would feel thankful toward a Creator, despite evil.)

THE FREE WILL DEFENSE VINDICATED

Put formally, you remember, the Free Will Defender's project was to show that

(1) God is omniscient, omnipotent, and wholly good

is consistent with

(3) There is evil.

What we have just seen is that

(35) It was not within God's power to create a world containing moral good but no moral evil

is possible and consistent with God's omnipotence and omniscience. But then it is clearly consistent with (1). So we can use it to show that (1) is consistent with (3). For consider

(1) God is omnipotent, omniscient, and wholly good
(35) It was not within God's power to create a world containing moral good without creating one containing moral evil

and

(36) God created a world containing moral good.

These propositions are evidently consistent—i.e., their conjunction is a possible proposition. But taken together they entail

(3) There is evil.

For (36) says that God created a world containing moral good; this together with (35) entails that He created one containing moral evil. But if it contains moral evil, then it contains evil. So (1), (35), and (36) are jointly consistent and entail (3); hence (1) is consistent with (3); . . . Remember: to serve in this argument (35) and (36) need not be known to be true, or likely on our evidence, or anything of the sort; they need only be consistent with (1). Since they are, there is no contradiction [between (1) and (3)]; so the Free Will Defense appears to be successful. . . .

IS GOD'S EXISTENCE COMPATIBLE WITH *NATURAL* EVIL?

Perhaps the atheologian can regroup once more. What about *natural* evil? Evil that can't be ascribed to the free actions of human beings? Suffering due to earthquakes, disease, and the like? Is the existence of evil of *this* sort compatible with (1) [God is omnipotent, omniscient, and morally perfect]? Here two lines of thought present themselves. On the one hand, it is conceivable that some natural evils and some persons are so related that the persons would have produced *less* moral good if the evils had been absent. Some people deal creatively with certain kinds of hardship or suffering, acting in such a way that on balance the whole state of affairs is valuable. And perhaps the response would have been less impressive and the total situation less valuable if the evil had not taken place. But a more traditional line of thought is indicated by St. Augustine, who attributes much of the evil we find to *Satan* or to Satan and his cohorts. Satan, so the traditional doctrine goes, is a mighty nonhuman spirit who, along with many other angels, was created long before God created man. Unlike most of his colleagues, Satan rebelled against God and has since been wreaking whatever havoc he can. The result is natural evil. So the natural evil we find is due to free actions of nonhuman spirits.

Augustine is presenting what I earlier called a *theodicy,* as opposed to a *defense.* He believes that *in fact* natural evil (except for what can be attributed to God's punishment) is to be ascribed to the activity of beings that are free and rational but nonhuman. The Free Will Defender, of course, does not assert that this is *true;* he says only that it is *possible* [and consistent with (1)]. He points to the possibility that natural evil is due to the actions of significantly free but nonhuman persons. We have noted that there is no inconsistency in the idea that God could not have created a world with a better balance of moral good over moral evil than this one displays. Something similar holds here; possibly natural evil is due to the free activity of nonhuman persons; and possibly it wasn't within God's power to create a set of such persons whose free actions produced a greater balance of good over evil. That is to say, it is possible that

> (40) Natural evil is due to the free actions of nonhuman persons; there is a balance of good over evil with respect to the actions of these nonhuman persons; and it was not within the power of God to create a world that contains a more favorable balance of good over evil with respect to the actions of the nonhuman persons it contains.

Again, it must be emphasized that (40) is not required to be *true* for the success of the Free Will Defense; it need only be compatible with (1). And it certainly looks as if it is. If (40) *is* true, furthermore, then *natural* evil significantly resembles *moral* evil in that, like the latter, it is the result of the activity of significantly free persons. In fact both moral and natural evil would then be special cases of what we might call *broadly moral evil*—evil resulting from the free actions of personal beings, whether human or not. Given this idea, we can combine (37) and (40) into one compendious statement:

> (41) All the evil in Kronos [the actual world] is broadly moral evil, and it was not within the power of God to create a world containing a better balance of broadly moral good and evil.

(41) appears to be consistent with (1) and

> (42) God creates a world containing as much broadly moral good as Kronos contains.

But (1), (41), and (42) together entail that there is as much evil as Kronos contains. So (1) is consistent with the proposition that there is as much evil as Kronos contains. I therefore conclude that the Free Will Defense successfully rebuts the charge of inconsistency brought against the theist.

The Karma and Rebirth Explanation

From *Brahma-sūtra Commentary* by Śaṅkara in *The Vedānta Sūtras of Bādarāyaṇa,* Georg Thibaut, translator, Max Müller, editor, *Sacred Books of the East,* Volumes 34 and 38, 1890–1904

The Absolutist view known as Advaita, Non-Dualism, was introduced earlier (see under Absolute Brahman), as was its chief classical proponent, Śaṅkara. Śaṅkara views the world as strictly an illusion, but he takes seriously, or pretty seriously, the theistic teachings of certain Hindu scriptures (namely, the Upanishads and the Gītā), as meditational aids, as will be explained. Scripture says that Brahman is the source of the world, and so since Brahman is unsullied value and bliss, whence evil? How could evil have its source in what is inherently its opposite?

Śaṅkara's explanation is complex. First there is the distinction between Brahman as "without" and "with qualities" (or "attributes"), nirguṇa *contrasting with* saguṇa *brahman. Brahman-without-qualities is supremely real; Brahman-with-qualities is talked about in scripture as an aid to meditation. Scripture is like a patient teacher (*guru*), and it is difficult to appreciate that Brahman as supremely real has no qualities. Scripture talks about God, that is, Brahman-with-qualities, as a preparatory to the austere truth—which is that nothing but Brahman-without-qualities is real. God, too, is part of a cosmic illusion, due to spiritual ignorance (*avidyā, translated in the text as "Nescience"*).*

Brahman-with-qualities is God, the Lord and Creator. How then could the Lord, who is perfect—much as in the Western conception—allow evil in the world? Śaṅkara asks this question in the text excerpted below. His answer is an Eastern version of a free-will theodicy, "Eastern" because of the prominence of assumptions about karma *and rebirth. There is also the supposition, that Śaṅkara shares with almost all classical Indian theists, that the transmigratory world is beginningless.*

As explained above in the general introduction, the word karma *in Sanskrit means "action." In Śaṅkara's usage, it is shorthand for a psychological theory and means something like "habit." As explained earlier, every action that one performs creates a psychological valence, or habit, to do that type of action again. Many habits are such fundamental dispositions of the soul that they carry over into and determine the course of a soul's next incarnation. To an extent, virtue and vice are their own reward, but also God's universe is moral. There is justly moral payback for bad karma, for bad habits, that is to say, for bad patterns of behavior. Much of what we see as natural evil is this payback, for which, then, the Lord cannot be blamed.*

But at the beginning of the universe there was no good or bad karma (what Śaṅkara calls in the text religious merit and demerit). At the time of creation, the Lord could not have acted with respect to the merit of souls. Śaṅkara answers that there is no beginning with respect to Nescience.

Here the deep question is, then, why is there Nescience, avidyā, *spiritual ignorance. If Brahman is the supreme reality, our own true self, why is it that we are unenlightened? We shall consider this question further with respect to the next two selections—from modern Eastern thought.*

[Śaṅkara]. . . the activity of the Lord also may be supposed to be mere sport, proceeding from his own nature[1], without reference to any purpose. For on the ground neither of reason nor of Scripture can we construe any other purpose of the Lord. Nor can his nature be questioned[2].— Although the creation of this world appears to us a weighty and difficult undertaking, it is mere play to the Lord, whose power is unlimited. And if in ordinary life we might possibly, by close scrutiny, detect some subtle motive, even for sportful action, we cannot do so with re-

---

[1] The nature (svabhāva) of the Lord is, the commentators say, Māyā joined with time and karman.

[2] This clause is an answer to the objection that the Lord might remain at rest instead of creating a world useless to himself and the cause of pain to others. For in consequence of his conjunction with Māyā the creation is unavoidable.

gard to the actions of the Lord, all whose wishes are fulfilled, as Scripture says.—Nor can it be said that he either does not act or acts like a senseless person; for Scripture affirms the fact of the creation on the one hand, and the Lord's omniscience on the other hand. And, finally, we must remember that the scriptural doctrine of creation does not refer to the highest reality; it refers to the apparent world only, which is characterised by name and form, the figments of Nescience, and it, moreover, aims at intimating that Brahman is the Self of everything.

[sūtra] Inequality (of dispensation) and cruelty (the Lord can)not (be reproached with), on account of his regarding (merit and demerit); for so (Scripture) declares.

[Śaṅkara] In order to strengthen the tenet which we are at present defending, we follow the procedure of him who shakes a pole planted in the ground (in order to test whether it is firmly planted), and raise another objection against the doctrine of the Lord being the cause of the world.—The Lord, it is said, cannot be the cause of the world, because, on that hypothesis, the reproach of inequality of dispensation and cruelty would attach to him. Some beings, viz. the gods and others, he renders eminently happy; others, as for instance the animals, eminently unhappy; to some again, as for instance men, he allots an intermediate position. To a Lord bringing about such an unequal condition of things, passion and malice would have to be ascribed, just as to any common person acting similarly; which attributes would be contrary to the essential goodness of the Lord affirmed by Sruti and Smriti [i.e. by scripture]. Moreover, as the infliction of pain and the final destruction of all creatures would form part of his dispensation, he would have to be taxed with great cruelty, a quality abhorred by low people even. For these two reasons Brahman cannot be the cause of the world.

The Lord, we reply, cannot be reproached with inequality of dispensation and cruelty, 'because he is bound by regards.' If the Lord on his own account, without any extraneous regards, produced this unequal creation, he would expose himself to blame; but the fact is, that in creating he is bound by certain regards, i.e. he has to look to merit and demerit. Hence the circumstance of the creation being unequal is due to the merit and demerit of the living creatures created, and is not a fault for which the Lord is to blame. The position of the Lord is to be looked on as analogous to that of Parjanya, the Giver of rain. For as Parganya is the common cause of the production of rice, barley, and other plants, while the difference between the various species is due to the various potentialities lying hidden in the respective seeds, so the Lord is the common cause of the creation of gods, men, &c., while the differences between these classes of beings are due to the different merit belonging to the individual souls. Hence the Lord, being bound by regards, cannot be reproached with inequality of dispensation and cruelty. And if we are asked how we come to know that the Lord, in creating this world with its various conditions, is bound by regards, we reply that Scripture declares that; compare, for instance, the two following passages, 'For he (the Lord) makes him, whom he wishes to lead up from these worlds, do a good deed; and the same makes him, whom he wishes to lead down from these worlds, do a bad deed' (Kaush. Up. III, 8)[1]; and 'A man becomes good by good work, bad by bad work' (Bri. Up. III, 2, 13). Smriti [i.e. scriptural] passages also declare the favour of the Lord and its opposite to

---

[1] From this passage we must not—the commentators say—infer injustice on the part of the Lord; for the previous merit or demerit of a being determines the specific quality of the actions which he performs in his present existence, the Lord acting as the common cause only (as Parjanya does).

depend on the different quality of the works of living beings; so, for instance, 'I serve men in the way in which they approach me' (Bha. Gî. IV, 11).

[sūtra] If it be objected that it (viz. the Lord's having regard to merit and demerit) is impossible on account of the non-distinction (of merit and demerit, previous to the first creation); we refute the objection on the ground of (the world) being without a beginning.

[Śaṅkara] But—an objection is raised—the passage, 'Being only this was in the beginning, one, without a second,' affirms that before the creation there was no distinction and consequently no merit on account of which the creation might have become unequal. And if we assume the Lord to have been guided in his dispensations by the actions of living beings subsequent to the creation, we involve ourselves in the circular reasoning that work depends on diversity of condition of life, and diversity of condition again on work. The Lord may be considered as acting with regard to religious merit after distinction had once arisen; but as before that the cause of inequality, viz. merit, did not exist, it follows that the first creation must have been free from inequalities.

This objection we meet by the remark, that the transmigratory world is without beginning. The objection would be valid if the world had a beginning; but as it is without beginning, merit and inequality are, like seed and sprout, caused as well as causes, and there is therefore no logical objection to their operation. To the question how we know that the world is without a beginning, the next Sūtra replies.

[sūtra] (The beginninglessness of the world) recommends itself to reason and is seen (from Scripture).

[Śaṅkara] The beginninglessness of the world recommends itself to reason. For if it had a beginning it would follow that, the world springing into existence without a cause, the released souls also would again enter into the circle of transmigratory existence; and further, as then there would exist no determining cause of the unequal dispensation of pleasure and pain, we should have to acquiesce in the doctrine of rewards and punishments being allotted, without reference to previous good or bad actions. That the Lord is not the cause of the inequality, has already been remarked. Nor can Nescience by itself be the cause, as it is of a uniform nature. On the other hand, Nescience may be the cause of inequality, if it be considered as having regard to merit accruing from action produced by the mental impressions of wrath, hatred, and other afflicting passions. Without merit and demerit nobody can enter into existence, and again, without a body merit and demerit cannot be formed; so that—on the doctrine of the world having a beginning—we are led into a logical see-saw. The opposite doctrine, on the other hand, explains all matters in a manner analogous to the case of the seed and sprout, so that no difficulty remains. . . .

[sūtra] And because all the qualities (required in the cause of the world) are present (in Brahman).

[Śaṅkara] The teacher has now refuted all the objections, such as difference of character, and the like, which other teachers have brought forward against what he had established as the real sense of the Veda, viz. that the intelligent Brahman is the cause and matter of this world.

Now, before entering on a new chapter, whose chief aim it will be to refute the (positive) opinions held by other teachers, he sums up the foregoing chapter, the purport of which it was to show why his view should be accepted.—Because, if that Brahman is acknowledged as the cause of the world, all attributes required in the cause (of the world) are seen to be present—Brahman being all-knowing, all-powerful, and possessing the great power of Māyā—on that account this our system, founded on the Upanishads, is not open to any objections.

Ego, Evolution, and Soul-Making

From *The Life Divine* by Sri Aurobindo, 1973

See the introduction to the selection from Aurobindo under Speculative Spiritual Metaphysics for a sketch of Aurobindo's life and an overview of his metaphysics. In the selection here, Aurobindo elaborates his sense of the direction of evolution, namely, toward our becoming spiritually transformed individuals who have a rather direct awareness of Brahman (i.e. God) but who remain embodied, each with a distinct personality and a transformed body, life, and mind. Aurobindo sees evil as instrumental to this process.

More precisely, he sees evil as growing out of egoistic awareness, which is of course our normal awareness, where we see ourselves as fundamentally other to everyone else and are not aware of Brahman. But Brahman, whose essential nature is Sachchidananda (Existence, Consciousness-Force, and Bliss), is everyone and everything. Brahman uses the ego as scaffolding, or as a mold, for the slow development of the spiritual individual.

Thus Aurobindo's view is like the soul-making theodicy of Western Romantics and John Hick. But where Hick has soul-making continuing past death into other worlds, Aurobindo embraces reincarnation, a series of births in this world, where the divine individual is forged. Now I should add that Aurobindo also has "other worlds," other manifestations of Brahman. These are not evolutionary in character, however, and contain, strictly speaking, no evil (though various limitations do define each world, or, as Aurobindo says, "plane of being"). Soul-development goes on only here in this world. (The idea matches the traditional saying in Hinduism that even a god has to take a human birth in order to make spiritual progress.)

Aurobindo has an answer to the question why, given Brahman and Sachchidananda as our true nature, we are not born enlightened. That would be impossible until we have sufficiently developed strength of personality to be able to maintain our individuality—unless one were to cash in his/her evolutionary chips. Aurobindo does say that some opt for Nirvana, or extinguishing of finite personality in a reabsorption in the One. But for most of us, a divine life is, apparently, our eventual destiny.

Apart from several factual matters, the deep question with this view seems to be whether Brahman is morally good in subjecting us as egos to pain and suffering so that divine individuals may develop. I see myself as a distinct person, with little joys and pains, who will die. Maybe some soul in me is profitting from my experiences. But what about me? On Aurobindo's view, it seems than we human egos get used.

If all is in truth Sachchidananda [Brahman as Existence-Consciousness-Bliss], death, suffering, evil, limitation can only be the creations, positive in practical effect, negative in essence, of a distorting consciousness which has fallen from the total and unifying knowledge of itself into some error of division and partial experience. This is the fall of man typified in the poetic parable of the Hebrew Genesis. That fall is his deviation from the full and pure acceptance of God and himself, or rather of God in himself, into a dividing consciousness which brings with it all the train of the dualities, life and death, good and evil, joy and pain, completeness and want, the fruit of a divided being. This is the fruit which Adam and Eve, Purusha and Prakriti, the soul tempted by Nature, have eaten. The redemption comes by the recovery of the universal in the individual and of the spiritual term in the physical consciousness. Then alone the soul in Nature can be allowed to partake of the fruit of the tree of life and be as the Divine and live for ever. For then only can the purpose of its descent into material consciousness be accomplished, when the knowledge of good and evil, joy and suffering, life and death has been accomplished through the recovery by the human soul of a higher knowledge which reconciles and identifies these opposites in the universal and transforms their divisions into the image of the divine Unity.

To Sachchidananda extended in all things in widest commonalty and impartial universality, death, suffering, evil and limitation can only be at the most reverse terms, shadow-forms of their luminous opposites. As these things are felt by us, they are notes of a discord. They formulate separation where there should be a unity, miscomprehension where there should be an understanding, an attempt to arrive at independent harmonies where there should be a self-adaptation to the orchestral whole. All totality, even if it be only in one scheme of the universal vibrations, even if it be only a totality of the physical consciousness without possession of all that is in movement beyond and behind, must be to that extent a reversion to harmony and a reconciliation of jarring opposites. On the other hand, to Sachchidananda transcendent of the forms of the universe the dual terms themselves, even so understood, can no longer be justly applicable. Transcendence transfigures; it does not reconcile, but rather transmutes opposites into something surpassing them that effaces their oppositions. . . .

. . . If life is in its nature individual phenomenon and not representation of a universal existence and the breathing of a mighty Life-Spirit, if the dualities which are the response of the individual to its contacts are not merely a response but the very essence and condition of all living, if limitation is the inalienable nature of the substance of which our mind and body are formed, disintegration of death the first and last condition of all life, its end and its beginning, pleasure and pain the inseparable dual stuff of all sensation, joy and grief the necessary light and shade of all emotion, truth and error the two poles between which all knowledge must eternally move, then transcendence is only attainable by the abandonment of human life in a Nirvana beyond all existence or by attainment to another world, a heaven quite otherwise constituted than this material universe.

It is not very easy for the customary mind of man, always attached to its past and present associations, to conceive of an existence still human, yet radically changed in what are now our fixed circumstances. We are in respect to our possible higher evolution much in the position of the original Ape of the Darwinian theory. It would have been impossible for that Ape leading his instinctive arboreal life in primeval forests to conceive that there would be one day an animal on the earth who would use a new faculty called reason upon the materials of his inner and outer existence, who would dominate by that power his instincts and habits, change the circumstances of his physical life, build for himself houses of stone, manipulate Nature's forces, sail the seas, ride the air, develop codes of conduct, evolve conscious methods for his mental and spiritual development. And if such a conception had been possible for the Ape-mind, it would still have been difficult for him to imagine that by any progress of Nature or long effort of Will and tendency he himself could develop into that animal. Man, because he has acquired reason and still more because he has indulged his power of imagination and intuition, is able to conceive an existence higher than his own and even to envisage his personal elevation beyond his present state into that existence. His idea of the supreme state is an absolute of all that is positive to his own concepts and desirable to his own instinctive aspiration,—Knowledge without its negative shadow of error, Bliss without its negation in experience of suffering, Power without its constant denial by incapacity, purity and plenitude of being without the opposing sense of defect and limitation. It is so that he conceives his gods; it is so that he constructs his heavens. But it is not so that his reason conceives of a possible earth and a possible humanity. His dream of God and Heaven is really a dream of his own perfection; but he finds the same difficulty in accepting its practical realisation here for his ultimate aim as would the ancestral Ape if called upon to believe in himself as the future Man. His imagination, his religious aspirations may hold that end before him; but when his reason asserts itself, rejecting imagination and transcendent intuition, he puts it by as a brilliant superstition contrary to the hard facts of the material universe. It becomes then only his inspiring vision of the impossible. All that is possible is a conditioned, limited and precarious knowledge, happiness, power and good.

Yet in the principle of reason itself there is the assertion of a Transcendence. For reason is in its whole aim and essence the pursuit of Knowledge, the pursuit, that is to say, of Truth by the elimination of error. Its view, its aim is not that of a passage from a greater to a lesser error, but it supposes a positive, preexistent Truth towards which through the dualities of right knowledge and wrong knowledge we can progressively move. If our reason has not the same instinctive certitude with regard to the other aspirations of humanity, it is because it lacks the same essential illumination inherent in its own positive activity. We can just conceive of a positive or absolute realisation of happiness, because the heart to which that instinct for happiness belongs has its own form of certitude, is capable of faith, and because our minds can envisage the elimination of unsatisfied want which is the apparent cause of suffering. But how shall we conceive of the elimination of pain from nervous sensation or of death from the life of the body? Yet the rejection of pain is a sovereign instinct of the sensations, the rejection of death a dominant claim inherent in the essence of our vitality. But these things present themselves to our reason as instinctive aspirations, not as realisable potentialities.

Yet the same law should hold throughout. The error of the practical reason is an excessive subjection to the apparent fact which it can immediately feel as real and an insufficient courage in carrying profounder facts of potentiality to their logical conclusion. What is, is the realisation of an anterior potentiality; present potentiality is a clue to future realisation. And here potentiality exists; for the mastery of phenomena depends upon a knowledge of their causes and processes and if we know the causes of error, sorrow, pain, death, we may labour with some hope towards their elimination. For knowledge is power and mastery.

In fact, we do pursue as an ideal, so far as we may, the elimination of all these negative or adverse phenomena. We seek constantly to minimise the causes of error, pain and suffering. Science, as its knowledge increases, dreams of regulating birth and of indefinitely prolonging life, if not of effecting the entire conquest of death. But because we envisage only external or secondary causes, we can only think of removing them to a distance and not of eliminating the actual roots of that against which we struggle. And we are thus limited because we strive towards secondary perceptions and not towards root-knowledge, because we know processes of things, but not their essence. We thus arrive at a more powerful manipulation of circumstances, but not at essential control. But if we could grasp the essential nature and the essential cause of error, suffering and death, we might hope to arrive at a mastery over them which should not be relative but entire. We might hope even to eliminate them altogether and justify the dominant instinct of our nature by the conquest of that absolute good, bliss, knowledge and immortality which our intuitions perceive as the true and ultimate condition of the human being.

The ancient Vedanta presents us with such a solution in the conception and experience of Brahman as the one universal and essential fact and of the nature of Brahman as Sachchidananda.

In this view the essence of all life is the movement of a universal and immortal existence, the essence of all sensation and emotion is the play of a universal and self-existent delight in being, the essence of all thought and perception is the radiation of a universal and all-pervading truth, the essence of all activity is the progression of a universal and self-effecting good.

But the play and movement embodies itself in a multiplicity of forms, a variation of tendencies, an interplay of energies. Multiplicity permits of the interference of a determinative and temporarily deformative factor, the individual ego; and the nature of the ego is a self-limitation of consciousness by a willed ignorance of the rest of its play and its exclusive absorption in one form, one combination of tendencies, one field of the movement of energies. Ego is the factor which determines the reactions of error, sorrow, pain, evil, death; for it gives these values to movements which would otherwise be represented in their right relation to the one Existence, Bliss, Truth and Good. By recovering the right relation we may eliminate the ego-determined reactions, reducing them eventually to their true values; and this recovery can be effected by the right participation of the individual in the consciousness of the totality and in the consciousness of the transcendent which the totality represents.

Into later Vedanta there crept and arrived at fixity the idea that the limited ego is not only the cause of the dualities, but the essential condition for the existence of the universe. By getting rid of the ignorance of the ego and its resultant limitations we do indeed eliminate the dualities, but we eliminate along with them our existence in the cosmic movement. Thus we return to the essentially evil and illusory nature of human existence and the vanity of all effort after perfection in the life of the world. A relative good linked always to its opposite is all that here we can seek. But if we adhere to the larger and profounder idea that the ego is only an intermediate representation of something beyond itself, we escape from this consequence and are able to apply Vedanta to fulfillment of life and not only to the escape from life. The essential cause and condition of universal existence is the Lord,

Ishwara or Purusha, manifesting and occupying individual and universal forms. The limited ego is only an intermediate phenomenon of consciousness necessary for a certain line of development. Following this line the individual can arrive at that which is beyond himself, that which he represents, and can yet continue to represent it, no longer as an obscured and limited ego, but as a centre of the Divine and of the universal consciousness embracing, utilising and transforming into harmony with the Divine all individual determinations.

We have then the manifestation of the divine Conscious Being in the totality of physical Nature as the foundation of human existence in the material universe. We have the emergence of that Conscious Being in an involved and inevitably evolving Life, Mind and Supermind as the condition of our activities; for it is this evolution which has enabled man to appear in Matter and it is this evolution which will enable him progressively to manifest God in the body,—the universal Incarnation. We have in egoistic formation the intermediate and decisive factor which allows the One to emerge as the conscious Many out of that indeterminate totality general, obscure and formless which we call the subconscient,—*hṛdaya samudra,* the ocean heart in things of the Rig Veda. We have the dualities of life and death, joy and sorrow, pleasure and pain, truth and error, good and evil as the first formations of egoistic consciousness, the natural and inevitable outcome of its attempt to realise unity in an artificial construction of itself exclusive of the total truth, good, life and delight of being in the universe. We have the dissolution of this egoistic construction by the self-opening of the individual to the universe and to God as the means of that supreme fulfilment to which egoistic life is only a prelude even as animal life was only a prelude to the human. We have the realisation of the All in the individual by the transformation of the limited ego into a conscious centre of the divine unity and freedom as the term at which the fulfilment arrives. And we have the outflowing of the infinite and absolute Existence, Truth, Good and Delight of being on the Many in the world as the divine result towards which the cycles of our evolution move. This is the supreme birth which maternal Nature holds in herself; of this she strives to be delivered.

Why Am I Not Enlightened?

From "Nishitani's Buddhist Response to Nihilism" by Stephen H. Phillips in *Journal of the American Academy of Religion,* Volume 55, Number 1, 1987

For necessary background, see the discussion of Nishitani's Zen philosophy under The Vibrant Void.

According to Buddhist philosophy, evil is not an intellectual problem to be explained but an existential problem to be eliminated. As mentioned in the general introduction, the Buddha himself—according to both Southern and the Northern traditions—was inspired to seek enlightenment by sight of the "three evils," disease, old age, and death. According to the Northern or Mahāyāna tradition, to become a Bodhisattva (see the Glossary) is to transcend evil.

Keiji Nishitani argues that evil, and in particular modern nihilism (a sense of mean-inglessness), is just what we should expect given that we are unenlightened. Evil and meaninglessness (which he calls nihility) are to be for us, as for the original Buddha, a spur to spiritual progress, and to an eventual enlightenment termed satori *in Japanese.*

In the excerpt from a journal article of mine below, I reconstruct and criticize Nishitani's reasoning. Note the similarity in structure, and in quite a few details, between Nishitani's position and that of the Advaitin, Śaṅkara. In particular, there is a common reliance on a presumed beginninglessness of avidyā, *"spiritual ignorance." This, it seems to me, is unsatisfactory.*

We confront an existential problem in cosmic meaninglessness, and are faced with despair when we ask, "What is my life *for?*" The solution, we are told, is living "appropriation" of *śūnyatā*. What would this mean in terms of personal action? It would mean that one would be naturally no longer self-centered, that one would live for others in a spirit of *agapē* and *karuṇā*, "compassion." What would one do for others? Apparently, the "enlightened" (a) help others achieve enlightenment and (b) play "in earnest," having become like a child, as well as "just sit," in that there is nothing personal to gain or protect. Thus, *śūnyatā* would uphold "play" and "just sitting" in a way distinct from its upholding of ourselves as we are now, with our petty desires and aims. The "life-affirmation" of *śūnyatā* and its value-conferral are tied to the attitudes of "play" and of "just sitting." What then should we think of the view that attitudes of "play" and of "just sitting" are in some preferred way underpinned by the reality of *śūnyatā*? Does Nishitani in this way provide a solution to the tension between religious faith and evil, or is this mere sleight of hand?

An easy rebuttal appears available in an appeal to social conscience—despite the talk of transcendence of self-regard—since "play" and "just sitting" are what the transformation is to amount to in a positive way. Are we to play and just sit while people are oppressed and nations with unenlightened leaders move closer to nuclear war? Are we to "just sit" while people in Africa, or anywhere, starve?[1] Clearly, play and just sitting do not seem to be crucial to survival in our day and age, and not only societally but also from the individual's perspective. Most of us enjoy playing. And "just sitting" might be luxurious. But there is rent to be paid. Yet these lines of objection may be superficial because they do not take into account "nihility."

One must appreciate how radical is Nishitani's condemnation of our everyday concerns, despite the talk of "life-affirmation." In our present state we are totally "corrupt." All our desires and goals are enveloped by nihility, the meaninglessness of self-regarding aims in the context of death and radical physical contingency. There is only one qualification. Nishitani says:

---

[1] Buddhism has long had to live with an ethical tension between the ideals of compassion and *samādhi* ("just sitting"). Nishitani believes that the tension is resolved in the emergence of Mahāyāna and is ideal of the Bodhisattva, an ideal opposed to the earlier (and Theravāda) ideal of the Arhat. But *how* does the Bodhisattva help others? He helps them win *nirvāṇa* for themselves; then he himself passes into the ultimate extinction of form and personality, and transcendent "bliss." The ideal thus remains "world-negational," although it is not, to be sure, as world-negational as the ideal of the Arhat who seeks above all his own salvation, for in Mahāyāna there is at least more of an acknowledgment of the importance of others.

Yet were complete corruption the last word on the actual condition of the *imago Dei* in man, we should still be left with some unanswered questions: How can man look for God, and how can he recognize when he has found him? How can man become conscious of sin? How can man hear when God calls out to him? It is not without reason, therefore, that [Emil] Brunner attempts to come up with some "point of contact." On the other hand, though, if we set any limit at all to the completeness of the corruption within man, we risk falling short of the full truth of human sinfulness. Therefore, the place of "contact" must be present, in some sense, *within* that complete corruption itself. It may be found, I think, in the very awareness of the fact of complete corruption itself.

Recall that to appreciate nihility is to be "authentic." Nihility is *the* religious attitude, Nishitani says. And this attitude has a special confirmational role in the Buddhist theory. It reflects the transcendence of *śūnyatā* in the sphere of values. Nishitani makes perhaps his most important contribution to Buddhist philosophy in the way in which he ties the transcendence of *śūnyatā* to "nihility." Nihility is something that we should expect, given the reality of *śūnyatā*. He suggests that nihility as a natural expression of the transcendence of *śūnyatā* protects that transcendence, as it were. The only way existentially to *śūnyatā* is through "nihility," as though this state of despair were some purifying spiritual fire burning away all self-regard.

There is thus a pronounced value-opposition between "nihility" and the transcendence of *śūnyatā* on the one hand and its "life-affirmation" on the other. Nihility is so radical that it is hard to make sense of the claim that Emptiness is life-affirmative. Moreover, the value-opposition is shuffled off, cosmologically, in a theory of *avidyā,* an "original" and beginningless "ignorance."

According to Nishitani, when we participate in the larger awareness of *śūnyatā*, a personal action ceases to be a "task;" we are no longer laden with a sense of a debt to be repaid through work (this is called "*karma*"). We have no sense of meaninglessness. There are no problems of choice. In fact, action happens spontaneously. We are rushed forward into the world by the dynamic nature of *śūnyatā,* yet with compassion as well as the attitudes of "play" and "just sitting." But is not something similar supposed to be what is already happening in reality? Nishitani's fundamental assumption is that *śūnyatā* is surpassingly real. "Emptiness" has been said to be omnipresent, to *sustain all forms right now,* whether or not we are aware of this. Why then are we not aware of this now? To this problem the theory of *avidyā* is put forth.

Nishitani appears to some extent to recognize the problem, but his "solution" moves very fast:

> As rational or personal beings, we grasp ourselves and thereby get caught by our reason or personality. While this is our own act, it is not something we are free to do as we please. The force of destiny is at work here, impelling us to be and to act in this manner.

What is this "destiny?" We are not told. Then again near the end of the book:

> At the home ground of Dasein [Nishitani's shorthand for the intrinsic "presence" guaranteed by *śūnyatā,* the cosmic but unconfinable "here and now"], where we find the wellspring of that infinite drive [to finite forms, acts, and personality], we become aware of an infinite self-enclosure, or what [Arnold] Toynbee calls "self-centeredness." The ancients took this elemental self-enclosure, this self-enclosure that is the wellspring of endless karmic activity, as the darkness of ignorance (*avidyā*) or "fundamental darkness."

This is the Eastern "non-solution" *par excellence*.[2] No explanation of the "infinite self-enclosure" or of *śūnyatā*'s "drive" away from itself into "ignorance" is given. These are thought to be, I suppose, just brute facts. Cosmic "ignorance" (*avidyā*) is said to be primal and "beginningless" (*anādi*);[3] but we are left in the dark about why things should be this way—a theoretical failure that is all the more grievous in the light of the possibility of *satori* (and the life-affirmation) putatively provided by *sunyatā*. Here lies perhaps the chief inadequacy of the theory of *śūnyatā*: *avidyā* is very mysterious in Nishitani's view. And since it is so mysterious, he does not resolve the tension between religious faith and evil, that is to say, he fails—to use his own terms—to find an alternative to nihility. He is not convincing that *śūnyatā* is a grand life-affirmation. Either it affirms too little, only "play" and "just sitting," or too much, all the evils of existence."[4]

DISCUSSION QUESTIONS

1. What is David Hume's argument—expressed by the character Philo—that what the empiricist theologian (viz., Cleanthes) calls God should be judged to be amoral?

2. Reconstruct Augustine's expansion of free-will theodicy to cover what seems to be (but isn't, on this view) natural evil.

3. What constraints are there to God's power, according to the process theodicy of David Griffin, and how do these help explain various evils? Provide at least one concrete example of evil beyond those taken up by Griffin, and explain how Griffin's theodicy would view it.

4. Outline the Irenaean, or "soul-making," theodicy of John Hick. Give a few examples of teleological evils. What is the ultimate goal of the creative process, according to Hick? Are there any evils that, in your opinion, such a goal would not redeem?

5. What is the difference between a defense and an explanation, in particular, a defense of God in the face of evil as opposed to a veritable theodicy or explanation of evil on theistic assumptions? What is Alvin Plantinga's defense of God in the face of evil? Is it (a) successful outright, (b) successful depending on the success of other theistic projects or arguments, or (c) outright unsuccessful? Elaborate.

---

[2] The theory of *avidyā* stands out in Vedānta, and does so more—in the Indian context—than in Buddhism.

[3] Compare the statement of Śaṅkara, the great Advaita Vedāntin, on *avidyā* (i.e., "nonawareness of the Absolute"): "[it is] a beginningless and endless, primal illusion . . ." *Brahmasūtrabhāṣya* 1.1.1: *anādir ananto naisargiko 'dhyāso . . . [avidyā]*.

[4] What horrible "play" is sustained by *śūnyatā,* war and all moral evils as well as all the natural evils of disease, pain, and death! "By means of its own dharma, this Existenz maintains dhāranī [sic] over all phenomena in their dharma-like nature, or suchness, within this world of transitoriness and uses them for its own enjoyment." If "Emptiness" may be conceived, with qualifications, as "God," as Nishitani often suggests, then God would hardly appear to be worthy of worship, "enjoying," as Nishitani here implies, even the phenomena of pain and suffering.

6. Rehearse the metaphysics of Advaita Vedānta, as expounded by Śaṅkara (see also under Absolute Brahman), in order to lay out Śaṅkara's explanation of evil. How do you think Śaṅkara might respond to the question of why is there spiritual ignorance (or Nescience, *avidyā*)?

7. Outline Aurobindo's theodicy. What do you see as its strongest and weakest points, and why?

8. What is Nishitani's Buddhist attitude toward evil? Does he successfully explain, or even defend, Buddhist teachings against a charge that evil would make them unlikely. Does evil make any Buddhist teaching seem unlikely? Explain.

CHAPTER SIX

Religious Language

Because a Divine Reality would in some way transcend the sphere of the everyday, philosophers have wondered how it is possible to talk about God, et cetera. How can human language, learned and used with respect to the finite and mundane, fittingly apply to the infinite and other-worldly? For example, when God is said to be loving, would this be in the same sense meant as when a human being is said to be loving? There are deep issues involved in the question. How in general do words mean? And how in particular would expressions have meaning with respect to a Divine Reality?

Some religious skeptics have claimed that the problem of religious language demolishes theology and all systems of religious belief. Often with a particular theory of meaning in hand, the skeptic finds religious language meaningless by that yardstick. The meaningfulness of religious language could then be defended by a counterattack on the particular theory of meaning at its core or its applicability.

However, even without a well worked-out general view of meaning guiding our reflection in these straits, we can see that the meaning of religious expressions is problematic insofar as we cannot point to what we mean. It is plausible that descriptive meaningfulness is tied to acquaintance with features designated by descriptive terms. The meaning of the term *red,* for example, can be learned through acquaintance with ripe apples, blood exposed to air, and so forth, along with appropriate pointings, for example, "That is red." Can religious language be learned similarly?

Some moderns see the function of religious language as non-cognitive, as not meant to describe anything or to assert facts. Clearly, they say, the language of poetry is evocative, not meant to say what is or how things are in fact. Religious language has a distinct function, too. It binds together a community, or expresses ethical ideals, or evokes religious feelings—such are some of the views of a non-cognitivist camp. Defenders of religious beliefs, especially of religious systems, see these views as anathema.

Classical writers both in the East and in the West also worried about religious language. We begin this section with selections on the appropriateness of negative predication one Eastern, from Śaṅkara, one Western, from Maimonides (representing the negative theological strand in classical Judaic, Christian, and Islamic thought)—that have had enormous influence in their respective traditions. Thomas Aquinas presents a less extreme view, where positive predicates can rightly be used of God, not in precisely the same sense predicates have when applied to everything things, but in a special sense that is analogical.

The final four selections are modern. Antony Flew judges (some) theistic assertion meaningless on a falsifiability criterion. J. H. Randall, seeing himself as sympathetic to religion, thinks that religious language has different functions than to assert (and, he assumes, there is no peculiarly religious or spiritual realm about which facts could be asserted). William Alston makes the cognitivist case, arguing for the meaningfulness of even literal predication, while showing that such deep issues emerge in this arena—requiring more deliberation than he (and we, I might add) feels can be managed in any moderate space—that he confines himself to a few particular problems involved with the meaning of *incorporeal* applied to God. Janet Martin Soskice takes an even bolder view: she sees terms like *God* as referential, with various descriptions of God (etc.) as metaphorical but as nonetheless possibly true. Literal language, says Soskice, is simply insufficiently rich when it comes to (e.g.) the sense of God found in Christianity.

Negative Predication

From *The Guide for the Perplexed* by Moses Maimonides, M. Friedländer, translator, 1904 • From *Commentary on the Bṛhadāraṇyaka Upaniṣad* by Śaṅkara, Swami Madhavananda, translator, 1975

Moses Maimonides (1135–1204) was born in Córdoba, in Spain, during the rule of Islamic Moors. Although a Jewish rabbi well-versed in Judaic Scripture and other works in Hebrew, Maimonides wrote in Arabic, the language of his immediate philosophic forebears, al-Farabī, Avicenna, and other Islamic thinkers.

Maimonides feels a tension between classical theism's postulation of Divine attributes (power, knowledge, and others, especially simplicity), on the one hand, and the meaning of these terms in application to things encountered in everyday life. A horse, for example, has attributes. "Being a horse" and "being an animal" are attributes that a horse has essentially; "being the property of Raphael" is an attribute that it has accidentally. The having of attributes makes certain statements true: for example, "That is a horse," made true by the horse's having the attribute "horsehood," and "That horse is Raphael's property," made true by the horse having the attribute "belonging to Raphael." The terms refer to attributes, and a thing's having the attributes makes a descriptive or assertive statement true. This metaphysical picture of how language hooks up with the world underlies Maimonides' concerns about language used with reference to God.

God is simple; that is to say, there can be no distinction among various attributes. Nor is God like anything in the earth or heavens (compare Philo's negative theology discussed earlier). Thus expressions have to be negative if they are at all to direct the mind to truths about God; positive expressions would imply that God possesses positive attributes in the fashion of ordinary things.

Śaṅkara (see the introductory discussion under Absolute Brahman) has similar worries about language used with regard to Brahman, and finds a scriptural statement (i.e. an Upanishadic statement) that addresses the worry and proclaims a solution to boot. (Brahman is transcendent of everything finite except the individual self, or, that too, though we are the infinite Brahman and must learn to see ourselves as divorced from all finite "adjuncts" or attributes.) But human language normally deals with the finite; specifically, positive characterization is confined to differentiating finite things. Thus there seems no way to refer to Brahman—except negatively, through the statement that Brahman is "not this, not this" (neti neti). These two words from the Bṛhadāraṇyaka Upaniṣad are probably the most frequently quoted of all scriptural passages throughout the long history of Advaita (Hindu Absolutism). Scripture's purpose is salvific, soteriological. If human language were entirely inadequate to communicate Brahman, then scripture, which is verbal, could not perform its task. Some of Śaṅkara's followers speculate (not very successfully) about the power of metaphor and indirect indication. But Śaṅkara himself thinks that this negative indication is sufficient to convey the transcendence of Brahman, who is one's true self and the "Truth of truth."

FROM *THE GUIDE FOR THE PERPLEXED*[1]

. . . It is now necessary to explain how negative expressions can in a certain sense be employed to designate attributes, and how negative designations of attributes are distinguished from the positive. Then I shall show that we cannot describe the Creator by any means except the negative. An attribute does not exclusively belong to the one object to which it is depicted as related; while qualifying one thing, it can also be mentioned as qualifying other things, and is in that case not peculiar to that one thing. [For example], if you see an object from a distance, and on enquiring what it is, are told that it is a living being, you have certainly learnt an attribute of the object seen, and although that attribute does not exclusively belong to the object perceived, designating it expresses that the object is not a plant or a mineral. Again, if a man is in a certain house, and you know that something is in the house, but not exactly what, you ask what is in the house, and you are told, not a plant nor a mineral. You have thereby obtained some special knowledge of the thing; you have learnt that it is a living being, although you do not yet know what kind of living being it is. The negative designations have this in common with the positive, that they (if true) circumscribe the object to some extent, although such circumscription consists only in the exclusion of what otherwise would not be excluded. In the following point, however, the negative designations are distinguished from the positive. The positive designations of attributes, although the attributes are not peculiar to one thing, describe a portion of what we desire to know, either some part of its essence or some of its accidents; the negative designations of attributes, on the other hand, do not, as regards the essence of the thing we

---

[1] For clarity, a few emendations of Friedländer's translation have been made—ed.

desire to know, in any way tell us what it is, except it be indirectly, as has been shown in the instance given by us.

After this introduction, I would observe that—as has already been shown—God's existence is absolute, that it includes no commonplace, as will be proved, and that we comprehend only the fact that He exists, not His essence. Consequently it is a false assumption to hold that He has any attribute to be designated by positive expressions; for He does not possess existence in addition to His essence; it therefore cannot be said that the one may be described as an attribute of the other; much less has He a compound essence, consisting of two constituent elements to which the designation of an attribute could refer; still less has He accidents, which could be described by expressions designating attributes. Hence it is clear that no expression whatsoever designating a positive attribute can apply to Him. The negative expressions, however, are those which are necessary to direct the mind to the truths which we must believe concerning God; for example, it has been established by proof that some being exists besides those things which can be perceived by the senses, or apprehended by the mind; when we say of this being, that it exists, we mean that its non-existence is impossible. We then perceive that such a being is not, for instance, like the four elements, which are inanimate, and we therefore say that it is living, expressing thereby that it is not dead. We call such a being incorporeal, because we notice that is unlike the heavens, which are living but material. Seeing also that it is different from the intellect, which, though incorporeal and living, owes its existence to some cause, we say it is the first, expressing thereby that its existence is not due to any cause. We further notice that the existence, that is, the essence, of this being is not limited to its own existence; many existences emanate from it, and its influence is not like that of the fire in producing heat, or that of the sun in sending forth light, but consists in constantly giving them stability and order by well-established rule, as we shall show: we say, on that account, it has power, wisdom, and will, that is, it is not feeble or ignorant, or hasty, and does not abandon its creatures; when we say it is not feeble, we mean that its existence is capable of producing the existence of many other things; by saying that it is not ignorant, we mean "it perceives" or "it lives"—for everything that perceives is living—by saying "it is not hasty, and does not abandon its creatures," we mean that all these creatures preserve a certain order and arrangement; they are not left to themselves; they are not produced aimlessly, but whatever condition they receive from that being is given with design and intention. We thus learn that there is no other being like unto God, and we say that He is One, that is, there are not more Gods than one.

FROM *COMMENTARY ON THE BŖHADĀRAŅYAKA UPANIŞAD*

. . . in order to ascertain the nature of what has been called 'the Truth of truth,' viz. Brahman, [scripture] introduces the text:

> *Now therefore the description (of Brahman): 'Not this, not this.' Because there is no other and more appropriate description than this 'Not this.' Now Its name: 'The Truth of truth.'*

since after ascertaining the nature of 'truth,' what remains is the Truth of truth, therefore the nature of that will be next ascertained. *Description* is a specific statement—about Brahman. What is this statement? *Not this, not this.*

How through these two terms 'Not this, not this' is it sought to describe the Truth of truth? By the elimination of all differences due to limiting adjuncts [or attributes], the words refer to something that has no distinguishing mark such as name, or form, or action, or heterogeneity, or species, or qualities. Words denote things through one or other of these. But Brahman has none of these distinguishing marks. Hence It cannot be described as, 'It is such and such,' as we can describe a cow by saying, 'There moves a white cow with horns.' Brahman is described by means of name, form and action superimposed on It, in such terms as, 'Knowledge, Bliss, Brahman' (III. ix. 28), and 'Pure Intelligence' (II. iv. 12), 'Brahman,' and 'Ātman.' When, however, we wish to describe Its true nature, free from all differences due to limiting adjuncts, then it is an utter impossibility. Then there is only one way left, viz. to describe It as 'Not this, not this,' by eliminating all possible specifications of It that have been known.

These two negative particles are for conveying all-inclusiveness through repetition so as to eliminate every specification whatsover that may occur to us. . . . When through the elimination of all limiting adjuncts the desire to know about space, time and everything else (that is not Brahman) is removed, one realises one's identity with Brahman, the Truth of truth, which is homogeneous like a lump of salt, and which is Pure Intelligence without interior or exterior; his desire to know is completely satisfied, and his intellect is centred in the Self alone. Therefore the two negative particles in 'Not this, not this' are used in an all-inclusive sense.

Objection: Well, after buckling with such ado is it fair to describe Brahman thus?

Reply: Yes. Why? *Because there is no other and more appropriate description* (of Brahman) *than this 'Not this, not this,'* therefore this is the only description of Brahman. The particle repeated twice covers all possible predications that are to be eliminated by the two negative particles, as when we say, 'Every village is beautiful.' It was said, 'Its secret name is: The Truth of truth' (II. i. 20); it is thus that the Supreme Brahman is the Truth of truth. Therefore the *name* of Brahman that has been mentioned is appropriate. What is it? *The Truth of truth.* . . .

Analogical Predication

From *Summa Theologica* by Thomas Aquinas in *Basic Writings of Saint Thomas Aquinas,* Anton C. Pegis, editor and translator, 1945

Thomas Aquinas (1225–1274), the enormously influential theologian whose a posteriori *arguments for God we reviewed under Arguments for a Divine Reality, puts forth a theory of religious language that, like his arguments, have been the focus of centuries of later commentary and reflection.*

Thomas sees negative theology—and the view that only negative expressions can lead the mind to comprehend truths about God—as defeatist, implying that nothing could be known about God. If names apply in entirely different senses to God and to creatures, then there could be no reasoning about God that did not commit the fallacy of equivocation. This is the fault of using the same word in more than one sense when the argument depends on a single sense (e.g., Brass is a metal; metals are elements on the periodic table; therefore, brass is an element on the periodic table). Nevertheless, a term like "wisdom" cannot mean the same thing when applied to God as it does when said of a human being. That would be the verbal equivalent of idolatry.

Thus Thomas is motivated to find and stake out middle ground between an equivocal (and defeatist) view of talk about God and a univocal (and idolatrous) view. His middle position has come to be called the doctrine of analogy. It has two parts.

First, some words carry as part of their signification the implication that the thing signified is corporeal, that is, finite and material. Such words applied to God can have only metaphorical meaning. Metaphorical meaning involves analogy or similarity in some respect but also distinctness. God is not corporeal, so such a word as stone *can be applied to God only analogically, with the dissimilarity being the corporeality of an actual stone as opposed to the incorporeality of God. Nevertheless, "God is a stone" is meaningful: God is like a stone in being steadfast and enduring.*

Second, some words designate perfections, or qualitative attributes, that admit of degrees, such as being, good, *and* living. *In such cases, application to God and to creatures is in the same general sense, since the words carry no implication of corporeality as part of their intrinsic meaning. God is perfectly good; creatures are good only imperfectly. So the meaning of* good *is not univocal, the same in each case but analogical, since its precise meaning (including how it signifies) depends on the nature of that to which it is applied.*

WHETHER ANY NAME CAN BE APPLIED TO GOD PROPERLY?

OBJECTION 1.

It seems that no name is applied properly to God. For all names which we apply to God are taken from creatures, as was explained above. But the names of creatures are applied to God metaphorically, as when we say, God is a stone, or a lion, or the like. Therefore names are applied to God in a metaphorical sense.

OBJ. 2.

Further, no name can be applied properly to anything if it should be more truly denied of it than given to it. But all such names as *good, wise,* and the like, are more truly denied of God than given to Him; . . . Therefore none of these names is said of God properly.

OBJ. 3.

Further, corporeal names are applied to God in a metaphorical sense only, since He is incorporeal. But all such names imply some kind of corporeal condition; for their meaning is bound up with time and composition and like corporeal conditions. Therefore all these names are applied to God in a metaphorical sense.

On the contrary, . . . Some names there are which express evidently the property of the divinity, and some which express the clear truth of the divine majesty; but others there are which are said of God metaphorically by way of similitude. Therefore not all names are applied to God in a metaphorical sense, but there are some which are said of Him properly.

I answer that, According to the preceding article, our knowledge of God is derived from the perfections which flow from Him to creatures; which perfections are in God in a more eminent way than in creatures. Now our intellect apprehends them as they are in creatures, and as it apprehends them thus does it signify them by names. Therefore, as to the names applied to God, there are two things to be considered—viz., the perfections themselves which they signify, such as goodness, life, and the like, and their mode of signification. As regards what is signified by these names, they belong properly to God, and more properly than they belong to creatures, and are applied primarily to Him. But as regards their mode of signification, they do not properly and strictly apply to God; for their mode of signification befits creatures.

REPLY OBJ. 1.

There are some names which signify these perfections flowing from God to creatures in such a way that the imperfect way in which creatures receive the divine perfection is part of the very signification of the name itself, as *stone* signifies a material being; and names of this kind can be applied to God only in a metaphorical sense. Other names, however, express the perfections themselves absolutely, without any such mode of participation being part of their signification, as the words *being, good, living,* and the like; and such names can be applied to God properly.

REPLY OBJ. 2.

Such names as these . . . are denied of God for the reason that what the name signifies does not belong to Him in the ordinary sense of its signification, but in a more eminent way. Hence . . . God is above all substance and all life.

REPLY OBJ. 3.

These names which are applied to God properly imply corporeal conditions, not in the thing signified, but as regards their mode of signification; whereas those which are applied to God metaphorically imply and mean a corporeal condition in the thing signified. . . .

On the contrary, Whatever is predicated of various things under the same name but not in the same sense is predicated equivocally. But no name belongs to God in the same sense that it belongs to creatures; for instance, wisdom in creatures is a quality, but not in God. Now a change in genus changes an essence, since the genus is part of the definition; and the same applies to other things. Therefore whatever is said of God and of creatures is predicated equivocally.

Further, God is more distant from creatures than any creatures are from each other. But the distance of some creatures makes any univocal predication of them impossible, as in the case of those things which are not in the same genus. Therefore much less can anything be predicated univocally of God and creatures; and so only equivocal predication can be applied to them.

I answer that, Univocal predication is impossible between God and creatures. The reason of this is that every effect which is not a proportioned result of the power of the efficient cause receives the similitude of the agent not in its full degree, but in a measure that falls short; so that what is divided and multiplied in the effects resides in the agent simply, and in an unvaried manner. For example, the sun by the exercise of its one power produces manifold and various forms in these sublunary things. In the same way, as was said above, all perfections existing in creatures divided and multiplied pre-exist in God unitedly. Hence, when any name expressing perfection is applied to a creature, it signifies that perfection as distinct from the others according to the nature of its definition; as, for instance, by this term *wise* applied to a man, we signify some perfection distinct from a man's essence, and distinct form his power and his being, and from all similar things. But when we apply *wise* to God, we do not mean to signify anything distinct from His essence or power or being. And thus when this term *wise* is applied to man, in some degree it circumscribes and comprehends the thing signified; whereas this is not the case when it is applied to God, but it leaves the thing signified as uncomprehended and as exceeding the signification of the name. Hence it is evident that this term *wise* is not applied in the same way to God and to man. The same applies to other terms. Hence, no name is predicated univocally of God and of creatures.

Neither, on the other hand, are names applied to God and creatures in a purely equivocal sense, as some have said. Because if that were so, it follows that from creatures nothing at all could be known or demonstrated about God; for the reasoning would always be exposed to the fallacy of equivocation. Such a view is against the Philosopher, who proves many things about God, and also against what the Apostle says: *The invisible things of God are clearly seen being understood by the things that are made* (*Rom.* i. 20). Therefore it must be said that these names are said of God and creatures in an *analogous* sense, that is, according to proportion.

This can happen in two ways: either according as many things are proportioned to one (thus, for example *healthy* is predicated of medicine and urine in relation and in proportion to health of body, of which the latter is the sign and the former the cause), or according as one thing is proportioned to another (thus, *healthy* is said of medicine and an animal, since medicine is the cause of health in the animal body). And in this way some things are said of God and creatures analogically, and not in a purely equivocal nor in a purely univocal sense. For we can name God only from creatures. Hence, whatever is said of God and creatures is said according as there is some relation of the creature to God as to its principle and cause, wherein all the perfections of things pre-exist excellently. Now this mode of community is a mean between pure equivocation and simple univocation. For in analogies the idea is not, as it is in univocals, one and the same; yet it is not totally diverse as in equivocals; but the name which is thus used in a multiple sense signifies various proportions to some one thing: *e.g., healthy,* applied to urine, signifies the sign of animal health; but applied to medicine, it signifies the cause of the same health.

What Does the Theist Assert?

From "Theology and Falsification" by Antony Flew in *New Essays in Philosophical Theology,* Antony Flew and Alasdair MacIntyre, editors, 1955

Antony Flew (born 1923), an English philosopher, has devoted most of a long and distinguished career to attacking the claims of theism. An advocate of conceptual atheism, *Flew holds that there is no possibility of the existence of God as traditionally conceived, no more than there is of a "square circle." Flew has contributed much to the debate over God's attributes and the question of the coherence of classical theism. But in the selection below, he challenges the meaningfulness of God talk from a different angle.*

Flew presents a parable that he takes to reflect the evidence—pro and con, a few indications of design (pro) but also natural evil (con)—for and against the existence of God, evidence that, as he represents it, seems, all told, to weigh against theism. Then focusing on the claim that God is loving, Flew wonders what could count for the committed theist as decisive counterevidence. What could definitely show that there was no loving God?

It is a simple matter of logic that an assertion is truth-functionally equivalent to a negation of its denial. That is, the truth of an assertion entails that its denial is false. Then if the theist's assertion that God is loving does not deny anything that one could hold up as counterevidence, it does not, Flew claims, really assert anything either. Without the possibility of counterevidence—or falsification—the assertion is meaningless.

An empirical verifiability—or even falsifiability—criterion of meaningfulness for an assertive statement has been discredited by such counterexamples as the question of the verifiability—or falsifiability—of the thesis, "Empirical verifiability (falsifiability) is the criterion of meaningfulness" (the thesis applied to itself would show that it itself is meaningless). Nevertheless, an assertion of fact should be connected to empirical evidence in some way. Has Flew shown that for the committed theist there is no possibility of such connection with the claim that God is loving?

Let us begin with a parable. It is a parable developed from a tale told by John Wisdom in his haunting and revelatory article 'Gods.' Once upon a time two explorers came upon a clearing in the jungle. In the clearing were growing many flowers and many weeds. One explorer says, 'Some gardener must tend this plot.' The other disagrees, 'There is no gardener.' So they pitch their tents and set a watch. No gardener is ever seen. 'But perhaps he is an invisible gardener.' So they set up a barbed-wire fence. They electrify it. They patrol with bloodhounds. (For they remember how H. G. Wells's *The Invisible Man* could be both smelt and touched though he could not be seen.) But no shrieks ever suggest that some intruder has received a shock. No movements of the wire ever betray an invisible climber. The bloodhounds never give cry. Yet still the Believer is not convinced. 'But there is a gardener, invisible, intangible, insensible to electric shocks, a gardener who has no scent and makes no sound, a gardener who comes secretly to look after the garden which he loves.' At last the Sceptic despairs, 'But what remains of your original assertion? Just how does what you call an invisible, intangible, eternally elusive gardener differ from an imaginary gardener or even from no gardener at all?'

In this parable we can see how what starts as an assertion, that something exists or that there is some analogy between certain complexes of phenomena, may be reduced step by step to an altogether different status, to an expression perhaps of a 'picture preference'. The Sceptic says there is no gardener. The Believer says there is a gardener (but invisible, etc.). One man talks about sexual behaviour. Another man prefers to talk of Aphrodite (but knows that there is not really a superhuman person additional to, and somehow responsible for, all sexual phenomena). The process of qualification may be checked at any point before the original assertion is completely withdrawn and something of that first assertion will remain (Tautology). Mr. Wells's invisible man could not, admittedly, be seen, but in all other respects he was a man like the rest of us. But though the process of qualification may be, and of course usually is, checked in time, it is not always judiciously so halted. Someone may dissipate his assertion completely without noticing that he has done so. A fine brash hypothesis may thus be killed by inches, the death by a thousand qualifications.

And in this, it seems to me, lies the peculiar danger, the endemic evil, of theological utterance. Take such utterances as 'God has a plan,' 'God created the world,' 'God loves us as a father loves his children.' They look at first sight very much like assertions, vast cosmological assertions. Of course, this is no sure sign that they either are, or are intended to be, assertions. But let us confine ourselves to the cases where those who utter such sentences intend them to express assertions. (Merely remarking parenthetically that those who intend or interpret such utterances as crypto-commands, expressions of wishes, disguised ejaculations, concealed ethics, or as anything else but assertions, are unlikely to succeed in making them either properly orthodox or practically effective).

Now to assert that such and such is the case is necessarily equivalent to denying that such and such is not the case.[1] Suppose then that we are in doubt as to what someone who gives vent to an utterance is asserting, or suppose that, more radically, we are sceptical as to whether he is really asserting anything at all, one way of trying to understand (or perhaps it will be to expose) his utterance is to attempt to find what he would regard as counting against, or as being incompatible with, its truth. For if the utterance is indeed an assertion, it will necessarily be equivalent to a denial of the negation of that assertion. And anything which would count against the assertion, or which would induce the speaker to withdraw it and to admit that it had been mistaken, must be part of (or the whole of) the meaning of the negation of that assertion. And to know the meaning of the negation of an assertion, is as near as makes no matter, to know the meaning of that assertion.[2] And if there is nothing which a putative assertion denies then there is nothing which it asserts either: and so it is not really an assertion. When the Sceptic in the parable asked the Believer, 'Just how does what you call an invisible, intangible, eternally elusive gardener differ from an imaginary gardener or even from no gardener at all?' he was suggesting that the Believer's earlier statement had been so eroded by qualification that it was no longer an assertion at all.

---

[1] For those who prefer symbolism: $p \equiv \sim \sim p$.

[2] For by simply negating $\sim p$ we get p: $\sim \sim p \equiv p$.

Now it often seems to people who are not religious as if there was no conceivable event or series of events the occurrence of which would be admitted by sophisticated religious people to be a sufficient reason for conceding 'There wasn't a God after all' or 'God does not really love us then'. Someone tells us that God loves us as a father loves his children. We are reassured. But then we see a child dying of inoperable cancer of the throat. His earthly father is driven frantic in his efforts to help, but his Heavenly Father reveals no obvious sign of concern. Some qualification is made—God's love is 'not a merely human love' or it is 'an inscrutable love', perhaps—and we realize that such sufferings are quite compatible with the truth of the assertion that 'God loves us as a father (but, of course, . . .)'. We are reassured again. But then perhaps we ask: what is this assurance of God's (appropriately qualified) love worth, what is this apparent guarantee really a guarantee against? Just what would have to happen not merely (morally and wrongly) to tempt but also (logically and rightly) to entitle us to say 'God does not love us' or even 'God does not exist'? I therefore put to the succeeding symposiasts the simple central questions, 'What would have to occur or to have occurred to constitute for you a disproof of the love of, or of the existence of, God?'

Religious Language as Symbolic

From *The Role of Knowledge in Western Religion* by John Herman Randall, Jr., 1958

J. H. Randall (born 1899), for many years a philosophy professor at Columbia University, agrees with Flew that much seemingly assertive religious speech fails to be informative (i.e., cognitive). But, unlike Flew, Randall has a sympathetic view of religion, and finds religious language to perform important functions both for individuals and society. Randall presupposes that there is no God, no Divine Reality of any type, and no spiritual realm of fact. However, people's believing there is, or at least engaging with religious symbols, is not simply to have false beliefs but has a fourfold positive function that he spells out.

Randall is not pellucidly clear whether he thinks it matters whether religious people actually believe to be true what are really symbolic myths. But it seems he does not. Randall seems to urge that those who, like himself, realize that ideas of God, etc., are just myths should nevertheless embrace religion, engage in religious practices.

The four positive functions Randall finds for talk about God and other such subjects are, first, provoking emotional response and appropriate action (need this be so benign?). Second, religious symbols "stimulate joint or cooperative activity." Third, they allow us to communicate aspects of experience that would otherwise be difficult or impossible to express. Fourth, religious symbols mediate an imaginative bringing out of perhaps what is the very best in human experience, and Randall waxes eloquent about what seems to be a mystical vision. But one must remember that for him this is much like imaginative transformations of experience through art, that mystical experiences are themselves not factually informative, and that there is no God. As he says, his own eloquent God talk "is a symbolic statement."

. . . religion and knowledge are clearly not rivals for our intellectual respect, though they may well be for our affections. This holds whether that "knowledge" be taken as the deliverances of the enterprise of science, as the findings of the thoughtful philosophical interpretation of experience, or as the opinions of mere sound common sense. These are the three major kinds of formulated assertions or propositions capable of being tested by evidence and of being judged to be true. As thus susceptible to verification, they are commonly agreed to constitute "knowledge"; they include both descriptions of facts and explanations of those facts, for both take the form of statements *that* such and such is the case. This is the sense of "knowledge" whose role in religion we are questioning. It is necessary to be precise about just what we mean by "knowledge," lest our arguments turn into quarrels about the mere use of words. It is beyond doubt, there can be no serious conflict between religion and "knowledge" in this sense, "knowledge" taken as factual descriptions or theoretical explanations of anything, as propositions that are "warrantedly assertible" or "true."

For religion offers no descriptions and no explanations . . .

We can assume, therefore, that all religious beliefs without exception are "mythology." That is, they are all religious "symbols." If such symbols can be said to possess any kind of "truth," they certainly do not possess the literal truth of the factual statements of the descriptive sciences or of common sense, or the "warranted assertibility" and explanatory value of the well founded theories of science and philosophy. . . .

If the function of religious beliefs is not to generate knowledge and truth, what is their function? Very early in every great religious tradition, reflective men came to see that the ordinary ideals entertained and used in worship, prayer and ritual could not be "literally" true. The idea of God, for example, employed by the unreflective in the actual practice of the religious arts, could not be adequate to the true nature of the Divine. God could not be "really" the animal, or natural force, or carved image, the imaginative picture, in which the average man conceives the Divine. He could not be even the highest human image, the "Father," or the kind of "person" who in the present fashion seems appropriately approached in terms of the "I-Thou" experience. Important and even indispensable in religious practice as are these ways of imagining the Divine, they are all, reflective men soon came to realize, attempts to fit the idea of God in somehow with the rest of men's experience. But they are not adequate definitions or descriptions of the religious dimension of that experience. They cannot be taken as literal accounts of the Divine. They are imaginative and figurative ways of conceiving the relations of men and their ideals to the nature of things, and to its religious dimension. . . .

All ideas of God, like all other religious beliefs, are without exception *religious symbols*. This means that they perform what is primarily a religious function. They are employed in religious experience, and serve to carry on the religious life. They are techniques, instruments, in terms of which ritual and the other religious arts are conducted.

[The functions religious symbols perform are] a complex matter difficult to formulate and state satisfactorily. In answering our questions as to the role of knowledge and truth in the religious life, it is necessary to dwell for a little on the positive functions of religious symbols, and on the way in which even those symbols whose primary role is clearly noncognitive nevertheless do contribute to what has always been described as a "revelation" of truth. In this attempt to elucidate a very complicated matter, I shall state some of the conclusions to which I have been led . . . as a result of various seminars I have been privileged to conduct jointly with Paul Tillich.

At the outset it is necessary to draw a sharp distinction between a symbol and a sign. A sign is something which provokes the same human response as some other thing, for which it can hence stand as a kind of surrogate or substitute. A sign hence stands for or represents something other than itself: it is always a sign *of* something else. In contrast, a symbol is in no sense representative: it does not stand for or take the place of anything other than itself. Rather, it *does* something in its own right: it provokes a characteristic response in men. The terminology is not yet settled on this point; but the distinction is fundamental, though the particular way of expressing it is in the present state of usage arbitrary. It is important to realize that religious symbols are not signs; they belong rather with the nonrepresentative symbols which function in various ways in both intellectual and practical life.

A further distinction is also necessary. Some symbols, without being themselves directly representative, or standing for any other identifiable thing, except, perhaps, for certain intellectual processes, nevertheless play an important part in activities that are cognitive, that is, which eventuate in knowledge and truth. The body of scientific concepts, hypotheses, and theories is full of such nonrepresentative but *cognitive* symbols. An instance is the notion of "velocity at an instant." In contrast, there are other symbols, like those that play a role in social processes and in art, whose function is not to participate in activities that eventuate in knowledge, but to lead to other kinds of consequences. What is important to recognize is that religious symbols belong with social and artistic symbols, in the group of symbols that are both *nonrepresentative* and *noncognitive*. Such noncognitive symbols can be said to symbolize not some external thing that can be indicated apart from their operation, but rather what they themselves *do,* their peculiar functions.

Just what is it that such noncognitive symbols do? In the first place, all of them, including religious symbols, provoke in men an emotional response, and stimulate appropriate human activities. In traditional terms, they act on the will rather than on the intellect. They act as motives, they lead to action on the part of the men who are influenced by them. They do not, like signs, merely lead the mind to other things; they produce results in conduct.

Secondly, they provoke in a group of men, the community for whom they serve as symbols, a common or shared response. They stimulate joint or cooperative activity. This response can become individualized; but even then its individual form is derivative from what is fundamentally a social or group response. The response is common or shared, although the "meaning" of the symbol, that is, its relation to other elements of men's experience, would receive a different intellectual interpretation from different members of the group or symbol community. Thus a physical social symbol, like the flag, or an intellectual social symbol, like the "state" or "liberty," would be fitted in quite differently with other ideas by different men, though all would be stimulated to patriotic emotions and activities, or to libertarian feelings and attitudes.

Thirdly, noncognitive symbols are able to communicate qualitative or "shared" experience, experience that is difficult to put into precise words or statements, and may well be ineffable. This is particularly clear with artistic symbols: they act powerfully in men's experience, but it is notoriously almost impossible to state exactly what they "mean." Needless to say, such artistic symbols must be carefully distinguished from what are often indeed called "symbols" in works of art, but what are really representative signs—signs of something else. It is just that element in a poetic metaphor that is lost through translation into common prose that distinguishes the symbol that is at work from the element of mere sign.

Religious symbols share with other noncognitive symbols these three characteristics. But in addition, and fourthly, religious symbols in particular can be said to "disclose" or "reveal" something about the world in which they function. It is at just this point that we come to the relation between religious symbols and what is usually called religious "knowledge," which is peculiarly close with those intellectual religious symbols that are religious beliefs or ideas. . . . Religious symbols are commonly said to "reveal" some "truth" about experience. If we ask what it is that such symbols do reveal or disclose about the world, it is clear that it is not what we should call in the ordinary sense "knowledge," in the sense already defined. This revelation can be styled "knowledge" or "truth" only in a sense that is "equivocal" or metaphorical. It is more like direct acquaintance than descriptive knowledge: it resembles what we call "insight" or "vision." Such symbols do not "tell" us anything that is verifiably so; they rather make us "see" something about our experience and our experienced world.

What such a symbol does disclose can be best approached by asking how it is that we gain "insight" into the character and nature of another human personality. By external observation of his behavior, by watching him act and listening to him talk, we can learn much "knowledge" about him that is clearly gained by methods not essentially different from those by which we gain "knowledge" about the behavior of other things in our natural world. But intimate acquaintance with another human personality acquired through a long experience of friendship or of love, can give us an "insight" into the essence of the man that cannot be won by any merely external observation of his behavior. When certain of his acts or words "reveal" to us what he "really is," as we put it, we often say that they are "symbols" of his true character and nature. The gifted biographer or historian often has such "insight" into the persons he is trying to grasp. Ernst Cassirer had a genius for this kind of insight, and he erected a whole theory of historical knowledge around this process of what he called "symbolic interpretation." What Wilhelm Dilthey called *Verstehen* has been grossly abused by many German sociologists, but it has a genuine application if anywhere to the knowledge of human personality.

Just what does this process of symbolic interpretation mean? It seems, first, that such symbolic acts or words concentrate and sum up and unify a long and intimate experience we have enjoyed of a person, or a long and close study we have made of a figure's activities. Secondly, they reveal possibilities and powers latent in his nature. For what a mean "really is" not exhausted in what he has already done, in his past behavior that is on the record. It is what he *can* do, the power he has in him. All knowledge of anything is ultimately a knowledge of its powers and possibilities. But clearly the distinction between what any being has done and what that being can do, is most striking and significant in the case of human personality.

The example of human personality has always seemed the best clue to the way of conceiving the Divine in the world, even when men have gone on to recognize that the religious dimension of existence ultimately transcends personality. Generalizing the function of symbols in coming to know persons, we may say that a religious symbol unifies and sums up and brings to a focus men's long and intimate experience of their universe and of what it offers to human life. As John Dewey says of the work of art in general, it "operates imaginatively rather than in the realm of physical existences. What it does is to concentrate and enlarge an immediate experience."[1]

In so doing, religious symbols seem to disclose or reveal powers and possibilities inherent in the nature of things. They serve, that is, not as instruments of a "knowledge" based on an experience of what the world has done, of how it has behaved and acted in the past, of the resources it has been found to provide for men, but rather as instruments of "insight" and "vision," of what it could do, of what it might offer, of what it might become and be. Religious symbols are thus like Platonic Ideas, which themselves developed from a refinement of the Pythagorean religious symbols: they do not tell us that anything is so, they rather make us see something. They enable us to discern possibilities beyond the actual, powers not yet fully realized; and in so doing they disclose what the nature of things "really is." Like Platonic Ideas, religious symbols are closely connected with the power of intellectual vision, *Nous,* the power of "imagination," if the imagination be the organ of intellectual vision.

And so religious symbols, through concentrating the long experience of a people, and the insights of its prophets and saints, seem to serve as instruments of revelation, of vision—of a vision of the powers and possibilities in the world. They disclose what Paul Tillich calls, in symbolic terms, "the power of Being." They lead to a vision of man in the world, of the human situation in its cosmic setting, and to use Tillich's term again, of man's "ultimate concern." Speaking most generally, they lead to a vision of the Divine, what the Christian symbol has called the *visio Dei* and the *fruitio Dei.* They serve the chief end of man, "to glorify God and enjoy Him forever." It is impossible even to state this function of religious symbols except in symbolic terms. For it is clear that all formulations of these visions, all ways of imagining and conceiving the Divine, all ideas of God, whether those employed in the practice of the religious arts, like worship or prayer, or the refined and subtle concepts of the great philosophical theologians, are religious symbols. Only through symbols can we approach the Divine, only thus can we indicate the religious dimension of life in the world. We cannot see God face to face. This latter is itself a symbolic statement.

Religious Truth Claims

From "Can We Speak Literally of God?" by William P. Alston in *Is God God?* Axel D. Steuer and James William McClendon, Jr., editors, 1981

William Alston, whom we encountered in the first section, argues that there is no reason to suppose that we cannot speak literally of God. Even positive personalistic predicates,

---

[1] John Dewey, *Art as Experience,* p. 273.

such as 'speaks,' 'acts,' and so forth, can be applied, in Alston's view, literally and truly of God. At least, the burden of proof must be carried by those who claim they cannot literally be applied.

Alston is thus opposed to just about every position that we have reviewed in this section (though not to Soskice's position, which may be viewed as making an even stronger case for the possibility of theological truth: see below). Contrary to Flew and Randall, Alston holds not only that some talk about God should be understood as assertive and cognitive but also that it may be true (is true). And in contrast with Maimonides and negative theology, Alston does not think that only negative expressions could possibly succeed in applying to God. Nor does he agree with Thomas and others about the role of analogy and metaphor in talking about God. On the other hand, since Thomas finds some terms to have the same general sense whether applied to God or creatures, the disagreement does not seem extreme.

Foremost Alston's point is that it is possible that some positive personalistic predicates be literally true of God. To show this he asks us to think imaginatively about what is strictly required for a basic (personalistic) action. It seems that it is at least imaginable that God act personalistically (such that personalistic predicates be true of God) even if God be incorporeal.

The upshot of Alston's discussion is that it would appear unwise to proceed glibly one way or another in theology, or atheology, on the basis of seeming discoveries about language use and language learning. Reflection on requirements for meaningfulness do not abrogate the deep questions of metaphysics.

In this essay we shall be concerned with only one stretch of talk about God, but a particularly central stretch—subject-predicate statements in which the subject-term is used to refer to God. I mean this to be limited to *statements* in a strict sense, utterances that are put forward with a "truth claim". This is a crucial stretch of the territory, because any other talk that involves reference to God presupposes the truth of one or more *statements* about God. For example, if I ask God to give me courage, I am presupposing that God is the sort of being to whom requests can be sensibly addressed. Thus our more specific topic concerns whether terms can be literally predicated of God.

According to contemporary Protestant theologians of a liberal cast, it is almost an article of faith that this is impossible. Let us be somewhat more explicit than people like that generally are, as to just what is being denied. When someone says that we cannot speak literally of God, that person does not mean to deny us the capacity to form a subject-predicate sentence that contains a subject-term used to refer to God, making a literal use of the predicate term and uttering the sentence with the claim that the predicate is true of the subject. I could easily refute that denial here and now—"God has commanded us to love one another." I have just done it. But presumably it is not that sort of ability that is in question. It is rather a question as to whether any such truth claim can succeed. What is being denied is that any predicate term, used literally, can be *truly applied* to God, or as we might say, that any predicate is *literally true* of God.

But even this is stronger than a charitable interpretation would require. Presumably, no one who thinks it possible to refer to God would deny that some negative predicates are literally true of God—for instance, incorporeal, immutable, or not-identical-with-Richard-Nixon. Nor would all extrinsic predicates be ruled out; it would be difficult to deny that 'thought of now by me' could be literally true of God. Now it is notoriously difficult to draw an exact line between positive and negative predicates; and the class of predicates I am calling "extrinsic" is hardly easier to demarcate. It is either very difficult or impossible to give a precise characterization of the class of predicates to which the deniers of literal talk should be addressing themselves. Here I shall confine myself to the following brief statement. The reason various predicates are obvious examples of "negative" or "extrinsic" predicates is that they do not "tell us anything" about the subject—about the nature or operations of the subject. Let us call predicates that do "tell us something" about such matters "intrinsic" predicates. We may then take it that an opponent of literal theological talk is denying that any *intrinsic* predicate can be literally true of God. It will be noted that "intrinsic" predicates include various *relational* predicates, such as "made the heavens and the earth" and "spoke to Moses." . . .

The question whether certain terms can be literally applied to God is often identified with the question whether those terms are literally true of God in senses they bear outside theology. Thus with respect to P[ersonalistic]-predicates, it is often supposed that God can be spoken of as literally having knowledge and intentions, as creating, commanding, and forgiving, only if those terms are literally true of God in the same senses as those in which they are literally true of human beings. The reason usually given for this supposition is that we first come to attach meaning to these terms by learning what it is for human beings to command, forgive, and so on, and that there is no other way we can proceed. We cannot begin by learning what it is for God to know, command, or forgive. I do not want to contest this claim about the necessary order of language learning, though there is much to be said on both sides. I will confine myself to pointing out that even if this claim is granted, it does *not* follow that terms can be literally applied to God only in senses in which they also are true of human beings and other creatures. For the fact that we must begin with creatures is quite compatible with the supposition that at some later stage terms take on special technical senses in theology. After all, that is what happens in science. There, too, it can be plausibly argued that we can learn theoretical terms in science only if we have already learned commonsense meanings of these and other terms—senses in which the terms are true of ordinary middle-sized objects. But even if that is true, it does not prevent such terms as 'force' and 'energy' from taking on new technical senses in the development of sophisticated theories. Why should not the same be true of theology? . . .

Whether certain predicates are literally true of God depends on both parties to the transaction; it depends both on what God is like and on the content of the predicates. To carry out a proper discussion of the present issue, I would need to (a) present and defend an account of the nature of God, and (b) present and defend an analysis of such P-predicates as will be considered. That would put us in a position to make some well-grounded judgments as to whether such predicates could be literally true of God. Needless to say, I will not have time for all that; I would not have had time, even if I had cut the preliminary cackle and buckled down to the job straight away. Hence I must scale down my aspirations.

Instead of trying "tell it like it is" with God, I shall simply pick one commonly recognized attribute of God—incorporeality—which has been widely thought to rule out personal agency, and I shall consider whether it does so. My main reasons for focusing on incorporeality, rather than on simplicity, infinity, timelessness, or immutability, are that it, much more than the others, is widely accepted today as a divine attribute and that it has bulked large in some recent arguments against the literal applicability of P-predicates. On the side of the predicates, I shall consider those types of analyses that are, in my judgment, the strongest contenders and ask what each of them implies as to literal applicability to an incorporeal being. . . .

Let us consider, then whether it is conceptually possible for an incorporeal being to perform overt actions. Our entrée to that discussion will be a consideration of the vulnerable premise in the argument, the thesis that overt behavior requires bodily movements.

To understand the grounds for this thesis, we must introduce the notion of a *basic action*. Roughly speaking, a basic action is one that is performed *not* by or in (simultaneously) performing some other action. Thus if I sign my name, *that* is done by moving my hand in a certain way, so the action is not basic; but if moving my hand is *not* done *by* doing something else, it will count as a basic action. Just where to locate basic human actions is philosophically controversial. If contracting muscles in my hand is something I *do* (in the intended sense of 'do'), then it seems that I move my hand *by* contracting my muscles, and moving my hand will not count as a basic action. Again, if sending neural impulses to the muscles is something I *do,* then it seems that I contract the muscles *by* sending neural impulses to them, and so the contraction of muscles will not count as a basic action. Since I do not have time to go into this issue, I shall simply follow a widespread practice and assume that all overt human basic actions consist in the movements of certain parts of the body which ordinarily would be thought to be under "voluntary control," such as the hand.

It follows from our explanation of the term 'basic action' that every nonbasic action is done *by* performing a basic action. If we are further correct in ruling that every human basic action consists in moving some part of one's body, then it follows that every human nonbasic action is built on, or presupposes, some bodily movement of the agent. The relationship differs in different cases: Sometimes the nonbasic action involves an effect of some bodily movement(s), as in the action of knocking over a vase; sometimes it involves the bodily movement's falling under a rule or convention of some kind, as in signaling a turn. But whatever the details, it follows from what has been laid down thus far that a human being cannot do anything overt without moving some part of the body. Either the action is basic, in which case it merely *consists* in moving some part of one's body; or it is not, in which case it is done *by* moving some part of one's body.

[The concept of a basic action] as we set it out initially, is simply the concept of an action that is not performed *by* or *in* (simultaneously) performing some other action. This general concept is quite neutral as to what kinds of actions have that status for one or another type of agent. It is just a fact about human beings (*not* a general constraint on action or basic action) that only movements of certain parts of their bodies are under their direct voluntary control and that anything else they bring off, they must accomplish *by* moving their bodies in certain ways. If *I* am to knock over a vase or make a soufflé or communicate with someone, I must do so by moving my hands, legs, vocal organs, or whatever. But that is only because of my limitations. We can conceive of agents, corporeal or otherwise, such that things other than their bodies (if any) are under their direct voluntary control. Some agents might be such that they could knock over a vase or bring a soufflé into being without doing something else in order to do so.[1]

What these considerations suggest is that it is conceptually possible for any change whatsoever to be the core of a basic action. Movements of an agent's body are only what we happen to be restricted to in the human case. Just what changes are within the basic action repertoire of a given incorporeal agent would depend upon the nature of that agent. But the main point is that since such changes are not necessarily restricted to bodily movements of the agent, a subject's bodilessness is no conceptual bar to the performance of basic actions by that subject.

I believe that the case in which we are particularly interested, divine action, can be thought of along the lines of the preceding discussion. Of course, one can think of God as creating light by saying to himself, "Let there be light", or as parting the sea of reeds by saying to himself, "Let the sea of reeds be parted". In that case the basic actions would be mental actions. But what the above discussion indicates is that we are not conceptually required to postulate this mental machinery. We could think just as well of the coming into being of light or of the parting of the sea of reeds as directly under God's voluntary control.

This further suggests that all God's actions might be basic actions. If any change whatsoever could conceivably be the core of a basic action, and if God is omnipotent, then clearly, God *could* exercise direct voluntary control over every change in the world which he influences by his activity. However, I do not claim to have done more than exhibit this as a possibility. It is equally possible that God chooses to influence some situations *indirectly*. He might choose to lead or inspire Cyrus to free the Israelites, thus using Cyrus as an instrument to bring about that result. In that case, freeing the Israelites would be a nonbasic action. I am quite willing to leave the decision on this one up to God.[2] . . .

---

[1] Be careful to envisage this situation just as I have described it. The agent knocks over the vase not by doing anything else—even anything mental. Telekinesis is often thought of as an agent saying to himself something like "Let the vase be knocked over", and *this* causes the vase to fall over. But that does not make knocking over the vase a basic action. It is still a matter of knocking over the vase *by* doing something else, albeit something mental. In order for knocking over a vase to be a basic action, it would have to be just as immediate as is my raising my arm in the normal case, where I do this not by saying to myself "Let the arm rise", whereupon it rises; but where I just raise the arm intentionally.

[2] It might be contended that if the physical universe, or any part thereof, is under God's direct voluntary control, this implies that the world is the body of God, which in turn implies that God is not an incorporeal being; that would mean that our case for *incorporeal* basic action fails. That is, the contention would be that in order to ascribe basic actions to S we have to pay the price of construing the changes in question as movements of S's body. This claim could be supported by the thesis that a sufficient condition for something to be part of my body is that it be under my direct voluntary control. So if the physical universe is under God's direct voluntary control, it is His body. Against this, I would argue that we have many different ways of picking out the body of a human being. In addition to the one just mentioned, my body is distinctive in that it is the perspective from which I perceive the world; it provides the immediate causal conditions of my consciousness; and it constitutes the phenomenological locus of my "bodily sensations". With multiple criteria there is room for maneuver. Holding the other criteria constant, we can envisage a state of affairs in which *something other than my body*, e.g., my wristwatch, is under my direct voluntary control. Thus I deny that my position requires God to have a body.

As indicated earlier, this paper constitutes but a fragment of a thoroughgoing discussion of the title question. Other fragments would go into the question as to whether timelessness, immutability, and other traditional attributes constitute a bar to the literal predication of one or another kind of predicate. And of course we would have to discuss whether God *is* timeless, immutable, and so on. Moreover, we would have to scrutinize the classical arguments for the denial that *any* intrinsic predicates can be literally predicated of God. But perhaps even this fragment has sufficed to show that the prospects for speaking literally about God are not as dim as if often supposed by contemporary thinkers.

Metaphor and Religious Realism

From *Metaphor and Religious Language* by Janet Martin Soskice, 1985

Janet Martin Soskice, a contemporary English philosopher, upholds a theological realism, finding the richness of the reality of God, as known through revelation, mystical experience, and rational (natural) theology, to require—and to have required (witness Scriptural statements as well as mystic writing)—metaphorical language to convey the human/Divine encounter. People may make mistakes in theology as in any intellectual enterprise. But there is no reason to assume that terms like "God" do not refer—their reference is established initially by revelation and mystical experience—nor that metaphorical descriptions of God are, as metaphorical, not possibly true. Thus just like common nouns and proper names, the reference of 'God' would be established through a kind of pointing, that is to say, experientially, and metaphorically phrased assertions would, like any assertion, be made true by facts.

Soskice argues that a person does not have to have a direct experience of a referent to understand what is meant by a referring expression, because of the power of language to convey an entire community's sense of a particular domain. Just as in science where experts fix meanings that pass into common use, so in the religious domain mystics and poets of the sacred are able to secure for an entire community, she maintains, an understanding of God mediated by language.

Soskice points to three factors crucial to such understanding: (a) experience, broadly construed to include appreciation of such general features of the world as the change that leads theologians like Thomas to reason to a First Cause, (b) community, where linguistic tasks are naturally apportioned to experts, and (c) an interpretive tradition (a hermeneutic tradition), providing categories and terms, sometimes irreducibly metaphoric, to be used to express on-going religious experience. Soskice upholds the importance of religious experience, but emphasizes—and makes a virtue of—the theory-ladenness of its reportage.

According to Soskice's analysis, descriptions of God (etc.) may have to be metaphorical, because literal language is not sufficiently rich to convey, for example, the sense of God conveyed in Christian tradition, but, she argues, this does not mean that the descriptions might not be true. Soskice stresses the importance of that type of metaphor called, technically, catechesis. (Alston makes a similar point when he says: "it can be plausibly argued that we can learn theoretical terms in science only if we have already learned commonsense meanings of these and other terms—senses in which the terms are true of ordinary middle-sized objects. But even if that is true, it does not prevent such terms as 'force' and 'energy' from taking on new technical senses in the development of sophisticated theories. Why should not the same be true of theology?") In sum, Soskice sees the appropriateness of metaphor to be grounded in the transcendence and infinity of God who cannot be perfectly described; she exults in the time-worn (time-proven) metaphors of tradition; and she finds nothing about non-literal speech to undercut the possibility of talk of a Divine Reality.

. . . Our concern is with conceptual possibility rather than proof, and with a demonstration that we may justly claim to speak of God without claiming to define him, and to do so by means of metaphor. Realism accommodates figurative speech which is reality depicting without claiming to be directly descriptive. Despite claims to the contrary, a reflective theological realism . . . need not do violence to genuine religious conviction by vulgar anthropomorphism—indeed, it is particularly well suited to a theology which wishes to preserve the sense of God's transcendence.

But this realism has even more to commend itself to the Christian than this, for it emphasizes . . . the importance to Christian belief of experience, community, and an interpretive tradition. Even in its scientific application, the realism which we have defended brings these three factors into play. Experience is essential, for ultimately it is in experience that reference is grounded—thus . . . this realism is an empirical theory. Community is essential because each speaker is a member of a particular community of interest, which provides the context for his referential claims. A great part of our referential activity depends on what [Hilary] Putman has called a "division of linguistic labour", that is, we rely on authoritative members of our community to ground referring expressions. We refer to Columbus when we mention his name, because we have heard the name from others, who heard it from others, etc., going back to Columbus himself. In a different example, we claim to refer to neutrinos when we speak of them, not in virtue of knowledge and experience which each of us has of them, but because we are members of a linguistic community containing experts whose experience is judged sufficiently immediate to ground a reference. Putnam's claim is that it is not words which refer, but speakers using words who refer, bears the gloss that each speaker is a member of a particular linguistic community and thus connected by means of his fellows to a range of experience far exceeding his own.

The descriptive vocabulary which any individual uses is, in turn, dependent on the community of interest and investigation in which he finds himself, and the descriptive vocabulary which a community has at its disposal is embedded in particular traditions of investigation and conviction; for example, the geneticist will assume that it is a biochemical mechanism which is responsible for trait inheritance and not magical spells or curses. His descriptive language is forged in a particular context of investigation where there is agreement on matters such as what constitutes evidence, what are genuine arguments, what counts as a fact, and so on, and while his claims may be genuinely referential, this does not mean that they escape from this contextuality. The realist position is not that we dispense with theoretical contexts or wider frameworks of assumption, but that the world informs our theory even though our theory may never adequately describe the world. . . .

The point that speakers use language according to precedents and established belief is not a new one, . . . but commonly it has been taken to imply a relativism like that of Nietzsche. What is different about the reassessment of reference we have given is that it allows that reference does indeed occur within a context of enquiry, within a particular tradition of investigation with its own descriptive vocabulary, yet insists that this contextuality does not deprive the descriptive vocabulary of its referential status—this is the point of the claim that terms can be coreferential across theories, and in this way it reinforces a realist, rather than relativist, argument.

Corresponding to the scientific communities of interest, there are religious communities of interest (Christians, for example) which are bound by shared assumptions, interests, and traditions of interpretation, and share a descriptive vocabulary.

The Christian, too, makes claims on the basis of experience which, although different from the kind on which scientific judgments are based, is experience none the less. It is important to clarify what we mean by 'experience' in this context; it is a portmanteau term to cover two sorts, the first being the dramatic or pointed religious experiences of the kind which might prompt one to say, 'whatever appeared to me on the mountain was God', or 'whatever caused me to change my life was God'. The second are the diffuse experiences which form the subject of subsequent metaphysical reflection, the kind on which Aquinas based his proofs for the existence of God; for example, the experience of contingency which prompts us to postulate the non-contingent, the experience of cause which prompts us to postulate the uncaused, the experience of order which prompts us to postulate an ordering agent, and so on. On this view, even the abstractions of natural theology are based, in the long run, on experience—although of a diffuse kind. When an individual, or the wider religious community, decides upon a particular model or image as a means of elucidating experience, pointed or diffuse, they do so as heirs to an established tradition of explanation and a common descriptive vocabulary. . . . This realist argument is possible because we dispense with the empiricist dogma that reference is fixed by unrevisable description and adopt instead a social theory where reference is established partly by senses of terms, but largely by speakers' use of those terms in particular situations. Experience does remain vital, but it is admitted to be experience assessed in the categories used by a particular community of interest and within a particular tradition of evaluation.

Consider accounts of religious or mystical experience; the mystic . . . often feels a crisis of descriptive language because there do not seem to be words and concepts in the common stock adequate to his or her experience. This straining of linguistic resources leads to the catachretical employment of metaphor, of phrases like 'the dark night', 'the spiritual marriage', and 'mystic union'. But the significance of these terms can be assessed, even by other theists, only in terms of the contexts in which they arise. Often, indeed almost always, the mystical writer is influenced by a particular tradition of descriptive imagery and philosophical presupposition. John of the Cross, for example, uses scholastic terminology (although not always with the sense the scholastic writers intended) and the theme of 'mystic night' and 'cloud of unknowing' is itself a biblical theme, harking back to the Cloud of the Exodus and to the Night of the Song of Songs. Often, too, it will be found that the mystic's remarks arise from particular patterns of devotional life; hence the common injunction that the neophyte follow a particular course of life, of reading and of prayer so that he may, by God's grace, be open to this 'night' or 'marriage'. Experience is vital to the mystic, but experience interpreted in the descriptive vocabulary of their particular community of interest and tradition of belief.

This emphasis on experience does not mean that only those privileged with mystical experiences can speak about them. The generality of Christians speak of the 'beatific vision' without having had experiences which they would describe as such. They do so because they belong to a community and tradition of faith which contains authoritative members for whom the term does denominate a particular experience. There is an element of trust involved in relying on others whose experience is wider than one's own, yet in almost all areas of life this is the perfectly rational enterprise of using the wider resources of the community to extend one's own, and necessarily limited, experience and expertise.

. . . there is no reason why the mystics' claims, although qualified and couched in the language of their particular mystical tradition, should not be referential. The essential claim, the 'dubbing event', is something like 'Whatever caused this experience is God.' The referential value of the claim is not, then, affected by being articulated in theory-laden terms like 'spiritual marriage' or 'descent of the cloud', though it must be emphasized that to show that the use of terms like 'spiritual marriage', 'beatific vision', or 'dark night' refers does not guarantee that these are experiences of the sort Christians have taken them to be. It does not demonstrate that they are experiences of the Christian God, or of any god at all; but this is only to say that realism involves the possibility of error, as the theological realist is willing to admit. The mystics and those following them may be sadly misguided as to the cause of their experience and so, of course, may be the physicist who speaks of 'black holes in space'. . . .

The mystic's case is a dramatic one, but in more commonplace theological reflections, and in the use of the more commonplace models and metaphors, . . . we see the same factors at work and the same realist presupposition. The religious teacher is not always privileged with experiences denied to the common run; he may equally be someone with the gift of putting into words what others have sensed. He may have the ability to find metaphors and choose models which illuminate the experience of others, for example, be the first to say that God's presence is like that of a powerful wind. The great divine and the great poet have this in common: both use metaphor to say that which can be said in no other way but which, once said, can be recognized by many. . . .

In Christian theology, . . . repetition of metaphor has often gone hand in hand with typological interpretation and the conviction that certain events in the Old Testament prefigure those in the New. We need not commit ourselves to this tenet of faith to make the essentially literary point that, in ways similar to the allusive techniques of any literary tradition, certain metaphors and models of God's presence and gracious acts, models which often can stand as significant in their own right without historical glosses, have been used and re-used in the central texts of Christianity and in subsequent expositions of those texts. So, to explain what it means to Christians to say that God is a fountain of living water, or a vine-keeper, or a rock, or fortress, or king requires an account not merely of fountains, rocks, vines, and kings but of a whole tradition of experiences and of the literary tradition which records and interprets them.

This, incidentally, is an answer to the frequently put question, 'on what basis are some of the Christian's models given priority over others?' Choice is not unconditioned; we do not choose the model of God as shepherd over that of God as poultry keeper or cattleman at random. A favoured model continues to be so in virtue of its own applicability certainly, but also because the history of its application makes it already freighted with meaning. To say that God is 'king' recalls a whole history of kingship and insubordination recorded in the biblical texts.

These metaphors retain their metaphorical nature but they have become more than simple metaphor—they are almost emblematic—and if one were to undertake a study, not of the use of metaphor as a conceptual vehicle in religious language, but of the specific senses of Christian metaphorical uses, it would, in a great part, be a study of gloss upon gloss, use and re-use of the figures which comprise an interweaving of meanings so complex that the possible readings are never exhausted. . . .

From the literary observation we return to the philosophical one, for the touchstone of these chronicles of faith is experience, experiences pointed or diffuse, the experience of individuals and of communities which are believed to be experiences of the activity of a transcendent God. The language used to account for them is metaphorical and qualified, it stands within a tradition of use and is theory-laden, yet in so far as it is grounded on experience it is referential, and it is the theological realist's conviction that that to which it refers, the source of these experiences, is God who is the source and cause of all that is.

John Donne's 'Hymne to Christ, at the Authors Last Going Into Germany' begins in this way,

In what torne ship soever I embarke,
That ship shall be my embleme of thy Arke;
What sea soever swallow mee, that flood
Shall be to mee an embleme of thy blood;

The ark, the flood, death—death in Christ's blood—water, baptism, death and rising again—in four lines, Donne brings together the sacred past and the author's present in one image at the centre of which is Christ's atonement. The author's experience is interpreted by his sacred texts, his sacred texts are reinterpreted by his own experience, the whole is founded upon centuries of devotional practice. If there is one insight to be taken from philosophical hermeneutics, it is this—that we interpret texts and they interpret us. But something needs to be added to this formula, for it is not simply that texts interpret us, they interpret our experiences; and it is not simply that we interpret texts, for we also interpret the experiences which they more or less obscurely chronicle.

It is a commonplace that in the twentieth century we have lost the living sense of the biblical metaphors which our forefathers had. Sometimes it is suggested that this is a consequence of urban life where few have any contact with the shepherds and sheep, kings, and vines. This simple view fails to see that the distinctively Christian reading of the metaphors of God as shepherd, or king, or vine keeper could never be had simply by knowing about sheep, kings, and vines, and forgets that the Scottish crofter of a previous generation who had no experience of grape vines or Temples had no trouble construing Jesus's claim to be the true vine or Temple. Other times, it is said that we have lost this living sense because we no longer read the Bible and there is much in this, yet it is not difficult to imagine that there are some Christians (extreme fundamentalists) who know the text word for word, yet for whom, precisely because they regard it as simply a book of historical fact, much of its allusive significance is lost. If it is true that biblical imagery is lifeless to modern man (and it is not obvious that this is so), this is more likely to be the legacy of historical criticism, of the search for the historical Jesus, and of attempts made by Christians both liberal and conservative to salvage his exact words and acts from the dross of allusion and interpretation with which the gospel writers surrounded them. It is the legacy of a literalism which equates religious truth with historical facts, whatever these might be. Christianity is indeed a religion of the book, but not of a book of this sort of fact. Its sacred texts are chronicles of experience, armouries of metaphor, and purveyors of an interpretive tradition. The sacred literature thus both records the experiences of the past and provides the descriptive language by which any new experience may be interpreted. If this is so, then experience, customarily regarded as the foundation of natural theology, is also the touchstone of the revealed. All the metaphors which we use to speak of God arise from experiences of that which cannot adequately be described. . . .

DISCUSSION QUESTIONS

1. Show the connection between Maimonides's negative theology and his view about the exclusive appropriateness of negative predication with respect to God; show also a parallel connection with respect to the thought of Śaṅkara.

2. Explain Thomas Aquinas's theory of analogical predication in theology.

3. Has Antony Flew shown that for the committed theist nothing could count as evidence against the claim that God is loving? Would this show that the claim is meaningless?

4. Present J. H. Randall's view of religious language. (Optionally, discuss the question of the extent to which Randall's view is continuous with that of sociologists of religion such as Durkheim: see under Religion Debunked.)

5. Contrast William Alston's view of religious language with that of at least two other authors reviewed in this section. Then explain how Alston would use the notion of a "basic action" to defend the thesis that personalistic predicates might be true of God. Does this consideration show decisively that Alston's view is better than the other views you have discussed?

6. Reconstruct the position and arguments of Janet Martin Soskice on metaphor and the possibility of a religious realism. Why is it, according to her view, that contextuality does not undermine referential realism in the religious (or another) domain? In what sense does she hold that a religious metaphor may be true? Do you find her analysis accurate?

CHAPTER SEVEN

Faith Against Reason

Fideism is the view that the nature of religious faith precludes rational or philosophic inquiry into the grounds (reasons), or lack thereof, for religious beliefs. Or, in some versions—where faith is not considered a matter of belief—fideism is the view that faith precludes philosophy, period. Where beliefs are involved, they are not held on defensible grounds but "on faith." There are several distinct types of fideism, many of which differ on what religious faith is.

Romantic fideism denies, in its most radical version, that faith has a belief component; faith is a kind of feeling or emotion informed by imagination, not reason. Romantics exalt the role of the imagination in the religious arena, usually also denouncing reason, as does William Blake in the selection below. While Blake admits—unlike some—an interpretive and belief dimension to faith, he does not see faith as appropriately subject to rational scrutiny.

Existentialist fideism stresses the absurdity of the universe, finding paradox at every turn. Faith is a blind leap, a criterionless choice of God or another life commitment. The nineteenth-century Danish thinker Søren Kierkegaard is probably the most famous religious existentialist, though the religious existentialist movement has been widespread.

Mystical fideism is the view that faith or trust in God (etc.) opens mystical doors, preparing one for mystical experience. This is a major theme of William James's *The Varieties of Religious Experience.*

Voluntarist fideism, which is similar to existentialist fideism though not as extremely anti-rational, insists on assent to religious propositions as an act of will or choice, undetermined or uninformed by evidence, but also not ruled out by other things we know. This type of fideism is propagated also by William James.

Wittgensteinian fideism is the view that religious faith is a whole way of life that can be understood only from the inside, only by actively participating in that life. Philosophers outside the religious circle do not, *ex hypothesi,* understand religious life and thus have no right to criticize it—understanding being a prerequisite to philosophic scrutiny. D. Z. Phillips is a leading proponent of this type of fideism, which has been popular among professional philosophers. Phillips develops in the religious arena ideas of the British (though Austrian-born) philosopher Ludwig Wittgenstein (1889–1951) on language and meaning.

Anti-evidentialism, championed by Alvin Plantinga, construes propositions such as "God is speaking to me," "God is evident in the beauty of a sunset" to be basic in appropriate circumstances in that they are (a) warranted but (b) no argument can be given for them. Plantinga rejects the fideist label for his position, but several have found it a way of avoiding debate about such fundamental theistic propositions as "God exists."

Fideists have in common a view of faith as guiding, or constituting, an entire way of life. This is an especially important theme with the Taoism of Lao Tzu, who is also anti-rational in the sense of being opposed to moralizing and the making of distinctions by the mind. Most fideists also agree that faith is, in part, an emotion or passion, though few go so far as to claim that neither does it shape nor is it shaped by the way one looks intellectually at the world. With regard to philosophy of religion, fideism is defined by its rejection of the relevance of evidence, philosophic canons of evidence, or philosophic scrutiny.

Taoist Virtuous Anti-Virtue

From *The Tao-te Ching* by Lao Tzu in *A Source Book in Chinese Philosophy,* Wing-Tsit Chan, translator and editor, 1963

As noted in the section Divine Reality, Lao Tzu opposes the Confucian emphasis on the social, promoting instead an individualistic perspective that eschews the divisiveness, and especially the moralizing, of discursive mentality. Lao Tzu recommends a profounder atunement to nature, as exhibited in one "fearing danger on all sides" who is at the same time serene and genuine "like a piece of uncarved wood." Taoism is at once pastoral and perfectionist. Taoist attitudes seem comparable both to the fideism of some Romantics such as Blake and to the mystical openness recommended by William James.

The twentieth-century French philosopher Michel Foucault was notorious for saying such things as "Before biology there was no life." Obviously, there were living beings before the science of biology developed. Foucault's point is that a science, or, more broadly, a mental attitude, shapes, in a sense creates, the objects of its purview. A similar notion is expressed by Lao Tzu. Before Confucian moralizing, people were not concerned with the petty and corrupting distinctions of virtue and vice. By returning to a psychic state more attuned to our true nature, people will be moral. It is only with the decline of the Tao that the virtues of humanity and righteousness arise. By having faith in our own true character, we return to the natural spontaneity of the Tao.

> When the great Tao declined,
> The doctrines of humanity (*jen*) and righteousness (*i*) arose.
> When knowledge and wisdom appeared,
> There emerged great hypocrisy.

When the six family relationships[1] are not in harmony,
There will be the advocacy of filial piety and deep love to children.
When a country is in disorder,
There will be praise of loyal ministers.

Abandon sageliness and discard wisdom;
Then the people will benefit a hundredfold.
Abandon humanity and discard righteousness;
Then the people will return to filial piety and deep love.
Abandon skill and discard profit;
Then there will be no thieves or robbers.
However, these three things are ornament (*wen*) and not adequate.
Therefore let people hold on to these:
 Manifest plainness,
 Embrace simplicity,
 Reduce selfishness,
 Have few desires.

Abandon learning and there will be no sorrow.
How much difference is there between "Yes, sir," and "Of course not"?
How much difference is there between "good" and "evil"?
What people dread, do not fail to dread.
But, alas, how confused, and the end is not yet.
The multitude are merry, as though feasting on a day of sacrifice,
Or like ascending a tower at springtime.
I alone am inert, showing no sign (of desires),
Like an infant that has not yet smiled.
Wearied, indeed, I seem to be without a home.
The multitude all possess more than enough,
I alone seem to have lost all.
Mine is indeed the mind of an ignorant man,
Indiscriminate and dull!
Common folks are indeed brilliant;
I alone seem to be in the dark.

Common folks see differences and are clear-cut;
I alone make no distinctions.
I seem drifting as the sea;
Like the wind blowing about, seemingly without destination.
The multitude all have a purpose;
I alone seem to be stubborn and rustic.
I alone differ from others,
And value drawing sustenance from Mother (Tao).

---

[1] Father, son, elder brother, younger brother, husband, and wife.

The all-embracing quality of the great virtue (*te*) follows alone from the Tao.
The thing that is called Tao is eluding and vague.
 Vague and eluding, there is in it the form.
 Eluding and vague, in it are things.
Deep and obscure, in it is the essence.
The essence is very real; in it are evidences.
From the time of old until now, its name (manifestations) ever remains,
By which we may see the beginning of all things.
How do I know that the beginnings of all things are so?
Through this (Tao).

To yield is to be preserved whole.
To be bent is to become straight.
To be empty is to be full.
To be worn out is to be renewed.
To have little is to possess.
To have plenty is to be perplexed.
Therefore the sage embraces the One
And becomes the model of the world.
He does not show himself; therefore he is luminous.
He does not justify himself; therefore he becomes prominent.
He does not boast of himself; therefore he is given credit.
He does not brag; therefore he can endure for long.
It is precisely because he does not compete that the world cannot compete with him.
Is the ancient saying, "To yield is to be preserved whole," empty words?
Truly he will be preserved and (prominence, etc.) will come to him.

Romantic Anti-Rationalism

From *The Poetry and Prose of William Blake,* David V. Erdman, editor, 1970

William Blake (1757–1827) is a Romantic poet who is still widely read. He is equally renowned for his visionary paintings and engravings, whose themes are religious and mystical. Blake, like many in the Romantic movement, was suspicious of the perspective of science, finding the confidence in reason of the philosophers of the preceding generation—now called the Age of Enlightenment, sometimes the Age of Reason—full of overweening pride. Blake saw reason as opposed to life, as dissecting to understand and to categorize things rigidly in boxes (coffins).

Faith, in contrast, is informed by poetic imagination. It provides a spiritual vision transcending the tools of reason. Faith, for Blake, may be viewed as a kind of "seeing as," a profound interpretation, or transformation, of experience by the imagination, which is the only appropriate faculty for appreciating the Divine, the faculty through which God and the angels are revealed. In the essay, "A Vision of the Last Judgment," Blake says, " 'What,' it will

*be Questiond, 'When the Sun rises do you not see a round Disk of fire somewhat like a
Guinea?' O no no, I see an Innumerable company of the Heavenly host crying 'Holy Holy
Holy is the Lord God Almighty.'" Newton and his crowd misinterpret what they see through
an overreliance on reason and a failure to use the Poetic faculty.*

*In the selection here, Blake is purposely ironic in casting his thought in argument
form. But he is serious about his conclusions. There is no legitimate natural religion, that
is, rational theology, but only revealed religion. Imagination allows us to transcend the
given. It thus provides direction.*

THERE IS NO NATURAL RELIGION

The Author & Printer W Blake

[a]

The Argument. Man has no notion of moral fitness but from Education. Naturally he is
only a natural organ subject to Sense.

I Man cannot naturally Percieve. but through his natural or bodily organs.

II Man by his reasoning power. can only compare & judge of what he has already perciev'd.

III From a perception of only 3 senses or 3 elements none could deduce a fourth or fifth

IV None could have other than natural or organic thoughts if he had none but organic
perceptions

V Mans desires are limited by his perceptions. none can desire what he has not perciev'd

VI The desires & perceptions of man untaught by any thing but organs of sense, must
be limited to objects of sense.

Conclusion. If it were not for the Poetic or Prophetic character, the Philosophic & Experimental would soon be at the ratio of all things, & stand still unable to do other than repeat the same dull round over again

THERE IS NO NATURAL RELIGION

[b]

I Mans perceptions are not bounded by organs of perception. he percieves more than
sense (tho' ever so acute) can discover.

II Reason or the ratio of all we have already known. is not the same that it shall be
when we know more.

[III lacking]

IV The bounded is loathed by its possessor. The same dull round even of a univer[s]e
would soon become a mill with complicated wheels

V If the many become the same as the few when possess'd, More! More! is the cry of
a mistaken soul, less than All cannot satisfy Man.

VI If any could desire what he is incapable of possessing, despair must be his eternal lot.

VII The desire of Man being Infinite the possession is Infinite & himself Infinite Application. He who sees the Infinite in all things sees God. He who sees the Ratio only sees himself only.

Therefore God becomes as we are, that we may be as he is. . . .

Theistic Existentialism

From *Philosophical Fragments/Johannes Climacus* by Søren Kierkegaard, Howard V. Hong and Edna H. Hong, editors and translators, 1985

Regarded as a founder of existentialism, the Danish philosopher Søren Kierkegaard (1813–1855) weaves Romantic strands into his theism—that is, the importance of passion—as well an emphasis on paradox and absurdity and a "leap of faith" associated with religious existentialism. Existentialist themes common to both religious and areligious varieties were introduced above with the selection from Albert Camus (see under Religion Debunked), who pointedly criticized Kierkegaard.

Unlike Camus, Kierkegaard finds the fundamental absurdity, the fundamental otherness that we confront whenever and wherever we deeply probe, to disclose itself as God, though not as "God" to our minds as an idea or an entity that we can comprehend. The term God itself (or, as the translator writes, god) is suspect. That other nevertheless can stir infinite passion, but can never be possessed by us, who would turn it into an idol, that is to say, who cannot transcend the anthropomorphic. Kierkegaard suggests that the right way to live is to throw ourselves at this "what" we cannot comprehend. But it is difficult to discern precisely what stance he recommends. As Camus says, Kierkegaard is enigmatic. One thing, however, is clear: the otherness is not amenable to comprehension by our minds.

Kierkegaard appears to take a voluntarist view of the emotions. Passions are not waves of feeling that break upon us but rather are intricately bound up with our wills. We make our passions, as we make our lives and values. Nothing is given except an absurd context, our freedom and individuality, and the openness of our lives.

THE ABSOLUTE PARADOX

(A Metaphysical Caprice)

Although Socrates did his very best to gain knowledge of human nature and to know himself—yes, even though he has been eulogized for centuries as the person who certainly knew man best—he nevertheless admitted that the reason he was disinclined to ponder the nature of such creatures as Pegasus and the Gorgons was that he still was not quite clear about himself, whether he (a connoisseur of human nature) was a more curious monster than Typhon or a friendlier and simpler being, by nature sharing something divine (see *Phaedrus,* 229 e).[1] This seems to be a paradox. But one must not think ill of the paradox, for the paradox is the passion of thought, and the thinker without the paradox is like the lover without passion: a mediocre fellow. But the ultimate potentiation of every passion is always to will its own downfall, and so it is also the ultimate passion of the understanding [*Forstand*] to will the collision, although in one way or another the collision must become its downfall. This, then, is the ultimate paradox of thought: to want to discover something that thought itself cannot think. This passion of thought is fundamentally present everywhere in thought, also in the single individual's thought insofar as he, thinking, is not merely himself. But because of habit we do not discover this. . . .

But what is this unknown against which the understanding in its paradoxical passion collides and which even disturbs man and his self-knowledge? It is the unknown. But it is not a human being, insofar as he knows man, or anything else that he knows. Therefore, let us call this unknown *the god.* It is only a name we give to it. It hardly occurs to the understanding to want to demonstrate that this unknown (the god) exists. If, namely, the god does not exist, then of course it is impossible to demonstrate it. But if he does exist, then it is foolishness to want to demonstrate it, since I, in the very moment the demonstration commences, would presuppose it not as doubtful—which a presupposition cannot be, inasmuch as it is a presupposition—but as decided, because otherwise I would not begin, easily perceiving that the whole thing would be impossible if he did not exist. If, however, I interpret the expression "to demonstrate the existence [*Tilværelse*] of the god" to mean that I want to demonstrate that the unknown, which exists, is the god, then I do not express myself very felicitously, for then I demonstrate nothing, least of all an existence, but I develop the definition of a concept. It is generally a difficult matter to want to demonstrate that something exists—worse still, for the brave souls who venture to do it, the difficulty is of such a kind that fame by no means awaits those who are preoccupied with it. The whole process of demonstration continually becomes something entirely different, becomes an expanded concluding development of what I conclude from having presupposed that the object of investigation exists. Therefore, whether I am moving in the world of sensate

---

[1] See Plato, *Phaedrus,* 229 d–230 a (Socrates speaking):

For my part, Phaedrus, I regard such theories [a scientific account of how Boreas seized Orythia from the river] as no doubt attractive, but as the invention of clever, industrious people who are not exactly to be envied, for the simple reason that they must then go on and tell us the real truth about the appearance of centaurs and the Chimera, not to mention a whole host of such creatures, Gorgons and Pegasuses and countless other remarkable monsters of legend flocking in on them. If our skeptic, with his somewhat crude science, means to reduce every one of them to the standard of probability, he'll need a deal of time for it. I myself have certainly no time for the business, and I'll tell you why, my friend. I can't as yet 'know myself,' as the inscription at Delphi enjoins, and so long as that ignorance remains it seems to me ridiculous to inquire into extraneous matters. Consequently I don't bother about such things, but accept the current beliefs about them, and direct my inquiries, as I have just said, rather to myself, to discover whether I really am a more complex creature and more puffed up with pride than Typhon, or a simpler, gentler being whom heaven has blessed with a quiet, un-Typhonic nature.

palpability or in the world of thought, I never reason in conclusion to existence, but I reason in conclusion from existence. For example, I do not demonstrate that a stone exists but that something which exists is a stone. The court of law does not demonstrate that a criminal exists but that the accused, who does indeed exist, is a criminal. Whether one wants to call existence an *accessorium* [addition], or the eternal *prius* [presupposition], it can never be demonstrated. . . .

If one wanted to demonstrate Napoleon's existence from Napoleon's works, would it not be most curious, since his existence certainly explains the works but the works do not demonstrate *his* existence unless I have already in advance interpreted the word "his" in such a way as to have assumed that he exists. But Napoleon is only an individual, and to that extent there is no absolute relation between him and his works—thus someone else could have done the same works. Perhaps that is why I cannot reason from the works to existence. If I call the works Napoleon's works, then the demonstration is superfluous, since I have already mentioned his name. If I ignore this, I can never demonstrate from the works that they are Napoleon's but demonstrate (purely ideally) that such works are the works of a great general etc. However, between the god and his works there is an absolute relation. God is not a name but a concept and perhaps because of that his *essentia involvit existentiam* [essence involves existence].

God's works, therefore, only the god can do. Quite correct. But, then, what are the god's works? The works from which I want to demonstrate his existence do not immediately and directly exist, not at all. Or are the wisdom in nature and the goodness or wisdom in Governance right in front of our noses? Do we not encounter the most terrible spiritual trials here, and is it ever possible to be finished with all these trials? But I still do not demonstrate God's existence from such an order of things, and even if I began, I would never finish and also would be obliged continually to live *in suspenso* lest something so terrible happen that my fragment of demonstration would be ruined. Therefore, from what works do I demonstrate it? From the works regarded ideally—that is, as they do not appear directly and immediately. But then I do not demonstrate it from the works, after all, but only develop the ideality I have presupposed; trusting in *that*,[2] I even dare to defy all objections, even those that have not yet arisen. By beginning, then, I have presupposed the ideality, have presupposed that I will succeed in accomplishing it, but what else is that but presupposing that the god exists and actually beginning with trust in him.

---

[2] See, for example, Anselm, *Proslogium,* II, where, trusting in the presupposed ideality, he proceeds to demonstrate its existence. *St. Anselm,* tr. Sidney N. Deane (Chicago: Open Court, 1930), p. 7:

Truly there is a God, although the fool hath said in his heart, There is no God.

And so, Lord, do thou, who dost give understanding to faith, give me, so far as thou knowest it to be profitable, to understand that thou art as we believe; and that thou art that which we believe. And, indeed, we believe that thou art a being than which nothing greater can be conceived. Or is there no such nature, since the fool hath said in his heart, there is no God? (Psalms xiv. 1). But, at any rate, this very fool, when he hears of this being of which I speak—a being than which nothing greater can be conceived—understands what he hears, and what he understands is in his understanding; although he does not understand it to exist.

And how does the existence of the god emerge from the demonstration? Does it happen straightway? Is it not here as it is with the Cartesian dolls?[3] As soon as I let go of the doll, it stands on its head. As soon as I let go of it—consequently, I have to let go of it. So also with the demonstration—so long as I am holding on to the demonstration (that is, continue to be one who is demonstrating), the existence does not emerge, if for no other reason than that I am in the process of demonstrating it, but when I let go of the demonstration, the existence is there. Yet this letting go, even that is surely something; it is, after all, *meine Zuthat* [my contribution]. Does it not have to be taken into account, this diminutive moment, however brief it is—it does not have to be long, because it is a *leap*. . . .

Therefore, anyone who wants to demonstrate the existence of God (in any other sense than elucidating the God-concept and without the *reservatio finalis* [ultimate reservation] that we have pointed out—that the existence itself emerges from the demonstration by a leap) proves something else instead, at times something that perhaps did not even need demonstrating, and in any case never anything better. For the fool says in his heart that there is no God, but he who says in his heart or to others: Just wait a little and I shall demonstrate it—ah, what a rare wise man he is. . . .

The paradoxical passion of the understanding is, then, continually colliding with this unknown, which certainly does exist but is also unknown and to that extent does not exist. The understanding does not go beyond this; yet in its paradoxicality the understanding cannot stop reaching it and being engaged with it, because wanting to express its relation to it by saying that this unknown does not exist will not do, since just saying that involves a relation. But what, then, is this unknown, for does not its being the god merely signify to us that it is the unknown? To declare that it is the unknown because we cannot know it, and that even if we could know it we could not express it,[4] does not satisfy the passion, although it has correctly perceived the unknown as frontier. But a frontier is expressly the passion's torment, even though it is also its incentive. And yet it can go no further, whether it risks a sortie through *via negationis* [the way of negation] or *via eminentiae* [the way of idealization].

What, then, is the unknown? It is the frontier that is continually arrived at, and therefore when the category of motion is replaced by the category of rest it is the different, the absolutely different. But it is the absolutely different in which there is no distinguishing mark. Defined as the absolutely different, it seems to be at the point of being disclosed, but

---

[3] An eccentrically weighted tumbler doll that rolls to its feet when released is misnamed for the so-called Cartesian devil (a hollow glass figure, weighted and open at the bottom and partially filled with air), which moves in a partially filled container of water when the pliable top of the container is pressed down.

[4] A reference to the formulation by Gorgias, a Sophist. See Sextus Empiricus, *Against the Logicians,* VII, 65; *Opera,* p. 149; Loeb, II, p. 35: "Gorgias of Leontini belonged to the same party as those who abolish the criterion, although he did not adopt the same line of attack as Protagoras. For in his book entitled *Concerning the Nonexistent* or *Concerning Nature* he tries to establish successively three main points—firstly, that nothing exists; secondly, that even if anything exists it is inapprehensible by man; thirdly, that even if anything is apprehensible, yet of a surety it is inexpressible and incommunicable to one's neighbour."

not so, because the understanding cannot even think the absolutely different; it cannot absolutely negate itself but uses itself for that purpose and consequently thinks the difference in itself, which it thinks by itself. It cannot absolutely transcend itself and therefore thinks as above itself only the sublimity that it thinks by itself. If the unknown (the god) is not solely the frontier, then the one idea about the different is confused with the many ideas about the different. The unknown is then in διασπορά [dispersion], and the understanding has an attractive selection from among what is available and what fantasy can think of (the prodigious, the ridiculous, etc.).

But this difference cannot be grasped securely. Every time this happens, it is basically an arbitrariness, and at the very bottom of devoutness there madly lurks the capricious arbitrariness that knows it itself has produced the god. If the difference cannot be grasped securely because there is no distinguishing mark, then, as with all such dialectical opposites, so it is with the difference and the likeness—they are identical. Adhering to the understanding, the difference has so confused the understanding that it does not know itself and quite consistently confuses itself with the difference. In the realm of fantastical fabrication, paganism has been adequately luxuriant. With respect to the assumption just advanced, which is the self-ironizing of the understanding, I shall merely trace it in a few lines without reference to whether it was historical or not. There exists [*existere*], then, a certain person who looks just like any other human being, grows up as do other human beings, marries, has a job, takes tomorrow's livelihood into account as a man should. It may be very beautiful to want to live as the birds of the air live, but it is not permissible, and one can indeed end up in the saddest of plights, either dying of hunger—if one has the endurance for that—or living on the goods of others. This human being is also the god. How do I know that? Well, I cannot know it, for in that case I would have to know the god and the difference, and I do not know the difference, inasmuch as the understanding has made it like unto that from which it differs. Thus the god has become the most terrible deceiver through the understanding's deception of itself. The understanding has the god as close as possible and yet just as far away.

Someone may now be saying, "I know full well that you are a capricemonger, but you certainly do not believe that it would occur to me to be concerned about a caprice so curious or so ludicrous that it probably has never occurred to anyone and, above all, is so unreasonable that I would have to lock everything out of my consciousness in order to think of it." That is exactly what you have to do, but then is it justifiable to want to keep all the presuppositions *you* have in your consciousness and still presume to think about your consciousness without any presuppositions? Most likely you do not deny the consistency of what has been developed—that in defining the unknown as the different the understanding ultimately goes astray and confuses the difference with likeness? But this seems to imply something different, namely, that if a human being is to come truly to know something about the unknown (the god), he must first come to know that it is different from him, absolutely different from him. The understanding cannot come to know this by itself (since, as we have seen, it is a contradiction); if it is going to come to know this, it must come to know this from the god, and if it does come to know this, it cannot understand this and consequently cannot come to know this, for how could it understand the absolutely different? If this is not immediately clear, then it will become more clear from the corollary, for if the god is absolutely different from a human being, then a human being is absolutely different from the god—but how is the understanding to grasp this? At this point we seem to stand at a paradox. Just to come to know that the god is the different, man needs the god and then comes to know that the god is absolutely different from him. But if the god is to be absolutely different from a human being, this can have its basis not in that which man owes to the god (for to that extent they are akin) but in that which he owes to himself or in that which he himself has committed. What, then, is the difference? Indeed, what else but sin, since the difference, the absolute difference, must have been caused by the individual himself. We stated this in the foregoing by saying that the individual is untruth and is this through his own fault, and we jestingly, yet earnestly, agreed that it is too much to ask him to find this out for himself. Now we have come to the same point again. The connoisseur of human nature became almost bewildered about himself when he came up against the different; he no longer knew whether he was a more curious monster than Typhon or whether there was something divine in him. What did he lack, then? The consciousness of sin, which he could no more teach to any other person than any other person could teach it to him. Only the god could teach it—if he wanted to be teacher. But this he did indeed want to be, as we have composed the story, and in order to be that he wanted to be on the basis of equality with the single individual so that he could completely understand him. Thus the paradox becomes even more terrible, or the same paradox has the duplexity by which it manifests itself as the absolute—negatively, by bringing into prominence the absolute difference of sin and, positively, by wanting to annul this absolute difference in the absolute equality.

But is a paradox such as this conceivable? We shall not be in a hurry; whenever the contention is over a reply to a question and the contending is not like that on the race track, it is not speed that wins but correctness. The understanding certainly cannot think it, cannot hit upon it on its own, and if it is proclaimed, the understanding cannot understand it and merely detects that it will likely be its downfall. To that extent, the understanding has strong objections to it; and yet, on the other hand, in its paradoxical passion the understanding does indeed will its own downfall. But the paradox, too, wills this downfall of the understanding, and thus the two have a mutual understanding, but this understanding is present only in the moment of passion. Let us consider the condition of erotic love [*Elskov*], even though it is an imperfect metaphor. Self-love lies at the basis of love [*Kjærlighed*], but at its peak its paradoxical passion wills its own downfall. Erotic love also wills this, and therefore these two forces are in mutual understanding in the moment of passion, and this passion is precisely erotic love. Why, then, should the lover not be able to think this, even though the person who in self-love shrinks from erotic love can neither comprehend it nor dare to venture it, since it is indeed his downfall. So it is with the passion of erotic love. To be sure, self-love has foundered, but nevertheless it is not annihilated but is taken captive and is erotic love's *spolia opima* [spoils of war]. But it can come to life again, and this becomes erotic love's spiritual trial. So also with the paradox's relation to the understanding, except that this passion has another name, or, rather, we must simply try to find a name for it.

Mystical Faith

From *The Varieties of Religious Experience* by William James, 1929

Selections from works by William James are included in the sections Polytheism and Henotheism, Speculative Spiritual Metaphysics, and Mystical Experience, but we have put off introducing the person and his most closely held views about religion until this section. These views are a pragmatism and a voluntarist fideism best expressed in the next selection, below—from James's essay "The Will to Believe." But I shall go on and say a few words about the life of the great American philosopher now.

James (1842–1910) was born and raised in New York City, though he spent several years in Europe. His father, Henry James, Sr., was a philosopher of some renown; his brother, Henry James, Jr., became his generation's leading novelist. William attended Harvard medical school, and began teaching anatomy there in 1873 (at age 31). James reports a personal crisis during his medical-school period concerning the possibility of free will. Scientific, or, as James called it, medical determinism seems to have been more prevalent in high intellectual circles then than now. James moved from medicine to philosophy with the goal of defending personal autonomy. He began teaching philosophy at Harvard at 1879 (at age 37). James remained at Harvard almost his entire professional life, retiring in 1907 (at age 65).

Many great names of late nineteenth- and early twentieth-century philosophy were James's friends and colleagues: Charles Peirce, F. H. Bradley, Josiah Royce, Henri Bergson, George Santayana, and John Dewey among others, all with considerable reputations. James for his part became famous for a terrific vitality. Public speaking was his forté. Most of his books are transcriptions of lectures, as is his classic, The Varieties of Religious Experience, *which was delivered in 1901/02 as the Gifford Lectures in Edinburgh.*

In the selection here, James makes two main points, both of which are psychological. First, religious faith is much more a matter of intuition and feeling than it is of intellectual commitment. James agrees with the Romantics in this. Systems of theology, etc., he sees as driven by subrational elements, and to be less important in a religious life than prereflective intuitions.

Second, James suggests that through faith a person opens himself or herself to the action of the supernatural; faith would thus be a prerequisite to the mystical life that James sees as most estimable in religion. He does not hold that the specific intellectual content of faith is very important; what is important is persistence. This view connects with James's pragmatism, more about which in the introduction to the next selection.

Were one asked to characterize the life of religion in the broadest and most general terms possible, one might say that it consists of the belief that there is an unseen order, and that our supreme good lies in harmoniously adjusting ourselves thereto. This belief and this adjustment are the religious attitude in the soul. I wish during this hour to call your attention to some of the psychological peculiarities of such an attitude as this, or belief in an object which we cannot see. All our attitudes, moral, practical, or emotional, as well as religious, are due to the "objects" of our consciousness, the things which we believe to exist, whether really or ideally, along with ourselves. Such objects may be present to our senses, or they may be present only to our thought. In either case they elicit from us a *reaction;* and the reaction due to things of thought is notoriously in many cases as strong as that due to sensible presences. It may be even stronger. The memory of an insult may make us angrier than the insult did when we received it. We are frequently more ashamed of our blunders afterwards than we were at the moment of making them; and in general our whole higher prudential and moral life is based on the fact that material sensations actually present may have a weaker influence on our action than ideas of remoter facts. . . .

. . . in the metaphysical and religious sphere, articulate reasons are cogent for us only when our inarticulate feelings of reality have already been impressed in favor of the same conclusion. Then, indeed, our intuitions and our reason work together, and great world-ruling systems, like that of the Buddhist or of the Catholic philosophy, may grow up. Our impulsive belief is here always what sets up the original body of truth, and our articulately verbalized philosophy is but its showy translation into formulas. The unreasoned and immediate is but a surface exhibition. Instinct leads, intelligence does but follow. If a person feels the presence of a living God after the fashion shown by my quotations [from mystic literature] your critical arguments, be they never so superior, will vainly set themselves to change his faith. . . .

. . . The further limits of our being plunge, it seems to me, into an altogether other dimension of existence from the sensible and merely 'understandable' world. Name it the mystical region, or the supernatural region, whichever you choose. So far as our ideal impulses originate in this region (and most of them do originate in it, for we find them possessing us in a way for which we cannot articulately account), we belong to it in a more intimate sense than that in which we belong to the visible world, for we belong in the most intimate sense wherever our ideals belong. Yet the unseen region in question is not merely ideal, for it produces effects in this world. When we commune with it, work is actually done upon our finite personality, for we are turned into new men, and consequences in the way of conduct follow in the natural world upon our regenerative change. But that which produces effects within another reality must be termed a reality itself, so I feel as if we had no philosophic excuse for calling the unseen or mystical world unreal.

God is the natural appellation, for us Christians at least, for the supreme reality, so I will call this higher part of the universe by the name of God. We and God have business with each other; and in opening ourselves to his influence our deepest destiny is fulfilled. The universe, at those parts of it which our personal being constitutes, takes a turn genuinely for the worse or for the better in proportion as each one of us fulfills or evades God's demands. As far as this goes I probably have you with me, for I only translate into schematic language what I may call the instinctive belief of mankind: God is real since he produces real effects. . . .

That the God with whom, starting from the hither side of our own extra-marginal self, we come at its remoter margin into commerce should be the absolute world-ruler, is of course a very considerable over-belief. Over-belief as it is, though, it is an article of almost every one's religion. Most of us pretend in some way to prop it upon our philosophy, but the philosophy itself is really propped upon this faith. . . .

What the more characteristically divine facts are, apart from the actual inflow of energy in the faith-state and the prayer-state, I know not. But the over-belief on which I am ready to make my personal venture is that they exist. . . . Who knows whether the faithfulness of individuals here below to their own poor over-beliefs may not actually help God in turn to be more effectively faithful to his own greater tasks?

Voluntarist Faith

From *The Will to Believe and Other Essays in Popular Philosophy* by William James, 1899

Although pragmatism, voluntarism, and fideism are the usual tags applied to James's philosophic and religious views, meliorism is also suitable (in French, melior *means "better"). Patients who believe they will recover, whatever the evidence, improve their chances. Without evidence that others will act cooperatively, strangers believing that others will do so improve the course of a collective action. Looters are able to rob a train only because the passengers do not take a meliorist attitude toward their fellow travellers. When evidence does not absolutely rule out some proposition* p, *then we have every right to believe* p, *without evidence, especially given that the belief could lead to an improvement in our lives. James thinks that many religious beliefs are like this.*

His pragmatism is a more formal philosophic stance, though its connection with his advocacy of mystic faith and of meliorism is readily apparent. James holds that there is no point in espousing a belief that does not make a difference in our lives. In fact, the worth (and, at places in his writing, the very truth) of a belief is to be judged pragmatically. Thus if religious beliefs have the potentiality to open mystic doors, and if mystical experience is the extreme value its advocates suppose, then religious beliefs score high pragmatically.

James's fideism is a voluntarism in the sense that, in the final analysis, it is a sheer choice—an act of will—whether we accept religious hypotheses. In this, James may be counted a forerunner of twentieth-century existentialism, or at least as similarly stressing the importance of choice unbridled by prior belief. However, unlike the existentialists, James finds evidentialist and other constraints upon the act of will involved in faith. Philosophically the most crucial of these, as he explains them in the following selection, is that the hypothesis must be live; that is to say, (a) it must not be ruled out by other things we know, and (b) it must make an appeal to our overall mindset—potentially cohere, we might say, with our overall outlook. Here James shows himself much the traditional philosopher, despite his championing of faith.

I have long defended to my own students the lawfulness of voluntarily adopted faith; but as soon as they have got well imbued with the logical spirit, they have as a rule refused to admit my contention to be lawful philosophically, even though in point of fact they were personally all the time chock-full of some faith or other themselves. I am all the while, however, so profoundly convinced that my own position is correct, that your invitation has seemed to me a good occasion to make my statements more clear. Perhaps your minds will be more open than those with which I have hitherto had to deal. I will be as little technical as I can, though I must begin by setting up some technical distinctions that will help us in the end.

Let us give the name of *hypothesis* to anything that may be proposed to our belief; and just as the electricians speak of live and dead wires, let us speak of any hypothesis as either *live* or *dead.* A live hypothesis is one which appeals as a real possibility to him to whom it is proposed. If I ask you to believe in the Mahdi, the notion makes no electric connection with your nature,—it refuses to scintillate with any credibility at all. As an hypothesis it is completely dead. To an Arab, however (even if he be not one of the Mahdi's followers), the hypothesis is among the mind's possibilities: it is alive. This shows that deadness and liveness in an hypothesis are not intrinsic properties, but relations to the individual thinker. They are measured by his willingness to act. The maximum of liveness in an hypothesis means willingness to act irrevocably. Practically, that means belief; but there is some believing tendency wherever there is willingness to act at all.

Next, let us call the decision between two hypotheses an *option.* Options may be of several kinds. They may be—1, *living* or *dead;* 2, *forced* or *avoidable;* 3, *momentous* or *trivial;* and for our purposes we may call an option a *genuine* option when it is of the forced, living, and momentous kind.

1. A living option is one in which both hypotheses are live ones. If I say to you: "Be a theosophist or be a Mohammedan," it is probably a dead option, because for you neither hypothesis is likely to be alive. But if I say: "Be an agnostic or be a Christian," it is otherwise: trained as you are, each hypothesis makes some appeal, however small, to your belief.

2. Next, if I say to you: "Choose between going out with your umbrella or without it," I do not offer you a genuine option, for it is not forced. You can easily avoid it by not going out at all. Similarly, if I say, "Either love me or hate me," "Either call my theory true or call it false," your option is avoidable. You may remain indifferent to me, neither loving nor hating, and you may decline to offer any judgment as to my theory. But if I say, "Either accept this truth or go without it," I put on you a forced option, for there is no standing place outside of the alternative. Every dilemma based on a complete logical disjunction, with no possibility of not choosing, is an option of this forced kind.

3. Finally, if I were Dr. Nansen and proposed to you to join my North Pole expedition, your option would be momentous; for this would probably be your only similar opportunity, and your choice now would either exclude you from the North Pole sort of immortality altogether or put at least the chance of it into your hands. He who refuses to embrace a unique opportunity loses the prize as surely as if he tried and failed. *Per contra,* the option is trivial when the opportunity is not unique, when the stake is insignificant, or when the decision is reversible if it later prove unwise. Such trivial options abound in the scientific life. A chemist finds an hypothesis live enough to spend a year in its verification: he believes in it to that extent. But if his experiments prove inconclusive either way, he is quit for his loss of time, no vital harm being done.

It will facilitate our discussion if we keep all these distinctions well in mind.

The next matter to consider is the actual psychology of human opinion. When we look at certain facts, it seems as if our passional and volitional nature lay at the root of all our convictions. When we look at others, it seems as if they could do nothing when the intellect had once said its say. Let us take the latter facts up first.

Does it not seem preposterous on the very face of it to talk of our opinions being modifiable at will? Can our will either help or hinder our intellect in its perceptions of truth? Can we, by just willing it, believe that Abraham Lincoln's existence is a myth, and that the portraits of him in *McClure's Magazine* are all of some one else? Can we, by any effort of our will, or by any strength of wish that it were true, believe ourselves well and about when we are roaring with rheumatism in bed, or feel certain that the sum of the two one-dollar bills in our pocket must be a hundred dollars? We can *say* any of these things, but we are absolutely impotent to believe them; and of just such things is the whole fabric of truths that we do believe in made up,—matters of fact, immediate or remote, as Hume said, and relations between ideas, which are either there or not there for us if we see them so, and which if not there cannot be put there by any action of our own. . . .

The talk of believing by our volition seems, then, from one point of view, simply silly. From another point of view it is worse than silly, it is vile. When one turns to the magnificent edifice of the physical sciences, and sees how it was reared; what thousands of disinterested moral lives of men lie buried in its mere foundations; what patience and postponement, what choking down of preference, what submission to the icy laws of outer fact are wrought into its very stones and mortar; how absolutely impersonal it stands in its vast augustness,—then how besotted and contemptible seems every little sentimentalist who comes blowing his voluntary smoke-wreaths, and pretending to decide things from out of his private dream! Can we wonder if those bred in the rugged and manly school of science should feel like spewing such subjectivism out of their mouths? The whole system of loyalties which grow up in the schools of science go dead against its toleration; so that it is only natural that those who have caught the scientific fever should pass over to the opposite extreme, and write sometimes as if the incorruptibly truthful intellect ought positively to prefer bitterness and unacceptableness to the heart in its cup.

> It fortifies my soul to know
> That, though I perish, Truth is so—

sings Clough. . . . And that delicious *enfant terrible* Clifford writes: "Belief is desecrated when given to unproved and unquestioned statements for the solace and private pleasure of the believer. . . . Whoso would deserve well of his fellows in this matter will guard the purity of his belief with a very fanaticism of jealous care, lest at any time it should rest on an unworthy object, and catch a stain which can never be wiped away. . . . If [a] belief has been accepted on insufficient evidence [even though the belief be true, as Clifford on the same page explains] the pleasure is a stolen one. . . . It is sinful because it is stolen in defiance of our duty to mankind. That duty is to guard ourselves from such beliefs as from a pestilence which may shortly master our own body and then spread to the rest of the town.

. . . It is wrong always, everywhere, and for every one, to believe anything upon insufficient evidence."

All this strikes one as healthy, even when expressed, as by Clifford, with somewhat too much of robustious pathos in the voice. Free-will and simple wishing do seem, in the matter of our credences, to be only fifth wheels to the coach. Yet if any one should thereupon assume that intellectual insight is what remains after wish and will and sentimental preference have taken wing, or that pure reason is what then settles our opinions, he would fly quite as directly in the teeth of the facts.

It is only our already dead hypotheses that our willing nature is unable to bring to life again. But what has made them dead for us is for the most part a previous action of our willing nature of an antagonistic kind. When I say 'willing nature,' I do not mean only such deliberate volitions as may have set up habits of belief that we cannot now escape from,—I mean all such factors of belief as fear and hope, prejudice and passion, imitation and partisanship, the circumpressure of our caste and set. As a matter of fact we find ourselves believing, we hardly know how or why. Mr. Balfour gives the name of 'authority' to all those influences, born of the intellectual climate, that make hypotheses possible or impossible for us, alive or dead. Here in this room, we all of us believe in molecules and the conservation of energy, in democracy and necessary progress, in Protestant Christianity and the duty of fighting for 'the doctrine of the immortal Monroe,' all for no reasons worthy of the name. We see into these matters with no more inner clearness, and probably with much less, than any disbeliever in them might possess. His unconventionality would probably have some grounds to show for its conclusions; but for us, not insight, but the *prestige* of the opinions, is what makes the spark shoot from them and light up our sleeping magazines of faith. Our reason is quite satisfied, in nine hundred and ninety-nine cases out of every thousand of us, if it can find a few arguments that will do to recite in case our credulity is criticised by some one else. Our faith is faith in some one else's faith, and in the greatest matters this is most the case. Our belief in truth itself, for instance, that there is a truth, and that our minds and it are made for each other,—what is it but a passionate affirmation of desire, in which our social system backs us up? We want to have a truth; we want to believe that our experiments and studies and discussions must put us in a continually better and better position towards it; and on this line we agree to fight out our thinking lives. But if a pyrrhonistic sceptic asks us *how we know* all this, can our logic find a reply? No! certainly it cannot. It is just one volition against another,—we willing to go in for life upon a trust or assumption which he, for his part, does not care to make.

As a rule we disbelieve all facts and theories for which we have no use. Clifford's cosmic emotions find no use for Christian feelings. Huxley belabors the bishops because there is no use for sacerdotalism in his scheme of life. Newman, on the contrary, goes over to Romanism, and finds all sorts of reasons good for staying there, because a priestly system is for him an organic need and delight. Why do so few 'scientists' even look at the evidence for telepathy, so called? Because they think, as a leading biologist, now dead, once said to me, that even if such a thing were true, scientists ought to band together to keep it suppressed and concealed. It would undo the uniformity of Nature and all sorts of other things without which scientists cannot carry on their pursuits. But if this very man had been shown something which as a scientist he might *do* with telepathy, he might not only have examined the evidence, but even have found it good enough. This very law which the logicians would impose upon us—if I may give the name of logicians to those who would rule out our willing nature here—is based on nothing but their own natural wish to exclude all elements for which they, in their professional quality of logicians, can find no use. . . .

Our next duty, having recognized this mixed-up state of affairs, is to ask whether it be simply reprehensible and pathological, or whether, on the contrary, we must treat it as a normal element in making up our minds. The thesis I defend is, briefly stated, this: *Our passional nature not only lawfully may, but must, decide an option between propositions, whenever it is a genuine option that cannot by its nature be decided on intellectual grounds; for to say, under such circumstances, "Do not decide, but leave the question open," is itself a passional decision,—just like deciding yes or no,—and is attended with the same risk of losing the truth.* The thesis thus abstractly expressed will, I trust, soon become quite clear. . . .

One more point, small but important, and our preliminaries are done. There are two ways of looking at our duty in the matter of opinion,—ways entirely different, and yet ways about whose difference the theory of knowledge seems hitherto to have shown very little concern. *We must know the truth;* and *we must avoid error,*—these are our first and great commandments as would-be knowers; but they are not two ways of stating an identical commandment, they are two separable laws. Although it may indeed happen that when we believe the truth *A,* we escape as an incidental consequence from believing the falsehood *B,* it hardly ever happens that by merely disbelieving *B* we necessarily believe *A.* We may in escaping *B* fall into believing other falsehoods, *C* or *D,* just as bad as *B;* or we may escape *B* by not believing anything at all, not even *A.*

Believe truth! Shun error!—these, we see, are two materially different laws; and by choosing between them we may end by coloring differently our whole intellectual life. We may regard the chase for truth as paramount, and the avoidance of error as secondary; or we may, on the other hand, treat the avoidance of error as more imperative, and let truth take its chance. Clifford, in the instructive passage which I have quoted, exhorts us to the latter course. Believe nothing, he tells us, keep your kind in suspense forever, rather than by closing it on insufficient evidence incur the awful risk of believing lies. You, on the other hand, may think that the risk of being in error is a very small matter when compared with the blessings of real knowledge, and be ready to be duped many times in your investigation rather than postpone indefinitely the chance of guessing true. I myself find it impossible to go with Clifford. We must remember that these feelings of our duty about either truth or error are in any case only expressions of our passional life. Biologically considered, our minds are as ready to grind out falsehood as veracity, and he who says, "Better go without belief forever than believe a lie!" merely shows his own preponderant private horror of becoming a dupe. He may be critical of many of his desires and fears, but this fear he slavishly obeys. He cannot imagine any one questioning its binding force. For my own part, I have also a horror of being duped; but I can believe that worse things than being duped may happen to a man in this world: so Clifford's exhortation has to my ears a thoroughly fantastic sound. It is like a general informing his soldiers that it is better to keep out of battle forever than to risk a single wound. Not so are victories either over enemies or over nature gained. Our errors are surely not such awfully solemn things. In a world where we are so certain to incur them in spite of all our caution, a certain lightness of heart seems healthier than this excessive nervousness on their behalf. At any rate, it seems the fittest thing for the empiricist philosopher.

And now, after all this introduction, let us go straight at our question. I have said, and now repeat it, that not only as a matter of fact do we find our passional nature influencing us in our opinions, but that there are some options between opinions in which this influence must be regarded both as an inevitable and as a lawful determinant of our choice.

I fear here that some of you my hearers will begin to scent danger, and lend an inhospitable ear. Two first steps of passion you have indeed had to admit as necessary,—we must think so as to avoid dupery, and we must think so as to gain truth; but the surest path to those ideal consummations, you will probably consider, is from now onwards to take no further passional step.

Well, of course, I agree as far as the facts will allow. Wherever the option between losing truth and gaining it is not momentous, we can throw the chance of *gaining truth* away, and at any rate save ourselves from any chance of *believing falsehood,* by not making up our minds at all till objective evidence has come. In scientific questions, this is almost always the case; and even in human affairs in general, the need of acting is seldom so urgent that a false belief to act on is better than no belief at all. Law courts, indeed, have to decide on the best evidence attainable for the moment, because a judge's duty is to make law as well as to ascertain it, and (as a learned judge once said to me) few cases are worth spending much time over: the great thing is to have them decided on *any* acceptable principle, and got out of the way. But in our dealings with objective nature we obviously are recorders, not makers, of the truth; and decisions for the mere sake of deciding promptly and getting on to the next business would be wholly out of place. Throughout the breadth of physical nature facts are what they are quite independently of us, and seldom is there any such hurry about them that the risks of being duped by believing a premature theory need be faced. The questions here are always trivial options, the hypotheses are hardly living (at any rate not living for us spectators), the choice between believing truth or falsehood is seldom forced. The attitude of sceptical balance is therefore the absolutely wise one if we would escape mistakes. What difference, indeed, does it make to most of us whether we have or have not a theory of the Röntgen rays, whether we believe or not in mind-stuff, or have a conviction about the causality of conscious states? It makes no difference. Such options are not forced on us. On every account it is better not to make them, but still keep weighing reasons *pro et contra* with an indifferent hand.

. . . The most useful investigator, because the most sensitive observer, is always he whose eager interest in one side of the question is balanced by an equally keen nervousness lest he become deceived. Science has organized this nervousness into a regular *technique,* her so-called method of verification; and she has fallen so deeply in love with the method that one may even say she has ceased to care for truth by itself at all. It is only truth as technically verified that interests her. The truth of truths might come in merely affirmative form, and she would decline to touch it. Such truth as that, she might repeat with Clifford, would be stolen in defiance of her duty to mankind. Human passions, however, are stronger than technical rules. "Le cœur a ses raisons," as Pascal says, "que la raison ne connaît pas;" and however indifferent to all but the bare rules of the game the umpire, the abstract intellect, may be, the concrete players who furnish him the materials to judge of are usually, each one of them, in love with some pet 'live hypothesis' of his own. Let us agree, however, that wherever there is no forced option, the dispassionately judicial intellect with no pet hypothesis, saving us, as it does, from dupery at any rate, ought to be our ideal.

The question next arises: Are there not somewhere forced options in our speculative questions, and can we (as men who may be interested at least as much in positively gaining truth as in merely escaping dupery) always wait with impunity till the coercive evidence shall have arrived? . . .

Moral questions immediately present themselves as questions whose solution cannot wait for sensible proof. A moral question is a question not of what sensibly exists, but of what is good, or would be good if it did exist. Science can tell us what exists; but to compare the *worths,* both of what exists and of what does not exist, we must consult not science, but what Pascal calls our heart. Science herself consults her heart when she lays it down that the infinite ascertainment of fact and correction of false belief are the supreme goods for man. Challenge the statement, and science can only repeat it oracularly, or else prove it by showing that such ascertainment and correction bring man all sorts of other goods which man's heart in turn declares. The question of having moral beliefs at all or not having them is decided by our will. Are our moral preferences true or false, or are they only odd biological phenomena, making things good or bad for *us,* but in themselves indifferent? How can your pure intellect decide? If your heart does not *want* a world of moral reality, your head will assuredly never make you believe in one. . . .

Turn now from these wide questions of good to a certain class of questions of fact, questions concerning personal relations, states of mind between one man and another. *Do you like me or not?*—for example. Whether you do or not depends, in countless instances, on whether I meet you half-way, am willing to assume that you must like me, and show you trust and expectation. The previous faith on my part in your liking's existence is in such cases what makes your liking come. But if I stand aloof, and refuse to budge an inch until I have objective evidence, until you shall have done something apt, as the absolutists say, *ad extorquendum assensum meum,* ten to one your liking never comes. How many women's hearts are vanquished by the mere sanguine insistence of some man that they *must* love him! He will not consent to the hypothesis that they cannot. The desire for a certain kind of truth here brings about that special truth's existence; and so it is in innumerable cases of other sorts. Who gains promotions, boons, appointments, but the man in whose life they are seen to play the part of live hypotheses, who discounts them, sacrifices other things for their sake before they have come, and takes risks for them in advance? His faith acts on the powers above him as a claim, and creates its own verification.

A social organism of any sort whatever, large or small, is what it is because each member proceeds to his own duty with a trust that the other members will simultaneously do theirs. Wherever a desired result is achieved by the co-operation of many independent persons, its existence as a fact is a pure consequence of the precursive faith in one another of those immediately concerned. A government, an army, a commercial system, a ship, a college, an athletic team, all exist on this condition, without which not only is nothing achieved, but nothing is even attempted. A whole train of passengers (individually brave enough) will be looted by a few highwaymen, simply because the latter can count on one another, while each passenger fears that if he makes a movement of resistance, he will be shot before any one else backs him up. If we believed that the whole car-full would rise at once with us, we should each severally rise, and train-robbing would never even be attempted. There are, then, cases where a fact cannot come at all unless a preliminary faith exists in its coming. *And where faith in a fact can help create the fact,* that would be an insane logic which should say that faith running ahead of scientific evidence is the 'lowest kind of immorality' into which a thinking being can fall. Yet such is the logic by which our scientific absolutists pretend to regulate our lives!

In truths dependent on our personal action, then, faith based on desire is certainly a lawful and possibly an indispensable thing.

But now, it will be said, these are all childish human cases, and have nothing to do with great cosmic matters, like the question of religious faith. Let us then pass on to that. Religions differ so much in their accidents that in discussing the religious question we must make it very generic and broad. What then do we now mean by the religious hypothesis? Science says things are; morality says some things are better than other things; and religion says essentially two things.

First, she says that the best things are the more eternal things, the overlapping things, the things in the universe that throw the last stone, so to speak, and say the final word. "Perfection is eternal,"—this phrase of Charles Secrétan seems a good way of putting this first affirmation of religion, an affirmation which obviously cannot yet be verified scientifically at all.

The second affirmation of religion is that we are better off even now if we believe her first affirmation to be true.

Now, let us consider what the logical elements of this situation are *in case the religious hypothesis in both its branches be really true.* (Of course, we must admit that possibility at the outset. If we are to discuss the question at all, it must involve a living option. If for any of you religion be a hypothesis that cannot, by any living possibility be true, then you need go no farther. I speak to the 'saving remnant' alone.) So proceeding, we see, first, that religion offers itself as a *momentous* option. We are supposed to gain, even now, by our belief, and to lose by our nonbelief, a certain vital good. Secondly, religion is a *forced* option, so far as that good goes. We cannot escape the issue by remaining sceptical and waiting for more light, because, although we do avoid error in that way *if religion be untrue,* we lose the good, *if it be true,* just as certainly as if we positively chose to disbelieve. It is as if a man should hesitate indefinitely to ask a certain woman to marry him because he was not perfectly sure that she would prove an angel after he brought her home. Would he not cut himself off from that particular angel-possibility as decisively as if he went and married some one else? Scepticism, then, is not avoidance of option; it is option of a certain particular kind of risk. *Better risk loss of truth than chance of error,—* that is your faith-vetoer's exact position. He is actively playing his stake as much as the believer is; he is backing the field against the religious hypothesis, just as the believer is backing the religious hypothesis against the field. To preach scepticism to us as a duty until 'sufficient evidence' for religion be found, is tantamount therefore to telling us, when in presence of the religious hypothesis, that to yield to our fear of its being error is wiser and better than to yield to our hope that it may be true. It is not intellect against all passions, then; it is only intellect with one passion laying down its law. And by what, forsooth, is the supreme wisdom of this passion warranted? Dupery for dupery, what proof is there that dupery through hope is so much worse than dupery through fear? I, for one, can see no proof; and I simply refuse obedience to the scientist's command to imitate his kind of option, in a case where my own stake is important enough to give me the right to choose my own form of risk. If religion be true and the evidence for it be still insufficient, I do not wish, by putting your extinguisher upon my nature (which feels to me as if it had after all some business in this matter), to forfeit my sole chance in life of getting upon the winning side,—that chance depending, of course, on my willingness to run the risk of acting as if my passional need of taking the world religiously might be prophetic and right.

All this is on the supposition that it really may be prophetic and right, and that, even to us who are discussing the matter, religion is a live hypothesis which may be true. Now, to most of us religion comes in a still further way that makes a veto on our active faith even more illogical. The more perfect and more eternal aspect of the universe is represented in our religions as having personal form. The universe is no longer a mere *It* to us, but a *Thou*, if we are religious; and any relation that may be possible from person to person might be possible here. For instance, although in one sense we are passive portions of the universe, in another we show a curious autonomy, as if we were small active centres on our own account. We feel, too, as if the appeal of religion to us were made to our own active goodwill, as if evidence might be forever withheld from us unless we met the hypothesis half-way. . . . I, therefore, for one, cannot see my way to accepting the agnostic rules for truth-seeking, or wilfully agree to keep my willing nature out of the game. I cannot do so for this plain reason, that *a rule of thinking which would absolutely prevent me from acknowledging certain kinds of truth if those kinds of truth were really there, would be an irrational rule.* That for me is the long and short of the formal logic of the situation, no matter what the kinds of truth might materially be.

I confess I do not see how this logic can be escaped. But sad experience makes me fear that some of you may still shrink from radically saying with me, *in abstracto,* that we have the right to believe at our own risk any hypothesis that is live enough to tempt our will. I suspect, however, that if this is so, it is because you have got away from the abstract logical point of view altogether, and are thinking (perhaps without realizing it) of some particular religious hypothesis which for you is dead. The freedom to 'believe what we will' you apply to the case of some patent superstition; and the faith you think of is the faith defined by the schoolboy when he said, "Faith is when you believe something that you know ain't true." I can only repeat that this is misapprehension. *In concreto,* the freedom to believe can only cover living options which the intellect of the individual cannot by itself resolve; and living options never seem absurdities to him who has them to consider. When I look at the religious question as it really puts itself to concrete men, and when I think of all the possibilities which both practically and theoretically it involves, then this command that we shall put a stopper on our heart, instincts, and courage, and *wait*—acting of course meanwhile more or less as if religion were *not* true—till doomsday, or till such time as our intellect and senses working together may have raked in evidence enough,—this command, I say, seems to me the queerest idol ever manufactured in the philosophic cave. Were we scholastic absolutists, there might be more excuse. If we had an infallible intellect with its objective certitudes, we might feel ourselves disloyal to such a perfect organ of knowledge in not trusting to it exclusively, in not waiting for its releasing word. But if we are empiricists, if we believe that no bell in us tolls to let us know for certain when truth is in our grasp, then it seems a piece of idle fantasticality to preach so solemnly our duty of waiting for the bell. Indeed we *may* wait if we will,—I hope you do not think that I am denying that,—but if we do so, we do so at our peril as much as if we believed. In either case we *act,* taking our life in our hands. No one of us ought to issue vetoes to the other, nor should we bandy words of abuse. We ought, on the contrary, delicately and profoundly to respect one another's mental freedom: then only shall we bring about the intellectual republic; then only shall we have that spirit of inner tolerance without which all our outer tolerance is soulless, and which is empiricism's glory; then only shall we live and let live, in speculative as well as in practical things.

Let me end by a quotation from [Fitz James Stephen]:

"What do you think of yourself? What do you think of the world? . . . These are questions with which all must deal as it seems good to them. They are riddles of the Sphinx, and in some way or other we must deal with them. . . . In all important transactions of life we have to take a leap in the dark. . . . If we decide to leave the riddles unanswered, that is a choice; if we waver in our answer, that, too, is a choice: but whatever choice we make, we make it at our peril. If a man chooses to turn his back altogether on God and the future, no one can prevent him; no one can show beyond reasonable doubt that he is mistaken. If a man thinks otherwise and acts as he thinks, I do not see that any one can prove that *he* is mistaken. Each must act as he thinks best; and if he is wrong, so much the worse for him. We stand on a mountain pass in the midst of whirling snow and blinding mist, through which we get glimpses now and then of paths which may be deceptive. If we stand still we shall be frozen to death. If we take the wrong road we shall be dashed to pieces. We do not certainly know whether there is any right one. What must we do? 'Be strong and of a good courage.' Act for the best, hope for the best, and take what comes. . . . If death ends all, we cannot meet death better."[1]

---

[1] *Liberty, Equality, Fraternity,* p. 353, 2d edition. London, 1874.

Wittgensteinian Fideism

From *Religion Without Explanation* by D. Z. Phillips, 1976

The Welsh philosopher, D. Z. Phillips, has been the leading spokesperson during the last generation for the defense of religion known as Wittgensteinian fideism. The position has been popular since the mid-fifties, inspired by Ludwig Wittgenstein's approach to language and meaning in his Philosophical Investigations *(published in English translation in 1953).*

Wittgenstein holds that meaning is a matter of usage, usages that depend, in turn, on our sharing common forms of life. "If a lion could speak, we could not understand him." It is not possible, says Wittgenstein, to give a comprehensive theory of meaningfulness, invoking a single or even a handful of criteria. Language games differ enormously according to the human activities of which they form a part. Words do not mean in the same way in different contexts. Thus the term God, *Phillips points out, is not to be taken as referential in the manner of a name or designation of a physical object. Christianity is a form of life, and Christian religious language has meaning as determined in that context.*

Thus Phillips's Wittgensteinian fideism involves at once a noncognitivist approach to religious language and an insistence on engagement in religious practices as key to the religious form of life. Philosophers misunderstand religious language when they take it out of the context in which it is alive, and play their games of philosophic scrutiny. Philosophy has a role, according to Phillips, in clarifying the boundaries of religious-language use, in bringing out what is distinctive about it. But when it tries to assimilate such statements as "There is a God" to assertions about everyday objects ("There is an airplane overhead"), it falls into grievous error. "Does God exist?" is not a theoretical question, nor should it be thought that philosophers, says Phillips, are able to answer it.

One question we are left with, then, is: Does this mean that philosophy has no role in evaluating religion, in helping us to decide whether to be religious, or which religion to choose?

. . . We have already seen . . . that talk of a completed life is importantly different in many respects from talk of a life which is still in progress. Belief in a final judgement is not a *means* of expressing thoughts about a completed life, but a form of language which makes it possible to have certain thoughts about a completed life. This is why two men who disagree about whether there is a final judgement are very different from two men who disagree about the truth of an empirical proposition. Wittgenstein brings out the differences quite neatly when he says:

> Suppose someone were a believer and said: 'I believe in a Last Judgement', and I said: 'Well, I'm not so sure. Possibly.' You would say that there is an enormous gulf between us.

If he said 'There is a German aeroplane overhead', and I said 'Possibly, I'm not so sure', you'd say we were fairly near.

What, then, does belief amount to here if it is not a matter of believing in the truth of certain empirical propositions? Wittgenstein suggests that

> Here believing obviously plays much more this role: suppose we said that a certain picture might play the role of constantly admonishing me, or I always think of it. Here, an enormous difference would be between those people for whom the picture is constantly in the foreground, and the others who just didn't use it at all. . . .

. . . In Christianity, reflection on death itself creates a new attitude to all earthly things, an attitude which, in Christianity, is closely bound up with the distinction between the eternal and the temporal. For the Christian, the necessity and unavoidability of death show the essential contingency of all things, his own creature-hood, that all things are a gift, that nothing is his by right. His response to this is one of humility and gratitude. For example, he sees each new day as a gift from God. If someone were to try to understand the notion of a gift in this context, the sense in which a day can be said to be given, in terms of one person making a gift to another, the sense in which a day can be seen as given would be destroyed. The same is true of the sense in which we speak of talents being given. Some people may speak of natural gifts and not be led to worship. For others, this sense of the given leads to prayer and worship. In face of what is given, the believer kneels. Talk of 'God' has its sense in this reaction. It is not the name of an individual; it does not refer to anything. No individual could give a day to men, since the sense in which a day can be said to be given depends on the absence of any such giving. The most commonly held secular counterpart to divine grace is called luck. The believer's sin is to behave in relation to people and things as if they were his by right. The Christian ideal is to see things as a gift of grace. Reflection on death is one expression of this ideal. Saint Paul connects the possibility of resurrection with dying daily. Christianity has, at its centre, a Cross—a divine self-renunciation. It is by dying to this world that the Christian finds the possibility in Christ of being glorified, transformed, raised up.

Here, briefly hinted at, one has different conceptions of eternity. But those who accuse such accounts of reductionism will want to ask what such conceptions refer to. They want to ask this sort of question: It is all very well saying that a belief in a last judgement can play a role in people's lives, but the question remains of whether in fact there is going to be a day of judgement. But . . . such questions [are] the product of confusion. A notion of reference is being imported into the beliefs which is quite alien to them. This can be brought out by considering Wittgenstein's remarks about the way in which the word 'God' enters people's lives:

> The word 'God' is amongst the earliest learnt—pictures and catechisms, etc. But not the same consequences as with pictures of aunts. I wasn't shown (that which the picture pictured).

People who ask, 'But does the picture or belief in a day of judgement refer to anything?' want to be shown that which the picture pictures. But if this could be done it would not be the same kind of picture. Wittgenstein says that he 'could show Moore the pictures of a tropical plant. There is a technique of comparison between picture and plant'. In this case, if someone used the pictures of the plants as proof of the reality of the plants someone might say, with justification, 'I shan't be convinced if you can only show me these pictures. I shall only be convinced when I see the plants'. If, on the other hand, having heard of people praising the Creator of heaven and earth, glorifying the Father of us all, feeling answerable to the One who sees all, someone were to say, 'But these are only religious perspectives, show me what they refer to', this would be a misunderstanding of the grammar of such perspectives. The pictures of the plants refer to their objects, namely, the plants. The religious pictures give one a language in which it is possible to think about human life in a certain way. The pictures (and here one should bear in mind that 'picture' here covers related terms such as 'model' or 'map') provide the logical space within which such thoughts can have a place. When these thoughts are found in worship, the praising and the glorifying does not refer to some object called God. Rather, the expression of such praise and glory is what we call the worship of God. . . .

. . . If a person believes in God this is something which shows itself in his praise and worship. 'I believe in God' is, above all, an expression of faith.

To ask whether God exists is not to ask a theoretical question. If it is to mean anything at all, it is to wonder about praising and praying; it is to wonder whether there is anything in all that. This is why philosophy cannot answer the question 'Does God exist?' with either an affirmative or a negative reply. For from whose mouth does the question come and how is it answered? Praising, thanking, confessing, asking, and adoring before God may have meant little to a man. Suddenly, it means everything to him. He says that God has become a reality in his life. Has this come about by his discovering an object? Hardly. What has happened is that he has found God *in* a praise, a thanksgiving, a confessing and an asking which were not his before. And if coming to God is not coming to see that an object one thought did not exist does in fact exist, neither is losing faith in God coming to see that an object one thought existed does not in fact exist. 'There is a God', though it appears to be in the indicative mood, is an expression of faith. One of its most characteristic forms is showing forth praise. 'There is no God' also appears to be in the indicative mood. But it is in fact a denial; it may indicate one of a number of possible negative relations in which a man may stand to the affirmation of faith.

The task of philosophy is to comment on the character of such affirmations and denials. Such philosophical comment may in fact clear the way or bar the way towards affirmation or denial for a person, but that is a consequence and not the purpose of the comment. . . . What we have done is to comment on the deep-going assumptions often involved in a philosopher's asking, 'Does God exist?' The worst misunderstanding is to think that this question is a theoretical one. Not far behind is the belief that philosophers should be able to answer it.

Modern Anti-Evidentialism

From "Reason and Belief in God" by Alvin Plantinga in *Faith and Rationality: Reason and Belief in God,* Nicholas Wolterstorff and Alvin Plantinga, editors, 1983

Alvin Plantinga, whom we first encountered in the section Evil, has done much work in the epistemology of religious belief, that is, in the area of philosophy concerned with the question of whether religious beliefs are justified and why. In the paper excerpted here, Plantinga challenges what he calls the evidentialist objection to theism by attacking the general epistemological theory known as foundationalism, which takes the justification of a belief to be a matter of inferential relation to "basic beliefs" or "basic propositions" and provides criteria for what beliefs are to count as basic. Only basic beliefs, as determined by these criteria, do not stand in need of justification. But Plantinga finds the criteria inadequate. He accepts the bifurcation of basic and non-basic beliefs, but disagrees about the conditions under which a belief is to count as basic.

According to Plantinga's reconstruction of classical foundationalism, basic beliefs would be (a) self-evident, (b) incorrigible, or (c) evident to the senses. But there are beliefs, argues Plantinga, that are basic but do not meet these standards. He favors a modified foundationalism (Reformed epistemology) where basic beliefs have grounds, that is, stand in relation to justification-conferring conditions as opposed to being justified by being related to other beliefs. (That is to say, not all justification is a matter of a belief or set of beliefs justifying some belief in question. There are justifying conditions that are not beliefs, sometimes called non-doxastic justification.) Unfortunately, Plantinga does not tell us much—in this paper—about just what counts as (non-doxastic) grounds for basic theistic beliefs. He does suggest, however, by the nature of his examples, something of what these would be.

At the end of the selection, Plantinga makes some general comments about fideism, differentiating his view from fideist positions as traditionally conceived. These remarks should prove helpful in forming an overview of the fideism surveyed here.

THE EVIDENTIALIST OBJECTION TO BELIEF IN GOD

My first topic, then, is the evidentialist objection to theistic belief. Many philosophers—W. K. Clifford, Brand Blanshard, Bertrand Russell, Michael Scriven, and Anthony Flew—to name a few—have argued that belief in God is irrational or unreasonable or not rationally acceptable or intellectually irresponsible or somehow noetically below par because, as they say, there is *insufficient evidence* for it. Bertrand Russell was once asked what he would say if, after dying, he were brought into the presence of God and asked why he had not been a believer. Russell's reply: "I'd say 'Not enough evidence God! Not enough evidence!'" We may have our doubts as to just how that sort of response would be received; but Russell, like many others, held that theistic belief is unreasonable because there is insufficient evidence for it. . . .

. . . Interesting is [Karl Barth's] view that belief in God need not be based on argument. Barth joins Calvin and Bavinck in holding that the believer in God is entirely within his rights in believing as he does even if he does not know of any good theistic argument (deductive or inductive), even if he does not believe there is any such argument, and even if in fact no such argument exists. Like Calvin, Kuyper, and Bavinck, Barth holds that belief in God is *properly basic*—that is, such that it is rational to accept it without accepting it on the basis of any other propositions or beliefs at all. In fact, they think the Christian ought not to accept belief in God on the basis of argument; to do so is to run the risk of a faith that is unstable and wavering, subject to all the wayward whim and fancy of the latest academic fashion. What the Reformers held was that a believer is entirely rational, entirely within his epistemic rights, in *starting with* belief in God, in accepting it as basic, and in taking it as premise for argument to other conclusions.

In rejecting natural theology, therefore, these Reformed thinkers mean to say first of all that the propriety or rightness of belief in God in no way depends upon the success or availability of the sort of theistic arguments that form the natural theologian's stock in trade. I think this is their central claim here, and their central insight. As these Reformed thinkers see things, one who takes belief in God as basic is not thereby violating any epistemic duties or revealing a defect in his noetic structure; quite the reverse. The correct or proper way to believe in God, they thought, was not on the basis of arguments from natural theology or anywhere else; the correct way is to take belief in God as basic.

I spoke earlier of classical foundationalism, a view that incorporates the following three theses:

1. In every rational noetic structure there is a set of beliefs taken as basic—that is, not accepted on the basis of any other beliefs,

2. In a rational noetic structure nonbasic belief is proportional to support from the foundations, and

3. In a rational noetic structure basic beliefs will be self-evident or incorrigible or evident to the senses.

Now I think these three Reformed thinkers should be understood as rejecting classical foundationalism. They may have been inclined to accept (1); they show no objection to (2); but they were utterly at odds with the idea that the foundations of a rational noetic structure can at most include propositions that are self-evident or evident to the senses or incorrigible. In particular, they were prepared to insist that a rational noetic structure can include belief in God as basic.

The *Ground* of Belief in God

My claim is that belief in God is properly basic; it does not follow, however, that it is *groundless*. Let me explain. Suppose we consider perceptual beliefs, memory beliefs, and beliefs ascribing mental states to other persons, such beliefs as:

3. I see a tree,

4. I had breakfast this morning, and

5. That person is in pain.

Although beliefs of this sort are typically taken as basic, it would be a mistake to describe them as *groundless*. Upon having experience of a certain sort, I believe that I am perceiving a tree. In the typical case I do not hold this belief on the basis of other beliefs; it is nonetheless not groundless. My having that characteristic sort of experience—to use Professor Chisholm's language, my being appeared treely to—plays a crucial role in the formation of that belief. It also plays a crucial role in its *justification*. Let us say that a belief is *justified* for a person at a time if (a) he is violating no epistemic duties and is within his epistemic rights in accepting it then and (b) his noetic structure is not defective by virtue of his then accepting it. Then my being appeared to in this characteristic way (together with other circumstances) is what confers on me the right to hold the belief in question; this is what justifies me in accepting it. We could say, if we wish, that this experience is what justifies me in holding it; this is the *ground* of my justification, and, by extension, the ground of the belief itself.

If I see someone displaying typical pain behavior, I take it that he or she is in pain. Again, I do not take the displayed behavior as *evidence* for that belief; I do not infer that belief from others I hold; I do not accept it on the basis of other beliefs. Still, my perceiving the pain behavior plays a unique role in the formation and justification of that belief; as in the previous case it forms the ground of my justification for the belief in question. The same holds for memory beliefs. I seem to remember having breakfast this morning; that is, I have an inclination to believe the proposition that I had breakfast, along with a certain past-tinged experience that is familiar to all but hard to describe. Perhaps we should say that I am appeared to pastly; but perhaps that insufficiently distinguishes the experience in question from that accompanying beliefs about the past not grounded in my own memory. The phenomenology of memory is a rich and unexplored realm; here I have no time to explore it. In this case as in the others, however, there is a justifying circumstance present, a condition that forms the ground of my justification for accepting the memory belief in question.

In each of these cases a belief is taken as basic, and in each case *properly* taken as basic. In each case there is some circumstance or condition that confers justification; there is a circumstance that serves as the *ground* of justification. So in each case there will be some true proposition of the sort

(6) In condition *C, S* is justified in taking *p* as basic.

Of course *C* will vary with *p*. For a perceptual judgment such as

(7) I see a rose-colored wall before me

C will include my being appeared to in a certain fashion. No doubt *C* will include more. If I am appeared to in the familiar fashion but know that I am wearing rose-colored glasses, or that I am suffering from a disease that causes me to be thus appeared to, no matter what the color of the nearby objects, then I am not justified in taking (7) as basic. Similarly for memory. Suppose I know that my memory is unreliable; it often plays me tricks. In particular, when I seem to remember having breakfast, then, more often than not, I have not had breakfast. Under these conditions I am not justified in taking it as basic that I had breakfast, even though I seem to remember that I did.

So being appropriately appeared to, in the perceptual case, is not sufficient for justification; some further condition—a condition hard to state in detail—is clearly necessary. The central point here, however, is that a belief is properly basic only in certain conditions; these conditions are, we might say, the ground of its justification and, by extension, the ground of the belief itself. In this sense basic beliefs are not, or are not necessarily, *groundless* beliefs.

Now similar things may be said about belief in God. When the Reformers claim that this belief is properly basic, they do not mean to say, of course, that there are no justifying circumstances for it, or that it is in that sense groundless or gratuitous. Quite the contrary. Calvin holds that God "reveals and daily discloses himself in the whole workmanship of the universe," and the divine art "reveals itself in the innumerable and yet distinct and well ordered variety of the heavenly host." God has so created us that we have a tendency or disposition to see his hand in the world about us. More precisely, there is in us a disposition to believe propositions of the sort *this flower was created by God* or *this vast and intricate universe was created by God* when we contemplate the flower or behold the starry heavens or think about the vast reaches of the universe.

Calvin recognizes, at least implicitly, that other sorts of conditions may trigger this disposition. Upon reading the Bible, one may be impressed with a deep sense that God is speaking to him. Upon having done what I know is cheap, or wrong, or wicked, I may feel guilty in God's sight and form the belief *God disapproves of what I have done.* Upon confession and repentence I may feel forgiven, forming the belief *God forgives me for what I have done.* A person in grave danger may turn to God, asking for his protection and help; and of course he or she then has the belief that God is indeed able to hear and help if he sees fit. When life is sweet and satisfying, a spontaneous sense of gratitude may well up within the soul; someone in this condition may thank and praise the Lord for his goodness, and will of course have the accompanying belief that indeed the Lord is to be thanked and praised.

There are therefore many conditions and circumstances that call forth belief in God: guilt, gratitude, danger, a sense of God's presence, a sense that he speaks, perception of various parts of the universe. A complete job would explore the phenomenology of all these conditions and of more besides. This is a large and important topic, but here I can only point to the existence of these conditions.

Of course none of the beliefs I mentioned a moment ago is the simple belief that God exists. What we have instead are such beliefs as:

8. God is speaking to me,

9. God has created all this,

10. God disapproves of what I have done,

11. God forgives me, and

12. God is to be thanked and praised.

These propositions are properly based in the right circumstances. But it is quite consistent with this to suppose that the proposition *there is such a person as God* is neither properly basic nor taken as basic by those who believe in God. Perhaps what they take as basic are such propositions as (8)–(12), believing in the existence of God on the basis of propositions such as those. From this point of view it is not wholly accurate to say that it is belief in God that is properly basic; more exactly, what are properly basic are such propositions as (8)–(12), each of which self-evidently entails that God exists. It is not the relatively high-level and general proposition *God exists* that is properly basic, but instead propositions detailing some of his attributes or actions. . . .

Fideism

I take up one final question. In *Reflections on Christian Philosophy* Ralph McInerny suggests that what I have been calling Reformed epistemology is *fideism.* Is he right? Is the Reformed epistemologist perforce a fideist? That depends: it depends, obviously enough, on how we propose to use the term "fideism." According to my dictionary fideism is "exclusive or basic reliance upon faith alone, accompanied by a consequent disparagement of reason and utilized especially in the pursuit of philosophical or religious truth." A fideist therefore urges reliance on faith rather than reason, in matters philosophical and religious; and he may go on to disparage and denigrate reason. We may thus distinguish at least two grades of fideism: moderate fideism, according to which we must rely upon faith rather than reason in religious matters, and extreme fideism, which disparages and denigrates reason.

Now let us ask first whether the Reformed epistemologist is obliged to be an extreme fideist. Of course there is more than one way of disparaging reason. One way to do it is to claim that to take a proposition on faith is higher and better than accepting it on the basis of reason. Another way to disparage reason is to follow Kant in holding that reason left to itself inevitably falls into paradox and antinomy on ultimate matters. According to Kant pure reason offers us conclusive argument for supposing that the universe had no beginning, but also, unfortunately, conclusive arguments for the denial of that proposition. I do not think any of the alleged arguments are anywhere nearly conclusive, but if Kant were right, then presumably reason would not deserve to be paid attention to, at least on this topic. According to the most common brand of extreme fideism, however, reason and faith *conflict* or *clash* on matters of religious importance; and when they do, faith is to be preferred and reason suppressed. Thus according to Kierkegaard faith teaches "the absurdity that the eternal is the historical." He means to say, I think, that this proposition is among the deliverances of faith but absurd from the point of view of reason; and it should be accepted despite this absurdity. The turn-of-the-century Russian theologian Shestov carried extreme fideism even further; he held that one can attain religious truth only by rejecting the proposition that $2 + 2 = 4$ and accepting instead $2 + 2 = 5$.

Now it is clear, I suppose, that the Reformed epistemologist need not be an extreme fideist. His views on the proper basicality of belief in God surely do not commit him to thinking that faith and reason conflict. So suppose we ask instead whether the Reformed epistemologist is committed to *moderate* fideism. And again that depends; it depends upon how we propose to use the terms "reason" and "faith." One possibility would be to follow Abraham Kuyper, who proposes to use these terms in such a way that one takes on faith whatever one accepts but does not accept on the basis of argument or inference or demonstration:

> There is thus no objection to the use of the term 'faith' for that function of the soul by which it attains certainty immediately or directly, without the aid of discursive demonstration. This places faith over against demonstration, but *not* over against knowing.

On this use of these terms, anything taken as basic is taken on faith; anything believed on the basis of other beliefs is taken on reason. I take *2 + 1 = 3* as basic; accordingly, I take it on faith. When I am appropriately appeared to, I take as basic such propositions as *I see a tree before me* or *there is a house over there;* on the present construal I take these things on faith. I remember that I had lunch this noon, but do not accept this belief on the basis of other propositions; this too, then, I take on faith. On the other hand, what I take on the basis of reason is what I believe on the basis of argument or inference from other propositions. Thus I take *2 + 1 = 3* on faith, but *21 × 45 = 945* by reason; for I accept the latter on the basis of calculation, which is a form of argument. Further, suppose I accept supralapsarianism or premillennialism or the doctrine of the virgin birth on the grounds that God proposes these doctrines for our belief and God proposes only truths; then on Kuyper's use of these terms I accept these doctrines not by faith but by reason. Indeed, if with Kierkegaard and Shestov I hold that the eternal is the historical and that 2 + 2 = 5 because I believe God proposes *these* things for my belief, then on the present construal I take them not on faith but on the basis of reason.

And here we can see, I think, that Kuyper's use of these terms is not the relevant one for the discussion of fideism. For consider Shestov. Shestov is an extreme fideist because he thinks faith and reason conflict; and when they do, he says, it is reason that must be suppressed. To paraphrase the poem, "When faith and reason clash, let reason go to smash!" But he is not holding that faith teaches something—*2 + 2 = 5*, for example—that conflicts with a belief—*2 + 2 = 4*—that one arrives at by reasoning from other propositions. On the contrary, the poignancy of the clash is just that what faith teaches conflicts with an *immediate* teaching of reason—a proposition that is apparently self-evident. On the Kuyperian use of these terms Shestov would be surprised to learn that he is not a fideist after all. For what he takes faith to conflict with here is not something one accepts by reason—that is, on the basis of other propositions. Indeed, on the Kuyperian account Shestov not only does not qualify as a fideist; he probably qualifies as an antifideist. Shestov probably did not recommend taking *2 + 2 = 5* as basic; he probably held that God proposes this proposition for our belief and that we should therefore accept it. On the other hand, he also believed, no doubt, that *2 + 2 = 4* is apparently self-evident. So given the Kuyperian use, Shestov would be holding that faith and reason conflict here, but it is *2 + 2 = 4* that is the deliverance of faith and *2 + 2 = 5* the deliverance of reason! Since he recommends accepting

2 + 2 = 5, the deliverance of reason, he thus turns out to be a rationalist or antifideist, at least on this point.

And this shows that Kuyper's use of these terms is not the relevant use. What we take on faith is not simply what we take as basic, and what we accept by reason is not simply what we take on the basis of other propositions. The deliverances of reason include propositions taken as basic, and the deliverances of faith include propositions accepted on the basis of others.

The Reformed epistemologist, therefore, is a fideist only if he holds that some central truths of Christianity are not among the deliverances of reason and must instead be taken on faith. But just what are the deliverances of reason? What do they include? First, clearly enough, self-evident propositions and propositions that follow from them by self-evidently valid arguments are among the deliverances of reason. But we cannot stop there. Consider someone who holds that according to correct scientific reasoning from accurate observation the earth is at least a couple of billion years old; nonetheless, he adds, the fact is it is no more than some 6000 years old, since that is what faith teaches. Such a person is a fideist, even though the proposition *the earth is more than 6000 years old* is neither self-evident nor a consequence of what is self-evident. So the deliverances of reason include more than the self-evident and its consequences. They also include basic perceptual truths (propositions "evident to the senses"), incorrigible propositions, certain memory propositions, certain propositions about other minds, and certain moral or ethical propositions.

But what about the belief that there is such a person as God and that we are responsible to him? Is that among the deliverances of reason or an item of faith? For Calvin it is clearly the former. "There is within the human mind, and indeed by natural instinct, an awareness of divinity. . . . God himself has implanted in all men a certain understanding of his divine majesty. . . . men one and all perceive that there is a God and that he is their Maker." (*Institutes* I, 3, 1) According to Calvin everyone, whether in the faith or not, has a tendency or nisus, in certain situations, to apprehend God's existence and to grasp something of his nature and actions. This natural knowledge can be and is suppressed by sin, but the fact remains that a capacity to apprehend God's existence is as much part of our natural noetic equipment as is the capacity to apprehend perceptual truths, truths about the past, and truths about other minds. Belief in the existence of God is in the same boat as belief in other minds, the past, and perceptual objects; in each case God has so constructed us that in the right circumstances we form the belief in question. But then the belief that there is such a person as God is as much among the deliverances of reason as those other beliefs.

From this vantage point we can see, therefore, that the Reformed epistemologist is not a fideist at all with respect to belief in God. He does not hold that there is any conflict between faith and reason here, and he does not even hold that we cannot attain this fundamental truth by reason; he holds, instead, that it is among the deliverances of reason.

Of course the nontheist may disagree; he may deny that the existence of God is part of the deliverances of reason. A former professor of mine for whom I had and have enormous respect once said that theists and nontheists have different conceptions of reason. At the time I did not know what he meant, but now I think I do. On the Reformed view I have been urging, the deliverances of reason include the existence of God just as much as perceptual truths, self-evident truths, memory truths, and the like. It is not that theist and nontheist agree as to what reason delivers, the theist then going on to accept the existence of God by faith; there is, instead, disagreement in the first place as to what are the deliverances of reason. But then the Reformed epistemologist is no more a fideist with respect to belief in God than is, for example, Thomas Aquinas. Like the latter, he will no doubt hold that there are other truths of Christianity that are not to be found among the deliverances of reason—such truths, for example, as that God was in Christ, reconciling the world to himself. But he is not a fideist by virtue of his views on our knowledge of God.

By way of summary: I have argued that the evidentialist objection to theistic belief is rooted in classical foundationalism; the same can be said for the Thomistic conception of faith and reason. Classical foundationalism is attractive and seductive; in the final analysis, however, it turns out to be both false and self-referentially incoherent. Furthermore, the Reformed objection to natural theology, unformed and inchoate as it is, may best be seen as a rejection of classical foundationalism. As the Reformed thinker sees things, being self-evident, or incorrigible, or evident to the senses is not a necessary condition of proper basicality. He goes on to add that belief in God is properly basic. He is not thereby committed to the idea that just any or nearly any belief is properly basic, even if he lacks a criterion for proper basicality. Nor is he committed to the view that argument is irrelevant to belief in God if such belief is properly basic. Furthermore, belief in God, like other properly basic beliefs, is not groundless or arbitrary; it is grounded in justification-conferring conditions. Finally, the Reformed view that belief in God is properly basic is not felicitously thought of as a version of fideism.

DISCUSSION QUESTIONS

1. Explain the anti-rationalism of Lao Tzu. What attitudes does Lao Tzu recommend?

2. What are the limitations of reason, according to William Blake, and what is the importance of poetic imagination?

3. Analyze the combination of existentialist fideism, Romanticism, and negative theology in the selection from Søren Kierkegaard. Find quotations that exhibit each of the themes that you identify.

4. Outline William James's views about the nature and importance of faith as expressed in the selection from his *The Varieties of Religious Experience.*

5. Explain James's views about how different attitudes toward evidence are appropriate in different spheres of human inquiry and practice. Just what constraints, according to James, apply to the religious sphere? Do you agree with him that we have the right to believe religious hypotheses in the hope that the belief will make our lives better?

6. What is distinctive about the Wittgensteinian fideism championed by D. Z. Phillips; in particular, what attitude would such a fideist take toward the non-religious philosopher wondering whether there are religious or spiritual truths such as, "God exists"? What avenues of response do you see as open to such a philosopher?

7. Rehearse Alvin Plantinga's criticism of traditional foundationalism. Why would this critique, according to Plantinga, place certain theistic beliefs in a favorable light, that is, for particular people in particular circumstances? What are the most important issues surrounding the question of just which beliefs are to count as basic for a given individual? (Optionally, how does Plantinga's position differ from other positions surveyed in this section?)

CHAPTER EIGHT

Religion and Ethics

A prevalent view is that there is a tight relation between religion and ethics, so tight, according to some, that to reject religion is to embrace an ethical nihilism. Others, admitting that living ethically does not require religious attitudes, find, however, a converse relation: religious attitudes are essentially ethical. Ethical intentions, they say, are at the core of adopting a Christian or another religious point of view. Or some say ethics provides a perspective from which religions can and should be reformed, bringing, for example, religious teachings into conformity with natural law or ridding a religion of sexist language and patriarchal societal forms. Amerindian religion brings with it an environmental ethics, still others claim, an ethics that could help abate environmental crises.

There is, further, the question of the relationship between mysticism and ethics, as well as normative issues from abortion to treatment of animals. Is a theocentric ethics a coherent option, in particular, a *divine command theory*? Most scholars see a divine command theory (commandments of God as setting ethical standards) as allied with mainstream Western theism. Does this view survive scrutiny? According to some, Plato shows why no divine command theory could be adequate.

In this section, these and other questions will be explored. We shall begin with a selection from David Hume, who attacks religious ethics. For Confucius, or the Confucian position, religious ritual and ceremony are key to developing good character. Zera Yacob, an Ethiopian philosopher of the seventeenth century, argues that an ethical sensibility, in particular an appreciation of God's natural law, provides a standpoint for criticizing religious teachings, and leverage on the competing ethical claims of competing religions—Islam and Christianity especially. R. B. Braithwaite, a non-cognivist who rejects the notion that there are religious facts, sees ethical intentions as the core of a religious commitment. For Aurobindo, there are religious or spiritual facts, to be mystically discovered, but all religious ethical teachings, indeed almost all ethical teachings, are too inflexible and system-bound to be of help to a mystic endeavor. The selections from Plato, from James Hanink and Gary Mar, and from Kai Nielsen address divine command theory. Next we shall take a brief look at an influential feminist critique of sexist God-talk and patriarchal religion, by Mary Daly, then survey the Jaina ethics of *non-injury,* which has been influential in Eastern civilizations, and conclude by reviewing Amerindian ethical attitudes as well as feminist ethics respecting the environment. Amerindian religion is championed by philosophers J. B. Callicott and Thomas Overholt as a possible solution to current crises concerning the environment. Rosemary Radford Ruether finds a nexus of religious, feminist, and ethical attitudes demanded by environmental problems.

"A Frivolous Species of Merit"

From *Dialogues Concerning Natural Religion* by David Hume

David Hume has the character Philo, in his classic dialogue, attack religion at its ethical junctions. (About Philo and other characters of Hume's, see the introductory discussion to the Hume selection entitled "The Teleological Argument" under Arguments for a Divine Reality.) Cleanthes, another character, defends a relationship between religion and ethics. At the end it seems the controversy has concerned only popular religion since Philo finally reveals that even he accepts "philosophic religious attitudes" as commendable with respect to ethical issues. (Is this a sop to Hume's peers, to his eighteenth-century intellectual community?)

Philo, who does most of the talking, rails against what he sees as the effects of religion on society historically, and on individuals, their behavior and character. Scholars tend to think that Philo voices Hume's own opinions. In any case, Philo presents important facets of the early modern debate, and several considerations, too, that seem relevant to contemporary concerns regarding the intersection of ethics and religion.

In particular, Philo finds fear of an afterlife a sentiment unconducive to societal welfare and to development of individual character. Sectarianism and attendant religious wars he cites as urging a negative estimation of the ethical effects of religion. Hume's own ethical theory—which is drawn on by Philo though it is not elaborated—is that the natural emotions of friendship and compassion should be fostered, not piety, which is a "frivolous species of merit."

My inclination, replied CLEANTHES, lies, I own, a contrary way. Religion, however corrupted, is still better than no religion at all. The doctrine of a future state is so strong and necessary a security to morals that we never ought to abandon or neglect it. For if finite and temporary rewards and punishments have so great an effect, as we daily find, how much greater must be expected from such as are infinite and eternal?

How happens it then, said PHILO, if vulgar superstition be so salutary to society, that all history abounds so much with accounts of its pernicious consequences on public affairs? Factions, civil wars, persecutions, subversions of government, oppression, slavery, these are the dismal consequences which always attend its prevalence over the minds of men. If the religious spirit be ever mentioned in any historical narration, we are sure to meet afterwards with a detail of the miseries which attend it. And no period of time can be happier or more prosperous than those in which it is never regarded or heard of.

The reason of this observation, replied CLEANTHES, is obvious. The proper office of religion is to regulate the heart of men, humanize their conduct, infuse the spirit of temperance, order, and obedience; and as its operation is silent and only enforces the motives of morality and justice, it is in danger of being overlooked and confounded with these other motives. When it distinguishes itself and acts as a separate principle over men, it has departed from its proper sphere and has become only a cover to faction and ambition.

And so will all religion, said PHILO, except the philosophical and rational kind. Your reasonings are more easily eluded than my facts. The inference is not just, because finite and temporary rewards and punishments have so great influence that therefore such as are infinite and eternal must have so much greater. Consider, I beseech you, the attachment which we have to present things, and the little concern which we discover for objects so remote and uncertain. When divines are declaiming against the common behavior and conduct of the world, they always represent this principle as the strongest imaginable (which indeed it is), and describe almost all human kind as lying under the influence of it, and sunk into the deepest lethargy and unconcern about their religious interests. Yet these same divines, when they refute their speculative antagonists, suppose the motives of religion to be so powerful that, without them, it were impossible for civil society to subsist; nor are they ashamed of so palpable a contradiction. It is certain, from experience, that the smallest grain of natural honesty and benevolence has more effect on men's conduct than the most pompous views suggested by theological theories and systems. A man's natural inclination works incessantly upon him; it is forever present to the mind, and mingles itself with every view and consideration; whereas religious motives, where they act at all, operate only by starts and bounds, and it is scarcely possible for them to become altogether habitual to the mind. The force of the greatest gravity, say the philosophers, is infinitely small in comparison of that of the least impulse, yet it is certain that the smallest gravity will, in the end, prevail above a great impulse, because no strokes or blows can be repeated with such constancy as attraction and gravitation.

Another advantage of inclination: it engages on its side all the wit and ingenuity of the mind, and when set in opposition to religious principles seeks every method and art of eluding them; in which it is almost always successful. Who can explain the heart of man, or account for those strange salvos and excuses with which people satisfy themselves when they follow their inclinations in opposition to their religious duty? This is well understood in the world; and none but fools ever repose less trust in a man because they hear that, from study and philosophy, he has entertained some speculative doubts with regard to theological subjects. And when we have to do with a man who makes a great profession of religion and devotion, has this any other effect upon several who pass for prudent than to put them on their guard, lest they be cheated and deceived by him?

We must further consider that philosophers, who cultivate reason and reflection, stand less in need of such motives to keep them under the restraint of morals, and that the vulgar, who alone may need them, are utterly incapable of so pure a religion as represents the Deity to be pleased with nothing but virtue in human behavior. The recommendations to the Divinity are generally supposed to be either frivolous observances or rapturous ecstasies or a bigoted credulity. We need not run back into antiquity or wander into remote regions to find instances of this degeneracy. Amongst ourselves, some have been guilty of that atrociousness, unknown to the Egyptian and Grecian superstitions, of declaiming, in express terms, against morality, and representing it as a sure forfeiture of the divine favor if the least trust or reliance be laid upon it.

But even though superstition or enthusiasm should not put itself in direct opposition to morality, the very diverting of the attention, the raising up a new and frivolous species of merit, the preposterous distribution which it makes of praise and blame, must have the most pernicious consequences, and weaken extremely men's attachment to the natural motives of justice and humanity.

Such a principle of action likewise, not being any of the familiar motives of human conduct, acts only by intervals on the temper, and must be roused by continual efforts in order to render the pious zealot satisfied with his own conduct and make him fulfil his devotional task. Many religious exercises are entered into with seeming fervor where the heart, at the time, feels cold and languid. A habit of dissimulation is by degrees contracted, and fraud and falsehood become the predominant principle. Hence the reason of that vulgar observation that the highest zeal in religion and the deepest hypocrisy, so far from being inconsistent, are often or commonly united in the same individual character.

The bad effects of such habits, even in common life, are easily imagined; but where the interests of religion are concerned, no morality can be forcible enough to bind the enthusiastic zealot. The sacredness of the cause sanctifies every measure which can be made use of to promote it.

The steady attention alone to so important an interest as that of eternal salvation is apt to extinguish the benevolent affections, and beget a narrow, contracted selfishness. And when such a temper is encouraged, it easily eludes all the general precepts of charity and benevolence.

Thus the motives of vulgar superstition have no great influence on general conduct, nor is their operation favorable to morality, in the instances where they predominate.

Is there any maxim in politics more certain and infallible than that both the number and authority of priests should be confined within very narrow limits, and that the civil magistrate ought, forever, to keep his *fasces* and *axes* from such dangerous hands? But if the spirit of popular religion were so salutary to society, a contrary maxim ought to prevail. The greater number of priests and their greater authority and riches will always augment the religious spirit. And though the priests have the guidance of this spirit, why may we not expect a superior sanctity of life and greater benevolence and moderation from persons who are set apart for religion, who are continually inculcating it upon others, and who must themselves imbibe a greater share of it? Whence comes it then, that in fact the utmost a wise magistrate can propose with regard to popular religions is, as far as possible, to make a saving game of it, and to prevent their pernicious consequences with regard to society? Every expedient which he tries for so humble a purpose is surrounded with inconveniences. If he admits only one religion among his subjects, he must sacrifice, to an uncertain prospect of tranquillity, every consideration of public liberty, science, reason, industry, and even his own independence. If he gives indulgence to several sects, which is the wiser maxim, he must preserve a very philosophical indifference to all of them, and carefully restrain the pretensions of the prevailing sect; otherwise he can expect nothing but endless disputes, quarrels, factions, persecutions, and civil commotions.

Confucius on Religious Ritual and Virtue

From *Disputers of the Tao* by A. C. Graham, 1989

As mentioned in the general introduction, Confucius (551–479 BCE) was the first great Chinese philosopher, so influential especially in his ethical and political philosophy that he is often said to be the father of Chinese civilization. His view of the proper relationship between ethics and religion is instructive in its own right but is also interesting for its contrasts and similarities with Western ideas about these matters.

There are several important ethical themes in Confucius's teaching, and scholars oversimplify when they point to a formulation of what Christians call the Golden Rule, or to jen *(humanity), or to ceremony and politeness, as a single key to his ethical system. These elements, and others, interlock in a complex teaching.*

A distinctive facet is nonetheless an emphasis on appropriateness, on what might be called good manners and an instinctual propriety. Learning music and practicing ceremony and religious ritual are viewed as ways a sense of appropriateness becomes native to one's character. This is what is meant by the contrast, often appearing in Confucius's texts, between learning and mere thinking. Learning involves following an established pattern; thinking does not.

Confucius has a humanist orientation; he is not interested in such questions as whether there is survival of death. Ideas of an afterlife have no place in his ethics. However, he apparently does see moral law as grounded in the pervasive spirituality he calls Heaven. But this grounding is not a matter of Divine commandments.

The selection is from A. C. Graham (1919–1991) who has been called the leading twentieth-century authority on classical Chinese thought. Graham quotes profusely from Confucius's Analects *while reconstructing Confucius's ethical and political philosophy.*

CEREMONY AND MUSIC

Let us start with Confucius as he sees himself, the preserver and restorer of a declining culture, who would not presume to invent anything.

"In transmitting but not originating, trusting in and loving the ancient, I would venture to compare myself to our old P'eng." (*Analects* 7/1)

In studying the *Documents* and *Songs* of early Chou, and the ceremonies and music, Confucius recognises the importance of thinking, but is inclined to put the stress rather on learning.

"To learn without thinking is stultifying, to think without learning is dangerous." (2/15)

"I used to go without food all day, without sleep all night, to think. No use, better to learn." (15/31)

"My disciples, why does none of you learn the *Songs?* The *Songs* may be used to stir imagination, to become observant, to get people together, to complain, at home in serving your father and abroad in serving your lord; and you will remember many names of birds, animals, plants and trees." (17/9)

This may seem an unpromising beginning to a philosophical tradition, but let us continue. The institutions which for Confucius are central to Chou culture are its ceremony and its music. The word *li* 'ceremony' embraces all rites, custom, manners, conventions, from the sacrifices to ancestors down to the detail of social etiquette. *Li* in social intercourse corresponds to a considerable extent with Western conceptions of good manners; the Confucian gentleman moves with an effortless grace within the framework of fixed convention, informing every action with consideration and respect for the other person. *Yüeh* ('music'), which embraces dance, is primarily the music and dance of sacred rites; correspondingly, ceremony is continuous with music in being conducted with style like an artistic performance. What above all distinguishes *li* from Western conceptions of good manners is that for Confucius it has everywhere the efficacy of sacred rite, an efficacy in transforming human relations which is independent of the powers to which explicitly religious rituals are addressed.

The enormous importance which Confucius ascribes to ceremony by no means implies that he identifies the ritual with the moral. He has a different word, *yi* (related to another *yi* 'fitting'), for the right, which is conceived as the conduct fitting to one's role or status, for example as father or son, ruler or minister.

"It is the right which the gentleman deems the substance, it is through ceremony that he performs it, through humility that he expresses it, through being trustworthy that he perfects it, the gentleman!" (15/18)

"If those above love ceremony, none of the people will presume to be irreverent; if they love the right, none will presume to disobey; if they love trustworthiness, none will presume to be insincere." (13/4)

The effect of ceremonial forms in the social hierarchy is, as this last passage implies, that instead of actions merely being fitted to each other as right (the people *obeying* the ruler) attitudes become harmonious (the people *revering* the ruler).

"The disciple Yu-tzu said 'In the employment of ceremony it is harmony which is most to be valued. In the Way of the former kings it is this which is most beautiful, follow it in small things and great. Where things are not on course, if you harmonise by the knowledge of harmony without regulating it by ceremony, they still cannot be put on course." (1/12)

Music no doubt also inspires this harmony, although Confucius never theorises about its overwhelming effect on himself.

"The Master while in Ch'i heard the Shao, and for three months did not notice the taste of meat. He said 'I did not conceive that making music had reached such heights.'" (7/14)

Chapter 10 of the *Analects* records detailed observations of the Master's own ceremonial performance.

"When summoned by his lord to serve as usher, his expression was serious, his step brisk. When with clasped hands he bowed to his colleagues on left and right, his robes moved evenly in front and behind. His hurrying advance was a glide. When the guest withdrew he would invariably announce, 'The guest no longer looks back.'" (10/2)

Although there are later ritualist texts which prescribe such details, Confucius himself never lays down rules about them. It may be presumed that his disciples noted points in the performance of the supreme artist in ceremony of which he would perhaps not himself be conscious, as refinements of a personal style from which one could learn without necessarily imitating him. There are items in the series in which his good manners plainly have nothing to do with prescribed forms.

"The stable caught fire. On returning from court the Master said 'Is anyone hurt?' He did not ask about the horses." (10/11)

The past to which Confucius looks back is not the beginning of things; there is no cosmogonic myth in pre-Han literature, merely a blank of pre-history before the first Emperors, who for Confucius are the pre-dynastic sages Yao and Shun. Although interested in the institutions of all the Three Dynasties which followed he draws primarily on the last, the Chou, the one of which the tradition is not yet extinct. Indeed he sees history down to the Chou not as regress but as progress.

"Chou had the two earlier dynasties as examples to it. How glorious is its culture! I follow Chou." (3/14)

In spite of this fidelity to Chou he sees the rebuilding of contemporary culture as a process of selecting and evaluating past and present models.

"The Master called the Shao music both perfectly beautiful and perfectly good. He called the Wu music perfectly beautiful but not perfectly good." (3/25)

"Lin Fang asked about the basic in ceremony. The Master said 'An excellent question! In ceremony prefer the thrifty to the extravagant, in mourning put grief before meticulousness.'" (3/4)

Elsewhere we see him applying the former of these critical principles to a traditional observance.

"To wear a hempen cap is the ceremony, but the blank silk cap of today is thriftier, so I follow the majority. To prostrate oneself before ascending the steps is the ceremony, but today people prostrate themselves at the top, which is lax; even at the cost of diverging from the majority I do it before ascending." (9/3)

GOVERNMENT AS CEREMONY

A pair of concepts first prominent in the *Analects* is *Tao* 'the Way' and *te* 'Potency'. In this text *Tao* is used only of the proper course of human conduct and of the organisation of government, which is the Way of 'antiquity', of 'the former kings', of 'the gentleman', of 'the good man' and of 'Wen and Wu' the founders of Chou, or else of what someone teaches as the Way ('my Way', and 'our master's Way'). Confucius does not use it, as Confucians as well as Taoists soon came to do, of the course of the natural world outside man. *Te*, which has often been translated as 'virtue' (to be understood as in 'The virtue of cyanide is to poison' rather than in 'Virtue is its own reward'), had been traditionally used of the power, whether benign or baleful, to move others without exerting physical force. Confucius uses it in this sense of the charisma of Chou which won it universal allegiance, but moralises and widens the concept, so that it becomes the capacity to act according to and bring others to the Way.

The two concepts are interdependent, as later in *Lao-tzu* (also entitled *Tao te ching* 'Classic of the Way and of Potency'); a person's *te* is his potentiality to act according to the *Tao*.

"One not persistent in maintaining Potency, not sincere in his trust in the Way, how can you tell whether he is there or he isn't?" (19/2)

"Be intent on the Way, be grounded in Potency, rely on nobility, take recreation in the arts." (7/6)

An extremely remarkable feature of Confucius' thought is his conviction that all government can be reduced to ceremony. In a state which has the Way the ruler wins the reverent submission of all by ceremony alone without the need of force, through the Potency which emanates from his person. In an age when government was detaching itself more and more from the ritual functions of kings this indeed looks like a reversion to an obsolete past of primitive magic . . . the early Chou *Documents* already give great weight to penal law.

"Are you capable of ruling the state by ceremony and deference? Then what difficulties will you have? If you are incapable of ruling the state by ceremony and deference, what have you to do with ceremony?" (4/13)

"If you guide them by government, hold them even by punishment, the people will elude you and have no shame. If you guide them by Potency, hold them even by ceremony, the people will both have shame and draw near you." (2/3)

Confucius accepts law as belonging to the apparatus of government, but measures success in ruling by how little it is necessary to apply it.

"In hearing litigation I am no different from others, but the point is surely to bring it about that there is no litigation!" (12/13)

"Chi-k'ang-tzu asked Confucius about government: 'What if we were to execute those without the Way to get nearer to those who have it?'

'When you engage in government,' Confucius answered, 'what need have you for executions? If you desire to be good the people will be good. The gentleman's Potency is the wind, the small man's Potency is the grass. The grass in the wind from above is sure to bend.'" (12/19)

Although Confucius protests at excessive taxation and recognises the need to enrich the people before expecting them to respond to teaching, he sees the radical cure of social ills, not indeed in simply returning to Chou institutions, but in arranging the ideal court ceremonial by a critical selection from the rituals of the Three Dynasties, Hsia, Yin or Shang, and Chou.

"Yen Yüan asked about ruling a state. The Master said 'Put into effect the calendar of Hsia, ride the carriage of Yin, wear the cap of Chou. For music, the Shao and Wu. Banish the airs of Cheng and keep glib people at a distance. The airs of Cheng are wanton, glib people are dangerous.'" (15/11)

Ideally the ruler should not have to do anything at all, simply trust to the Potency which radiates from him. Confucius once even uses the term *wu wei* 'doing nothing' later to become characteristic of Taoism.

"One who put in order by doing nothing, would not that be Shun? What is there that he did? Just assumed a respectful posture and faced south." (15/5)

"One who engages in government by Potency may be compared to the North Star; it occupies its place and all the stars pay homage to it." (2/1)

This can hardly be intended as practical politics, but there is no question of his confidence in Potency as a universal civilizing influence.

"The Master wished to live among the barbarian Nine Tribes. Someone said 'They're uncouth, what about that?' He said 'If a gentleman lived among them what uncouthness would there be?'" (9/14)

This is not quite the faith in the universal influence of the good man which Mencius was later to support by his doctrine of the goodness of human nature. It is rather a faith in the power of trained manners, customs, and rituals to harmonise attitudes and open the inferior to the influence of the superior. His single reference to human nature emphasises not man's goodness but his malleability.

"The Master said 'By nature we are near to each other, by habituation we diverge.' The Master said 'Only the highest wisdom and lowest folly do not shift.'" (17/2)

HEAVEN AND THE SPIRITS

When in the 17th and 18th centuries Confucius first attracted attention in the West many saw him as a rationalist sceptical of the existence of supernatural beings. To Westerners preoccupied with the emerging conflict between reason and religion this seemed the obvious interpretation. It took some time to appreciate that, except for the Mohists, no one in ancient China much cared whether consciousness survives death or whether Heaven is a personal God or impersonal principle, issues of overwhelming importance to Jesuits and *philosophes*. The attitude of Confucius is that we should not be diverted from human affairs by matters which do not concern us. There is no reason to question that he recognises the sacrifices to Heaven, mountain and river gods, and ghosts of ancestors, as the greatest of ceremonies, harmonising not only man with man but man with cosmos. But for him the value of ceremony is in the harmony itself and does not depend on anything outside. He is not interested in how the sacrifices relate us to cosmos; our business is with man, and to speculate about the realm of the numinous is idle curiosity. It is not so much that he is a sceptic as that he does not care whether you are a sceptic or not.

"The Master did not talk about marvels, feats of strength, irregularities, gods." (7/21)

"Chi-lu asked about serving the ghosts and gods. The master said, 'Until you can serve men how can you serve the ghosts?'

'Permit me to ask about death.'

'Until you know about life how can you know about death?'" (11/12)

"Fan Ch'ih asked about wisdom. The Master said 'To work at doing right for the people, and to be reverent to the ghosts and gods but keep them at a distance, may be called wisdom." (6/22)

"He sacrificed as though they were present, sacrificed to gods as though the gods were present. The Master said 'Unless I involve myself in the sacrifice it is as though I did not sacrifice.'" (3/12)

A story in a Han anthology of largely pre-Han material, unlikely to be genuine but very typically Confucian, has the Master judging the propriety of questions about the spirits entirely by the consequences for human behaviour.

"Tzu-kung asked Confucius whether the dead have knowledge or not. Confucius said: 'If I preferred to say that they do have knowledge, I am afraid that filial sons and obedient grandsons would hinder life to send off the dead. If I preferred to say that they do not, I am afraid that unfilial offspring would abandon the dead without burial. If you wish to know whether the dead have knowledge or not, delaying until death to know it for yourself you still won't be too late.'"

The shift of attention to the human realm, and refusal to speculate outside its range, became general throughout the age of the philosophers. The question whether "the dead have knowledge" is raised occasionally, but in terms of whether ghosts can harm the living, not of personal survival; the only kind of immortality welcomed, when the prospect of it was conceived in the 3rd century B.C., is the prolongation of life by elixirs, not survival as a ghost. Some, including the Confucian Hsün-tzu, take it for granted that consciousness ends at death. Otherwise, except by the Mohists, who do argue at length that the dead are conscious, the issue is left open and treated as a theme for wit rather than serious argument. Thus in a story which turns up in the 3rd century B.C. a king of Ch'u is about to sacrifice two prisoners of war in order to smear his battle drums with their blood; they escape this fate by arguing

"If the dead lack knowledge, it will be pointless to use us to smear the drums; if they do have knowledge, when you are about to go into battle we shall stop the drums sounding." . . .

THE THREAD WHICH UNIFIES MORALITY

Until very recently most Western readers of Confucius tried to detach his moral thinking from its bedding in ceremony, which they discarded if not as dross then at any rate as significant only within Chinese society. The major Confucian virtue *jen,* commonly translated 'benevolence', an unselfish concern for the welfare of others, can indeed from Mencius onwards be understood in detachment from ceremony. But the translation 'benevolence' is not appropriate to the *Analects* itself, where Confucius is forming a new concept by adapting an old word to his own insights. *Jen* had been the stative verb corresponding to the noun *jen* which the aristocratic clans of Chou used to distinguish themselves from the common people. Thus in two of the *Songs* a lady admires a man riding out to hunt as "handsome and martial", "handsome and strong", "Handsome and *jen* (noble, lordly)". By the time of Confucius the noun *jen* was widening to the ordinary word for a human being. But throughout the history of Imperial China there was some hesitation in applying the noun to include barbarians, although it was always understood (as already by Confucius) that they are civilizable by the adoption of Chinese customs; genetically they are *jen,* but until civilized they tend to be classed rather with the beasts and birds. The noble, civilized, fully human, pride themselves on their manners and conventions, but above all on the virtues which give these meaning and which distinguish themselves from the boors and savages who do not know how to behave. The stative verb *jen*, as it was inherited by Confucius, covers like English 'noble' the whole range of superior qualities distinctive of the man of breeding. Granted that it is coming to mean 'human, humane' rather than 'noble', it may be convenient to stay with 'noble' as the *ad hoc* equivalent in the present chapter; being nearer to the older meaning, it suggests the sort of concept which Confucius is narrowing in the direction of benevolence. In any case he finds human qualities at their full flower only in the *chün-tzu* ('lord's son'), a word with very much the same social and moral range as English 'gentleman'. Its opposite is *hsiao-jen* 'small man', 'vulgar man'.

Confucius more than once joins the stative verb with the noun, for example,

"A noble who is ignoble (= a human who is inhuman), what has he to do with ceremony? A noble who is ignoble, what has he to do with music?" (3/3)

At the source of the varied qualities which distinguish the noble is a disinterested concern for the other person.

"Chung-kung asked about being noble (= human). The master said 'Behave abroad as though welcoming an important guest, employ the people as though conducting an important sacrifice. What you do not yourself desire do not do to others. No one in the state will resent you, no one in the family will resent you." (12/2)

Here, in the middle of the usual ceremonial references, we come on the grand generalisation, "What you do not yourself desire do not do to others", the negative form of the Golden Rule at the heart of ethics, which in the West too sprang from a mind not much inclined to analysis, that of Jesus. Confucius, who generally gives the impression of synthesising a view of life from the contemplation of rites, texts, pieces of music, persons in legend or history rather than of abstracting ideas, does have a universal pattern running through his teaching.

"The Master said 'Tzu-kung, do you think of me as someone who has learned a lot and retained it?'

'Yes,' he answered, 'Is that wrong?'

'Wrong, I have one thread running through it.'" (15/3)

"Tzu-kung asked 'Is there a single word which one could act on all one's life?' The Master said 'Wouldn't it be likening-to-oneself (*shu*)? What you do not yourself desire do not do to others.'" (15/24)

Shu is one of the phonetic cognates of *ju* 'be like' which are basic to analogical thinking in Chinese, and is written with the same graph distinguished by the 'heart' radical which tends to mark verbs of thinking and feeling ('thinking of [self and other] as alike'). The art of definition developed only gradually throughout the classical period, but towards the end of it we find it neatly defined in the syncretistic *Shih-tzu*.

"Likening-to-oneself is using one's own person to measure. What you do not yourself desire do not do to others, what you dislike in others reject in yourself, what you desire in others seek in yourself, this is likening-to-oneself."

Also illuminating are Hsün-tzu's three rhymed slogans for *shu*.

"For the gentleman there are three sorts of likening-to-oneself.

Being unable to serve your lord
Yet expecting obedience from a servant
is failure to liken-to-oneself.

Being unable to give parents their due
Yet expecting sons to be filial
is failure to liken-to-oneself.

Being unable to be respectful to an elder brother
Yet expecting a younger to take orders from you
is failure to liken-to-oneself.

If a knight is clear about these three sorts of likening-to-oneself it will be possible for him to correct his person."

Although only the negative side of the Golden Rule is included in the formulation the positive is also affirmed.

"The Master said: 'Tseng-tzu, I have one thread running through my Way.' Tseng-tzu assented. When the master went out the disciples asked 'What did he mean?'

'The Master's Way', said Tseng-tzu, 'is nothing but doing-one's-best-for-others (*chung*) and likening-to-oneself (*shu*).'" (4/15)

Chung is used especially of devoted loyalty to a ruler, but also of wholeheartedness on behalf of inferiors. It is a phonetic cognate of *chung* 'centre', the graph as with *shu* being distinguished by the 'heart' radical. The fullest collection of early Confucian definitions, by Chia Yi in the 2nd century B.C., has

"Concern for and benefiting issuing right from the centre of you is called *chung*."

While *shu* is not a virtue but a form of analogical thinking, *chung* is one of the Confucian virtues, displayed on behalf of others in general and of one's prince in particular. For the disciple Tseng-tzu at least, the one thread cannot be quite reduced to a single concept; there has to be both the wholeheartedness on behalf of others and the act of putting oneself in their places by which one learns what to do for them.

It is this single thread which unifies courage, reverence, and the other dispositions which are distinctively noble or human.

"Fan Ch'ih asked about being noble. The Master said 'One is concerned for others.' He asked about being wise. The Master said 'One knows others.' (12/22)

Jen as such does not imply knowledge; indeed, in observing that all virtues go astray without learning, Confucius gives as one illustration,

"To love nobility more than learning deludes one into foolishness." (17/8)

Jen is not sufficient for sagehood, which requires knowledge and ability as well.

"Tzu-kung said 'What of someone who by his bounty to all the people is capable of helping everyone? May he be called noble?'

'Is that to do with being noble?', said the Master. 'With sagehood surely. Even Yao and Shun would have trouble with that. As for the noble, himself desiring to stand up he stands others up, himself desiring to get through he gets others through. The ability to find the analogy in the nearest may be called the secret of nobility.'" (6/30)

Here the attitude to others which springs from likening them to oneself is presented not in negative but in positive terms.

A striking feature of Confucius' treatment of *jen* is that he does not see it as a matter of degree. Either you have it or you don't; and even in most of the best of us it is only intermittent. He says of his own disciples:

"In the case of Yen Yüan, his heart for three months at a time does not go off course from being noble. As for the rest of them, they attain it only for a day or a month." (6/7)

One should perhaps see *jen* as the orientation which makes right action effortless, following attainment of just the right balance between self and others, a precarious balance which hardly anyone is able to sustain. The perfectly and permanently disinterested person being a very rare creature, Confucius is cautious in recognising even the greatest men as *jen*, and disclaims it of himself. It seems however that since it is a matter of attuning the desires on behalf of self and others, when you do have *jen* it comes effortlessly and instantaneously:

"Is nobility so far away? As soon as I desire to be noble, nobility arrives." (7/30)

To identify the one thread unifying the ceremonial raises the possibility of treating it as a principle wholly detached from ceremony, which becomes mere social convention. This was what Mo-tzu was soon to do, subjecting all conventions to the principle of concern for everyone and the test of practical utility. But such a detachment from tradition and custom always remained foreign to Confucianism. For Confucius the instant in which you conquer self to see self and others in perfect proportion is an instant in which accord with conventions becomes effortless and the exercise of style within fixed forms is an uninterrupted flow. The achievement of *jen* results immediately from 'return to ceremony' (*fu li*), which may be understood as the recovery of the meaning of ceremony by which it ceases to be mere formality.

"Yen Yüan asked about the noble. The Master said 'By conquest of self returning to ceremony one becomes noble. If by conquest of self you return to ceremony for a single day, the whole world will acknowledge you as noble. Becoming noble derives from oneself, not from others!'

'I would ask you to itemise it'.

'What isn't according to ceremony don't look at, don't listen to, don't say, don't do.'" (12/1)

God and the Natural Good

From *The Treatise of Zera Yacob* by Zera Yacob in *The Source of African Philosophy* by Claude Sumner, 1986

Ethiopia has a rich ancient civilization, in evidence not only, as with the rest of sub-Saharan Africa, in stores of folklore and traditional wisdom and practices but also in old inscriptions and slightly less ancient texts—written in Sabaean (first century CE) and Geez (from the third century). Geez literature spans more than fifteen hundred years and is continuous with contemporary Amharic, the language of central Ethiopia and its capital,

Addis Ababa. A great flowering of Geez literature, particularly poetry, occurred in the sixteenth century. The philosopher Zera Yacob (1599–1692) was steeped in the tradition of qene, *poems and hymns usually devotional in content.*

Zera Yacob's seventeenth century in Ethiopia was marked by political and religious strife. Competing traditions of Christianity, some sponsored by European states, along with incursions of Judaism and Islam, fed open political conflicts. At age 27, Zera Yacob was denounced by a Catholic advisor to a recently converted prince and had to flee for his life. For two years he hid in a cave. Returning to society, Yacob found a merchant patron, tutored his sons, and married his maidservant. One of the sons, Walda Heywat, asked Zera Yacob to write down his philosophical views; The Treatise of Zera Yacob *was the result.*

The book's Geez title, Hatäta, *means inquiry. Yacob inquires into the grounds of religious and ethical teachings and practices. He finds these to be the law of God as evident in the constitution of nature. The proposition that God's creation is good is Yacob's guiding light. Or, we may say, his guiding light is human reason, the faculty that, on this view, God has given humans to discern what is right. Human reason tracks God's law as revealed in nature, not in books. Zera Yacob upholds natural law against religious teachings deriving from special revelations. Religious teachings often contradict one another, but human reason is capable of figuring out what is the right course to follow, that is, on the assumption, itself supported by natural evidence, that God's arrangement of nature is good. For example, religions have enjoined fasting and other forms of asceticism. But in being opposed to the grain of nature, such teachings cannot be correct.*

THE LAW OF MOSES AND THE MEDITATION OF MOHAMMED

To the person who seeks it, truth is immediately revealed. Indeed he who investigates with the pure intelligence set by the creator in the heart of each man and scrutinizes the order and laws of creation will discover the truth. Moses said: "I have been sent by God to proclaim to you his will and his law"; but those who came after him added stories of miracles that they claimed had been wrought in Egypt and on Mount Sinai and attributed them to Moses. But to an inquisitive mind they do not seem to be true. For in the Books of Moses, one can find a wisdom that is shameful and that fails to agree with the wisdom of the creator or with the order and the laws of creation. Indeed by the will of the creator, and the law of nature, it has been ordained that man and woman would unite in a carnal embrace to generate children, so that human beings will not disappear from the earth. Now this mating, which is willed by God in his law of creation, cannot be impure since God does not stain the work of his own hands. But Moses considered that act as evil; but our intelligence teaches us that he who says such a thing is wrong and makes his creator a liar. Again they said that the law of Christianity is from God, and miracles are brought forth to prove it. But our intelligence tells and confirms to us with proofs that marriage springs from the law of the creator; and yet monastic law renders this wisdom of the creator ineffectual, since it prevents the generation of children and extinguishes mankind. The law of Christians which propounds the superiority of monastic life over marriage is false and cannot come from

God. How can the violation of the law of the creator stand superior to his wisdom, or can man's deliberation correct the word of God? Similarly Mohammed said: "The orders I pass to you are given to me by God"; and there was no lack of writers to record miracles proving Mohammed's mission, and people believed in him. But we know that the teaching of Mohammed could not have come from God; those who will be born both male and female are equal in number; if we count men and women living in an area, we find as many women as men; we do not find eight or ten women for every man; for the law of creation orders one man to marry one woman. If one man marries ten women, then nine men will be without wives. This violates the order of creation and the laws of nature and it ruins the usefulness of marriage; Mohammed, who taught in the name of God, that one man could marry many wives, is not sent from God. These few things I examined about marriage.

Similarly when I examine the remaining laws, such as the Pentateuch, the law of the Christians and the law of Islam, I find many things which disagree with the truth and the justice of our creator that our intelligence reveals to us. God indeed has illuminated the heart of man with understanding by which he can see the good and evil, recognize the licit and the illicit, distinguish truth from error, "and by your light we see the light, oh Lord"! If we use this light of our heart properly, it cannot deceive us; the purpose of this light which our creator gave us is to be saved by it, and not to be ruined by it. Everything that the light of our intelligence shows us comes from the source of truth, but what men say comes from the source of lies and our intelligence teaches us that all that the creator established is right. The creator in his kind wisdom has made blood to flow monthly from the womb of women. And the life of a woman requires this flow of blood in order to generate children; a woman who has no menstruation is barren and cannot have children, because she is impotent by nature. But Moses and Christians have defiled the wisdom of the creator; Moses even considers impure all the things that such a woman touches; this law of Moses impedes marriage and the entire life of a woman and it spoils the law of mutual help, prevents the bringing up of children and destroys love. Therefore this law of Moses cannot spring from him who created woman. Moreover, our intelligence tells us that we should bury our dead brothers. Their corpses are impure only if we follow the wisdom of Moses; they are not, however, if we follow the wisdom of our creator who made us out of dust that we may return to dust. God does not change to impurity the order he imposes on all creatures with great wisdom, but man attempts to render it impure that he may glorify the voice of falsehood.

The gospel also declares: "He who does not leave behind father, mother, wife and children is not worthy of God." This forsaking corrupts the nature of man. God does not accept that his creature destroy itself, and our intelligence tells us that abandoning our father and our mother helpless in their old age is a great sin; the Lord is not a god that loves malice; those who desert their children are worse than the wild animals, that never forsake their offspring. He who abandons his wife abandons her to adultery and thus violates the order of creation and the laws of nature. Hence what the Gospel says on this subject cannot come from God. Likewise the Mohammedans said that it is right to go and buy a man as if he were an animal. But with our intelligence we understand that this Mohammedan law cannot come from the creator of man who made us equal, like brothers, so that we call our creator our father. But Mohammed made the weaker man the possession of the stronger and equated a rational creature with irrational animals; can this depravity be attributed to God?

God does not order absurdities, nor does he say: "Eat this, do not eat that; today eat, tomorrow do not eat; do not eat meat today, eat it tomorrow," unlike the Christians who follow the laws of fasting. Neither did God say to the Mohammedans: "Eat during the night, but do not eat during the day," nor similar and like things. Our reason teaches us that we should eat of all things which do no harm to our health and our nature, and that we should eat each day as much as is required for our sustenance. Eating one day, fasting the next endangers health; the law of fasting reaches beyond the order of the creator who created food for the life of man and wills that we eat it and be grateful for it; it is not fitting that we abstain from his gifts to us. If there are people who argue that fasting kills the desire of the flesh, I shall answer them: "The concupiscence of the flesh by which a man is attracted to a woman and a woman to a man springs from the wisdom of the creator; it is improper to do away with it; but we should act according to the well-known law that God established concerning legitimate intercourse. God did not put a purposeless concupiscence into the flesh of men and of all animals; rather he planted it in the flesh of man as a root of life in this world and a stabilizing power for each creature in the way destined for it. In order that this concupiscence lead us not to excess, we should eat according to our needs, because overeating and drunkenness result in ill health and shoddiness in work. A man who eats according to his needs on Sunday and during the fifty days does not sin, similarly he who eats on Friday and on the days before Easter does not sin. For God created man with the same necessity for food on each day and during each month. The Jews, the Christians and the Mohammedans did not understand the work of God when they instituted the law of fasting; they lie when they say that God imposed fasting upon us and forbade us to eat; for God our creator gave us food that we support ourselves by it, not that we abstain from it.

THE LAW OF GOD AND THE LAW OF MAN

I said to myself: "Why does God permit liars to mislead his people?" God has indeed given reason to all and everyone so that they may know truth and falsehood, and the power to choose between the two as they will. Hence if it is truth we want, let us seek it with our reason which God has given us so that with it we may see that which is needed for us from among all the necessities of nature. We cannot, however, reach truth through the doctrine of man, for all men are liars. If on the contrary we prefer falsehood, the order of the creator and the natural law imposed on the whole of nature do not perish thereby, but we ourselves perish by our own error. God sustains the world by his order which he himself has established and which man cannot destroy, because the order of God is stronger than the order of men. Therefore those who believe that monastic life is superior to marriage are they themselves drawn to marriage because of the might of the order of the creator; those who believe the fasting brings righteousness to their soul eat when they feel hungry; and those who believe that he who has given up his goods is perfect are drawn to seek them again on account of their usefulness, as many of our monks have done. Likewise all liars would like to break the order of nature: but it is not possible that they do not see their lie broken down. But the creator laughs at them, the Lord of creation derides them. God knows the right way to act, but the sinner is caught in the snare set by himself. Hence a monk who holds the order of marriage as impure will be caught in the snare of fornication and of other carnal sins against nature and of grave sickness. Those who despise riches will show their hypocrisy in the presence of kings and of wealthy persons in order to acquire these goods. Those who desert their relatives for the sake of God lack temporal assistance in times of difficulty and in their old age, they begin to blame God and man and to blaspheme. Likewise all those who violate the law of the creator fall into the trap made by their own hands. God permits error and evil among men because our souls in this world live in a land of temptation, in which the chosen ones of God are put to the test, as the wise Solomon said: "God has put the virtuous to the test and proved them worthy to be with him; he has tested them like gold in a furnace, and accepted them as a holocaust." After our death, when we go back to our creator, we shall see how God made all things in justice and great wisdom and that all of his ways are truthful and upright. It is clear that our soul lives after the death of our flesh; for in this world our desire for happiness is not fulfilled; those in need desire to possess, those who possess desire more, and though man owned the whole world, he is not satisfied and craves for more. This inclination of our nature shows us that we are created not only for this life, but also for the coming world; there the souls which have fulfilled the will of the creator will be perpetually satisfied and will not look for other things. Without this inclination the nature of man would be deficient and would not obtain that of which it has the greatest need. Our soul has the power of having the concept of God and of seeing him mentally; likewise it can conceive of immortality. God did not give this power purposelessly; as he gave the power, so did he give the reality. In this world complete justice is not achieved: wicked people are in possession of the goods of this world in a satisfying degree, the humble starve; some wicked men are happy, some good men are sad, some evil men exult with joy; some righteous men weep. Therefore, after our death there must needs be another life and another justice, a perfect one, in which retribution will be made to all according to their deeds, and those who have fulfilled the will of the creator revealed through the light of reason and have observed the law of their nature will be rewarded. The law of nature is obvious, because our reason clearly propounds it, if we examine it. But men do not like such inquiries; they choose to believe in the words of men rather than to investigate the will of their creator.

THE NATURE OF KNOWLEDGE

The will of God is known by this short statement from our reason that tells us: "Worship God your creator and love all man as yourself." Moreover our reason says: "Do not do unto others that which you do not like done to you, but do unto others as you would like others to do unto you." The decalogue of the Pentateuch expresses the will of the creator excepting the precept about the observance of the Sabbath, for our reason says nothing of the observance of the Sabbath. But the prohibitions of killing, stealing, lying, adultery: our reason teaches us these and similar ones. Likewise the six precepts of the Gospel are the will of the creator. For indeed we desire that men show mercy to us; it therefore is fitting that we ourselves show the same mercy to the others, as much as it is within our power. It is the will of God that we keep our life and existence in this world. It is the will of the creator that we come into and remain in this life, and it is not right for us to leave it against his holy will. The creator himself wills that we adorn our life with science and work; for such an end did he give us reason and power. Manual labour comes from the will of God, because without it the necessities of our life cannot be fulfilled. Likewise marriage of one man with one woman and education of children. Moreover there are many other things which agree with our reason and are necessary for our life or for the existence of mankind. We ought to observe them, because such is the will of our creator, and we ought to know that God does not create us perfect but creates us with such a reason as to know that we are to strive for perfection as long as we live in this world, and to be worthy for the reward that our creator has prepared for us in his wisdom. It was possible for God to have created us perfect and to make us enjoy beatitude on earth; but he did not will to create us in this way; instead he created us with the capacity of striving for perfection, and placed us in the midst of the trials of the world so that we may become perfect and deserve the reward that our creator will give us after our death; as long as we live in this world we ought to praise our creator and fulfil his will and be patient until he draws us unto him, and beg from his mercy that he will lessen our period of hardship and forgive our sins and faults which we committed through ignorance, and enable us to know the laws of our creator and to keep them.

Now as to prayer, we always stand in need of it because our rational nature requires it. The soul endowed with intelligence that is aware that there is a God who knows all, conserves all, rules all, is drawn to him so that it prays to him and asks him to grant things good and to be freed from evil and sheltered under the hand of him who is almighty and for whom nothing is impossible, God great and sublime who sees all that is above and beneath him, holds all, teaches all, guides all, our Father, our creator, our Protector, the reward for our souls, merciful, kind, who knows each of our misfortunes, takes pleasure in our patience, creates us for life and not for destruction, as the wise Solomon said: "You, Lord, teach all things, because you can do all things and overlook men's sins so that they can repent. You love all that exists, you hold nothing of what you have made in abhorrence, you are indulgent and merciful to all." God created us intelligent so that we may meditate on his greatness, praise him and pray to him in order to obtain the needs of our body and soul. Our reason which our creator has put in the heart of man teaches all these things to us. How can they be useless and false?

Religion as Ethics

From *An Empiricist's View of the Nature of Religious Belief* by R. B. Braithwaite, 1955

Like J. H. Randall, Jr. (see under Religious Language), R. B. Braithwaite finds religious language to be non-cognitive. In an endowed lectureship at Cambridge in 1955, Braith-

waite, a longtime Cambridge professor of philosophy, put forth an interpretation of reli-
gious assertions as intentions to behave in a certain way. The lecture was published as a
book, from which the selection here is excerpted.

Braithwaite says that he takes "the typical meaning of the body of Christian asser-
tions as being given by their proclaiming intentions to follow an agapeistic way of life."
Such ethical proclamations he views as, in turn, themselves non-cognitive in that they are
not factually assertive but rather show a person's attitude toward his/her own future be-
havior. They are, then, something like promises.

The intentions are supported, as a matter of psychology, by stories, such as the
parables found in the Bible. Braithwaite points out that the clearly fictional Pilgrim's
Progress, *by John Bunyan, plays an important role in English religious life. It does not*
seem to matter, he concludes, whether biblical stories are considered true. They play
their reinforcing role with regard to ethical intentions whether regarded as fact or
fiction.

Apart from the question of the adequacy of this interpretation of religion, there is the
issue of the satisfactoriness of Braithwaite's understanding of ethics. One problem appears
to be that if ethical judgments are statements of intentions then it should be impossible for
a person to judge that a particular promise should be kept—that keeping it would be
morally right—while intending to break it anyway. A similar problem does not arise for
Braithwaite's interpretation of religious assertions, because he is not claiming that all reli-
gious people actually see their assertions in his way. He would admit that to an extent his
view is continuous with the debunking perspective of the sociology of religion and that not
much hangs on whether religious persons would agree with him. His claim is that he has
saved the best in religion without having to admit a realm of peculiar facts.

The meaning of any statement, then, will be taken as being given by the way it is used. The
kernel for an empiricist of the problem of the nature of religious belief is to explain, in empirical terms, how a religious statement is used by a man who asserts it in order to express
his religious conviction.

Since I shall argue that the primary element in this use is that the religious assertion is
used as a moral assertion, I must first consider how moral assertions are used. According to
the view developed by various moral philosophers since the impossibility of regarding
moral statements as verifiable propositions was recognized, a moral assertion is used to express an *attitude* of the man making the assertion. It is not used to assert the proposition
that he has the attitude—a verifiable psychological proposition; it is used to show forth or
evince his attitude. The attitude is concerned with the action which he asserts to be right or
to be his duty, or the state of affairs which he asserts to be good . . .

The advantage this account of moral assertions has over all others, emotive non-
propositional ones as well as cognitive propositional ones, is that it alone enables a satisfactory answer to be given to the question: What is the reason for my doing what I think I
ought to do? The answer it gives is that, since my thinking that I ought to do the action is
my intention to do it if possible, the reason why I do the action is simply that I intend to do
it, if possible. On every other ethical view there will be a mysterious gap to be filled somehow

between the moral judgment and the intention to act in accordance with it: there is no such gap if the primary use of a moral assertion is to declare such an intention.

Let us now consider what light this way of regarding moral assertions throws upon assertions of religious conviction. The idealist philosopher McTaggart described religion as 'an emotion resting on a conviction of a harmony between ourselves and the universe at large',[1] and many educated people at the present time would agree with him. If religion is essentially concerned with emotion, it is natural to explain the use of religious assertions on the lines of the original emotive theory of ethics and to regard them as primarily evincing religious feelings or emotions. The assertion, for example, that God is our Heavenly Father will be taken to express the asserter's feeling secure in the same way as he would feel secure in his father's presence. But explanations of religion in terms of feeling, and of religious assertions as expressions of such feelings, are usually propounded by people who stand outside any religious system; they rarely satisfy those who speak from inside. Few religious men would be prepared to admit that their religion was a matter merely of feeling: feelings—of joy, of consolation, of being at one with the universe—may enter into their religion, but to evince such feelings is certainly not the primary use of their religious assertions.

This objection, however, does not seem to me to apply to treating religious assertions in the conative way in which recent moral philosophers have treated moral statements—as being primarily declarations of adherence to a policy of action, declarations of commitment to a way of life. That the way of life led by the believer is highly relevant to the sincerity of his religious conviction has been insisted upon by all the moral religions, above all, perhaps, by Christianity. 'By their fruits ye shall know them.' The view which I put forward for your consideration is that the intention of a Christian to follow a Christian way of life is not only the criterion for the sincerity of his belief in the assertions of Christianity; it is the criterion for the meaningfulness of his assertions. Just as the meaning of a moral assertion is given by its use in expressing the asserter's intention to act, so far as [it] in him lies, in accordance with the moral principle involved, so the meaning of a religious assertion is given by its use in expressing the asserter's intention to follow a specified policy of behaviour. To say that it is belief in the dogmas of religion which is the cause of the believer's intending to behave as he does is to put the cart before the horse: it is the intention to behave which constitutes what is known as religious conviction.

But this assimilation of religious to moral assertions lays itself open to an immediate objection. When a moral assertion is taken as declaring the intention of following a policy, the form of the assertion itself makes it clear what the policy is with which the assertion is concerned. For a man to assert that a certain policy ought to be pursued, which on his view is for him to declare his intention of pursuing the policy, presupposes his understanding what it would be like for him to pursue the policy in question. I cannot resolve not to tell a lie without knowing what a lie is. But if a religious assertion is the declaration of an intention to carry out a certain policy, what policy does it specify? The religious statement itself will not explicitly refer to a policy, as does a moral statement; how then can the

---

[1] J. M. E. McTaggart, *Some Dogmas of Religion* (1906), p. 3.

asserter of the statement know what is the policy concerned, and how can he intend to carry out a policy if he does not know what the policy is? I cannot intend to do something I know not what.

The reply to this criticism is that, if a religious assertion is regarded as representative of a large number of assertions of the same religious system, the body of assertions of which the particular one is a representative specimen is taken by the asserter as implicitly specifying a particular way of life. It is no more necessary for an empiricist philosopher to explain the use of a religious statement taken in isolation from other religious statements than it is for him to give a meaning to a scientific hypothesis in isolation from other scientific hypotheses. We understand scientific hypotheses, and the terms that occur in them, by virtue of the relation of the whole system of hypotheses to empirically observable facts; and it is the whole system of hypotheses, not one hypothesis in isolation, that is tested for its truth-value against experience. So there are good precedents, in the empiricist way of thinking, for considering a system of religious assertions as a whole, and for examining the way in which the whole system is used. . . .

The way to find out what are the intentions embodied in a set of religious assertions, and hence what is the meaning of the assertions, is by discovering what principles of conduct the asserter takes the assertions to involve. These may be ascertained both by asking him questions and by seeing how he behaves, each test being supplemental to the other. If what is wanted is not the meaning of the religious assertions made by a particular man but what the set of assertions would mean were they to be made by anyone of the same religion (which I will call their *typical* meaning), all that can be done is to specify the form of behaviour which is in accordance with what one takes to be the fundamental moral principles of the religion in question. . . . I myself take the typical meaning of the body of Christian assertions as being given by their proclaiming intentions to follow an agapeistic way of life, and for a description of this way of life—a description in general and metaphorical terms, but an empirical description nevertheless—I should quote most of the Thirteenth Chapter of I Corinthians. . . .

My contention then is that the primary use of religious assertions is to announce allegiance to a set of moral principles: without such allegiance there is no 'true religion'. This is borne out by all the accounts of what happens when an unbeliever becomes converted to a religion. The conversion is not only a change in the propositions believed—indeed there may be no specifically intellectual change at all; it is a change in the state of will. An excellent instance is C. S. Lewis's recently published account of his conversion from an idealist metaphysic—'a religion [as he says] that cost nothing'—to a theism where he faced (and he quotes George MacDonald's phrase) 'something to be neither more nor less nor other than *done*'. There was no intellectual change, for (as he says) 'there had long been an ethic (theoretically) attached to my Idealism': it was the recognition that he had to do something about it, that 'an attempt at complete virtue must be made'.[2] His conversion was re-orientation of the will. . . .

---

[2] C. S. Lewis, *Surprised by Joy* (1955), pp. 198, 212–13.

A[n] . . . important difference between religious and purely moral principles is that, in the higher religions at least, the conduct preached by the religion concerns not only external but also internal behaviour. The conversion involved in accepting a religion is a conversion, not only of the will, but of the heart. Christianity requires not only that you should behave towards your neighbour as if you loved him as yourself: it requires that you should love him as yourself. And though I have no doubt that the Christian concept of *agape* refers partly to external behaviour—the agapeistic behaviour for which there are external criteria—yet being filled with *agape* includes more than behaving agapeistically externally: it also includes an agapeistic frame of mind. I have said that I cannot regard the expression of a feeling of any sort as the primary element in religious assertion; but this does not imply that intention to feel in a certain way is not a primary element, nor that it cannot be used to discriminate religious declarations of policy from declarations which are merely moral. Those who say that Confucianism is a code of morals and not, properly speaking, a religion are, I think, making this discrimination.

Many Christians will, no doubt, behave in a specifically Christian manner in that they will follow ritual practices which are Christian and neither Jewish nor Buddhist. But though following certain practices may well be the proper test for membership of a particular religious society, a church, not even the most ecclesiastically-minded Christian will regard participation in a ritual as the fundamental characteristic of a Christian way of life. There must be some more important difference between an agapeistically policied Christian and an agapeistically policied Jew than that the former attends a church and the latter a synagogue.

The really important difference, I think, is to be found in the fact that the intentions to pursue the behaviour policies, which may be the same for different religions, are associated with thinking of different *stories* (or sets of stories). By a story I shall here mean a proposition or set of propositions which are straightforwardly empirical propositions capable of empirical test and which are thought of by the religious man in connexion with his resolution to follow the way of life advocated by his religion. On the assumption that the ways of life advocated by Christianity and by Buddhism are essentially the same, it will be the fact that the intention to follow this way of life is associated in the mind of a Christian with thinking of one set of stories (the Christian stories) while it is associated in the mind of a Buddhist with thinking of another set of stories (the Buddhist stories) which enables a Christian assertion to be distinguished from a Buddhist one.

A religious assertion will, therefore, have a propositional element which is lacking in a purely moral assertion, in that it will refer to a story as well as to an intention. The reference to the story is not an assertion of the story taken as a matter of empirical fact: it is a telling of the story, or an alluding to the story, in the way in which one can tell, or allude to, the story of a novel with which one is acquainted. To assert the whole set of assertions of the Christian religion is both to tell the Christian doctrinal story and to confess allegiance to the Christian way of life. . . .

What I am calling a *story* Matthew Arnold called a *parable* and a *fairy-tale.* Other terms which might be used are *allegory, fable, tale, myth.* I have chosen the word 'story' as being the most neutral term, implying neither that the story is believed nor that it is disbelieved. The Christian stories include straightforward historical statements about the life and death of Jesus of Nazareth; a Christian (unless he accepts the unplausible Christ-myth theory) will naturally believe some or all of these. Stories about the beginning of the world and of the Last Judgment as facts of past or of future history are believed by many unsophisticated Christians. But my contention is that belief in the truth of the Christian stories is not the proper criterion for deciding whether or not an assertion is a Christian one. A man is not, I think, a professing Christian unless he both proposes to live according to Christian moral principles and associates his intention with thinking of Christian stories; but he need not believe that the empirical propositions presented by the stories correspond to empirical fact.

But if the religious stories need not be believed, what function do they fulfil in the complex state of mind and behaviour known as having a religious belief? How is entertaining the story related to resolving to pursue a certain way of life? My answer is that the relation is a psychological and causal one. It is an empirical psychological fact that many people find it easier to resolve upon and to carry through a course of action which is contrary to their natural inclinations if this policy is associated in their minds with certain stories. And in many people the psychological link is not appreciably weakened by the fact that the story associated with the behaviour policy is not believed. Next to the Bible and the Prayer Book the most influential work in English Christian religious life has been a book whose stories are frankly recognized as fictitious—Bunyan's *Pilgrim's Progress;* and some of the most influential works in setting the moral tone of my generation were the novels of Dostoevsky. It is completely untrue, as a matter of psychological fact, to think that the only intellectual considerations which affect action are beliefs: it is *all* the thoughts of a man that determine his behaviour; and these include his phantasies, imaginations, ideas of what he would wish to be and do, as well as the propositions which he believes to be true.

The Ethics of Self-Transformation

From *The Synthesis of Yoga* by Sri Aurobindo, 1973

For an introduction to the life and thought of the modern Indian mystic philosopher, Aurobindo, see the discussion under Speculative Spiritual Metaphysics.

Aurobindo's urging of mystical opportunities leads him to take a dim view of religious ethical prescriptions—indeed all ethical prescriptions—since mystic transformation requires, he suggests, a more profound and individually tailored treatment of a person's nature. This treatment, he believes, is a process actually occurring through spiritual evolution, but is also a process that can be speeded up through yogic practice. Yoga involves what he takes to be general principles of spiritual transformation, principles which he is unwilling to call ethical.

Aurobindo admits that spiritual evolution requires general prescriptions for conduct. And he does not seem to think that practicing yoga requires behavior that would be unethical according to common norms. He is nevertheless suspicious of societal rules, apparently out of a fear that they might impede an individual's yogic initiative.

. . . there is, above society's external law and man's moral law and beyond them, though feebly and ignorantly aimed at by something within them, a larger truth of a vast unbound consciousness, a law divine towards which both these blind and gross formulations are progressive faltering steps that try to escape from the natural law of the animal to a more exalted light or universal rule. That divine standard, since the godhead in us is our spirit moving towards its own concealed perfection, must be a supreme spiritual law and truth of our nature. Again as we are embodied beings in the world with a common existence and nature and yet individual souls capable of direct touch with the Transcendent, this supreme truth of ourselves must have a double character. It must be a law and truth that [discloses] the perfect movement, harmony, rhythm of a great spiritualised collective life and determines perfectly our relations with each being and all beings in Nature's varied oneness. It must be at the same time a law and truth that [discloses] to us at each moment the rhythm and exact steps of the direct expression of the Divine in the soul, mind, life, body of the individual creature.[1] And we find in experience that this supreme light and force of action in its highest expression is at once an imperative law and an absolute freedom. It is an imperative law because it governs by immutable Truth our every inner and outer movement. And yet at each moment and in each movement the absolute freedom of the Supreme handles the perfect plasticity of our conscious and liberated nature.

The ethical idealist tries to discover this supreme law in his own moral data, in the inferior powers and factors that belong to the mental and ethical formula. And to sustain and organise them he selects a fundamental principle of conduct essentially unsound and constructed by the intellect, utility, hedonism, reason, intuitive conscience or any other generalised standard. All such efforts are foredoomed to failure. Our inner nature is the progressive expression of the eternal Spirit and too complex a power to be tied down by a single dominant mental or moral principle. Only the supramental consciousness can reveal to its differing and conflicting forces their spiritual truth and harmonise their divergences.

The later religions endeavor to fix the type of a supreme truth of conduct, erect a system and declare God's law through the mouth of Avatar or prophet. These systems, more powerful and dynamic than the dry ethical idea, are yet for the most part no more than idealistic glorifications of the moral principle sanctified by religious emotion and the label of a superhuman origin. Some, like the extreme Christian ethic, are rejected by Nature because they insist unworkably on an impracticable absolute rule. Others prove in the end to be evolutionary compromises and become obsolete in the march of Time. The true divine law, unlike these mental counterfeits, cannot be a system of rigid ethical determinations that press into their cast-iron moulds all our life-movements. The Law divine is truth of life and truth of the spirit and must take up with a free living plasticity and inspire with the direct touch of its eternal light each step of our action and all the complexities of our life-issues. It must act not as a rule and for-

---

[1] Therefore the Gita defines "Dharma", an expression which means more than either religion or morality, as action controlled by our essential manner of self-being.

mula but as an enveloping and penetrating conscious presence that determines all our thoughts, activities, feelings, impulsions of will by its infallible power and knowledge. . . .

The higher ethical law is discovered by the individual in his mind and will and psychic sense and then extended to the race. The supreme law also must be discovered by the individual in his spirit. Then only, through a spiritual influence and not by the mental idea, can it be extended to others. A moral law can be imposed as a rule or an ideal on numbers of men who have not attained that level of consciousness or that fineness of mind and will and psychic sense in which it can become a reality to them and a living force. As an ideal it can be revered without any need of practice. As a rule it can be observed in its outsides even if the inner sense is missed altogether. The supramental and spiritual life cannot be mechanised in this way; it cannot be turned into a mental idea or an external rule. It has its own great lines, but these must be made real, must be the workings of an active Power felt in the individual's consciousness and the transcriptions of an eternal Truth powerful to transform mind, life and body. . . .

Divine Command Theory Attacked

From *Euthyphro* by Plato, F. J. Church, translator, 1956

The Euthyphro *is an early dialogue of Plato's, one in which, scholars believe, the views of the historical Socrates are reflected. Throughout the early dialogues of Plato, the character Socrates is concerned with right conduct, along with the question of the standards of right conduct.*

Plato seems to use the dialogue for another purpose as well, a theological purpose. The setting is that Socrates, who has been indicted for false religious teachings and corrupting the youth of Athens and who will soon stand trial, meets Euthyphro on the steps of the courthouse. Euthyphro, a man renowned for piety, is prosecuting his father for a dubious murder: the father, who is unnamed, had caught and tied up an actual murderer who died while he was seeking the help of authorities. Astounded, Socrates asks why Euthyphro is prosecuting is very own father, especially when the action seems questionably a crime. Euthyphro replies that piety requires it. Then Socrates begins examining Euthyphro's understanding of piety. A first definition—that piety is what is loved by the gods— does not withstand scrutiny, because Euthyphro believes in a polytheism, and holds that what is loved by Hera, for example, might not be loved by Zeus. It is at this point that Socrates shows that he does not accept that there are quarrels and the like among the gods, suggesting a kind of monotheism (see the discussion of Plato in the section Divine Reality).

Our excerpt begins with a second definition, that piety is what all *the gods love. Philosophers have taken this to suggest a divine command theory against a backdrop of monotheism. To behave piously is to behave justly. And the canons or standards determining which types of actions count as pious and just are determined by the love of the gods, that is, all the gods, or God.*

Socrates then proposes what has been called the Euthyphro dilemma: "Do the gods love piety because it is pious, or is it pious because they love it?" Does God command what God commands because God sees what is just and unjust by nature, or do God's commands determine the very standards of the just and the unjust, right and wrong? This dilemma is discussed in the next selection, from James Hanink and Gary Mar.

Socrates' own examination hinges on a distinction between (a) a motivating reason for doing a particular action and (b) a reason for labelling something as in a particular state of being acted upon. There are in the text two corresponding senses of the word because. *Socrates apparently believes that, on analogy with other acts, loving requires a motivating reason, and thus that there must be something in the nature of an act that is a reason for the gods to love it. Piety is, then, loved by the gods because it is pious, though something may be said to be in a state of being loved by the gods simply by virtue of their loving it.*

EUTHYPHRO: Well, I should say that piety is what all the gods love, and that impiety is what they all hate.

SOCRATES: Are we to examine this definition, Euthyphro, and see if it is a good one? Or are we to be content to accept the bare statements of other men or of ourselves without asking any questions? Or must we examine the statements?

EUTHYPHRO: We must examine them. But for my part I think that the definition is right this time.

SOCRATES: We shall know that better in a little while, my good friend. Now consider this question. Do the gods love piety because it is pious, or is it pious because they love it?

EUTHYPHRO: I do not understand you, Socrates.

SOCRATES: I will try to explain myself: we speak of a thing being carried and carrying, and being led and leading, and being seen and seeing; and you understand that all such expressions mean different things, and what the difference is.

EUTHYPHRO: Yes, I think I understand.

SOCRATES: And we talk of a thing being loved, of a thing loving, and the two are different?

EUTHYPHRO: Of course.

SOCRATES: Now tell me, is a thing which is being carried in a state of being carried because it is carried, or for some other reason?

EUTHYPHRO: No, because it is carried.

SOCRATES: And a thing is in a state of being led because it is led, and of being seen because it is seen?

EUTHYPHRO: Certainly.

SOCRATES: Then a thing is not seen because it is in a state of being seen: it is [said to be] in a state of being seen because it is seen; and a thing is not led because it is in a state of being led: it is [said to be] in a state of being led because it is led; and a thing is not carried because it is in a state of being carried: it is [said to be] in a state of being carried because it is carried. Is my meaning clear now, Euthyphro? I mean this: if anything becomes or is affected, it does not become because it is in a state of becoming: it is [said to be] in a state of becoming because it becomes; and it is not affected because it is in a state of being affected: it is [said to be] in a state of being affected because it is affected. Do you not agree?

EUTHYPHRO: I do.

SOCRATES: Is not that which is being loved in a state either of becoming or of being affected in some way by something?

EUTHYPHRO: Certainly.

SOCRATES: Then the same is true here as in the former cases. A thing is not loved by those who love it because it is in a state of being loved; it is [said to be] in a state of being loved because they love it.

EUTHYPHRO: Necessarily.

SOCRATES: Well, then, Euthyphro, what do we say about piety? Is it not loved by all the gods, according to your definition?

EUTHYPHRO: Yes.

SOCRATES: Because it is pious, or for some other reason?

EUTHYPHRO: No, because it is pious.

SOCRATES: Then it is loved by the gods because it is pious; it is not pious because it is loved by them?

EUTHYPHRO: It seems so.

SOCRATES: But, then, what is pleasing to the gods is pleasing to them, and is [said to be] in a state of being loved by them, because they love it?

EUTHYPHRO: Of course.

SOCRATES: Then piety is not what is pleasing to the gods, and what is pleasing to the gods is not pious, as you say, Euthyphro. They are different things.

EUTHYPHRO: And why, Socrates?

SOCRATES: Because we are agreed that the gods love piety because it is pious, and that it is not pious because they love it. Is not this so?

EUTHYPHRO: Yes.

SOCRATES: And that what is pleasing to the gods because they love it, is pleasing to them by reason of this same love, and that they do not love it because it is pleasing to them.

EUTHYPHRO: True.

SOCRATES: Then, my dear Euthyphro, piety and what is pleasing to the gods are different things. If the gods had loved piety because it is pious, they would also have loved what is pleasing to them because it is pleasing to them; but if what is pleasing to them had been pleasing to them because they loved it, then piety, too, would have been piety because they loved it. But now you see that they are opposite things, and wholly different from each other. For the one is of a sort to be loved because it is loved, while the other is loved because it is of a sort to be loved. My question, Euthyphro, was, What is piety? But it turns out that you have not explained to me the essential character of piety; you have been content to mention an affect which belongs to it—namely, that all the gods love it. You have not yet told me what its essential character is. Do not, if you please, keep from me what piety is; begin again and tell me that. Never mind whether the gods love it, or whether it has other effects: we shall not differ on that point. Do your best to make clear to me what is piety and what is impiety.

Divine Command Theory Defended

From "What Euthyphro Couldn't Have Said" by James G. Hanink and Gary R. Mar in *Faith and Philosophy*, Volume 4, Number 3, 1987

*James Hanink and Gary Mar take it upon themselves to defend divine command theory (called by them Divine Command Morality, DCM) against a dilemma: on one horn (**A**) God's commands are dispensable—thus DCM is false—and on the other (**B**) God's commands are arbitrary. This reading of Socrates' challenge to Euthyphro in Plato's dialogue is stretched, but the problem seems pressing enough. It is indeed often cited by philosophers to show divine command theory inadequate.*

If God—presuming God to exist—bases commands on what is right and wrong by nature (e.g. murder's being wrong because it is the killing of something, a human being, with an intrinsic right to live), then we would like to know on what the commands are based, what it is in the nature of an action (or its objects, its effects, or the motivations for it) that makes it right or wrong. The criteria for moral rightness would lie in actions, or agents, themselves. God could be then a moral advisor, who out of perfect wisdom would be able to give perfect advice and thus infallible commandments in the sense of moral dicta based on a perfect comprehension of the nature of right and wrong. This option has been embraced by several eminent theologians through the long history of Western theism. But Hanink and Mar are nevertheless correct that this is not what they call DCM because God would then not set the standards for right and wrong (except, perhaps, in creating everything). The rightness and wrongness of actions would be logically independent of God's moral advice, that is, commands.

*The common philosophic objection to the dilemma's other horn (**B**) (that God's commandments set moral standards externally to the nature of agents and acts) is that morality would be arbitrary. If God had commanded baby torture ("Go out and torture all infants"), then baby torture would be morally right. (And it does not seem that baby torture could by any stretch of the imagination be morally right.) Hanink and Mar, however, embrace this option, arguing that God commands only that which is in accordance with God's nature as Perfect Righteousness. Perfect Righteousness is an essential attribute of God. It is only by ignoring the constraints of God's nature as Perfect Righteousness that philosophers have been able to imagine God commanding heinous acts such as baby torture.*

*Does this move show that Hanink and Mar understand righteousness independently from God's commands? If so, they would seem to be embracing horn (**A**) of the dilemma. In the next selection, Kai Nielsen argues that an understanding of the morally right (or goodness) is independent of an understanding of God as righteousness (i.e., that God is good). We shall reconsider Hanink and Mar's position after reviewing what Nielsen has to say.*

[Abstract:] In this paper we argue for a simple version of Divine Command Morality, namely that an act's being morally right consists in its being in accord with God's will, and an act's being morally wrong consists in its being contrary to God's will. In so arguing, we contend that this simple version of Divine Command Morality is not subject to the Euthyphro dilemma, either as Plato or as contemporary critics have ordinarily proposed it. Nor, we maintain, is our position incompatible with the most adequate formulation of natural law ethics. Finally we explain why Euthyphro could not have made a better case for his own position.

> Where is the wise man? Where is the scholar? Where is the philosopher of this age? Has not God made foolish the wisdom of the world? For since in the wisdom of God the world through its wisdom did not know him, God was pleased through the foolishness of what was preached to save those who believe. I Cor. 1:20-21

What is it to be a "simple believer?" In part, it is to see in God's will the standard of what is morally right and morally wrong. This ethical stance doubtless contributes to the annoyed dismissal simple believers often receive in both public and philosophical forums. How important philosophy has been in bringing about the marginal status of the simple believer and his ethical stance is hard to say. If conceptual analysis counts as much as philosophers like to think, then the role of philosophy has been a major one. Certainly there are grounds for the general claim that the teaching of philosophy is seldom kind to the thesis that God's will is the standard of what is right and wrong. This ethical stance, usually termed Divine Command Morality (hereafter, DCM), has been given rough handling from Plato to Frankena, with any number of hostile critics in between. Although contemporary defenses of DCM have appeared in philosophical journals and colloquia, these defenses have employed sophisticated metaethical, causal, or 'paradigmatic' versions of DCM that the simple believer might well fail to recognise. Our first question, then, is whether there is a philosophically defensible version of DCM that a simple believer could both recognize and embrace.

I

The generally negative assessment of DCM from Plato's time to our own is largely due to Socrates' famous challenge to Euthyphro. This challenge, known as the Euthyphro dilemma, is perhaps the most serious and sophisticated challenge to the coherence of any DCM.

Let us begin, appropriately, with a simple version of DCM.

(V.1) An act's being morally right consists in its being in accord with God's will, and an act's being morally wrong consists in its being contrary to God's will.

Admittedly, the use of 'consists' in (V.1) is vague, and we will say more about this in subsequent sections. But our present concern is to formulate the Euthyphro dilemma for (V.1).

Euthyphro's original version of DCM, namely,

(V.2) An act is holy if all the gods love it, and an act is unholy if all the gods hate it,

differs in three conspicuous ways form (V.1). First, Euthyphro's (V.2) is stated with respect to the gods of Homer, whereas the cornerstone of the simple believer's (V.1) is the God of Judaism and Christianity. This sharp transition from Hellenism to Hebraism will be essential to our defense of DCM. Secondly, following the tenor of modern philosophy, (V.1) is stated in terms of 'right' and 'wrong' rather than in terms of 'holy' and 'unholy.' Finally, Euthyphro's (V.2), unlike (V.1), is compatible with a merely extensional equivalence between God's willing or forbidding an act and that act's being right or wrong. And, of course, Socrates devises his dilemma to underscore just this point.

According to received philosophical doctrine, none of the above modifications in the transition from (V.2) to (V.1) succeeds in dulling the pointedness of the Euthyphro dilemma. Thus, most philosophers conclude that the dilemma, as directed against the simple believer's (V.1), shows morality's conceptual independence from the God. And many, like Socrates, following only the authority of argument, see in this dilemma a dialectical weapon against any hint of "authoritarianism" in ethics. But lest we acquiesce in any hasty conclusions, let us examine the supposed cogency of the Euthyphro dilemma—as directed against (V.1).

We can state the dilemma as follows:

(P1) Either an act is right because God wills it, or God wills an act because it is right.

(P2) If an act is right because God wills it, then morality is arbitrary.

(P3) If God wills an act because it is right, then DCM is false.

(P4) Therefore, either morality is arbitrary or DCM is false.

We might best appreciate the force of this dilemma if we next elaborate the supporting arguments for (P2) and (P3).

(P2), which expresses the first horn of the Euthyphro dilemma, is the claim that DCM makes right and wrong arbitrary. For suppose that an act is right or wrong just because God wills or forbids it. If so, then it seems that there is nothing intrinsic to the act itself that makes it right or wrong. Instead, whether it is right or wrong depends on a single decisive, but extrinsic, factor: God's will. Worse still for the simple believer, if God were now to forbid what had hitherto been a right act and to will what had hitherto been a wrong act, then right becomes wrong and wrong becomes right. Even if what God approves of is—as a matter of fact—what is right and what God disapproves of is—as a matter of fact—what is wrong, it seems that God's will could not, without flirting with arbitrariness, be the *standard* of morality.

So staunch an apologist as C. S. Lewis, writing about DCM, voices this very worry.

> There were in the eighteenth century terrible theologians who held that 'God did not command certain things because they are right, but certain things are right because God commanded them.' To make the position perfectly clear, one of them even said that though God has, as it happens, commanded us to love Him and one another, He might equally well

have commanded us to hate Him and one another, and hatred would have been right. It was apparently a mere toss-up which he decided to do. Such a view in effect makes God a mere arbitrary tyrant. It would be better and less irreligious to believe in no God and to have no ethics than to have such an ethics and such a theology as this. [*Reflections on the Psalms* (New York: 1958)]

Does the faith of the simple believer that the heart of morality is to be found in God's will indeed implicate God in a scheme of moral arbitrariness?

The simple believer, of course, will want to block the accusation of arbitrariness. But how? The Commandments, he insists, are not merely arbitrary rules, enjoined upon even the non-believer. Rather the Commandments are, as it were, fundamental directives that tell us how we might respect and fulfill the nature that our Creator has given us.

But if this answer is made, then further conceptual problems arise. For isn't the simple believer holding that: (a) an act is right because God wills it, and (b) God wills the act because it contributes to human flourishing? Yet it follows from (a) and (b), the critic charges, that an act is right, ultimately, because of its relation to human flourishing. If so, then haven't we arrived at some form of naturalism? But, if this is the case, why not avoid the detour through DCM and its attendant conundrums?

We have seen something, then, of the force of the first horn of the Euthyphro dilemma. The second horn, to which we now turn, will seem just as daunting. If DCM's account of right and wrong is not to be viciously circular, then it would seem that if God wills an act because it is right, the rightness of the act could not consist in God's willing it. The critic argues that 'because,' when used univocally, is an antisymmetric relation. Thus, for any propositions p and q,

(1) if p because q, then it is not the case that q because p.

Now, the critic claims, we can see why (P3), the second horn of the dilemma, is true. For suppose we admit the antecedent of (P3), namely, that

(P3.a) God wills an act because it is right.

Using the minimal assumption that 'consists' implies 'because,' namely that

(V.1.a) an act's being morally right *consists* in being in accord with God's will

at least implies that

(2) an act is right *because* God wills it,

we can apply (1), the principle of the antisymmetry of 'because,' to (P3.a) to infer the negation of (2) and so conclude that DCM, as expressed by (V.1.a), is false. Thus, if God wills an act because it is right, then it cannot be right because God wills it. Hence an act's being right cannot simply consist in God's willing it.

There is, moreover, still another way of arguing for the second horn of the Euthyphro dilemma. This added argument rests on the claim that the believer must first justify his confidence about what God in fact wills by an appeal to ethical norms. James Cornman and Keith Lehrer have put their case plainly enough.

Consider what we would do if we read that Moses had returned with such commandments as 'make love to thy neighbor's wife,' 'Steal thy neighbor's goods,' and 'Take advantage of thy parents.' We would decide that whatever was revealed to Moses, it was not the will of God, because these are immoral commandments. We do not justify that something is moral by showing that it expresses God's will, because the only available way to evaluate conflicting claims about what God wills is by finding which one is in accordance with what is moral. [*Philosophical Problems and Arguments* (New York: 1974), p. 429.]

If we know that something is God's will because we know that it is right, is it not circular to claim that the act is right because God wills it?

Traditional philosophical wisdom, then, seems to have shown that the simple believer is far too simple. And yet we recall that the foolishness of God is wiser than the wisdom of the world. So perhaps we should not just yet dismiss the view of the simple believer.

II

But what can we say in defense of the simple believer? With his account of morality caught on the apparently well-supported horns of the Euthyphro dilemma, how are we to proceed?

Might one try to slip between those horns? Perhaps the alternatives posed in the dilemma's first premise

(P1) Either an act is right because God wills it or God wills it because it is right

are not exhaustive. But how could this be? One way is if the alternatives 'p because q' and 'q because p' (where p and q are propositions) are both false because p turns out, in some sense, to be equivalent to q. An analogy might be useful. Suppose one were asked whether measurement is quantitative because it uses numbers or whether measurement uses numbers because it is quantitative. Here the alternatives are, of course, spurious because in using numbers for measurement, one is engaged in a quantitative activity. Measurement's being quantitative just consists in its use of numbers. We cannot take the use of numbers in measurement to be the cause or the reason or the explanation of that activity's being quantitative, or conversely.

Now the simple believer reminds us that God personifies Perfect Righteousness. Part of what it means to say that God is righteous is that it is God's nature to act according to what is right, a righteousness we see in His fulfilling of His covenant with His people. To say that God *personifies* righteousness is to say that He is *Righteousness*. Hence, His acts are righteous simply by being in accord with His will. Finally, to say that God is *Perfect* Righteousness is to say that God's righteousness is complete in and of itself. Thus, to say that God personifies Perfect Righteousness is to say that his actions are completely and self-sufficiently righteous in that they are in accord with His will. God is not righteous because God conforms (however perfectly) to some higher standard of righteousness. Rather, God's will is not only the measure, but also the personal substance, of Perfect Righteousness. Expressing this understanding of God requires, to be sure, that the simple believer begin to develop a "philosophy of God." So, to an extent, the simple believer now becomes, if not so already, something of a philosopher. But this philosophy articulates, rather than supplants, simple belief. . . .

. . . we shall call [our strategy for defending DCM] the "moral perfection as person" strategy. This strategy, we have seen, insists that God *is* Perfect Righteousness. On this view the charge, that it must be the case that *either* God wills an act because it is right *or* that an act is right because God wills it, breaks down. Neither disjunct is true, since 'because' fails to capture the insight that God personifies Righteousness. And the righteousness of one's action just is its sharing in the Perfect Righteousness who is God. The disjunctive first premise, then, of the Euthyphro dilemma betrays a deep misconception of the nature of God, and so the believer can rightly reject that premise.

The Autonomy of Ethics

From *Ethics without God* by Kai Nielsen, 1990

The Canadian philosopher Kai Nielsen has published widely on ethics and in defense of philosophic atheism. In this selection, he gives no indication that he has read the paper by Hanink and Mar excerpted here, but he seems to be mindful of their position. In fact, Nielsen presents a full-bodied attack on divine command theory, including but not restricted to the defense offered by Hanink and Mar.

 Nielsen presents examples of theistic statements to show that "moral goodness" is a notion that can be understood independently of God's commands. Unless "I ought to do what God wills" is a tautology, then such independence is shown. Nielsen continues by arguing that the theist must begin with an assumption of God as perfectly good in order to have a truly moral obligation to do what God commands. In this way, Nielsen's focus shifts to the logical status of the claim, "God is good."

 First, if "God is good" is not what Nielsen calls a truth of language, not a matter of what God by definition is, or is essentially, then, presumably, assuming its truth, it would be a discovery. God might have turned out not to have been good, but evidence indicates the contrary, that God is good. "God is good" would be then synthetic, *a statement whose predicate does not apply to its subject as a mere matter of definition. But if it is discovered that God is good, there must be criteria for determining goodness that are independent of what is required to understand God.*

 On the other hand, "God is good" may be analytic, *what Nielsen calls a truth of language, a statement whose predicate defines its subject—where what the subject term refers to (namely, God) is essentially what the predicate says (namely, good). Apart from natural theologians such as Hume's Cleanthes (see under Arguments for a Divine Reality), this construal of "God is good" seems to accord best with what mainstream theists believe. Surely, Hanink and Mar's "simple believer" could endorse this interpretation. But since there is linguistic evidence, Nielsen argues, that "God is good" is not a statement of complete identity (the terms are not interchangeable), at best the statement would reflect a partial identity, where goodness would be partially constitutive of God. On analogy to "Puppies are young" and our need to have an independent understanding of "young" to understand that puppies are young—though being young is partially constitutive of a puppy's essential nature—we must have an independent understanding of "good," Nielsen argues.*

If this reasoning is correct, would it show that the canons of morality are independent of God (as reflected in God's commands), and that Hanink's and Mar's defense of their version of a divine command theory fails? Nielsen has carried us deep into metaphysical issues (though he apparently thinks he is talking only about language), where the issue of God's simplicity or other relation among God's attributes has been raised. Furthermore, it seems possible that there be independent routes to learning morality—so that we need not be apprised of God's commands to know right and wrong and the meaning of "x is good"—while God's commands set absolutely the standards of right and wrong anyway. Similarly, water seems to be necessarily H_2O (and being H_2O is the absolute standard or test for water) though we come to identify water in different ways and indeed discover that water is H_2O. Surely water was discovered to be H_2O, but also, some philosophers have argued (notably Saul Kripke), water is essentially, necessarily H_2O. Contra an assumption of Nielsen's then, the necessary truth "Water is H_2O" would be synthetic. Thus "God is good" would be a necessary truth, a matter of what God is essentially, but also a discovery.

Theologians like [Karl] Barth and [Emil] Brunner claim that ethical principles gain their justification because they are God's decrees. But as [A.C.] Ewing points out, if "being obligatory" means just "willed by God," it becomes unintelligible to ask why God wills one thing rather than another. In fact, there can be no reason for his willing one thing rather than another, for his willing it *eo ipso* makes whatever it is he wills good, right or obligatory. "God wills it because it ought to be done" becomes "God wills it because God wills it"; but the first sentence, even as used by the most ardent believer, is not a tautology. "If it were said in reply that God's commands determine what we ought to do but that these commands were only issued because it was good that they should be or because obedience to them did good, this would still make judgments about the good, at least, independent of the will of God, and we should not have given a definition of all fundamental ethical concepts in terms of God or made ethics dependent on God."[1] Furthermore, it becomes senseless to say what the believer very much wants to say, namely, "I ought always to do what God wills" if "what I ought to do" and "what God wills" have the same meaning. And to say I ought to do what God wills because I love God makes the independent assumption that I ought to love God and that I ought to do what God wills if I love him.

Suppose we say instead that we ought to do what God wills because God will punish us if we do not obey him. This may indeed be a cogent, self-interested or prudential reason for doing what God commands, but it is hardly a morally good reason for doing what he commands since such considerations of self-interest cannot be an adequate basis for morality. A powerful being—an omnipotent and omniscient being—speaking out of the

---

[1] A. C. Ewing, "The Autonomy of Ethics," in Ian Ramsey (ed.), *Prospect for Metaphysics* (London: Allen & Unwin, 1961), p. 39.

whirlwind cannot by his mere commands create an obligation. Ewing goes on to assert: "Without a prior conception of God as good or his commands as right, God would have no more claim on our obedience than Hitler or Stalin except that he would have more power than even they had to make things uncomfortable for those who disobey him." Unless we assume that God is morally perfect, unless we assume the perfect goodness of God, there can be no necessary "relation between being commanded or willed by God and being obligatory or good."

To this it is perfectly correct to reply that as believers we must believe that God is wholly and completely good, the most perfect of all conceivable beings. It is not open for a Jew or a Christian to question the goodness of God. He must start with that assumption. Any man who seriously questions God's goodness or asks why he should obey God's commands shows by this very response that he is not a Jew or a Christian. Believers must claim that God is wholly and utterly good and that what he wills or commands is of necessity good, though this does not entail that the believer is claiming that the necessity here is a logical necessity. For a believer, God is all good; he is the perfect good. This being so, it would seem that the believer is justified in saying that he and we—if his claim concerning God is correct—ought to do what God wills and that our morality is after all grounded in a belief in God. But this claim of his is clearly dependent on his assumption that God is good. Yet I shall argue that even if God is good, indeed, even if God is the perfect good, it does not follow that morality can be based on religion and that we can know what we ought to do simply by knowing what God wishes us to do.

To come to understand the grounds for this last, rather elliptical claim, we must consider the logical status of "God is good." Is it a nonanalytic and in some way substantive claim, or is it analytic? (Can we say that it is neither?) No matter what we say, we get into difficulties.

Let us try to claim that it is nonanalytic, that it is in some way a substantive statement. So understood, God cannot then be by definition good. If the statement is synthetic and substantive, its denial cannot be self-contradictory; that is, it cannot be self-contradictory to assert that X is God but X is not good. It would always in fact be wrong to assert this, for God is the perfect good, but the denial of this claim is not self-contradictory, it is just false or in some way mistaken. The *is* in "God is the perfect good" is not the *is* of identity; perfect goodness is being predicated of God in some logically contingent way. It is the religious experience of the believer and the events recorded in the Bible that lead the believer to the steadfast conviction that God has a purpose or vocation for him which he can fulfill only by completely submitting to God's will. God shall lead him and guide him in every thought, word and deed. Otherwise he will be like a man shipwrecked, lost in a vast and indifferent universe. Through careful attention to the Bible, he comes to understand that God is a wholly good being who has dealt faithfully with his chosen people. God is not by definition perfectly good or even good, but in reality, though not of logical necessity, he never falls short of perfection.

Assuming that "God is good" is not a truth of language, how, then, do we know that God is good? Do we know or have good grounds for believing that the remarks made at the end of the above paragraph are so? The believer can indeed make such a claim, but how do we or how does he know that this is so? What grounds have we for believing that God is good? Naïve people, recalling how God spoke to Job out of the whirlwind may say that

God is good because he is omnipotent and omniscient. But this clearly will not do, for, as [Ronald] Hepburn points out, there is nothing logically improper about saying "X is omnipotent and omniscient and morally wicked." Surely in the world as we know it there is no logical connection between being powerful and knowledgeable and being good. As far as I can see, all that God proved to Job when he spoke to him out of the whirlwind was that God was an immeasurably powerful being; but he did not prove his moral superiority to Job and he did nothing at all even to exhibit his moral goodness. (One might even argue that he exhibited moral wickedness.) We need not assume that omnipotence and omniscience bring with them goodness or even wisdom.

What other reason could we have for claiming that God is good? We might say that he is good because he tells us to do good in thought, word and deed and to love one another. In short, in his life and in his precepts God exhibits for us his goodness and love. Now one might argue that children's hospitals and concentration camps clearly show that such a claim is false. But let us assume that in some way God does exhibit his goodness to man. Let us assume that if we examine God's works we cannot but affirm that God is good.[2] We come to understand that he is not cruel, callous or indifferent. But in order to make such judgments or to gain such an understanding, we must use our own logically independent moral criteria. In taking God's goodness as not being true by definition or as being some kind of conceptual truth, we have, in asserting "God is good," of necessity made a moral judgment, a moral appraisal, using a criterion that cannot be based on a knowledge that God exists or that he issues commands. We call God good because we have experienced the goodness of his acts, but in order to do this, in order to know that he is good or to have any grounds for believing that he is good, we must have an independent moral criterion which we use in making this predication of God. So if "God is good" is taken to be synthetic and substantive, then morality cannot simply be based on a belief in God. We must of logical necessity have some criterion of goodness that is not derived from any statement asserting that there is a deity.

Let us alternatively, and more plausibly, take "God is good" to be a truth of language. Now some truths of language (some analytic statements) are statements of identity, such as "puppies are young dogs" or "a father is a male parent." Such statements are definitions and the *is* indicates identity. But "God is good" is clearly not such a statement of identity, for [the fact] that *God* does not have the same meaning as *good* can easily be seen from the following case: Jane says to Betsy, after Betsy helps an old lady across the street, "That was good of you" most certainly does not mean "that was God of you." And when we say "conscientiousness is good" we do not mean to say "conscientiousness is God." To say, as a believer does, that God is good is not to say that God is God. This clearly indicates that the word *God* does not have the same meaning as the word *good*. When we are talking about God we are not talking simply about morality.

"God is the perfect good" is somewhat closer to "a father is a male parent," but even here *God* and *the perfect good* are not identical in meaning. "God is the perfect good" in

---

[2] This is surely to assume a lot.

some important respects is like "a triangle is a trilateral." Though something is a triangle if and only if it is a trilateral, it does not follow that *triangle* and *trilateral* have the same meaning. Similarly, something is God if and only if that something is the perfect good, but it does not follow that *God* and *the perfect good* have the same meaning. When we speak of God we wish to say other things about him as well, though indeed what is true of God will also be true of the perfect good. Yet what is true of the evening star will also be true of the morning star, since they both refer to the same object, namely Venus, but, as Frege has shown, it does not follow that the two terms have the same meaning if they have the same referent.

Even if it could be made out that "God is the perfect good" is in some way a statement of identity, (1) it would not make "God is good" a statement of identity, and (2) we could know that X is the perfect good only if we already knew how to decide that X is good. So even on the assumption that "God is the perfect good" is a statement of identity, we need an independent way of deciding whether something is good; we must have an independent criterion for goodness.

Surely the alternative presently under consideration is more plausible than the alternative considered [earlier]. "God is good" most certainly appears to be analytic in the way "puppies are young," "a bachelor is unmarried" or "unjustified killing is wrong" are analytic. These statements are not statements of identity; they are not definitions, though they all follow from definitions and to deny any of them is self-contradictory.

In short, it seems to me correct to maintain that "God is good," "puppies are young" and "triangles are three-sided" are all truths of language; the predicates partially define their subjects. That is to say— to adopt for a moment, a Platonic-sounding idiom—goodness is partially definitive of Godhood, as youngness is partially definitive of puppyhood and as three-sidedness is partially definitive of triangularity.

To accept this is not at all to claim that we can have no understanding of good without an understanding of God; and the truth of the above claim that God is good will not show that God is the, or even a, fundamental criterion for goodness. Let us establish first that and then how the fact of such truths of language does not show that we could have no understanding of good without having an understanding of God. We could not understand the full religious sense of what is meant by God without knowing that whatever is denoted by this term is said to be good; but, as *young* or *three-sided* are understood without reference to puppies or triangles, though the converse cannot be the case, so *good* is also understood quite independently of any reference to God. We can intelligibly say, "I have a three-sided figure here that is most certainly not a triangle" and "colts are young but they are not puppies." Similarly, we can well say "conscientiousness, under most circumstances at least, is good even in a world without God." Such an utterance is clearly intelligible, to believer and nonbeliever alike. It is a well-formed English sentence with a use in the language. Here we can use the word *good* without either asserting or assuming the reality of God. Such linguistic evidence clearly shows that good is a concept which can be understood quite independently of any reference to the deity, that morality without religion, without theism is quite possible. In fact, just the reverse is the case. Christianity, Judaism and theistic religions of that sort could not exist if people did not have a moral understanding that was, logically speaking, quite independent of such religions. We could have no understanding of the truth of "God is good" or of the concept God unless we had an independent understanding of goodness.

That this is so can be seen from the following considerations. If we had no understanding of the word *young,* and if we did not know the criteria for deciding whether a dog
was young, we could not know how correctly to apply the word *puppy.* Without such a
prior understanding of what it is to be young, we could not understand the sentence
"puppies are young." Similarly, if we had no understanding of the use of the word *good,*
and if we did not know the criteria for deciding whether a being (or if you will, a power
or a force) was good, we could not know how correctly to apply the word *God.* Without
such a prior understanding of goodness, we could not understand the sentence "God is
good." This clearly shows that our understanding of morality and knowledge of goodness
are independent of any knowledge that we may or may not have of the divine. Indeed,
without a prior and logically independent understanding of good and without some nonre-
ligious criterion for judging something to be good, the religious person could have no
knowledge of God, for he could not know whether that powerful being who spoke out of
the whirlwind and laid the foundations of the earth was in fact worthy of worship and perfectly good.

From my argument we should conclude that we cannot decide whether something is good
or whether it ought to be done simply from finding out (assuming that we can find out)
that God commanded it, willed it, enjoined it. Furthermore, whether "God is good" is synthetic
(substantive) or analytic (a truth of language), the concept of good must be understood as something distinct from the concept of God; that is to say, a man could know how to use *good* properly and still not know how to use *God.* Conversely, a man could not know how to use *God*
correctly unless he already understood how to use *good.* An understanding of goodness is logically prior to, and is independent of, any understanding or acknowledgment of God.

Feminist Critique of "God-talk"

From *Beyond God the Father: Toward a Philosophy of Women's Liberation* by Mary
Daly, 1973

*According to Mary Daly, a leading feminist theorist and a professor of theology at Boston
College, religion—mainstream Western religion in particular—has been used to subjugate women and, especially, to keep them quiet. The modern refusal of women to submit
any longer to patriarchal societal forms has involved a recognition of male dominion
over patterns of speech, falsely sacralized speech in the case of calling God exclusively
Father (and not Mother) and pronominally referring to God through the masculine, 'He',
'Him', and 'His'. Matters have in fact been worse: such implicit patriarchy in speech has
been coupled with the explicit in, for example, the Pauline text that denies women the
right to teach religious matters and the consonant policy concerning women and the
priesthood in Roman Catholicism, et cetera.*

*Women, then, have been forced to develop other modes of communication, what
Daly calls the sounds of silence, and other modes of worship and communion, what*

she calls the Antichurch. But Daly does not restrict herself to pointing out forms of opposition male domination has brought about; she offers a vision of non-subjugational forms of society and of people, both men and women, who no longer instinctively be-have in patriarchal modes. She sees much good having come out of sexist religion, de-spite its sexism, such as people being helped to achieve "a kind of autonomy, charity, and peace." She does not want to reject religion entirely, but to help push it into non-subjugational forms. With the last selection of this section, we shall see another feminist, Rosemary Radford Ruether, arguing similarly for a non-sexist, ecological religious sensitivity to help us resolve current crises especially concerning the environment.

ANTICHURCH AND THE SOUNDS OF SILENCE

Male religion entombs women in sepulchres of silence in order to chant its own eternal and dreary dirge to a past that never was. The silence *imposed* upon women echoes the struc-tures of male hierarchies. It is important to listen to the structures of this imposed silence in order to hear the flow of the new sounds of free silence that are the voice of sisterhood as Antichurch.

Durkheim wrote of the Warramunga tribe in Australia which imposed absolute silence upon women for long mourning periods (as long as two years). As a result, he claimed, the women developed communication through gestures. Some preferred to remain silent even for years after the imposed period of silence. One woman was said to have been silent for twenty-four years. One wonders if the continuation of silence is because the women dis-cover a better means of communication, an underground language of silence that men can-not understand.

The Pauline text screamed (it doesn't matter at all whether this was written by Paul or some pseudo-Paul): "I permit no woman to teach . . . she is to keep silent." The point, it seems, was that women cannot "officially" speak—a claim still shrilly proclaimed by Roman Catholicism and orthodox Judaism and affirmed only a bit more subtly by Reform Judaism and Protestant Christianity. For the "sacred" words were all written by men and can only be repeated and echoed. In religions that cling to the past, whether by Bibliolatry or by tradition or both, no woman can break out of imposed silence.

In modern times academia and the printed secular word have partially moved in on the territory of the sacred church and its sacred word. Here too women have been entombed in imposed silence, in the gross and obvious way of simply being excluded and in the more subtle way of only being allowed to echo male words. One may not dare to think out loud women's words—at least, not too much. We know the penalties for that.

As a result the new sounds of free silence may be hard for many to understand. They are many-faceted. We speak forth shapes and colors, utter textures, flash forth to each other in a flow of understanding what is too awesome to be understood: our own self-birth in sis-terhood. Robin Morgan paints the silence:

And I will speak less and less to you
And more and more in crazy gibberish you cannot understand:
witches' incantations, poetry, old women's mutterings . . . .[1]

This multi-faced communication that is being born among women in the modern tech-nological jungle of America is nonspeech in the terms of our culture, just as truly as the gestures of the "primitive" Warramunga women were nonspeech to their men. Multi-leveled communication is of course not unknown to all men, but the rules of patriarchy try to write it out as much as possible. What is new when it happens with women is that it is the interflow of our own being, our affirmation of process that is our own process over and against sepulchral forms that almost but never quite did quench our fire.

Women are starting to know now the defects of language because it is not ours. It reflects the structures blessed by male religion. In order to say that women's speech breaks out of these bounds I have called it silence. It is silence in the sense of going beyond inau-thentic speech, but to those who know only inauthentic speech it is meaningless. "Logical positivists" have claimed that one can ask only whatever questions language clearly ex-presses. To go outside this pre-established box is, supposedly, to use "pseudo-propositions," to say the unthinkable, the meaningless. What the logical positivists did not point out was that the pre-established box is patriarchal, which would mean that our new anti-patriarchal questions are *a priori* pseudo-questions. Other academicians, and non-academicians, though they would not call themselves logical positivists, share this view. To such persons, who crush thought and language into patriarchal space and time past, the new sounds are unhear-able. A sexist language-bound world is deaf to these.

Suzanne Langer wrote of the restriction on discourse that sets bounds to the complex-ity of speakable ideas. She saw this as an inherent defect of language, which is a poor medium for expressing emotions, ever-moving patterns, the ambivalences and intricacies of inner experience, the interplay of feelings and thought, memories and echoes of memo-ries. The fine arts compensate for this built-in defect of language, she maintained.[2] But I would point out that poetry and the fine arts have been *individual* expressions of ontologi-cal reason—granting that in the case of great art many people can resonate to such expres-sions. They have remained by and large within patriarchy, which has neatly labeled them "fine arts," and entombed them in its museums and universities. Contained, they have not made planetary rebellion. Indeed most art and poetry in our culture expresses patriarchal feelings. (Look at the flabby, unathletic bodies of Renaissance Madonnas; read the diar-rheic outpourings of misogynism in Milton, Kipling, Claudel.) By contrast, the new sounds of silence, sparking forth a network of boundary communication, is the dawning of communal New Being. This is neither "public" nor "private," neither "objective" nor "sub-jective." It is intersubjective silence, the vibrations of which are too high for the patriarchal hearing mechanism. It is, then, ultrasonic.

---

[1] Robin Morgan, *Monster* (New York: Vintage), p. 85.
[2] Suzanne Langer, *Philosophy in a New Key* (New York: New American Library).

BEYOND THE ANTICHURCH

I have already indicated that the merging of feeling and thought, of the personal and the political in the new space being created by the second wave of feminism is a widespread spiritual event. It implies conflict with sexist religion as such, but it also portends transcendence, not only of the sexism, but also of the conflict. This is partially due to the paradoxical fact that there is an *élan* toward transcendence discernible in the women I have called spiritual expatriates, which is at least in part traceable to the influence of religion upon their lives. This influence has been both direct and indirect, that is, by way of direct participation in organized religion and by way of a general cultural climate that has in large measure been shaped by the Judeo-Christian heritage.

A purely negative evaluation of the effects of religion would be inaccurate. It cannot be denied that many people, women and men, have achieved with the help of religion a kind of autonomy, charity, and peace. I have pointed out that these qualities, and particularly this peace, have been attained at too high a price, that is, by leaping over inequities instead of working through these. Certainly, there is something deficient in harmony bought at the expense of insight, in solving problems by not seeing them. Yet it is the human condition always to have only partial insight, and it would be foolish and insensitive to deny all authenticity to the deep experience, the values, and the commitment of those whose religious conditioning rendered them opaque to its own negative aspects. Those who have abandoned institutional religion—or to be more accurate, *been abandoned by institutional religion*—because of these negative elements have often retained a fundamentally spiritual insight, although in many cases they would be reluctant and even hostile to the idea of calling it "religious." At any rate, there is a remarkable radicalization of consciousness among these spiritual exiles, which often manifests itself in refusal to stop short at limited goals and particular issues, however valid and important—such as legalization of abortion, free day care centers, or the equal rights amendment—and constantly seek to understand the deep implications of liberation.

This deeply radicalized consciousness is by no means the unique property of those who at some time have been personally related to the churches, however. It is one of the developing dimensions of sisterhood—a dynamic toward spiritualization of consciousness and communal incarnation of that consciousness. To call this reality Antichurch is good, but we should not stop with this name alone. To say this word and to stop here is to be caught in a mode of expression that leaves us with an "opposition of opposites." "Opposites" are open to seductive advances, to offers of cooptation, as radical women know. This is illustrated by the many incidences of being invited to speak to obviously nonfeminist gatherings, or to be on panels that are carefully "balanced to represent both extreme points of view" (the assumption being that "truth" must lie in between somewhere). "Opposites" are open to seduction not because they are perceived as radical, but because they are perceived as similar to, in the same category with, the "opponent." To recognize this is not to renounce our identity as Antichurch, nor, on the pragmatic level, does it mean that we must always renounce such offers of a forum. It does mean that we have to be wary and that we have to reach toward something *beyond* opposition.

The Jain Ethics of Non-Injury

From *Āyāro (Ācārāṅga Sūtra),* Muni Mahendra Kumar, translator, 1981

Just as an ethical orientation taken from God's commands according to scripture is integral to the mainstream philosophies of Judaism, Christianity, and Islam, so an ethics of non-injury (Sanskrit: ahiṃsā), tied to a mystic attainment, has been integral to much Eastern religion and philosophy, particularly Buddhism. In the context of classical India, it is, however, a smaller religious group called Jains (or Jainas) who should be most closely identified with the ethics of non-injury.

Mahāvīra, the founder of Jainism, lived in the sixth century BCE. He was roughly contemporary with the Buddha. Mahāvīra is also known as the Jina, "the Victor" (over passion). His teaching of non-injury stems from a sense of the pervasiveness of consciousness throughout the realm of the living (especially animals). Not only are Jains vegetarians, but Jain monks have been known to wear masks to prevent injury to insects from breathing. Regarding even vegetable life as forms of sentience, some Jain monks have starved themselves to death not to harm others.

Like Buddhist scriptures, the Jain Canon is immense. This selection, from the Ācārāṅga Sūtra, concerns ahiṃsā and its justification. The practice is not said simply to be conducive to one's own good or to be the teaching of Mahāvīra. Non-injury is defended by an idea of equality of soul. Everything that is conscious hates injury, and so realizing that others are like oneself in being conscious and hating all forms of harm, one should refrain from injuring others. Some commentators have identified this teaching with Christianity's Golden Rule.

THE TRUE DOCTRINE: NON-VIOLENCE

1. I say—

The *Arhats* (Venerable Ones) of the past, those of the present and the future narrate thus, discourse thus, proclaim thus, and asserverate thus:
One should not injure, subjugate, enslave, torture or kill any animal, living being, organism or sentient being.
2. This Doctrine of Non-violence (viz. *Ahiṃsā-dharma*) is immaculate, immutable and eternal.
The Self-realised *Arhats*, having comprehended the world (of living beings), have propounded this (Doctrine).

3. (The *Arhats* have propounded the Doctrine of Non-violence for one and all, equally for)

those who are intent on practising it and those who are not;
those who are desirous to practise it and those who are not;
those who have eschewed violence and those who have not;

those who are acquisitive and those who are not;

those who are deeply engrossed in worldly ties and those who are not.

4. This Doctrine of *Ahiṃsā* is Truth. It is truely [truly] axiomatic. It is rightly enunciated here (i.e. in the Teachings of the *Arhats*).

5. Having accepted this (Great vow of Non-violence), one should neither vitiate it nor forsake it.

Comprehending the true spirit of the Doctrine, (one should practise it till one's last breath).

6. He should be dispassionate towards sensual objects.

7. He should refrain from worldly desires.

8. How can one who is bereft of the knowledge of this (Doctrine of *Ahiṃsā*), have the knowledge of other (Doctrines)?

9. This (Doctrine of Non-violence) which is being expounded has been perceived, heard, deliberated upon and thoroughly understood.

10. Those who resort to and remain engrossed in violence suffer (the miseries of) transmigration again and again.

11. O *Sādhaka*!* You, who are endeavouring day and night; discern that those who are stupefied are outside the sphere of the Doctrine (of Non-violence). You should, therefore, be alert and always sedulous. . . .

20. Some put forth mutually . . . contradictory doctrines in the field (of philosophy).

Some of them contend: "The following doctrine has been perceived, heard, reflected upon, thoroughly, comprehended and scrutinized in all directions—upwards, downwards and lateral: 'All animals, living beings, organisms and sentient creatures may be injured, governed, enslaved, tortured and killed: Know that there is no sin in committing violence.'

21. This (approval of violence) is the doctrine of the ignoble ones.

22. Those who are Noble Ones assert thus: "O Protagonists of the doctrine of violence! Whatever you have perceived, heard, reflected upon, thoroughly comprehended and scrutinized in all directions—upwards, downwards and lateral, is fallacious, and hence, you say, speak, assert and preach: 'All animals, living beings, organisms and sentient creatures may be injured, governed, enslaved, tortured and killed: Know that there is no sin in committing violence.'"

23. We, on the other hand, say, speak, assert and preach: "All animals, living beings, organisms and sentient creatures should not be injured, governed, enslaved, tortured and killed: Know that it is non-violence which is (completely) free from sin."

24. This (approval of non-violence) is the doctrine of the Noble ones.

25. First, we shall ask (each philosopher) to enunciate his own doctrine and then put the following question to him: "O philosophers! Is suffering pleasing to you or painful?

26. "(If you say that suffering is pleasing to you, your answer is contradictory to what is self-evident. And if you, on the other hand, say that suffering is painful to you, then) your answer is valid. Then, we want to tell you that just as suffering is painful to you, in the same way it is painful, disquieting and terrifying to all animals, living beings, organisms and sentient beings."

---

* A person following the Path.—ed.

122. Through observation and scrutiny find out for yourself that inquietude is distasteful to, highly terrifying and painful for all animals, all beings, all those throbbing with life and all souls. So do I say. . . .

123. (Being overwhelmed by grief), the creatures are scared from (all) directions and intermediate directions. . . .

133. He (true ascetic), comprehending it (i.e. consequences of an act of violence), becomes vigilant over the practice of self-discipline.

134. Hearing from the Bhagavān Mahāvīra Himself or from the monks, one comes to know:—It (i.e. causing violence . . . , in fact, is the knot of bondage,

it, in fact, is the delusion,

it, in fact, is the death,

it, in fact, is the hell.

146. It is he who perceives (that violence causes) terror (and that it would be to) his own detriment (becomes competent to practise non-violence).

147. One who knows the inner-self knows the external (world) as well: One who knows the external (world) knows the inner-self as well. . . .

148. Try to realise the significance of this 'equality'. . . .

171. Those (who do not rejoice in the practice of the ethical code), while indulging in violence, preach (to others) the ethical code.

174. One who is rich in the enlightenment (i.e. one who practices non-violence) should not indulge in any sinful action (i.e. causing violence and self-indulgence) through his conscience (guided) by the intellect fully illuminated with Truth. . . .

Reënchanted Nature

From "Traditional American Indian Attitudes toward Nature" by J. D. Callicott and Thomas Overholt in *From Africa to Zen,* Robert C. Solomon and Kathleen M. Higgins, editors, 1993

Central to the religious attitudes of traditional Amerindian peoples is a reverence for nature, and, especially, a sense of animals as persons. This does not mean that hunting is looked upon with moral disapprobation but that in hunting, and in numerous other activities, the traditional Amerindian typically shows deep respect for whatever he or she is engaged with, not elevating the human over the natural and not vaunting a sense of superiority.

In several publications, philosophers J. B. Callicott and Thomas Overholt have championed such attitudes as part of an attempt to forge a new environmental ethic. It is not sufficient, they say, to recognize current crises; we need to renounce the attitudes that have led to them and adopt new attitudes, similar to the traditional Amerindian, of profound respect for nature. These attitudes should be based on the realization that, fundamentally, we are not different from other life forms. Moreover, if matter is spiritualized with us, then it is also all over the planet.

Callicott and Overholt sense that, as they say, "The modern mechanistic worldview and its technological expression are collapsing. A new, more organic ecological worldview and a corresponding technological esprit are beginning to take shape." They see traditional Amerindian religious notions as great resources for clothing the new perspective and popularizing it. They are hopeful that a revitalization of traditional Amerindian religious attitudes—which some see as already widespread in North America—will have, in sum, positive ecological consequences.

Let us now explore . . . the suggestion made . . . that in its *practical* consequences the traditional American Indian view of nature was on the whole more productive of a coöperative symbiosis of people with their environment than is the view of nature predominant in the prevailing Western European and Euro-American tradition.

Respecting the latter, Ian McHarg writes that "it requires little effort to mobilize a sweeping indictment of the physical environment which is [Western] man's creation [and] it takes little more to identify the source of the value system which is the culprit.[1] According to McHarg, the culprit is "the Judeo-Christian-Humanist view which is so unknowing of nature and of man, which has bred and sustained his simple-minded anthropocentricism."[2]

Since the early 1960s popular ecologists and environmentalists (perhaps most notably Rachel Carson and Barry Commoner, along with McHarg and Lynn White, Jr., and, more recently, Norman Myers, Paul Ehrlich, and Bill McKibben) have, with a grim fascination, recited a litany of environmental ills. They have spoken of "polychlorinated biphenyls," "chlorofluorocarbons," "nuclear tinkering," "acid rain," and "the gratified bulldozer" in language once reserved for detailing the precincts of Hell and abominating its seductive Prince. Given the frequency with which we are reminded of the symptoms of strain in the global biosphere and the apocalyptic rhetoric in which they are usually cast we may be excused if we omit this particular step from the present argument. Let us stipulate that modern technological civilization (European in its origins) has been neither restrained nor especially delicate in manipulating the natural world.

With somewhat more humor than other advocates of environmental reform, Aldo Leopold characterized the modern Western approach to nature thus: "By and large our present problem is one of attitudes and implements. We are remodeling the Alhambra with a steam shovel, and we are proud of our yardage. We shall hardly relinquish the shovel, which after all has many good points, but we are in need of gentler and more objective criteria for its successful use."[3] So far as the historical roots of the environmental crisis are concerned, we have here suggested that the much maligned attitudes arising out of the Judaic aspect of the Judeo-Christian tradition (man's God-given right to subdue nature, and so forth) have not been so potent a force in the work of remodeling as the tradition of Western natural philosophy that originated among the ancient Greeks, insidiously affected Christianity, and fully flowered in modern classical scientific thought. At least Western

---

[1] Ian McHarg, "Values, Process, Form," from *The Fitness of Man's Environment* (Washington, D.C.: Smithsonian Institution Press, 1968), reprinted in Robert Disch, ed., *The Ecological Conscience* (Englewood Cliffs, N.J.: Prentice-Hall, 1970), p. 25.

[2] Ibid., p. 98.

[3] Leopold, *Sand County,* pp. 263–64.

natural philosophy has been as formative of the cultural milieu (one artifact of which is the steam shovel itself) as have Genesis and the overall Old Testament worldview. In any case, mixed and blended together, they create a mentality in which unrestrained environmental exploitation and degradation could almost have been predicted in advance.

It seems obvious (especially to philosophers and historians of ideas) that attitudes and values *do* directly "determine" behavior by setting goals (for example, to subdue the Earth, to have dominion) and, through a conceptual representation of the world, by providing means (for example, mechanics, optics, and thermodynamics) expressed in technologies (for example, steam shovels and bulldozers). . . .

At the one extreme, it seems incredible to think that *all* our conceptualizations, our representations of the nature of nature, are, as it were, mere entertainment, a sort of Muzak for the mind, while our actions proceed in some blind way from instinctive or genetically programmed sources. After all, our picture of nature defines our theater of action. It defines both the possibilities and the limitations that circumscribe human endeavor. We attempt to do only what we think is possible, while we leave alone what we think is not. Moveover, what we believe human nature to be, and what we take to be our proper place and role in the natural world, represents an ideal that, consciously or not, we strive to realize. At the other extreme, the facts of history and everyday experience do not support any simple cause-and-effect relationship between a given conceptual and valuational set and how people actually behave. Notoriously, we often act in ways that conflict with our sincere beliefs, especially our moral beliefs, and with our values.

Here is our suggestion for understanding the relationship between human environmental attitudes and values, on the one hand, and actual human behavior in respect to nature, on the other. Inevitably, human beings must consume other living things and modify the natural environment. Representations of the order of nature and the proper relationship of people to that order may have either a tempering, restraining effect on our manipulative and exploitative tendencies or an accelerating, exacerbating effect. They also give form and direction to these inherently human drives and thus provide different cultures with their distinctive styles of doing things. It appears, further, that in the case of the predominant European mentality, shaped both by Judeo-Christian and by Greco-Roman images of nature and man, the effect was to accelerate the inherent human disposition to consume "resources" and modify surroundings. A kind of "takeoff" or (to mix metaphors) "quantum leap" occurred, and Western European civilization was propelled—for better or worse—into its industrial, technological stage, with a proportional increase in ecological and environmental distress. The decisive ingredient, the sine qua non, may have been the particulars of the European worldview.

If the predominant traditional Chinese view of nature and man has been characterized by Yi-Fu Tuan and others as quiescent and adaptive, the American Indian view of the world has been characterized as in essence "ecological"—for example, by Stewart Udall in *The Quiet Crisis*. The general American Indian worldview (at least the one central part of it to which we have called attention) deflected the inertia of day-to-day, year-to-year subsistence in a way that resulted, on the average, in conservation. Pre-Columbian American

Indian conservation of resources may have been a *consciously* posited goal. But probably it was not. Probably conservation was neither a personal ideal nor a tribal policy because the "wise use" of "natural resources" would, ironically, appear to be inconsistent with the spiritual and personal attributes that the Indians regarded as belonging to nature and natural things. So-called natural resources are represented by most conservationists, whose philosophy was shaped by Gifford Pinchot, the nation's first chief forester, as only commodities, subject to scarcity, and therefore in need of prudent "development" and "management." The American Indian posture toward nature was, we suggest, more moral or ethical. Animals, plants, and minerals were treated as persons, and conceived to be coequal members of a natural social order.

Our cautious claim that the American Indian worldview supported and included a distinctly ethical attitude toward nature and the myriad variety of natural entities is based on the following basic points. The American Indians, on the whole, viewed the natural world as enspirited. Natural beings therefore felt, perceived, deliberated, and responded voluntarily as persons. Persons are members of a social order (that is, part of the operational concept of *person* is the capacity for social interaction). Social interaction is limited by (culturally variable) behavioral restraints—rules of conduct—which we call, in sum, good manners, morals, and ethics. Thus, as N. Scott Momaday maintains: "Very old in the Native American world view is the conviction that the earth is vital, that there is a spiritual dimension to it, a dimension in which man rightly exists. It follows logically that there are ethical imperatives in this matter.[4] The American Indians, more particularly, lived in accordance with an "ecological conscience" that was structurally similar to Aldo Leopold's "land ethic."

Examples of wastage—buffalo rotting on the plains under high cliffs or beaver all but trapped out during the fur trade—are supposed to deliver the coup de grace to all romantic illusions of the American Indian's reverence for nature. But examples of murder and war also abound in European history. Must we conclude therefrom that Europeans were altogether without a humanistic ethic of any sort?[5] Hardly. What confounds such facile arguments is a useful understanding of the function of ethics in human affairs.

As philosophers point out, ethics bear a normative relation to behavior. They do not describe how people actually behave. Rather, they set out how people *ought* to behave. People remain free to act either in accordance with a given ethic or not. The fact that on some occasions some do not scarcely proves that, in a given culture, ethical norms do not exist, or that ethics are not on the whole influential and effective behavioral restraints.

The familiar Christian ethic, with its emphasis on the dignity and intrinsic value of human beings, has long been a very significant element of Western culture, and has exerted a decisive influence within European and Euro-American civilization. Certainly, it has

---

[4] Momaday, "First American Views," p. 18.

[5] The most scurrilous example of this sort of argument with which we are acquainted is Daniel A. Guthrie's "Primitive Man's Relationship to Nature," *BioScience* 21 (July 1971): 721–23. In addition to rotting buffalo, Guthrie cites alleged extirpation of Pleistocene megafauna by Paleo-Indians, ca. 10,000 B.P. (as if that were relevant), and his cheapest shot of all, "the litter of bottles and junked cars to be found on Indian reservations today."

inspired noble and even heroic deeds both by individuals and by whole societies. The documented existence and influence of the Christian ethic are not in the least diminished by monstrous crimes on the part of individual Europeans. Nor do shameful episodes of national depravity, like the Spanish Inquisition, and genocide, as in Nazi Germany, refute the assertion that a human-centered ethic has palpably affected average behavior among members of the European culture and substantially shaped the character of Western civilization.

By parity of reasoning, examples of occasional destruction of nature on the pre-Columbian American continent and even the extirpation of species, especially during periods of enormous cultural stress, as in the fur trade era, do not, by themselves, refute the assertion that American Indians lived not only by a trial ethic but by a land ethic as well. The overall and usual effect of such an ethic was to establish a greater harmony between the aboriginal American peoples and their environment than that enjoyed by their Euro-American successors.

We are living today in a very troubling time, but also a time of great opportunity. The modern mechanistic worldview and its technological expression are collapsing. A new, more organic ecological worldview and a corresponding technological esprit are beginning to take shape. But how can we translate this essentially scientific realization and its techno-social analogue into terms easily grasped by ordinary people so that we may all begin to see ourselves as a part of nature and as dependent on it for our sustenance? Only then can we hope to evolve a sustainable society.

The Indians were hardly evolutionary ecologists, but their outlook on nature was, albeit expressed in the imagery of myth, remarkably similar to the concept of nature emerging from contemporary biology. They saw themselves as plain members and citizens of their respective biotic communities, humbly and dependently participating in the local economy of nature. Hence one way to help popularize the emerging new ecological worldview and its associated life-style would be to turn for help to the indigenous wisdom of the North American continent. American Indian mythology could put imaginative flesh and blood on the dry skeleton of the abstract environmental sciences.

American Indian thought remains an untapped intellectual resource for all contemporary Americans. Euro-Americans cannot undo the past injustices that our forebears inflicted on American Indians. What we can do, however, is to recognize and fully incorporate the cognitive cultural achievements evolved in this hemisphere. So doing would engender respect and honor for the peoples who created them and for their contemporary custodians.

Some may say that "mining" the so-far "untapped" intellectual "resource" represented by traditional American Indian cognitive cultures would only perpetuate the history of exploitation of Native Americans by Euro-Americans.[6] After appropriating Indian lands, now we propose to add insult to injury by appropriating Indian ideas. We disagree. Things

---

[6] A similar complaint about Western intellectual colonialism of Asian traditions of thought has been registered by Gerald James Larson, "'Conceptual Resources' in South Asia for 'Environmental Ethics,'" in Callicott and Ames, *Nature in Asian Traditions of Thought,* pp. 267–77.

of the mind are not diminished when they are shared. Teachers do not diminish their knowledge by sharing it with students. Quite the contrary. Similarly, American Indian thought could only be enlarged and enriched should it become a principal tributary to the mainstream of contemporary North American culture and civilization. And, vice versa, North American culture and civilization could at last become something more than an extension of its European matrix should it mix and merge with the rich legacy of its native peoples.

Ecofeminism

From *Gaia and God* by Rosemary Radford Ruether, 1992

Rosemary Radford Ruether, a leading theologian and feminist theorist who has held positions at Harvard and Yale and other distinguished universities, sees environmental crises as symptomatic of the philosophic and religious illness of a false regard toward nature, a regard deeply embedded in Western culture and enshrined, sanctified in Christianity especially. She has much in common with Callicott and Overholt in her analyses, and, like them, is far from sanguine about the idea of any "technological fix" to current environmental crises. Ruether sees destructive patterns of human relationship to nature as continuous with patterns of gender, class, and racial domination. We need, she says, "a social reordering" to bring about justice and a new, healed relationship to the earth, which she symbolizes as Gaia, the Divine Mother.

Ruether holds that we need not, indeed should not, abandon a sense of transcendence to bring religion in line with the ethics demanded by environmental crises. On the contrary, she asks us to listen to two Divine voices, one of God, the other of Gaia, the one found in a covenantal tradition, the other in a sacramental. However, the covenantal tradition in particular needs to be reshaped and cleansed, she suggests, from "patriarchal constructions."

Ruether also asks us to rededicate ourselves to "base communities" which would nurture a new biophilic consciousness. She sees the change of consciousness (metanoia) required to be furthered less by professional, costly therapies than by community interaction, which in most cases would be simple and free. It would be in such communities, with new liturgies and religious practices, that we would be able to develop societal patterns and norms appropriate to living in harmony with our Mother, the earth, and all her many offspring.

Critics are likely to see these suggestions as impractical or insufficiently concrete. Moreover, some environmental problems, such as global warming and depletion of atmospheric ozone, are planetary, and it is argued that international political policies hold the only promise for progress toward their resolution. Many experts are dubious whether small (base) communities, however noble their intentions as judged in a local context, could make decisions that would add up to a wise environmental policy regarding the earth as a whole. But Ruether to her credit sees her small communities as aware of global problems and as self-constraining, even self-guiding in their light, as eager to comply and to inaugurate practices in accordance with the best environmental wisdom concerning the whole earth, who, it bears repeating, would be revered as Gaia, the Divine Mother.

Gaia and God, ecofeminism, and earth healing: these vast concepts point to the wide-ranging agenda that I seek to explore. . . . Are Gaia, the living and sacred earth, and God, the monotheistic deity of the biblical traditions, on speaking terms with each other? Ecology and feminism, brought together in the unified perspective of ecofeminism, provide the critical perspective from which I seek to evaluate the heritage of Western Christian culture. The goal of this quest is earth healing, a healed relationship between men and women, between classes and nations, and between humans and the earth. Such healing is possible only through recognition and transformation of the way in which Western culture, enshrined in part in Christianity, has justified such domination.

It would be useful to define the sense in which I use the terms *ecology, feminism,* and *ecofeminism.* The word *ecology* comes from the biological science of natural environmental communities. It examines how these natural communities function to sustain a healthy web of life and how they become disrupted, causing death to plant and animal life. Human intervention is the major cause of such disruption. Thus ecology, in the expanded sense of a combined socioeconomic and biological science, emerged in the last several decades to examine how human misuse of "nature" is causing pollution of soils, water, and air, and the destruction of plant and animal communities, thereby threatening the base of life upon which the human species itself depends.

Deep ecology took this study of ecology to another level. It examined the symbolic, psychological, and ethical patterns of destructive relations of humans with nature. It particularly saw Western culture, sanctified in Christianity, as a major cause of this destructive culture. It explored ways to create new, more holistic consciousness and culture.

Feminism also has many dimensions of meaning. As liberal feminism, it seeks equality of women with men in liberal, democratic societies; as socialist feminism, it declares that such equality is not possible without a transformation of the social relations of ownership of the means of production and reproduction. Radical feminism declared that the issue was deeper, that we had to look at the patterns of culture and consciousness that sustain male domination over and violence to women.

Ecofeminism brings together these two explorations of ecology and feminism, in their full, or deep forms, and explores how male domination of women and domination of nature are interconnected, both in cultural ideology and in social structures. . . .

If dominating and destructive relations to the earth are interrelated with gender, class, and racial domination, then a healed relation to the earth cannot come about simply through technological "fixes." It demands a social reordering to bring about just and loving interrelationship between men and women, between races and nations, between groups presently stratified into social classes, manifest in great disparities of access to the means of life. In short, it demands that we must speak of eco-justice, and not simply of domination of the earth as though that happened unrelated to social domination.

Classical Western cultural traditions, which were codified between 500 B.C.E. and 800 C.E., and of which Christianity is a major expression, have justified and sacralized these relationships of domination. Thus we inherit not only a legacy of systems of domination, but also cultures that teach us to see such relations as the "natural order" and as the will of God.

In particular, the way these cultures have construed the idea of the male monotheistic God, and the relation of this God to the cosmos as its Creator, have reinforced symbolically the relations of domination of men over women, masters over slaves, and (male ruling-class) humans over animals and over the earth. Domination of women has provided a key link, both socially and symbolically, to the domination of earth, hence the tendency in patriarchal cultures to link women with earth, matter, and nature, while identifying males with sky, intellect, and transcendent spirit.

But these classical traditions did not only sacralize patriarchal hierarchy over women, workers, and the earth. They also struggled with what they perceived to be injustice and sin and sought to create just and loving relations between people in their relation to the earth and to the divine. Some of this effort to name evil and struggle against it reinforced relations of domination and created victim-blaming spiritualities and ethics. But there are also glimpses in this heritage of transformative, biophilic relationships.

These glimpses are a precious legacy that needs to be separated from the toxic waste of sacralized domination. We do not need to and should not totalize negative judgment against past biblical and Christian cultures. It would be surprising indeed if there were no positive insights that could be reclaimed from three thousand years of collective human struggle about the meaning of life and the way to live justly and well. Ecofeminist critics of classical culture are surely not the first humans to have positive sensibilities.

A healed relation to each other and to the earth then calls for a new consciousness, a new symbolic culture and spirituality. We need to transform our inner psyches and the way we symbolize the interrelations of men and women, humans and earth, humans and the divine, the divine and the earth. Ecological healing is a theological and psychic-spiritual process. Needless to say, spirituality or new consciousness will not transform deeply materialized relations of domination by themselves. We must be wary of new forms of privatized intrapsychic activity, divorced from social systems of power. Rather we must see the work of eco-justice and the work of spirituality as interrelated, the inner and outer aspects of one process of conversion and transformation. . . .

Gaia is the word for the Greek Earth Goddess, and it is also a term adopted by a group of planetary biologists, such as James Lovelock and Lynn Margulis, to refer to their thesis that the entire planet is a living system, behaving as a unified organism.

The term *Gaia* has caught on among those seeking a new ecological spirituality as a religious vision. Gaia is seen as a personified being, an immanent divinity. Some see the Jewish and Christian male monotheistic God as a hostile concept that rationalizes alienation from and neglect of the earth. Gaia should replace God as our focus of worship. I agree with much of this critique, yet I believe that merely replacing a male transcendent deity with an immanent female one is an insufficient answer to the "god-problem."

We need a vision of a source of life that is "yet more" than what presently exists, continually bringing forth both new life and new visions of how life should be more just and more caring. The human capacity for ethical reason is not rootless in the universe, but expresses this deeper source of life "beyond" the biological. Consciousness and altruistic care are qualities that have some reflection in other animals, and indeed are often too poorly developed in our own species. To believe in divine being means to believe that those qualities in ourselves are rooted in and respond to the life power from which the universe itself arises. . . .

. . . [There are] two lines of biblical and Christian tradition that I seek to reclaim for an ecofeminist theology and spirituality, the covenantal tradition and the sacramental tradition. These two traditions seem to me to be complementary rather than alternatives to each other. The one tradition shapes our relation to nature and each other in terms of law and ethical responsibility. The other tradition ecstatically experiences the divine bodying forth in the cosmos, and beckons us into communion.

Neither of these traditions can be accepted simply in its traditional form, however. Both traditions were shaped in patriarchal, slave-holding societies and also reflect ancient geocentric cosmologies. Christians need to reshape these ideas in ways that free them from patriarchal constructions. We also need to bring these modes of relating to nature into dialogue with contemporary scientific knowledge and global realities. . . .

In these two traditions, covenantal and sacramental, we hear two voices of divinity from nature. One speaks from the mountaintops in the thunderous masculine tones of "thou shalt" and "thou shalt not." It is the voice of power and law, but speaking (at its most authentic) on behalf of the weak, as a mandate to protect the powerless and to restrain the power of the mighty. There is another voice, one that speaks from the intimate heart of matter. It has long been silenced by the masculine voice, but today is finding again her own voice. This is the voice of Gaia. Her voice does not translate into laws or intellectual knowledge, but beckons us into communion.

Both of these voices, of God and of Gaia, are our own voices. We need to claim them as our own, not in the sense that there is "nothing" out there, but in the sense that what is "out there" can only be experienced by us through the lenses of human existence. We are not the source of life, but are latecomers to the planet. Our minds didn't fall from the skies, but are the flowering of organic body and its capacities to know itself. We can touch our fellow beings, and intuit the source of all life and thought that lies behind the whole. This contact, though humanly imaged, can be true. Its truth lies in the test of relationships; do our metaphors bear the fruits of compassion or of enmity?

We need both of these holy voices. We cannot depend on volunteerism alone to save rain forests and endangered species, set limits to the exploitation of animals and sanction abusers. We need organized systems and norms of ecological relations. Otherwise, not only will most people not comply, but will not be able to comply, because they have no way of fulfilling their daily needs except through the exigencies of the present system. But, without the second voice, our laws have no heart, no roots in compassion and fellow feeling. They fail to foster a motivating desire for biophilic living. . . .

How do we carry on a struggle to heal the world and to build a new biospheric community in the face of this intransigent system of death? It is my belief that those who want to carry on this struggle in a sustained way must build strong base communities of celebration and resistance. By "base communities" I mean local face-to-face groups with which one lives, works, and prays. I do not mean that all these functions would necessarily come together for most people in one base community. Most people will find these different forms of support in a variety of groups and networks, although it is important that these many groups recognize their interconnections in one unified struggle.

There are three interrelated aspects of the work of such local communities. One is shaping the personal therapies, spiritualities, and corporate liturgies by which we nurture and symbolize a new biophilic consciousness. Second, there is the utilization of local institutions over which we have some control, our homes, schools, churches, farms, and locally controlled businesses, as pilot projects of ecological living. Third, there is the building of organizational networks that reach out, regionally, nationally, and internationally, in a struggle to change the power structures that keep the present death system in place.

We must start by recognizing that *metanoia,* or change of consciousness, begins with us. This does not happen all at once, but is an ongoing process. We all have been shaped to misname evil, to seek invulnerable power, or else to capitulate to such power demands in the hands of male authorities. We are tied to present systems of consumption and can hardly imagine alternatives to them that might give us greater peace and wholeness, even though the scramble to "keep up" in the present systems leaves us ever more insecure, anxious, and exhausted.

We need healing therapies and spiritualities of inner growth to let go of fears and open up to each other and to the world around us, to learn how to *be,* rather than to *strive.* The struggle to change the death system must be deeply rooted in joy in the goodness of life. Making healing and inner growth available to us all means unhooking them from professionalized "help," which comes with credentials and high price tags. Although there is a place for skilled people, most of what we need is fairly simple and "free."

We can survey ideas from a few good books, gather a group on a regular basis to discuss the ideas from "experts," and then begin to open up to each other and learn to become good "ears" for hearing each other's story. We also need to recover our body-psyche-spirit nexus, to learn to breathe again, to feel our life energy. Small groups can learn, perhaps with initial expert advice, and teach each other techniques of breathing, biofeedback, meditation, and massage.

We need to take the time to sit under trees, look at water, and at the sky, observe small biotic communities of plants and animals with close attention, get back in touch with the living earth. We can start to release the stifled intuitive and creative powers of our organism, to draw and to write poetry, and to know that we stand on holy ground.

In addition to personal therapies and spirituality, we need corporate liturgies as well, to symbolize and express our altered consciousness. Unfortunately most of our institutional forms of worship are tied to alienated, patriarchal consciousness. Much of their worship is literally "deadly," although some are open to partial transformation. Thus communities of new being and consciousness need to become their own liturgists. They need to learn to shape corporate liturgies to mourn together for violated lives, to midwife healing and new birth, and to taste a new creation already present.

Such communities can also learn to carry liturgy to the streets, in protest marches and demonstrations that cry out against the death system and visualize renewed life in ways that can catch the imagination of others who participate with them or watch them. We can call on all the arts—song and music, dance and mime, posters and banners, costumes and puppetry—to shape the public liturgies of biospheric politics. . . .

The time is short for major changes, if we are to save much of the biotic system of the earth that is in danger. The Worldwatch Institute estimates that we have about forty years for major global shifts to be carried out voluntarily (until 2030). After that time major disasters of famine and collapse of life systems, under the pressures of exploitative use, will take place, and there could well be very dangerous militarist and totalitarian responses from threatened elites, as indeed is already happening.

In speaking about the urgency of the situation before audiences, I am often asked if I am "optimistic" about the possibilities for change. The assumption behind this question seems to be that we have two ideational stances toward these crises: optimism or pessimism. But I am inclined to think that both these stances get us off the hook. If we are "optimistic," it suggests that change is inevitable and will happen in the "natural" course of things, and so we need not make much effort ourselves. Someone else will take care of it. If we are "pessimistic," change is impossible, and therefore it is useless to try. In either case we have the luxury, as critical but comfortable elites in the United States, to question the present system without being responsible for it.

What we need is neither optimism nor pessimism, in these terms, but committed love. This means that we remain committed to a vision and to concrete communities of life no matter what the "trends" may be. Whether we are immediately "winning" or "losing" cannot shake our rooted understandings of what biophilic life is and should be, although we need to adapt our strategies to the changing fortunes of the struggle. We also remain clear that life is not made whole "once and for all," in some static millennium of the future. It is made whole again and again, in the renewed day born from night and in the new spring that rises from each winter.

Being rooted in love for our real communities of life and for our common mother, Gaia, can teach us patient passion, a passion that is not burnt out in a season, but can be renewed season after season. Our revolution is not just for us, but for our children, for the generations of living beings to come. What we can do is to plant a seed, nurture a seed-bearing plant here and there, and hope for a harvest that goes beyond the limits of our powers and the span of our lives.

DISCUSSION QUESTIONS

1. According to David Hume's discussion in his *Dialogues,* what seem to be the moral effects of religion on, first, individual character and, second, society? Try to present the two sides he suggests, and say which side you suspect Hume himself favors.

2. Trace the Confucian views on ceremony and religious ritual as important to individual character development and relations in society. Do you find such views to be relevant to our times?

3. Outline the ethical views of Zera Yacob. By what criteria would he decide ethical and religious disputes?

4. Explain the connection between religious stories and parables, on the one hand, and ethical intentions, on the other, that R. B. Braithwaite sees. Do you agree that as far as the way one leads one's life is concerned it is immaterial whether one regards religious stories as true?

5. Explain Aurobindo's attitude toward traditional ethical teachings, religious and otherwise.

6. Reconstruct Plato's argument (voiced by the character Socrates) in favor of an ethical objectivism, that is, in favor of something's being loved by the gods because it is pious, as opposed to its being pious because it is loved by the gods.

7. What is the "Euthyphro dilemma" that James Hanink and Gary Mar examine in the course of defending a divine command theory of ethics (DCM)? What are the dilemma's two horns, and why is one of these, but not the other, unacceptable to Hanink and Mar? How do they defend DCM against the charge that moral principles would be arbitrary?

8. Reconstruct Kai Nielsen's attack on divine command theory, an attack that may also be called a defense of the independence of ethics. What considerations, if any, might possibly dull the edge of his critique, or do you see his as a knock-down argument? Explain.

9. Present Mary Daly's criticism of patriarchal religion and God-talk. Do you agree? What do you think of the alternatives she envisages?

10. What is the Jain teaching of non-injury (*ahiṃsā*), and how far, do you think, may it legitimately be extended? Reconstruct and evaluate the non-injury argument of the *Ācārāṅga Sūtra*.

11. To what do J. B. Callicott and Thomas Overholt attribute current environmental crises? What solutions do they recommend? Do you agree with their analysis and recommendations?

12. Present the views of Rosemary Radford Ruether concerning current environmental crises and traditional religion, especially Christianity. What reforms does she recommend? Are they practical? Would they solve environmental problems?

CHAPTER NINE

Personal Destiny

A teaching of individual survival of death is included in the doctrines of each world religion; religious thinkers denying an afterlife in the interest of another message (e.g., a Christian social ethic) have been, all told, quite rare. As we have seen, debunkers of religion, such as Freud and Marx, try to make the tag "wishful thinking" stick to all religious beliefs, but normally it is survival claims that are targeted to best make the overall case. People both instinctively and consciously try to avoid death, and the death of a loved one is often life's most painful event. It is surely true that many find consolation in an afterlife teaching. Critics say that religion provides a false though understandable comfort.

Until recently in the West, the positive reasons cited for accepting religious views about survival were pretty much limited to revelation. Doubtless there have been popular stories of communion with the dead, but a citing of natural evidence in support of an afterlife doctrine has not been mainstream within the religious philosophies associated with the major Western religious traditions, Judaism, Christianity, and Islam. Beliefs about personal survival and the nature of an afterlife have been determined principally by interpretations of scripture.

With Eastern (Hindu and Buddhist) views of reincarnation, in contrast, there are long traditions of considering certain natural phenomena as best explained by supposing a series of previous lives. (Of course, several Hindu and Buddhist scriptures also declare reincarnation.) M. Hiriyanna presents some of the best-explanationist arguments in an excerpt in this section.

Lack of evidence has been the main reason cited by a line of Western skeptical philosophers—from David Hume to F. H. Bradley and Bertrand Russell—why an afterlife seems unlikely. But recently, accounts of "near-death" experiences have been interpreted as suggesting that individual consciousness does survive the death of the body. Raymond Moody, a physician, presents some of these accounts—more precisely, a paradigmatic story based on many accounts—in the last selection of this section.

Much of the recent philosophic discussion of personal survival has focused on questions about possibility. Integral to mainstream Christianity—and most Judaism, too—has been belief in bodily resurrection, with, in some versions, a time gap between death and the assumption of a new, or restored, body in paradise. Philosophers have challenged the coherence of such conceptions. In the first selection below, George Mavrodes attempts to meet the challenges and to defend the possibility of resurrection.

Possibility is also the guiding light in C. J. Ducasse's discussion, where not the likelihood but rather the conceivability of reincarnation is what primarily gets aired. Building on common knowledge about a person's memory—and the lack of it with respect to early childhood—and about deep psychological dispositions or inclinations (a topic continuous with the theory of *karma* that Hiriyanna discusses), Ducasse sketches what he sees as an account of how reincarnation might occur.

The selections from Hume, Bradley, and Russell address the evidential question in the main, deciding that survival is highly unlikely. Russell also talks about emotional attitudes toward death, arguing, with a characteristically honest and high-minded sensibility, that we, out of pride in what we think and love, in facing death should reject fear. Bradley, too, in a footnote, says fear is out of place, claiming that since we cannot imagine our own death, fearing it would stem from an illusion.

Resurrection

From "The Life Everlasting and the Bodily Criterion of Identity" by George I. Mavrodes in *Nous,* Volume XI, Number 1, 1977

George Mavrodes, a philosophy professor at the University of Michigan, defends the possibility of a bodily resurrection against the objection that since there would be no bodily continuity (the physical body, after all, clearly decays), then any new body in paradise would belong to a new person, not to the person who died. The objection rests on a bodily criterion of personal identity, such that if a person A and a person B are the same person, then they must have the same body at all times. Mavrodes accepts the criterion but argues that it does not eliminate the possibility envisioned in Christian teachings about resurrection.

Mavrodes's strategy is to examine closely bodily continuity. It turns out that it is not so easy to specify precisely what bodily continuity amounts to. Insofar as attributes, such as hair color, are time-indexed—as, indeed, it seems they should be, since Mavrodes with brown hair in his youth as opposed to Mavrodes with grey hair in his maturity is the same person—and insofar as a single person is not thought to have two bodies (one in the grave, one restored), there does not seem to be any particular problem simply with diachronous differences. The rub is in the problem of continuity. Mavrodes's hair presumably changed gradually from brown to grey. But it proves so difficult to specify precisely what is required here (series of spatio-temporal points) that it seems that there is plenty of room for God (who is the required agent for resurrection on this view) to restore the person to a glorious body while maintaining her or his identity—so Mavrodes concludes.

Or it may be, he admits, that a continuity test does rule out the afterlife possibility envisioned. But in that case, Mavrodes points out, we have a serious problem with all personal identity, as well as the identity of things, from day to day, or moment to moment, on this side of the grave. In other words, the intractability of the problem of identity through change in our everyday world works to the benefit of the defender of the Christian teaching.

"I believe in . . . the resurrection of the body and the life everlasting. Amen." With these words the Apostle's Creed comes to a close, and with them also it expresses, I think, an important element in the orthodox Christian faith. As a very minimum this element involves the claim that the lives of at least some human beings do not come to a permanent end with their bodily deaths here, but that these individuals will either continue their lives beyond the incident of death or else that they will resume their lives at some point in the future, and that this continued or resumed life will be everlasting. An additional element seems to be the claim that this continued or resumed life will be a bodily life, and that it involves the resurrection—presumably somehow or other a reconstitution—of the body which died here.

Naturally, one might think of critical questions to ask about this belief, such as that of what reason or justification might be given in favor of supposing that it is true, or that of how such an apparently difficult operation might be accomplished. I think that Christians have usually been inclined to answer the former of these questions by saying that one knows of such things primarily by the revelation of God. And they usually have not thought of much of interest to say about the second question beyond saying that the resurrection of the body and the life everlasting are gifts of God, who is presumably able to do such things. In this paper I do not intend to pursue these questions at all, and so I will say nothing either in support or in criticism of such answers.

I turn, instead, to a somewhat different question, one which some philosophers apparently think is somehow prior to the questions I have just mentioned. This is the question of what, if any, sense can be made out of the identification of the persons who live the life everlasting with persons who began their careers in this world and died here. Some philosophers not only think that this question is prior to the others I have just mentioned—they apparently think it is the only philosophical question about immortality and similar topics. John Passmore, for example, writes, "As for immortality, there have often been doubts about whether this is really a question for philosophy. But insofar as it is, the question is whether it is possible to identify the being who is said to live after death with the living being by any of the ordinary means used in identification—that is, the means by which we determine whether we are both talking about the same person."

Antony Flew asserts both the priority and the enormity of the difficulty involved in this question. He writes, "Any reconstitution doctrine is confronted with the question 'How is the reconstituted person on the last day to be identified as the original me, as opposed to a mere replica, an appropriately brilliant forgery?' There seems to be no satisfactory answer to this question at least for a pure reconstitution theory. This question is, however, logically prior to all questions about the reasons, if any, that might be brought forward in support of such a doctrine.

"This decisive objection seems rarely to have been raised, and when it has been, its force has not usually been felt. . . . Notwithstanding the form of the original question, the difficulty is not one of 'How do you know?' but of 'What do you know?' The objection is that the reconstituted people could only be mere replicas of and surrogates for their earthly predecessors. Neither the appeal to the cognitive and executive resources of Omnipotence nor the appeal to the supposed special status of the person in question does anything at all to meet this contention. . . ."

If we were to put the objection we are here considering in its bluntest form it would come to something like this: We can know from the outset, and before we get into questions and claims about revelation, omnipotence, and the like, that the beliefs to which I referred in the first paragraph of this paper are false. Not even the omnipotence of God can bring about the state of affairs envisioned in those beliefs. For that state of affairs is conceptually impossible. That is a blunt statement of the position but it is perhaps not exactly accurate. More accurately, this position holds that there is a conceptual incompatibility between the state of affairs envisioned in this belief and some empirical facts about this world, facts which we know to be plainly true. While therefore it is abstractly possible that an omnipotent God could actualize the state of affairs in question, it is not possible for him to do so *given what actually happens in the world.* And it may also be held that it is now too late for God to alter the course of this world in such a way as to make possible the life of the world to come, at least in a way which would be importantly relevant to these Christian beliefs.

The conceptual incompatibility alleged here is supposed to be generated by a criterion of personal identity. . . .

This . . . probably reminds us of what is sometimes called "Leibniz's Law," and it is intended to do so. A first stab at formulating that law might go like this:

(4) For any entities x and y, x is identical with y IF [if and only if] x has every property which y has, and vice versa.

As it stands, this has some difficulties. First, it may suggest, in conjunction with certain empirical facts, that I had no youth. For one of my properties is that of being gray-haired. But the only plausible candidate for Mavrodes-as-youth did not have gray hair. So perhaps this formulation entails that I am not identical with that candidate. This difficulty can be remedied. While it is true of me now that I have gray hair it is also true of me now that in 1950 I had brown hair. It is also true of the candidate for Mavrodes-as-youth that he had brown hair in 1950, and there is no empirical reason to think that it is not true of him that he has gray hair now. Probably if we want a version of Leibniz's Law which applies to diachronic, as well as synchronic, identity then we need to formulate it in terms of properties such as these.

Some properties are such that even if a given thing has them at some time it need not have them at every time at which it has any property at all (i.e., at any time at which it exists). Having brown hair is apparently such a property. Let us call these the "time-variable properties." There are other properties such that if an entity has one of them at some time then it has that property at all times that is has any properties at all. Call these the "time-stable properties." Now we can propound the thesis that to every property which a thing has at an arbitrarily chosen time, t, there corresponds a time-stable property which it has at all times. For take any arbitrarily chosen property, P, which the thing has a t. If P is time-stable then it is itself the corresponding property, and the thing will have P whenever it exists. If P is time-variable, then *having P at t* is the corresponding time-stable property which the thing will have as long as it exists. And if we want a version of Leibniz's Law which will apply to diachronic identity then we should formulate it in terms of time-stable properties only. . . .

. . . Many Christians, at least . . . profess to believe in the resurrection of the body, the body which ran through its career in this world and then died, and not merely in the production of a new body for the world to come. So they believe that if y, in the world to come, is identical with some this-worldly x then the body which y has in that world to come *is,* in some sense, the same body which x had in this world. Does this improve their position *vis à vis* the Criterial Sceptic?

Such a sceptic, I think, is likely to say that the believer's position is not thereby strengthened, at least not with respect to many of those who are supposed to share in the life everlasting. For as a matter of fact they have already died, long ago, and their bodies have already decayed and totally ceased from existing. And so it is not possible that there should be a body, now or in the future, which is identical with the one they had during their earthly career. But why should this last consequence be thought to follow upon the former undisputed facts? Why should it be impossible that a certain body should perish, decay, and cease from existing, and then that later on that same body should be resurrected and take its place again in the realm of existing things?

The Sceptic will not be embarrassed by these questions, and will take them as a welcome opportunity to clarify further his sense of the diachronic identity of bodies. He has a criterion for such identity. The relevant part of it is as follows:

(7) For any x and y, x is the same body as y only if x is spatio-temporally continuous with y.

But if a body has decayed and ceased to exist by t_1 then there is a time immediately after t_1 during which it does not exist. If it were to be resurrected and brought again into existence at some later time, t_2, then it would suffer from a temporal gap between t_1 and t_2. The body which existed at t_2 would not be spatio-temporally continuous with the body which existed before t_1. And so, according to (7), they could not be identical. . . .

Perhaps we could state this necessary condition more formally as follows:

(8) For any x and y, if x and y are bodies, then x is spatio-temporally continuous with y if and only if there is a spatio-temporal point, ST_1, at which x is located, and a point, ST_2, at which y is located, and there is a compact series of points including ST_1 and ST_2 such that there is a body located at every point in this series.

Well, perhaps so. This explanation does not seem to have escaped from technicality, but maybe if we work through it carefully it will be clear enough. Except for one point. Or perhaps even that is clear enough. At any rate it is this. The expression "ST_1" appears twice in the formula above. What is the relation between the point referred to in its first occurrence and that referred to in its second occurrence?

But of course the answer is obvious, isn't it? These two uses of "ST$_1$" refer to the same point. Of course they do. But this answer, though obvious, is crucial. For if we allow these two uses to refer to two different points then (8) will not rule out the claim that the resurrection body is spatio-temporally continuous with some long perished earthly body. So it would seem that the sceptic cannot afford to abandon this answer. And this reply invited us to ask about the criterion of identity for spatio-temporal points. This question bodes more embarrassment for the sceptic than did the earlier ones.

It may be important to notice here that we cannot avoid this question merely by stylistic changes which eliminate the word "same" from the answer, or which eliminate the double use of "ST$_1$" in (8). I suppose that we can make such changes. (We can, for that matter, restate the Christian hope of enjoying the life everlasting so that it does not require the word "same.") These words are not crucial, but the fact which lies behind them is. If (8) is to be applicable to the diachronic identity of bodies then we must say two things about a single point. We must state its relation to the body in question and we must state its relation to another point. And in doing this we must understand that we are saying these two things about the very same point. And so, it would seem, we must understand what it is for something to be "the very same point."

Here, I think, the line of inquiry which we have been following begins to draw to a close. For it is hard to think of a criterion of identity for spatio-temporal points which will be attractive to the Criterial Sceptic. What seem to be the options? Well, I suppose that a feeble step forward might be taken by saying that x and y are the same point if and only if they have the same spatio-temporal coordinates. But of course the question will be asked again, and the sceptic will be wedged even more tightly in the constricting corner. Or the sceptic may simply opt for a Leibnizian account of sameness here. But surely the believer will seize on this to justify his reliance on Leibniz's Law from the beginning, If, after all, even the sceptic comes to nothing better than this is in the end. . . .

On the other hand, the sceptic may here formulate a criterion which does not depend on bodies, times and spaces, but which makes use of some other notions. I do not know what such a criterion might be. But any such attempt seems likely to give aid and comfort to the believer. For if there is such a criterion for points, and if the identity of bodies depends in the end upon such a criterion, then why should there not also be a non-spatio-temporal, non-physical criterion for persons too, thus avoiding all the difficulties which the Criterial Sceptic has raised? Or, finally, the sceptic may simply say that no criterion is available here, nor is any needed. Spatio-temporal points, he might say, are "criterially primitive." We understand what is meant by "same" here without the use of criteria. Point x just is the same as y, and there is no more to be said about it. I suspect that this is correct. But correct or not, will it not almost surely incite the believer to reply that we understand "same person" at least as well as "same spatio-temporal point"? And if we understand the one without criteria then why should we not also understand the other in the same way? It looks suddenly as though whatever the sceptic says opens up a plausible position for the believer to occupy.

This concludes the body of my argument. In some sense, I have not solved the problem posed by people such as Flew [and] Passmore. . . . I have not shown that the resurrection body satisfies the continuity criterion for identity with the this-worldly body, and hence I have not shown that the resurrected person satisfies the bodily identity criterion for identity with some pre-mortem person. What I have argued, essentially, is that the problem cannot have the gravity which philosophers such as these are inclined to assign to it. Either it must be much more serious, infecting all of our ordinary judgments about the identity of this-worldly persons with the incoherence or arbitrariness which they ascribe to resurrection judgments, or it is less serious, having, in all likelihood, the same sort of solution which validates our ordinary judgments. In the first case the Christian's faith, though perhaps rather bad off, would not be worse off than the more prosaic faith of his non-religious colleagues, and he and they could survey the dismal logical prospects together. In the second case, too, the Christian's faith would seem to be no worse off than that of his secular counterparts. But in the second case the prospects, or some of them at least, are more cheerful. The believer might even invite his counterpart to consider some of them with him. But who knows whether that is philosophy?

Karma and Rebirth

From *Indian Conception of Values* by M. Hiriyanna, 1975

Professor Hiriyanna (1871–1950) was, during the middle part of this century, a leading expositor of Indian philosophic conceptions, with two popular textbooks to his credit. In this excerpt, he explains the relation between karma *and rebirth as it was typically understood in classical times. The key idea is that of deep psychological disposition, or* saṃskāra *in Sanskrit. C. J. Ducasse, in the following selection, may be taken to provide a modern gloss of the notion: deep dispositions are such things as a musical ear or a mathematical talent or an extraordinary sensitivity to animals. (Compare the discussion of* karma *under Hinduism in the general introduction; see also the Glossary entry.)*

Hiriyanna voices a few time-honored arguments found in classical Indian traditions in favor of rebirth. How is it that a new-born baby knows to reach for its mother's breast? And why do some fall in love at first sight? These and some other phenomena are said to be best explained by deep dispositions formed in previous lives.

Finally, there is the moral dimension of the doctrines of karma *and rebirth. Though the inclinations, or dispositions, that one builds up through choices may be strong, one can always resist them and make new* karma. Karma *seem a lot like habits, which are self-rewarding or self-punishing (compare the notion that virtue is its own reward). According to much Hindu and Buddhist philosophy, there is added justice in that the habits one has built up in this life (and previous lives) determine one's talents or deep dispositions in the next lifetime. C. J. Ducasse may be taken as expanding on this aspect of reincarnation theory, too—as well as on the nature of dispositions, or* saṃskāra, *already mentioned.*

THE DOCTRINE OF KARMA

The doctrine of *karma*[1] has had a profound influence on the life of the Indian people. It signifies that nothing can happen without a sufficient cause in the moral as in the physical world—that each life with all its pains and pleasures is the necessary result of the actions of past lives and becomes in its turn the cause, through its own activities, of future births. What we have been makes us what we are. According to it, the future, as we shall soon explain, lies entirely in our own hands so that belief in this doctrine serves as a perpetual incentive to right conduct. . . .

. . . There is no contradiction in . . . pointing to both freedom and necessity as the implications of the doctrine, for they refer to different aspects of karma. Every deed that we do leads to a double result. It not only produces what may be termed its direct result (*phala*) the pain or pleasure following from it, according to the nature of the deed done; it also establishes in us a disposition (*saṁskāra*) or tendency to repeat the same deed in the future. The necessity involved in the karma doctrine is only in so far as the former of these results, viz., the pain or the pleasure is concerned. As regards the latter, viz. the tendencies, they are entirely under our control; and our moral progress depends wholly upon the success with which we regulate them, as they tend to express themselves in action. . . .

Now as regards the arguments in support of transmigration commonly met with in Indian philosophical literature. One of them starts from the fact that all men are born with certain predilections and deduces from it that, not being traceable to the present life, they necessarily point back to the experiences of another but forgotten existence as their source. And, as the same argument can be extended to that existence and also to every other preceding existence, it is concluded . . . that there should have been in the case of every one a series of lives, which has had no beginning in time. The readiness to suck the mother's milk, found in a new-born babe, is the example usually given to illustrate this conclusion.[2] It involves a psychological factor, viz., the manifestation of will (*saṁkalpa*), in however rudimentary a form it may be. Nobody has taught it in this life that by sucking the milk its life will be sustained; and it should therefore imply, it is urged, a reminiscence, albeit unconscious, of similar manifestations of will in earlier lives. It may be thought that such dispositions can be traced to heredity, but we shall then be only pushing back the difficulty farther, for that principle leaves unexplained why a particular child should be born of particular parents. If the connection between the two is not to be a matter of sheer accident, it can be explained only by assuming a certain affinity between them and by admitting in the very act of doing so, the pre-existence of the self. Even if we grant that such innate aptitudes are due to heredity, there are other facts of experience like what is described as

---

[1] The word *karma* is wider in its significance than *dharma* [righteous acts] and includes *adharma* [sin] also. *Dharma* and *adharma* are together designated as *karma,* 'deed', because their essence consists in doing.

[2] Another example is given: man's inborn fear of death, which is explained as a consequence of the many sufferings undergone on occasions of former death.

'loving at first sight' . . . with which the principle of heredity can obviously have nothing to do. It is in reference to such love between king Aja and his bride Indumati that Kālidāsa, for instance, observes that the unconscious mind can discover the hidden kinship between two souls.

There are other arguments like the ethical one based on the observed inequalities of human fortunes . . . ; but these being familiar, we may pass on to mention another, which is more in the nature of a suggestion than an argument. Kālidāsa, to whom we have just referred, refers in his famous play of *Śākuntalam* to the strange fact that sometimes, when every circumstance favours a state of peace and contentment, the sight of a beautiful thing or the hearing of sweet music makes a person rather wistful, instead of serving as a source of pleasure to him. This apparent exception to the rule that a thing of beauty is a joy for ever, the poet explains as the consequence of recalling, though only subconsciously . . . , of some love or friendship of a former life which, now being past, gives rise to a feeling of melancholy. 'The longing sometimes felt by even a happy person at the sight of a beautiful thing and the hearing of sweet sounds implies, to be sure, a dim reminiscence of the affections of a former birth which are deeply rooted in the heart'. The gates of memory are opened, as it were, then and 'the shades of the past come through it before his saddened eyes'. This phenomenon cannot be explained as a mere reaction to external stimulus or on any other general principle of that kind, for it does not occur in the case of all persons and may not occur even in the case of the same person whenever he is in the presence of beautiful things.

Reincarnation

From *Nature, Mind, and Death* by C. J. Ducasse, 1951

C. J. Ducasse (1881–1969), a distinguished American philosopher who received the honor of being elected President of the American Philosophical Association, is unusual in having been influenced early in his career by Eastern thought. In the selection here, he defends the possibility of reincarnation within the confines of science and everyday knowledge.

Although Ducasse does present one instance of testimony of recollection of a previous lifetime, his purpose is not to argue that reincarnation occurs in fact but rather to show that there can be evidence in its favor and just what sort of evidence this would be. (Ian Stevenson, in several books, has gathered many such stories of apparent recollection—also cases of hypnotic regression where apparently an event from a past life has been "relived." Some of the accounts, both of unaided memory and of hypnotic recall, Stevenson claims have been confirmed by material evidence: see the list of his books in the Guide to Further Reading.) As mentioned, it is the possibility of reincarnation that Ducasse aims to establish, not its actuality. He argues that we may think of the deeper substratum of personal identity—what he calls a person's individuality, as opposed to the more superficial stratum that he calls personality—as surviving death and determining talents and proclivities in a future lifetime.

Unfortunately, there has been little contemporary philosophic response to Ducasse and in general to Eastern religious claims of reincarnation. Several issues need to be aired. For example, how would an advocate of reincarnation view the phenomenon of population growth? Not every human being alive today could have had a previous human lifetime: there would not be enough previous human births to go around. Is there any easy translation between animal and human forms? What would be the ramification of that for Ducasse's points about individuality, or what Hiriyanna calls saṃskāra*, karmic dispositions?*

The most detailed theory of reincarnation among pre-moderns appears within Tibetan literature (it is, however, couched in esoteric terms, and is difficult to understand); Aurobindo, among moderns, expresses a fairly detailed (and more easily comprehended) view: see the Guide to Further Reading.

The hypothesis of survival as rebirth (whether immediate or delayed) in a material world (whether the earth or some other planet) is of course not novel. It has been variously called reincarnation, transmigration, metempsychosis, or palingenesis; and, as W. R. Alger declares, "No other doctrine has exerted so extensive, controlling, and permanent an influence upon mankind as that of the metempsychosis—the notion that when the soul leaves the body it is born anew in another body, its rank, character, circumstances, and experience in each successive existence depending on its qualities, deeds, and attainments in its preceding lives."[1] . . .

. . . This conception of survival, moreover, is the most concrete. Because what it supposes is so like the life we know, it can be imagined most clearly.

Not only has it had wide popular acceptance, but it has also commended itself to some of the most eminent thinkers not only in the East but also in the West. Among these have been Pythagoras, Plato, and Plotinus; and Origen and some others of the early Christian fathers. Indeed, the statement twice reported of Jesus[2] that John the Baptist was the prophet Elijah who was to come, suggests that Jesus himself perhaps held the doctrine. In more recent times, David Hume, although not himself professing it, asserts that it is the only conception of survival that philosophy can hearken to.[3] Schopenhauer's contention that death of the body is not death of the will, and that so long as the will-to-live persists it will gain bodily objectification, amounts to acceptance of the idea of rebirth. McTaggart regards earthly rebirth as "the most probable form of the doctrine of immortality."[4] . . .

---

[1] W. R. Alger, *A Critical History of the Doctrine of a Future Life,* p. 475.

[2] Matt. 11:14; 17:12.

[3] Hume, *Essay on Immortality,* III.

[4] McTaggart, *Some Dogmas of Religion,* p. xiii, and Chap. IV.

The hypothesis of survival as rebirth—let us say, on this earth—at once raises the question whether one's present life is not itself a rebirth; for logically, even if not in point of practical interest, the hypothesis of earlier lives is exactly on a par with that of later lives. Hence, assuming transmigration, to suppose that one's present life would be as arbitrary as to suppose that it is going to be the last, *i.e.,* that one will not survive the death of it although it is a survival of earlier deaths.

Now, the supposition that one's present life not only will have successors but also has had predecessors, immediately brings up the objection that we have no recollection of having lived before. But . . . if absence of memory of having existed at a certain time proved that we did not exist at that time, it would then prove far too much; for it would prove that we did not exist during the first few years of the life of our present body, nor on most of the days since then, for we have no memories whatever of the great majority of them, nor of those first few years. Lack of memory of lives earlier than our present one is therefore no evidence at all that we did not live before.

Moreover, there is occasional testimony of recollection of a previous life, where the recollection is quite circumstantial and even alleged to have been verified. One such case may be cited here without any claim that it establishes preexistence, but only to substantiate the assertion that specific testimony of this kind exists. Evidently, testimony cannot be dismissed here any more than elsewhere merely because it happens to clash with an antecedent belief the empirical basis of which is only that we have not met before with such testimony. So to proceed would be to become guilty of *argumentatum ad ignorantiam* [argument based merely on our not having evidence]. If preexistence should happen to be a fact, it is obvious that the only possible empirical evidence of it would consist of verifiable recollections such as testified to in the case about to be described.

It is that of "The Rebirth of Katsugoro," recorded in detail and with many affidavits respecting the facts, in an old Japanese document translated by Lafcadio Hearn.[5] The story is, in brief, that a young boy called Katsugoro, son of a man called Genzo in the village of Nakanomura, declared that in his preceding life a few years before he had been called Tozo; that he was then the son of a farmer called Kyubei and his wife Shidzu in a village called Hodokubo; that his father had died and had been replaced in the household by a man called Hanshiro; and that he himself, Tozo, had died of smallpox at the age of six, a year after his father. He described his burial, the appearance of his former parents, and their house. He eventually was taken to their village, where such persons were found. He himself led the way to their house and recognized them; and they confirmed the facts he had related. Further, he pointed to a shop and a tree, saying that they had not been there before; and this was true.

Testimony of this kind is directly relevant to the question of rebirth. The recollections related in this case are much too circumstantial to be dismissed as instances of the familiar and psychologically well-understood illusion of *déja vu,* and although the testimony that they were verified is not proof that they were, it cannot be rejected *a priori.* Its reliability

---

[5] L. Hearn, *Gleanings in Buddha Fields,* Chap. X.

has to be evaluated in terms of the same standards by which the validity of testimonial evidence concerning anything else is appraised. . . .

. . . the rebirth [McTaggart's] supposition allows is . . . not personal rebirth if, by man's personality, one means . . . .the habits, the skills, the knowledge, character, and memories he gradually acquires during life on earth. These . . . may conceivably persist for a longer or shorter time after death, but, if our present birth is indeed a rebirth, they certainly are not brought to a new earth life; for we know very well that we are not born with the knowledge, habits, and memories we now have, but gained them little by little as a result of the experiences and efforts of our present lifetime.

But this brings up another difficulty, namely, what then is there left which could be supposed to be reborn? A possible solution of it, which at the same time would provide empirical content for [C. D.] Broad's postulated but undescribed "psychic factor," is definable in terms of the difference familiar in psychology between, on the one hand, *acquired* skills, habits, and memories, and on the other *native* aptitudes, instincts, and proclivities; that is, in what a human being is at a given time we may distinguish two parts, one deeper and more permanent, and an other more superficial and transient. The latter consists of everything he has acquired since birth: habits, skills, memories, and so on. This is his personality.[6] The other part, which somewhat arbitrarily for lack of a better name we may here agree to call his individuality, comprises the aptitudes and dispositions which are native in him. These include not only the simple ones, such as aptitude for tweezer dexterity, which have been studied in laboratories because they so readily lend themselves to it, but also others more elusive: intellectual, social, and esthetic aptitudes, dispositions, and types of interest or of taste. Here the task of discriminating what is innate from what is acquired is much more difficult, for it is complicated by the fact that some existent aptitudes may only become manifest after years have passed, or perhaps never, simply because not until then, or never, did the external occasion present itself for them to be exercised—just as aptitude for tweezer dexterity, for instance, in those who have it, must remain latent so long as they are not called upon to employ tweezers.

There can be no doubt that each of us, on the basis of his same individuality—that is, of his same stock of innate latent capacities and incapacities—would have developed a more or less different empirical mind and personality if, for instance, he had been put at birth in a different family, or had later been thrust by some external accident into a radically different sort of environment, or had had a different kind of education, or had met and married a very different type of person, and so on. Reflection on this fact should cause one to take his present personality with a large grain of salt, viewing it no longer humorlessly as his absolute self, but rather, in imaginative perspective, as but one of the various personalities which his individuality was equally capable of generating had it happened to enter phenomenal history through birth in a different environment. Thus, to the question: What is it that could be supposed to be reborn? an intelligible answer may be returned by

---

[6] Lat. *persona* = a mask for actors (*per* = through, and *sonus* = sound); thus, the mask or appearance through which the voice speaks.

saying that it might be the core of positive and negative aptitudes and tendencies which we have called a man's individuality, as distinguished from his personality. And the fact might further be that, perhaps as a result of persistent striving to acquire a skill or trait he desires, but for which he now has but little gift, aptitude for it in future births would be generated and incorporated into his individuality.

A man's individuality, as we have here defined it, would to some extent function as would Broad's "psychic factor": it would be what remains of a man after not only the death of his body but also after the disintegration of his lifetime-acquired "personal" mind, whether at bodily death or at some longer or shorter time thereafter. . . .

. . . [Some have argued, however, that] without the awareness of identity which memory provides, rebirth would not be discernibly different from the death of one person followed by the birth of another. In this connection, [Corliss] Lamont quotes Leibniz's question: "Of what use would it be to you, sir, to become king of China, on condition that you forgot what you have been? Would it not be the same as if God, at the same time he destroyed you, created a king in China?"[7]

But continuousness of memory, rather than preservation of a comprehensive span of memories, is what is significant for consciousness of one's identity. Thus, for example, none of us finds his sense of identity impaired by the fact that he has no memories of the earliest years of his present life. And if, on each day, he had a stock of memories relating to, let us say, only the then preceding ten years, or some other perhaps even shorter period, this would provide all that would be needed for a continuous sense of identity. The knowledge he would have of his personal history would, it is true, comprise a shorter span than it now does, but the span in either case would have an earliest term, and in either case the personality known would have a substantial amount of historical dimension. That the sense of identity depends on *gradualness of change* in ourselves, rather than on preservation unchanged of any specific part of ourselves, strikes one forcibly when he chances to find letters, perhaps, which he wrote thirty or forty years before. Many of them may awaken no recollections whatever, even of the existence of the persons to whom they were addressed or whom they mentioned, and it sometimes seems incredible also that the person who wrote the things they contain should be the same as his present self. In truth, it is not the same in any strict sense, but only continuous with the former person. The fact, as the Buddha insisted, is that one's personality, like everything else that exists in time, changes as time passes—some constituents of it remaining for shorter or longer periods, the while others are being lost and others acquired. Yet, because of the gradualness and diverse speeds of the changes between one's earlier and one's present personality, the sense of identity is at no time lacking. . . .

. . . In attempting . . . to take into account the survival possibilities described in earlier sections of this chapter, we have gradually defined a form of survival which appears possible and which, if it should be a fact, would have significance for the living. The main features of that conception may now be summarily recited. They would be:

---

[7] Corliss Lamont, *The Illusion of Immortality,* p. 22; Leibniz, *Philosophische Schriften,* ed. Gerhardt, IV, 300.

(*a*) That in the mind of man two comprehensive constituents are to be discerned—one, acquired during his lifetime and most obvious, which we have called his *personality* or the personal part of his mind; and another, less obvious but more basic, which exists in him from birth, and which for lack of a better name we have called his *individuality* or the individual part of his mind;

(*b*) That this part, consisting of aptitudes, instincts, and other innate dispositions or tendencies, is the product gradually distilled from the actions, experiences, and strivings of the diverse personalities which developed by union of it with the bodies of a succession of earlier lives on earth (or possibly elsewhere);

(*c*) That, between any two such successive lives, there is an interval during which some parts of the personality of the preceding life persist—consciousness then being more or less dreamlike, but perhaps gradually learning to discriminate between images of subjective origin and memory images, and between either of these and images of objective, *i.e.,* of telepathic or clairvoyant, origin, if any;

(*d*) That some time during the interval is occupied by more or less complete recollection of the acts and events of the preceding life, and of their discernible consequences; and that dispositions of various apposite sorts are generated thereby, in some such automatic way as that in which, during life, deep changes of attitude are sometimes generated in us by our reading or seeing and hearing performed a tragedy or other impressive drama, or indeed by witnessing highly dramatic real events;

(*e*) That, partly because the specific nature of a man's individuality automatically shapes to some extent the external circumstances as well as the nature of the personality he develops from a given birth, and perhaps partly also because what his individuality has become may determine automatically—through some such affinity as McTaggart suggests—where and when and from whom he will be reborn, justice is immanent in the entire process. . . .

In conclusion, however, let it be emphasized again that no claim is made that this conception of survival is known to be true, or even known to be more probably true than not; but only (1) that it is possible in the threefold sense stated earlier; (2) that belief or disbelief of it has implications for conduct; (3) that, if true, it would satisfy pretty well most of the demands which make the desire for survival so widespread; and (4) that, notwithstanding some gaps in that conception due to our ignorance of mechanisms such as certain of those it postulates, it is yet clear and definite enough to refute, namely, that no life after death both possible and significant can be imagined.

Immortality

From *David Hume: The Philosophical Works,* Thomas Hill Green and Thomas Hodge Grose, editors, 1964

David Hume, the eighteenth-century critic of religious claims whom we have encountered several times previously, argues that the rules of analogy weigh heavily against a view of the soul's immortality: similarities between classes of phenomena in one respect suggest that similarities obtain in other respects, too. Thus if (a) we have two buckets equally full of liquid and (b) a glass of each quenches thirst while (c) the first bucket puts out a moderate-sized fire, then (d) we have every reason to expect that the second bucket would extinguish a similar-sized fire. Hume with this analytic tool surveys the relations between physical phenomena, such as bodily weaknesses in infancy, and psychological phenomena, such as mental weakness in infancy, and concludes, from a host of proportional relationships, that the mind or soul perishes when the body perishes. Clearly, consciousness as we know it diminishes through the physical action of a drug or a spinal cord injury. It would seem then natural that when the body has ceased to function as a living organism, individual consciousness would cease, too.

Moreover, there are conceptual problems with the immortality thesis, says Hume, overpopulation of afterlife worlds, for example. And we should be particularly suspicious, he urges, of any doctrine which is "favored by our passions."

Hume's arguments are difficult to counter on their own grounds. Possibly, however, as even Bertrand Russell points out (see below), evidence from so-called psychical research could make a contrary case.

. . . arguments from the analogy of nature are strong for the mortality of the soul: and these are really the only philosophical arguments, which ought to be admitted with regard to this question, or indeed any question of fact.

Where any two objects are so closely connected, that all alterations, which we have ever seen in the one, are attended with proportionable alterations in the other: we ought to conclude, by all rules of analogy, that, when there are still greater alterations produced in the former, and it is totally dissolved, there follows a total dissolution of the latter.

Sleep, a very small effect on the body, is attended with a temporary extinction: at least, a great confusion in the soul.

The weakness of the body and that of the mind in infancy are exactly proportioned; their vigour in manhood, their sympathetic disorder in sickness, their common gradual decay in old age. The step further seems unavoidable; their common dissolution in death.

The last symptoms, which the mind discovers, are disorder, weakness, insensibility, and stupidity; the forerunners of its annihilation. The further progress of the same causes, encreasing the same effects, totally extinguish it.

Judging by the usual analogy of nature, no form can continue, when transferred to a condition of life very different from the original one, in which it was placed. Trees perish in the water; fishes in the air; animals in the earth. Even so small a difference as that of climate is often fatal. What reason then to imagine, that an immense alteration, such as is made on the soul by the dissolution of its body, and all its organs of thought and sensation, can be effected without the dissolution of the whole?

Every thing is in common between soul and body. The organs of the one are all of them the organs of the other. The existence therefore of the one must be dependent on the other.

The souls of animals are allowed to be mortal; and these bear so near a resemblance to the souls of men, that the analogy from one to the other forms a very strong argument.

Their bodies are not more resembling: yet no one rejects the argument drawn from comparative anatomy. The *Metempsychosis* is therefore the only system of this kind, that philosophy can so much as hearken to.

Nothing in this world is perpetual. Every thing, however, seemingly firm, is in continual flux and change: The world itself gives symptoms of frailty and dissolution: How contrary to analogy, therefore, to imagine, that one single form, seeming the frailest of any, and from the objects and causes subject to the greatest disorders, is immortal and indissoluble? What a daring theory is that! How lightly, not to say how rashly, entertained!

How to dispose of the infinite number of posthumous existences ought also to embarrass the religious theory. Every planet, in every solar system, we are at liberty to imagine peopled with intelligent, mortal beings: At least we can fix on no other supposition. For these, then, a new universe must, every generation, be created beyond the bounds of the present universe; or one must have been created at first so prodigiously wide as to admit of this continual influx of beings. Ought such bold suppositions to be received by any philosophy: and that merely on the pretext of a bare possibility?

When it is asked, whether *Agamemnon, Thersites, Hannibal, Nero,* and every stupid clown, that ever existed in *Italy, Scythia, Bactria,* or *Guinea,* are now alive; can any man think, that a scrutiny of nature will furnish arguments strong enough to answer so strange a question in the affirmative? The want of argument, without revelation, sufficiently establishes the negative. . . .

All doctrines are to be suspected which are favoured by our passions. And the hopes and fears which give rise to this doctrine, are very obvious.

It is an infinite advantage in every controversy, to defend the negative. If the question be out of the common experienced course of nature, this circumstance is almost, if not altogether, decisive. By what arguments or analogies can we prove any state of existence, which no one ever saw, and which no wise resembles any that ever was seen? Who will repose such trust in any pretended philosophy, as to admit upon its testimony the reality of so marvellous a scene? Some new species of logic is requisite for that purpose; and some new faculties of the mind, that they may enable us to comprehend that logic.

Survival

From *Appearance and Reality* by F. H. Bradley, 1897

English philosopher F. H. Bradley (1846–1924) held a lifelong fellowship at Oxford that did not require teaching with the result that Bradley was able to devote an entire career to philosophical research and writing. He wrote important works in logic and in ethics. But it was his idealist metaphysics for which Bradley became most renowned.

In the selection excerpted here, which is taken from the last portion of his principal metaphysical work, Appearance and Reality *(first published in 1893), Bradley takes up a topic that he calls initially the "Immortality of the Soul" but would more rightly be called*

*survival. ("I shall assume that what is meant is an existence after death which is con-
scious of its identity with our life here and now.") The context of Bradley's reflection is
interesting:* Appearance and Reality *is devoted to upholding an idealist or spiritual metaphysics, and specifically, the reality of an Absolute, a spiritual reality underlying all appearances. For Bradley, reality is so thoroughly endowed with the characteristics
commonly attributed to God that one might expect him to favor a survival thesis. However, he considers the question with a cold eye.*

*Bradley does not seem to think that there are implications of metaphysics for this
topic; "even on the ground of common crude Materialism" survival, he thinks, is possible. We must turn, then, to the available evidence. But unfortunately we find little and
none that is decisive. The question becomes a matter of probabilities. And like Hume,
Bradley judges the likelihood of survival, based on the known evidence, to be slim
(though he does not say clearly what this evidence is).*

*Here we may note that another camp of spiritual metaphysics—the process camp that
we surveyed with Charles Hartshorne, Alfred North Whitehead, and David Griffin—also
does not uphold a survival thesis. For Hartshorne and company, the only survival is
through the vivid memory of God. Yet God's memory is so vivid, some process theologians
speculate, that events of one's life are immortalized, the movie of one's life being constantly witnessed. More traditional theologians, on the other hand, typically see personal
survival not only as scripturally based but also as key to the theistic response to evil, that
is, to their theodicies.*

I will end this chapter with a few remarks on a subject which lies near. I refer to that which
is commonly called the Immortality of the Soul. This is a topic on which for several reasons I would rather keep silence, but I think that silence here might fairly be misunder-
stood. It is not easy, in the first place, to say exactly what a future life means. The period of
personal continuance obviously need not be taken as endless. And again precisely in what
sense, and how far, the survival must be personal is not easy to lay down. I shall assume
here what is meant is an existence after death which is conscious of its identity with our
life here and now. And the duration of this must be taken as sufficient to remove any idea
of unwilling extinction or of premature decease. Now we seem to desire continuance (if we
do desire it) for a variety of reasons, and it might be interesting elsewhere to set these out
and to clear away confusions.[1] I must however pass at once to the question of possibility.

. . . There is no way of proving, first, that a body is required for a soul. . . . And though
a soul, when bodiless, might (for all we know) be even more subject to mortality, yet obviously here we have passed into a region of ignorance. And to say that in this region a

---

[1] The so-called fear of extinction seems to rest on a confusion, and I do not believe that, in a proper form, it exists
at all. It is really merely shrinking from defeat and from injury and pain. For we can think of our own total
surcease, but we cannot imagine it. Against our will, and perhaps unconsciously, there creeps in the idea of a reluctant and struggling self, or of a self disappointed, or wearied, or in some way discontented. And this is certainly not a self completely extinguished. There is no fear of death at all, we may say, except either incidentally
or through an illusion.

personal continuance could not be, appears simply irrational. And the same result holds, even if we take a body as essential to every soul, and, even if we insist also (as we cannot) that this body must be made of our everyday substance. A future life is possible even on the ground of common crude Materialism.[2] After an interval, no matter how long, another nervous system sufficiently like our own might be developed; and in this case memory and a personal identity must arise. The event may be as improbable as you please, but I at least can find no reason for calling it impossible. And we may even go a step further still. It is conceivable that an indefinite number of such bodies should exist, not in succession merely, but all together and all at once. But, if so, we might gain a personal continuance not single but multiform, and might secure a destiny on which it would be idle to enlarge. In ways like the above it is clear that a future life is possible, but, on the other hand, such possibilities are not worth much.

A thing is impossible absolutely when it contradicts the known nature of Reality. It is impossible relatively when it collides with some idea which we have found good cause to take as real. A thing is possible, first, as long as it is not quite meaningless. It must contain some positive quality belonging to the universe; and it must not at the same time remove this and itself by some destructive addition. A thing is possible further, according as its meaning contains without discrepancy more and more of what is held to be real. We, in other words, consider anything more possible as it grows in probability. And 'Probability', we are rightly told, 'is the guide of life'. We want to know, in short, not whether a thing is merely and barely possible, but how much ground we have for expecting it and not something else.

In a case like the present, we cannot, of course, hope to set out the chances, for we have to do with elements the value of which is not known. . . .

. . . But, if we may not deal with [these elements], the possibility of a future life is, on this ground, quite unknown; and, if so, we have no right to consider it at all. And the general result to my mind is briefly this. When you add together the chances of a life after death—a life taken as bodiless, and again as diversely embodied—the amount is not great. The balance of hostile probability seems so large that the fraction on the other side to my mind is not considerable. And we may repeat, and may sum up our conclusion thus. If we appeal to blank ignorance, then a future life may even have no meaning, and may fail wholly to be possible. Or if we avoid this worst extreme, a future life may be but barely possible. But a possibility, in this sense, stands unsupported face to face with an indefinite universe. And its value, so far, can hardly be called worth counting. If, on the other hand, we allow ourselves to use what knowledge we possess, and if we judge fairly of future life by all the grounds we have for judging, the result is not much modified. Among those grounds we certainly find a part which favours continuance; but, taken at its highest, that part appears to be small. Hence a future life must be taken as decidedly improbable.

---

[2] I have attempted to show this in an article on the "Evidences of Spiritualism," *Fortnightly Review,* December, 1885. It may perhaps be worth while to add here that apparently even a high organism is possible, which apart from accidents would never die. Apparently this could not be termed impossible in principle, at least within our present knowledge.

Survival

From *Why I Am Not a Christian* by Bertrand Russell, 1967

Probably the best-known English philosopher of this century, Bertrand Russell (1872–1970), was also one of the most accomplished, having pioneered much in philosophical logic as well as in epistemology and the world-bound metaphysical projects of what has come to be known as the analytic movement. A collection of early philosophic essays that Russell deemed elementary, Problems of Philosophy, *has been hailed as the best introduction to the discipline overall ever composed. Russell's prose is commonly viewed as a model of lucidity, as eminently readable, and is largely free from technical jargon despite his accomplishments in logic.*

Russell does not subscribe to a bodily criterion of personal identity. He sees the person as principally a collection of habits and memories—in a word, a mind. So in principle a survival thesis would seem more congenial from such a perspective than to those who identify the person with a body. He does say, later in this selection, that he sees the mind, like the body, as a "matter of organization, not of primal substance." But he does not readily identify the mind with a physical organization. The question of mind-body identity he wishes to leave open, it seems. In any case, Russell finds the possibility of continuity, past the body's death, of personal memory (and habit?) "very unlikely." His main reason is the way habits are formed, namely, by, as he says, frequent similar occurrences—of a physical nature, we might add. For Russell, memories and patterns of behavior are somehow tied to structures of the brain. He admits that the evidence of "psychical research" could someday prove overwhelming, and a survival view be established. It is not conceptually impossible, Russell says. But the evidence of a tight, albeit unknown, relation between mind and body in conception, gestation, infancy, and so on convinces Russell that the life of the soul ends with the death of the body.

Russell also addresses the question of why so many are prone to believe in an afterlife. The answer, he says, is fear. But this is a fear that is, he argues, ignoble, despite the utility of belief in an afterlife in certain earlier periods of history. Now with science informing us about what there is and how it is, we need no longer brook superstition, and can turn to ourselves and our own effort to make this world "a fit place to live in."

Before we can profitably discuss whether we shall continue to exist after death, it is well to be clear as to the sense in which a man is the same person as he was yesterday. Philosophers used to think that there were definite substances, the soul and the body, that each lasted on from day to day, that a soul, once created, continued to exist throughout all future time, whereas a body ceased temporarily from death till the resurrection of the body.

The part of this doctrine which concerns the present life is pretty certainly false. The matter of the body is continually changing by processes of nutriment and wastage. Even if it were not, atoms in physics are no longer supposed to have continuous existence; there is no sense in saying: this is the same atom as the one that existed a few minutes ago. The continuity of a human body is a matter of appearance and behavior, not of substance.

The same thing applies to the mind. We think and feel and act, but there is not, in addition to thoughts and feelings and actions, a bare entity, the mind or the soul, which does or suffers these occurrences. The mental continuity of a person is a continuity of habit and memory: there was yesterday one person whose feelings I can remember, and that person I regard as myself of yesterday; but, in fact, myself of yesterday was only certain mental occurrences which are now remembered and are regarded as part of the person who now recollects them. All that constitutes a person is a series of experiences connected by memory and by certain similarities of the sort we call habit.

If, therefore, we are to believe that a person survives death, we must believe that the memories and habits which constitute the person will continue to be exhibited in a new set of occurrences.

No one can prove that this will not happen. But it is easy to see that it is very unlikely. Our memories and habits are bound up with the structure of the brain, in much the same way in which a river is connected with the riverbed. The water in the river is always changing, but it keeps to the same course because previous rains have worn a channel. In like manner, previous events have worn a channel in the brain, and our thoughts flow along this channel. This is the cause of memory and mental habits. But the brain, as a structure, is dissolved at death, and memory therefore may be expected to be also dissolved. There is no more reason to think otherwise than to expect a river to persist in its old course after an earthquake has raised a mountain where a valley used to be.

All memory, and therefore (one may say) all minds, depend upon a property which is very noticeable in certain kinds of material structures but exists little if at all in other kinds. This is the property of forming habits as a result of frequent similar occurrences. For example: a bright light makes the pupils of the eyes contract; and if you repeatedly flash a light in a man's eyes and beat a gong at the same time, the gong alone will, in the end, cause his pupils to contract. This is a fact about the brain and nervous system—that is to say, about a certain material structure. It will be found that exactly similar facts explain our response to language and our use of it, our memories and the emotions they arouse, our moral or immoral habits of behavior, and indeed everything that constitutes our mental personality, except the part determined by heredity. The part determined by heredity is handed on to our posterity but cannot, in the individual, survive the disintegration of the body. Thus both the hereditary and the acquired parts of a personality are, so far as our experience goes, bound up with the characteristics of certain bodily structures. We all know that memory may be obliterated by an injury to the brain, that a virtuous person may be rendered vicious by encephalitis lethargica, and that a clever child can be turned into an idiot by lack of iodine. In view of such familiar facts, it seems scarcely probable that the mind survives the total destruction of brain structure which occurs at death.

It is not rational arguments but emotions that cause belief in a future life.

The most important of these emotions is fear of death, which is instinctive and biologically useful. If we genuinely and wholeheartedly believed in the future life, we should cease completely to fear death. The effects would be curious, and probably such as most of us would deplore. But our human and subhuman ancestors have fought and exterminated their enemies throughout many geological ages and have profited by courage; it is therefore an advantage to the victors in the struggle for life to be able, on occasion, to overcome the natural fear of death. Among animals and savages, instinctive pugnacity suffices for this purpose; but at a certain stage of development, as the Mohammedans first proved, belief in Paradise has considerable military value as reinforcing natural pugnacity. We should therefore admit that militarists are wise in encouraging the belief in immortality, always supposing that this belief does not become so profound as to produce indifference to the affairs of the world. . . .

Religion is based, I think, primarily and mainly upon fear. It is partly the terror of the unknown and partly, as I have said, the wish to feel that you have a kind of elder brother who will stand by you in all your troubles and disputes. Fear is the basis of the whole thing—fear of the mysterious, fear of defeat, fear of death. Fear is the parent of cruelty, and therefore it is no wonder if cruelty and religion have gone hand in hand. It is because fear is at the basis of those two things. In this world we can now begin a little to understand things, and a little to master them by help of science, which has forced its way step by step against the Christian religion, against the churches, and against the opposition of all the old precepts. Science can help us to get over this craven fear in which mankind has lived for so many generations. Science can teach us, and I think our own hearts can teach us, no longer to look around for imaginary supports, no longer to invent allies in the sky, but rather to look to our own efforts here below to make this world a fit place to live in, instead of the sort of place that the churches in all these centuries have made it. . . .

The question of personal immortality stands on a somewhat different footing [than religious dogmas]. Here evidence either way is possible. Persons are part of the everyday world with which science is concerned, and the conditions which determine their existence are discoverable. A drop of water is not immortal; it can be resolved into oxygen and hydrogen. If, therefore, a drop of water were to maintain that it had a quality of aqueousness which would survive its dissolution we should be inclined to be skeptical. In like manner we know that the brain is not immortal, and that the organized energy of a living body becomes, as it were, demobilized at death and therefore not available for collective action. All the evidence goes to show that what we regard as our mental life is bound up with brain structure and organized bodily energy. Therefore it is rational to suppose that mental life ceases when bodily life ceases. The argument is only one of probability, but it is as strong as those upon which most scientific conclusions are based.

There are various grounds upon which this conclusion might be attacked. Psychical research professes to have actual scientific evidence of survival and undoubtedly its procedure is, in principle, scientifically correct. Evidence of this sort might be so overwhelming that no one with a scientific temper could reject it. The weights to be attached to the evidence, however, must depend upon the antecedent probability of the hypothesis of survival. There are always different ways of accounting for any set of phenomena, and of these we should prefer the one which is antecedentally least improbable. Those who already think it likely that we survive death will be ready to view this theory as the best explanation of psychical phenomena. Those who, on other grounds, regard this theory as implausible will seek for other explanations. For my part, I consider the evidence so far adduced by psychical research in favor of survival much weaker than the physiological evidence on the other side. But I fully admit that it might at any moment become stronger, and in that case it would be unscientific to disbelieve in survival.

Survival of bodily death is, however, a different matter from immortality: it may only mean a postponement of psychical death. It is immortality that men desire to believe in. Believers in immortality will object to physiological arguments, such as I have been using, on the ground that soul and body are totally disparate, and that the soul is something quite other than its empirical manifestations through our bodily organs. I believe this to be a metaphysical superstition. Mind and matter alike are for certain purposes convenient terms but are not ultimate realities. Electrons and protons, like the soul, are logical fictions; each is really a history, a series of events, not a single persistent entity. In the case of the soul, this is obvious from the facts of growth. Whoever considers conception, gestation, and infancy cannot seriously believe that the soul is an indivisible something, perfect and complete throughout this process. It is evident that it grows like the body, and that it derives both from the spermatozoon and from the ovum, so that it cannot be indivisible. This is not materialism: it is merely the recognition that everything interesting is a matter of organization, not of primal substance. . . .

Religion, since it has its source in terror, has dignified certain kinds of fear and made people think them not disgraceful. In this it has done mankind a great disservice: *all* fear is bad. I believe that when I die I shall rot, and nothing of my ego will survive. I am not young, and I love life. But I should scorn to shiver with terror at the thought of annihilation. Happiness is [not the less] true happiness because it must come to an end, nor do thought and love lose their value because they are not everlasting. Many a man has borne himself proudly on the scaffold; surely the same pride should teach us to think truly about man's place in the world.

Survival

From *Life after Life* by Raymond A. Moody, Jr., and from the foreword by Elisabeth Kübler-Ross, 1975

Dr. Raymond Moody provides all the introduction that is needed in the excerpt here from his book on "near-death experiences": he tells us about the history of his own interest in the topic and the methodology that has resulted in his paradigmatic account. The account itself follows.

At the end of the selection is excepted part of the Forward to Moody's book written by the person who has been perhaps the leading researcher into the process of dying, Dr. Elisabeth Kübler-Ross. Moody's work is beyond all suspicion of psychic charlatanism, of any "cooking the data" that has vitiated some research within parapsychology (see Foundations of Parapsychology, *by Hoyt Edge, Robert Morris, John Plamer, and Joseph Rush, listed in the Guide to Further Reading, in particular their discussion of the controversy over evidence of "communion with the dead"). Nevertheless, it is difficult to know how to interpret near-death experiences. Could they be compared to a dream? Is the inter-subjectivity of the experiences itself alone an indication of objectivity? Maybe. But collective illusions do occur.*

During the past few years I have encountered a large number of persons who were involved in what I shall call "near-death experiences." I have met these persons in many ways. At first it was by coincidence. In 1965, when I was an undergraduate student studying philosophy at the University of Virginia, I met a man who was a clinical professor of psychiatry in the School of Medicine. I was struck from the beginning with his warmth, kindliness and humor. It came as a great surprise when I later learned a very interesting fact about him, namely, that he had been dead—not just once but on two occasions, about ten minutes apart—and that he had given a most fantastic account of what happened to him while he was "dead." I later heard him relate his story to a small group of interested students. At the time, I was most impressed, but since I had little background from which to judge such experiences, I "filed it away," both in my mind and in the form of a tape recording of his talk.

Some years later, after I had received my Ph.D. in philosophy, I was teaching in a university in eastern North Carolina. In one course I had my students read Plato's *Phaedo,* a work in which immortality is among the subjects discussed. In my lectures I had been emphasizing the other doctrines which Plato presents there and had not focused upon the discussion of life after death. After class one day a student stopped by to see me. He asked whether we might discuss the subject of immortality. He had an interest in the subject because his grandmother had "died" during an operation and had recounted a very amazing experience. I asked him to tell me about it, and much to my surprise, he related almost the same series of events which I had heard the psychiatry professor describe some years before.

At this time my search for cases became a bit more active, and I began to include readings on the subject of human survival of biological death in my philosophy courses. However, I was careful not to mention the two death experiences in my courses. I adopted, in effect, a wait-and-see attitude. If such reports were fairly common, I thought, I would probably hear of more if I just brought up the general topic of survival in philosophical discussions, expressed a sympathetic attitude toward the question, and waited. To my amazement, I found that in almost every class of thirty or so students, at least one student would come to me afterwards and relate a personal near-death experience.

What has amazed me since the beginning of my interest are the great similarities in the reports, despite the fact that they come from people of highly varied religious, social, and educational backgrounds. By the time I entered medical school in 1972, I had collected a sizable number of these experiences and I began mentioning the informal study I had been doing to some of my medical acquaintances. Eventually, a friend of mine talked me into giving a report to a medical society, and other public talks followed. Again, I found that after every talk someone would come up to tell me of an experience of his own.

As I became more widely known for this interest, doctors began to refer to me persons whom they had resuscitated and who reported unusual experiences. Still others have written to me with reports after newspaper articles about my studies appeared.

At the present time, I know of approximately 150 cases of this phenomenon. The experiences which I have studied fall into three distinct categories:

1. The experiences of persons who were resuscitated after having been thought, adjudged, or pronounced clinically dead by their doctors.
2. The experiences of persons who, in the course of accidents or severe injury or illness, came very close to physical death.
3. The experiences of persons who, as they died, told them to other people who were present. Later, these other people reported the content of the death experience to me.

From the vast amount of material that could be derived from 150 cases, selection obviously has occurred. Some of it has been purposeful. For example, although I have found reports of the third type to complement and to agree very well with experiences of the first two types, I have for the most part dropped them from consideration for two reasons. First, it helps to reduce the number of cases studied to a more manageable level, and second, it enables me to stick as close as possible to firsthand reports. Thus, I have interviewed in great detail some fifty persons upon whose experiences I am able to report. Of these, the cases of the first type (those in which an apparent clinical death actually occurs) are certainly more *dramatic* than those of the second type (in which only a close brush with death occurs). Indeed, whenever I have given public talks on this phenomenon, the "death" episodes have invariably drawn most of the interest. Accounts in the press have sometimes been written so as to suggest they are the *only* type of case with which I have dealt.

However, in selecting the cases to be presented in this book, I have avoided the temptation to dwell only on those cases in which a "death" event took place. For, as will become obvious, cases of the second type are not different from, but rather form a continuum with, cases of the first type. Also, though the near-death experiences themselves are remarkably similar, both the circumstances surrounding them and the persons describing them vary widely. Accordingly, I have tried to give a sample of experiences which adequately reflects this variation. . . .

Despite the wide variation in the circumstances surrounding close calls with death and in the types of persons undergoing them, it remains true that there is a striking similarity among the accounts of the experiences themselves. In fact, the similarities among various reports are so great that one can easily pick out about fifteen separate elements which recur again and again in the mass of narratives that I have collected. On the basis of these points of likeness, let me now construct a brief, theoretically "ideal" or "complete" experience which embodies all of the common elements, in the order in which it is typical for them to occur.

A man is dying and, as he reaches the point of greatest physical distress, he hears himself pronounced dead by his doctor. He begins to hear an uncomfortable noise, a loud ringing or buzzing, and at the same time feels himself moving very rapidly through a long dark tunnel. After this, he suddenly finds himself outside of his own physical body, but still in the immediate physical environment, and he sees his own body from a distance, as though he is a spectator. He watches the resuscitation attempt from this unusual vantage point and is in a state of emotional upheaval.

After a while, he collects himself and becomes more accustomed to his odd condition. He notices that he still has a "body," but one of a very different nature and with very different powers from the physical body he has left behind. Soon other things begin to happen. Others come to meet and to help him. He glimpses the spirits of relatives and friends who have already died, and a loving, warm spirit of a kind he has never encountered before—a being of light—appears before him. This being asks him a question, nonverbally, to make him evaluate his life and helps him along by showing him a panoramic, instantaneous playback of the major events of his life. At some point he finds himself approaching some sort of barrier or border, apparently representing the limit between earthly life and the next life. Yet, he finds that he must go back to the earth, that the time for his death has not yet come. At this point he resists, for by now he is taken up with his experiences in the afterlife and does not want to return. He is overwhelmed by intense feelings of joy, love, and peace. Despite his attitude, though, he somehow reunites with his physical body and lives.

Later he tries to tell others, but he has trouble doing so. In the first place, he can find no human words adequate to describe these unearthly episodes. He also finds that others scoff, so he stops telling other people. Still, the experience affects his life profoundly, especially his views about death and its relationship to life.

It is important to bear in mind that the above narrative is not meant to be a representation of any one person's experience. Rather, it is a "model," a composite of the common elements found in very many stories. I introduce it here only to give a preliminary, general idea of what a person who is dying may experience. Since it is an abstraction rather than an actual account, in the present chapter I will discuss in detail each common element, giving many examples.

Before doing that, however, a few facts need to be set out in order to put the remainder of my exposition of the experience of dying into the proper framework.

1. Despite the striking similarities among various accounts, no two of them are precisely identical (though a few come remarkably close to it).

2. I have found no one person who reports every single component of the composite experience. Very many have reported most of them (that is, eight or more of the fifteen or so) and a few have reported up to twelve.

3. There is no one element of the composite experience which every single person has reported to me, which crops up in every narrative. Nonetheless, a few of these elements come fairly close to being universal.

4. There is not one component of my abstract model which has appeared in only one account. Each element has shown up in many separate stories.

5. The order in which a dying person goes through the various stages briefly delineated above may vary from that given in my "theoretical model." To give one example, various persons have reported seeing the "being of light" before, or at the same time, they left their physical bodies, and not as in the "model," some time afterward. However, the order in which the stages occur in the model is a very typical order, and wide variations are unusual.

6. How far into the hypothetical complete experience a dying person gets seems to depend on whether or not the person actually underwent an apparent clinical death, and if

so, on how long he was in this state. In general, persons who were "dead" seem to report more florid, complete experiences than those who only came close to death, and those who were "dead" for a longer period go deeper than those who were "dead" for a shorter time.

7. I have talked to a few people who were pronounced dead, resuscitated, and came back reporting none of these common elements. Indeed, they say that they don't remember anything at all about their "deaths." Interestingly enough, I have talked with several persons who were actually adjudged clinically dead on separate occasions years apart, and reported experiencing nothing on one of the occasions, but having had quite involved experiences on the other.

8. It must be emphasized that I am writing primarily about reports, accounts, or narratives, which other persons have given to me verbally during interviews. Thus, when I remark that a given element of the abstract, "complete" experience does not occur in a given account, I do not mean necessarily to imply that it did not happen to the person involved. I only mean that this person did not tell me that it did occur, or that it does not definitely come out in his account that he experienced it. . . .

FOREWORD

I have had the privilege of reading the pre-publication copy of Dr. Moody's *Life After Life,* and I am delighted that this young scholar has the courage to put his findings together and make this new type of research available to the general public.

Since I have worked with terminally ill patients over the last two decades, I have become more and more preoccupied with looking into the phenomena of death itself. We have learned a lot about the process of dying, but we still have many questions with regard to the moment of death and to the experience our patients have when they are pronounced medically dead.

It is research such as Dr. Moody presents in his book that will enlighten many and will confirm what we have been taught for two thousand years—that there is life after death. Though he does not claim to have studied death itself, it is evident from his findings that the dying patient continues to have a conscious awareness of his environment after being pronounced clinically dead. This very much coincides with my own research, which has used the accounts of patients who have died and made a comeback, totally against our expectations and often to the surprise of some highly sophisticated, well-known and certainly accomplished physicians.

All of these patients have experienced a floating out of their physical bodies, associated with a great sense of peace and wholeness. Most were aware of another person who helped them in their transition to another plane of existence. Most were greeted by loved ones who had died before them, or by a religious figure who was significant in their life and who coincided, naturally, with their own religious beliefs. . . .

ELISABETH KÜBLER-ROSS, M.D.

DISCUSSION QUESTIONS

1. What is the bodily criterion of personal identity? Explain how George Mavrodes accepts it and goes on to defend the possibility of bodily resurrection.

2. Present the classical Indian arguments in favor of *karma* and rebirth as sketched by M. Hiriyanna. How might these arguments be evaluated?

3. Elaborate the distinction, expressed by C. J. Ducasse, between individuality and personality. Do you see it as valid? Would it help make a case in favor of the possibility of reincarnation? What considerations might count for, or against, the actuality of reincarnation?

4. Present and elaborate with fresh examples David Hume's arguments against the thesis of the immortality of the soul. Which of the considerations he mentions do you see as carrying the most weight? Could it be countered? Explain.

5. Discuss the relation, or lack thereof, between the survival hypothesis and a religious or spiritual metaphysics. Would the reality of God (etc.), in your view, insure survival? Ground your response with references to the work of F. H. Bradley, process philosophers such as Whitehead and Hartshorne, and/or theologians who articulate theodicies such as Hick or Aurobindo.

6. Is personal survival possible according to Bertrand Russell? What criteria of personal identity does he espouse? What reasons does Russell provide in support of his belief that survival is unlikely? What is wrong with the typical religious view in these straits, according to this philosopher? Do you agree?

7. Assess the evidence provided by Dr. Raymond Moody. Does it establish the likelihood of survival?

CHAPTER TEN

Religious Pluralism

Although, as we have seen, there are concurrences at an abstract level in the beliefs associated with all the major religions, there also are beliefs that conflict. Some philosophers argue that the positions of the various religious traditions worldwide are mutually exclusive, and with no consideration decisive in favor of any single religious view that they cancel each other out. When there is conflicting testimony and opinions in other domains, to suspend judgment seems reasonable. If a person surveying the global religious scene hadn't a clue about which religion to believe, would not the reasonable position be here, too, not to believe anything?

The six authors presented in this section all answer no. However, while they agree that the conflict among religious claims does not undercut the warrant of at least some religious belief, they do not agree about why. And it is important for us to realize the degree of difficulty of the problem that they are addressing. William Alston, our first author, in fact does a good job in bringing out the sharpness of some of the conflicts among even theistic religious belief systems, all of which have much in common in their understandings of God. Religious wars—between Christians and Muslims, Protestants and Catholics, Muslims and Hindus, and so on—show that doctrinal incompatibilities are often felt deeply. There is no author in this section representing the religious debunkers again, but we can readily appreciate why many who argue against religion find religious pluralism and the doctrinal dissension that goes with it decisive evidence against the truth of all religious claims.

Incommensurable Perspectives

From *Perceiving God: The Epistemology of Religious Experience* by William P. Alston, 1991

William Alston, a philosopher whom we have encountered twice before (under God and Religious Language), takes up the pluralism problem in the context of a defense of Christian beliefs on the basis of Christian mystical experience. Like William Wainwright (see under Mysticism), Alston upholds an epistemological parallelism between sense and mystical experience: the practice of forming beliefs about physical objects according to sense perceptions proves reliable, and so, too, he argues, is the practice of forming religious beliefs according to mystical experience. We may recall, however, that Steven Katz (see under Mysticism) and others—including William James (see under Faith Against Reason)—have argued that it is precisely the conflicts of doctrines putatively based on mystical experiences—the conflicts between what Buddhist and Christian mystics say, et cetera—that vitiate such a defense. William James proposes his "piecemeal supernaturalism" and philosophic polytheism just to avoid this problem. According to James, there is, beyond a drastically minimalist core, no system of religious belief that is warranted by mystical experiences; full-bodied religious beliefs must be held on faith.

Unlike James, Alston does not consider the conflicts from a perspective outside of a "Christian mystical perceptual practice" (CMP). What Alston means here is a doxastic practice, *a practice of forming beliefs within a culturally mediated religious framework (itself based, he contends, on records of earlier mystical experiences as well as theoretical reflection: revelation is interpreted by him as mystical experience). The point is that from within a Christian mystical doxastic practice the fact that there is no neutral, independent way (no non-question-begging argument) to show the wrongness of a religious doxastic practice that issues in beliefs incompatible with Christian beliefs, is no reason why the Christian should not continue with his or her full-fledged belief-forming practice. A simple analogy would be a situation where you have witnessed an event and feel you know precisely what has happened but where another gives testimony contradicting yours. Should the conflict just in itself mean that you should not take yourself to be warranted in your belief about what happened? Alston suggests that one should stick to one's guns.*

This analogy is perhaps too simple, and Alston provides another. He asks us to imagine two sensory perceptual practices that deliver beliefs contradicting the issue of our "Aristotelian" sensory practice of encountering discrete physical objects. First, there might be a "Cartesian" sensory practice of "seeing what is visually perceived as an indefinitely extended medium that is more or less concentrated at various points," or, second, a "Whiteheadian" practice of perceiving "momentary events growing out of each other in a continuous process." In a footnote Alston insists that we imagine that these conflicting practices are not mere interpretations of common experience but different ways of perceiving: the raw presentations simply are different. In that case, he argues, there would be no neutral, independent way (no non-question-begging-argument) to show the wrongness of the alternative sensory belief-forming practices. Should we "Aris-totelians" then not continue with our own practice? It would seem it would be practically impossible for us to stop. And Alston argues that the same holds for a Christian mystical perceptual practice, that is to say, that it is rational for the Christian "to continue to ac-cept, and operate in accordance with, the system of Christian belief." The practitioner belonging to a competing religious or mystical tradition would be viewed, like an Aris-totelian viewing the Cartesian or Whiteheadian sensory practitioner, simply as an out-sider. (Compare the fideist position of D. Z. Phillips under Faith Against Reason.)

An issue not addressed by Alston is that of the warrant of religious or mystical testi-mony from the perspective of someone not engaged in a particular religious or mystical pursuit. Here religious pluralism and the accompanying conflicts of doctrine cannot be dismissed as belonging to an incomprehensible "other" while a single mystical belief-forming practice remains privileged. And the deep question with Alston's approach seems to be whether even from inside a religious tradition the conflicts with other religions are so difficult to understand as he suggests.

. . . one's conception of the Ultimate will differ in different religions. Even where the broad outlines of the conception is the same, as it is among the various theistic religions, the de-tails will differ. After all, a religiously very important feature of the Christian, Jewish, and Moslem conceptions of the Ultimate has to do with God's purposes for mankind and His work in history; and the account of this varies drastically from one of these traditions to an-other.[1] And all these will diverge sharply from the conception of the Ultimate in Buddhism and certain forms of Hinduism, where the Ultimate is not thought of as a personal agent. Let's further note that one's conception of God (the Ultimate) enters, to a greater or lesser degree, into a particular subject's identification of the perceived object as God (Brahman . . .). When I take *God* to be present to me I will, if I am a Christian, but not if I am Moslem or a Hindu, most likely take it that *He who became man in the person of Jesus Christ to save us from our sins* is present to me. Indeed, it is generally true we make use of what we be-lieve about perceived objects when we perceptually identify them. When I take the person I see across the room to be Joe Walker, I thereby take him to be the person with whom I went to college, who lives two blocks from me, and so on. . . .

. . . the existence of a plurality of mutually incompatible forms of MP [mystical per-ceptual practice] poses some difficulty for the claim of any one of them to be a source of justified belief about Ultimate Reality. Yes, I think it does. Let's see if we can do better by way of saying just how. Since each form of MP is, to a considerable extent, incompatible with all the others, not more than one such form can be (sufficiently) reliable as a way of forming beliefs about the Ultimate. For if one is reliable, then most of the beliefs that issue

---

[1] It is, I take it, obvious that I do not restrict a *conception* of the Ultimate to the most basic beliefs concerning its nature, in which case all theistic religions would share the same conception, but think of it as embracing all the beliefs about the Ultimate that play a major role in the religion.

from it are true; and hence, because of the incompatibility, a large proportion of the beliefs issuing from each of the others will be false; and so none of those others is a reliable practice. Now why should I suppose that CMP [Christian mystical perceptual practice] is the one that is reliable (if any are)? No doubt, *within* CMP there are weighty reasons for supposing it to be much more reliable than its rivals; in the practice of CMP we find God telling people things that imply this. It is claimed from within the Christian tradition that God has assured us that His Holy Spirit will guide the church in its decisions, will keep it from error, will provide a "testimony" to the accuracy of the words of Christ, and so on. But, of course, each of the competing traditions can also produce conclusive internal reasons in support of its claims. Hence, if it is to be rational for me to take CMP to be reliable, I will have to have sufficient *independent* reasons for supposing that CMP is reliable, or more reliable or more likely to be reliable, than its alternatives. But no such reasons are forthcoming. Hence, it cannot be rational to engage in CMP; and by the same reasoning it cannot be rational to engage in any other particular form of MP. . . .

Now this line of argument assumes that there are no independent reasons for *epistemically* preferring one form of MP to the others. And this may well be challenged. . . . But all that is a very long story, and I will not embark on it in this book. Instead I shall adopt a "worst case scenario" and consider the prospects for the rationality of CMP on the assumption that there are no significant independent reasons for epistemically preferring it to its rivals. I shall seek to show that even on those assumptions, the justificatory efficacy of CMP is by no means dissipated, though it may be significantly weakened. . . .

. . . Suppose that in certain cultures there were a well established "Cartesian" practice of seeing what is visually perceived as an indefinitely extended medium that is more or less concentrated at various points, rather than, as in our "Aristotelian" practice, as made up of more or less discrete objects scattered about in space. In other cultures we find a "Whiteheadian" SP [sense-perceptual practice] to be equally socially established; here the visual field is seen as made up of momentary events growing out of each other in a continuous process.[2] Let's further suppose that each of these practices serves its practitioners equally well in their dealings with the environment. We may even suppose that each group has developed physical science, in its own terms, to about as high a pitch as the others. But suppose further that, in this imagined situation, we are as firmly wedded to our "Aristotelian" form of SP as we are in fact. The Cartesian and Whiteheadian *ausländer* seem utterly outlandish to us, and we find it difficult to take seriously the idea that they may be telling it like it is. Nevertheless, we can find no neutral grounds on which to argue effectively for the greater accuracy of our way of doing it. In such a situation would it be clear

---

[2] Note that as we are envisaging the situation, it is not that the world *looks* the same to people in all these different cultures and they only apply different higher-level theories as to the real nature of what they are seeing. No, the world *looks* different to them in the ways I have been specifying. What is seen *presents* itself, phenomenologically, as a continuous medium to the Cartesians and as a flux of momentary events to the Whiteheadians. Thus my imagined situation is on all fours with the situation of religious diversity as it bears on the perception of the Ultimate and the formation of perceptual beliefs therefrom.

that it is irrational for us to continue to form perceptual beliefs in our "Aristotelian" way, given that the practice is proving itself by its fruits? It seems to me that quite the opposite is clear. In the absence of any external reason for supposing that one of the competing practices is more accurate than my own, the only rational course for me is to sit tight with the practice of which I am a master and which serves me so well in guiding my activity in the world. But our actual situation here with regard to CP is precisely parallel to the one we have been imagining. Hence, by parity of reasoning, the rational thing for a practitioner of CP to do is to continue to form Christian M-beliefs [manifestation beliefs: beliefs about God's appearing in certain ways], and, more generally, to continue to accept, and operate in accordance with, the system of Christian belief. . . .

. . . I have been arguing that the existence of a plurality of uneliminated interpractice competitors does not damage the credibility of any one of them to nearly the same extent as a plurality of uneliminated intrapractice competitors. Nevertheless, I do not wish to deny that the situation does have significant adverse consequences for the epistemic status of CMP and other forms of MP. It can hardly be denied that if we were not faced with such persistent incompatibilities the participants in CMP (at least those who reflect seriously on the facts of religious diversity) would feel much more confident in CMP and would be justified in so feeling. Even if it is true, as suggested above, that the mere possibility of this kind of diversity poses problems for the epistemic status of a particular practice, it still remains true that whether or not the possibility is realized is significant for the issue. This is so, if for no other reason, because an actual plurality of incompatible perceptual practices shows that the possibility in question is genuine, that the reality in question does admit of being perceived in incompatible fashions; and this forces on us the question of which, if any, of these ways can best lay claim to represent that reality as it is. Thus it can hardly be denied that the fact of religious diversity reduces the rationality of engaging in CMP (for one who is aware of the diversity) below what it would be if this problem did not exist. Just how much it is reduced I cannot say. We do not have the conceptual resources to quantify degrees of rationality or justification in this area (and perhaps in any area).

Religions as (Better and Worse) Worldviews

From *Philosophy of Religion* by William J. Wainwright, 1988

Alston's argument is premised on there being no neutral, independent way to decide among conflicting religious belief systems. William Wainwright, a philosopher whom we first encountered in the section Mysticism, indicates, in contrast, that there well might be. Wainwright thinks that a cumulative case might be made that showed one religious belief system to be superior to its rivals—and superior to an areligious naturalism, too. The crucial move making possible this approach is to regard a religious belief system as a worldview, as a metaphysical system, an abstract theory purporting to unify our understanding of all there is, including our experiences. Wainwright would apply to religious belief systems the criteria that philosophers have identified as relevant to evaluating worldviews. First, he says a lot about just what these criteria are.

*Wainwright discusses eleven general tests of a worldview's adequacy. The best metaphysical system—and the best religious belief system—would be the one that best meets these tests. However, to make that determination requires judgment, since it may be easily imagined that, by one criterion, system **A** does better, while by another, system **B** proves superior. Are all the criteria commensurable? That is, can a single score deriving from all the tests plausibly be determined? Just how are the different tests to be comparatively weighted? Still, even if there are difficult questions about such a procedure, Wainwright's chief point is that in principle such comparative judgments can be—and are—made.*

. . . A type of reasoning is employed in diverse forms of human inquiry that is neither deductive nor inductive but an inference to the best explanation. Conclusions are drawn from a variety of independent considerations. None is itself sufficient to establish the conclusion. They can't always be fully articulated. Nevertheless, when taken together, they entitle us to conclude that some hypothesis or interpretation makes more sense of a range of facts than its alternatives do. There are general rules and guidelines for inferences of this kind. Their application, however, requires judgment. The quality of a person's judgment is affected by learning and experience, familiarity with the subject matter, and, in some cases, character or taste.

How is this relevant to the philosophy of religion? Basil Mitchell suggests that the "intellectual aspect" of a traditional religion "may be regarded as a world-view or metaphysical system"—a comprehensive picture that attempts to make sense of human experience as a whole.[1] In this respect, systems of religious belief resemble world-views like Marxism and philosophical systems such as stoicism or platonism. Metaphysical systems are supported and attacked by cumulative case reasoning. Their advocates insist they make more sense of the relevant facts than their alternatives do. Critics attempt to show that they don't.

Can *religious* world-views be supported by this sort of reasoning? . . .

A variety of criteria are used to assess rival metaphysical systems. We will discuss the most important ones and illustrate their application by examining the dispute between theism and naturalism.

Good metaphysical systems must meet a number of criteria. For example, (1) *the facts that the system explains must actually exist.* Some metaphysical systems, for instance, offer explanations of the objectivity of moral and aesthetic values. If values *aren't* objective, these systems are defective.

In addition, (2) *a good metaphysical system should be compatible with well-established facts and theories.* For example, philosophical accounts of the mind-body relation mustn't contradict the findings of biology and psychology. Generally speaking,

---

[1] Basil Mitchell, *The Justification of Religious Belief,* p. 99.

metaphysical systems should be compatible with accepted theories in other disciplines. If they aren't, the burden of proof is on the metaphysician to show why those theories are inadequate. Systems that are incompatible with the theory of biology evolution, for instance, begin with a strike against them.

An adequate system must also meet four formal criteria. (3) *It must be logically consistent,* and (4) *it shouldn't be "self-stultifying."* While most world-views meet the first formal requirement, some seem to fail the second. A view is self-stultifying if its assertion implies that it can't be known to be true, or its assertion implies that it is false or can't be expressed. Mādhyamika Buddhism and Advaita Vedānta may fail this test. Mādhyamika, for example, seems to assert that all views are false. But if *all* views are false, then its own view is false (that is, it is false that all views are false). Advaita maintains that reality is inexpressible. If reality is inexpressible, however, one can't *express* this by saying "Reality is inexpressible." . . .

(5) *Adequate metaphysical systems should also be coherent.* Their parts ought to "hang together." A system should thus display a certain amount of interconnectedness and systematic articulation. Monotheism, for example, seems more coherent than polytheisms that posit a number of gods but don't clearly explain the connections between them.

Other things being equal, (6) *simpler systems are preferable to complex ones.* A system may be simpler because it employs fewer basic concepts or makes fewer basic assumptions, or because it uses fewer explanatory principles or isn't committed to as many kinds of reality. For example, physicalism and idealism posit only one kind of reality (bodies and minds respectively). They are thus simpler than dualisms that assert that matter and mind are equally real and can't be reduced to each other. Monotheism is simpler than polytheism in the sense that it posits fewer explanatory principles.

But good metaphysical systems not only must meet formal criteria. They must also possess explanatory power. This involves several things—avoiding ad hoc hypotheses, precision, scope, fruitfulness, and a system's ability to "illuminate" the facts it explains.

(7) *Good metaphysical systems should avoid ad hoc hypotheses.* An ad hoc hypothesis has no independent plausibility and it is neither implied by the theory nor naturally suggested by it. Its only function is to explain away apparent counter-evidence. For example, when confronted with evidence of geological and biological evolution, some nineteenth-century biblical literalists tried to preserve their version of Christianity by adding a hypothesis. They suggested that God had deliberately created a world containing fossil traces and other misleading indications of geological and biological evolution; the empirical evidence points to evolution but the evidence is deceptive.

(8) *Metaphysical explanations should be precise.* An explanation is more precise when it accounts for more features of a phenomenon or provides a more detailed explanation of the mechanisms responsible for them. For example, a theory of art that explains various kinds of aesthetic value (beauty, expressiveness, sublimity, and so on) is more precise than one that only accounts for aesthetic value in general. Or suppose two metaphysical theories trace phenomena back to an absolute mind. One is more precise than the other if it provides a more detailed account of the absolute spirit and its relation to other things.

(9) *A system's scope is also important.* Other things being equal, metaphysical theories are better when they explain a wider range of phenomena. A system that illuminates

humanity's scientific, moral, aesthetic, and religious experience, for example, is superior to one that only illuminates science.

Furthermore, (10) *one should consider a system's fruitfulness.* There are several ways in which theories can be fruitful. They may predict new phenomena or previously unnoticed aspects of known phenomena. They may also generate interesting new problems and solutions or suggest illuminating interpretations of facts the theories didn't anticipate. Metaphysical theories don't generate predictions. However, they can generate new problems and solutions and interesting interpretations of new facts. Platonism, for example, was used to illuminate the data of Christian revelation and romantic love, although it didn't anticipate either of these phenomena.

(11) *Good metaphysical systems provide illuminating explanations of the phenomena within their explanatory range.* There are several ways in which theories can illuminate facts. A puzzling phenomenon can sometimes be subsumed under general principles. The phenomenon is explained by showing how it follows from the system's postulates and theorems or from hypotheses that are either suggested by the system or are easily incorporated in it. For example, classical theists make sense of revelation by inferring the likelihood of a revelation from God's desire to enter into relations with His creatures and humanity's weakness and need for God. Theists frequently attempt to illuminate evil by showing how its occurrence follows from hypotheses that easily cohere with theism (the lawfulness of the created order, for instance, or the desirability of moral growth and independence). If the theist's postulates, theorems, and hypotheses are plausible, the puzzling phenomenon is "illuminated."

When a metaphysical theory integrates a set of apparently unrelated phenomena, it sometimes illuminates them. For example, a system may interpret historical, sociological, psychological, and moral facts as diverse expressions of humanity's drive towards transcendence. Other systems interpret the same facts as expressions of sinful self-reliance. Still others think it more helpful to view them as products of the interaction between an innately good human nature and a corrupt social environment. . . .

In short, a good metaphysical system explains real facts, is consistent with other things we know, meets formal criteria, and possesses explanatory power. It may also have to satisfy a pragmatic criterion.

Paul Tillich argues that (12) *philosophical theories should be judged by "their efficacy in the life-process of mankind."*[2] According to Frederick Ferré, an adequate metaphysical system must be "capable of 'coming to life' for individuals . . . becoming . . . a usable instrument for our coping with the total environment." It must have a "capacity for ringing true with respect to" those who use it, enabling them to "cope successfully with the challenges of life."[3] William James makes a similar point. Adequate metaphysical systems must meet practical as well as intellectual demands. . . .

The best metaphysical system, then, is that which best satisfies these criteria. One should note that the criteria are comparative; they are used in deciding *between* competing theories.

---

[2] Paul Tillich, *Systematic Theology,* Vol. 1, p. 105.

[3] Frederick Ferré and Kent Bendall, *Exploring the Logic of Faith,* p. 171.

The question, therefore, is "*On the whole,* does theory A satisfy the criteria better than theory B?" Theory A might do this even if it doesn't fully satisfy *some* of the criteria (perhaps it includes some ad hoc hypotheses) and even if B satisfies a few criteria better than A. . . .

On the whole, religious world-views are consistent and reasonably coherent. However, a few may be self-stultifying. Mādhyamika Buddhism appears to assert that all views are false. But if *all* views are false, its own view is false. Advaita maintains that reality is inexpressible. Yet if reality *is* inexpressible, one can't express this by *saying* "Reality is inexpressible." . . . These world-views thus seem self-stultifying. But both have responses to this charge. Mādhyamika denies that it really is asserting that all views are false. It neither denies nor asserts that all views are false. Nor does it deny or assert the opposite (that some views are true). Mādhyamika insists it has *no* views of its own and thus isn't asserting *anything!* Advaita can evade the charge by qualifying the claim that reality is inexpressible. For example, it can withdraw to the position that reality can only be expressed by negations (saying what it is not). Since "Reality is not expressible by affirmative statements" is a negation, its assertion isn't inconsistent with the truth of what it says. In spite of appearances, then, Mādhyamika and Advaita may not be self-stultifying. In any case, most religious world-views are free from this defect.

The major religious world-views are also more or less equally precise, comprehensive, and fruitful. Nor does one seem more ad hoc than the others. But some systems might seem simpler. Jewish and Muslim monotheism is simpler than the Christian doctrine that one divine nature exists in three "presentations" or "persons" (Father, Son, and Holy Spirit). Hīnayāna Buddhists say little about Nirvāna except that it is real, totally unlike the space-time world or its constituents, and the end of suffering. Hīnayāna's description of ultimate reality is thus simpler than the more elaborate descriptions of other systems.

But religious world-views aren't just accounts of ultimate reality. They are also interpretations of reality as a whole. For example, Hīnayāna Buddhism provides elaborate analyses of the constituents of the space-time world and their interconnections. One must understand these to grasp the nature of human existence and the causes of suffering. What is crucial, then, isn't the comparative simplicity of different accounts of ultimate reality but the comparative simplicity of entire systems. It isn't clear that any religious view, *as a whole,* is simpler than others.

Religious Inclusivism

From *The Complete Works of Swami Vivekananda,* 1907

Swami Vivekananda (1863–1902) was a follower of Sri Ramakrishna, the leading nineteenth-century Indian mystic and spiritual leader (see under Mysticism). Learned in English and Western disciplines as well as in Sanskrit and traditional Indian philosophy, Vivekananda became the great popularizer of Hindu ideas in the West during the latter part of the nineteenth century. He travelled widely, first in the United States, where in

1893 he attended the Parliament of World Religions in Chicago, and then in England and Europe. At the Chicago Parliament, Vivekananda had great success, establishing a reputation for wit, eloquence, and intellectual depth. We may note that William James attended the Parliament, and that James refers several times to Vivekananda in his Varieties *(first published in 1902).*

Vivekananda finds it a virtue of Hinduism that it is inclusivist, that it accepts "all religions as true." Of course, that acceptance cannot include the exclusivist claims of other religions, but it does include, Vivekananda explains, even the impersonalism of Buddhism. For Vivekananda, God (or Brahman) as infinite is capable of revealing diverse Divine truths, and does so. However, Vivekananda apparently also endorses a hierarchy among religious teachings, ranging from the religious notions and practices of the "savage" to those of the "highest man" whose virtues make "society stand in awe of him and doubt his human nature." Does Hinduism, as Vivekananda understands it, sacrifice egalitarianism to win its breadth and inclusivism?

The hierarchy explains some of the contradictions among religious teachings. But more fundamentally, Vivekananda suggests, the requirements of God's reaching out to touch everyone, along with the diversity of human nature and cultural circumstance, result in apparent contradictions. Thus by properly indexing religious claims—with a "for me" or a "for that time and culture"—the contradictions would be resolved. Similar moves are made by our remaining three authors, Huston Smith, Seyyed Nasr, and John Hick.

RESPONSE TO WELCOME

At the World's Parliament of Religions, Chicago
11th September, 1893

Sisters and Brothers of America,

It fills my heart with joy unspeakable to rise in response to the warm and cordial welcome which you have given us. I thank you in the name of the most ancient order of monks in the world; I thank you in the name of the mother of religions; and I thank you in the name of millions and millions of Hindu people of all classes and sects.

My thanks, also, to some of the speakers on this platform who, referring to the delegates from the Orient, have told you that these men from far-off nations may well claim the honour of bearing to different lands the idea of toleration. I am proud to belong to a religion which has taught the world both tolerance and universal acceptance. We believe not only in universal toleration, but we accept all religions as true. I am proud to belong to a nation which has sheltered the persecuted and the refugees of all religions and all nations of the earth. I am proud to tell you that we have gathered in our bosom the purest remnant of the Israelites, who came to Southern India and took refuge with us in the very year in which their holy temple was shattered to pieces by Roman tyranny. I am proud to belong to the religion which has sheltered and is still fostering the remnant of the grand Zoroastrian nation. I will quote to you, brethren, a few lines from a hymn which I remember to have repeated from my earliest boyhood, which is every day repeated by millions of human beings: *"As the different streams having their sources in different places all mingle their water in the sea, so, O Lord, the different paths which men take through different tendencies, various though they appear, crooked or straight, all lead to Thee."*

The present convention, which is one of the most august assemblies ever held, is in itself a vindication, a declaration to the world of the wonderful doctrine preached in the Gita: *"Whosoever comes to Me, through whatsoever form, I reach him; all men are struggling through paths which in the end lead to me."* Sectarianism, bigotry, and its horrible descendant, fanaticism, have long possessed this beautiful earth. They have filled the earth with violence, drenched it often and often with human blood, destroyed civilisation and sent whole nations to despair. Had it not been for these horrible demons, human society would be far more advanced than it is now. But their time is come ; and I fervently hope that the bell that tolled this morning in honour of this convention may be the death-knell of all fanaticism, of all persecutions with the sword or with the pen, and of all uncharitable feelings between persons wending their way to the same goal.

WHY WE DISAGREE

15th September, 1893

I will tell you a little story. You have heard the eloquent speaker who has just finished say, "Let us cease from abusing each other," and he was very sorry that there should be always so much variance.

But I think I should tell you a story which would illustrate the cause of this variance. A frog lived in a well. It had lived there for a long time. It was born there and brought up there, and yet was a little, small frog. Of course the evolutionists were not there then to tell us whether the frog lost its eyes or not, but, for our story's sake, we must take it for granted that it had its eyes, and that it every day cleansed the water of all the worms and bacilli that lived in it with an energy that would do credit to our modern bacteriologists. In this way it went on and became a little sleek and fat. Well, one day another frog that lived in the sea came and fell into the well.

"Where are you from?"

"I am from the sea."

"The sea! How big is that? Is it as big as my well?" and he took a leap from one side of the well to the other.

"My friend," said the frog of the sea, "how do you compare the sea with your little well?"

Then the frog took another leap and asked, "Is your sea so big?"

"What nonsense you speak, to compare the sea with your well!"

"Well, then," said the frog of the well, "nothing can be bigger than my well; there can be nothing bigger than this; this fellow is a liar, so turn him out."

That has been the difficulty all the while.

I am a Hindu. I am sitting on my own little well and thinking that the whole world is my little well. The Christian sits in his little well and thinks the whole world is his well. The Mohammedan sits in his little well and thinks that is the whole world. I have to thank you of America for the great attempt you are making to break down the barriers of this little world of ours, and hope that, in the future, the Lord will help you to accomplish your purpose.

PAPER ON HINDUISM

Read at the Parliament on 19th September, 1893

Three religions now stand in the world which have come down to us from time prehistoric—Hinduism, Zoroastrianism and Judaism. They have all received tremendous shocks and all of them prove by their survival their internal strength. But while Judaism failed to absorb Christianity and was driven out of its place of birth by its all-conquering daughter, and a handful of Parsees is all that remains to tell the tale of their grand religion, sect after sect arose in India and seemed to shake the religion of the Vedas to its very foundations, but like the waters of the seashore in a tremendous earthquake it receded only for a while, only to return in an all-absorbing flood, a thousand times more vigorous, and when the tumult of the rush was over, these sects were all sucked in, absorbed, and assimilated into the immense body of the mother faith.

From the high spiritual flights of the Vedanta philosophy, of which the latest discoveries of science seem like echoes, to the low ideas of idolatry with its multifarious mythology, the agnosticism of the Buddhists, and the atheism of the Jains, each and all have a place in the Hindu's religion.

Where then, the question arises, where is the common centre to which all these widely diverging radii converge? Where is the common basis upon which all these seemingly hopeless contradictions rest? And this is the question I shall attempt to answer.

The Hindus have received their religion through revelation, the Vedas. They hold that the Vedas are without beginning and without end. It may sound ludicrous to this audience, but a book can be without beginning or end. But by the Vedas no books are meant. They mean the accumulated treasury of spiritual laws discovered by different times. Just as the law of gravitation existed before its discovery, and would exist if all humanity forgot it, so is it with the laws that govern the spiritual world. The moral, ethical, and spiritual relations between soul and soul and between individual spirits and the Father of all spirits, were there before their discovery, and would remain even if we forgot them.

The discoverers of these laws are called Rishis, and we honour them as perfected beings. I am glad to tell this audience that some of the very greatest of them were women. Here it may be said that these laws as laws may be without end, but they must have had a beginning. The Vedas teach us that creation is without beginning or end. Science is said to have proved that the sum total of cosmic energy is always the same. Then, if there was a time when nothing existed, where was all this manifested energy? Some say it was in a potential form in God. In that case God is sometimes potential and sometimes kinetic, which would make Him mutable. Everything mutable is a compound, and everything compound must undergo that change which is called destruction. So God would die, which is absurd. Therefore there never was a time when there was no creation.

If I may be allowed to use a simile, creation and creator are two lines, without beginning and without end, running parallel to each other. God is the ever active providence, by whose power systems after systems are being evolved out of chaos, made to run for a time and again destroyed. This is what the Brâhmin boy repeats every day: *"The sun and the moon, the Lord created like the suns and moons of previous cycles."* And this agrees with modern science.

Here I stand and if I shut my eyes, and try to conceive my existence, "I", "I", "I", what is the idea before me? The idea of a body. Am I, then, nothing but a combination of material substances? The Vedas declare, "No". I am a spirit living in a body. I am not the body. The body will die, but I shall not die. Here am I in this body; it will fall, but I shall go on living. I had also a past. The soul was not created, for creation means a combination which means a certain future dissolution. If then the soul was created, it must die. Some are born happy, enjoy perfect health, with beautiful body, mental vigour and all wants supplied. Others are born miserable, some are without hands or feet, others again are idiots and only drag on a wretched existence. Why, if they are all created, why does a just and merciful God create one happy and another unhappy, why is He so partial? Nor would it mend matters in the least to hold that those who are miserable in this life will be happy in a future one. Why should a man be miserable even here in the reign of a just and merciful God?

In the second place, the idea of a creator God does not explain the anomaly, but simply expresses the cruel fiat of an all-powerful being. There must have been causes, then, before his birth, to make a man miserable or happy and those were his past actions.

Are not all the tendencies of the mind and the body accounted for by inherited aptitude? Here are two parallel lines of existence—one of the mind, the other of matter. If matter and its transformations answer for all that we have, there is no necessity for supposing the existence of a soul. But it cannot be proved that thought has been evolved out of matter, and if a philosophical monism is inevitable, spiritual monism is certainly logical and no less desirable than a materialistic monism; but neither of these is necessary here.

We cannot deny that bodies acquire certain tendencies from heredity, but those tendencies only mean the physical configuration, through which a peculiar mind alone can act in a peculiar way. There are other tendencies peculiar to a soul caused by its past actions. And a soul with a certain tendency would by the laws of affinity take birth in a body which is the fittest instrument for the display of that tendency. This is in accord with science, for science wants to explain everything by habit, and habit is got through repetitions. So repetitions are necessary to explain the natural habits of a new-born soul. And since they were not obtained in this present life, they must have come down from past lives.

There is another suggestion. Taking all these for granted, how is it that I do not remember anything of my past life? This can be easily explained. I am now speaking English. It is not my mother tongue, in fact no words of my mother tongue are now present in my consciousness; but let me try to bring them up, and they rush in. That shows that consciousness is only the surface of the mental ocean, and within its depths are stored up all our experiences. Try and struggle, they would come up and you would be conscious even of your past life.

This is direct and demonstrative evidence. Verification is the perfect proof of a theory, and here is the challenge thrown to the world by the Rishis. We have discovered the secret by which the very depths of the ocean of memory can be stirred up—try it and you would get a complete reminiscence of your past life.

So then the Hindu believes that he is a spirit. Him the sword cannot pierce—him the fire cannot burn—him the water cannot melt—him the air cannot dry. The Hindu believes that every soul is a circle whose circumference is nowhere, but whose centre is located in the body, and that death means the change of this centre from body to body. Nor is the soul bound by the conditions of matter. In its very essence it is free, unbounded, holy, pure, and perfect. But somehow or other it finds itself tied down to matter, and thinks of itself as matter.

Why should the free, perfect, and pure being be thus under the thraldom of matter, is the next question. How can the perfect soul be deluded into the belief that it is imperfect? We have been told that the Hindus shirk the question and say that no such question can be there. Some thinkers want to answer it by positing one or more quasi-perfect beings, and use big scientific names to fill up the gap. But naming is not explaining. The question remains the same. How can the perfect become the quasi-perfect; how can the pure, the absolute, change even a microscopic particle of its nature? But the Hindu is sincere. He does not want to take shelter under sophistry. He is brave enough to face the question in a manly fashion ; and his answer is: "I do not know. I do not know how the perfect being, the soul, came to think of itself as imperfect, as joined to and conditioned by matter." But the fact is a fact for all that. It is a fact in everybody's consciousness that one thinks of oneself as the body. The Hindu does not attempt to explain why one thinks one is the body. The answer that it is the will of God is no explanation. This is nothing more than what the Hindu says, "I do not know."

Well, then, the human soul is eternal and immortal, perfect and infinite, and death means only a change of centre from one body to another. The present is determined by our past actions, and the future by the present. The soul will go on evolving up or reverting back from birth to birth and death to death. But here is another question: Is man a tiny boat in a tempest, raised one moment on the foamy crest of a billow and dashed down into a yawning chasm the next, rolling to and fro at the mercy of good and bad actions—a powerless, helpless wreck in an ever-raging, ever-rushing, uncompromising current of cause and effect; a little moth placed under the wheel of causation which rolls on crushing everything in its way and waits not for the widow's tears or the orphan's cry? The heart sinks at the idea, yet this is the law of Nature. Is there no hope? Is there no escape?—was the cry that went up from the bottom of the heart of despair. It reached the throne of mercy, and words of hope and consolation came down and inspired a Vedic sage, and he stood up before the world and in trumpet voice proclaimed the glad tidings: "Hear, ye children of immortal bliss! even ye that reside in higher spheres! I have found the Ancient One who is beyond all darkness, all delusion: knowing Him alone you shall be saved from death over again." "Children of immortal bliss"—what a sweet, what a hopeful name! Allow me to call you, brethren, by that sweet name—heirs of immortal bliss—yea, the Hindu refuses to call you sinners. Ye are the Children of God, the sharers of immortal bliss, holy and perfect beings. Ye divinities on earth—sinners! It is a sin to call a man so; it is a standing libel on human nature. Come up, O lions, and shake off the delusion that you are sheep; you are souls immortal, spirits free, blest and eternal; ye are not matter, ye are not bodies; matter is your servant, not you the servant of matter.

Thus it is that the Vedas proclaim not a dreadful combination of unforgiving laws, not an endless prison of cause and effect, but that at the head of all these laws, in and through every particle of matter and force, stands One "by whose command the wind blows, the fire burns, the clouds rain, and death stalks upon the earth."

And what is His nature?

He is everywhere, the pure and formless One, the Almighty and the All-merciful. "Thou art our father, Thou art our mother, Thou art our beloved friend, Thou art the source of all strength; give us strength. Thou art He that beareth the burdens of the universe; help me bear the little burden of this life." Thus sang the Rishis of the Vedas. And how to worship Him? Through love. "He is to be worshipped as the one beloved, dearer than everything in this and the next life." . . .

Science is nothing but the finding of unity. As soon as science would reach perfect unity, it would stop from further progress, because it would reach the goal. Thus Chemistry could not progress farther when it would discover one element out of which all others could be made. Physics would stop when it would be able to fulfil its services in discovering one energy of which all the others are but manifestations, and the science of religion become perfect when it would discover Him who is the one life in a universe of death, Him who is the constant basis of an ever-changing world. One who is the only Soul of which all souls are but delusive manifestations. Thus is it, through multiplicity and duality, that the ultimate is reached. Religion can go no farther. This is the goal of all science.

All science is bound to come to this conclusion in the long run. Manifestation, and not creation, is the word of science today, and the Hindu is only glad that what he has been cherishing in his bosom for ages is going to be taught in more forcible language, and with further light from the latest conclusions of science.

Descend we now from the aspirations of philosophy to the religion of the ignorant. At the very outset, I may tell you that there is no *polytheism* in India. In every temple, if one stands by and listens, one will find the worshippers applying all the attributes of God, including omnipresence, to the images. It is not polytheism, nor would the name henotheism explain the situation. "The rose called by any other name would smell as sweet." Names are not explanations.

I remember, as a boy, hearing a Christian missionary preach to a crowd in India. Among other sweet things he was telling them was that if he gave a blow to their idol with his stick, what could it do? One of his hearers sharply answered, "If I abuse your God, what can He do?" "You would be punished," said the preacher, "when you die." "So my idol will punish you when you die," retorted the Hindu.

The tree is known by its fruits. When I have seen amongst them that are called idolators, men, the like of whom in morality and spirituality and love I have never seen anywhere, I stop and ask myself, "Can sin beget holiness?"

Superstition is a great enemy of man, but bigotry is worse. Why does a Christian go to church? Why is the cross holy? Why is the face turned toward the sky in prayer? Why are there so many images in the Catholic Church? Why are there so many images in the minds of Protestants when they pray? My brethren, we can no more think about anything without a mental image than we can live without breathing. By the law of association, the material image calls up the mental idea and *vice versa.* This is why the Hindu uses an external symbol when he worships. He will tell you, it helps to keep his mind fixed on the Being to whom he prays. He knows as well as you do that the image is not God, is not omnipresent. After all, how much does omnipresence mean to almost the whole world? It stands merely as a word, a symbol. Has God superficial area? If not, when we repeat the word "omnipresent", we think of the extended sky or of space, that is all.

As we find that somehow or other, by the laws of our mental constitution, we have to associate our ideas of infinity with the image of the blue sky, or of the sea, so we naturally connect our idea of holiness with the image of a church, a mosque, or a cross. The Hindus have associated the idea of holiness, purity, truth, omnipresence, and such other ideas with different images and forms. But with this difference that while some people devote their whole lives to their idol of a church and never rise higher, because with them religion means an intellectual assent to certain doctrines and doing good to their fellows, the whole religion of the Hindu is centred in realisation. Man is to become divine by realising the divine. Idols or temples or churches or books are only the supports, the helps, of his spiritual childhood: but on and on he must progress.

He must not stop anywhere. *"External worship, material worship,"* say the scriptures, *"is the lowest stage; struggling to rise high, mental prayer is the next stage, but the highest stage is when the Lord has been realised."* Mark, the same earnest man who is kneeling before the idol tells you, *"Him the sun cannot express, nor the moon, nor the stars, the lightning cannot express Him, nor what we speak of as fire; through Him they shine."* But he does not abuse any one's idol or call its worship sin. He recognises in it a necessary stage of life. *"The child is father of the man."* Would it be right for an old man to say that childhood is a sin or youth is a sin?

If a man can realise his divine nature with the help of an image, would it be right to call that a sin? Nor even when he has passed that stage, should he call it an error. To the Hindu, man is not travelling from error to truth, but from truth to truth, from lower to higher truth. To him all the religions, from the lowest fetishism to the highest absolutism, mean so many attempts of the human soul to grasp and realise the Infinite, each determined by the conditions of its birth and association, and each of these marks a stage of progress; and every soul is a young eagle soaring higher and higher, gathering more and more strength, till it reaches the Glorious Sun.

Unity in variety is the plan of nature, and the Hindu has recognised it. Every other religion lays down certain fixed dogmas, and tries to force society to adopt them. It places before society only one coat which must fit Jack and John and Henry, all alike. If it does not fit John or Henry, he must go without a coat to cover his body. The Hindus have discovered that the absolute can only be realised, or thought of, or stated, through the relative, and the images, crosses, and crescents are simply so many symbols—so many pegs to hang the spiritual ideas on. It is not that this help is necessary for every one, but those that do not need it have no right to say that it is wrong. Nor is it compulsory in Hinduism.

One thing I must tell you. Idolatry in India does not mean anything horrible. It is not the mother of harlots. On the other hand, it is the attempt of undeveloped minds to grasp high spiritual truths. The Hindus have their faults, they sometimes have their exceptions; but mark this, they are always for punishing their own bodies, and never for cutting the throats of their neighbours. If the Hindu fanatic burns himself in the pyre, he never lights the fire of Inquisition. And even this cannot be laid at the door of his religion any more than the burning of witches can be laid at the door of Christianity.

To the Hindu, then, the whole world of religions is only a travelling, a coming up, of different men and women, through various conditions and circumstances, to the same goal. Every religion is only evolving a God out of the material man, and the same God is the inspirer of all of them. Why, then, are there so many contradictions? They are only apparent, says the Hindu. The contradictions come from the same truth adapting itself to the varying circumstances of different natures.

It is the same light coming through glasses of different colours. And these little variations are necessary for purposes of adaptation. But in the heart of everything the same truth reigns. The Lord has declared to the Hindu in His incarnation as Krishna, *"I am in every religion as the thread through a string of pearls. Wherever thou seest extraordinary holiness and extraordinary power raising and purifying humanity, know thou that I am there."* And what has been the result? I challenge the world to find, throughout the whole system of Sanskrit philosophy, any such expression as that the Hindu alone will be saved and not others. Says Vyasa, *"We find perfect men even beyond the pale of our caste and creed."* One thing more. How, then, can the Hindu, whose whole fabric of thought centres in God, believe in Buddhism which is agnostic, or in Jainism which is atheistic?

The Buddhists or the Jains do not depend upon God; but the whole force of their religion is directed to the central truth in every religion, to evolve a God out of man. They have not seen the Father, but they have seen the Son. And he that hath seen the Son hath seen the Father also.

This, brethren, is a short sketch of the religious ideas of the Hindus. The Hindu may have failed to carry out all his plans, but if there is ever to be a universal religion, it must be one which will have no location in place or time; which will be infinite like the God it will preach, and whose sun will shine upon the followers of Krishna and of Christ, on saints and sinners alike; which will not be Brahminic or Buddhistic, Christian or Mohammedan, but the sum total of all these, and still have infinite space for development; which in its catholicity will embrace in its infinite arms, and find a place for, every human being, from the lowest grovelling savage not far removed from the brute, to the highest man towering by the virtues of his head and heart almost above humanity, making society stand in awe of him and doubt his human nature. It will be a religion which will have no place for persecution or intolerance in its polity, which will recognise divinity in every man and woman, and whose whole scope, whose whole force, will be created in aiding humanity to realise its own true, divine nature.

Offer such a religion, and all the nations will follow you. Asoka's council was a council of the Buddhist faith. Akbar's, though more to the purpose, was only a parlour-meeting.

It was reserved for America to proclaim to all quarters of the globe that the Lord is in every religion.

May He who is the Brahman of the Hindus, the Ahura-Mazda of the Zoroastrians, the Buddha of the Buddhists, the Jehovah of the Jews, the Father in Heaven of the Christians, give strength to you to carry out your noble idea! The star arose in the East; it travelled steadily towards the West, sometimes dimmed and sometimes effulgent, till it made a circuit of the world; and now it is again rising on the very horizon of the East, the borders of the Sanpo, a thousandfold more effulgent than it ever was before.

Hail, Columbia, motherland of liberty! It has been given to thee, who never dipped her hand in her neighbour's blood, who never found out that the shortest way of becoming rich was by robbing one's neighbours, it has been given to thee to march at the vanguard of civilisation with the flag of harmony.

Primordial (Perennial) Philosophy

From *Forgotten Truth: The Primordial Tradition* by Huston Smith, 1976

A different approach, which is nonetheless hierarchical as well as inclusivist in a way, is perennial philosophy. A perennialist—such as Professor Huston Smith, formerly of M.I.T. and the University of California, Berkeley, who was, among academic highbrows, a leader of the sixties counterculture, helping to navigate the straits of spiritual theory— finds the highest teaching to be esoteric, *and obscured by the official doctrines of the major religions. But the true view also radiates through the accretions of religious traditions, and one can catch glints of truth within each religion if one has patience and discernment.*

Perennial philosophy per se *has not fared well under professional scrutiny, though in a sense perennialism is quite common philosophically. Many philosophers are realists about truth, for example, including metaphysical and ethical truths, and believe that perennially people get things right. The facts are often hidden when it comes to questions of philosophic import, and often misconceptions reign. But if, say, one held that pleasure is the criterion of the ethically good, then, knowing that an ethical hedonism has been espoused from time to time in various cultures, one could be both a perennialist in ethics and a hedonist. A more fully perennial philosophy would tell us a story about why the truth only on occasion emerges.*

To his credit, Huston Smith provides such a story—in broad outline. Religion is key both to the disclosure and to the concealment of spiritual truth. Smith's view is that a revelation founds a religion that through time comes to hide, or distort, the original, primordial truth revealed. The concealing and distorting brought about by religious institutionalization and other factors important to a religion's prosperity in this world account for the conflicts and contradictions in religious doctrines considered worldwide.

The doctrinal conflicts are, then, in Smith's view an evil rooted in the accommodations religions must make to the world. This may be right, but Smith does not provide much of a theodicy, and not much at all by way of making his sense of the spiritual reality and its relation to the world less vague, and thus more open to scrutiny. In his defense, it might be said that the sense of the reality that he wants to convey is not primarily intellectual but rather mystical. Nevertheless, several burning intellectual questions remain.

The reader will recognize the affinity of [my] thesis with what has been called "the perennial philosophy." I am not unhappy with that phrase, but to bring out the fact that this particular philosophy nowhere originated, nor has it succeeded in maintaining itself operatively, save in a cultic context—a context that works to transform lives as well as minds—I prefer the less exclusively intellectual designation "the primordial tradition" (primordial: "existing . . . from the beginning; fundamental," *Oxford English Dictionary*). . . .

As the all-empowering but impalpable essence that creates each snowflake of existence and causes it to settle in its own proper place, the mathematical point is in everything. Kabbalists call it the Inward or Holy Palace; in Islam it is the Divine Station that combines contrasts and antinomies. In China it is the Chung Yung, the Invariable Middle, the Taoist Void that unites the spokes and makes of them a wheel. Though nothing could exist without it, in the realm of the Ten Thousand Things only man can be aware of it and identify with it intentionally. The awareness can be cultivated directly through meditation or indirectly through the "meditation of everyday life," which aims at reducing the tension between the contraries of human existence. Practicing detachment, the aspirant undercuts the vicissitudes of the stream of forms and attains peace in emptiness. To connote the point where the opposites of space and time are resolved, Blake wrote of "infinity in the palm of your hand / And eternity in an hour"; the phrase "holy indifference," for its part, tokens the fact that in that selfsame point the opposition between good and evil likewise collapses:

> One to me is fame and shame,
> One to me is loss and gain,
> One to me is pleasure, pain.
>
> *Bhagavad-Gita*

Passage through the "gateless gate" (Mu Mon Kan) that guards the holy center can be disorienting. If it takes the form of a powerful satori it can feel as if one has been sucked into a "black hole" where physical laws are destroyed. When eyes have accustomed themselves to the new, ethereal light, however, one sees that no movement has occurred. Length and breadth had already withdrawn into the cross's horizontal center; now the vertical axis too collapses. Renouncing the space it had embodied to make an important but provisional point, that axis now withdraws the ontic, value distinctions that once it metered. *Sub species aeternitatis* phenomena are themselves noumena; samsara, nirvana.

> The perfect way knows no difficulties
> Only it refuses to make distinctions.
> A hair's breadth difference
> And heaven and hell are set apart.

Seng-ts'an

. . . If we have left the impression that the primordial philosophy counsels reversion, we should speak more plainly. The needed return—a kind of homecoming—is in outlook only; it is in world view and sense of reality, and even here phrases such as "going back" are imprecise. For the issue does not really concern time at all; it concerns truth, truth of the kind that is time*less*. If we have appealed to past ages it is because we see them as having been bathed in such truth to a degree that we are not. In this respect we would indeed be pleased to see life on earth recover a lost dimension, and are grateful for persons who are working to reknit the rich coherence of a fully human consciousness which the cramped and aggressive rationality of modernity has bruised so badly. But our opportunity is not in any literal sense to go back, a move that in a thousand ways is impossible even if it were desirable. Bygone days really are gone, and many species of "the good old days" would not be good in our context. . . .

"Originality is thus related to inspiration, and above all to revelation, for the origins are transcendent, being beyond this world, in the domains of Spirit. Ultimately the origin is nothing less than the Absolute, the Infinite and Eternal,"[1] and originality a guarantor of both authenticity and effectuality. In this fundamental sense of the word, a sense that carries the prospect of a progressive awakening in the direction of man's root and source, our book is a call for originality at all costs.

Developments will occur, of course; on the terrestrial plane nothing escapes change, and this holds as much for religions as for individuals and civilizations. Nor are changes in all respects deleterious. Respecting religions, change often involves a double movement whose aspects to some extent balance one another. On the one hand the collectivity degenerates in proportion to its distance from the Revelation that launched it, while on the other hand, with respect to doctrine, the tradition blooms, values that were implicit from the start being now articulated. Thus a progressive and compensating unfolding occurs within the very framework of a general decline.[2] Five hundred years after the initial Vedic revelation, Brahmanism was in danger of ossifying in formalism and privilege: at precisely that moment the Upanishads appeared. Implicit wisdom was made explicit and rishis devel-

---

[1] Martin Lings, *What Is Sufism?* (Berkeley: University of California Press, 1975), p. 15.

[2] A similar pattern can often be seen in the history of art. "Strange as it may seem, it has always happened in the history of art, that by the time perfection of technique has been attained, inspiration has declined. It was so in Greece, and in Europe after the Renaissance. It almost seems as if concentration upon technique hindered the free working of the imagination a little; if so, however much we desire both, do not let us make any mistake as to which is first." A. K. Coomaraswamy, "The Aims of Indian Art," *Studies in Comparative Religion,* Winter 1975, p. 7.

oped the techniques of yoga. Five hundred years after Buddha, his tradition stood in like danger; it was on the verge of shriveling to a monasticism without possibility of expanding radiation. It was then that the Mahayana burgeoned, overlaying the "holy selfishness" of the Pratyeka Buddhas with the ideal of the compassionate Bodhisattva, and again the day was saved. In Judaism the time of the Psalms and the Song of Solomon could not possibly have been that of the Pentateuch, any more than the Kabbalah could have unfolded before the Middle Ages. The Christianity of the desert fathers flowers in the Middle Ages more gently under the sign of the Virgin Mother and gives rise in turn to pure gnosis in the Rhineland mystics and aspects of Scholasticism. In Islam the successive disintegration of empires and the sundering rift between Sunnis and Shi'ites are redeemed by the progressive unfolding of Sufism and the growth of its invigorating orders. It would be wrong to conclude from these examples that religions never decline and die. History shows that they do and logic that they must; belonging as they do to the order of finitude, their days are numbered from the start. . . .

. . . It happened to have been Muhammad's destiny to penetrate versatilely an exceptionally wide range of earthy experience: not only was he shepherd, merchant, hermit, exile, soldier, law-giver, and prophet-priest-king; he was also orphan (but with a remarkably loving grandfather and uncle), for many years the husband of one wife much older than himself, a many times bereaved father, a widower, and finally the husband of many wives, some much younger than himself.[3] What sanctified this earthly plenitude was the degree to which it was dominated by acute and unswerving sensitivity to the magnetism of the Hereafter. "Do for this world," he said, "as if thou wert to live a thousand years and for the next as if thou wert to die tomorrow." On the one hand this Hadith "enjoins the perfection—the patient thoroughness we might say—incumbent upon man as representative of God on earth; and on the other hand it demands that he shall be ready to leave this world at a moment's notice."[4] Inasmuch as this terrestrial plane is our current lot, it is not only natural but appropriate for us to feel concern for our daily problems and those of our neighbors. We build our sand castles because we need them, and in their small way they are beautiful, reflecting in their fragile moats and turrets the patterns of another place, a more enduring realm. But every man and woman is infinitely more than the child that plays thus in salt and sand, even as a seed contains in virtuality a great tree: "O high-born race of foreigners on earth . . . you do not belong here, you belong somewhere else."[5] Moreover, our entire visible cosmos rests on an invisible volcano. We imagine that our earth, its mountain ranges and unplumbed seas, can be destroyed only by forces of its own kind, by masses and energies that are in some way physical, but in this we are mistaken. The world, in appearance so resilient, so substantial, can withdraw "from within." Matter can flow back to the immaterial source from which it came, causing the entire space-time field to collapse

---

[3] Margin Lings, *What is Sufism?* p. 34.

[4] *Ibid.*

[5] Augustine, *Enarrationes in Psalmos,* 136.13.

like a balloon that is emptied of air. Our marvel consists in the fact that, possessed as we are of souls and Spirit, we can escape this collapse by retreating, or rather advancing, into the mathematical point, our unchanging Center which is non-spatial. All discussion of social problems and the dangers that press upon us should proceed in the context of this realization. They must be given their fair measure of concern but not more.

A Common Ground

From *Knowledge and the Sacred* by Seyyed Hossein Nasr, 1981

Another globalist who champions the esoteric in religions is Seyyed Hossein Nasr, a distinguished contemporary scholar, the author of more than twenty well-received books, and an Islamic mystic. By his early forties Professor Nasr, having mastered much traditional Islamic learning and Western as well (with a Harvard Ph.D.), had been named Chancellor of Aryamehr University in Teheran. Now he is University Professor of Islamic Studies at George Washington University in Washington, D.C. The selection here is from Nasr's 1981 Gifford Lectures, the prestigious series staged in Edinburgh, where William James first presented the talks that became The Varieties of Religious Experience.

Nasr says that the "multiplicity of sacred forms" found in the world's religious traditions "is the most definitive evidence of the reality of the sacred." But the uninitiate (modern scholars of religion, logic-touting philosophers, psychologists, social scientists, and company) with their profane outlooks insensitive to the subtleties of sacred forms find in the differences of sacred traditions contradictions that make religious claims suspect. Nasr holds that it is not possible to appreciate the sacred in another tradition without being steeped in the esoteric wisdom, or mysticism, of one's own.

Abstractly considered, the point is that the Absolute as transcendent of all finite manifestations is capable of expressing or manifesting itself in diverse and seemingly opposed sacred forms, and does so. All revelations of the supreme Logos or Word, considered from the side of the human, can only be partial and not exhaustive. Within traditional Islamic theology, it is said that the Koran itself is but a portion of the heavenly Book, which is infinite.

Nasr urges that such inclusivism need not lead to an abandonment of the absolutist claims of one's own tradition. One can and should hold that the revelation in one's own tradition is indeed privileged. When one has been steeped in the delights of sacred science, one will have the eyes to behold the wonders of other revelations, themselves entirely special, too. Nasr stresses that it is not the abstract metaphysical conception of an Absolute capable of diverse expressions that is of the essence but rather the individual sacred disciplines whereby people have been led to lead renewed spiritual lives.

Both Nasr and Smith invite questions about the esoteric in religions. The esoteric is to be distinguished from the exoteric not so much as the secret versus the public but as the province of an elite. Nasr in particular emphasizes that the elite savants of the sacred

wish that everyone would share in their knowledge. They do not want to keep anything se-
cret, he says. But sacred science requires discipline, and without it sacred forms become
cheapened, profaned.

Turning to evaluative issues, we find that a common defense of esotericism is that the
evaluating philosopher stands outside a putatively privileged circle. (Again, compare the
fideist position by D. Z. Phillips under Faith Against Reason.) But insofar as the abstract
principles that supposedly link esoteric truths to more common pursuits are made ex-
plicit, a philosopher should find grist for his or her mill. And if they are not made explicit,
it seems one could speculate about what appears to be presupposed, and still carry out
an intellectual assessment.

PRINCIPIAL KNOWLEDGE AND THE MULTIPLICITY OF SACRED FORMS

Verily, to every people there has been sent a prophet.
Quran

I meditated upon religions, making great effort to understand them,
And I came to realize that they are a unique Principle with numerous ramifications.
Ḥallāj

They worship me as One and as many, because they see that all is in me.
Bhagavad Gītā

One of the paradoxes of our age is that the manifestation of religion in different worlds of form and meaning has been used by the already desacralized type of knowledge, which has dominated the mental outlook of Western man in recent times, to destroy further what little remains of the sacred in the contemporary world. Modern man is encountering the other worlds of sacred forms and meaning in their full reality at the very moment when sacred knowledge and an interiorizing intelligence, which would be able to penetrate into the inner meaning of alien forms, having become so inaccessible. The result is that the multiplicity of sacred forms, which is itself the most definitive evidence of the reality of the sacred and the universality of the truth that each universe of form and meaning transmits in its own manner, has been employed, by those who deny the reality of the sacred as such, to relativize what has survived of the Christian tradition. The multiplicity of sacred forms has been used as an excuse to reject all sacred forms, as well as the *scientia sacra* which lies behind and beyond these forms. Had the West encountered other religions in a serious manner while a veritable intellectual tradition in the sense understood here still survived in its midst, the results would have been very different from the spectacle that "comparative religion" presents to the modern world. For an intelligence which has been illuminated by the Intellect and a knowledge which is already blessed with the perfume of the sacred sees in the multiplicity of sacred forms, not contradictions which relativize, but a confirmation of the universality of the Truth and the infinite creative power of the Real that unfolds Its inexhaustible possibilities in worlds of meaning which, although different, all reflect the unique Truth. That is why the revival of tradition in modern times and the attempt to re-sacralize knowledge have been accompanied from the beginning with concern with the multiplicity of traditions and their inner unity.

What is remarkable is that even in the study of the sacred, the principle that only the like can know the like has been forgotten and the secularized mind has adopted every possible path and method to study the phenomenon and reality of religion and religions, provided the nature of the sacred as sacred is not considered seriously. That is why despite all the light that the traditional perspective brings to bear upon the study of religions, it is so widely neglected. Hardly anyone in Western theological circles has made use of the keys which tradition alone provides to unlock the door of the understanding of other worlds of sacred form and meaning without destroying the absoluteness of religion; for traditional metaphysics alone is able to see each religion as *a* religion and *the* religion, "absolute" within its own universe, while reconfirming that ultimately only the Absolute is absolute. . . .

Tradition studies religions from the point of view of *scientia sacra* which distinguishes between the Principle and manifestation, Essence and form, Substance and accident, the inward and the outward. It places absoluteness at the level of the Absolute, asserting categorically that only the Absolute is absolute. It refuses to commit the cardinal error of attributing absoluteness to the relative, the error which Hinduism and Buddhism consider as the origin and root of all ignorance. Hence every determination of the Absolute is already in the realm of relativity. The unity of religions is to be found first and foremost in this Absolute which is at once Truth and Reality and the origin of all revelations and of all truth. When the Sufis exclaim that the doctrine of Unity is unique (*al-tawḥīdᵘ wāḥid*), they are asserting this fundamental but often forgotten principle. Only at the level of the Absolute are the teachings of the religions the same. Below that level there are correspondences of the most profound order but not identity. The different religions are like so many languages speaking of that unique Truth as it manifests itself in different worlds according to its inner archetypal possibilities, but the syntax of these languages is not the same. Yet, because each religion comes from the Truth, everything in the religion in question which is revealed by the Logos is sacred and must be respected and cherished while being elucidated rather than being discarded and reduced to insignificance in the name of some kind of abstract universality.

The traditional method of studying religions, while asserting categorically the "transcendent unity of religion" and the fact that "all paths lead to the same summit," is deeply respectful of every step on each path, of every signpost which makes the journey possible and without which the single summit could never be reached. It seeks to penetrate into the meaning of rites, symbols, images, and doctrines which constitute a particular religious universe but does not try to cast aside these elements or to reduce them to anything other than what they are within that distinct universe of meaning created by God through a particular revelation of the Logos.

A Common Ground

From "Religious Pluralism and Salvation" by John Hick in *Faith and Philosophy,*
Volume 5, Number 4, 1988

We encountered John Hick in studying his Irenaean or "soul-making" theodicy in the sec-
tion entitled Evil. Here the philosopher tries to articulate what he sees as the metaphysi-
cal underpinnings of religious pluralism, underpinnings that would authenticate each of
the major traditions.
    There are two key moves that Hick makes. First, he identifies as central to the claims
of world religions their purporting to be effective contexts for salvation, for a reorienting
of a person away from a natural egoism, or self-centeredness, toward what Hick calls the
divine Reality (God, Brahman, śūnyatā). Second, Hick uses the "Kantian insight" of sub-
jective shaping of appearances along with the Kantian distinction of (a) the noumenal, or
in itself (an sich), versus (b) the phenomenal, or received (für uns), to explain the differ-
ences in religious traditions as issuing out of one and the same divine Reality.
    With regard to the identification of salvation as religiously central, we should note
that Hick gives a sufficiently broad definition of the (Christian) term that the transforma-
tional views of all the major religions are included. Also important is Hick's judgment
that each tradition is as effective as any of the others in providing salvation, or a context
for salvation, so understood. Some, of course, would want to challenge this judgment—
and some the presupposition that a religious orientation is itself desirable. At the end of
the selection, Hick cites theological movements as well as papal statements that show
support for his soteriological inclusivism.
    The metaphysical move is also at once contentious and expressive of ideas found in
several prominent spiritual thinkers, as we have seen even in our short study. How much
play, or give, so to say, is there in the relation between what the Real is in itself and its
appearances? Enough to account for all the discrepancies in the belief systems of world
religions? If there is enough to accomplish all that, what could possibly be excluded? Are
there to be no constraints on spiritually metaphysical theorizing? With everyday things,
such as a table or chair, there is a correlation between the physical configuration and our
experiences. The table projects itself in my experience in ways that reflect what it really
is. Is there to be no such relation between the divine Real and its appearances? What
about the particularist worries within even theistic conceptions that, as we saw, William
Alston (among others) expresses? But despite the difficulty of these and like questions,
Hick has sketched a theory in broad outline that would promote religious harmony and
undercut objections based on religious dissension.

The fact that there is a plurality of religious traditions, each with its own distinctive beliefs,
spiritual practices, ethical outlook, art forms and cultural ethos, creates an obvious problem for those of us who see them, not simply as human phenomena, but as responses to the
Divine. For each presents itself, implicitly or explicitly, as in some important sense

absolute and unsurpassable as rightly claiming a total allegiance. The problem of the relationship between these different streams of religious life has often been posed in terms of their divergent belief-systems. For whilst there are various overlaps between their teachings there are also radical differences: is the divine reality (let us refer to it as the Real) personal or non-personal; if personal, is it unitary or triune; is the universe created, or emanated, or itself eternal; do we live only once on this earth or are we repeatedly reborn? and so on and so on. When the problem of understanding religious plurality is approached through these rival truth-claims it appears particularly intractable.

I want to suggest, however, that it may more profitably be approached from a different direction, in terms of the claims of the various traditions to provide, or to be effective contexts of, salvation. 'Salvation' is primarily a Christian term, though I shall use it here to include its functional analogues in the other major world traditions. In this broader sense we can say that both Christianity and these other faiths are paths of salvation. For whereas pre-axial religion was (and is) centrally concerned to keep life going on an even keel, the post-axial traditions, originating or rooted in the 'axial age' of the first millennium B.C.E.—principally Hinduism, Judaism, Buddhism, Christianity, Islam—are centrally concerned with a radical transformation of the human situation.

It is of course possible, in an alternative approach, to define salvation in such a way that it becomes a necessary truth that only one particular tradition can provide it. If, for example, from within Christianity we define salvation as being forgiven by God because of Jesus' atoning death, and so becoming part of God's redeemed community, the church, then salvation is by definition Christian salvation. If on the other hand, from within Mahayana Buddhism, we define it as the attainment of *satori* or awakening, and so becoming an ego-free manifestation of the eternal Dharmakaya, then salvation is by definition Buddhist liberation. And so on. But if we stand back from these different conceptions to compare them we can, I think, very naturally and properly see them as different forms of the more fundamental conception of a radical change from a profoundly unsatisfactory state to one that is limitlessly better because rightly related to the Real. Each tradition conceptualizes in its own way the wrongness of ordinary human existence—as a state of fallenness from paradisal virtue and happiness, or as a condition of moral weakness and alienation from God, or as the fragmentation of the infinite One into false individuals, or as a self-centeredness which pervasively poisons our involvement in the world process, making it to us an experience of anxious, unhappy unfulfillment. But each at the same time proclaims a limitlessly better possibility, again conceptualized in different ways—as the joy of conforming one's life to God's law; as giving oneself to God in Christ, so that 'it is no longer I who live, but Christ who lives in me' (Galatians 2:20), leading to eternal life in God's presence; as a complete surrender (*islam*) to God, and hence peace with God, leading to the bliss of paradise; as transcending the ego and realizing oneness with the limitless being-consciousness-bliss (*sat-chitananda*) of Brahman; as overcoming the ego point of view and entering into the serene selflessness of nirvana. I suggest that these different conceptions of salvation are specifications of what, in a generic formula, is the transformation of human existence from self-centeredness to a new orientation, centered in the divine Reality. And in each case the good news that is proclaimed is that this limitlessly better possibility is actually available and can be entered upon, or begin to be entered upon, here and

Each rel? has a way to attain the great good.

now. Each tradition sets forth the way to attain this great good: faithfulness to the Torah, discipleship to Jesus, obedient living out of the Qur'anic way of life, the Eightfold Path of the Buddhist dharma, or the three great Hindu *margas* of mystical insight, activity in the world, and self-giving devotion to God. . . .

. . . I have suggested that if we identify the central claim of each of the great religious traditions as the claim to provide, or to be an effective context of, salvation; and if we see salvation as an actual change in human beings from self-centeredness to a new orientation centered in the ultimate divine Reality; and if this new orientation has both a more elusive 'spiritual' character and a more readily observable moral aspect—then we arrive at the modest and largely negative conclusion that, so far as we can tell, no one of the great world religions is salvifically superior to the rest.

If this is so, what are we to make of the often contradictory doctrines of the different traditions? In order to make progress at this point, we must distinguish various kinds of levels of doctrinal conflict.

There are, first, conceptions of the ultimate as Jahweh, or the Holy Trinity, or Allah, or Shiva, or Vishnu, or as Brahman, or the Dharmakaya, the Tao, and so on.

If salvation is taking place, and taking place to about the same extent, within the religious systems presided over by these various deities and absolutes, this suggests that they are different manifestations to humanity of a yet more ultimate ground of all salvific transformation. Let us then consider the possibility that an infinite transcendent divine reality is being differently conceived, and therefore differently experienced, and therefore differently responded to from within our different religio-cultural ways of being human. This hypothesis makes sense of the fact that the salvific transformation seems to have been occurring in all the great traditions. Such a conception is, further, readily open to philosophical support. For we are familiar today with the ways in which human experience is partly formed by the conceptual and linguistic frameworks within which it occurs. The basically Kantian insight that the mind is active in perception, and that we are always aware of our environment as it appears to a consciousness operating with our particular conceptual resources and habits, has been amply confirmed by work in cognitive psychology and the sociology of knowledge and can now be extended with some confidence to the analysis of religious awareness. If, then, we proceed inductively from the phenomenon of religious experience around the world, adopting a religious as distinguished from a naturalistic interpretation of it, we are likely to find ourselves making two moves. The first is to postulate an ultimate transcendent divine reality (which I have been referring to as the Real) which, being beyond the scope of our human concepts, cannot be directly experienced by us as it is in itself but only as it appears through our various human thought-forms. And the second is to identify the thought-and-experienced deities and absolutes as different manifestations of the Real within different historical forms of human consciousness. In Kantian terms, the divine noumenon, the Real *an sich,* is experienced through different human receptivities as a range of divine phenomena, in the formation of which religious concepts have played an essential part.

These different 'receptivities' consist of conceptual schemas within which various personal, communal and historical factors have produced yet further variations. The most basic concepts in terms of which the Real is humanly thought-and-experienced are those of (personal) deity and of the (non-personal) absolute. But the Real is not actually experienced either as deity in general or as the absolute in general. Each basic concept becomes (in Kantian terminology) schematized in more concrete form. It is at this point that individual and cultural actors enter the process. The religious tradition of which we are a part, with its history and ethos and its great exemplars, its scriptures feeding our thoughts and emotions, and perhaps above all its devotional or meditative practices, constitutes an uniquely shaped and coloured 'lens' through which we are concretely aware of the Real specifically as the personal Adonai, or as the Heavenly Father, or as Allah, or Vishnu, or Shiva . . . or again as the non-personal Brahman, or Dharmakaya, or the Void or the Ground . . . Thus, one who uses the forms of Christian prayer and sacrament is thereby led to experience the Real as the divine Thou, whereas one who practices advaitic yoga or Buddhist zazen is thereby brought to experience the Real as the infinite being-consciousness-bliss of Brahman, or as the limitless emptiness of *sunyata* which is at the same time the infinite fullness of immediate reality as 'wondrous being.'

. . . to suppose that the experienced deities and absolutes which are the intentional objects of worship or content of religious meditation, are appearances or manifestations of the Real, rather than each being itself the Real *an sich,* is not to suppose that they are illusions—any more than the varying ways in which a mountain may appear to a plurality of differently placed observers are illusory. That the same reality may be variously experienced and described is true even of physical objects. But in the case of the infinite, transcendent divine reality there may well be much greater scope for the use of varying human conceptual schemas producing varying modes of phenomenal experience. Whereas the concepts in terms of which we are aware of mountains and rivers and houses are largely (though by no means entirely) standard throughout the human race, the religious concepts in terms of which we become aware of the Real have developed in widely different ways within the different cultures of the earth. . . .

. . . why postulate an ineffable and unobservable divine-reality-in-itself? If we can say virtually nothing about it, why affirm its existence? The answer is that the reality or non-reality of the postulated noumenal ground of the experienced religious phenomena constitutes the difference between a religious and a naturalistic interpretation of religion. If there is no such transcendent ground, the various forms of religious experience have to be categorized as purely human projections. If on the other hand there is such a transcendent ground, then these phenomena may be joint products of the universal presence of the Real and of the varying sets of concepts and images that have crystallized within the religious traditions of the earth. To affirm the transcendent is thus to affirm that religious experience is not solely a construction of the human imagination but is a response—though always culturally conditioned—to the Real. . . .

. . . the picture that I am suggesting can be outlined as follows: our human religious experience, variously shaped as it is by our sets of religious concepts, is a cognitive re-

sponse to the universal presence of the ultimate divine Reality that, in itself, exceeds human conceptuality. This Reality is however manifested to us in ways formed by a variety of human concepts, as the range of divine personae and metaphysical impersonae witnessed to in the history of religions. Each major tradition, built around its own distinctive way of thinking-and-experiencing the Real, has developed its own answers to the perennial questions of our origin and destiny, constituting more or less comprehensive and coherent cosmologies and eschatologies. These are human creations which have, by their association with living streams of religious experience, become invested with a sacred authority. However they cannot all be wholly true; quite possibly none is wholly true; perhaps all are partly true. But since the salvific process has been going on through the centuries despite this unknown distribution of truth and falsity in our cosmologies and eschatologies, it follows that it is not necessary for salvation to adopt any one of them. We would therefore do well to learn to tolerate unresolved, and at present unresolvable, differences concerning these ultimate mysteries.

One element, however, to be found in the belief-systems of most of the traditions raises a special problem, namely that which asserts the sole salvific efficacy of that tradition. I shall discuss this problem in terms of Christianity because it is particularly acute for those of us who are Christians. We are all familiar with such New Testament texts as 'There is salvation in no one else [than Jesus Christ], for there is no other name under heaven given among men by which we must be saved' (Acts 4:12), and with the Catholic dogma *Extra ecclesiam nulla salus* (No salvation outside the church) and its Protestant equivalent—never formulated as an official dogma but nevertheless implicit within the 18th and 19th century Protestant missionary expansion—no salvation outside Christianity. Such a dogma differs from other elements of Christian belief in that it is not only a statement about the potential relationship of Christians to God but at the same time about the actual relationship of non-Christians to God. It says that the latter, in virtue of being non-Christian, lack salvation. Clearly such a dogma is incompatible with the insight that the salvific transformation of human existence is going on, and so far as we can tell going on to a more or less equal extent, within all the great traditions. Insofar, then, as we accept that salvation is not confined to Christianity we must reject the old exclusivist dogma.

This has in fact now been done by most thinking Christians, though exceptions remain, mostly within the extreme Protestant fundamentalist constituencies. The *Extra ecclesiam* dogma, although not explicitly repealed, has been outflanked by the work of such influential Catholic theologians as Karl Rahner, whose new approach was in effect endorsed by Vatican II. Rahner expressed his more inclusivist outlook by suggesting that devout people of other faiths are 'anonymous Christians,' within the invisible church even without knowing it, and thus within the sphere of salvation. The present Pope, in his Encyclical *Redemptor Hominis* (1979) has expressed this thought even more comprehensively by saying that 'every man without exception has been redeemed by Christ' and 'with every man without any exception whatever Christ is in a way united, even when man is unaware of it' (para. 14). And a number of Protestant theologians have advocated a comparable position.

DISCUSSION QUESTIONS

1. Examine the position and arguments of William Alston in support of the right of a Christian mystic to form beliefs in accordance with Christian tradition and experience, ignoring conflicting claims of rival religious and mystic traditions. Is Alston right to find incommensurability here?

2. How would William Wainwright resolve the doctrinal conflicts associated with religious pluralism? Discuss the evaluative criteria he presents. Has he successfully sidestepped the question of incommensurability?

3. Outline Vivekananda's views concerning religious pluralism. Does he successfully find a way of regarding "all religions as true"? How might Vivekananda respond to an advocate of a religious belief system who denied his inclusivism?

4. What is the perennialist position of Huston Smith? Why, in his view, does spiritual truth become concealed and distorted? Do you think that the answer he provides to this question could be expanded to explain all important doctrinal conflicts among religions? Discuss what you see as the central issues here.

5. What are S. N. Nasr's views concerning religious pluralism? In particular, how would he defend even the exclusivism of religious traditions? Does this amount to revisionist reinterpretation out of line with traditional teachings? What is your assessment of Nasr's position?

6. Evaluate the position of John Hick concerning religious pluralism, his identification of salvation as religiously central, and his (Kantian) metaphysics of a divine Reality. What are some important problems that Hick faces? Do you think that they can be resolved?

Pronunciation Guide

GUIDE TO SANSKRIT PRONUNCIATION

a	like *u* in *mum*	e	like *a* in *maze*
ā	like *a* in *father*	ai	like *i* in *mine*
i	like *i* in *bit*	o	like *o* in *go*
ī	like *ee* in *feed*	au	like *ow* in *cow*
u	like *u* in *pull*		
ū	like *oo* in *moon*		
ṛ	You won't pronounce this correctly; try *rea* in *really* (while turning the tip of the tongue up to touch the palate)		

SEMIVOWELS (BEST UNDERSTOOD AS A PARTICULAR CLASS OF CONSONANTS)*

y	like *y* in *yonder*	l	like *l* in *luck*
r	like *r* in *ram*	v	like *v* in *clover*

CONSONANTS

Guttural class

k	like *ck* in *sack*	gh	another aspirate, same principle as with *kh; g* pronounced while breathing out
kh	like *k* in Sanskrit, except aspirated, that is, pronounced while breathing out, as in *keel*		
g	like *g* in *gun*	ṅ	like *n* in *trunk,* except more guttural

Palatal class

c	like *ch* in *churn*	j	like *j* in *joy*
ch	another aspirate, same principle	jh	aspirated *j,* like *jay*
		ñ	like *n* in *canyon*

---

*By convention, the names of the consonants add an *a* (Sanskrit *a*) in pronunciation. Thus y is pronounced *ya* (like *yu* in *yummy*). Vowels, in contrast, are pronounced exactly as written. Note also each vowel corresponds to only one sound, unlike in English. (With a few exceptions, this is true of consonants as well.)

Lingual class

ṭ	There is no English equivalent: a *t* sound (as in *tough*) but with the tip of the tongue touching the roof of the mouth	ṭh	aspirated *ṭ*
		ḍ	like *d* in *deer*, but "lingualized" as with *ṭ*
		ḍh	aspirated *ḍ*
		ṇ	lingualized *n* sound

Dental class

t	like *t* in *tough*	dh	aspirated *d*
th	aspirated *t* (not like *th* in *thumb*)	n	like *n* in *now*
d	like *d* in *dove*		

Labial class

p	like *p* in *pun*	b	like *b* in *buck*
ph	aspirated *p* as in *pin* (not like *ph* in *philosophy*)	bh	aspirated *b*
		m	like *m* in *meal*

Sibilants

ś	like *sh* in *shove*	s	like *s* in *sun*
ṣ	lingualized *sh* sound		

And in a class alone

h	like *h* in *heart*

SPECIAL CHARACTERS AND SOUNDS

ḥ	Visarga: calls for breath following a vowel. For example, *duḥkha* ("pain") is pronounced *du* followed by a breath (very short) and then *kha*
ṃ	This is shorthand for all nasals, the particular type of which is determined by the class of the following consonant. For example, the *ṃ* in *sāṃkhya* ("analysis") is equivalent in *ñ*, since *kh* belongs to the guttural class. (Do not try to remember this rule; just nasalize.)

GUIDE TO CHINESE PRONUNCIATION

This guide is written for native speakers of English within North America. In many cases, similar sounds are only rough approximations. Also, Chinese dialects differ among each other significantly in pronunciation.

VOWELS _____

a	like *a* in *far*		n	like *n* in *no*
ai	like *ai* in *aisle*		p	like *b* in *baby*
ao	like *ou* in *loud*		p'	like *p* in *pin,* said emphatically
e	like *e* in *her*		r	like *r* in *rare*
ei	like *ei* in *weight*		s	like *s* in *so*
i	like *i* in *machine,* except as part of *ing*		sh	like *sh* in *shoe*
			t	like *d* in *doll*
ing	like *ing* in *wing*		t'	like *t* in *tell,* said emphatically
o	like *o* in *open*		ts, tz	like *dz* in *adze*
u	like *oo* in *rule*		ts', tz'	like *ts* in *tsetse,* said emphatically
ü	like *oo* in *rule,* or better, like French *u*		w	like *w* in *water*

CONSONANTS _____

ch	like *j* in *jam*
ch'	like *ch* in *change,* said emphatically
f	like *f* in *faint*
h	like *h* in *how,* or, better, like *j* or *g* in Spanish *Jorge*
hs	like *sh* in *whoosh*
j	like *r* in *rare*
k	like *g* in *go*
k'	like *k* in *kill,* said emphatically
l	like *l* in *like*
m	like *m* in *moon*

Thus:

Hsün Tzu	"shoon dzoo"
Lao Tzu	"lao dzoo"
Chuang Tzu	"jwong dzoo"
Seng-chao	"seng jao"
Hsüan-tsang	"shwawn dzong"
Fa-tsang	"faw dzong"
I-hsüan	"ee shwawn"
Chu Hsi	"joo shee"
Wang Fu-chih	"wang foo jee"
jen	"ren"

GUIDE TO ARABIC PRONUNCIATION

This guide is written for native speakers of English within North America. In many cases, similar sounds are only rough approximations; Arabic contains several consonants for which there is no close English equivalent.

VOWELS

a	(in unaccented syllables) like *a* in *about*	i	like *ee* in *beet*
a	(in accented syllables) like *a* in *father*	ī	more elongated, like *ee* in *see*
		o	like *o* in *open*
ā	like *a* in *bah!*	ō	more elongated, like *o* in *so*
e	like *e* in *egg*	u	like *oo* in *room*
ē	more elongated, like *ay* in *bay*	ū	more elongated, like *ue* in *sue*

CONSONANTS

'	like *tt* in *button,* or the sound between the syllables of *uh-uh*	j	like *j* in *judge*
		k	like *k* in *kick*
'	like the sound between the *a*'s in *baa,* when imitating the sound of sheep	kh	like *j* and *g* in Spanish *Jorge*
		l	like *l* in *like*
		m	like *m* in *moon*
b	like *b* in *baby*	n	like *n* in *no*
ch	like *ch* in *church*	q	like *k* in *Luke*
d	like *d* in *dog*	r	like *r* in Spanish *pero*
dh	like *th* in *there*	s	like *s* in *so*
f	like *f* in *faint*	sh	like *sh* in *shoe*
gh	like *g* in *agua,* in some Spanish dialects; like Parisian *r*	t	like *t* in *tot*
		th	like *th* in *thick*
		w	like *w* in *water*
h	like *h* in *how*	z	like *z* in *zebra*

Glossary

a posteriori See *knowledge a posteriori.*

a priori See *knowledge a priori.*

Advaita Vedānta Non-Dual Vedānta; a prominent school of classical Indian philosophy based on scriptures called Upanishads; a monistic view ("All is Brahman"), including—or especially—the seemingly individual consciousness or self; sometimes called Illusionism because of its claim that all appearance of fundamental diversity is illusory.

aesthetic theodicy A view that denies that what seems evil is really evil, at least in an ultimate sense: all apparent evil is necessary to the great beauty (and diversity) of God's creation and is thus really good.

agnosticism Suspension of judgment regarding the existence of God and other religious issues; the position that there is insufficient evidence either to affirm or to deny the existence of God, etc.

ahiṃsā (Sanskrit) Non-injury.

analytic A proposition (q.v.) is said to be analytic when whatever it says about something *x*—its subject—is contained within the concept, or idea, of what *x* is (e.g. 'A triangle is a figure with three angles'). Compare *synthetic.*

anātman (Sanskrit) "No self," or "no soul"; an important Buddhist doctrine.

animism The so-called "primitive" outlook that attributes consciousness or spirit to natural objects.

anthropic principle In physics, the principle that were nature not to exhibit certain features or laws, human observation and science (physics) would not be possible.

anti-evidentialism The position that there are basic propositions in religion, such as "God is speaking to me" and "The sunset shows the glory of God," that cannot be established by argument from other propositions, but may nonetheless be (non-propositionally) justified or warranted.

apriorist theology A view of God arrived at by deducing attributes of God from a definition of God (usually God as Perfect) and a few other premises.

argument A set of one or more propositions, called premises, advanced as proof or evidence for another proposition called the conclusion.

Arhat The "saint" who, according to Theravāda, or Southern, Buddhism, has realized Nirvāṇa.

aseity Self-existence; necessity of being; self-causality; "having within itself the grounds of its own explanation" and "having its own cause or reason for existence within itself." Such a characteristic has been attributed to God, and indeed used to differentiate God from everything else.

atheism The view that there is no God. See also: *conceptual atheism* and *factual atheism*.

ātman (Sanskrit) Self or soul; the Upanishadic term for an individual's true or most basic consciousness.

avatāra (Sanskrit) God incarnate; according to much Indian theism, God takes birth as a divine man or woman whenever world events demand, e.g., Krishna as portrayed in the *Gītā*.

avidyā Spiritual ignorance; in much Vedānta, lack of direct awareness of *brahman* (q.v.) or God.

Bhagavad-Gītā "Song of God"; an important text—considered revealed—in Indian theism.

bhakti (Sanskrit) Love of God.

Bible Scriptural revelation, according to Christianity.

Bodhisattva According to Northern (i.e., Mahāyāna) Buddhism, an enlightened person (a Buddha) who turns back to the world in a spirit of compassion.

Brahman The Absolute, the One, God in much Hindu thought (Brahman, in distinction to the classical Western concept of God, is not thought to create *ex nihilo,* but to be rather the "Ground" of all being).

brahma-vidyā (Sanskrit) knowledge of the Absolute (or, of God).

Brāhminism The most conversative strand of Hinduism, centering on rituals and liturgies performed by priests called Brāhmins, who are the highest of four principal Hindu castes.

Buddha The awakened; an epithet of Siddhārtha Gautama, the founder of Buddhism, after his enlightenment.

Cārvāka A materialist and skeptical school of classical Indian philosophy also known as Lokāyata, "those who follow the way of the world."

cathexis According to Sigmund Freud, our desires or instincts drive us (or our dreams, etc.) to have experiences whereby they may release their "energy" or "force." This release is thought to be pleasurable, and is called cathexis.

ch'i (Chinese) A vital force important in Taoist mysticism.

classical theism The mainstream theology of Judaism, Christianity, and Islam, articulated by Philo, Christian Church Fathers, Avicenna, and others within Western religious traditions; a view of God emphasizing God's perfection, simplicity, and timelessness.

cogency An evaluative term for arguments. A cogent argument must meet three conditions. If any one of the three conditions is not met, the argument is fallacious: (a) the reasoner(s) must be warranted in believing the premises; (b) the argument must proceed according to a correct principle of reasoning; (c) one must argue in good faith and thus not suppress any relevant evidence. If these three conditions are met, one is warranted, or justified, in believing the argument's conclusion. In other words, a cogent argument forces a (rational) person to believe the conclusion (again, given that she is warranted in believing the premises).

cognitive/non-cognitive Informative/uninformative; a contrast applied both to questions of the import of mystical experience (Is a mystical experience informative concerning an objective reality?) and religious claims or beliefs (Does a religious claim purport to inform us about an objective reality?).

coherence A standard for evaluating theories: a satisfactory theory would not contain any contradictions among its central propositions themselves or among them and some fact about the world. Also a coherent theory would exhibit categories that interlock. (For example, some have claimed that pain and suffering are incompatible with a conception of God as Perfect. Accordingly, to claim the existence of God while admitting the reality of evil would be like saying both "a cat is an animal" and "a cat is not an animal." But others claim that theism is an especially coherent theory since its central categories, "God," "aseity," "creativity," "creatures with free will," and so on, tightly interlock.)

common consent argument The argument for the existence of God premised on an assumption that (nearly?) everyone (perhaps unconsciously or inchoately) has a belief that there is (something like) a God.

compatibility A logical term for the possibility that two assertions can both be true.

conceptual atheism The view that God could not possibly exist because the concept of God is incoherent (like the concept of a round square).

(God's) consequent nature In Whiteheadian or process theology, this is God's physical pole contrasting with God's mental pole, or *primordial nature,* that is, God's concrete feeling of every material being's feeling immediately after it occurs. Whitehead calls this aspect of God "consequent" because it is immediately consequent to all the (sentient) happenings in the world.

contingent existence Existence that need not be (contrasting with *aseity*).

contingent truth A true proposition that could conceivably be false.

cosmological arguments These are arguments that focus on a feature of things, or certain facts in the world, or certain natural events, and assert that this feature etc. can only be understood by supposing the existence of God.

(*the*) **cosmological argument** An argument purporting to prove the existence of God from the premises (1) that everything in the universe that exists is contingent (and the universe as a whole), and (2) that these contingencies, or the universe as a whole, can only be explained in reference to a necessary being, namely God. (See also: *first-cause argument.*)

creation *ex nihilo* A theory of Divine creation according to which God creates our material world "out of nothing." On some interpretations, there is thus an "ontological gulf" between God and the world (a view sometimes coupled with *negative theology*).

cumulative case A type of argument that would collect evidence or considerations of several different types to establish, in particular, a metaphysics or *worldview.*

debunking A debunking effort vis-à-vis a belief *p* involves not only argument against the truth of *p* but also explanation why someone would hold *p* in spite of its falsity and a lack of good grounds.

deism The view that God created the universe and established natural law *ab initio,* but thereafterwards does not intervene in worldly events.

dharma The key ethical concept in Hinduism, (Sanskrit) "right practice."

dharmakāya In personalistic forms of Mahāyāna Buddhism, the "Buddha-body" or "body of righteousness" that is the divine reality underlying the world.

dialectic The process, or the investigation of the process, whereby a concept or its social realization passes over first into its negation and then a synthesis preserving the best of the two earlier stages; the method of Hegelian philosophy (see under Speculative Spiritual Metaphysics).

divine command theory The position in ethics that God's commands form the criteria, or standards, for right and wrong behavior, and for ethical judgments in general.

doxastic practice A belief-forming practice, such as the forming of beliefs about one's immediate physical environment on the basis of current sensory experience.

dual transcendence In the theology proposed by Charles Hartshorne, God transcends everything else atemporally, and also transcends temporally—by increasing in value—the immediately preceding state of itself.

emanationism The theory of Divine creation that the world emerges or emanates out of God's own self, who is conceived as the Ground of being.

empiricism A view emphasizing experience and experimental method for all factual knowledge.

Emptiness The "(vibrant) Void," *śūnyatā,* the reality that *nirvāṇa* experience is thought to reveal, according to Buddhist teachings; a state of consciousness totally devoid of self-regard, according to some interpretations.

epistemology Theory of knowledge and justification of beliefs.

esotericism In religion, practices or beliefs of an elite.

ex nihilo nihil fit The metaphysical principle that, according to some philosophers, "nothing comes out of nothing" (Latin).

existentialism A philosophic stance stressing individual freedom and choice, the absurdity of the universe or its ultimate incomprehensibility in scientific terms, and each person's making religious or other meaningfulness for himself or herself. Religious existentialists also stress the importance of blind faith.

factual atheism The view that God, though possibly existing, does not exist in fact (compare *conceptual atheism*).

fideism The view that the logic of faith precludes rational inquiry and the citing of evidence for or against beliefs in question, which are held, then, "on faith." *Romantic* fideism denies (in its most radical version) that faith has propositional content; faith is a kind of feeling or emotion. *Existentialist* fideism insists on assent to propositions as an act of will or choice, unguided or uninformed by evidence. *Anti-evidentialism* construes propositions such as "God is speaking to me," "God is evident in the beauty of a sunset" to be basic in appropriate circumstances in that they are (a) justified but (b) no argument can be given for them. See also: *Wittgensteinian fideism.*

first-cause argument An argument purporting to prove the existence of God from the premises (1) that every worldly existent is caused (or causality is universal) and (2) that this fact (that everything has a cause) can only be explained with reference to a "first cause," namely God.

free-will theodicy In its most radical form, the view that all evil in the world is the result of choices by free agents, and that God in creating free agents does something good. Accordingly, God would not be responsible for evil. Two major subdivisions of this view are: (a) interpretation of natural evil as the work of superhuman personal forces (e.g., Satan), and (b) interpretation of natural evil as "reaction" or "righting the balance" resulting from the wrong actions of free beings. (b is a doctrine of Augustinian theodicy, which is overall an *aesthetic theodicy.*)

Gemara In Judaism, commentary on the Mishnah (q.v.) and forming part of the Talmud (q.v.).

genetic fallacy According to some philosophers, this is the faulty reasoning that would find a belief false solely because of circumstances of its origin.

Gītā See *Bhagavad-Gītā.*

hadīth (Arabic) "Sayings"; in Islam, the statements of the prophet Mohammed that are not part of the Koran, or God's word, but constitute a second level of religious authority.

henotheism The view found in several Indian religious works that there is one God who appears as (or is conceived in) several divine forms, for example, as the Hindu pantheon.

hermeneutics The science, or techniques, of interpretation.

historicism Skepticism based on the view that (in particular, philosophic) claims are conditioned by vagaries of historical circumstance (and thus need not be taken at face value). Karl Marx is commonly credited with the insight.

(Divine) immanence An attribute often equated with omnipresence (q.v.); God as immanent would everywhere in-dwell.

incompatibility A logical term for the impossibility that two assertions can be true.

Indian theism Also called theistic Vedānta. Hindu and classical Indian views holding forth God (Sanskrit: *īśvara*) as the Divine Reality, and usually purporting to be grounded teachings of the *Bhagavad-Gītā* as well as various Upanishads.

infinity A commonly attributed property, or characteristic, of God, often said to include God's eternity (infinity with respect to time) and omnipresence (infinity with respect to place).

islam (Arabic) "Surrender"; in Islam, surrender to God's will as revealed to Mohammed.

iṣṭa-devatā (Sanskrit) "Preferred divinity."

īśvara (Sanskrit) God, the Lord.

jen (Chinese) The virtue of love and humanity; fellow-concern nobility.

karma (Sanskrit) "Action"; psychological dispositions to act in a certain manner acquired through previous actions; habit.

kaivalya (Sanskrit) "Aloneness"; the true state of the individual self, as aloof from nature and blissfully self-rapt, according to Yoga philosophy (as articulated, e.g., in the *Yoga-sūtra*).

knowledge *a priori* Knowledge had apart from experience (e.g., of mathematical and logical truths). Deductive knowledge. Knowledge of necessary truths (according to many philosophers).

knowledge *a posteriori* Knowledge acquired through experience; knowledge of contingent truths (according to many philosophers).

Koran Islamic scripture. In Arabic, literally "recitation." Also written "Quran."

li (Chinese) rule, principle, ceremony, ritual.

Lokāyata See *Cārvāka.*

logos (Greek) "Word," "reason"; God's mind or wisdom according to Philo and other classical Western theists; identified with the second Person, or Christ, according to Christian trinitarians.

Mahābhārata The Great Indian Epic; a poem of over 100,000 verses depicting a conflict over royal succession. The *Bhagavad-Gītā* constitutes a small portion of this epic.

Mahāyāna Northern Buddhism; the "Great Vehicle."

materialism The view that physical matter is the only, or fundamental, reality, and that everything can, in principle, be explained in terms referring only to physical things.

māyā (Sanskrit) "illusion," cosmic illusion; finite delimitation.

metaphysics (1) The area of philosophy concerned with the questions of what things are real and of the most general relations among them; (2) worldview (q.v.).

metaphysical evil According to some philosophers and theologians, everything other than God is evil in this sense, namely, that everything except God is not Perfect.

Mishnah In Judaism, the collection of traditional laws and precepts made by Judah the Prince, forming the basis of the Talmud or the authoritative source for Judaic tradition.

modal ontological argument A type of argument purporting to prove the existence of God from the definition of God as Perfect—having among the Divine perfections *aseity* or necessary existence.

monotheism The view that there is only one God or Perfect Being, usually considered to be the Creator of the universe or its Ground of being. This view is usually taken to entail the unity of God, that is, that God is single.

moral evil Evil perpetrated by free (human) beings out of their own choices.

(the) mysticism argument An argument purporting to prove the existence of a spiritual reality, God, Brahman, "Emptiness" (or *nirvāṇa*), from the occurrence of certain special experiences that are said to be like sense experiences in revealing realities but unlike sense experiences in revealing something spiritual rather than physical things.

natural evil Evils, such as diseases, pain, death, that are part of the world order and not the result of actions freely undertaken.

naturalism The view that the physical universe is a closed system, with no supernatural entities or agencies operative in it. A naturalist might admit non-material things (such as minds or persons), but would see these as part of nature, not as belonging to a transcendent realm.

necessary truth A proposition whose falsity cannot be imagined; one true in "all possible worlds" (e.g., $2 + 3 = 5$).

negative theology The view that nothing positive can be known about God; God is known only by such formulae as "God is not this" and "God is not that." A view that stresses the transcendence of God; God is thought "Wholly Other."

neti neti (Sanskrit) "Not this, not this"; an Upanishadic statement taken to underscore the transcendence and indescribility of Brahman.

nibbāna The Pāli word for *nirvāṇa*.

nirvāṇa (Sanskrit) Literally, "extinction" or "blowing out." In Buddhism, the experience thought to be the personal *summum bonum;* "enlightenment," "salvation."

omnibenevolence An attribute of God according to classical Western theism: God is "All-Loving." In process theology, God is understood to be "maximally loving."

omnipresence A controversial Divine attribute entailing that God pervades everything. There would be nowhere God is not. Deists, in particular, deny this attribute.

omnipotence An attribute of God according to classical Western theism: there is nothing that God could not do (even to make $2 + 2 = 5$, according to a radical interpretation). In process theology, in contrast, God is understood to have "maximal power," but power constrained by certain logical, metaphysical, and self-imposed limits.

omniscience An attribute of God according to classical Western theism: there is nothing that God does not know (even future events that humans normally consider the result of their own choices, according to a radical interpretation). In process theology, God is understood to have "maximal knowledge," but knowledge constrained by certain logical, metaphysical, and self-imposed limits.

ontological argument An *a priori* argument purporting to prove the existence of God from the concept of God together with other premises.

overdetermination A causal doctrine about the possibility of a single event having more than one sufficient cause.

pantheism The view that God somehow is everything; the theology that equates Nature and God.

panentheism See *process theology.*

parama-puruṣa-artha (Sanskrit) Supreme personal good.

pāramitā Perfection; there are six moral and spiritual perfections exhibited by a Bodhisattva (q.v.), according to Mahāyāna Buddhism.

perennial philosophy A view that the right outlook periodically appears and reappears, an outlook usually thought of as spiritual and esoteric.

philosophy The discipline concerned with claims about what is real (metaphysics), how we know (epistemology), and how we should live (ethics). Philosophy also includes evaluative efforts concerning the most general or abstract concepts and claims of other disciplines including individual sciences and religious systems, in particular purported ties among them.

polytheism A view that there is more than one divine being.

prajñā-pāramitā The "perfection of wisdom" belonging to a Bodhisattva.

pratītya-samutpāda Interdependent origination; an important Buddhist doctrine.

(God's) primordial nature In Whiteheadian or process theology, this is God's mental pole contrasting with God's physical pole, or *consequent nature;* that is, God's grasping all possibilities of creation before they occur. God's primordial nature does not, strictly speaking, change, but God does, according to process theology, ever renew a vision of harmonious possibilities on the basis of what actually occurs. (Compare the classical theistic notion of *logos.*)

principle of credulity According to some philosophers, the principle concerning testimony that one ought to "give the benefit of doubt" unless there is a reason why one should not. In other words, acceptance of someone's testimony would be the default position, with refusal to accept it requiring special justification.

process theology The view that God includes the processes of the world, changing as the world changes; also known as "panentheism," which is to be distinguished from "pantheism" by the former's upholding a version of divine transcendence.

process theodicy The view that particular evils are to be explained as (a) moral evil, (b) chance occurrences, with general indeterminacy to be explained as a necessary condition for finite beings to act freely, or (c) direct results of the conditions that make possible free finite beings (especially the nature of matter).

proposition The bearer of the truth-values (a) truth and (b) falsity; the information conveyed by a declarative sentence.

psychology of religion The attempt to understand religious beliefs and practices as outgrowths of psychological forces.

rational theology The view that religious beliefs—specifically, the beliefs that God exists and has such and such a nature—have grounds that can be rationally discovered and formulated; the individual enterprises aimed to show those grounds.

revelation According to some theologies ("buddhologies" as well), the source of right belief about God or the Supreme Reality; commonly identified with scripture (the *Bible,* the *Koran,* the *Bhagavad-Gītā,* for example).

Ṛg Veda The oldest text in Sanskrit, a collection of poems and hymns to various Indo-European gods and goddesses.

saccidānanda (Absolute) Existence-Consciousness-Bliss, a popular Vedāntic characterization of Brahman.

satori In Zen Buddhism, enlightenment or the supreme experience that is the goal of Zen practice.

(Divine) simplicity According to some theologians, God's properties are all mutually entailed, with no division among them. Thus talking of Divine attributes would not be meant to imply that there is complexity in what God is or that God could lose some characteristic.

sociology of religion The attempt to understand religious beliefs and practices as outgrowths of social conditions (cf., *historicism*).

soul-making theodicy Like aesthetic theodicy, this theory finds positive value in evil. Suffering, limitations, pain and death are *intrinsically* evil but *instrumentally* good—in spurring us to personal growth, or "soul-making." (Also called Romantic theodicy.)

spiritual philosophy A view, contrasting with a materialism, finding the fundamental reality as conscious or, as with Buddhism, promoting the value of consciousness or particular conscious states.

śūnyatā See *Emptiness.*

sūra (Arabic) "Verse" or "chapter"; verses of the Koran.

synthetic A proposition (q.v.) is said to be synthetic when whatever it says about something *x*—its subject—is not contained within the concept, or idea, of what *x* is (e.g., 'My dog has long ears'). Compare *analytic*.

Talmud The authoritative source for Judaic tradition, comprised of the Mishnah and Gemara. There are two Talmudim, one compiled in Babylon and one in Palestine.

tao The "suprarational" Way of both Heaven and Earth, according to the ancient Chinese teaching of Lao Tzu. Taoism has much in common with Western *negative theology,* but the Tao is considered much more immanent, present in all things, than Western negative theologians typically conceive of God. With Confucius and Confucianists, *tao* seems to mean moral system or moral truth.

te In classical Chinese philosophy, a thing's "virtue" in the sense of its deeply individual power and nature.

teleological argument A cosmological argument purporting to prove the existence of God from the premises that (1) the world exhibits design, (2) everything that is designed has a designer, and (3) the designer of the world is God.

theodicy That branch of rational theology concerned with defending the view that God exists as omnibenevolent ("all-loving") despite the appearance of evil in the world.

Tipiṭaka (Pāli) "Three Baskets," an epithet for the Canon of Southern Buddhism.

Theravāda "The Doctrine of the (Buddhist) Elders"; an early school of philosophic Buddhism, appearing in the Southern Canon.

Torah In Hebrew, "law"; Judaic scripture. Sometimes "Torah" is used to refer only to the Pentateuch or first five books of Judaic scripture.

(Divine) transcendence God's being beyond, or other to, everything in heaven and earth; an attribute often insisted on by *negative theology.* According to some, this attribute is compatible with Divine immanence; according to others, it is not.

trinitarianism In Christianity, the doctrine that God, though one, is also three persons, namely, the Father, the Son or Christ (also said to be the Logos), and the Holy Spirit.

Upanishads Mystic and speculative treatises regarded as sacred by many Hindus and forming the source texts for the classical Indian philosophic schools of Vedānta (q.v.).

Vedānta Originally an epithet for the Upanishads; in the classical period, any of several schools defending Upanishadic views, e.g., Advaita (q.v.) and Indian theism (q.v.).

voluntarist fideism A view that stresses that the acceptance of religious claims is a matter of will or choice not entirely determined by evidence. (Compare *fideism,* especially existentialist fideism.)

wish-fulfillment In Sigmund Freud's psychological theory, a source of religious beliefs and practices. Freud sees human instincts (or desires or wishes) as unconscious psychological forces that can be fulfilled (or *cathected*) in dreams and artistic productions when they do not find expression in everyday waking experience. Freud sees religious beliefs as originating in certain instincts, such as a desire for immortality, that cannot be satisfied in life. Thus religious beliefs would be mere fantasy, or wishful thinking.

Wittgensteinian fideism The view that a religious faith and practice is a "form of life" that cannot be understood from the outside. (See the introductory discussion under Faith Against Reason.)

worldview A comprehensive theory or philosophy whose categories and claims would account for all experience and reality.

wu-wei (Chinese) "non-action"; with Chuang Tzu and other Taoists, the principle of passive perfection, of perfect response as opposed to original action.

yoga (1) Self-discipline, mystic discipline. (2) A classical Indian school of philosophy (expressed in the *Yoga-sūtra* and other texts) holding that the individual conscious being is utterly distinct from nature, and that through yogic practice a blissful and utter aloneness, *kaivalya,* is realized.

Yoga-sūtra See *yoga,* the second definition.

yogin A practitioner of yoga.

zazen In Japanese, meditation.

Guide to Further Reading

This bibliography has been compiled with needs of the advanced undergraduate in mind. Its organization mirrors that of the book as a whole, with the addition of two categories of textbooks at the beginning. In some cases, descriptive remarks are included in parentheses.

TEXTBOOKS IN PHILOSOPHY OF RELIGION

M. J. Charlesworth, *Philosophy of Religion: The Historic Approaches.* New York: Herder and Herder, 1972. (Traces historically the attitudes philosophers in the West have taken toward religion.)

John H. Hick, *Philosophy of Religion,* 4th ed. Englewood Cliffs, New Jersey: Prentice Hall, 1990.

Ed. L. Miller, *God and Reason.* Englewood Cliffs, New Jersey: Prentice Hall, 1994.

William J. Wainwright, *Philosophy of Religion.* Belmont, California: Wadsworth, 1988.

TEXTBOOKS IN RELIGIOUS STUDIES

Denise Lardner Carmody and John Tully Carmody, *Shamans, Prophets, & Sages: A Concise Introduction to World Religions.* Belmont, California: Wadsworth, 1985.

Mircea Eliade, *A History of Religious Ideas.* 4 vols. Chicago: University of Chicago Press, 1978. (An impressive, virtuoso study, wide-ranging and insightful though not entirely free of an interpretive agenda.)

Lewis M. Hopke, *Religions of the World,* 6th ed. New York: Macmillan, 1994.

S. A. Nigosian, *World Faiths.* New York: St. Martin's, 1990.

Ninian Smart, *The Religious Experience of Mankind,* 2nd ed. New York: Charles Scribner's, 1976. (A detailed study by a distinguished philosopher.)

Huston Smith, *The Religions of Man.* New York: Harper & Row, 1965. (A little out of date but extremely interesting especially for those disposed to take the perennialist perspective: see the discussion of Professor Smith's views under Religious Pluralism.)

JUDAISM

Louis Finkelstein, *The Jews: Their History, Culture, and Religion,* 3rd ed. 3 vols. New York: Harper, 1960. (A detailed, scholarly work.)

Meyer Levin, *Classic Hassidic Tales.* New York: Penguin, 1975.

Jacob Neusner, *The Way of the Torah.* Belmont, California: Wadsworth, 1979. (A text written for undergraduates.)

Gershom Scholem, *The Messianic Idea in Judaism.* New York: Schocken, 1971. (Written by the leading scholar of Jewish mysticism in this century.)

CHRISTIANITY

Howard Clark Kee, *The Origins of Christianity: Sources and Documents.* Englewood Cliffs, New Jersey: Prentice-Hall, 1973.

Hans Joachim Hillerbrad, *The Reformation: A Narrative History Related by Contemporary Observers and Participants.* Grand Rapids, Michigan: Baker, 1978.

Jaroslav Pelikan, *The Christian Tradition: A History of the Development of Doctrine.* 5 vols. Chicago: University of Chicago Press, 1971–1989. (Written by an intellectual historian; too detailed for most undergraduates.)

Kenneth Scott Latourette, *A History of Christianity,* rev. ed. 2 vols. New York: Harper & Row, 1975.

Harry Wolfson, *The Philosophy of the Church Fathers,* 3rd ed. Cambridge, Massachusetts: Harvard University Press, 1970. (Written by a philosopher and historian with a wonderfully lively style; a classic.)

ISLAM

Frederick Denny, *Islam and the Muslim Community.* San Francisco: Harper & Row, 1987.

Fazlur Rahman, *Islam.* New York: Holt, Rinehart and Winston, 1966. (A well-written text in a history of religion series.)

Anne-Marie Schimmel, *Mystical Dimensions of Islam.* Chapel Hill, North Carolina: University of North Carolina Press, 1975. (A definitive and sympathetic study that finds Sufism growing out of the teachings of the Koran.)

Harry Wolfson, *The Philosophy of the Kalām.* Cambridge, Massachusetts: Harvard University Press, 1976. (Wolfson's style is lucid and entertaining; his sensibilities are those of a philosopher; the book is highly recommended for those wishing to know more about Arabic philosophy.)

HINDUISM

A. L. Basham, *The Wonder That Was India.* New York: Hawthorn, 1963. (A historical study of many dimensions of classical Indian civilization before the Muslim invasions; the offensiveness of the title does not indicate the quality of the book.)

Nirad C. Chaudhuri, *Hinduism: A Religion to Live By.* New York: Oxford University Press, 1979.

Surendranath Dasgupta, *A History of Indian Philosophy,* 5 vols. Cambridge: Cambridge University Press, 1922–1955. (Volume 1 is particularly good for an overview of the different classical philosophical systems.)

John M. Koller, *The Indian Way.* New York: Macmillan, 1982.

Louis Renou, *Religions of Ancient India.* New York: Schocken, 1968. (A classic study of the religion of the Vedic and early Upanishadic periods.)

BUDDHISM

Kenneth Ch'en, *Buddhism: The Light of Asia.* Woodbury, New York: Barron's Educational Series, 1968. (A well-written textbook treatment.)

Heinrich Dumoulin, *A History of Zen Buddhism.* Boston: Beacon, 1963. (Detailed, definitive.)

David J. Kalupahana, *Buddhist Philosophy: A Historical Analysis.* Honolulu: The University Press of Hawaii, 1976.

Hajime Nakamura, *Indian Buddhism.* Delhi: Motilal Banarsidass, 1987. (Focuses on texts; probably too complex for almost all undergraduates but contains an excellent bibliography.)

CHINESE RELIGION

John Blofield, *Taoism: The Road to Immortality.* Boston: Shambala, 1978.

Kenneth Ch'en, *Buddhism in China: A Historical Survey.* Princeton, New Jersey: Princeton University Press, 1964.

Clifford H. Plopper, *Chinese Religion Seen Through the Proverbs.* New York: Paragon Reprint, 1969. (An interesting angle on Chinese religion including Buddhism and Taoism but not limited to them.)

Laurence G. Thompson, *Chinese Religion: An Introduction.* Belmont, California: Wadsworth, 1989.

Holmes Welch, *Taoism: The Parting of the Way.* Boston: Beacon, 1966. (A delightfully written, short but fairly comprehensive exposition of Taoism mainly as a religion.)

AFRICAN AND AMERINDIAN RELIGION

Joseph Epes Brown, *The Spiritual Legacy of the American Indian.* New York: Crossroad, 1982. (An overview by a longtime student and sympathizer.)

Wade Davis, *The Serpent and the Rainbow.* New York: Warner, 1985. (A fascinating account of Haitian *voudoun,* with suggestions about prehistoric African religious practices.)

Ake Hultkrantz, *Belief and Worship in Native North America.* Syracuse, New York: Syracuse University Press, 1981.

Edward Geoffrey Parrinder, *African Traditional Religion,* 3rd ed. New York: Harper & Row, 1976.

Benjamin C. Ray, *African Religions: Symbol, Ritual, and Community.* Englewood Cliffs, New Jersey: Prentice-Hall, 1976.

GOD

Stephen T. Davis, *Logic and the Nature of God.* Grand Rapids, Michigan: Eerdmans, 1983.

Lewis S. Ford, "The Infinite God of Process Theism," *Proceedings of the Catholic Philosophic Association* 55 (1981), pp. 84–90.

David Griffin, "Charles Hartshorne's Postmodern Philosophy," in *Hartshorne, Process Philosophy and Theology* (Robert Kane and Stephen H. Phillips, eds.). Albany, New York: State University of New York Press, 1989.

Michael Morgan, *Platonic Piety.* New Haven: Yale University Press, 1990.

Alvin Plantinga, *Does God Have a Nature?* Milwaukee: Marquette University Press, 1980. (A contemporary philosophic defense of classical theism.)

Frederick Sontag and M. Darrol Bryant (eds.), *God: The Contemporary Discussion.* Barrytown, New York: Unification Theological Seminary, 1982. (A globalist collection of essays by leading philosophers and scholars of religion.)

A. E. Taylor, "Theism," in the *Encyclopedia of Religion and Ethics* (James Hastings, ed.). New York: Scribner, 1961. (A classic exposition.)

Harry Wolfson, *Philo: Foundations of Religious Philosophy in Judaism, Christianity, and Islam.* Cambridge, Massachusetts: Harvard University Press, 1968.

ABSOLUTE BRAHMAN

Eliot Deutsch, *Advaita Vedānta: A Philosophical Reconstruction.* Honolulu: The University of Hawaii Press, 1973.

Robert E. Hume (tr.), *The Thirteen Principle Upanishads,* 2nd ed. Oxford: Oxford University Press, 1932. (Remains the best English translation; Hume's introduction is also good if slightly tilted toward the Advaita interpretation.)

Karl H. Potter (ed.), *Advaita Vedānta.* Princeton: Princeton University Press, 1983. (Chapter 5 of Potter's lucid introduction explicates the Advaita metaphysics of Brahman.)

A. G. Krishna Warrier, *God in Advaita.* Simla: Indian Institute of Advanced Study, 1977.

THE VIBRANT VOID, "EMPTINESS"

T. V. R. Murti, *The Central Philosophy of Buddhism.* London: Allen and Unwin, 1955.

Ninian Smart, *Doctrine and Argument in Indian Philosophy.* New York: Humanities Press, 1964. (Chapter II, on Buddhist metaphysics, is an adept philosophical discussion of the *śūnyatā* concept, rendered by Smart as the "Void.")

Henry Clarke Warren, *Buddhism in Translation.* New York: Atheneum, 1973. (Translations from the Pāli Canon.)

THE TAO

Stephen Addiss and Stanley Lombardo (tr.), *Tao te ching.* Indianapolis: Hackett, 1993. (A new translation; contains a useful introduction by Burton Watson.)

Victor H. Mair (ed.), *Experimental Essays on Chuang-tzu.* Honolulu: The University Press of Hawaii, 1983.

POLYTHEISM AND HENOTHEISM

Nancy Frankenberry, *Religion and Radical Empiricism.* Albany, New York: State University of New York Press, 1987. (Contains competent discussion of James's spiritual minimalism and philosophic polytheism.)

John Hick, *God Has Many Names.* Philadelphia: Westminster, 1980.

Johannes Maringer, *The Gods of Prehistoric Man.* New York: Knopf, 1960.

Michiko Yusa, "Henotheism," in the *Encyclopedia of Religion* (Mircea Eliade, ed.). New York: Macmillan, 1987.

SPECULATIVE SPIRITUAL METAPHYSICS

Charles Hartshorne, *Whitehead's View of Reality.* New York: Pilgrim Press, 1981.

John Passmore, *A Hundred Years of Philosophy.* New York: Penguin, 1978. (Contains lucid discussion of James's and others' criticisms of Hegel's speculations.)

Stephen H. Phillips, *Aurobindo's Philosophy of Brahman.* Leiden: Brill, 1986.

Robert C. Solomon, *In the Spirit of Hegel.* New York: Oxford University Press, 1983.

ARGUMENTS FOR A DIVINE REALITY

Arindam Chakrabarti and B. K. Matilal (eds.), *Knowing from Words: Western and Indian Philosophical Analysis of Understanding and Testimony.* Dordrecht: Kluwar Academic, 1994. (Contains essays by several distinguished philosophers.)

George Chemparathy, *An Indian Rational Theology: Introduction to Udayana's Nyāyakusumāñjali.* Vienna: De Nobili Research Library, 1972.

William Lane Craig, *The Cosmological Argument from Plato to Leibniz.* New York: Barnes and Noble, 1980.

William Lane Craig, *The Kalām Cosmological Argument.* London: Macmillan, 1979.

Antony Flew, *God and Philosophy.* New York: Dell, 1967. (Contains excellent rehearsals of failings of rational theology.)

John Hick (ed.), *The Existence of God.* New York: Macmillan, 1964. (Classical and contemporary examinations of several arguments of rational theology.)

John Hick and Arthur C. McGill (eds.), *The Many-Faced Argument.* New York: Macmillan, 1967. (Classical and contemporary studies of the ontological argument.)

Robert Kane, "The Modal Ontological Argument," *Mind,* Vol. 93 (1984), pp. 336–350.

Anthony Kenny, *The Five Ways: Saint Thomas Aquinas' Proofs of God's Existence.* London: Routledge & Kegan Paul, 1969.

Hugo A. Meynell, *The Intelligible Universe: A Cosmological Argument.* London: Macmillan, 1982.

Alvin Plantinga, *The Nature of Necessity.* Oxford: Oxford University Press, 1974. (Contains sophisticated championing of a modal ontological argument.)

Karl H. Potter, *Nyāya-Vaiśeṣika* (Encyclopedia of Indian Philosophies, Vol. II). Princeton: Princeton University Press, 1977. (Pages 100ff are a readily comprehensible examination of Udayana's and other Indian theists' arguments for God.)

F. R. Tennant, *Philosophical Theology,* Vol. II. Cambridge: Cambridge University Press, 1956. (Sustained championing of the teleological argument.)

MYSTICAL EXPERIENCE

William Alston, "Religious Experience and Religious Belief," *Nous,* Vol. 16 (1982), pp. 3–12. (Expression of ideas seminal to Alston's *Perceiving God,* which is excerpted under Religious Pluralism.)

Sobharini Basu, *Modern Indian Mysticism.* 3 vols. Varanasi: K. S. Mitra, 1974.

C. D. Broad, *Religion, Philosophy and Psychical Research.* London: Routledge & Kegan Paul, 1930.

Mircea Eliade, *Shamanism: Archaic Techniques of Ecstasy.* Princeton: Princeton University Press, 1972.

Rudolf Otto, *The Idea of the Holy.* London: Oxford University Press. (A classic defense of theistic mysticism.)

Nelson Pike, *Mystic Union: An Essay in the Phenomenology of Mysticism.* Ithaca, New York: Cornell University Press, 1992. (Penetrating discussion of Ruysbroeck and monistic mysticism in general.)

Wayne Proudfoot, *Religious Experience.* Berkeley, California: University of California Press, 1985. (Critical of several philosophic defenses of mysticism.)

W. T. Stace, *Mysticism and Philosophy.* London: Macmillan, 1960. (A classic; particularly sympathetic to monistic mysticism.)

Frits Staal, *Exploring Mysticism.* London: Penguin, 1975. (Mainly an introduction to ways of studying mysticism.)

D. T. Suzuki, *Mysticism: Christian and Buddhist.* New York: Harper, 1957.

Richard Woods (ed.), *Understanding Mysticism.* Garden City, New York: Doubleday, 1980. (An anthology of useful papers, some by psychologists and social scientists.)

Religion Debunked

Peter Angeles (ed.), *Critiques of God.* Buffalo: Prometheus, 1976. (Diverse essays united in the theme of rejection of religion.)

Debiprasad Chattopadhyaya (ed.), *Cārvāka/Lokāyata.* New Delhi: Indian Council of Philosophical Research, 1990. (Contains a historical survey of classical Indian materialism.)

Erik H. Erikson, *Young Man Luther: A Study in Psychoanalysis and History.* New York: Norton, 1962. (A model effort of psychological debunking.)

Clifford Geertz, "Religion as a Cultural System," in *Reader in Comparative Religion* (ed. W. Lessa and E. Vogt). New York: Harper & Row, 1972.

Kai Nielson, *Contemporary Critiques of Religion.* New York: Herder and Herder, 1971.

Bertrand Russell, *Science and Religion.* London: Oxford University Press, 1961.

Ninian Smart, *The Science of Religion and the Sociology of Knowledge: Some Methodological Questions.* Princeton: Princeton University Press, 1973. (A thoughtful probe.)

Evil

Wendy Doniger, *The Origins of Evil in Hindu Mythology.* Berkeley, California: University of California Press, 1976.

Antony Flew, *The Presumption of Atheism.* London: Elek/Pemberton, 1976.

David Ray Griffin, *Evil Revisited: Responses and Considerations.* Albany, New York: State University of New York Press, 1991. (Griffin responds to various criticisms of his process theodicy.)

Arthur L. Herman, *The Problem of Evil and Indian Thought.* Delhi: Motilal Banarsidass, 1976.

John Hick, "The Problem of Evil," in *Encyclopedia of Philosophy* (Paul Edwards, ed.). New York: Macmillan, 1967. (Contains an excellent, historically organized bibliography of the Western discussion.)

Gottfried Wilhelm Leibniz, *Theodicy* (edited and introduced by Diogenes Allen). Indianapolis: Bobbs-Merrill, 1966.

Keiji Nishitani, *The Self-Overcoming of Nihilism.* Graham Parkes, translator. Albany, New York: State University of New York Press, 1991. (An early work of Nishitani's.)

Nelson Pike (ed.), *God and Evil: Readings on the Theological Problem of Evil.* Englewood Cliffs, New Jersey: Prentice-Hall, 1964.

Alvin Plantinga, *The Nature of Necessity.* Oxford: Oxford University Press, 1974. (Contains a more sophisticated version of a free-will defense than that presented here.)

Religious Language

William Alston, "Ineffability," in *Philosophy of Religion* (Steven M. Cahn, ed.). New York: Harper & Row, 1970.

A. J. Ayer, *Language, Truth, and Logic.* New York: Dover, 1952. (Classic exposition of the verificationalist position.)

E. L. Mascall, *Existence and Analogy.* London: Longmans, Green & Co., 1949. (Extended discussion of the Thomist doctrine of analogy.)

Sallie McFague, *Metaphorical Theology: Models of God in Religious Language.* Philadelphia: Fortress, 1982.

Ronald E. Santoni (ed.), *Religious Language and the Problem of Religious Knowledge.* Bloomington, Indiana: Indiana University Press, 1968. (Several essays in this collection are classics.)

FAITH AGAINST REASON

Lorraine Clark, *Blake, Kierkegaard, and the Spectre of Dialectic.* Cambridge: Cambridge University Press, 1991.

Gary Gutting, *Religious Belief and Religious Skepticism.* Notre Dame: University of Notre Dame Press, 1982. (A Wittgensteinian approach.)

Gerald D. McCarthy (ed.), *The Ethics of Belief Debate.* Atlanta: Scholars Press, 1986.

Terence Penelhum, *God and Skepticism: A Study in Skepticism and Fideism.* Dordrecht: D. Reidel, 1983. (Lucid discussion by a top philosopher.)

Louis P. Pojman, *The Logic of Subjectivity: Kierkegaard's Philosophy of Religion.* University, Alabama: University of Alabama Press, 1984. (Four of seven chapters concern Kierkegaard's views of faith; invariably helpful.)

Bennett Ramsey, *Submitting to Freedom: The Religious Vision of William James.* New York: Oxford University Press, 1993.

RELIGION AND ETHICS

Christopher Chappel, *Nonviolence to Animals, Earth, and Self in Asian Traditions.* Albany, New York: State University of New York Press, 1993.

Arthur C. Danto, *Mysticism and Morality: Oriental Thought and Moral Philosophy.* New York: Harper & Row, 1973.

Greta Gaard (ed.), *Ecofeminism: Women, Animals, Nature.* Philadelphia: Temple University Press, 1993.

Herbert Fingarette, *Confucius—The Secular as Sacred.* New York: Harper & Row, 1972.

James R. Horne, *The Moral Mystic.* Waterloo, Ontario: Winfred Laurier University Press, 1983. (A critical survey of views on the relation between mysticism and morality.)

Paul T. Jersild and Dale A. Johnson (eds.), *Moral Issues & Christian Response,* 5th ed. Fort Worth: Harcourt Brace Jovanovich, 1993.

Gene Outka and John P. Reeder, Jr. (eds.), *Religion and Morality.* Garden City, New York: Anchor, 1973. (Includes papers on divine command theory.)

Rajendra Prasad, *Karma, Causation and Retributive Morality: Conceptual Essays in Ethics and Metaethics.* New Delhi: Indian Council of Philosophical Research, 1989.

Rosemary Radford Ruether, *Sexism and God-Talk: Toward a Feminist Theology.* Boston: Beacon, 1983.

Mary Evelyn Tucker and John A. Grim (eds.), *Worldviews and Ecology.* Lewisburg, Pennsylvania: Bucknell University Press, 1993. (A globalist collection, including essays on Taoism and Confucianism, Islam, and Amerindian views with respect to environmental ethics.)

PERSONAL DESTINY

Aurobindo, *The Life Divine.* Pondicherry: Sri Aurobindo Ashram Trust, 1973. (Aurobindo's theory of rebirth is laid out in Book Two, Part Two, Chapters 20 through 22.)

David Chidester, *Patterns of Transcendence: Religion, Death, and Dying.* Belmont, California: Wadsworth, 1990. (A globalist treatment.)

Hoyt Edge, Robert Morris, John Plamer, and Joseph Rush (eds.), *Foundations of Parapsychology.* London: Routledge & Kegan Paul, 1986. (A well-written, balanced textbook treatment of the history, methods, and findings of parapsychology.)

Francesco Fremantle and Chögyam Trungpa (trs.), *The Tibetan Book of the Dead.* Boulder, Colorado: Shambala, 1975. (Includes an introductory commentary.)

Hermann Haring and Johann-Baptist Metz (eds.), *Reincarnation or Resurrection?* London: SCM Press, 1993. (Essays by religious-studies scholars.)

Thomas Nagel, "Death," in his *Mortal Questions.* Cambridge: Cambridge University Press, 1979. (Argues that although there is no survival and no experience of death, it is nonetheless an evil as depriving us of a good.)

Terence Penelhum (ed.), *Immortality.* Belmont, California: Wadsworth, 1973. (Philosophic essays by classical Western authors and contemporary philosophers.)

Ian Stevenson, *Cases of the Reincarnation Type.* 4 vols. Charlottesville, Virginia: University Press of Virginia, 1975-1983.

Ian Stevenson, *Children Who Remember Previous Lives.* Charlottesville, Virginia: University Press of Virginia, 1987.

RELIGIOUS PLURALISM

David Ray Griffin and Huston Smith, *Primordial Truth and Postmodern Theology.* Albany, New York: State University of New York Press, 1989. (A dialogue between Griffin and Smith on process and perennialist views.)

Basil Mitchell, *The Justification of Religious Belief.* London: Macmillan, 1973. (Champions cumulative case arguments.)

Seyyed Hossein Nasr, *The Need for a Sacred Science.* Albany, New York: State University of New York Press, 1993.

Nicholas Rescher, *Pluralism.* Oxford: Oxford University Press, 1993. (A sophisticated defense of pluralism in various domains.

Wilfred Cantwell Smith, *The Meaning and End of Religion.* San Francisco: Harper & Row, 1978. (Explores historical interactions among faiths.)

Wilfred Cantwell Smith, *Towards a World Theology.* Philadelphia Westminster, 1981.

CREDITS

William P. Alston   From *Perceiving God: The Epistemology of Religious Experience* by William P. Alston. Copyright © 1991 by Cornell University. Used by permission of the publisher, Cornell University Press.

William P. Alston   From "Hartshorne and Aquinas: A Via Media" from *Existence and Actuality* edited by John B. Cobb, Jr. and Franklin I. Gamwell © 1984 by The University of Chicago. Reprinted with permission of the University of Chicago Press.

William P. Alston   From "Can We Speak Literally of God?" from *Is God God?*, Axel D. Steuer and James Wm. McClendon, Jr., editors. Copyright © 1981 by Abingdon. Used by permission.

Saint Thomas Aquinas   From "Five Ways" and *Summa Theologica* by Thomas Aquinas in *Basic Writings of Saint Thomas Aquinas* by Anton C. Pegis, editor and translator © 1945. Used by permission of the Anton C. Pegis Estate.

Arthur J. Arberry   From "On the Nature of God" from *Avicenna on Theology* translated by Arthur J. Arberry © 1951 John Murray (Publishers) Ltd. Reprinted with permission of the publisher.

Augustine   From "The Nature of the Good: Against the Manichees" by Augustine in *Augustine: Earlier Writings* edited by John H. S. Burleigh (The Library of Christian Classics Series). Used by permission of Westminster/John Knox Press.

Sri Aurobindo   From *The Synthesis of Yoga* by Sri Aurobindo © 1955 Sri Aurobindo Ashram Trust.

Sri Aurobindo   From *The Life Divine* by Sri Aurobindo. © 1987 Sri Aurobindo Ashram Trust.

R. B. Braithwaite   From *An Empiricist's View of the Nature of Religious Belief* by R. B. Braithwaite. Copyright © 1955. Reprinted with the permission of Cambridge University Press.

Martin Buber   Reprinted with permission of Charles Scribner's Sons, an imprint of Macmillan Publishing from *I and Thou* by Martin Buber, translated by Walter Kaufmann. Translation copyright © 1970 Charles Scribner's Sons.

J. D. Callicott and Thomas Overholt   From "Traditional American Indian Attitudes Toward Nature" by J. D. Callicott and Thomas Overholt in *From Africa to Zen*, Robert C. Solomon and Kathleen M. Higgins, editors. Copyright © 1993 by Rowman & Littlefield Publishers. Reprinted by permission.

Albert Camus   From *The Myth of Sisyphus and Other Essays* by Albert Camus, translator Justin O'Brien. Copyright © 1955 by Alfred A. Knopf, Inc. Reprinted by permission of the publisher.

M. A. Corey   From *God and the New Cosmology*. Copyright © 1993 by M. A. Corey, Reprinted by permission of Rowman & Littlefield Publishers.

William Lane Craig and Quentin Smith   From "The Caused Beginning of the Universe" in *Theism, Atheism, and Big Bang Cosmology* by William Lane Craig and Quentin Smith © 1993 William Lane Craig and Quentin Smith. Reprinted by permission of Oxford University Press.

Mary Daly   Reprinted from *Beyond God the Father: Toward a Philosophy of Women's Liberation* by Mary Daly © 1973 Mary Daly. Reprinted with permission of Beacon Press.

Alain Daniélou   From *Hindu Polytheism* (Bollingen Series 73) by Alain Daniélou © 1964, renewed 1992 Princeton University Press. Reprinted with permission of Princeton University Press.

C. J. Ducasse   Reprinted from *Nature, Mind, and Death* by C. J. Ducasse with permission of Open Court Publishing Company, LaSalle, Illinois © 1951 Open Court Publishing Company.

Mircea Eliade   Reprinted from *Yoga: Immortality and Freedom* (Bollingen Series 56) by Mircea Eliade, translated by Willard R. Trask © 1958, renewed 1969 Princeton University Press. Reprinted with permission of Princeton University Press.

Antony Flew and Alasdair MacIntyre   From "Theology and Falsification" by Antony Flew reprinted with the permission of Macmillan Publishing Company from *New Essays in Philosophical Theology* by Antony Flew and Alasdair MacIntyre, editors. Copyright 1955, renewed 1983 by Antony Flew and Alasdair MacIntyre.

Sigmund Freud   Printed from *The Future of An Illusion* by Sigmund Freud, translated from the German by James Strachey, with the permission of W.W. Norton & Company, Inc. Copyright © 1961 by James Strachey, renewed 1989 by Alix Strachey.

Richard M. Gale   From *On the Nature and Existence of God* by Richard M. Gale © 1991 Cambridge University Press with permission of Cambridge University Press.

Dwight Goddard   From "Surangama Sūtra" from *A Buddhist Bible* by Dwight Goddard, editor. Copyright 1938, renewed © 1966 by E.P. Dutton. Used by permission of Dutton Signet, a division of Penguin Books USA, Inc.

A. C. Graham   Reprinted from *Disputers of the Tao* by A. C. Graham with permission of Open Court Publishing Company, LaSalle, Illinois © 1989 Open Court Publishing.

David R. Griffin   From "Creation Out of Chaos and the Problem of Evil" by David R. Griffin in *Encountering Evil: Live Options in Theodicy* by Stephen T. Davis. Copyright © 1981 Stephen T. Davis. Used by permission of Westminster/John Knox Press.

Kwame Gyekye   Reprinted from *An Essay on African Philosophical Thought* by Kwame Gyekye © 1987 Cambridge University Press with permission of Cambridge University Press.

James G. Hanink and Gary R. Mar   From "What Euthyphro Couldn't Have Said" reprinted from *Faith and Philosophy*, Volume 4, No. 3, (July 1987): pp. 241-245, 246-247 © 1987 The Society of Christian Philosophers. Reprinted with permission of the editor.

Charles Hartshorne   From *Omnipotence and Other Theological Mistakes* by Charles Hartshorne by permission of the State University of New York Press © 1984 State University of New York.

John Hick   From *Evil and the God of Love*, Revised Edition by John Hick. Copyright © 1966, 1977 by John H. Hick. Reprinted by permission of HarperCollins Publishers, Inc.

John Hick   From "Religious Pluralism and Salvation" by John Hick from *Faith and Philosophy*, Volume 5, No. 4, October 1988, Philip L. Quinn, Editor. Copyright © 1988.

M. Hiriyanna   Reprinted from *Indian Conception of Values* by M. Hiriyanna. Used by permission of Kavyalaya Publishers, Jayanagar Mysore © 1975 Kavyalaya Publishers.

Robert H. Kane   From "Anselm's Second, or Modal, Ontological Argument" by Robert H. Kane © 1994 by Robert H. Kane. Reprinted with permission of the author.

Philip Kapleau   From *The Three Pillars of Zen* by Philip Kapleau. Copyright © 1965, 1989 by Philip Kapleau. Copyright © 1980 by The Zen Center, Inc. Used by permission of Doubleday, a division of Bantam Doubleday Dell Publishing Group, Inc.

Steven T. Katz   From "Language, Epistemology, and Mysticism" from *Mysticism and Philosophical Analysis*, edited by Steven T. Katz © 1978 by Steven T. Katz. Reprinted with permission of Oxford University Press, Inc.

Søren Kierkegaard   Reprinted from *Philosophical Fragments/Johannes Climacus* by Søren Kierkegaard, edited and translated by Howard V.

Hong and Edna H. Hong © 1985 Reprinted with permission of Princeton University Press.

Sallie B. King   From "Two Epistemological Models for the Interpretation of Mysticism" by Sallie B. King reprinted from *Journal of the American Academy of Religion*, Volume 56, Number 2, William Scott Green, editor. © 1988.

Muni Mahendra Kumar, editor   From *Āyāro (Ācārāṅga Sūtra)* © 1981 by Jain Vishra Bharati and Today & Tomorrow's Printers and Publishers.

C. B. Martin   Reprinted from *Religious Belief* by C. B. Martin © 1959 Cornell University Press. Used by permission of C. B. Martin.

George I. Mavrodes   Reprinted from "The Life Everlasting and the Bodily Criterion of Identity" by George I. Mavrodes in *Noûs*, Volume IX, No. 1 (March 1977) © Blackwell Publishers, Cambridge, MA.

Raymond A. Moody, Jr.   From *Life after Life* by Raymond A. Moody © 1975 Bantam Books (by arrangement with MBB, Inc.)

Seyyed Hossein Nasr   Reprinted from *Knowledge and the Sacred* by Seyyed Hossein Nasr © 1981 with permission of Edinburgh University Press.

Kai Nielsen   From *Ethics Without God* by Kai Nielsen (Buffalo, NY: Prometheus Books). Copyright © 1990 by Kai Nielsen. Reprinted by permission of the publisher.

Keiji Nishitani   From *Religion and Nothingness* (Jan Van Bragt, Translator/Editor) © 1982 The University of California.

Robert Nozick   Reprinted by permission of the publishers from *Philosophical Explanations* by Robert Nozick, Cambridge, MA: Harvard University Press, Copyright © 1981 by Robert Nozick.

D. Z. Phillips   From *Religion Without Explanation* by D. Z. Phillips © 1976 Basil Blackwell Ltd. Reprinted with permission of the publisher.

Stephen H. Phillips   "Nishitani's Buddhist Response to Nihilism" by Stephen H. Phillips reprinted from *Journal of the American Academy of Religion* 55/1, William Scott Green, Editor. Copyright © 1987.

Alvin Plantinga   Reprinted from *God, Freedom, and Evil* by Alvin Plantinga. Copyright © 1974 by Alvin Plantinga. First published by Harper and Row © 1974. Present edition © 1977 by Wm. B. Eerdmans Publishing Co.

Alvin Plantinga   From "Reason and Belief in God" by Alvin Plantinga in *Faith and Rationality: Reason and Belief in God*, N. Wolterstorff and A. Plantinga, editors. Copyright © 1983 by University of Notre Dame Press. Used by permission.

Plato   *Symposium* by Plato, translated by Alexander Nehemas and Paul Woodruff. © 1989 Hackett Publishing Company, Inc.

Plato   Reprinted with permission of Macmillan College Publishing Company from *Euthyphro, Apology,*

INDEX